323/MX-3/626/MILLENIA/PR
FORD PROBE (1993-97)
1990-98 REPAIR MAN

Covers all U.S. and Cana
Mazda 323, MX-3, 626, M
Protege and Ford Probe (1993-97)

by **Todd W. Stidham**, A.S.E.

PUBLISHED BY **HAYNES NORTH AMERICA.** Inc.

Manufactured in USA
© 1999 Haynes North America, Inc.
ISBN 0-8019-9130-7
Library of Congress Catalog Card No. 99-072477
3456789012 9876543210

Haynes Publishing Group
Sparkford Nr Yeovil
Somerset BA22 7JJ England

Haynes North America, Inc
861 Lawrence Drive
Newbury Park
California 91320 USA

ABCDE
FGHIJ

11E1

Contents

Contents

SAFETY NOTICE

Proper service and repair procedures are vital to the safe, reliable operation of all motor vehicles, as well as the personal safety of those performing repairs. This manual outlines procedures for servicing and repairing vehicles using safe, effective methods. The procedures contain many NOTES, CAUTIONS and WARNINGS which should be followed, along with standard procedures to eliminate the possibility of personal injury or improper service which could damage the vehicle or compromise its safety.

It is important to note that repair procedures and techniques, tools and parts for servicing motor vehicles, as well as the skill and experience of the individual performing the work vary widely. It is not possible to anticipate all of the conceivable ways or conditions under which vehicles may be serviced, or to provide cautions as to all possible hazards that may result. Standard and accepted safety precautions and equipment should be used when handling toxic or flammable fluids, and safety goggles or other protection should be used during cutting, grinding, chiseling, prying, or any other process that can cause material removal or projectiles.

Some procedures require the use of tools specially designed for a specific purpose. Before substituting another tool or procedure, you must be completely satisfied that neither your personal safety, nor the performance of the vehicle will be endangered.

Although information in this manual is based on industry sources and is complete as possible at the time of publication, the possibility exists that some car manufacturers made later changes which could not be included here. While striving for total accuracy, the authors or publishers cannot assume responsibility for any errors, changes or omissions that may occur in the compilation of this data.

PART NUMBERS

Part numbers listed in this reference are not recommendations by Haynes North America, Inc. for any product brand name. They are references that can be used with interchange manuals and aftermarket supplier catalogs to locate each brand supplier's discrete part number.

SPECIAL TOOLS

Special tools are recommended by the vehicle manufacturer to perform their specific job. Use has been kept to a minimum, but where absolutely necessary, they are referred to in the text by the part number of the tool manufacturer. These tools can be purchased, under the appropriate part number, from your local dealer or regional distributor, or an equivalent tool can be purchased locally from a tool supplier or parts outlet. Before substituting any tool for the one recommended, read the SAFETY NOTICE at the top of this page.

ACKNOWLEDGMENTS

The publisher expresses appreciation to Mazda Motor Corporation for their generous assistance.

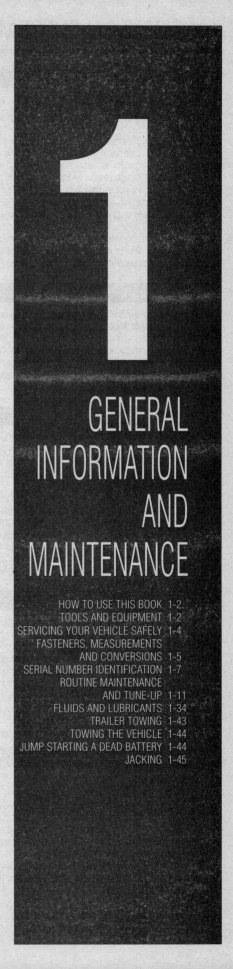

1

GENERAL INFORMATION AND MAINTENANCE

HOW TO USE THIS BOOK

This Chilton's Total Car Care manual is intended to help you learn more about the inner workings of your vehicle while saving you money on its upkeep and operation.

The beginning of the book will likely be referred to the most, since that is where you will find information for maintenance and tune-up. The other sections deal with the more complex systems of your vehicle. Systems (from engine through brakes) are covered to the extent that the average do-it-yourselfer can attempt. This book will not explain such things as rebuilding a differential because the expertise required and the special tools necessary make this uneconomical. It will, however, give you detailed instructions to help you change your own brake pads and shoes, replace spark plugs, and perform many more jobs that can save you money and help avoid expensive problems.

A secondary purpose of this book is a reference for owners who want to understand their vehicle and/or their mechanics better.

Where to Begin

Before removing any bolts, read through the entire procedure. This will give you the overall view of what tools and supplies will be required. So read ahead and plan ahead. Each operation should be approached logically and all procedures thoroughly understood before attempting any work.

If repair of a component is not considered practical, we tell you how to remove the part and then how to install the new or rebuilt replacement. In this way, you at least save labor costs.

Avoiding Trouble

Many procedures in this book require you to label and disconnect . . . " a group of lines, hoses or wires. Don't be think you can remember where everything goes—you won't. If you hook up vacuum or fuel lines incorrectly, the vehicle may run poorly, if at all. If you hook up electrical wiring incorrectly, you may instantly learn a very expensive lesson.

You don't need to know the proper name for each hose or line. A piece of masking tape on the hose and a piece on its fitting will allow you to assign your own label. As long as you remember your own code, the lines can be reconnected by matching your tags. Remember that tape will dissolve in gasoline or solvents; if a part is to be washed or cleaned, use another method of identification. A permanent felt-tipped marker or a metal scribe can be very handy for marking metal parts. Remove any tape or paper labels after assembly.

Maintenance or Repair?

Maintenance includes routine inspections, adjustments, and replacement of parts which show signs of normal wear. Maintenance compensates for wear or deterioration. Repair implies that something has broken or is not working. A need for a repair is often caused by lack of maintenance. for example: draining and refilling automatic transmission fluid is maintenance recommended at specific intervals. Failure to do this can shorten the life of the transmission/transaxle, requiring very expensive repairs. While no maintenance program can prevent items from eventually breaking or wearing out, a general rule is true: MAINTENANCE IS CHEAPER THAN REPAIR.

Two basic mechanic's rules should be mentioned here. First, whenever the left side of the vehicle or engine is referred to, it means the driver's side. Conversely, the right side of the vehicle means the passenger's side. Second, screws and bolts are removed by turning counterclockwise, and tightened by turning clockwise unless specifically noted.

Safety is always the most important rule. Constantly be aware of the dangers involved in working on an automobile and take the proper precautions. Please refer to the information in this section regarding SERVICING YOUR VEHICLE SAFELY and the SAFETY NOTICE on the acknowledgment page.

Avoiding the Most Common Mistakes

Pay attention to the instructions provided. There are 3 common mistakes in mechanical work:

1. Incorrect order of assembly, disassembly or adjustment. When taking something apart or putting it together, performing steps in the wrong order usually just costs you extra time; however, it CAN break something. Read the entire procedure before beginning. Perform everything in the order in which the instructions say you should, even if you can't see a reason for it. When you're taking apart something that is very intricate, you might want to draw a picture of how it looks when assembled in order to make sure you get everything back in its proper position. When making adjustments, perform them in the proper order. One adjustment possibly will affect another.

2. Overtorquing (or undertorquing). While it is more common for overtorquing to cause damage, undertorquing may allow a fastener to vibrate loose causing serious damage. Especially when dealing with aluminum parts, pay attention to torque specifications and utilize a torque wrench in assembly. If a torque figure is not available, remember that if you are using the right tool to perform the job, you will probably not have to strain yourself to get a fastener tight enough. The pitch of most threads is so slight that the tension you put on the wrench will be multiplied many times in actual force on what you are tightening.

There are many commercial products available for ensuring that fasteners won't come loose, even if they are not torqued just right (a very common brand is Loctite®. If you're worried about getting something together tight enough to hold, but loose enough to avoid mechanical damage during assembly, one of these products might offer substantial insurance. Before choosing a threadlocking compound, read the label on the package and make sure the product is compatible with the materials, fluids, etc. involved.

3. Crossthreading. This occurs when a part such as a bolt is screwed into a nut or casting at the wrong angle and forced. Crossthreading is more likely to occur if access is difficult. It helps to clean and lubricate fasteners, then to start threading the bolt, spark plug, etc. with your fingers. If you encounter resistance, unscrew the part and start over again at a different angle until it can be inserted and turned several times without much effort. Keep in mind that many parts have tapered threads, so that gentle turning will automatically bring the part you're threading to the proper angle. Don't put a wrench on the part until it's been tightened a couple of turns by hand. If you suddenly encounter resistance, and the part has not seated fully, don't force it. Pull it back out to make sure it's clean and threading properly.

Be sure to take your time and be patient, and always plan ahead. Allow yourself ample time to perform repairs and maintenance.

TOOLS AND EQUIPMENT

▶ **See Figures 1 thru 15**

Without the proper tools and equipment it is impossible to properly service your vehicle. It would be virtually impossible to catalog every tool that you would need to perform all of the operations in this book. It would be unwise for the amateur to rush out and buy an expensive set of tools on the theory that he/she may need one or more of them at some time.

The best approach is to proceed slowly, gathering a good quality set of those tools that are used most frequently. Don't be misled by the low cost of bargain tools. It is far better to spend a little more for better quality. Forged wrenches, 6 or 12-point sockets and fine tooth ratchets are by far preferable to their less expensive counterparts. As any good mechanic can tell you, there are few worse experiences than trying to work on a vehicle with bad tools. Your monetary savings will be far outweighed by frustration and mangled knuckles.

Begin accumulating those tools that are used most frequently: those associated with routine maintenance and tune-up. In addition to the normal assortment of screwdrivers and pliers, you should have the following tools:

• Wrenches/sockets and combination open end/box end wrenches in sizes ⅛–¾ in. and/or 3mm–19mm ¹³⁄₁₆ in. or ⅝ in. spark plug socket (depending on plug type).

➡**If possible, buy various length socket drive extensions. Universal-joint and wobble extensions can be extremely useful, but be careful when using them, as they can change the amount of torque applied to the socket.**

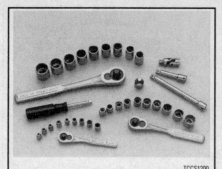

Fig. 1 All but the most basic procedures will require an assortment of ratchets and sockets

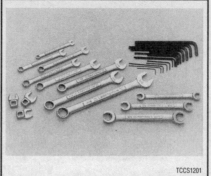

Fig. 2 In addition to ratchets, a good set of wrenches and hex keys will be necessary

Fig. 3 A hydraulic floor jack and a set of jackstands are essential for lifting and supporting the vehicle

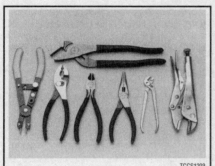

Fig. 4 An assortment of pliers, grippers and cutters will be handy for old rusted parts and stripped bolt heads

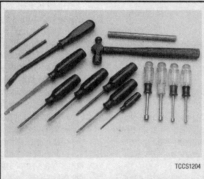

Fig. 5 Various drivers, chisels and prybars are great tools to have in your toolbox

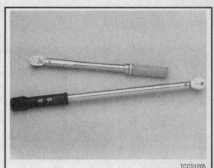

Fig. 6 Many repairs will require the use of a torque wrench to assure the components are properly fastened

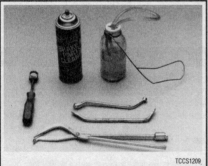

Fig. 7 Although not always necessary, using specialized brake tools will save time

Fig. 8 A few inexpensive lubrication tools will make maintenance easier

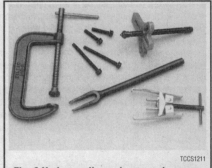

Fig. 9 Various pullers, clamps and separator tools are needed for many larger, more complicated repairs

Fig. 10 A variety of tools and gauges should be used for spark plug gapping and installation

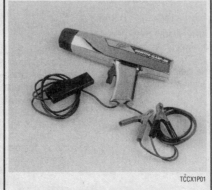

Fig. 11 Inductive type timing light

Fig. 12 A screw-in type compression gauge is recommended for compression testing

Fig. 13 A vacuum/pressure tester is necessary for many testing procedures

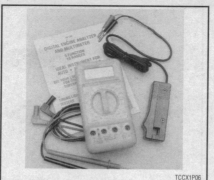

Fig. 14 Most modern automotive multimeters incorporate many helpful features

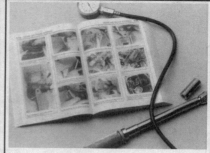

Fig. 15 Proper information is vital, so always have a Chilton Total Car Care manual handy

- Jackstands for support.
- Oil filter wrench.
- Spout or funnel for pouring fluids.
- Grease gun for chassis lubrication (unless your vehicle is not equipped with any grease fittings)
- Hydrometer for checking the battery (unless equipped with a sealed, maintenance-free battery).
- A container for draining oil and other fluids.
- Rags for wiping up the inevitable mess.

In addition to the above items there are several others that are not absolutely necessary, but handy to have around. These include an equivalent oil absorbent gravel, like cat litter, and the usual supply of lubricants, antifreeze and fluids. This is a basic list for routine maintenance, but only your personal needs and desire can accurately determine your list of tools.

After performing a few projects on the vehicle, you'll be amazed at the other tools and non-tools on your workbench. Some useful household items are: a large turkey baster or siphon, empty coffee cans and ice trays (to store parts), a ball of twine, electrical tape for wiring, small rolls of colored tape for tagging lines or hoses, markers and pens, a note pad, golf tees (for plugging vacuum lines), metal coat hangers or a roll of mechanic's wire (to hold things out of the way), dental pick or similar long, pointed probe, a strong magnet, and a small mirror (to see into recesses and under manifolds).

A more advanced set of tools, suitable for tune-up work, can be drawn up easily. While the tools are slightly more sophisticated, they need not be outrageously expensive. There are several inexpensive tach/dwell meters on the market that are every bit as good for the average mechanic as a professional model. Just be sure that it goes to a least 1200–1500 rpm on the tach scale and that it works on 4, 6 and 8-cylinder engines. The key to these purchases is to make them with an eye towards adaptability and wide range. A basic list of tune-up tools could include:

- Tach/dwell meter.
- Spark plug wrench and gapping tool.
- Feeler gauges for valve adjustment.
- Timing light.

The choice of a timing light should be made carefully. A light which works on the DC current supplied by the vehicle's battery is the best choice; it should have a xenon tube for brightness. On any vehicle with an electronic ignition system, a timing light with an inductive pickup that clamps around the No. 1 spark plug cable is preferred.

In addition to these basic tools, there are several other tools and gauges you may find useful. These include:

- Compression gauge. The screw-in type is slower to use, but eliminates the possibility of a faulty reading due to escaping pressure.
- Manifold vacuum gauge.
- 12V test light.
- A combination volt/ohmmeter
- Induction Ammeter. This is used for determining whether or not there is current in a wire. These are handy for use if a wire is broken somewhere in a wiring harness.

As a final note, you will probably find a torque wrench necessary for all but the most basic work. The beam type models are perfectly adequate, although the newer click types (breakaway) are easier to use. The click type torque wrenches tend to be more expensive. Also keep in mind that all types of torque wrenches should be periodically checked and/or recalibrated. You will have to decide for yourself which better fits your pocketbook, and purpose.

Special Tools

Normally, the use of special factory tools is avoided for repair procedures, since these are not readily available for the do-it-yourself mechanic. When it is possible to perform the job with more commonly available tools, it will be pointed out, but occasionally, a special tool was designed to perform a specific function and should be used. Before substituting another tool, you should be convinced that neither your safety nor the performance of the vehicle will be compromised.

Special tools can usually be purchased from an automotive parts store or from your dealer. In some cases special tools may be available directly from the tool manufacturer.

SERVICING YOUR VEHICLE SAFELY

▶ **See Figures 16, 17 and 18**

It is virtually impossible to anticipate all of the hazards involved with automotive maintenance and service, but care and common sense will prevent most accidents.

The rules of safety for mechanics range from ìdon't smoke around gasoline,î to ìuse the proper tool(s) for the job.î The trick to avoiding injuries is to develop safe work habits and to take every possible precaution.

Do's

- Do keep a fire extinguisher and first aid kit handy.
- Do wear safety glasses or goggles when cutting, drilling, grinding or prying, even if you have 20–20 vision. If you wear glasses for the sake of vision, wear safety goggles over your regular glasses.
- Do shield your eyes whenever you work around the battery. Batteries

contain sulfuric acid. In case of contact with, flush the area with water or a mixture of water and baking soda, then seek immediate medical attention.

- Do use safety stands (jackstands) for any undervehicle service. Jacks are for raising vehicles; jackstands are for making sure the vehicle stays raised until you want it to come down.
- Do use adequate ventilation when working with any chemicals or hazardous materials. Like carbon monoxide, the asbestos dust resulting from some brake lining wear can be hazardous in sufficient quantities.
- Do disconnect the negative battery cable when working on the electrical system. The secondary ignition system contains EXTREMELY HIGH VOLTAGE. In some cases it can even exceed 50,000 volts.
- Do follow manufacturer's directions whenever working with potentially hazardous materials. Most chemicals and fluids are poisonous.
- Do properly maintain your tools. Loose hammerheads, mushroomed punches and chisels, frayed or poorly grounded electrical cords, excessively

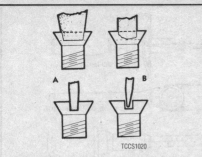

Fig. 16 Screwdrivers should be kept in good condition to prevent injury or damage which could result if the blade slips from the screw

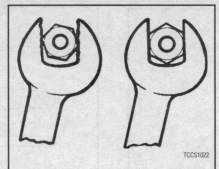

Fig. 17 Using the correct size wrench will help prevent the possibility of rounding off a nut

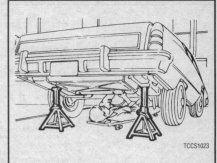

Fig. 18 NEVER work under a vehicle unless it is supported using safety stands (jackstands)

worn screwdrivers, spread wrenches (open end), cracked sockets, slipping ratchets, or faulty droplight sockets can cause accidents.

• Likewise, keep your tools clean; a greasy wrench can slip off a bolt head, ruining the bolt and often harming your knuckles in the process.

• Do use the proper size and type of tool for the job at hand. Do select a wrench or socket that fits the nut or bolt. The wrench or socket should sit straight, not cocked.

• Do, when possible, pull on a wrench handle rather than push on it, and adjust your stance to prevent a fall.

• Do be sure that adjustable wrenches are tightly closed on the nut or bolt and pulled so that the force is on the side of the fixed jaw.

• Do strike squarely with a hammer; avoid glancing blows.

• Do set the parking brake and block the drive wheels if the work requires a running engine.

Don'ts

• Don't run the engine in a garage or anywhere else without proper ventilation—EVER! Carbon monoxide is poisonous; it takes a long time to leave the human body and you can build up a deadly supply of it in your system by simply breathing in a little at a time. You may not realize you are slowly poisoning yourself. Always use power vents, windows, fans and/or open the garage door.

• Don't work around moving parts while wearing loose clothing. Short sleeves are much safer than long, loose sleeves. Hard-toed shoes with neoprene soles protect your toes and give a better grip on slippery surfaces. Watches and jewelry is not safe working around a vehicle. Long hair should be tied back under a hat or cap.

• Don't use pockets for toolboxes. A fall or bump can drive a screwdriver deep into your body. Even a rag hanging from your back pocket can wrap around a spinning shaft or fan.

• Don't smoke when working around gasoline, cleaning solvent or other flammable material.

• Don't smoke when working around the battery. When the battery is being charged, it gives off explosive hydrogen gas.

• Don't use gasoline to wash your hands; there are excellent soaps available. Gasoline contains dangerous additives which can enter the body through a cut or through your pores. Gasoline also removes all the natural oils from the skin so that bone dry hands will suck up oil and grease.

• Don't service the air conditioning system unless you are equipped with the necessary tools and training. When liquid or compressed gas refrigerant is released to atmospheric pressure it will absorb heat from whatever it contacts. This will chill or freeze anything it touches.

• Don't use screwdrivers for anything other than driving screws! A screwdriver used as an prying tool can snap when you least expect it, causing injuries. At the very least, you'll ruin a good screwdriver.

• Don't use an emergency jack (that little ratchet, scissors, or pantograph jack supplied with the vehicle) for anything other than changing a flat! These jacks are only intended for emergency use out on the road; they are NOT designed as a maintenance tool. If you are serious about maintaining your vehicle yourself, invest in a hydraulic floor jack of at least a 1½ ton capacity, and at least two sturdy jackstands.

FASTENERS, MEASUREMENTS AND CONVERSIONS

Bolts, Nuts and Other Threaded Retainers

▶ See Figures 19 and 20

Although there are a great variety of fasteners found in the modern car or truck, the most commonly used retainer is the threaded fastener (nuts, bolts, screws, studs, etc.). Most threaded retainers may be reused, provided that they are not damaged in use or during the repair. Some retainers (such as stretch bolts or torque prevailing nuts) are designed to deform when tightened or in use and should not be reinstalled.

Whenever possible, we will note any special retainers which should be replaced during a procedure. But you should always inspect the condition of a retainer when it is removed and replace any that show signs of damage. Check all threads for rust or corrosion which can increase the torque necessary to achieve the desired clamp load for which that fastener was originally selected. Additionally, be sure that the driver surface of the fastener has not been compromised by rounding or other damage. In some cases a driver surface may become only partially rounded, allowing the driver to catch in only one direction. In many of these occurrences, a fastener may be installed and tightened, but the driver would not be able to grip and loosen the fastener again.

If you must replace a fastener, whether due to design or damage, you must ALWAYS be sure to use the proper replacement. In all cases, a retainer of the same design, material and strength should be used. Markings on the heads of most bolts will help determine the proper strength of the fastener. The same

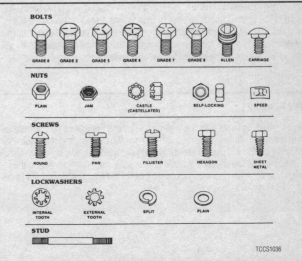

Fig. 19 There are many different types of threaded retainers found on vehicles

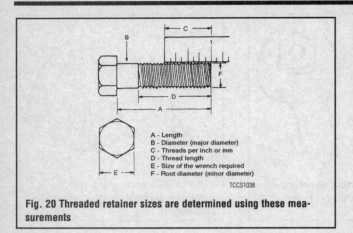

A - Length
B - Diameter (major diameter)
C - Threads per inch or mm
D - Thread length
E - Size of the wrench required
F - Root diameter (minor diameter)

TCCS1038

Fig. 20 Threaded retainer sizes are determined using these measurements

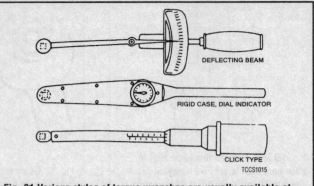

DEFLECTING BEAM

RIGID CASE, DIAL INDICATOR

CLICK TYPE

TCCS1015

Fig. 21 Various styles of torque wrenches are usually available at your local automotive supply store

material, thread and pitch must be selected to assure proper installation and safe operation of the vehicle afterwards.

Thread gauges are available to help measure a bolt or stud's thread. Most automotive and hardware stores keep gauges available to help you select the proper size. In a pinch, you can use another nut or bolt for a thread gauge. If the bolt you are replacing is not too badly damaged, you can select a match by finding another bolt which will thread in its place. If you find a nut which threads properly onto the damaged bolt, then use that nut to help select the replacement bolt.

✳✳ WARNING

Be aware that when you find a bolt with damaged threads, you may also find the nut or drilled hole it was threaded into has also been damaged. If this is the case, you may have to drill and tap the hole, replace the nut or otherwise repair the threads. NEVER try to force a replacement bolt to fit into the damaged threads.

Torque

Torque is defined as the measurement of resistance to turning or rotating. It tends to twist a body about an axis of rotation. A common example of this would be tightening a threaded retainer such as a nut, bolt or screw. Measuring torque is one of the most common ways to help assure that a threaded retainer has been properly fastened.

When tightening a threaded fastener, torque is applied in three distinct areas, the head, the bearing surface and the clamp load. About 50 percent of the measured torque is used in overcoming bearing friction. This is the friction between the bearing surface of the bolt head, screw head or nut face and the base material or washer (the surface on which the fastener is rotating). Approximately 40 percent of the applied torque is used in overcoming thread friction. This leaves only about 10 percent of the applied torque to develop a useful clamp load (the force which holds a joint together). This means that friction can account for as much as 90 percent of the applied torque on a fastener.

TORQUE WRENCHES

▶ See Figure 21

In most applications, a torque wrench can be used to assure proper installation of a fastener. Torque wrenches come in various designs and most automotive supply stores will carry a variety to suit your needs. A torque wrench should be used any time we supply a specific torque value for a fastener. Again, the general rule of "if you are using the right tool for the job, you should not have to strain to tighten a fastener" applies here.

Beam Type

The beam type torque wrench is one of the most popular types. It consists of a pointer attached to the head that runs the length of the flexible beam (shaft) to a scale located near the handle. As the wrench is pulled, the beam bends and the pointer indicates the torque using the scale.

Click (Breakaway) Type

Another popular design of torque wrench is the click type. To use the click type wrench you pre-adjust it to a torque setting. Once the torque is reached, the wrench has a reflex signaling feature that causes a momentary breakaway of the torque wrench body, sending an impulse to the operator's hand.

Pivot Head Type

▶ See Figure 22

Some torque wrenches (usually of the click type) may be equipped with a pivot head which can allow it to be used in areas of limited access. BUT, it must be used properly. To hold a pivot head wrench, grasp the handle lightly, and as you pull on the handle, it should be floated on the pivot point. If the handle comes in contact with the yoke extension during the process of pulling, there is a very good chance the torque readings will be inaccurate because this could alter the wrench loading point. The design of the handle is usually such as to make it inconvenient to deliberately misuse the wrench.

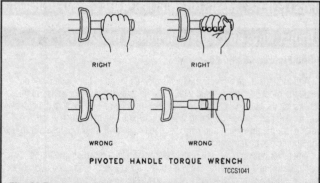

RIGHT   RIGHT

WRONG   WRONG

PIVOTED HANDLE TORQUE WRENCH

TCCS1041

Fig. 22 Torque wrenches with pivoting heads must be grasped and used properly to prevent an incorrect reading

➡️It should be mentioned that the use of any U-joint, wobble or extension will have an effect on the torque readings, no matter what type of wrench you are using. For the most accurate readings, install the socket directly on the wrench driver. If necessary, straight extensions (which hold a socket directly under the wrench driver) will have the least effect on the torque reading. Avoid any extension that alters the length of the wrench from the handle to the head/driving point (such as a crow's foot). U-joint or wobble extensions can greatly affect the readings; avoid their use at all times.

Rigid Case (Direct Reading)

A rigid case or direct reading torque wrench is equipped with a dial indicator to show torque values. One advantage of these wrenches is that they can be held at any position on the wrench without affecting accuracy. These wrenches are often preferred because they tend to be compact, easy to read and have a great degree of accuracy.

TORQUE ANGLE METERS

Because the frictional characteristics of each fastener or threaded hole will vary, clamp loads which are based strictly on torque will vary as well. In most applications, this variance is not significant enough to cause worry. But, in certain applications, a manufacturer's engineers may determine that more precise clamp loads are necessary (such is the case with many aluminum cylinder heads). In these cases, a torque angle method of installation would be specified. When installing fasteners which are torque angle tightened, a predetermined seating torque and standard torque wrench are usually used first to remove any compliance from the joint. The fastener is then tightened the specified additional portion of a turn measured in degrees. A torque angle gauge (mechanical protractor) is used for these applications.

Standard and Metric Measurements

▶ **See Figure 23**

Throughout this manual, specifications are given to help you determine the condition of various components on your vehicle, or to assist you in their installation. Some of the most common measurements include length (in. or cm/mm), torque (ft. lbs., inch lbs. or Nm) and pressure (psi, in. Hg, kPa or mm Hg). In most cases, we strive to provide the proper measurement as determined by the manufacturer's engineers.

Though, in some cases, that value may not be conveniently measured with what is available in your toolbox. Luckily, many of the measuring devices which are available today will have two scales so the Standard or Metric measurements may easily be taken. If any of the various measuring tools which are available to you do not contain the same scale as listed in the specifications, use the accompanying conversion factors to determine the proper value.

SERIAL NUMBER IDENTIFICATION

Vehicle

▶ **See Figures 24 and 25**

The Vehicle Identification Number (VIN) is stamped on a metal plate that is riveted to the instrument panel adjacent to the windshield. It can be seen by looking through the lower corner of the windshield on the driver's side. The VIN number is also stamped on the firewall directly behind the engine.

The VIN is a 17 digit combination of numbers and letters. The first 3 digits represent the world manufacturer identifier which is Mazda. The 5th digit is a passenger car identifier, indicating the vehicle is imported from outside North America or built by another manufacturer in North America for Mazda. The 9th digit is a check digit for all vehicles. The 10th digit indicates the model year: L for 1990, M for 1991, N for 1992, P for 1993, etc. The 11th digit is the assembly plant code. The 12th through 17th digits indicate the production sequence number.

CONVERSION FACTORS

LENGTH–DISTANCE

Inches (in.)	x 25.4	= Millimeters (mm)	x .0394	= Inches
Feet (ft.)	x .305	= Meters (m)	x 3.281	= Feet
Miles	x 1.609	= Kilometers (km)	x .0621	= Miles

VOLUME

Cubic Inches (in3)	x 16.387	= Cubic Centimeters	x .061	= in3
IMP Pints (IMP pt.)	x .568	= Liters (L)	x 1.76	= IMP pt.
IMP Quarts (IMP qt.)	x 1.137	= Liters (L)	x .88	= IMP qt.
IMP Gallons (IMP gal.)	x 4.546	= Liters (L)	x .22	= IMP gal.
IMP Quarts (IMP qt.)	x 1.201	= US Quarts (US qt.)	x .833	= IMP qt.
IMP Gallons (IMP gal.)	x 1.201	= US Gallons (US gal.)	x .833	= IMP gal.
Fl. Ounces	x 29.573	= Milliliters	x .034	= Ounces
US Pints (US pt.)	x .473	= Liters (L)	x 2.113	= Pints
US Quarts (US qt.)	x .946	= Liters (L)	x 1.057	= Quarts
US Gallons (US gal.)	x 3.785	= Liters (L)	x .264	= Gallons

MASS–WEIGHT

Ounces (oz.)	x 28.35	= Grams (g)	x .035	= Ounces
Pounds (lb.)	x .454	= Kilograms (kg)	x 2.205	= Pounds

PRESSURE

Pounds Per Sq. In. (psi)	x 6.895	= Kilopascals (kPa)	x .145	= psi
Inches of Mercury (Hg)	x .4912	= psi	x 2.036	= Hg
Inches of Mercury (Hg)	x 3.377	= Kilopascals (kPa)	x .2961	= Hg
Inches of Water (H₂O)	x .07355	= Inches of Mercury	x 13.783	= H₂O
Inches of Water (H₂O)	x .03613	= psi	x 27.684	= H₂O
Inches of Water (H₂O)	x .248	= Kilopascals (kPa)	x 4.026	= H₂O

TORQUE

Pounds–Force Inches (in–lb)	x .113	= Newton Meters (N·m)	x 8.85	= in–lb
Pounds–Force Feet (ft–lb)	x 1.356	= Newton Meters (N·m)	x .738	= ft–lb

VELOCITY

Miles Per Hour (MPH)	x 1.609	= Kilometers Per Hour (KPH)	x .621	= MPH

POWER

Horsepower (Hp)	x .745	= Kilowatts	x 1.34	= Horsepower

FUEL CONSUMPTION*

Miles Per Gallon IMP (MPG)	x .354	= Kilometers Per Liter (Km/L)	
Kilometers Per Liter (Km/L)	x 2.352	= IMP MPG	
Miles Per Gallon US (MPG)	x .425	= Kilometers Per Liter (Km/L)	
Kilometers Per Liter (Km/L)	x 2.352	= US MPG	

*It is common to covert from miles per gallon (mpg) to liters/100 kilometers (1/100 km), where mpg (IMP) x 1/100 km = 282 and mpg (US) x 1/100 km = 235.

TEMPERATURE

Degree Fahrenheit (°F)	= (°C x 1.8) + 32
Degree Celsius (°C)	= (°F – 32) x .56

TCCS1044

Fig. 23 Standard and metric conversion factors chart

The conversion factor chart is used by taking the given specification and multiplying it by the necessary conversion factor. For instance, looking at the first line, if you have a measurement in inches such as "free-play should be 2 in." but your ruler reads only in millimeters, multiply 2 in. by the conversion factor of 25.4 to get the metric equivalent of 50.8mm. Likewise, if the specification was given only in a Metric measurement, for example in Newton Meters (Nm), then look at the center column first. If the measurement is 100 Nm, multiply it by the conversion factor of 0.738 to get 73.8 ft. lbs.

89541P72

Fig. 24 The VIN number plate can be found on the on the driver side of the dash board, near the windshield

Fig. 25 The VIN number can also be found stamped on the firewall, under the hood

Vehicle Certification Label

The Vehicle Certification Label is attached to the left hand door jamb below the latch striker. The label contains the name of the manufacturer, month and year of manufacture, Gross Vehicle Weight Rating (GVWR), Gross Axle Weight Rating (GAWR), and the certification statement. The vehicle certification label also contains the VIN and the paint color code.

Engine Identification Label

▶ See Figure 26

The engine identification number label is located on the engine block.

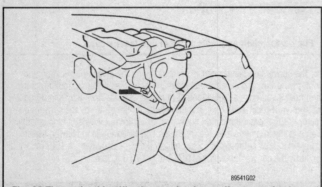

Fig. 26 The engine identification number is usually stamped onto a machined flat surface of the engine block

Transaxle

▶ See Figures 27 and 28

The transaxle identification label can be found either on the top of the transaxle or on the right side.

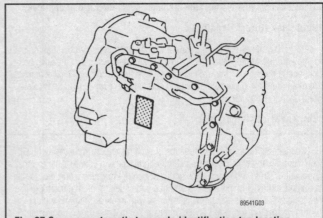

Fig. 27 Common automatic transaxle identification tag location

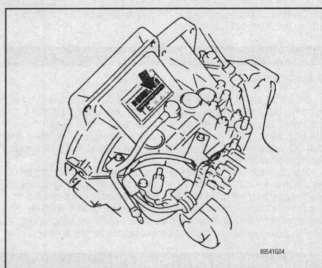

Fig. 28 Common manual transaxle identification tag location

VEHICLE IDENTIFICATION CHART

Engine Code						Model Year	
Code	Liters	Cu. In. (cc)	Cyl.	Fuel Sys.	Eng. Mfg.	Code	Year
Z5D	1.5	90.8 (1489)	4	MPFI	Mazda	L	1990
B6E	1.6	97.4 (1597)	4	MPFI	Mazda	M	1991
B6ZE	1.6	97.4 (1597)	4	MPFI	Mazda	N	1992
BPE	1.8	112.2 (1839)	4	MPFI	Mazda	P	1993
BPD	1.8	112.2 (1839)	4	MPFI	Mazda	R	1994
K8D	1.8	112.4 (1844)	6	MPFI	Mazda	S	1995
FSD	2.0	121.5 (1991)	4	MPFI	Mazda	T	1996
F2	2.2	133.2 (2184)	4	MPFI	Mazda	V	1997
KJS	2.3	137.2 (2254)	6	MPFI	Mazda	W	1998
KLD	2.5	152.3 (2496)	6	MPFI	Mazda		

MPFI: Multi-Point Fuel Injection

89541C20

ENGINE IDENTIFICATION

Year	Model	Engine Displacement Liters (cc)	Engine Series (ID/VIN)	Fuel System	No. of Cylinders	Engine Type
1995	Protege	1.5 (1489)	Z5D	MPFI	4	DOHC
	MX-3	1.8 (1839)	BPD	MPFI	4	DOHC
		1.6 (1597)	B6ZE	MPFI	4	DOHC
	626	1.8 (1844)	K8D	MPFI	6	DOHC
		2.0 (1991)	FSD	MPFI	4	DOHC
		2.5 (2496)	KLD	MPFI	6	DOHC
	MX-6/Probe	2.0 (1991)	FSD	MPFI	4	DOHC
		2.5 (2496)	KLD	MPFI	6	DOHC
	Millenia	2.5 (2496)	KLD	MPFI	6	DOHC
		2.3 (2254)	KJS	MPFI	6	DOHC
1996	Protege	1.5 (1489)	Z5D	MPFI	4	DOHC
		1.8 (1839)	BPD	MPFI	4	DOHC
	626	2.0 (1991)	FSD	MPFI	4	DOHC
		2.5 (2496)	KLD	MPFI	6	DOHC
	MX-6/Probe	2.0 (1991)	FSD	MPFI	4	DOHC
		2.5 (2496)	KLD	MPFI	6	DOHC
	Millenia	2.5 (2496)	KLD	MPFI	6	DOHC
		2.3 (2254)	KJS	MPFI	6	DOHC
1997	Protege	1.5 (1489)	Z5D	MPFI	4	DOHC
		1.8 (1839)	BPD	MPFI	4	DOHC
	626	2.0 (1991)	FSD	MPFI	4	DOHC
		2.5 (2496)	KLD	MPFI	6	DOHC
	MX-6/Probe	2.0 (1991)	FSD	MPFI	4	DOHC
		2.5 (2496)	KLD	MPFI	6	DOHC
	Millenia	2.5 (2496)	KLD	MPFI	6	DOHC
		2.3 (2254)	KJS	MPFI	6	DOHC
1998	Protege	1.5 (1489)	Z5D	MPFI	4	DOHC
		1.8 (1839)	BPD	MPFI	4	DOHC
	626	2.0 (1991)	FSD	MPFI	4	DOHC
		2.5 (2496)	KLD	MPFI	4	DOHC
	Millenia	2.5 (2496)	KLD	MPFI	6	DOHC
		2.3 (2254)	KJS	MPFI	6	DOHC

89541C22

ENGINE IDENTIFICATION

Year	Model	Engine Displacement Liters (cc)	Engine Series (ID/VIN)	Fuel System	No. of Cylinders	Engine Type
1990	323	1.6 (1597)	B6E	MPFI	4	SOHC
	Protege	1.8 (1839)	BPE	MPFI	4	SOHC
		1.8 (1839)	BPD	MPFI	4	DOHC
	626	2.2 (2184)	F2	MPFI	4	SOHC
		2.2 (2184)	F2	Turbo	4	SOHC
	MX-6	2.2 (2184)	F2	MPFI	4	SOHC
		2.2 (2184)	F2	Turbo	4	SOHC
1991	323	1.6 (1597)	B6E	MPFI	4	SOHC
	Protege	1.8 (1839)	BPE	MPFI	4	SOHC
		1.8 (1839)	BPD	MPFI	4	DOHC
	626	2.2 (2184)	F2	MPFI	4	SOHC
		2.2 (2184)	F2	Turbo	4	SOHC
	MX-6	2.2 (2184)	F2	MPFI	4	SOHC
		2.2 (2184)	F2	Turbo	4	SOHC
1992	323	1.6 (1597)	B6E	MPFI	4	SOHC
	Protege	1.8 (1839)	BPE	MPFI	4	SOHC
		1.8 (1839)	BPD	MPFI	4	DOHC
	MX-3	1.6 (1597)	B6E	MPFI	4	SOHC
		1.8 (1844)	K8D	MPFI	6	DOHC
	626	2.2 (2184)	F2	MPFI	4	SOHC
		2.2 (2184)	F2	Turbo	4	SOHC
	MX-6	2.2 (2184)	F2	MPFI	4	SOHC
		2.2 (2184)	F2	Turbo	4	SOHC
1993	323	1.6 (1597)	B6E	MPFI	4	SOHC
	Protege	1.8 (1839)	BPE	MPFI	4	SOHC
		1.8 (1839)	BPD	MPFI	4	DOHC
	MX-3	1.6 (1597)	B6E	MPFI	4	SOHC
		1.8 (1844)	K8D	MPFI	6	DOHC
	626	2.0 (1991)	FSD	MPFI	4	DOHC
		2.5 (2496)	KLD	MPFI	6	DOHC
	MX-6/Probe	2.0 (1991)	FSD	MPFI	4	DOHC
		2.5 (2496)	KLD	MPFI	6	DOHC
1994	323	1.6 (1597)	B6E	MPFI	4	SOHC ①
	Protege	1.8 (1839)	BPE	MPFI	4	SOHC
		1.8 (1839)	BPD	MPFI	4	DOHC
	MX-3	1.6 (1597)	B6E	MPFI	4	DOHC
		1.8 (1844)	K8D	MPFI	6	DOHC
	626	2.0 (1991)	FSD	MPFI	4	DOHC
		2.5 (2496)	KLD	MPFI	6	DOHC
	MX-6/Probe	2.0 (1991)	FSD	MPFI	4	DOHC
		2.5 (2496)	KLD	MPFI	6	DOHC

MPFI: Multi-Point Fuel Injection
SOHC: Single OverHead Camshaft
DOHC: Double OverHead Camshaft
① California models are B6ZE DOHC engines

89541C21

GENERAL ENGINE SPECIFICATIONS

Year	Engine ID/VIN	Engine Displacement Liters (cc)	Fuel System Type	Net Horsepower @ rpm	Net Torque @ rpm (ft. lbs.)	Bore x Stroke (in.)	Compression Ratio	Oil Pressure (lbs. @ rpm)
1998	Z5D	1.5 (1489)	MPFI	92 @ 5500	96 @ 4000	2.96 x 3.29	9.4:1	43-57 @ 3000
	BPD	1.8 (1839)	MPFI	122 @ 6000	117 @ 4000	3.27 x 3.35	9.0:1	43-57 @ 3000
	FSD	2.0 (1991)	MPFI	125 @ 5000	127 @ 3000	3.30 x 3.60	9.0:1	57-71 @ 3000
	KLD	2.5 (2496)	MPFI	[6]	[7]	3.30 x 2.90	9.2:1	49-71 @ 3000
	KJS	2.3 (2254)	MPFI	210 @ 5300	210 @ 3500	3.16 x 2.92	10.0:1	44-66 @ 3000

MPFI: Multi-Port Fuel Injection

[1] 323 Models = 82 @ 5000
MX-3 Model = 88 @ 5000
[2] 323 Models = 92 @ 2500
[3] 323 Models = 98 @ 2500
[4] 323 Federal models: 82 @ 5000
323 California models: 88 @ 5000
MX-3 Model = 105 @ 6200
[5] 323 Federal models: 92 @ 2500
323 California models: 98 @ 2500
MX-3 Model = 100 @ 3700

Turbo: Turbocharged

[1] M x -626 Models = 164 @ 5600
Millenia Models = 170 @ 5800
[6] M x -626 Models = 170 @ 6000
Millenia Models = 170 @ 5800
[7] M x -626 Models = 163 @ 5000
Millenia Models = 160 @ 4800

89541C05

GENERAL ENGINE SPECIFICATIONS

Year	Engine ID/VIN	Engine Displacement Liters (cc)	Fuel System Type	Net Horsepower @ rpm	Net Torque @ rpm (ft. lbs.)	Bore x Stroke (in.)	Compression Ratio	Oil Pressure (lbs. @ rpm)
1990	B6E	1.6 (1597)	MPFI	82 @ 5000	92 @ 2500	3.07 x 3.29	9.3:1	43-57 @ 3000
	BPE	1.8 (1839)	MPFI	103 @ 5500	111 @ 4000	3.27 x 3.35	8.9:1	43-57 @ 3000
	BPD	1.8 (1839)	MPFI	125 @ 6500	114 @ 4500	3.27 x 3.35	9.0:1	43-57 @ 3000
	F2	2.2 (2184)	MPFI	110 @ 4700	130 @ 3000	3.39 x 3.70	8.6:1	43-57 @ 3000
	F2	2.2 (2184)	Turbo	145 @ 4300	190 @ 3500	3.39 x 3.70	7.8:1	43-57 @ 3000
1991	B6E	1.6 (1597)	MPFI	82 @ 5000	92 @ 2500	3.07 x 3.29	9.3:1	43-57 @ 3000
	BPE	1.8 (1839)	MPFI	103 @ 5500	111 @ 4000	3.27 x 3.35	8.9:1	43-57 @ 3000
	BPD	1.8 (1839)	MPFI	125 @ 6500	114 @ 4500	3.27 x 3.35	9.0:1	43-57 @ 3000
	F2	2.2 (2184)	MPFI	110 @ 4700	130 @ 3000	3.39 x 3.70	8.6:1	43-57 @ 3000
	F2	2.2 (2184)	Turbo	145 @ 4300	190 @ 3500 [2]	3.39 x 3.70	7.8:1	43-57 @ 3000
1992	B6E	1.6 (1597)	MPFI	[1]	92 @ 2500	3.07 x 3.29	9.3:1	43-57 @ 3000
	BPE	1.8 (1839)	MPFI	103 @ 5500	111 @ 4000	3.27 x 3.35	8.9:1	43-57 @ 3000
	BPD	1.8 (1839)	MPFI	125 @ 6500	114 @ 4500	3.27 x 3.35	9.0:1	43-57 @ 3000
	K8D	1.8 (1844)	MPFI	130 @ 6500	115 @ 4500	2.95 x 2.74	9.2:1	48-71 @ 3000
	F2	2.2 (2184)	MPFI	110 @ 4700	130 @ 3000	3.39 x 3.70	8.6:1	43-57 @ 3000
	F2	2.2 (2184)	Turbo	145 @ 4300	190 @ 3500 [2]	3.39 x 3.70	7.8:1	43-57 @ 3000
1993	B6E	1.6 (1597)	MPFI	[1]	92 @ 2500	3.07 x 3.29	9.3:1	43-57 @ 3000
	BPE	1.8 (1839)	MPFI	103 @ 5500	111 @ 4000	3.27 x 3.35	8.9:1	43-57 @ 3000
	BPD	1.8 (1839)	MPFI	125 @ 6500	114 @ 4500	3.27 x 3.35	9.0:1	43-57 @ 3000
	K8D	1.8 (1844)	MPFI	130 @ 6500	115 @ 4500	2.95 x 2.74	9.2:1	48-71 @ 3000
	FSD	2.0 (1991)	MPFI	118 @ 5500	127 @ 4500	3.30 x 3.60	9.0:1	57-71 @ 3000
	KLD	2.5 (2496)	MPFI	164 @ 5600	160 @ 4800	3.30 x 2.90	9.2:1	49-71 @ 3000
1994	B6E/B6ZE	1.6 (1597)	MPFI	[4]	92 @ 2500	3.07 x 3.29	9.3:1	43-57 @ 3000
	BPE	1.8 (1839)	MPFI	103 @ 5500	111 @ 4000	3.27 x 3.35	8.9:1	43-57 @ 3000
	BPD	1.8 (1839)	MPFI	125 @ 6500	114 @ 4500	3.27 x 3.35	9.0:1	43-57 @ 3000
	K8D	1.8 (1844)	MPFI	130 @ 6500	115 @ 4500	2.95 x 2.74	9.2:1	48-71 @ 3000
	FSD	2.0 (1991)	MPFI	118 @ 5500	127 @ 4500	3.30 x 3.60	9.0:1	57-71 @ 3000
	KLD	2.5 (2496)	MPFI	164 @ 5600	160 @ 4800	3.30 x 2.90	9.2:1	49-71 @ 3000
1995	Z5D	1.5 (1489)	MPFI	92 @ 5500	96 @ 4000	2.96 x 3.29	9.4:1	44-66 @ 3000
	B6ZE	1.6 (1597)	MPFI	105 @ 6200	100 @ 3700	3.07 x 3.29	9.0:1	43-57 @ 3000
	BPD	1.8 (1839)	MPFI	122 @ 6000	117 @ 4000	3.27 x 3.35	9.0:1	43-57 @ 3000
	K8D	1.8 (1844)	MPFI	130 @ 6500	115 @ 4500	2.95 x 2.74	9.2:1	48-71 @ 3000
	FSD	2.0 (1991)	MPFI	118 @ 5500	127 @ 4500	3.30 x 3.60	9.2:1	49-71 @ 3000
	KJS	2.5 (2496)	MPFI	164 @ 5600	160 @ 4800	3.30 x 2.90	9.2:1	49-71 @ 3000
1996	KLD	2.3 (2254)	MPFI	210 @ 5300	210 @ 3500	3.16 x 2.92	10.0:1	44-66 @ 3000
	Z5D	1.5 (1489)	MPFI	92 @ 5500	96 @ 4000	2.96 x 3.29	9.4:1	43-57 @ 3000
	BPD	1.8 (1839)	MPFI	122 @ 6000	117 @ 4000	3.27 x 3.35	9.0:1	43-57 @ 3000
	FSD	2.0 (1991)	MPFI	114 @ 5500	124 @ 4500	3.30 x 3.60	9.0:1	57-71 @ 3000
	KLD	2.5 (2496)	MPFI	[5]	160 @ 4800	3.30 x 2.90	9.2:1	49-71 @ 3000
	KJS	2.3 (2254)	MPFI	210 @ 5300	210 @ 3500	3.16 x 2.92	10.0:1	44-66 @ 3000
1997	Z5D	1.5 (1489)	MPFI	92 @ 5500	96 @ 4000	2.96 x 3.29	9.4:1	43-57 @ 3000
	BPD	1.8 (1839)	MPFI	122 @ 6000	117 @ 4000	3.27 x 3.35	9.0:1	43-57 @ 3000
	FSD	2.0 (1991)	MPFI	114 @ 5500	124 @ 4500	3.30 x 3.60	9.0:1	57-71 @ 3000
	KLD	2.5 (2496)	MPFI	[5]	160 @ 4800	3.30 x 2.90	9.2:1	49-71 @ 3000
	KJS	2.3 (2254)	MPFI	210 @ 5300	210 @ 3500	3.16 x 2.92	10.0:1	44-66 @ 3000

89541C04

ROUTINE MAINTENANCE AND TUNE-UP

UNDERHOOD MAINTENANCE COMPONENT LOCATIONS

1. Windshield washer tank
2. Radiator cap
3. Power steering pump reservoir
4. Engine oil dipstick
5. Spark plug and wire

6. Distributor cap
7. PCV valve
8. Engine oil fill cap
9. Transmission fluid dipstick
10. Air filter housing

11. Brake fluid reservoir
12. Battery
13. Coolant overflow tank

89541P00

Proper maintenance and tune-up is the key to long and trouble-free vehicle life, and the work can yield its own rewards. Studies have shown that a properly tuned and maintained vehicle can achieve better gas mileage than an out-of-tune vehicle. As a conscientious owner and driver, set aside a Saturday morning, say once a month, to check or replace items which could cause major problems later. Keep your own personal log to jot down which services you performed, how much the parts cost you, the date, and the exact odometer reading at the time. Keep all receipts for such items as engine oil and filters, so that they may be referred to in case of related problems or to determine operating expenses. As a do-it-yourselfer, these receipts are the only proof you have that the required maintenance was performed. In the event of a warranty problem, these receipts will be invaluable.

The literature provided with your vehicle when it was originally delivered includes the factory recommended maintenance schedule. If you no longer have this literature, replacement copies are usually available from the dealer. A maintenance schedule is provided later in this section, in case you do not have the factory literature.

Air Cleaner

The air cleaner is a paper element contained in a housing located in the engine compartment. The air filter element should be serviced according to the Maintenance Intervals Chart at the end of this Section.

➥Check the air filter element more often if the vehicle is operated under severe dusty conditions and replace, as necessary

REMOVAL & INSTALLATION

▶ See Figures 29 thru 34

1. Ensure that the ignition is in the **OFF** position.
2. If necessary, loosen the air intake hose clamp.
3. Disconnect the airflow meter electrical connector from the cover.

4. Remove the air cleaner housing cover bolts and/or unclip the air cleaner housing cover clips.
5. Carefully lift the air cleaner housing cover upward to gain access to the filter.
6. If necessary for access, remove the housing cover.
7. Remove the air cleaner element from the housing.
8. Inspect the air cleaner element and replace as necessary.
To install:
9. Clean any dirt or other foreign material from the air filter housing.
10. Install the air filter element and the air filter cover.
11. Install and tighten the housing cover bolts and/or fasten the housing cover clips.
12. Connect the electrical connector to the air flow meter.

Fuel Filter

On all models except the Millenia, the fuel filter is attached to a bracket located in the left rear of the engine compartment, next to or beneath the brake master cylinder fluid reservoir.

On the Millenia, the fuel filter is located beneath an access cover in the trunk. Access to the cover is achieved by removing the trunk mat to expose the cover.

The fuel filter should be serviced according to the Maintenance Intervals Chart at the end of this Section.

REMOVAL & INSTALLATION

✳✳ CAUTION

Do not allow fuel spray or fuel vapors to come in contact with a spark or open flame. Keep a dry chemical fire extinguisher nearby. Never store fuel in an open container due to risk of fire or explosion.

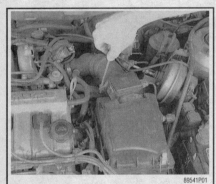

Fig. 29 To remove the air cleaner filter, first loosen the air intake hose clamp

Fig. 30 Detach any electrical wire harness connectors from the air cleaner housing cover . . .

Fig. 31 . . . then unbolt, or unclip, the covers fasteners

Fig. 32 Carefully lift the housing cover upwards then slide the cover sideways to disengage any retaining tabs (arrow)

Fig. 33 If necessary, detach the housing cover from the air intake tube by pulling it outward

Fig. 34 Remove the old air filter element from the housing and inspect it. Clean the inside of the housing of dirt/debris

Except Millenia models

▶ **See Figures 35 and 36**

1. Properly relieve the fuel system pressure.
2. Disconnect the negative battery cable.
3. If necessary, remove the air intake hose and/or filter housing.
4. If equipped, remove the fuel line clamps.
5. Disconnect the fuel lines from the filter and plug the ends to prevent leakage.
6. Loosen the bolt and nut and remove the fuel filter from its mounting bracket. Note the direction of the flow arrow on the filter so the replacement filter can be installed in the correct position.

To install:

7. Install the fuel filter in its mounting bracket, making sure the flow arrow is pointing in the proper direction. Tighten the bracket bolt and nut.
8. Unplug the fuel lines and connect them to the fuel filter.
9. If equipped, install the fuel line clamps.
10. If removed, install the air intake hose and/or filter housing.
11. Connect the negative battery cable.
12. Pressurize the fuel system and check all connections for leaks.

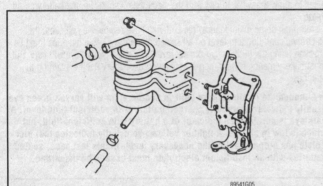

Fig. 35 Exploded view of a common fuel filter and related components

Fig. 36 Access to the fuel filter (arrow) can be difficult. Remove any obstructing components to ease replacement

Millenia Models

▶ **See Figure 37**

1. Insure the ignition is **OFF**. Relieve the fuel system pressure.
2. Disconnect the negative battery cable.
3. Open the trunk, and remove the trunk mat.
4. Remove the service hole cover.
5. Disconnect the fuel lines from both ends of the fuel filter. Plug the lines to prevent leakage.
6. Remove the nut from the fuel filter bracket, and remove the filter and bracket from the vehicle.
7. Remove the filter from the mounting bracket.

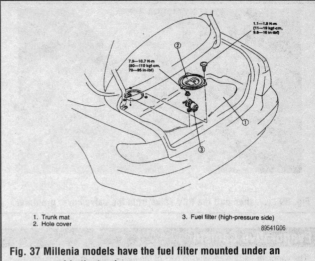

1. Trunk mat
2. Hole cover
3. Fuel filter (high-pressure side)

89541G06

Fig. 37 Millenia models have the fuel filter mounted under an access panel in the trunk

To install:

8. Position the filter in the mounting bracket.
9. Install and tighten the bracket nut to 70–95 inch lbs. (8–11 Nm).
10. Unplug the fuel lines and connect them to the filter.
11. Install the service hole cover.
12. Replace the trunk mat, and close the trunk.
13. Connect the negative battery cable.
14. Run the engine and check for any fuel leaks.

PCV Valve

The PCV valve is located in a grommet attached to the valve cover. For crankcase ventilation system testing, refer to Section 4.

REMOVAL & INSTALLATION

▶ **See Figures 38 and 39**

1. Remove the PCV valve from the valve cover grommet.
2. Disconnect the hose from the PCV valve and remove it from the vehicle.
3. Check the PCV valve for deposits and clogging. If the valve rattles when shaken, it is okay. If the valve does not rattle, clean the valve with solvent until the plunger is free, or replace it.
4. Check the PCV hose and the valve cover grommet for clogging and signs of wear or deterioration. Replace, as necessary.

To install:

5. Connect the PCV hose to the PCV valve.
6. Install the PCV valve in the valve cover grommet.

Fig. 38 To remove the PCV valve, first detach the vacuum hose from the valve . . .

Fig. 39 . . . then pull the PCV valve from the valve cover grommet

Evaporative Canister

The vapor, or carbon canister is part of the evaporative emission control system. It is located in the right rear of the engine compartment.

SERVICING

Servicing the carbon canister is only necessary if it is clogged or contains liquid fuel, indicated by odor or by excessive weight. Remove the canister and blow into the air vent in the bottom of the canister. If air passes from the fuel vapor inlet and the canister does not contain liquid fuel, it is okay. If replacement is necessary, the canister must be replaced as a unit; it cannot be disassembled. For further evaporative emission control system testing, refer to Section 4.

Battery

PRECAUTIONS

Always use caution when working on or near the battery. Never allow a tool to bridge the gap between the negative and positive battery terminals. Also, be careful not to allow a tool to provide a ground between the positive cable/terminal and any metal component on the vehicle. Either of these conditions will cause a short circuit, leading to sparks and possible personal injury.

Do not smoke or all open flames/sparks near a battery; the gases contained in the battery are very explosive and, if ignited, could cause severe injury or death.

All batteries, regardless of type, should be carefully secured by a battery hold-down device. If not, the terminals or casing may crack from stress during vehicle operation. A battery which is not secured may allow acid to leak, making it discharge faster. The acid can also eat away at components under the hood.

Always inspect the battery case for cracks, leakage and corrosion. A white corrosive substance on the battery case or on nearby components would indicate a leaking or cracked battery. If the battery is cracked, it should be replaced immediately.

GENERAL MAINTENANCE

Always keep the battery cables and terminals free of corrosion. Check and clean these components about once a year.

Keep the top of the battery clean, as a film of dirt can help discharge a battery that is not used for long periods. A solution of baking soda and water may be used for cleaning, but be careful to flush this off with clear water. DO NOT let any of the solution into the filler holes. Baking soda neutralizes battery acid and will de-activate a battery cell.

Batteries in vehicles which are not operated on a regular basis can fall victim to parasitic loads (small current drains which are constantly drawing current from the battery). Normal parasitic loads may drain a battery on a vehicle that is in storage and not used for 6–8 weeks. Vehicles that have additional acces-

sories such as a phone or an alarm system may discharge a battery sooner. If the vehicle is to be stored for longer periods in a secure area and the alarm system is not necessary, the negative battery cable should be disconnected to protect the battery.

Remember that constantly deep cycling a battery (completely discharging and recharging it) will shorten battery life.

BATTERY FLUID

♦ See Figure 40

Check the battery electrolyte level at least once a month, or more often in hot weather or during periods of extended vehicle operation. On non-sealed batteries, the level can be checked either through the case (if translucent) or by removing the cell caps. The electrolyte level in each cell should be kept filled to the split ring inside each cell, or the line marked on the outside of the case.

If the level is low, add only distilled water through the opening until the level is correct. Each cell must be checked and filled individually. Distilled water should be used, because the chemicals and minerals found in most drinking water are harmful to the battery and could significantly shorten its life.

If water is added in freezing weather, the vehicle should be driven several miles to allow the water to mix with the electrolyte. Otherwise, the battery could freeze.

Although some maintenance-free batteries have removable cell caps, the electrolyte condition and level on all sealed maintenance-free batteries must be checked using the built-in hydrometer "eye." The exact type of eye will vary. But, most battery manufacturers, apply a sticker to the battery itself explaining the readings.

➡**Although the readings from built-in hydrometers will vary, a green eye usually indicates a properly charged battery with sufficient fluid level. A dark eye is normally an indicator of a battery with sufficient fluid, but which is low in charge. A light or yellow eye usually indicates that electrolyte has dropped below the necessary level. In this last case, sealed batteries with an insufficient electrolyte must usually be discarded.**

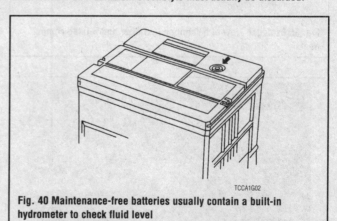

Fig. 40 Maintenance-free batteries usually contain a built-in hydrometer to check fluid level

Checking the Specific Gravity

♦ See Figures 41, 42 and 43

A hydrometer is required to check the specific gravity on all batteries that are not maintenance-free. On batteries that are maintenance-free, the specific gravity is checked by observing the built-in hydrometer "eye" on the top of the battery case.

✳✳ CAUTION

Battery electrolyte contains sulfuric acid. If you should splash any on your skin or in your eyes, flush the affected area with plenty of clear water. If it lands in your eyes, get medical help immediately.

Fig. 41 On non-sealed batteries, the fluid level can be checked by removing the cell caps

Fig. 42 If the fluid level is low, add only distilled water until the level is correct

Fig. 43 Check the specific gravity of the battery's electrolyte with a hydrometer

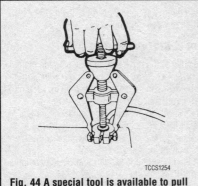

Fig. 44 A special tool is available to pull the clamp from the post

Fig. 45 The underside of this special battery tool has a wire brush to clean post terminals

Fig. 46 Place the tool over the battery posts and twist to clean until the metal is shiny

The fluid (sulfuric acid solution) contained in the battery cells will tell you many things about the condition of the battery. Because the cell plates must be kept submerged below the fluid level in order to operate, the fluid level is extremely important. And, because the specific gravity of the acid is an indication of electrical charge, testing the fluid can be an aid in determining if the battery must be replaced. A battery in a vehicle with a properly operating charging system should require little maintenance, but careful, periodic inspection should reveal problems before they leave you stranded.

At least once a year, check the specific gravity of the battery. It should be between 1.20 and 1.26 on the gravity scale. Most auto stores carry a variety of inexpensive battery hydrometers. These can be used on any non-sealed battery to test the specific gravity in each cell.

The battery testing hydrometer has a squeeze bulb at one end and a nozzle at the other. Battery electrolyte is sucked into the hydrometer until the float is lifted from its seat. The specific gravity is then read by noting the position of the float. If gravity is low in one or more cells, the battery should be slowly charged and checked again to see if the gravity has come up. Generally, if after charging, the specific gravity between any two cells varies more than 50 points (0.50), the battery should be replaced, as it can no longer produce sufficient voltage to guarantee proper operation.

CABLES

▶ **See Figures 44, 45, 46 and 47**

Once a year (or as necessary), the battery terminals and the cable clamps should be cleaned. Loosen the clamps and remove the cables, negative cable first. On top post batteries, the use of a puller specially made for this purpose is recommended. These are inexpensive and available in most parts stores. Side terminal battery cables are secured with a small bolt.

Clean the cable clamps and the battery terminal with a wire brush, until all corrosion, grease, etc., is removed and the metal is shiny. It is especially important to clean the inside of the clamp thoroughly (an old knife is useful here), since a small deposit of oxidation there will prevent a sound connection and

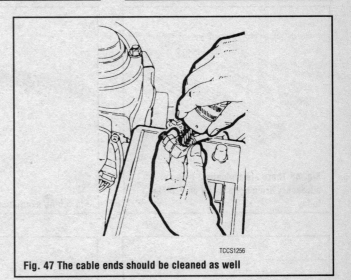

Fig. 47 The cable ends should be cleaned as well

inhibit starting or charging. Special tools are available for cleaning these parts, one type for conventional top post batteries and another type for side terminal batteries. It is also a good idea to apply some dielectric grease to the terminal, as this will aid in the prevention of corrosion.

After the clamps and terminals are clean, reinstall the cables, negative cable last; DO NOT hammer the clamps onto battery posts. Tighten the clamps securely, but do not distort them. Give the clamps and terminals a thin external coating of grease after installation, to retard corrosion.

Check the cables at the same time that the terminals are cleaned. If the cable insulation is cracked or broken, or if the ends are frayed, the cable should be replaced with a new cable of the same length and gauge.

CHARGING

☼☼ CAUTION

The chemical reaction which takes place in all batteries generates explosive hydrogen gas. A spark can cause the battery to explode and splash acid. To avoid personal injury, be sure there is proper ventilation and take appropriate fire safety precautions when working with or near a battery.

A battery should be charged at a slow rate to keep the plates inside from getting too hot. However, if some maintenance-free batteries are allowed to discharge until they are almost ìdead," they may have to be charged at a high rate to bring them back to ìlife." Always follow the charger manufacturer's instructions on charging the battery.

REPLACEMENT

When it becomes necessary to replace the battery, select one with an amperage rating equal to or greater than the battery originally installed. Deterioration and just plain aging of the battery cables, starter motor, and associated wires makes the battery's job harder in successive years. This makes it prudent to install a new battery with a greater capacity than the old.

Belts

INSPECTION

▶ **See Figures 48, 49, 50, 51 and 52**

Inspect the belts for signs of glazing or cracking. A glazed belt will be perfectly smooth from slippage, while a good belt will have a slight texture of fabric visible. Cracks will usually start at the inner edge of the belt and run outward. All worn or damaged drive belts should be replaced immediately. It is best to replace all drive belts at one time, as a preventive maintenance measure, during this service operation.

ADJUSTMENT

▶ **See Figures 53, 54, 55 and 56**

1990–94 1.6L and 1.8L 4-Cylinder Engines

ALTERNATOR BELT

1. Position a ruler perpendicular to the drive belt midway between the pulleys on the longest accessible belt span. Press firmly on the belt with your thumb to test the belt tension. The belt should deflect 0.31–0.35 in. (8–9mm) if it is new or 0.35–0.39 in. (9–10mm) for a used belt.
2. If the belt tension is not as specified in Step 1, loosen the alternator adjustment bolt and the through bolt. Turn the alternator adjustment screw to adjust the belt tension.
3. After adjustment, tighten the through bolt to 27–38 ft. lbs. (37–52 Nm) and the adjusting bolt to 14–19 ft. lbs. (19–25 Nm).

POWER STEERING AND AIR CONDITIONING BELT

1. Position a ruler perpendicular to the drive belt midway between the pulleys on the longest accessible belt span. Press firmly on the belt with your thumb to test the belt tension. The belt should deflect 0.31–0.35 in. (8–9mm) if it is new or 0.35–0.39 in. (9–10mm) if it is used.
2. If the belt tension is not as specified in Step 1, loosen the upper and lower air conditioning compressor through bolts.
3. Using a suitable prybar against the compressor body, move the compressor until the belt tension is as specified in Step 1.
4. After adjustment, tighten the upper and lower air conditioning compressor through bolts.

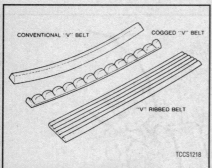

Fig. 48 There are typically 3 types of accessory drive belts found on vehicles today

Fig. 49 An example of a healthy drive belt

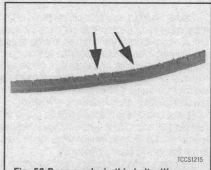

Fig. 50 Deep cracks in this belt will cause flex, building up heat that will eventually lead to belt failure

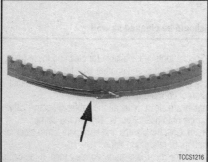

Fig. 51 The cover of this belt is worn, exposing the critical reinforcing cords to excessive wear

Fig. 52 Installing too wide a belt can result in serious belt wear and/or breakage

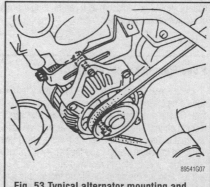

Fig. 53 Typical alternator mounting and drive belt adjustment points

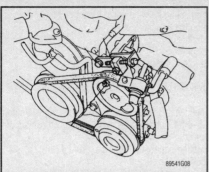

Fig. 54 Typical power steering and A/C compressor mounting and drive belt adjustment points

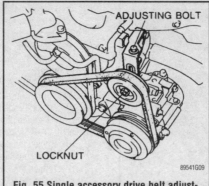

Fig. 55 Single accessory drive belt adjustment points with idler pulley

Fig. 56 Measure the belt deflection between two pulleys along the longest span

AIR CONDITIONING BELT

1. Position a ruler perpendicular to the drive belt midway between the pulleys on the longest accessible belt span. Press firmly on the belt with your thumb to test the belt tension. The belt should deflect 0.31–0.35 in. (8–9mm) if it is new or 0.35–0.39 in. (9–10mm) if it is used.

2. If the belt tension is not as specified in Step 1, loosen the upper and lower air conditioning compressor through bolts.

3. Using a suitable prybar against the compressor body, move the compressor until the belt tension is as specified in Step 1.

4. After adjustment, tighten the upper and lower air conditioning compressor through bolts.

1995 1.6L Engines

POWER STEERING

➡This belt includes the air conditioner compressor, if equipped.

1. Turn the ignition **OFF** and remove the key. Allow the engine to cool.
2. Remove the power steering pump belt shield.
3. Without A/C, loosen the adjusting bolt, lockbolt, and through-bolt. With A/C, loosen the adjusting bolt and the locknut.
4. Remove the power steering belt.

To install:

5. Install the power steering belt and make sure it is correctly lined up on the pulley.

6. Adjust the power steering belt tension/deflection by turning the adjusting bolt. A new belt should deflect 0.32–0.35 inch (8–9mm), and a used belt should deflect 0.36–0.39 inch (9–10mm).

7. Without A/C, tighten the lockbolt to 24–33 ft. lbs. (32–46 Nm). Tighten the through-bolt to 14–18 ft. lbs. (19–25 Nm). With A/C, tighten the locknut to 24–25 ft. lbs. (32–34 Nm).

8. Install the belt shield and tighten the attaching bolts to 61–86 inch lbs. (7–9 Nm).

ALTERNATOR

1. Turn the ignition **OFF** and remove the key. Allow the engine to cool.
2. Remove the power steering belt.
3. Loosen the alternator adjusting bolt and upper mounting bolt.
4. Raise and safely support the vehicle.
5. Remove the right splash shield.
6. Loosen the lower through-bolt.
7. Lower the vehicle and remove the alternator belt.

To install:

8. Install the alternator belt and make sure it is correctly lined up on the pulley.

9. Adjust the alternator belt deflection by turning the adjusting bolt. A new belt should deflect 0.22–0.27 inch (6–7mm), and a used belt should deflect 0.24–0.29 inch (6–8mm).

10. Tighten the upper mounting bolt to 14–18 ft. lbs. (19–25 Nm).
11. Raise and safely support the vehicle.
12. Tighten the lower through-bolt to 28–38 ft. lbs. (38–51 Nm).
13. Install the right splash shield and tighten the bolts to 71–88 inch lbs. (8–10 Nm).
14. Lower the vehicle.
15. Install the power steering belt.

1993–97 2.0L (FS) Engines

POWER STEERING AND A/C COMPRESSOR

▶ **See Figures 57, 58, 59, 60 and 61**

➡This belt includes the air conditioner compressor, if equipped.

1. Disconnect the negative battery cable.
2. Remove the power steering pump belt shield.
3. Loosen the through-bolt, lockbolt and adjusting bolt.
4. Remove the power steering belt.

Fig. 57 To remove the power steering/A/C compressor belt, first remove the belt shield attaching bolts (arrows) and shield

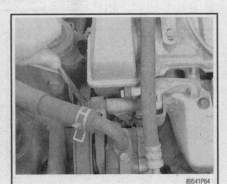

Fig. 58 Next, loosen the power steering pump through or upper pivot bolt . . .

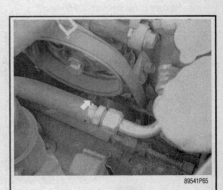

Fig. 59 . . . and the adjuster lockbolt (arrow)

Fig. 60 Loosen the adjuster bolt and relieve the tension from the drive belt

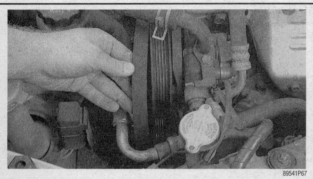

Fig. 61 Remove the power steering/A/C compressor drive belt by disengaging it from all related engine pulleys

To install:

5. Install the power steering belt and make sure it is correctly lined up on the pulley.

6. Adjust the power steering belt tension/deflection. A new belt should deflect 0.30–0.35 inch (8–9 mm), and a used belt should deflect 0.32–0.37 inch (8–10 mm).

7. Tighten the lockbolt to 24–34 ft. lbs. (32–46 Nm).

8. Tighten the through-bolt to 32–44 ft. lbs. (44–60 Nm).

9. Install the belt shield and tighten the attaching bolts to 61–86 inch lbs. (7–9 Nm).

10. Connect the negative battery cable.

ALTERNATOR

▶ See Figures 62, 63, 64 and 65

1. Disconnect the negative battery cable.
2. Remove the power steering belt.

3. Loosen the alternator adjusting bolt and upper mounting bolt.
4. Raise and safely support the vehicle.
5. Remove the RH splash shield.
6. Loosen the lower through-bolt.
7. Lower the vehicle and remove the alternator belt.

To install:

8. Install the alternator belt and make sure it is correctly lined up on the pulley.

9. Adjust the alternator belt tension/deflection by turning the adjusting bolt. A new belt should deflect 0.26–0.27 inch (6.5–7.0 mm), and a used belt should deflect 0.27–0.35 inch (7–9 mm).

10. Tighten the upper mounting bolt to 14–18 ft. lbs. (19–25 Nm).

11. Raise and safely support the vehicle.

12. Tighten the lower through-bolt to 28–38 ft. lbs. (38–51 Nm).

13. Install the RH splash shield and tighten the bolts to 71–88 inch lbs. (8–10 Nm).

14. Lower the vehicle.

15. Install the power steering belt.

16. Connect the negative battery cable.

2.2L Engine

ALTERNATOR BELT

1. Position a ruler perpendicular to the drive belt midway between the pulleys on the longest accessible belt span. Press firmly on the belt with your thumb to test the belt tension. The belt should deflect 0.24–0.31 in. (6–8mm) if it is new or 0.27–0.35 in. (7–9mm) if it is used.

2. If the belt tension is not as specified in Step 1, loosen the alternator adjustment bolt and the through bolt. Turn the alternator adjustment screw to adjust the belt tension.

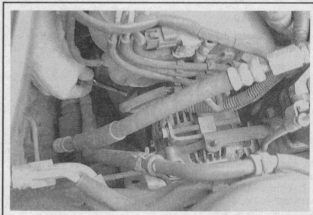

Fig. 62 To remove the alternator belt, first remove the power steering belt, then loosen the lower alternator pivot bolt

Fig. 63 Next loosen the adjuster lockbolt . . .

Fig. 64 . . . then the adjuster bolt and relieve the tension from the alternator drive belt

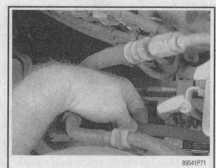

Fig. 65 Remove the alternator drive belt by disengaging it from all related engine pulleys

3. After adjustment, tighten the through bolt to 27–38 ft. lbs. (37–52 Nm) and the adjusting bolt to 13–18 ft. lbs. (18–25 Nm).

POWER STEERING AND AIR CONDITIONING BELT

1. Position a ruler perpendicular to the drive belt midway between the pulleys on the longest accessible belt span. Press firmly on the belt with your thumb to test the belt tension. The belt should deflect 0.27–0.35 in. (7–9mm) if it is new or 0.31–0.39 in. (8–10mm) if it is used.
2. If the belt tension is not as specified in Step 1, loosen the upper and lower air conditioning compressor through bolts.
3. Using a suitable prybar against the compressor body, move the compressor until the belt tension is as specified in Step 1.
4. After adjustment, tighten the upper and lower air conditioning compressor through bolts.

1.8L and 2.5L V6 Engines

ALTERNATOR AND POWER STEERING BELT

1. Position a ruler perpendicular to the drive belt midway between the pulleys on the longest accessible belt span. Press firmly on the belt with your thumb to test the belt tension. The belt should deflect 0.24–0.28 in. (6–7mm) if it is new or 0.28–0.31 in. (7–8mm) if it is used.
2. If the belt tension is not as specified in Step 1, loosen the idler pulley locknut. Turn the alternator adjustment bolt to adjust the belt tension.
3. After adjustment, tighten the idler pulley locknut to 23–41 ft. lbs. (31–46 Nm).

ALTERNATOR AND AIR CONDITIONING BELT

1. Position a ruler perpendicular to the drive belt midway between the pulleys on the longest accessible belt span. Press firmly on the belt with your thumb to test the belt tension. The belt should deflect 0.22–0.26 in. (5.5–6.5mm) if it is new or 0.26–0.30 in. (6.5–7.5mm) if it is used.
2. If the belt tension is not as specified in Step 1, loosen the idler pulley locknut. Turn the adjustment bolt to adjust the belt tension.
3. After adjustment, tighten the idler pulley locknut to 23–34 ft. lbs. (31–46 Nm).

1995–97 2.3L Engines

ALTERNATOR, A/C AND VACUUM PUMP

➡️If the belt is to be reused, mark the direction of normal belt rotation.

1. Switch the ignition **OFF** and remove the key. Allow the engine to cool.
2. Disconnect the negative battery cable.
3. Remove the right-hand splash shield and dust cover.
4. Using a wrench, turn the tensioner pulley locknut clockwise to remove tension on the belt.
5. Remove the belt from each of the pulleys, remove from the vehicle and inspect the belt.

To install:
6. Route the alternator belt around the pulleys.
7. Install the right-hand splash shield and dust cover.
8. Connect the negative battery cable.

POWER STEERING, SUPERCHARGER AND WATER PUMP

➡️If the belt is to be reused, mark the direction of normal belt rotation.

1. Disconnect the negative battery cable.
2. Switch the ignition **OFF** and remove the key. Allow the engine to cool.
3. Remove the right-hand splash shield and dust cover.
4. Remove the alternator belt.
5. Using a wrench, turn the tensioner pulley locknut clockwise to remove tension on the belt.
6. Remove the belt from each of the pulleys, remove from the vehicle and inspect the belt.

To install:
7. Route the power steering drive belt around the pulleys.
8. Install the alternator belt.
9. Install the right-hand splash shield and dust cover.
10. Connect the negative battery cable.

REMOVAL & INSTALLATION

➡️**When removing a belt from the engine, pay attention to its routing (over and under pulleys, etc.) before removing it. Drawing a quick picture may also help.**

Follow the adjustment procedure to loosen the accessory drive belt. Once loose, simply remove the belt from the pulleys. If there is a belt in front of the one you need to remove, follow the adjustment procedures for that accessory as well.

Timing Belts

INSPECTION

◆ **See Figures 66 thru 72**

All Mazda engines covered by this manual, utilize a timing belt to drive the camshaft from the crankshaft's turning motion and to maintain proper valve timing. Some manufacturer's schedule periodic timing belt replacement to assure optimum engine performance, to make sure the motorist is never stranded should the belt break (as the engine will stop instantly) and for some (manufacturer's with interference motors) to prevent the possibility of severe internal engine damage should the belt break.

Although some of these engines are not listed as an interference motor (it is not listed by the manufacturer as a motor whose valves might contact the pistons if the camshaft was rotated separately from the crankshaft) the first 2 reasons for periodic replacement still apply. Mazda recommends replacement every 60,000 miles (96,000 km) for most of their engines. In addition, most belt manufacturers recommend intervals anywhere from 45,000 miles (72,500 km) to 90,000 miles (145,000 km). You will have to decide for yourself if the peace of mind offered by a new belt is worth it on higher mileage engines.

But whether or not you decide to replace it, you would be wise to check it periodically to make sure it has not become damaged or worn. Generally speaking, a severely worn belt may cause engine performance to drop dramatically,

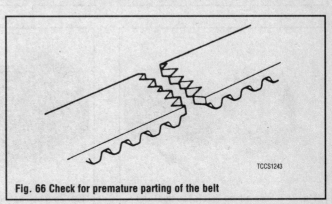

TCCS1243

Fig. 66 Check for premature parting of the belt

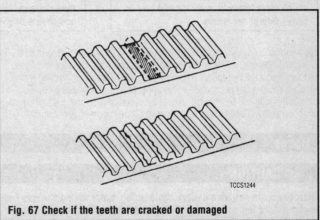

TCCS1244

Fig. 67 Check if the teeth are cracked or damaged

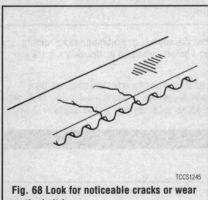

Fig. 68 Look for noticeable cracks or wear on the belt face

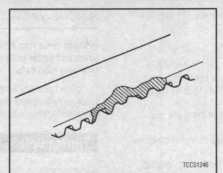

Fig. 69 You may only have damage on one side of the belt; if so, the guide could be the culprit

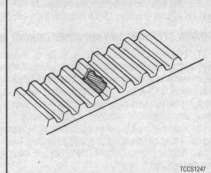

Fig. 70 Foreign materials can get in between the teeth and cause damage

Fig. 71 Inspect the timing belt for cracks, fraying, glazing or damage of any kind

Fig. 72 ALWAYS replace the timing belt at the interval specified by the manufacturer

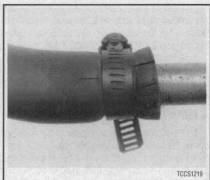

Fig. 73 The cracks developing along this hose are a result of age-related hardening

Fig. 74 A hose clamp that is too tight can cause older hoses to separate and tear on either side of the clamp

Fig. 75 A soft spongy hose (identifiable by the swollen section) will eventually burst and should be replaced

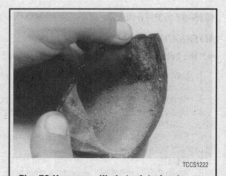

Fig. 76 Hoses are likely to deteriorate from the inside if the cooling system is not periodically flushed

but a damaged belt (which could give out suddenly) may not give as much warning. In general, any time the engine timing cover(s) is(are) removed you should inspect the belt for premature parting, severe cracks or missing teeth. Also, an access plug is provided in the upper portion of the timing cover so that camshaft timing can be checked without cover removal. If timing is found to be off, cover removal and further belt inspection or replacement is necessary.

Hoses

✳✳ CAUTION

Disconnect the negative battery cable or fan motor wiring harness connector before replacing any radiator/heater hose. The fan may come on, under certain circumstances, even though the ignition is off.

INSPECTION

▶ See Figures 73, 74, 75 and 76

Upper and lower radiator hoses along with the heater hoses should be checked for deterioration, leaks and loose hose clamps at least every 30,000 miles (48,000 km). It is also wise to check the hoses periodically in early spring and at the beginning of the fall or winter when you are performing other maintenance. A quick visual inspection could discover a weakened hose which might have left you stranded if it had remained unrepaired.

Whenever you are checking the hoses, make sure the engine and cooling system are cold. Visually inspect for cracking, rotting or collapsed hoses, and replace as necessary. Run your hand along the length of the hose. If a weak or swollen spot is noted when squeezing the hose wall, the hose should be replaced.

REMOVAL & INSTALLATION

1. Remove the radiator pressure cap.

❊❊ CAUTION

Never remove the pressure cap while the engine is running, or personal injury from scalding hot coolant or steam may result. If possible, wait until the engine has cooled to remove the pressure cap. If this is not possible, wrap a thick cloth around the pressure cap and turn it slowly to the stop. Step back while the pressure is released from the cooling system. When you are sure all the pressure has been released, use the cloth to turn and remove the cap.

2. Position a clean container under the radiator and/or engine draincock or plug, then open the drain and allow the cooling system to drain to an appropriate level. For some upper hoses, only a little coolant must be drained. To remove hoses positioned lower on the engine, such as a lower radiator hose, the entire cooling system must be emptied.

❊❊ CAUTION

When draining coolant, keep in mind that cats and dogs are attracted by ethylene glycol antifreeze, and are quite likely to drink any that is left in an uncovered container or in puddles on the ground. This will prove fatal in sufficient quantity. Always drain coolant into a sealable container. Coolant may be reused unless it is contaminated or several years old.

3. Loosen the hose clamps at each end of the hose requiring replacement. Clamps are usually either of the spring tension type (which require pliers to squeeze the tabs and loosen) or of the screw tension type (which require screw or hex drivers to loosen). Pull the clamps back on the hose away from the connection.

4. Twist, pull and slide the hose off the fitting, taking care not to damage the neck of the component from which the hose is being removed.

➡ **If the hose is stuck at the connection, do not try to insert a screwdriver or other sharp tool under the hose end in an effort to free it, as the connection and/or hose may become damaged. Heater connections especially may be easily damaged by such a procedure. If the hose is to be replaced, use a single-edged razor blade to make a slice along the portion of the hose which is stuck on the connection, perpendicular to the end of the hose. Do not cut deep so as to prevent damaging the connection. The hose can then be peeled from the connection and discarded.**

5. Clean both hose mounting connections. Inspect the condition of the hose clamps and replace them, if necessary.
To install:
6. Dip the ends of the new hose into clean engine coolant to ease installation.
7. Slide the clamps over the replacement hose, then slide the hose ends over the connections into position.

8. Position and secure the clamps at least ¼ in. (6.35mm) from the ends of the hose. Make sure they are located beyond the raised bead of the connector.

9. Close the radiator or engine drains and properly refill the cooling system with the clean drained engine coolant or a suitable mixture of ethylene glycol coolant and water.

10. If available, install a pressure tester and check for leaks. If a pressure tester is not available, run the engine until normal operating temperature is reached (allowing the system to naturally pressurize), then check for leaks.

❊❊ CAUTION

If you are checking for leaks with the system at normal operating temperature, BE EXTREMELY CAREFUL not to touch any moving or hot engine parts. Once temperature has been reached, shut the engine OFF, and check for leaks around the hose fittings and connections which were removed earlier.

CV-Boots

INSPECTION

▶ **See Figures 77 and 78**

The CV (Constant Velocity) boots should be checked for damage each time the oil is changed and any other time the vehicle is raised for service. These boots keep water, grime, dirt and other damaging matter from entering the CV-joints. Any of these could cause early CV-joint failure which can be expensive to repair. Heavy grease thrown around the inside of the wheel(s) and on the brake caliper/drum can be an indication of a torn boot. Thoroughly check the boots for missing clamps and tears. If the boot is damaged, it should be replaced immediately. Please refer to Section 7 for procedures.

➡ **Mazda recommends inspecting the CV-boots every 30,000 miles (48,000 km).**

Spark Plugs

▶ **See Figures 79 and 80**

A typical spark plug consists of a metal shell surrounding a ceramic insulator. A metal electrode extends downward through the center of the insulator and protrudes a small distance. Located at the end of the plug and attached to the side of the outer metal shell is the side electrode. The side electrode bends in at a 90° angle so that its tip is just past and parallel to the tip of the center electrode. The distance between these two electrodes (measured in thousandths of an inch or hundredths of a millimeter) is called the spark plug gap.

The spark plug does not produce a spark, but instead provides a gap across which the current can arc. The coil produces anywhere from 20,000 to 50,000 volts (depending on the type and application) which travels through the wires to the spark plugs. The current passes along the center electrode and jumps the gap to the side electrode, and in doing so, ignites the air/fuel mixture in the combustion chamber.

TCCS1011

Fig. 77 CV-boots must be inspected periodically for damage

TCCS1010

Fig. 78 A torn boot should be replaced immediately

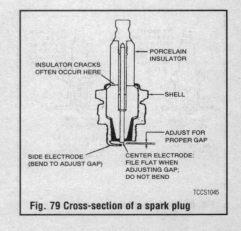

TCCS1045

Fig. 79 Cross-section of a spark plug

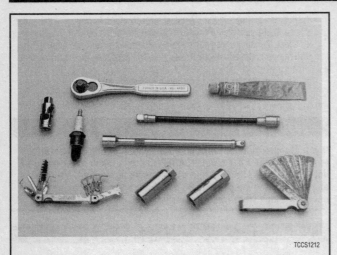

Fig. 80 A variety of tools and gauges are needed for spark plug service

SPARK PLUG HEAT RANGE

▶ See Figure 81

Spark plug heat range is the ability of the plug to dissipate heat. The longer the insulator (or the farther it extends into the engine), the hotter the plug will operate; the shorter the insulator (the closer the electrode is to the block's cooling passages) the cooler it will operate. A plug that absorbs little heat and remains too cool will quickly accumulate deposits of oil and carbon since it is not hot enough to burn them off. This leads to plug fouling and consequently to misfiring. A plug that absorbs too much heat will have no deposits but, due to the excessive heat, the electrodes will burn away quickly and might possibly lead to preignition or other ignition problems. Preignition takes place when plug tips get so hot that they glow sufficiently to ignite the air/fuel mixture before the actual spark occurs. This early ignition will usually cause a pinging during low speeds and heavy loads.

The general rule of thumb for choosing the correct heat range when picking a spark plug is: if most of your driving is long distance, high speed travel, use a colder plug; if most of your driving is stop and go, use a hotter plug. Original equipment plugs are generally a good compromise between the 2 styles and most people never have the need to change their plugs from the factory-recommended heat range.

REMOVAL & INSTALLATION

▶ See Figures 82, 83 and 84

A normal set of spark plugs usually requires replacement after about 20,000–30,000 miles (32,000–48,000 km), depending on your style of driving. In normal operation plug gap increases about 0.001 in. (0.025mm) for every

2500 miles (4000 km). As the gap increases, the plug's voltage requirement also increases. It requires a greater voltage to jump the wider gap and about two to three times as much voltage to fire the plug at high speeds than at idle. The improved air/fuel ratio control of modern fuel injection combined with the higher voltage output of modern ignition systems will often allow an engine to run significantly longer on a set of standard spark plugs, but keep in mind that efficiency will drop as the gap widens (along with fuel economy and power).

➡**Platinum tipped spark plugs usually require replacement after about 50,000–60,000 miles (80,000–96,000 km). However, some manufacturers have recommended replacement at 100,000 miles (160,000 km).**

When you're removing spark plugs, work on one at a time. Don't start by removing the plug wires all at once, because, unless you number them, they may become mixed up. Take a minute before you begin and number the wires with tape.

1. Disconnect the negative battery cable, and if the vehicle has been run recently, allow the engine to thoroughly cool.

2. On all engines except the 2.3L V6, carefully twist the spark plug wire boot to loosen it, then pull upward and remove the boot from the plug. Be sure to pull on the boot and not on the wire, otherwise the connector located inside the boot may become separated.

3. On 2.3L V6 engines, remove the ignition coil as follows:

   a. For the front bank of spark plugs, remove the charge air cooler.

   b. For the rear bank of spark plugs, remove the solenoid bracket assembly.

   c. Detach the ignition coil 4-pin connector.

   d. Remove the ignition coil attaching screws and remove the coil by pulling it straight up.

4. Using compressed air, blow any water or debris from the spark plug well to assure that no harmful contaminants are allowed to enter the combustion chamber when the spark plug is removed. If compressed air is not available, use a rag or a brush to clean the area.

➡**Remove the spark plugs when the engine is cold, if possible, to prevent damage to the threads. If removal of the plugs is difficult, apply a few drops of penetrating oil or silicone spray to the area around the base of the plug, and allow it a few minutes to work.**

5. Using a spark plug socket that is equipped with a rubber insert to properly hold the plug, turn the spark plug counterclockwise to loosen and remove the spark plug from the bore.

✳✳ WARNING

Be sure not to use a flexible extension on the socket. Use of a flexible extension may allow a shear force to be applied to the plug. A shear force could break the plug off in the cylinder head, leading to costly and frustrating repairs.

To install:

6. On all engines except the 2.3L V6, inspect the spark plug boot for tears or damage. If a damaged boot is found, the spark plug wire must be replaced.

7. On 2.3L V6 engines, inspect the coil-to-spark plug connection area for cracks or damage. If damage to the coil is found, replace the assembly.

8. Using a wire feeler gauge, check and adjust the spark plug gap. When

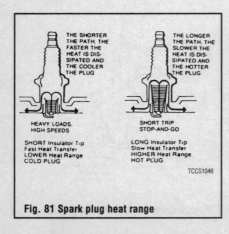

Fig. 81 Spark plug heat range

Fig. 82 To remove a spark plug, first remove the plug wire attached to the plug. Only detach one wire at a time

Fig. 83 Then, using a spark plug socket with a rubber insert, loosen the plug by turning it counterclockwise

using a gauge, the proper size should pass between the electrodes with a slight drag. The next larger size should not be able to pass while the next smaller size should pass freely.

9. Carefully thread the plug into the bore by hand. If resistance is felt before the plug is almost completely threaded, back the plug out and begin threading again. In small, hard to reach areas, an old spark plug wire and boot could be used as a threading tool. The boot will hold the plug while you twist the end of the wire and the wire is supple enough to twist before it would allow the plug to crossthread.

⁕⁕ WARNING

Do not use the spark plug socket to thread the plugs. Always carefully thread the plug by hand or using an old plug wire to prevent the possibility of crossthreading and damaging the cylinder head bore.

10. Carefully tighten the spark plug. If the plug you are installing is equipped with a crush washer, seat the plug, then tighten about ¼ turn to crush the washer. If you are installing a tapered seat plug, tighten the plug to specifications provided by the vehicle or plug manufacturer.

11. On all engines except the 2.3L V6, apply a small amount of silicone dielectric compound to the end of the spark plug lead or inside the spark plug boot to prevent sticking, then install the boot to the spark plug and push until it clicks into place. The click may be felt or heard, then gently pull back on the boot to assure proper contact.

12. On 2.3L V6 engines, install the ignition coil as follows:
   a. Position the ignition coil over the spark plug and press it down firmly to ensure full engagement.
   b. Align the mounting holes and install the coil attaching screws. Tighten the screws to 40–57 inch lbs. (4.5–6.4 Nm).
   c. Attach the ignition coil 4-pin connector.
   d. For the front bank of spark plugs, lubricate the sealing washers and install the charge air cooler. Tighten the attaching nuts to 12–16 ft. lbs. (16–22 Nm).
   e. For the rear bank of spark plugs, install the solenoid bracket assembly.

INSPECTION & GAPPING

▶ **See Figures 85, 86, 87 and 88**

Check the plugs for deposits and wear. If they are not going to be replaced, clean the plugs thoroughly. Remember that any kind of deposit will decrease the efficiency of the plug. Plugs can be cleaned on a spark plug cleaning machine, which can sometimes be found in service stations, or you can do an acceptable job of cleaning with a stiff brush. If the plugs are cleaned, the electrodes must be filed flat. Use an ignition points file, not an emery board or the like, which will leave deposits. The electrodes must be filed perfectly flat with sharp edges; rounded edges reduce the spark plug voltage by as much as 50%.

Check spark plug gap before installation. The ground electrode (the L-shaped one connected to the body of the plug) must be parallel to the center electrode and the specified size wire gauge (please refer to the Tune-Up Specifications chart for details) must pass between the electrodes with a slight drag.

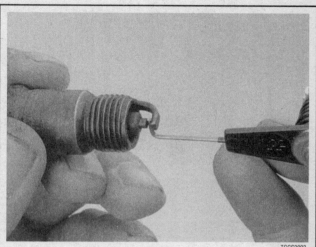

Fig. 85 Checking the spark plug gap with a feeler gauge

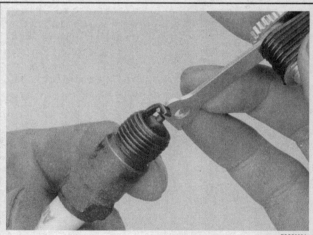

Fig. 86 Adjusting the spark plug gap

Fig. 84 Finally, remove the socket, with plug retained by the insert, and inspect the spark plug

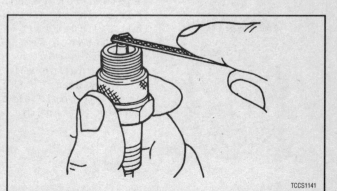

Fig. 87 If the standard plug is in good condition, the electrode may be filed flat—WARNING: do not file platinum plugs

A normally worn spark plug should have light tan or gray deposits on the firing tip.

A carbon fouled plug, identified by soft, sooty, black deposits, may indicate an improperly tuned vehicle. Check the air cleaner, ignition components and engine control system.

This spark plug has been **left in the engine too long,** as evidenced by the extreme gap- Plugs with such an extreme gap can cause misfiring and stumbling accompanied by a noticeable lack of power.

An oil fouled spark plug indicates an engine with worn poston rings and/or bad valve seals allowing excessive oil to enter the chamber.

A physically damaged spark plug may be evidence of severe detonation in that cylinder. Watch that cylinder carefully between services, as a continued detonation will not only damage the plug, but could also damage the engine.

A bridged or almost bridged spark plug, identified by a build-up between the electrodes caused by excessive carbon or oil build-up on the plug.

TCCA1P40

Fig. 88 Inspect the spark plug to determine engine running conditions

➡**NEVER adjust the gap on a used platinum type spark plug.**

Always check the gap on new plugs as they are not always set correctly at the factory. Do not use a flat feeler gauge when measuring the gap on a used plug, because the reading may be inaccurate. A round-wire type gapping tool is the best way to check the gap. The correct gauge should pass through the electrode gap with a slight drag. If you're in doubt, try one size smaller and one larger. The smaller gauge should go through easily, while the larger one shouldn't go through at all. Wire gapping tools usually have a bending tool attached. Use that to adjust the side electrode until the proper distance is obtained. Absolutely never attempt to bend the center electrode. Also, be careful not to bend the side electrode too far or too often as it may weaken and break off within the engine, requiring removal of the cylinder head to retrieve it.

Spark Plug Wires

TESTING

▸ **See Figure 89**

At every tune-up/inspection, visually check the spark plug cables for burns cuts, or breaks in the insulation. Check the boots and the nipples on the distributor cap and/or coil. Replace any damaged wiring.

Every 60,000 miles (96,000 Km) or 60 months, the resistance of the wires should be checked with an ohmmeter. Wires with excessive resistance will cause misfiring, and may make the engine difficult to start in damp weather.

To check resistance, use an ohmmeter and attach the leads to each end of the plug wires connector and read the resistance. The reading should not exceed 16 kohms per 3.28 ft. (1 m). Replace any wires that do not meet the specification.

REMOVAL & INSTALLATION

Except Millenia S Models with 2.3L Engines

▸ **See Figure 90**

Replace the spark plug wires one at a time when installing a new set so there will be no mixup. The longest cable should be replaced first. Make sure that the boot is installed firmly over the spark plug. The wire routing should be exactly the same as the original. Insert the nipple into the tower on the distributor cap and/or coil. Repeat the process for each wire.

Millenia S Models with 2.3L Engines

The Millenia S uses a 2.3L Miller-cycle supercharged engine which utilizes individual coils for each spark plug. There are no plug wires to inspect or change.

Distributor Cap and Rotor

REMOVAL & INSTALLATION

Distributor Cap

▸ **See Figures 91, 92 and 93**

1. As a precaution, label all of the spark plug wires with their perspective cylinder number. Also, matchmark the cap to the distributor body.
2. As necessary, remove any shrouds or air intake piping which may inhibit cap removal.

Fig. 89 Checking individual plug wire resistance with a digital ohmmeter

Fig. 90 Remove plug wires by grasping its boot, not the wire, and, while twisting slightly, pull straight upwards

Fig. 91 To remove the distributor cap, first label the spark plug wires attached to the cap with their cylinder numbers

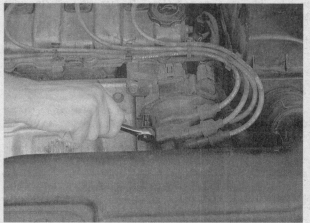

Fig. 92 Loosen the distributor cap attaching bolts. Use care to not drop and possibly loose them

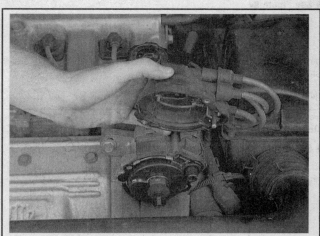

Fig. 93 Lift the cap, wires still attached, from the distributor

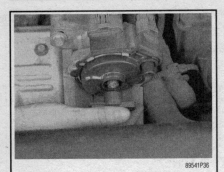

Fig. 94 To remove the distributor rotor, first remove the cap, then pull the rotor straight off the shaft

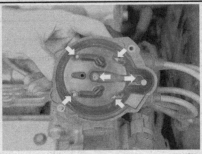

Fig. 95 Thoroughly inspect the cap for signs of damage, wear or corrosion, especially the electrical terminals (arrows)

Fig. 96 Inspect the rotor for signs of damage, wear or corrosion, especially the electrical terminals (arrows)

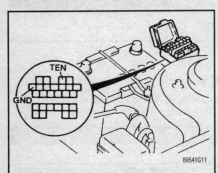

Fig. 97 On all models except 1994–98 626/MX-6/Probe with ATX, jumper the connections shown on the data link

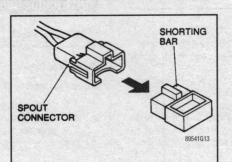

Fig. 98 On 1994–98 626/MX-6/Probe with ATX, remove the shorting bar from the spout connector

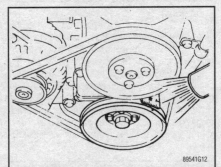

Fig. 99 Connect an inductive timing light and aim it at the crankshaft pulley. Read the pulley mark against the scale

3. Loosen the cap hold-down screws.
4. Remove the cap by lifting straight out to prevent damage to the rotor blade and spring.

➡ If the plug wires do not have enough slack to allow cap removal, confirm that they are properly labeled and remove them from the cap.

5. Installation is the reverse of the removal procedure. Note the position of the square alignment locator and tighten the hold-down screws to 18–23 inch pounds (2.0–2.6Nm)

Distributor Rotor

▶ See Figure 94

1. Remove the distributor cap.
2. Pull straight out on the rotor to disengage it from the shaft and armature.
3. Installation is the reverse of the removal procedure. Align the locating boss on the rotor with the hole on the armature, then insure that it is fully seated on the shaft.

INSPECTION

Distributor Cap

▶ See Figure 95

1. Wash the inside and outside surfaces of the cap with soap and water then dry it with compressed air.
2. Inspect the cap for cracks, broken or worn carbon button, or carbon tracks. Also inspect the cap terminals for dirt and corrosion.
3. Replace the cap if any of the above conditions are observed.

Distributor Rotor

▶ See Figure 96

1. Wash the rotor with soap and water then dry with it compressed air.
2. Inspect the rotor for cracks, carbon tracks, burns or damage to the blade or spring.
3. Replace the rotor if any of the above conditions are observed.

Ignition Timing

➡ If the information given in the following procedures differs from that on the emission information label located in the engine compartment, follow the directions given on the label. The label often reflects production running changes made during the model year.

CHECKING & ADJUSTMENT

Except 2.2L and 2.3L Engines

▶ See Figures 97, 98, 99 and 100

1. Apply the parking brake. If equipped with a manual transaxle, place the shifter in the neutral position. If equipped with an automatic transaxle, place the shift lever in **P**.
2. Locate the timing marks on the crankshaft pulley and timing belt lower cover. The engine may have to be cranked slightly to see the mark on the crankshaft pulley.
3. Start the engine and allow it to come to normal operating temperature. Make sure all accessories are **OFF**.
4. Check the idle speed and adjust, if necessary.

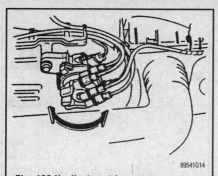

Fig. 100 If adjustment is necessary, loosen the distributor lockbolts and rotate it until the mark is aligned

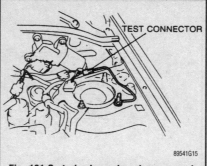

Fig. 101 On turbocharged engines, ground the single wire test connector to set the ignition timing

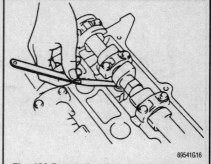

Fig. 102 Ensure that the cam lobe faces away from the follower when checking the valve clearance

5. Turn the engine off.

6. On all engines except 1994–98 2.0L (FS) engines with an automatic transaxle, connect a jumper wire between the TEN terminal and the GND terminal at the underhood diagnosis connector.

7. On 1994–98 2.0L (FS) engines with an automatic transaxle, remove the shorting bar from the double wire SPOUT connector.

8. Connect an inductive timing light according to the manufacturers instructions.

9. Start the engine and allow the idle to stabilize. Aim the timing light at the timing marks.

10. The mark on the crankshaft pulley should align with the specified BTDC degree mark on the timing cover scale, plus or minus 1 degree. If the marks are within alignment proceed with step 12. If the marks are not aligned, proceed to Step 11.

11. Loosen the distributor lock bolts just enough to turn the distributor. While aiming the timing light at the timing marks, turn the distributor until the marks are aligned. Tighten the distributor lock bolts to 14–19 ft. lbs. (19–25 Nm) and recheck the timing.

12. The ignition timing is now set. Disconnect the jumper wire from the underhood diagnosis connector or install the shorting bar from the double wire SPOUT connector.

13. Remove all test equipment.

2.2L Engines

▶ **See Figures 99, 100 and 101**

1. Apply the parking brake. If equipped with manual transaxle, place the shift lever in neutral. If equipped with automatic transaxle, place the shift lever in **P**.

2. Locate the timing marks on the crankshaft pulley and timing belt cover. You may have to crank the engine slightly to see the mark on the crankshaft pulley. If the marks are hard to see, clean them off with some degreasing cleaner and a wire brush.

3. Start the engine and allow it to come to normal operating temperature. Make sure all accessories are **OFF**.

4. Check the idle speed and adjust, if necessary.

5. Shut off the engine.

6. On non-turbocharged engines, disconnect and plug the vacuum hoses at the distributor vacuum diaphragm.

7. On turbocharged engines, connect a jumper wire between the single wire test connector, located near the left strut tower, and ground.

8. Connect an inductive timing light according to the manufacturers instructions.

9. Start the engine and allow the idle to stabilize.

10. The mark on the crankshaft pulley should align with the specified BTDC degree mark on the timing cover scale, plus or minus 1 degree. If the marks are within alignment proceed with step 12. If the marks are not aligned, proceed to Step 11.

11. Loosen the distributor lock bolt just enough to turn the distributor housing. While aiming the timing light at the timing marks, turn the distributor until the marks are aligned. Tighten the distributor lock bolt to 14–19 ft. lbs. (19–25 Nm) and recheck the timing.

12. Initial timing is now set. Disconnect the timing light from the engine.

13. On non-turbocharged engines, remove the plugs from the vacuum hoses and reconnect them to the distributor vacuum diaphragm.

14. On turbocharged engines, disconnect the jumper wire at the test connector.

2.3L Engines

The 2.3L engine (VIN KJ) utilizes individual ignition coils for each cylinder and the timing is controlled by the computer. Ignition timing adjustment is not possible or necessary.

Valve Lash

ADJUSTMENT

Except 1.5L, 2.3L, 1997–98 1.8L (BPD) and 1998 2.0L and 2.5L Engines

The valve lash on all engines is kept in adjustment hydraulically. No adjustment is necessary, or possible.

1.5L, 2.3L, 1997–98 1.8L (BPD) and 1998 2.0L and 2.5L Engines

These engines use solid cam followers with a removable adjustment shim. The valve lash clearance is measured with the original shim installed and checked against the specification. If adjustment is necessary, the original shim is removed, and a thicker or thinner shim is installed to obtain the proper clearance. Special tools are required in order to adjust the shim without removing the camshaft.

1.5L, 1997–98 1.8L (BPD) and 1998 2.0L Engines

▶ **See Figures 102, 103, 104, 105 and 106**

➡**With the engine cold, standard valve clearance is 0.010ñ0.012 in. (0.25–0.31mm) on intake and exhaust sides.**

1. Remove the cylinder head cover.

2. Measure the valve clearance by turning the crankshaft clockwise until the No. 1 piston is at TDC.

3. Measure the valve clearance at **A**. If the clearance exceeds specifications, replace the adjustment shim.

4. Turn the crankshaft clockwise 360 degrees until the No. 4 piston is at TDC. Measure the valve clearance at **B**. If the clearance exceeds specifications, replace the adjustment shim.

5. Repeat this procedure for all the camshafts.

6. Turn the crankshaft clockwise until the cam on the camshaft requiring the adjustment is positioned straight up.

7. Remove the camshaft cap bolts as follows:

8. For exhaust side No. 1, 2, and 3 cylinder adjustment shim removal use **A**.

9. For intake side No. 1, 2, and 3 cylinder adjustment shim removal use **B**.

10. For exhaust side No. 2, 3, and 4 cylinder adjustment shim removal use **C**.

11. For intake side No. 2, 3, and 4 cylinder adjustment shim removal use **D**.

12. Install special tools 49-T012-002 and 003, using the camshaft cap bolt holes. Torque the bolts to 100–125 inch lbs. (11–14 Nm).

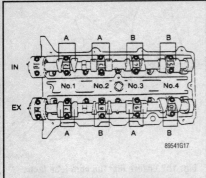

Fig. 103 Mazda 4-cylinder engines valve clearance checking positions

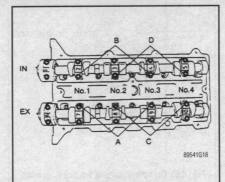

Fig. 104 Mazda 4-cylinder engines cam cap bolt removal positions—refer to text

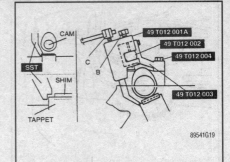

Fig. 105 Mount the tappet depressor tool onto the shaft above the tappet which needs adjustment

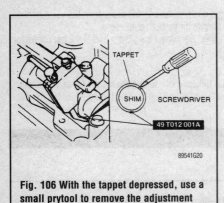

Fig. 106 With the tappet depressed, use a small prytool to remove the adjustment shim

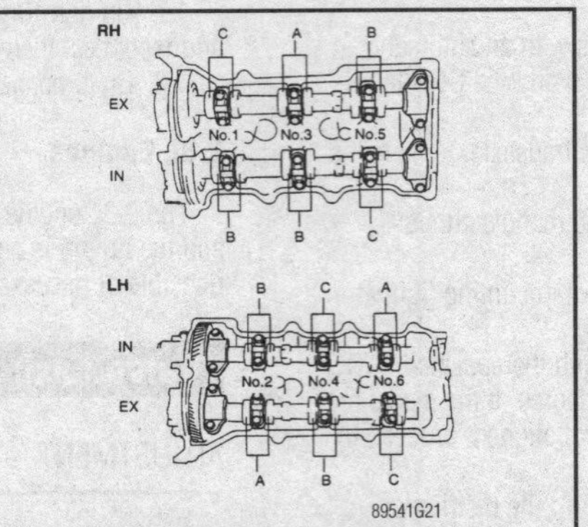

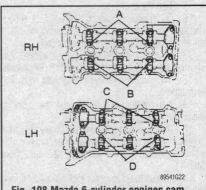

Fig. 107 Mazda 6-cylinder engine valve clearance checking positions

Fig. 108 Mazda 6-cylinder engines cam cap bolt removal positions—refer to text

13. Align the mark on the 49-T012-002 (shaft) with the mark on the 49-T012-003 (clamp). Tighten special tool 49-T012-004 (bolt) to secure the shaft.

14. Position special tool 49-T012-001A toward the center of the cylinder head, and mount it on the shaft where the adjustment shim needs replacement.

15. Position the notch of the tappet to allow a small pry tool to be inserted.

16. Set the special tool on the tappet by its notch. Tighten the mounting bolt **B** securing it on the shaft.

17. Tighten bolt **C**, and press down the tappet.

18. Using a small pry tool, pry the adjustment shim upwards through the notch on the tappet. Remove the shim with a magnet.

19. Select and install the proper adjustment shim. Loosen bolt **C** to allow the tappet to move up, and loosen bolt **B** to remove special tool 49-T012-001A.

20. Remove special tools 49-T012-002, 003 and 004, and tighten the camshaft cap bolts to 100–125 inch lbs. (11–14 Nm).

21. Repeat the procedure for all necessary adjustment shims. Check the valve clearance.

2.3L and 1998 2.5L Engines

▶ **See Figures 105, 106, 107 and 108**

➡ **With the engine cold, standard valve clearance is 0.011–0.012 in. (0.27–0.31mm) on intake and exhaust sides.**

1. Measure the valve clearance by turning the crankshaft clockwise until the No. 1 piston is at TDC.

2. Measure the valve clearance at **A**. Turn the crankshaft clockwise 240 degrees until the No. 3 piston is at TDC. Measure the valve clearance at **B**. Turn the crankshaft clockwise 240 degrees until the No. 5 piston is at TDC. Measure the valve clearance at **C**.

➡ **If the valve clearance exceeds the standard, replace the adjustment shim.**

3. Turn the crankshaft clockwise until the cam, on the camshaft requiring the adjustment shim replacement, is positioned straight up.

4. Remove the camshaft cap bolts as follows:

a. For right-hand (RH) exhaust side shim removal use **1**.
b. For right-hand (RH) intake side shim removal use **2**.
c. For left-hand (LH) intake side shim removal use **3**.
d. For left-hand (LH) exhaust side shim removal use **4**.

5. Install special tools 49-T012-002 and 003, using the camshaft cap bolt holes.

6. Align the mark on the 49-T012-002 (shaft) with the mark on the 49-T012-003 (clamp).

7. Position special tool 49-T012-001 toward the center of the cylinder head, and mount it on the shaft where the adjustment shim needs replacement.

8. Position the notch of the tappet to allow a small pry tool to be inserted.

9. Set the special tool on the tappet by its notch. Tighten the mounting bolt **B** securing it on the shaft.

10. Tighten bolt **C**, and press down the tappet.

11. Using a small pry tool, pry the adjustment shim upwards through the notch on the tappet. Remove the shim with a magnet.

12. Select and install the proper adjustment shim. Loosen bolt **C** to allow the tappet to move up, and loosen bolt B to remove special tool 49-T012-001.

13. Remove special tools 49-T012-002, 003 and 004, and tighten the camshaft cap bolts to 100–125 inch lbs. (11–14 Nm).

14. Repeat the procedure for all necessary adjustment shims. Check the valve clearance.

Idle Speed And Mixture Adjustments

IDLE SPEED ADJUSTMENT

▶ **See Figure 109**

➡ **Idle speed is controlled automatically by the ECU through the Idle Speed Control (ISC) solenoid valve. Idle speed adjustment is usually not necessary.**

1. Check the ignition timing and adjust to specification, if necessary.

2. Turn off all lights and other unnecessary electrical loads. Idle speed adjustment must be done while the radiator cooling fan is not operating.

TUNE-UP SPECIFICATIONS

Year	Engine ID/VIN	Engine Displacement Liters (cc)	Spark Plugs Gap (in.)	Ignition Timing (deg.) MT	AT	Fuel Pump (psi)	Idle Speed (rpm) MT	AT	Valve Clearance In.	Ex.
1990	B6E	1.6 (1597)	0.039-0.043	7B	7B [1]	30-37	750	750 [1]	HYD	HYD
	BPE	1.8 (1839)	0.039-0.043	5B	5B [1]	30-37	750	750 [1]	HYD	HYD
	BPD	1.8 (1839)	0.039-0.043	10B	10B [1]	30-37	750	[2]	HYD	HYD
	F2	2.2 (2184)	0.039-0.043	[3]	[3]	27-33	750 [1]	750	HYD	HYD
1991	B6E	1.6 (1597)	0.039-0.043	7B	7B [1]	30-37	750	750 [1]	HYD	HYD
	BPE	1.8 (1839)	0.039-0.043	5B	5B [1]	30-37	750	750 [1]	HYD	HYD
	BPD	1.8 (1839)	0.039-0.043	10B	10B [1]	30-37	750	750 [1]	HYD	HYD
	F2	2.2 (2184)	0.039-0.043	[3]	[3]	27-33	750 [1]	750	HYD	HYD
1992	B6E	1.6 (1597)	0.039-0.043	[4]	[4]	30-37	750 [1]	750 [1]	HYD	HYD
	BPE	1.8 (1839)	0.039-0.043	5B [1]	5B [1]	30-37	750 [1]	750 [1]	HYD	HYD
	BPD	1.8 (1839)	0.039-0.043	10B [1]	10B [1]	30-37	750 [1]	750 [1]	HYD	HYD
	K8D	1.8 (1844)	0.039-0.043	10B [1]	10B [1]	30-38	670	670	HYD	HYD
	F2	2.2 (2184)	0.039-0.043	[3]	[3]	27-33	750 [1]	750 [1]	HYD	HYD
1993	B6E	1.6 (1597)	0.039-0.043	[4]	[4]	30-37	750 [1]	750 [1]	HYD	HYD
	BPE	1.8 (1839)	0.039-0.043	5B [1]	5B [1]	30-37	750 [1]	750 [1]	HYD	HYD
	BPD	1.8 (1839)	0.039-0.043	10B [1]	10B [1]	30-37	750 [1]	750 [1]	HYD	HYD
	K8D	1.8 (1844)	0.039-0.043	10B [1]	10B [1]	30-38	670	670	HYD	HYD
	FSD	2.0 (1991)	0.039-0.043	10B [1]	10B [1]	37-46	700 [1]	700 [1]	HYD	HYD
	KLD	2.5 (2496)	0.039-0.043	10B [1]	10B [1]	30-36	650 [1]	650 [1]	HYD	HYD
1994	B6E	1.6 (1597)	0.039-0.043	[4]	[4]	30-37	750 [1]	750 [1]	HYD	HYD
	BPE	1.8 (1839)	0.039-0.043	5B [1]	5B [1]	30-37	750 [1]	750 [1]	HYD	HYD
	BPD	1.8 (1839)	0.039-0.043	10B [1]	10B [1]	30-37	750 [1]	750 [1]	HYD	HYD
	K8D	1.8 (1844)	0.039-0.043	10B [1]	10B [1]	30-38	670	670	HYD	HYD
	FSD	2.0 (1991)	0.039-0.043	10B [1]	10B [1]	37-46	700 [1]	700 [1]	HYD	HYD
	KLD	2.5 (2496)	0.039-0.043	10B [1]	10B [1]	30-36	650 [1]	650 [1]	HYD	HYD
1995	Z5D	1.5 (1489)	0.040-0.043	TDC [1]	TDC [1]	29-34	700 [1]	750 [1]	0.010-0.012 in.	[5]
	B6ZE	1.6 (1597)	0.039-0.043	[4]	[4]	30-37	750 [1]	750 [1]	HYD	HYD
	BPD	1.8 (1839)	0.039-0.043	TDC [1]	TDC [1]	29-34	750 [1]	750 [1]	HYD	HYD
	K8D	1.8 (1844)	0.039-0.043	10B [1]	10B [1]	30-38	670	670	HYD	HYD
	FSD	2.0 (1991)	0.040-0.043	10B [1]	10B [1]	37-46	700 [1]	700 [1]	HYD	HYD
	KLD	2.5 (2496)	0.040-0.043	10B [1]	10B [1]	30-36	650 [1]	650 [1]	HYD	HYD
	KJS	2.3 (2254)	0.028-0.031	7B [1]	7B [1]	30-48	650 [1]	650 [1]	0.011-0.012 in.	[5]
1996	Z5D	1.5 (1489)	0.040-0.043	TDC [1]	TDC [1]	29-34	700 [1]	750 [1]	0.010-0.012 in.	[5]
	BPD	1.8 (1839)	0.039-0.043	TDC [1]	TDC [1]	29-34	750 [1]	750 [1]	HYD	HYD
	FSD	2.0 (1991)	0.040-0.043	12B [1]	12B [1]	37-46	700 [1]	700 [1]	HYD	HYD
	KLD	2.5 (2496)	0.040-0.043	10B [1]	10B [1]	30-36	650 [1]	650 [1]	HYD	HYD
	KJS	2.3 (2254)	0.028-0.031	7B [1]	7B [1]	30-48	650 [1]	650 [1]	0.011-0.012 in.	[5]
1997	Z5D	1.5 (1489)	0.040-0.043	TDC [1]	TDC [1]	29-34	700 [1]	750 [1]	0.010-0.012 in.	[5]
	BPD	1.8 (1839)	0.039-0.043	TDC [1]	TDC [1]	29-34	750 [1]	750 [1]	HYD	HYD
	FSD	2.0 (1991)	0.039-0.043	10B [1]	10B [1]	37-46	700 [1]	700 [1]	HYD	HYD
	KLD	2.5 (2496)	0.039-0.043	10B [1]	10B [1]	30-36	650 [1]	650 [1]	HYD	HYD
	KJS	2.3 (2254)	0.028-0.031	7B [1]	7B [1]	30-48	650 [1]	650 [1]	0.011-0.012 in.	[5]

89541C06

TUNE-UP SPECIFICATIONS

Year	Engine ID/VIN	Engine Displacement Liters (cc)	Spark Plugs Gap (in.)	Ignition Timing (deg.) MT	AT	Fuel Pump (psi)	Idle Speed (rpm) MT	AT	Valve Clearance In.	Ex.
1998	Z5D	1.5 (1489)	0.040-0.043	TDC [1]	TDC [1]	29-43	700 [1]	750 [1]	0.010-0.012 in.	[5]
	BPD	1.8 (1839)	0.039-0.043	TDC [1]	TDC [1]	29-34	750 [1]	750 [1]	HYD	HYD
	FSD	2.0 (1991)	0.039-0.043	10B [1]	10B [1]	37-46	700 [1]	700 [1]	HYD	HYD
	KLD	2.5 (2496)	0.039-0.043	10B [1]	10B [1]	30-36	650 [1]	650 [1]	HYD	HYD
	KJS	2.3 (2254)	0.028-0.031	7B [1]	7B [1]	30-48	650 [1]	650 [1]	0.011-0.012 in.	[5]

B   Before Top Dead Center
TDC   Top Dead Center or 0 degrees
[1]   With test connector grounded
[2]   Except Canada = 750 with test connector grounded
    Canada = 800 with test connector grounded
[3]   Non-Turbo = 6B with vacuum hoses disconnected
    Turbo = 9B with test connector grounded
[4]   323 = 7B
    MX-3 = 10B
[5]   Specification is for both intake and exhaust valves - engine COLD

89541C07

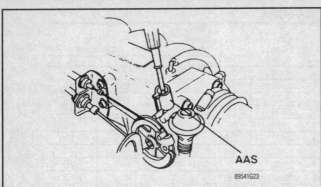

AAS

89541G23

Fig. 109 To adjust the idle speed, turn the Air Adjustment Screw (AAS), NOT the throttle stop

3. Set the parking brake and place the transaxle selector lever in neutral on manual transaxle vehicles or **P** on automatic transaxle vehicles. Warm up the engine.

4. On all engines except 1995–98 2.0L (FS) engines with automatic transaxle, connect a jumper wire between the TEN terminal and the GND terminal at the underhood test connector.

5. On 1995–98 2.0L (FS) engines with automatic transaxle, remove the shorting bar from the double wire SPOUT connector.

6. Attach a suitable tachometer according to the manufacturer's instructions.

7. Check the idle speed. It should be within specifications.

8. If the idle speed is not correct, adjust the idle speed by turning the air adjusting screw.

❄❄ WARNING

Do not tamper with any other adjustment screws. Doing so may result in damage to the throttle body.

9. After adjusting the idle speed, disconnect the jumper wire from the test connector or install the shorting bar.

10. Remove the tachometer from the engine.

MIXTURE ADJUSTMENT

On all Mazda engines, the air/fuel mixture is controlled by the Electronic Control Unit (ECU), therefore no idle mixture adjustment is possible or necessary.

Air Conditioning System

SYSTEM SERVICE & REPAIR

➡**It is recommended that the A/C system be serviced by an EPA Section 609 certified automotive technician utilizing a refrigerant recovery/recycling machine.**

The do-it-yourselfer should not service his/her own vehicle's A/C system for many reasons, including legal concerns, personal injury, environmental damage and cost.

According to the U.S. Clean Air Act, it is a federal crime to service or repair (involving the refrigerant) a Motor Vehicle Air Conditioning (MVAC) system for money without being EPA certified. It is also illegal to vent R-12 and R-134a refrigerants into the atmosphere. State and/or local laws may be more strict than the federal regulations, so be sure to check with your state and/or local authorities for further information.

➡**Federal law dictates that a fine of up to $25,000 may be levied on people convicted of venting refrigerant into the atmosphere.**

When servicing an A/C system you run the risk of handling or coming in contact with refrigerant, which may result in skin or eye irritation or frostbite. Although low in toxicity (due to chemical stability), inhalation of concentrated refrigerant fumes is dangerous and can result in death; cases of fatal cardiac arrhythmia have been reported in people accidentally subjected to high levels of refrigerant. Some early symptoms include loss of concentration and drowsiness.

➡**Generally, the limit for exposure is lower for R-134a than it is for R-12. Exceptional care must be practiced when handling R-134a.**

Also, some refrigerants can decompose at high temperatures (near gas heaters or open flame), which may result in hydrofluoric acid, hydrochloric acid and phosgene (a fatal nerve gas).

It is usually more economically feasible to have a certified MVAC automotive technician perform A/C system service on your vehicle.

R-12 Refrigerant Conversion

If your vehicle still uses R-12 refrigerant, one way to save A/C system costs down the road is to investigate the possibility of having your system converted to R-134a. The older R-12 systems can be easily converted to R-134a refrigerant by a certified automotive technician by installing a few new components and changing the system oil.

The cost of R-12 is steadily rising and will continue to increase, because it is no longer imported or manufactured in the United States. Therefore, it is often possible to have an R-12 system converted to R-134a and recharged for less than it would cost to just charge the system with R-12.

If you are interested in having your system converted, contact local automotive service stations for more details and information.

PREVENTIVE MAINTENANCE

Although the A/C system should not be serviced by the do-it-yourselfer, preventive maintenance should be practiced to help maintain the efficiency of the vehicle's A/C system. Be sure to perform the following:

• The easiest and most important preventive maintenance for your A/C system is to be sure that it is used on a regular basis. Running the system for five minutes each month (no matter what the season) will help ensure that the seals and all internal components remain lubricated.

➡**Some vehicles automatically operate the A/C system compressor whenever the windshield defroster is activated. Therefore, the A/C system would not need to be operated each month if the defroster was used.**

• In order to prevent heater core freeze-up during A/C operation, it is necessary to maintain proper antifreeze protection. Be sure to properly maintain the engine cooling system.

• Any obstruction of or damage to the condenser configuration will restrict air flow which is essential to its efficient operation. Keep this unit clean and in proper physical shape.

➡**Bug screens which are mounted in front of the condenser (unless they are original equipment) are regarded as obstructions.**

• The condensation drain tube expels any water which accumulates on the bottom of the evaporator housing into the engine compartment. If this tube is obstructed, the air conditioning performance can be restricted and condensation buildup can spill over onto the vehicle's floor.

SYSTEM INSPECTION

Although the A/C system should not be serviced by the do-it-yourselfer, system inspections should be performed to help maintain the efficiency of the vehicle's A/C system. Be sure to perform the following:

The easiest and often most important check for the air conditioning system consists of a visual inspection of the system components. Visually inspect the system for refrigerant leaks, damaged compressor clutch, abnormal compressor drive belt tension and/or condition, plugged evaporator drain tube, blocked condenser fins, disconnected or broken wires, blown fuses, corroded connections and poor insulation.

A refrigerant leak will usually appear as an oily residue at the leakage point

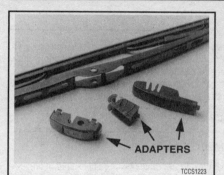

Fig. 110 Most aftermarket blades are available with multiple adapters to fit different vehicles

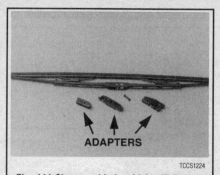

Fig. 111 Choose a blade which will fit your vehicle, and that will be readily available next time you need blades

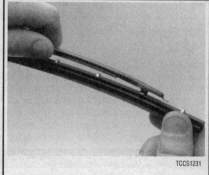

Fig. 112 When installed, be certain the blade is fully inserted into the backing

in the system. The oily residue soon picks up dust or dirt particles from the surrounding air and appears greasy. Through time, this will build up and appear to be a heavy dirt impregnated grease.

For a thorough visual and operational inspection, check the following:
• Check the surface of the radiator and condenser for dirt, leaves or other material which might block air flow.
• Check for kinks in hoses and lines. Check the system for leaks.
• Make sure the drive belt is properly tensioned. During operation, make sure the belt is free of noise or slippage.
• Make sure the blower motor operates at all appropriate positions, then check for distribution of the air from all outlets.

➡ **Remember that in high humidity, air discharged from the vents may not feel as cold as expected, even if the system is working properly. This is because moisture in humid air retains heat more effectively than dry air, thereby making humid air more difficult to cool.**

Windshield Wipers

ELEMENT (REFILL) CARE & REPLACEMENT

▶ **See Figures 110, 111 and 112**

For maximum effectiveness and longest element life, the windshield and wiper blades should be kept clean. Dirt, tree sap, road tar and so on will cause streaking, smearing and blade deterioration if left on the glass. It is advisable to wash the windshield carefully with a commercial glass cleaner at least once a month. Wipe off the rubber blades with the wet rag afterwards. Do not attempt to move wipers across the windshield by hand; damage to the motor and drive mechanism will result.

To inspect and/or replace the wiper blade elements, place the wiper switch in the **LOW** speed position and the ignition switch in the **ACC** position. When the wiper blades are approximately vertical on the windshield, turn the ignition switch to **OFF**.

Examine the wiper blade elements. If they are found to be cracked, broken or torn, they should be replaced immediately. Replacement intervals will vary with usage, although ozone deterioration usually limits element life to about one year. If the wiper pattern is smeared or streaked, or if the blade chatters across the glass, the elements should be replaced. It is easiest and most sensible to replace the elements in pairs.

If your vehicle is equipped with aftermarket blades, there are several different types of refills and your vehicle might have any kind. Aftermarket blades and arms rarely use the exact same type blade or refill as the original equipment.

Regardless of the type of refill used, be sure to follow the part manufacturer's instructions closely. Make sure that all of the frame jaws are engaged as the refill is pushed into place and locked. If the metal blade holder and frame are allowed to touch the glass during wiper operation, the glass will be scratched.

Tires and Wheels

Common sense and good driving habits will afford maximum tire life. Make sure that you don't overload the vehicle or run with incorrect pressure in the tires. Either of these will increase tread wear. Fast starts, sudden stops and sharp cornering are hard on tires and will shorten their useful life span.

➡ **For optimum tire life, keep the tires properly inflated, rotate them often and have the wheel alignment checked periodically.**

Inspect your tires frequently. Be especially careful to watch for bubbles in the tread or sidewall, deep cuts or underinflation. Replace any tires with bubbles in the sidewall. If cuts are so deep that they penetrate to the cords, discard the tire. Any cut in the sidewall of a radial tire renders it unsafe. Also look for uneven tread wear patterns that may indicate the front end is out of alignment or that the tires are out of balance.

TIRE ROTATION

▶ **See Figure 113**

Tires must be rotated periodically to equalize wear patterns that vary with a tire's position on the vehicle. Tires will also wear in an uneven way as the front steering/suspension system wears to the point where the alignment should be reset.

Rotating the tires will ensure maximum life for the tires as a set, so you will not have to discard a tire early due to wear on only part of the tread. Regular rotation is required to equalize wear.

When rotating "unidirectional tires," make sure that they always roll in the same direction. This means that a tire used on the left side of the vehicle must not be switched to the right side and vice-versa. Such tires should only be rotated front-to-rear or rear-to-front, while always remaining on the same side of the vehicle. These tires are marked on the sidewall as to the direction of rotation; observe the marks when reinstalling the tire(s).

Some styled or "mag" wheels may have different offsets front to rear. In these cases, the rear wheels must not be used up front and vice-versa. Furthermore, if these wheels are equipped with unidirectional tires, they cannot be rotated unless the tire is remounted for the proper direction of rotation.

➡ **The compact or space-saver spare is strictly for emergency use. It must never be included in the tire rotation or placed on the vehicle for everyday use.**

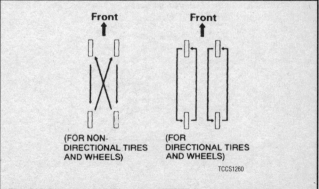

Fig. 113 Compact spare tires must NEVER be used in the rotation pattern

TIRE DESIGN

◆ **See Figure 114**

For maximum satisfaction, tires should be used in sets of four. Mixing of different brands or types (radial, bias-belted, fiberglass belted) should be avoided. In most cases, the vehicle manufacturer has designated a type of tire on which the vehicle will perform best. Your first choice when replacing tires should be to use the same type of tire that the manufacturer recommends.

When radial tires are used, tire sizes and wheel diameters should be selected to maintain ground clearance and tire load capacity equivalent to the original specified tire. Radial tires should always be used in sets of four.

✳✳ CAUTION

Radial tires should never be used on only the front axle.

When selecting tires, pay attention to the original size as marked on the tire. Most tires are described using an industry size code sometimes referred to as P-Metric. This allows the exact identification of the tire specifications, regardless of the manufacturer. If selecting a different tire size or brand, remember to check the installed tire for any sign of interference with the body or suspension while the vehicle is stopping, turning sharply or heavily loaded.

Snow Tires

Good radial tires can produce a big advantage in slippery weather, but in snow, a street radial tire does not have sufficient tread to provide traction and control. The small grooves of a street tire quickly pack with snow and the tire behaves like a billiard ball on a marble floor. The more open, chunky tread of a snow tire will self-clean as the tire turns, providing much better grip on snowy surfaces.

To satisfy municipalities requiring snow tires during weather emergencies, most snow tires carry either an M + S designation after the tire size stamped on the sidewall, or the designation "all-season." In general, no change in tire size is necessary when buying snow tires.

Most manufacturers strongly recommend the use of 4 snow tires on their vehicles for reasons of stability. If snow tires are fitted only to the drive wheels, the opposite end of the vehicle may become very unstable when braking or turning on slippery surfaces. This instability can lead to unpleasant endings if the driver can't counteract the slide in time.

Note that snow tires, whether 2 or 4, will affect vehicle handling in all non-snow situations. The stiffer, heavier snow tires will noticeably change the turning and braking characteristics of the vehicle. Once the snow tires are installed, you must re-learn the behavior of the vehicle and drive accordingly.

➡**Consider buying extra wheels on which to mount the snow tires. Once done, the "snow wheels" can be installed and removed as needed. This eliminates the potential damage to tires or wheels from seasonal removal and installation. Even if your vehicle has styled wheels, see if inexpensive steel wheels are available. Although the look of the vehicle will change, the expensive wheels will be protected from salt, curb hits and pothole damage.**

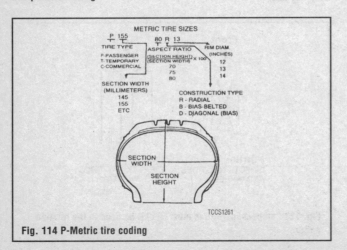

Fig. 114 P-Metric tire coding

TIRE STORAGE

If they are mounted on wheels, store the tires at proper inflation pressure. All tires should be kept in a cool, dry place. If they are stored in the garage or basement, do not let them stand on a concrete floor; set them on strips of wood, a mat or a large stack of newspaper. Keeping them away from direct moisture is of paramount importance. Tires should not be stored upright, but in a flat position.

INFLATION & INSPECTION

◆ **See Figures 115 thru 120**

The importance of proper tire inflation cannot be overemphasized. A tire employs air as part of its structure. It is designed around the supporting strength of the air at a specified pressure. For this reason, improper inflation drastically reduces the tireís ability to perform as intended. A tire will lose some air in day-to-day use; having to add a few pounds of air periodically is not necessarily a sign of a leaking tire.

Two items should be a permanent fixture in every glove compartment: an accurate tire pressure gauge and a tread depth gauge. Check the tire pressure (including the spare) regularly with a pocket type gauge. Too often, the gauge on the end of the air hose at your corner garage is not accurate because it suffers too much abuse. Always check tire pressure when the tires are cold, as pressure increases with temperature. If you must move the vehicle to check the tire inflation, do not drive more than a mile before checking. A cold tire is generally one that has not been driven for more than three hours.

A plate or sticker is normally provided somewhere in the vehicle (door post, hood, tailgate or trunk lid) which shows the proper pressure for the tires. Never counteract excessive pressure build-up by bleeding off air pressure (letting some air out). This will cause the tire to run hotter and wear quicker.

Fig. 115 Tires with deep cuts, or cuts which bulge, should be replaced immediately

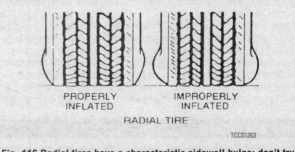

Fig. 116 Radial tires have a characteristic sidewall bulge; don't try to measure pressure by looking at the tire. Use a quality air pressure gauge

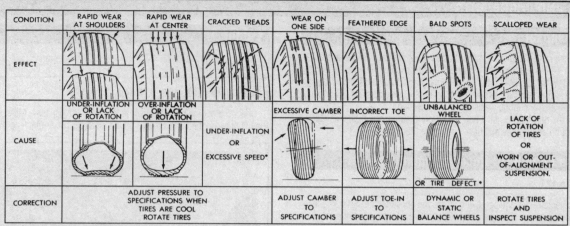

CONDITION	RAPID WEAR AT SHOULDERS	RAPID WEAR AT CENTER	CRACKED TREADS	WEAR ON ONE SIDE	FEATHERED EDGE	BALD SPOTS	SCALLOPED WEAR
EFFECT							
CAUSE	UNDER-INFLATION OR LACK OF ROTATION	OVER-INFLATION OR LACK OF ROTATION	UNDER-INFLATION OR EXCESSIVE SPEED*	EXCESSIVE CAMBER	INCORRECT TOE	UNBALANCED WHEEL OR TIRE DEFECT *	LACK OF ROTATION OF TIRES OR WORN OR OUT-OF-ALIGNMENT SUSPENSION.
CORRECTION	ADJUST PRESSURE TO SPECIFICATIONS WHEN TIRES ARE COOL ROTATE TIRES			ADJUST CAMBER TO SPECIFICATIONS	ADJUST TOE-IN TO SPECIFICATIONS	DYNAMIC OR STATIC BALANCE WHEELS	ROTATE TIRES AND INSPECT SUSPENSION

*HAVE TIRE INSPECTED FOR FURTHER USE.

TCCS1267

Fig. 117 Common tire wear patterns and causes

✴✴ CAUTION

Never exceed the maximum tire pressure embossed on the tire! This is the pressure to be used when the tire is at maximum loading, but it is rarely the correct pressure for everyday driving. Consult the owner's manual or the tire pressure sticker for the correct tire pressure.

Once you've maintained the correct tire pressures for several weeks, you'll be familiar with the vehicle's braking and handling personality. Slight adjustments in tire pressures can fine-tune these characteristics, but never change the cold pressure specification by more than 2 psi. A slightly softer tire pressure will give a softer ride but also yield lower fuel mileage. A slightly harder tire will give crisper dry road handling but can cause skidding on wet surfaces. Unless you're fully attuned to the vehicle, stick to the recommended inflation pressures.

All automotive tires have built-in tread wear indicator bars that show up as ½ in. (13mm) wide smooth bands across the tire when 1/16 in. (1.5mm) of tread remains. The appearance of tread wear indicators means that the tires should be replaced. In fact, many states have laws prohibiting the use of tires with less than this amount of tread.

You can check your own tread depth with an inexpensive gauge or by using a Lincoln head penny. Slip the Lincoln penny (with Lincoln's head upside-down) into several tread grooves. If you can see the top of Lincoln's head in 2 adjacent grooves, the tire has less than 1/16 in. (1.5mm) tread left and should be replaced. You can measure snow tires in the same manner by using the "tails" side of the Lincoln penny. If you can see the top of the Lincoln memorial, it's time to replace the snow tire(s).

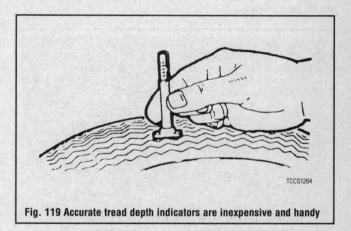

Fig. 119 Accurate tread depth indicators are inexpensive and handy

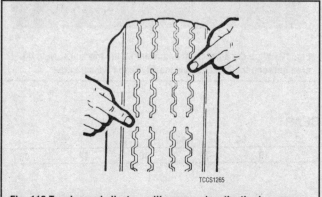

Fig. 118 Tread wear indicators will appear when the tire is worn

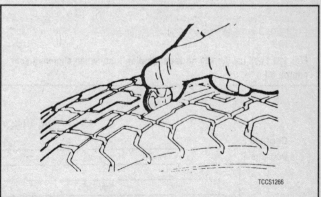

Fig. 120 A penny works well for a quick check of tread depth

FLUIDS AND LUBRICANTS

Fluid Disposal

Used fluids such as engine oil, transmission fluid, antifreeze and brake fluid are hazardous wastes and must be disposed of properly. Before draining any fluids, consult with your local authorities; in many areas waste oil, etc. is being accepted as a part of recycling programs. A number of service stations and auto parts stores are also accepting waste fluids for recycling.

Be sure of the recycling center's policies before draining any fluids, as many will not accept different fluids that have been mixed together.

Fuel and Engine Oil Recommendations

▶ **See Figure 121**

All Mazda vehicles are equipped with a catalytic converter, necessitating the use of unleaded gasoline. The use of leaded gasoline will damage the catalytic converter. Most Mazda vehicles are designed to use unleaded gasoline with an octane rating of 87, which usually means regular unleaded. The turbo models are designed to use unleaded gasoline with an octane rating of 91, which usually means mid-grade or super unleaded.

Oil must be selected with regard to the anticipated temperatures during the period before the next oil change. Using the chart, select the oil viscosity for the lowest expected temperature and you will be assured of easy cold starting and sufficient engine protection. The oil you pour into your engine should have the designation SG marked on the container. For maximum fuel economy benefits, use an oil with the Roman Numeral II next to the words Energy Conserving in the API Service Symbol.

Fig. 121 Look for the API oil identification label when choosing your engine oil

Engine

OIL LEVEL CHECK

▶ **See Figures 122, 123, 124 and 125**

Check the engine oil level every time you fill the gas tank. Make sure the oil level is between the **F** and **L** marks on the dipstick. The engine and oil must be

Fig. 122 To check the engine oil level, park the vehicle on a level surface and remove the engine oil dipstick

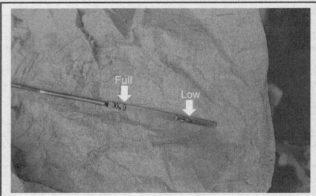

Fig. 123 Wipe the dipstick off and examine the markings. Note the area between the Full and Low marks, this is the safe area

OIL VISCOSITY CHART

Degrees F		-20	0	20	40	60	80	100	120	
Degrees C		-30	-20	-10	0	10	20	30	40	50
Oil		5W-30								
				10W-30						

89541C12

Fig. 124 Reinsert the clean dipstick, ensuring it is fully seated, then remove it again

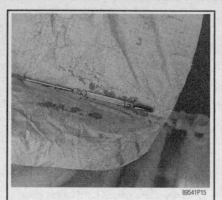

Fig. 125 Read the level on the dipstick

Fig. 126 Lightly coat the rubber gasket on the new oil filter with clean engine oil

warm and the vehicle parked on level ground to get an accurate reading. Also, allow a few minutes after turning off the engine for the oil to drain back into the pan before checking, or an inaccurate reading will result. Check the engine oil level as follows:

1. Open the hood and locate the engine oil dipstick.
2. If the engine is hot, you may want to wrap a rag around the dipstick handle before removing it.
3. Remove the dipstick and wipe it with a clean, lint-free rag, then reinsert it into the dipstick tube. Make sure it is inserted all the way or an inaccurate reading will result.
4. Pull out the dipstick and note the oil level. It should be between the marks, as stated above.
5. If the oil level is below the lower mark, replace the dipstick and add fresh oil to bring the level within the proper range. Do not overfill.
6. Recheck the oil level and close the hood.

OIL & FILTER CHANGE

◆ **See Figures 126 thru 133**

➡**Mazda recommends changing the oil and filter on non-turbo equipped vehicles every 7,500 miles (12,000 km) and turbo equipped vehicles every 5,000 miles (8,000 km). However, we here at Chilton believe that due to the relatively low-cost, in addition to the added longevity of your engine, this service should be performed every 3,000 miles (4,800 km).**

The engine oil and oil filter should be changed at the same time, at the recommended interval on the Maintenance Intervals chart. If the vehicle is being operated under extreme conditions or in very dusty areas, the oil should be changed more frequently. Before draining the oil, make sure the engine is at operating temperature. Hot oil holds more impurities in suspension and will flow better, allowing the removal of more oil and dirt.

Change the oil and filter as follows:

➡**Mazda recommends replacing the oil pan drain plug sealing washer any time it is removed.**

1. Run the engine until it reaches the normal operating temperature.
2. Raise and safely support the front of the vehicle securely on jackstands.
3. Wipe clean engine oil onto the rubber seal of the new oil filter. Also, if possible, pre-fill the filter with clean engine oil but note the following:
   a. If the filter is oriented vertically, with the seal facing upwards, fill the filter completely but use care when installing so as not to spill the oil and create a mess.
   b. If the filter is oriented vertically, with the seal facing downwards, do not pre-fill the filter. There would be no way to keep the oil in the filter when you install it.
   c. If the filter is oriented horizontally, only partially fill the filter. When you install the filter, some oil may start to spill out.
4. Slide a drain pan under the oil pan drain plug.
5. Before sliding under the vehicle, also gather the needed tools (wrenches, filter wrench, etc.), the new oil filter and a couple of rags (just in case!).

☀ CAUTION

The EPA warns that prolonged contact with used engine oil may cause a number of skin disorders, including cancer. You should make every effort to minimize your exposure to used engine oil. Protective gloves should be worn when changing the oil. Wash your hands and any other exposed skin areas as soon as possible after exposure to used engine oil. Soap and water, or waterless hand cleaner should be used.

6. Wipe the drain plug and the surrounding area clean. Loosen the drain plug with a socket or box wrench, and then remove it by hand. If necessary, use a rag to shield your fingers from the heat. Push in on the plug as you turn it out, so that oil does not leak out until the plug is completely removed.

Fig. 127 With the front of the vehicle raised and drain pan in position, loosen the oil drain plug . . .

Fig. 128 . . . then unscrew it, holding inward pressure on the plug

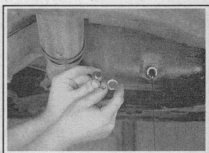

Fig. 129 While the oil is draining, clean the drain plug and replace its sealing washer with a new one

Fig. 130 Locate the engine oil filter (arrow) and remove it. Be careful around any hot engine or exhaust components!

Fig. 131 Install the new filter hand-tight. Once the rubber gasket contacts the block, turn the filter an additional ½ turn

Fig. 132 Ensure that the oil drain plug is tight, then remove the engine oil fill cap . . .

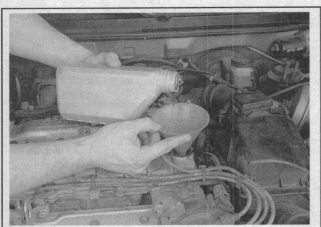

Fig. 133 . . . and, using a funnel to avoid spills, add the proper amount and grade of engine oil to the crankcase

7. Allow the oil to drain into the pan. Be very careful; if the engine is at operating temperature, the oil is hot enough to burn you.

8. Clean and install the drain plug complete with a new drain plug washer. Tighten the drain plug to 15 ft. lbs. (20 Nm).

9. Slide the drain pan under the oil filter. Slip an oil filter wrench onto the filter and turn it counterclockwise to loosen it. Wrap a rag around the filter and unscrew it the rest of the way. Be careful of oil running down the side of the filter.

10. Clean the oil filter adapter on the engine with a clean rag.

11. Place the new filter in position on the adapter fitting and screw it on by hand. After the rubber gasket contacts the sealing surface, turn the filter ½ turn, by hand.

12. Pull the drain pan from under the vehicle and lower the vehicle to the ground.

13. Remove the oil filler cap and fill the crankcase with the proper type and quantity of engine oil.

14. Turn the ignition to the **ON** position, but do not start the engine. Check the following:
   a. If equipped with an oil indicator lamp, ensure that the light is on.
   b. If equipped with an oil pressure gauge, ensure that it is reading zero pressure or LOW (L).
   c. If any of the above conditions are not met, DO NOT start the engine and repair the fault.

15. On the turbocharged engine, it is necessary to pre-lube the lubricating system before starting the engine to ensure an adequate supply of oil to the turbocharger bearings. This is done as follows:
   a. Detach the ignition coil electrical connector from the ignition coil.
   b. Crank the engine for approximately 20 seconds. Doing this will generate a fault code in the Self-Diagnostic portion of the Electronic Control Assembly.
   c. Reattach the electrical connector to the ignition coil.

16. Start the engine and run it at idle for approximately 30 seconds.

17. While the engine is running perform the following:
   a. If equipped with an oil indicator lamp, ensure that the light has gone out.
   b. If equipped with an oil pressure gauge, ensure that it is reading within the normal zone.
   c. Check the engine for any leaks.
   d. If any of the above conditions are not met, stop the engine immediately and repair the fault.

18. Stop the engine.

19. On the turbocharged engine, disconnect the negative battery cable and depress the brake pedal for approximately 5 seconds in order to cancel the fault code. Reconnect the negative battery cable.

20. Check and, if necessary, adjust the oil level.

Manual Transaxle (MTX)

FLUID RECOMMENDATIONS

For 1990–92 vehicles, Mazda recommends using SAE 75W-90 (GL-4 or GL-5) or Dexron®II Automatic Transmission Fluid (ATF) for all-season protection and SAE 80W-90 (GL-4 or GL-5) for use in sustained temperatures above 0°F (-18°C).

For 1993–98 vehicles Mazda recommends using SAE 75W-90 (GL-4 or GL-5) for all-season protection and SAE 80W-90 (GL-4 or GL-5) for use in sustained temperatures above 50°F (10°C).

LEVEL CHECK

1990–93 Vehicles Except MX-3 with G5M-R Transaxle, 323 4WD and 1993 626/MX-6/Probe

◗ See Figures 134 and 135

1. Park the car on a level surface. Apply the parking brake.

2. If equipped with a digital instrument cluster, disconnect the harness from the speed sensor assembly located on the transaxle housing.

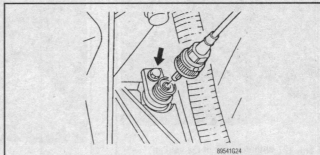

Fig. 134 Remove the speedometer cable or speed sensor harness plug from the driven gear assembly, as well as the retaining bolt (arrow)

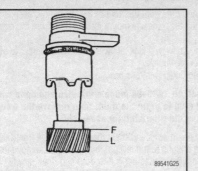

Fig. 135 Pull the speedometer driven gear assembly from the transaxle and, using the gear as a dipstick, read the fluid level

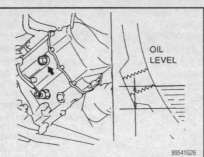

Fig. 136 To check the fluid level, remove the inspection/fill plug from the side of the case. If the level is below the plug, add oil until full

Fig. 137 To drain the transaxle, position a drain pan and loosen the transaxle drain plug

Fig. 138 Remove the drain plug, using care to not burn yourself with the hot fluid, and allow the fluid to drain into the pan

Fig. 139 Thoroughly clean the drain plug . . .

Fig. 140 . . . and replace the sealing washer with a new one

3. If equipped with an analog instrument cluster, disconnect the speedometer cable from the speedometer driven gear assembly located on the transaxle housing.

4. Remove the retaining bolt and pry out the speedometer driven gear assembly or the vehicle speed sensor from the transaxle housing.

5. Check the fluid level on the speedometer driven gear assembly or the vehicle speed sensor assembly. The level should be at the full mark, just above the gear teeth.

6. If the level is low, place a funnel in the driven gear or sensor opening in the transaxle and pour in the necessary amount of fluid. Recheck the fluid level.

7. Install the speedometer driven gear or speed sensor and connect the cable or harness.

MX-3 with G5M-R Transaxle, 323 4WD, 1993 626/MX-6/Probe and All 1994–98 vehicles

▶ See Figure 136

1. Park the vehicle on level ground.
2. Remove the oil level plug and washer.
3. Using a cotton swab or similar item, verify that the oil is near the bottom of the plug port.
4. If the oil level is low, add oil through the oil level plug hole.
5. Install a new washer to the oil level plug and tighten the plug to 29–43 ft. lbs. (40–58 Nm).

DRAIN & REFILL

▶ See Figures 137, 138, 139 and 140

1990–93 Vehicles Except MX-3 with G5M-R Transaxle, 323 4WD and 1993 626/MX-6/Probe

1. Raise and safely support the front of the vehicle securely on jackstands.
2. Slide a drain pan under the transaxle. Remove the speedometer driven gear or speed sensor on the top of the transaxle case.

3. Remove the drain plug on the bottom of the transaxle case.
4. When the fluid has been completely drained, install the drain plug and tighten to 29–43 ft. lbs. (39–59 Nm).
5. Fill the transaxle to the proper level.
6. Install the speedometer driven gear or speed sensor. Lower the vehicle.

MX-3 with G5M-R Transaxle, 323 4WD, 1993 626/MX-6/Probe and All 1994–98 vehicles

1. Raise and safely support the front of the vehicle securely on jackstands.
2. Slide a drain pan under the transaxle. Remove the drain plug and the washer and drain the oil into the drain pan.
3. Remove the oil level plug and the washer from the side of the transaxle case.
4. When the fluid has been completely drained, install the drain plug with a new washer and tighten to 29–43 ft. lbs. (40–58 Nm).
5. Fill the transaxle through the oil level plug hole until the fluid level reaches the bottom of the oil level plug hole.
6. Install the oil level plug with a new washer and tighten to 29–43 ft. lbs. (40–58 Nm).
7. Lower the vehicle.

Automatic Transaxle (ATX)

FLUID RECOMMENDATIONS

DEXRON®II or M-III® automatic transmission fluid is required.

LEVEL CHECK

▶ See Figures 141, 142 and 143

1. Park the car on a level surface and apply the parking brake. Run the engine to warm up the transaxle fluid.
2. Shift the transaxle through all ranges and return the lever to the **P** position.

3. With the engine still idling, remove the dipstick and wipe it clean, then insert it firmly. Be certain that it has been pushed fully home. Remove the dipstick and check the fluid level while holding the dipstick horizontally. The level should be at or near the high mark. The dipstick has a high and low mark on both sides, which are accurate for level indications when the fluid is hot (normal operating temperature), or at other than normal operating temperature.

4. If the fluid level is below the low mark, place a funnel on the dipstick tube and add Dexron®II or M-III® type automatic transmission fluid, one half pint (0.23L) at a time. Check the level often between additions, being careful not to overfill the transmission.

DRAIN, REFILL & FILTER SERVICE

▶ **See Figures 137, 138, 139, 140 and 144 thru 151**

1. Raise and safely support the front of the vehicle securely on jackstands.
2. Support the left-hand crossmember with a screw-type jack, or equivalent.

3. Remove the bolts and nuts from the front of the left-hand crossmember.
4. Remove the nuts and the transaxle mount through bolt from the rear of the crossmember.
5. Carefully lower the screw-type jack, allowing the crossmember to swing toward the left-hand side of the vehicle.
6. Position a drain pan under the transaxle.

➥**Some 1995 models and all 1996–98 models are also equipped with a drain plug. Remove the plug to drain the fluid, then remove the transmission oil pan to service the filter/strainer assembly.**

7. Loosen the pan retaining bolts and drain the fluid from the transaxle.
8. When the fluid has drained to the level of the pan flange, remove the pan retaining bolts, working from the rear, to allow it to drop and drain slowly.
9. When all the fluid has been drained, remove the pan and clean it thoroughly. Discard the pan gasket.
10. Remove and discard the transmission fluid filter and the filter-to-body

89541P18

Fig. 141 To check the ATX fluid level, first remove the dipstick, wipe it clean then reinsert it and remove it again

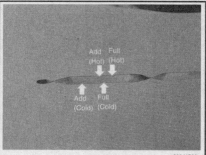

89541P38

Fig. 142 Read the fluid level on the dipstick. Ensure that it reads Full (hot or cold), if not . . .

89541P20

Fig. 143 . . . place a funnel into the dipstick tube and add the proper grade of fluid

89541P48

Fig. 144 Remove all but two transmission pan retaining bolts, then loosen the two remaining bolts . . .

89541P49

Fig. 145 . . . and carefully break the seal between the pan and transmission case, and allow the fluid to drain

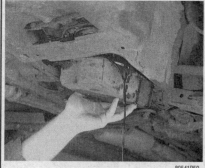

89541P50

Fig. 146 Remove the two remaining bolts and carefully lower the fluid pan

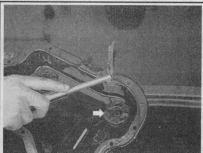

89541P54

Fig. 147 Thoroughly clean the fluid pan. Also inspect and clean the debris magnet (arrow)

89541P55

Fig. 148 Also remove the old gasket from the transmission case

89541P51

Fig. 149 Remove the filter attaching screws . . .

Fig. 150 . . . then lower the filter assembly and discard it

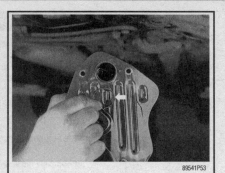

Fig. 151 Ensure that the old filter O-ring (arrow) did not stick in the transmission case

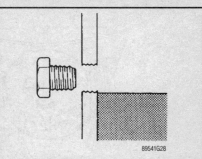

Fig. 152 Remove the fluid level check plug from the side of the transfer case to inspect the fluid level. The level should be as shown

gasket. The filter should not be reused or cleaned as the element material could contaminate the transaxle.

11. Install a new filter assembly using a new gasket. Tighten the retaining bolts to 69–95 inch lbs. (8–11 Nm).

12. Position a new gasket on the pan and install the pan. Tighten the pan retaining bolts to 69–95 inch lbs. (8–11 Nm).

13. Swing the left side crossmember into position and support it with the screw-type jack.

14. Install the 2 nuts and the left-hand transaxle mount through bolt to the rear of the left-hand crossmember. Tighten the nuts and through bolt to 49–69 ft. lbs. (67–93 Nm).

15. Install the 4 bolts and 1 nut to the front of the left-hand crossmember. Tighten the bolts to 27–40 ft. lbs. (36–54 Nm) and the nut to 55–69 ft. lbs. (79–93 Nm).

16. Remove the drain pan from under the vehicle. Remove the screw-type jack and then lower the vehicle to the ground.

17. Add approximately 7.2 qts. (6.8 liters) of fluid to the transaxle through the filler tube.

18. Run the engine and check for leaks. Check the fluid level according to the procedure described earlier.

Transfer Case

➡️Only the 1990–91 323 models with 4-wheel drive use a transfer case.

FLUID RECOMMENDATIONS

API Service GL-5 SAE 80–90 W oil is required. Total fluid capacity is 0.53 quart (0.5 liter).

LEVEL CHECK

▶ **See Figure 152**

1. Park the car on a level surface and apply the parking brake.
2. Remove the check plug from the side of the transfer carrier.
3. Check to see if oil level is at the bottom of the check plug hole.
4. If the fluid level is below the low mark, place a funnel into the plug hole and add the specified oil.
5. Install the check plug and tighten the plug to 28–43 ft. lbs. (39–58 Nm).

DRAIN & REFILL

▶ **See Figure 153**

1. Raise and safely support the vehicle.
2. Place a drain pan below the transfer unit.

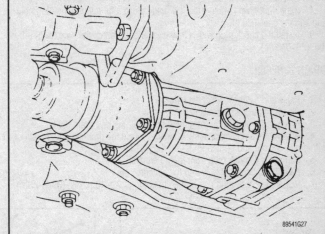

Fig. 153 Remove the transfer case drain plug to drain the fluid. The fill plug is located above and slightly behind the drain plug

3. Remove the drain plug from the transfer unit and drain the oil.
4. When the fluid is completely drained, install the drain plug with a new washer intact. Tighten the drain plug to 28–43 ft. lbs. (39–58 Nm).
5. Remove the check plug from the side of the transfer carrier.
6. Refill the transfer unit with the specified oil.
7. Install the check plug and tighten the plug to 28–43 ft. lbs. (39–58 Nm).

Rear Drive Axle

➡️Only the 1990–91 323 models with 4-wheel drive use a rear drive axle.

FLUID RECOMMENDATIONS

API Service GL-5 SAE 80–90 W oil is required. Total fluid capacity is 0.69 quart (0.65 liter).

LEVEL CHECK

▶ **See Figure 154**

1. Park the car on a level surface and apply the parking brake.
2. Remove the check plug from the differential.

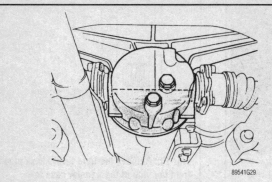

Fig. 154 Typical rear axle fluid level and drain plug locations for AWD vehicles

3. Check to see if oil level is at the bottom of the check plug hole.
4. If the fluid level is below the low mark, place a funnel into the plug hole and add the specified oil.
5. Install the check plug with a new washer and tighten the plug to 29–40 ft. lbs. (39–54 Nm).

DRAIN & REFILL

1. Raise and safely support the vehicle.
2. Place a drain pan below the differential.
3. Remove the drain plug from the differential unit and drain the oil.
4. When the fluid is completely drained, replace the drain plug complete with a new washer and tighten to 29–40 ft. lbs. (39–54 Nm).
5. Remove the check plug from the differential.
6. Refill the differential unit with the specified oil.
7. Install the check plug and tighten the plug to 29–40 ft. lbs. (39–54 Nm).

Cooling System

▶ **See Figures 155 and 156**

Check the cooling system at the interval specified in the Maintenance Intervals chart at the end of this section.

Hose clamps should be tightened, and defective hoses replaced. Damp spots, or accumulations of rust or dye near hoses, water pump or other areas, indicate areas of possible leakage. Check the radiator cap for a worn or cracked gasket. If the cap doesn't seal properly, fluid will be lost and the engine will overheat. A worn cap should be replaced with a new one.

Periodically clean any debris from the radiator fins. Pick the large pieces off by hand. The smaller pieces can be washed away with water pressure from a hose.

Carefully straighten any bent radiator fins with a pair of needle nose pliers. Be careful—the fins are very soft. Don't move the fins back and forth too much. Straighten them once and try not to move them again.

FLUID RECOMMENDATIONS

The recommended fluid is a 50/50 mixture of ethylene glycol antifreeze and water for year round use. Use a good quality antifreeze with water pump lubricants, rust inhibitors and other corrosion inhibitors along with acid neutralizers. Use only antifreeze that is SAFE FOR USE WITH AN ALUMINUM RADIATOR.

LEVEL CHECK

▶ **See Figures 157, 158, 159 and 160**

Coolant level should be checked at least once a month. With the engine cold, the coolant level should be even with the FULL mark on the coolant expansion tank. On some models, there is a coolant level dipstick.

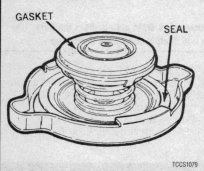

Fig. 155 Be sure the rubber gasket on the radiator cap has a tight seal

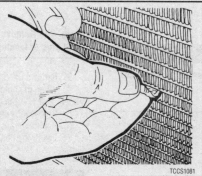

Fig. 156 Periodically remove all debris from the radiator fins

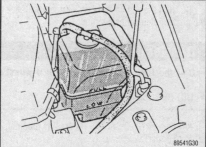

Fig. 157 On vehicles with see-through expansion or overflow tanks, the coolant level should read at the FULL line with the engine HOT

Fig. 158 On vehicles equipped with a dipstick in the overflow tank, remove the tank cap, which is also the dipstick

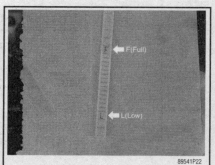

Fig. 159 Read the level on the dipstick. It should read at the F (Full) mark with the engine HOT, if not . . .

Fig. 160 . . . place a funnel in the tank opening and add a 50/50 mixture of water/coolant

DRAIN & REFILL

▶ See Figures 161, 162, 163 and 164

1. Remove the radiator cap.

❊❊ CAUTION

Never remove the radiator cap while the engine is running or personal injury from scalding hot coolant or steam may result. If possible, wait until the engine has cooled to remove the radiator cap. If this is not possible, wrap a thick cloth around the radiator cap and turn it slowly to the first stop. Step back while the pressure is released from the cooling system. When you are sure all the pressure has been released, press down on the cap, still with the cloth, and turn and remove it.

2. Position a suitable container under the radiator and open the draincock to drain the radiator.

❊❊ CAUTION

When draining the coolant, keep in mind that cats and dogs are attracted by the ethylene glycol antifreeze, and are quite likely to drink any that is left in an uncovered container or in puddles on the ground. This will prove fatal in sufficient quantity. Always drain the coolant into a sealable container.

3. Clean the cooling system by flushing with clear water.
4. Close the radiator draincock.

Fig. 161 Before draining the cooling system, allow it to completely cool, then remove the radiator cap. This will aid in draining the coolant

5. Refill the system with a 50/50 mixture of antifreeze and water. Fill to the FULL mark on the reservoir and install the radiator cap only to the first stop.
6. Start the engine and run it at fast idle until the upper radiator hose feels warm, indicating the thermostat has opened and coolant is flowing throughout the system.
7. Stop the engine. Carefully remove the radiator cap and top off the radiator with the water/antifreeze mixture, if required.
8. Install the radiator cap securely and fill the coolant reservoir to the FULL mark.

FLUSHING & CLEANING THE SYSTEM

Radiator and Engine Flush

1. Drain the cooling system. Remove the thermostat and reinstall the thermostat housing.
2. Disconnect the radiator overflow hose from the expansion tank and plug the end of the hose.
3. Disconnect the intake manifold outlet hose from the manifold nipple and plug both the nipple and the hose.
4. Disconnect the lower radiator hose from the radiator and position the hose to drain clear of the vehicle.
5. Connect a high pressure hose to the radiator lower hose outlet. Back flush the radiator and engine until water runs clear out of the lower radiator hose. Turn the water on and off several times to pulse the flow and help loosen sludge deposits.

❊❊ WARNING

The flushing water flow must be limited so that pressure inside the radiator does not exceed 15 psi (103.4kpa).

6. When the system drains clear, unplug the radiator overflow hose. When water flows clear from the hose, reinstall the plug.
7. Before reconnecting the cooling system hoses, disconnect all of the hoses installed for the radiator and engine back flush procedure. The heater coolant loop must be backflushed separately to prevent loosened sediment from lodging in the heater core.

Heater Core Back Flush

1. Install and clamp a garden hose female end fitting in the heater return hose, disconnected from the bypass nipple.
2. Connect a garden hose to the hose fitting in the heater return hose and flush the heater core circuit until the drain water runs clear. Pulse the flow by turning the water on and off several times. Allow full flow for approximately 5 minutes.
3. Shut off the flushing water and remove all adapters and plugs installed for the flushing operation. Reconnect all cooling system connections and tighten the hose clamps to 22–31 inch lbs. (2.5–3.5 Nm).
4. Install the thermostat with a new housing gasket. Tighten the retaining nuts.
5. Fill the cooling system and check for leaks.

Fig. 162 If equipped, open the access door in the lower splash shield to access the radiator drain petcock

Fig. 163 Position a large drain pan beneath the petcock, then open it and allow the coolant to drain

Fig. 164 Once the cooling system is drained, close the petcock and refill the radiator

Brake Master Cylinder

FLUID RECOMMENDATIONS

The brake fluid master cylinder requires brake fluid that meets or exceeds DOT 3 standards.

※※ WARNING

Clean, high quality brake fluid is essential to the safe and proper operation of the brake system. You should always buy the highest quality brake fluid that is available. If the brake fluid becomes contaminated, drain and flush the system, then refill the master cylinder with new fluid. Never reuse any brake fluid. Any brake fluid that is removed from the system should be discarded. Also, do not allow any brake fluid to come in contact with a painted surface; it will damage the paint.

LEVEL CHECK

▶ See Figures 165, 166, 167, 168 and 169

※※ CAUTION

Brake fluid contains polyglycol ethers and polyglycols. Avoid contact with the eyes and wash your hands thoroughly after handling brake fluid. If you do get brake fluid in your eyes, flush your eyes with clean, running water for 15 minutes. If eye irritation persists, or if you have taken brake fluid internally, IMMEDIATELY seek medical assistance.

Except 1990–92 MX-6 and 626 Models

All Mazda vehicles except the 1990–92 626 and MX-6 are equipped with a combination brake/clutch fluid reservoir. The fluid level should be between the MIN and MAX lines located on the side of the reservoir.

If it is necessary to add fluid, first wipe away any accumulated dirt or grease from the reservoir. Then remove the reservoir cap by twisting counterclockwise. Add fluid to the proper level. Avoid spilling fluid on any painted surface as it will harm the paint finish. Replace the reservoir cap.

1990–92 MX-6 and 626 Models

The brake master cylinder has a translucent reservoir which enables the fluid level to be checked without removing the reservoir cap. The brake fluid level should be between the MIN and MAX lines located on the side of the reservoir.

If it is necessary to add fluid, first wipe away any accumulated dirt or grease from the reservoir. Then remove the reservoir cap by twisting counterclockwise. Add fluid to the proper level. Avoid spilling brake fluid on any painted surface as it will harm the paint finish. Replace the reservoir cap.

Clutch Master Cylinder

FLUID RECOMMENDATIONS

The clutch fluid master cylinder requires brake fluid that meets or exceeds DOT 3 standards.

LEVEL CHECK

※※ CAUTION

Brake fluid contains polyglycol ethers and polyglycols. Avoid contact with the eyes and wash your hands thoroughly after handling brake fluid. If you do get brake fluid in your eyes, flush your eyes with clean, running water for 15 minutes. If eye irritation persists, or if you have taken brake fluid internally, IMMEDIATELY seek medical assistance.

Except 1990–92 MX-6 and 626 Models

All Mazda vehicles except the 1990–92 626 and MX-6 are equipped with a combination brake/clutch fluid reservoir. Refer to the brake master cylinder fluid level checking procedures.

1990–92 MX-6 and 626 Models

The clutch master cylinder has a translucent reservoir which enables the fluid level to be checked without removing the reservoir cap. The clutch fluid level should be between the MIN and MAX lines located on the side of the reservoir.

If it is necessary to add fluid, first wipe away any accumulated dirt or grease from the reservoir. Then remove the reservoir cap by twisting counterclockwise. Add fluid to the proper level. Avoid spilling brake fluid on any painted surface as it will harm the paint finish. Replace the reservoir cap.

Power Steering Pump

FLUID RECOMMENDATIONS

ATF Dexron®II or M-III® fluid should be used.

LEVEL CHECK

All Models Except 1993–98 626 and MX-6 Models

All models are equipped with a power steering fluid reservoir. The reservoir is translucent with FULL (**F**) and LOW (**L**) fluid level markings. The fluid should be kept filled to the FULL mark at all times.

89541G31

Fig. 165 Inspect the brake fluid level by simply looking through the fluid reservoir. The level should be maintained at a MAX (full) reading

89541P07

Fig. 166 Before removing the brake fluid reservoir cap, wipe the area clean to ensure no debris falls into the reservoir

89541P09

Fig. 167 Remove the fluid reservoir cap by turning it counterclockwise

Fig. 168 Add the proper grade of clean, fresh brake fluid from an unopened container until the full mark is achieved

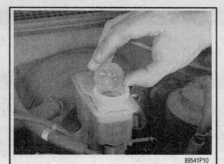

Fig. 169 Inspect this screen for any debris which may have fallen into the reservoir and clean it as necessary

Fig. 170 To check the power steering fluid level, remove the combination cap/dipstick from the reservoir

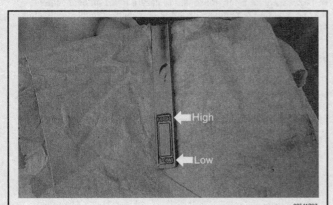

Fig. 171 Read the fluid level on the dipstick. It should read at or just below the HIGH mark, if not . . .

Fig. 172 . . . add enough of the proper grade of fluid until a HIGH reading is achieved

1993–98 626 and MX-6 Models

▶ See Figures 170, 171 and 172

1. Park the vehicle on level ground and apply the parking brake.
2. Turn the engine OFF and allow it to cool.
3. Remove the combination filler cap and dipstick.
4. Wipe the dipstick clean and reinstall.
5. Remove the combination filler cap and dipstick and inspect the fluid level.
6. The fluid level should be between the **H** and **L** marks on the dipstick. Add fluid as necessary.

Steering Gear

The manual steering gear has no provisions for checking and/or adding lubricant. It is a sealed unit and requires no maintenance.

Chassis Greasing

The ball joints and tie rod ends on Mazda vehicles are sealed at the factory and cannot be lubricated.

Body Lubrication and Maintenance

The hood latch, auxiliary catch, door, hatchback and liftgate hinges should be lubricated with multi-purpose grease and the door and window weatherstripping should be lubricated with silicone lubricant at least once a year. The body water drain holes located on the underside of each rocker panel, quarter panel and door should also be cleaned at this time.

To preserve the appearance of your car, it should be washed periodically with a mild detergent and water solution. Only wash the vehicle when the metal feels cool and the vehicle is in the shade. Rinse the entire vehicle with cold water, then wash and rinse one panel at a time, beginning with the roof and upper areas. After washing is complete, rinse the vehicle one final time and dry with a soft cloth or chamois.

Periodic waxing will remove harmful deposits from the vehicles surface and protect the finish. If the finish has dulled due to age or neglect, polishing may be necessary to restore the original gloss.

There are many specialized products available at your local auto parts store to care for the appearance of painted metal surfaces, plastic, chrome, wheels and tires as well as the interior upholstery and carpeting. Be sure to follow the manufacturers instructions before using them.

Wheel Bearings

REPACKING

All Mazda vehicles covered by this book use sealed bearing assemblies. There are no provisions for repacking the bearing.

TRAILER TOWING

It is not recommended to tow a trailer with any Mazda passenger car.

TOWING THE VEHICLE

If towing is required, the vehicle should be flat bedded, or towed with the front wheels off of the ground to prevent damage to the transaxle. If it is necessary to tow the vehicle from the rear, a wheel dolly should be placed under the front tires.

JUMP STARTING A DEAD BATTERY

▶ **See Figure 173**

Whenever a vehicle is jump started, precautions must be followed in order to prevent the possibility of personal injury. Remember that batteries contain a small amount of explosive hydrogen gas which is a by-product of battery charging. Sparks should always be avoided when working around batteries, especially when attaching jumper cables. To minimize the possibility of accidental sparks, follow the procedure carefully.

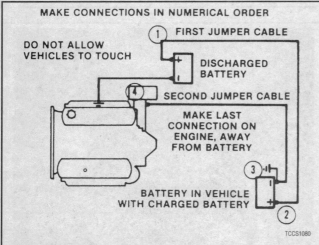

MAKE CONNECTIONS IN NUMERICAL ORDER
FIRST JUMPER CABLE
DO NOT ALLOW VEHICLES TO TOUCH
DISCHARGED BATTERY
SECOND JUMPER CABLE
MAKE LAST CONNECTION ON ENGINE, AWAY FROM BATTERY
BATTERY IN VEHICLE WITH CHARGED BATTERY
TCCS1080

Fig. 173 Connect the jumper cables to the batteries and engine in the order shown

✳✳ CAUTION

NEVER hook the batteries up in a series circuit or the entire electrical system will go up in smoke, including the starter!

Vehicles equipped with a diesel engine may utilize two 12 volt batteries. If so, the batteries are connected in a parallel circuit (positive terminal to positive terminal, negative terminal to negative terminal). Hooking the batteries up in parallel circuit increases battery cranking power without increasing total battery voltage output. Output remains at 12 volts. On the other hand, hooking two 12 volt batteries up in a series circuit (positive terminal to negative terminal, positive terminal to negative terminal) increases total battery output to 24 volts (12 volts plus 12 volts).

Jump Starting Precautions

• Be sure that both batteries are of the same voltage. Vehicles covered by this manual and most vehicles on the road today utilize a 12 volt charging system.
• Be sure that both batteries are of the same polarity (have the same terminal, in most cases NEGATIVE grounded).
• Be sure that the vehicles are not touching or a short could occur.
• On serviceable batteries, be sure the vent cap holes are not obstructed.
• Do not smoke or allow sparks anywhere near the batteries.
• In cold weather, make sure the battery electrolyte is not frozen. This can occur more readily in a battery that has been in a state of discharge.
• Do not allow electrolyte to contact your skin or clothing.

Jump Starting Procedure

1. Make sure that the voltages of the 2 batteries are the same. Most batteries and charging systems are of the 12 volt variety.
2. Pull the jumping vehicle (with the good battery) into a position so the jumper cables can reach the dead battery and that vehicle's engine. Make sure that the vehicles do NOT touch.
3. Place the transmissions/transaxles of both vehicles in **Neutral** (MT) or **P** (AT), as applicable, then firmly set their parking brakes.

➡ **If necessary for safety reasons, the hazard lights on both vehicles may be operated throughout the entire procedure without significantly increasing the difficulty of jumping the dead battery.**

4. Turn all lights and accessories OFF on both vehicles. Make sure the ignition switches on both vehicles are turned to the **OFF** position.
5. Cover the battery cell caps with a rag, but do not cover the terminals.
6. Make sure the terminals on both batteries are clean and free of corrosion or proper electrical connection will be impeded. If necessary, clean the battery terminals before proceeding.
7. Identify the positive (+) and negative (−) terminals on both batteries.
8. Connect the first jumper cable to the positive (+) terminal of the dead battery, then connect the other end of that cable to the positive (+) terminal of the booster (good) battery.
9. Connect one end of the other jumper cable to the negative (−) terminal on the booster battery and the final cable clamp to an engine bolt head, alternator bracket or other solid, metallic point on the engine with the dead battery. Try to pick a ground on the engine that is positioned away from the battery in order to minimize the possibility of the 2 clamps touching should one loosen during the procedure. DO NOT connect this clamp to the negative (−) terminal of the bad battery.

✳✳ CAUTION

Be very careful to keep the jumper cables away from moving parts (cooling fan, belts, etc.) on both engines.

10. Check to make sure that the cables are routed away from any moving parts, then start the donor vehicle's engine. Run the engine at moderate speed for several minutes to allow the dead battery a chance to receive some initial charge.
11. With the donor vehicle's engine still running slightly above idle, try to start the vehicle with the dead battery. Crank the engine for no more than 10 seconds at a time and let the starter cool for at least 20 seconds between tries. If the vehicle does not start in 3 tries, it is likely that something else is also wrong or that the battery needs additional time to charge.
12. Once the vehicle is started, allow it to run at idle for a few seconds to make sure that it is operating properly.
13. Turn ON the headlights, heater blower and, if equipped, the rear defroster of both vehicles in order to reduce the severity of voltage spikes and subsequent risk of damage to the vehicles' electrical systems when the cables are disconnected. This step is especially important to any vehicle equipped with computer control modules.
14. Carefully disconnect the cables in the reverse order of connection. Start with the negative cable that is attached to the engine ground, then the negative cable on the donor battery. Disconnect the positive cable from the donor battery and finally, disconnect the positive cable from the formerly dead battery. Be careful when disconnecting the cables from the positive terminals not to allow the alligator clips to touch any metal on either vehicle or a short and sparks will occur.

JACKING

◆ **See Figures 174, 175, 176, 177 and 178**

The vehicle is supplied with a scissors jack for emergency road repairs. The scissors jack may be used to raise the car via the notches on either side at the front and rear of the doors. Do not attempt to position the jack in any other place. Always block the diagonally opposite wheel when using a jack.

When using stands, use the side members at the front or trailing axle front mounting crossmember at the rear for placement points.

Whenever you plan to work under the car, you must support it on jackstands or ramps. Never use cinder blocks or stacks of wood to support the car, even if you're only going to be under it for a few minutes. Never crawl under the car when it is supported only by the tire-changing jack.

Small hydraulic, screw, or scissors jacks are satisfactory for raising the car. Drive-on trestles or ramps are also a handy and safe way to both raise and support the car. Never support the car on any suspension member or underbody panel.

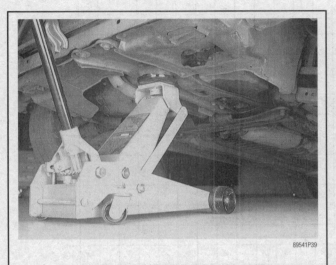

Fig. 174 Jack position for lifting the front of the vehicle

Fig. 175 Position the jackstands, to support the front end, under the sub-frame sections as shown

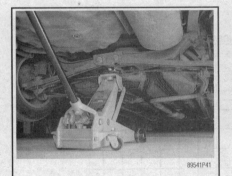

Fig. 176 Jack position for lifting the rear of the vehicle

Fig. 177 Position the jackstands, to support the rear of the vehicle, under the rear trailing arm-to-frame support

Fig. 178 A closer look at the rear jackstand positioned under the rear trailing arm-to-frame support

MANUFACTURER RECOMMENDED NORMAL MAINTENANCE INTERVALS

VEHICLE MILEAGE INTERVAL (x1000)

TO BE SERVICED		7.5	15	22.5	30	37.5	45	52.5	60	67.5	75	82.5	90	97.5	105	112.5	120	127.5	135	142.5	150	157.5	165	172.5	180
Change engine oil and filter	A	✓	✓	✓	✓	✓	✓	✓	✓	✓	✓	✓	✓	✓	✓	✓	✓	✓	✓	✓	✓	✓	✓	✓	✓
Replace air filter					✓				✓				✓				✓				✓				✓
Replace fuel filter									✓								✓								✓
Replace spark plugs					✓				✓				✓				✓				✓				✓
Replace engine timing belt	B								✓								✓								✓
Change engine coolant					✓				✓				✓				✓				✓				✓
Inspect valve clearance	C								✓								✓								✓
Inspect accessory drive belt tension					✓				✓				✓				✓				✓				✓
Inspect idle speed and fuel lines					✓				✓				✓				✓				✓				✓
Inspect engine cooling system					✓				✓				✓				✓				✓				✓
Inspect brake lines and hoses					✓				✓				✓				✓				✓				✓
Inspect front brake pads					✓				✓				✓				✓				✓				✓
Inspect rear brake pads/shoes					✓				✓				✓				✓				✓				✓
Inspect steering operation and components					✓				✓				✓				✓				✓				✓
Inspect front suspension					✓				✓				✓				✓				✓				✓
Inspect drive shaft boots					✓				✓				✓				✓				✓				✓
Inspect and tighten body bolts and nuts					✓				✓				✓				✓				✓				✓
Lubricate all locks and hinges		✓	✓	✓	✓	✓	✓	✓	✓	✓	✓	✓	✓	✓	✓	✓	✓	✓	✓	✓	✓	✓	✓	✓	✓

A The engine oil and filter should be changed every 7,500 miles (12,000 km) or 6 months, which ever occurs first.
B Except California models, inspect at 60,000 and 90,000 miles (96,000 and 144,000 km) and replace every 105,000 miles (168,000 km).
C For vehicles without hydraulic lash adjusters

89541C08

MANUFACTURER RECOMMENDED SEVERE MAINTENANCE INTERVALS

VEHICLE MILEAGE INTERVAL (x1000)

TO BE SERVICED		5	10	15	20	25	30	35	40	45	50	55	60	65	70	75	80	85	90	95	100	105	110	115	120
Change engine oil and filter	A	✓	✓	✓	✓	✓	✓	✓	✓	✓	✓	✓	✓	✓	✓	✓	✓	✓	✓	✓	✓	✓	✓	✓	✓
Replace air filter							✓						✓						✓						✓
Replace fuel filter													✓												✓
Replace spark plugs							✓						✓						✓						✓
Replace engine timing belt	B												✓												✓
Change engine coolant							✓						✓						✓						✓
Inspect valve clearance	C												✓												✓
Inspect accessory drive belt tension							✓						✓						✓						✓
Inspect idle speed and fuel lines							✓						✓						✓						✓
Inspect engine cooling system							✓						✓						✓						✓
Inspect brake lines and hoses							✓						✓						✓						✓
Inspect front brake pads				✓			✓			✓			✓			✓			✓			✓			✓
Inspect rear brake pads/shoes							✓						✓						✓						✓
Inspect steering operation and components							✓						✓						✓						✓
Inspect front suspension							✓						✓						✓						✓
Inspect drive shaft boots							✓						✓						✓						✓
Inspect and tighten body bolts and nuts				✓			✓			✓			✓			✓			✓			✓			✓
Lubricate all locks and hinges		✓	✓	✓	✓	✓	✓	✓	✓	✓	✓	✓	✓	✓	✓	✓	✓	✓	✓	✓	✓	✓	✓	✓	✓

A The engine oil and filter should be changed every 5,000 miles (8,000 km) or 4 months, which ever occurs first.
B Interval is for non-California vehicles. For California models, inspect at 60,000 and 90,000 miles (96,000 and 144,000 km) and replace every 105,000 miles (168,000 km).
C For vehicles without hydraulic lash adjusters

89541C09

CAPACITIES

89541C24

Year	Model	Engine ID/VIN	Engine Displacement Liters (cc)	Engine Oil with Filter (qts.)	Transmission Man ①	Transmission Auto. ①	Transfer Case (pts.)	Drive Axle Front (pts.)	Drive Axle Rear (pts.)	Fuel Tank (gal.)	Cooling System wo/AC (qts.)	Cooling System w/AC (qts.)
1995	Protege	Z5D	1.5 (1489)	3.7	2.8	5.7	—	—	—	13.2	6.3	6.3
	Protege	BPD	1.8 (1839)	4.0	2.8	5.7	—	—	—	13.2	6.3	6.3
	MX-3	B6ZE	1.6 (1597)	3.6	2.9	6.7	—	—	—	13.2	6.3	6.3
	MX-3	K8D	1.8 (1844)	4.2	2.9	6.1	—	—	—	13.2	7.9	7.9
	626	FSD	2.0 (1991)	3.7	2.9	9.3	—	—	—	15.5	7.4	7.4
	626	KLD	2.5 (2496)	4.2	2.9	9.3	—	—	—	15.5	7.9	7.9
	MX-6/Probe	FSD	2.0 (1991)	3.7	2.9	8.7	—	—	—	15.5	7.4	7.4
	MX-6/Probe	KLD	2.5 (2496)	4.2	2.9	9.3	—	—	—	15.5	7.9	7.9
	Millenia	KLD	2.5 (2496)	4.2	—	8.2	—	—	—	18.0	7.9	7.9
	Millenia	KJS	2.3 (2254)	4.3	—	8.2	—	—	—	18.0	7.9	7.9
1996	Protege	Z5D	1.5 (1489)	3.7	2.8	5.7	—	—	—	13.2	6.3	6.3
	Protege	BPD	1.8 (1839)	4.0	2.8	5.7	—	—	—	13.2	6.3	6.3
	626	FSD	2.0 (1991)	3.7	2.9	9.3	—	—	—	15.5	7.4	7.4
	626	KLD	2.5 (2496)	4.2	2.9	9.3	—	—	—	15.5	7.9	7.9
	MX-6/Probe	FSD	2.0 (1991)	3.7	2.9	8.7	—	—	—	15.5	7.4	7.4
	MX-6/Probe	KLD	2.5 (2496)	4.2	2.9	9.3	—	—	—	15.5	7.9	7.9
	Millenia	KLD	2.5 (2496)	4.2	—	8.2	—	—	—	18.0	7.9	7.9
	Millenia	KJS	2.3 (2254)	4.3	—	8.2	—	—	—	18.0	7.9	7.9
1997	Protege	Z5D	1.5 (1489)	3.7	2.8	5.7	—	—	—	13.2	6.3	6.3
	Protege	BPD	1.8 (1839)	4.0	2.8	5.7	—	—	—	13.2	6.3	6.3
	626	FSD	2.0 (1991)	3.7	2.9	9.3	—	—	—	15.5	7.9	7.9
	626	KLD	2.5 (2496)	4.2	2.9	9.3	—	—	—	15.5	7.9	7.9
	MX-6/Probe	FSD	2.0 (1991)	3.7	2.9	8.7	—	—	—	15.5	7.4	7.4
	MX-6/Probe	KLD	2.5 (2496)	4.2	2.9	9.3	—	—	—	15.5	7.9	7.9
	Millenia	KLD	2.5 (2496)	4.2	—	8.2	—	—	—	18.0	7.9	7.9
	Millenia	KJS	2.3 (2254)	4.3	—	8.2	—	—	—	18.0	7.9	7.9
1998	Protege	Z5D	1.5 (1489)	3.7	2.8	5.7	—	—	—	13.2	6.3	6.3
	Protege	BPD	1.8 (1839)	4.0	2.8	5.7	—	—	—	13.2	6.3	6.3
	626	FSD	2.0 (1991)	3.7	2.9	9.3	—	—	—	15.5	7.4	7.4
	626	KLD	2.5 (2496)	4.2	2.9	9.3	—	—	—	15.5	7.9	7.9
	Millenia	KLD	2.5 (2496)	4.2	—	8.2	—	—	—	18.0	7.9	7.9
	Millenia	KJS	2.3 (2254)	4.3	—	8.2	—	—	—	18.0	7.9	7.9

① All Measurements given are in quarts (qts.)
② Manual transmission = 5.3
   Automatic transmission = 6.3
③ Manual transmission without all wheel drive = 2.9
   Manual transmission with all wheel drive = 2.6
④ Automatic transmission without all wheel drive = 6.1
   Automatic transmission with all wheel drive = 7.0

CAPACITIES

89541C23

Year	Model	Engine ID/VIN	Engine Displacement Liters (cc)	Engine Oil with Filter (qts.)	Transmission Man ①	Transmission Auto. ①	Transfer Case (pts.)	Drive Axle Front (pts.)	Drive Axle Rear (pts.)	Fuel Tank (gal.)	Cooling System wo/AC (qts.)	Cooling System w/AC (qts.)
1990	323	B6E	1.6 (1597)	3.4	2.9	6.1	—	—	—	13.2	②	②
	Protege	BPE	1.8 (1839)	4.0	2.9	6.1	—	—	—	14.5	②	②
	Protege	BPD	1.8 (1839)	4.0	3.6	6.1	—	—	—	14.5	②	②
	626	F2	2.2 (2184)	4.3	3.5	7.2	—	—	—	15.9	7.9	7.9
	626 Turbo	F2	2.2 (2184)	4.3	3.9	7.2	—	—	—	15.9	7.9	7.9
	MX-6	F2	2.2 (2184)	4.3	3.5	7.2	—	—	—	15.9	7.9	7.9
	MX-6 Turbo	F2	2.2 (2184)	4.3	3.9	7.2	—	—	—	15.9	7.9	7.9
1991	323	B6E	1.6 (1597)	3.4	2.9	6.1	—	—	—	13.2	②	②
	Protege	BPE	1.8 (1839)	4.0	③	④	2.0	—	2.76	14.5	②	②
	Protege	BPD	1.8 (1839)	4.0	3.6	6.1	—	—	—	14.5	②	②
	626	F2	2.2 (2184)	4.3	3.5	7.2	—	—	—	15.9	7.9	7.9
	626 Turbo	F2	2.2 (2184)	4.3	3.9	7.2	—	—	—	15.9	7.9	7.9
	MX-6	F2	2.2 (2184)	4.3	3.5	7.2	—	—	—	15.9	7.9	7.9
	MX-6 Turbo	F2	2.2 (2184)	4.3	3.9	7.2	—	—	—	15.9	7.9	7.9
1992	323	B6E	1.6 (1597)	3.4	2.9	6.1	—	—	—	13.2	②	②
	Protege	BPE	1.8 (1839)	4.0	2.9	6.1	—	—	—	14.5	②	②
	Protege	BPD	1.8 (1839)	4.0	3.6	6.1	—	—	—	14.5	②	②
	MX-3	B6E	1.6 (1597)	3.4	2.9	6.7	—	—	—	13.2	6.3	6.3
	MX-3	K8D	1.8 (1844)	4.2	2.9	6.1	—	—	—	13.2	7.9	7.9
	626	F2	2.2 (2184)	4.3	3.5	7.2	—	—	—	15.9	7.9	7.9
	626 Turbo	F2	2.2 (2184)	4.3	3.9	7.2	—	—	—	15.9	7.9	7.9
	MX-6	F2	2.2 (2184)	4.3	3.5	7.2	—	—	—	15.9	7.9	7.9
	MX-6 Turbo	F2	2.2 (2184)	4.3	3.9	7.2	—	—	—	15.9	7.9	7.9
1993	323	B6E	1.6 (1597)	3.4	2.8	6.6	—	—	—	13.2	②	②
	Protege	BPD	1.8 (1839)	4.0	2.8	6.6	—	—	—	13.2	②	②
	MX-3	B6E	1.6 (1597)	3.4	2.8	6.6	—	—	—	13.2	6.3	6.3
	MX-3	K8D	1.8 (1844)	4.2	2.9	6.1	—	—	—	13.2	7.9	7.9
	626	FSD	2.0 (1991)	3.7	2.9	9.3	—	—	—	15.5	7.9	7.9
	MX-6/Probe	FSD	2.0 (1991)	3.7	2.9	8.7	—	—	—	15.5	7.4	7.4
	MX-6/Probe	KLD	2.5 (2496)	4.2	2.9	9.3	—	—	—	15.5	7.4	7.4
1994	323	B6ZE	1.6 (1597)	3.4	2.8	6.6	—	—	—	13.2	②	②
	Protege	BPE	1.8 (1839)	4.0	2.8	6.6	—	—	—	13.2	②	②
	Protege	BPD	1.8 (1839)	4.0	2.8	6.6	—	—	—	13.2	6.3	6.3
	MX-3	B6ZE	1.6 (1597)	3.6	2.9	6.7	—	—	—	13.2	6.3	6.3
	MX-3	K8D	1.8 (1844)	4.2	2.9	6.1	—	—	—	13.2	7.9	7.9
	626	FSD	2.0 (1991)	3.7	2.9	9.3	—	—	—	15.5	7.4	7.4
	626	KLD	2.5 (2496)	4.2	2.9	9.3	—	—	—	15.5	7.9	7.9
	MX-6/Probe	FSD	2.0 (1991)	3.7	2.9	8.7	—	—	—	15.5	7.4	7.4
	MX-6/Probe	KLD	2.5 (2496)	4.2	2.9	9.3	—	—	—	15.5	7.9	7.9

ENGLISH TO METRIC CONVERSION: MASS (WEIGHT)

Current mass measurement is expressed in pounds and ounces (lbs. & ozs.). The metric unit of mass (or weight) is the kilogram (kg). Even although this table does not show conversion of masses (weights) larger than 15 lbs, it is easy to calculate larger units by following the data immediately below.

To convert ounces (oz.) to grams (g): multiply th number of ozs. by 28
To convert grams (g) to ounces (oz.): multiply the number of grams by .035

To convert pounds (lbs.) to kilograms (kg): multiply the number of lbs. by .45
To convert kilograms (kg) to pounds (lbs.): multiply the number of kilograms by 2.2

lbs	kg	lbs	kg	oz	kg	oz	kg
0.1	0.04	0.9	0.41	0.1	0.003	0.9	0.024
0.2	0.09	1	0.4	0.2	0.005	1	0.03
0.3	0.14	2	0.9	0.3	0.008	2	0.06
0.4	0.18	3	1.4	0.4	0.011	3	0.08
0.5	0.23	4	1.8	0.5	0.014	4	0.11
0.6	0.27	5	2.3	0.6	0.017	5	0.14
0.7	0.32	10	4.5	0.7	0.020	10	0.28
0.8	0.36	15	6.8	0.8	0.023	15	0.42

ENGLISH TO METRIC CONVERSION: TEMPERATURE

To convert Fahrenheit (°F) to Celsius (°C): take number of °F and subtract 32; multiply result by 5; divide result by 9

To convert Celsius (°C) to Fahrenheit (°F): take number of °C and multiply by 9; divide result by 5; add 32 to total

Fahrenheit (F)	Celsius (C)			Fahrenheit (F)	Celsius (C)			Fahrenheit (F)	Celsius (C)		
°F	°C	°C	°F	°F	°C	°C	°F	°F	°C	°C	°F
−40	−40	−38	−36.4	80	26.7	18	64.4	215	101.7	80	176
−35	−37.2	−36	−32.8	85	29.4	20	68	220	104.4	85	185
−30	−34.4	−34	−29.2	90	32.2	22	71.6	225	107.2	90	194
−25	−31.7	−32	−25.6	95	35.0	24	75.2	230	110.0	95	202
−20	−28.9	−30	−22	100	37.8	26	78.8	235	112.8	100	212
−15	−26.1	−28	−18.4	105	40.6	28	82.4	240	115.6	105	221
−10	−23.3	−26	−14.8	110	43.3	30	86	245	118.3	110	230
−5	−20.6	−24	−11.2	115	46.1	32	89.6	250	121.1	115	239
0	−17.8	−22	−7.6	120	48.9	34	93.2	255	123.9	120	248
1	−17.2	−20	−4	125	51.7	36	96.8	260	126.6	125	257
2	−16.7	−18	−0.4	130	54.4	38	100.4	265	129.4	130	266
3	−16.1	−16	3.2	135	57.2	40	104	270	132.2	135	275
4	−15.6	−14	6.8	140	60.0	42	107.6	275	135.0	140	284
5	−15.0	−12	10.4	145	62.8	44	112.2	280	137.8	145	293
10	−12.2	−10	14	150	65.6	46	114.8	285	140.6	150	302
15	−9.4	−8	17.6	155	68.3	48	118.4	290	143.3	155	311
20	−6.7	−6	21.2	160	71.1	50	122	295	146.1	160	320
25	−3.9	−4	24.8	165	73.9	52	125.6	300	148.9	165	329
30	−1.1	−2	28.4	170	76.7	54	129.2	305	151.7	170	338
35	1.7	0	32	175	79.4	56	132.8	310	154.4	175	347
40	4.4	2	35.6	180	82.2	58	136.4	315	157.2	180	356
45	7.2	4	39.2	185	85.0	60	140	320	160.0	185	365
50	10.0	6	42.8	190	87.8	62	143.6	325	162.8	190	374
55	12.8	8	46.4	195	90.6	64	147.2	330	165.6	195	383
60	15.6	10	50	200	93.3	66	150.8	335	168.3	200	392
65	18.3	12	53.6	205	96.1	68	154.4	340	171.1	205	401
70	21.1	14	57.2	210	98.9	70	158	345	173.9	210	410
75	23.9	16	60.8	212	100.0	75	167	350	176.7	215	414

TCCS1C01

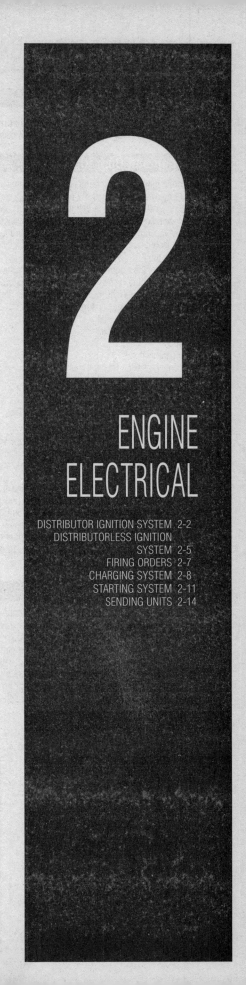

2

ENGINE
ELECTRICAL

DISTRIBUTOR IGNITION SYSTEM

➡For information on understanding electricity and troubleshooting electrical circuits, please refer to Section 6 of this manual.

Description and Operation

The electronic ignition on the normally aspirated engines is a fully transistorized, high energy system. On 1990–92 non-turbo 2.2L engines, it is a conventional electronic ignition system in that it operates with both centrifugal and vacuum advance mechanisms controlling ignition advance. The ignition timing is advanced by vacuum at low speeds and by the centrifugal mechanism at higher speeds. Proper engine performance and satisfactory exhaust emissions are controlled by the ECU.

The ECU controls the electronic ignition on all other engines including, the turbocharged 2.2L engine. The system is entirely electronic. The ECU sends the spark timing signal through the ignition module to the distributor based on its triggering signal from various sensors and switches. The sensors and switches include the following:

- Vane or mass air flow meter
- Idle switch
- Neutral gear switch
- Clutch engage switch (manual transmissions)
- EGR valve position sensor
- Knock sensor
- Throttle position sensor
- Engine coolant temperature sensor
- Engine coolant temperature switch

Other non-electronic components in the system include the starter interlock switch, battery, distributor, spark plugs, high tension leads and ignition module. The distributor provides a signal to the ECU to indicate crankshaft top dead center by means of its cylinder TDC sensors.

Both systems operate in the same manner. The power relay closes and changes the coil primary windings when the ignition switch is turned **ON**. When the engine is running, the ignition module grounds the negative side of the coil primary circuit which induces spark. This results in an inductive charge built up in the secondary circuit. Then the spark is sent to the distributor where the rotor and distributor cap work together to deliver spark to each spark plug.

Diagnosis and Testing

Before beginning any diagnosis and testing procedures, visually inspect the components of the ignition system and check for a possible discharged battery, damaged or loose electrical connections, blown fuses or damaged vacuum hoses. Also inspect the rotor and distributor cap for excessive wear, the spark plugs for damage and make sure that the distributor cap, rotor and spark plug wires are properly seated. Check the spark plug wires and boots for signs of poor insulation that could cause cross firing. Turn all accessories off during diagnosis and testing. Make sure the idle speed is within specification.

IGNITION COIL SPARK TEST

♦ See Figure 1

➡This test is only possible with engines using an external coil.

1. Disconnect the distributor lead wire from the distributor.
2. Hold the distributor lead wire with insulated pliers approximately 0.20–0.39 in. (5–10mm) from a ground.
3. While holding the wire in position, crank the engine.
4. A strong blue spark should be seen. If there is no spark, the ignition coil or pickup coil may be bad.
5. Replace the pickup coil or the ignition coil and test again.

DISTRIBUTOR SPARK TEST

♦ See Figure 1

1. Disconnect the spark plug wires from each spark plug.
2. Hold the end of the spark plug wire with insulated pliers 0.20–0.39 in. (5–10mm) from a ground. A spark tester may be connected to the plug wire end.
3. While holding the wire in position, crank the engine.
4. A strong blue spark should be seen. If there is no spark, the plug wires (refer to Section 1) and the distributor and/or coil should be checked.

Ignition Coil

IGNITION COIL RESISTANCE TEST

External Coils

♦ See Figures 2, 3 and 4

1. Disconnect the distributor wire from the coil.
2. Disconnect the electrical connector from the coil.
3. Check the resistance of the ignition coil primary by connecting an ohmmeter to both electrical terminals on the coil.
4. Check the resistance of the ignition coil secondary windings by connecting an ohmmeter to coil positive terminal and the coil-to-distributor wire tower terminal.
5. The resistance for all coils, except on 2.2L engines, should be as follows:
   a. Primary coil winding—0.81–0.99 ohms.
   b. Secondary coil winding—10–16 kilo ohms.
6. The resistance for the coil on 2.2L engines, should be as follows:
   a. Primary coil winding (turbo)—0.72–0.88 ohms.
   b. Primary coil winding (non-turbo)—0.77–0.95 ohms.
   c. Secondary coil winding—10.3–13.9 kilo-ohms.
7. If the ignition coil resistance is not within specifications, replace the ignition coil.

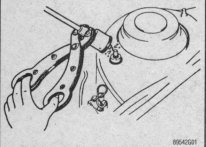

Fig. 1 To perform a spark test, hold the coil or spark plug wire 0.20–0.39 in. (5–10mm) from a ground and observe the spark

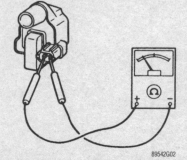

Fig. 2 Connect an ohmmeter on both terminals of the ignition coil and measure the primary resistance

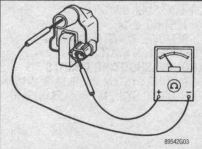

Fig. 3 Connect an ohmmeter on to the positive terminal of the ignition coil and the coil wire tower to check the secondary resistance

8. If the ignition coil is within the specified limits, connect a voltmeter to the ignition coil wire harness connectors positive terminal and a ground. Turn the ignition on and verify that you have battery voltage at the connector.

9. If voltage is present, perform a spark test.

10. If voltage is not present, check the wire harness and fuses for shorts or breaks.

Integral with Distributor Coil

▶ See Figures 4, 5 and 6

1. Disconnect the distributor wire from the coil.
2. Disconnect the 3 pin electrical connector from the coil.
3. Use an ohmmeter and check the resistance of the ignition coil primary winding. Connect the ohmmeter to the two outside terminals on the distributor (A and C). Terminal A is the closest terminal to the 6-pin connector, terminal B is in the middle and terminal C is the last terminal.
4. The resistance should be 0.58–0.86 ohms.
5. If the resistance is not within specifications, replace the distributor assembly. If the resistance is within specifications, proceed with step 6.
6. Remove the distributor cap and use an ohmmeter to measure the secondary coil resistance. Connect the ohmmeter to terminal C and the coil tower connector.
7. The resistance should be 11.5–18.5 ohms.
8. If the ignition coil resistance is not within specifications, replace the distributor.
9. If the ignition coil is within the specified limits, connect a voltmeter to the ignition coil wire harness connectors positive terminal (terminal C) and a ground. Turn the ignition on and verify that you have battery voltage at the connector.
10. If voltage is present, perform a spark test.
11. If voltage is not present, check the wire harness and fuses for shorts or breaks.

REMOVAL & INSTALLATION

External Coil except 1990–92 626 and MX-6

1. Disconnect the negative battery cable.
2. Disconnect the distributor lead wire from the coil.
3. Disconnect the electrical connector from the coil.
4. Remove the coil attaching bolts and remove the coil.
5. Installation is the reverse of the removal procedure.

1990–92 626 and MX6

NORMALLY ASPIRATED ENGINE

1. Disconnect the negative battery cable.
2. Disconnect the high tension lead from the coil by first twisting, then pulling it from the coil terminal.
3. Disconnect the distributor wiring harness from the coil. Tag the wires so they can be reinstalled in their original positions.
4. Remove the 2 mounting nuts and remove the coil and bracket assembly.
5. Loosen the clamp screw at the coil bracket and remove the coil.
6. Installation is the reverse of the removal procedure.

TURBOCHARGED ENGINE

1. Disconnect the negative battery cable.
2. Disconnect the high tension lead from the coil by first twisting, then pulling it from the coil terminal.
3. Disconnect the igniter wiring harness and remove the 2 nuts.
4. Lift the coil and igniter assembly and disconnect the coil and noise suppressor wiring harness. Tag the wires so they can be reinstalled in their original positions.
5. Slide the protective cover back and disconnect the coil wiring harness. Tag the wires so they can be reinstalled in their original positions.
6. Remove the noise suppressor. Remove the 2 screws and the ignitor module.
7. Remove the ignitor module mounting bracket and the coil.
8. Installation is the reverse of the removal procedure.

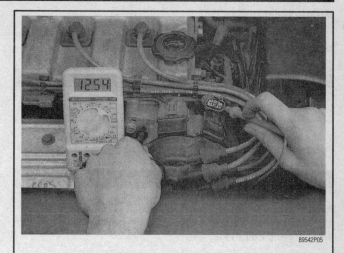

Fig. 4 Use a voltmeter in the ignition coil wire harness connector positive terminal to check for voltage to the coil

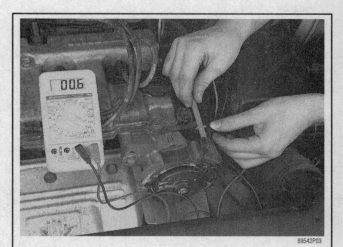

Fig. 5 Connect an ohmmeter on terminals A and C of the ignition coil distributor connector and measure the primary resistance

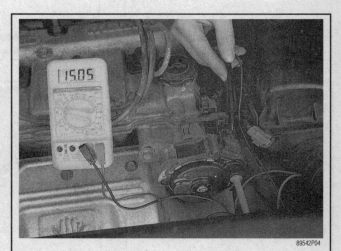

Fig. 6 Connect an ohmmeter to the positive terminal of the ignition coil connector and the coil tower to check the secondary resistance

Integral with Distributor Coil

The ignition coil is integrated within the distributor assembly and cannot be replaced. If the coil malfunctions, the distributor must be replaced.

Ignition Module

REMOVAL & INSTALLATION

The ignition module is integrated within the distributor and cannot be replaced. If the module has malfunctioned, the distributor must be replaced.

Distributor

REMOVAL

◆ **See Figures 7 thru 15**

1. Disconnect the negative battery cable.
2. Remove the distributor cap and position it aside, leaving the ignition wires connected.
3. On SOHC engines, remove the air intake hose from it's position next to the distributor.
4. Disconnect the distributor electrical connector(s) from the side of the distributor.
5. Using a wrench on the crankshaft pulley, rotate the crankshaft to position the No. 1 piston on Top Dead Center (TDC) of the compression stroke; the crankshaft pulley mark should align with the timing indicator and the distributor rotor should point towards the No 1. spark plug wire tower position of the cap.
6. Using chalk or paint, mark the position of the distributor housing on the cylinder head. Also mark the position of the distributor rotor in relation to the distributor housing.

7. Remove the distributor hold-down bolt(s).
8. On distributors attached to the end of the cylinder head (or inline with the camshaft), remove it by pulling it straight outward.
9. On distributors attached to the side of the cylinder head (or perpendicular with the camshaft), slowly pull it outward while watching the rotor. These distributors are gear driven and as you remove it, the gears will unmesh inside the engine, causing the rotor to rotate. when the rotor stops moving, stop pulling outward. Re-align the distributor body-to-cylinder head matchmark (do not push it back in to do this, simply rotate the body to align the marks). Place a third mark indicating the new rotor position-to-distributor body relation. When installing the distributor, align this mark and the body-to-head mark to properly position the distributor.
10. Inspect the O-ring on the distributor housing and replace it, if it is damaged or worn.

INSTALLATION

Engine Not Rotated

1. Using engine oil, lubricate the O-ring.
2. Install the distributor, aligning the marks that were made in Step 6 of the removal procedure. Be sure to engage the drive gear or tangs with the camshaft gear or slot in the camshaft.
3. Tighten the distributor hold-down bolt(s).
4. Connect the electrical connector(s) and, if equipped, air intake hose. Install the distributor cap.
5. Connect the negative battery cable. Start the engine and check or adjust the ignition timing. Refer to Section 1.

Engine Rotated

1. Disconnect the spark plug wire from the No. 1 cylinder spark plug. Remove the spark plug from the No. 1 cylinder and press a thumb over the spark plug hole.

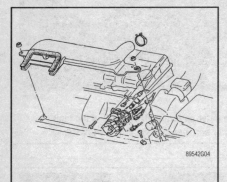

Fig. 7 Exploded view of a typical side mounted distributor

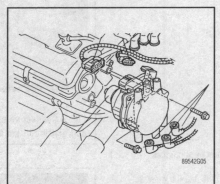

Fig. 8 Exploded view of a typical end or inline mounted distributor

Fig. 9 To remove the distributor, first label the spark plug wires attached to the cap with their cylinder numbers and disconnect them . . .

Fig. 10 . . . as well as the distributor wire harness plugs

Fig. 11 Matchmark the distributor body to the cylinder head

Fig. 12 Remove the distributor retaining bolts and cap. Ensure that the matchmark made earlier is still in alignment

Fig. 13 Make another matchmark on the distributor body to show the direction the rotor is pointing

Fig. 14 On gear driven distributors (see text), pull out slowly and make a third matchmark where the rotor points (as it will rotate slowly)

Fig. 15 Remove the distributor from the engine

2. Using a wrench on the crankshaft pulley, rotate the crankshaft until pressure is felt at the spark plug hole, indicating the piston is approaching TDC on the compression stroke. Continue rotating the crankshaft until the crankshaft pulley mark aligns with the timing cover indicator.

3. Place the distributor rotor in position so that it aligns with the No. 1 spark plug wire tower on the distributor cap.

4. Using engine oil, lubricate the O-ring.

5. Install the distributor. Be sure to engage the drive gear or tangs with the camshaft gear or slot. Align the mark that was made on the distributor housing with the mark that was made on the cylinder head. Tighten the distributor hold-down bolt(s).

6. Connect the electrical connector(s) and, if equipped, the air intake hose. Install the distributor cap.

7. Install the spark plug in the No. 1 cylinder and connect the spark plug wire.

8. Connect the negative battery cable. Start the engine and check or adjust the ignition timing. Refer to Section 1.

Crankshaft and Camshaft Position Sensors

Refer to Section 4, Driveability and Emission Controls, for service procedures.

DISTRIBUTORLESS IGNITION SYSTEM

General Information

➡The 1995–98 Mazda Millenia S with the 2.3L Miller-cycle supercharged engine and the 1998 2.0L and 2.5L engines use a distributorless ignition system.

The 2.3L engine utilizes an individual coil for each spark plug. Which means it has six separate coils which are all controlled by the engine computer.

The 1998 2.0L and 2.5L (except Millenia) engines utilize a coil pack, with 4 or 6 terminals on it. The system is known as a waste spark system since two plug wires are fired at the same time; one for a cylinder on compression, the other for a cylinder on exhaust.

The ECU sends the spark timing signal through the ignition module in the coil based on its triggering signal from various sensors and switches. The sensors and switches include the following:

- Vane or Mass Air Flow (MAF or MAS) meter
- Manifold Absolute Pressure (MAP) sensor
- Idle switch
- Neutral gear switch
- EGR valve position sensor
- Knock sensor
- Throttle Position Sensor (TPS)
- CranKshaft Position (CKP) sensor
- CaMshaft Position (CMP) sensor
- Engine Coolant Temperature (ECT) sensor
- Engine coolant temperature switch

The CrankShaft Position (CKP) sensor provides a signal to the ECU to indicate crankshaft Top Dead Center (TDC). The CaMshaft Position (CMP) sensor provides a signal to the ECU to indicate whether the engine is at TDC compression, or TDC exhaust.

Both systems operate in the same manner. The power relay closes and changes the coil primary windings when the ignition switch is turned **ON**. When the engine is running, each ignition module grounds the negative side of its coil primary circuit which induces spark. This results in an inductive charge built up in the secondary circuit. The spark is then sent directly to the spark plug that the coil assembly rests on top of (2.3L engines) or through the spark plug wire connected to that coil pack (1998 2.0L and 2.5L engines).

Other non-electronic components in the system include the starter interlock switch, battery and spark plugs.

Diagnosis and Testing

Before beginning any diagnosis and testing procedures, visually inspect the components of the ignition system and check for a possible discharged battery, damaged or loose electrical connections, blown fuses or damaged vacuum hoses. Also inspect the spark plugs for damage and make sure that the coils are properly seated. Check the spark plug towers and boots for signs of poor insulation that could cause spark grounding. Turn all accessories off during diagnosis and testing. Make sure the idle speed is within specification.

The following tools are required; a quality digital volt-ohmmeter, a remote starter and a spark tester for checking the ignition system. A spark tester resembles a spark plug without threads and the side electrode removed. Do not attempt to use a modified spark plug.

IGNITION COIL SPARK TEST

2.3L Engine

1. Remove one of the ignition coils, but leave the 4-wire connector plugged in.
2. Hold the coil with insulated pliers approximately 0.20–0.39 in. (5–10mm) from a ground.
3. While holding the coil in position, crank the engine.
4. A strong blue spark should be seen.
5. Repeat the test for each of the coils mounted on the engine.
6. If a spark is seen from some of the coils, and no trouble codes or check engine light is present, proceed as follows:

   a. Replace the faulty ignition coil with a known good unit and test again.

   b. If there is a spark visible, replace the defective coil.

   c. If there is still no spark, check the following ECM terminals for proper voltage (0 volts with ignition switch on, or 0.05 volts with engine idling):
- Cylinder No. 1: terminal 4S
- Cylinder No. 2: terminal 4W
- Cylinder No. 3: terminal 4AA
- Cylinder No. 4: terminal 4AE
- Cylinder No. 5: terminal 4AI
- Cylinder No. 6: terminal 4AM

   d. If the voltages are not normal, inspect and repair the ignition coil related wiring harnesses, connectors, power supply and grounds.

e. If the voltages are normal, Mazda recommends replacing the ECM. However, due to the cost of an ECM, Chilton recommends having the vehicle professionally tested with a scan tool designed specifically for the vehicle, before purchasing the ECM for replacement.

7. If no spark is seen from any of the coils or a trouble code or check engine light is present, proceed as follows:

a. Check to see if the following diagnostic trouble codes are present (refer to Section 4 for trouble code retrieval instructions):
- P0335—CranKshaft Position sensor (CKP) circuit malfunction
- P1345—SGC signal

b. If either of the two codes were found, carry out an inspection of the circuits related to the trouble code. Refer to Section 4.

c. If no codes are present, repair or replace the wiring harness connector between the ignition coil and ignition switch.

8. If a spark is seen from all coils, the system is normal.

1998 2.0L and 2.5L (except Millenia) Engines

▶ See Figure 16

1. Disconnect the spark plug wires from each spark plug.
2. Hold the end of the spark plug wire with insulated pliers 0.20–0.39 in. (5–10mm) from a ground. A spark tester may be connected to the plug wire end.
3. While holding the wire in position, crank the engine.
4. A strong blue spark should be seen. If there is no spark, the plug wires (refer to Section 1) and the coil pack should be checked.

Ignition Coil

TESTING

2.3L Engine

Because the ignition control module is integrated with the ignition coil, it is difficult to simply test the coil assembly itself. Refer to the ignition coil spark test given earlier in this section.

1998 2.0L and 2.5L (except Millenia) Engines

PRIMARY COIL WINDING RESISTANCE

▶ See Figures 17 and 18

1. Detach the coil pack wire harness connector.
2. On 2.0L engines, measure the resistance between the terminals as follows:
a. Connect an ohmmeter to terminals A and B and record the reading.
b. Connect an ohmmeter to terminals C and B and record the reading.
3. On 2.5L engines, measure the resistance between the terminals as follows:
a. Connect an ohmmeter to terminals A and D and record the reading.
b. Connect an ohmmeter to terminals B and D and record the reading.
c. Connect an ohmmeter to terminals C and D and record the reading.

4. The resistance specification is 0.45–0.55 ohms at 68°F (20°C).
5. If any of the readings are not within specification, replace the coil pack.

SECONDARY COIL WIRE RESISTANCE

▶ See Figures 19 and 20

1. Label and detach the spark plug wires from the coil pack.
2. On 2.0L engines, measure the resistance between the spark plug terminals as follows:
a. Connect an ohmmeter to terminals 1 and 4 and record the reading.
b. Connect an ohmmeter to terminals 2 and 3 and record the reading.
3. On 2.5L engines, measure the resistance between the spark plug terminals as follows:
a. Connect an ohmmeter to terminals 1 and 4 and record the reading.
b. Connect an ohmmeter to terminals 2 and 5 and record the reading.
c. Connect an ohmmeter to terminals 3 and 6 and record the reading.
4. The resistance specification is 11.5–15.5k ohms at 68°F (20°C).
5. If any of the readings are not within specification, replace the coil pack.

REMOVAL & INSTALLATION

2.3L Engine

▶ See Figures 21 and 22

1. For the front bank of spark plugs, remove the charge air cooler.
2. For the rear bank of spark plugs, remove the solenoid bracket assembly.
3. Detach the ignition coil 4-pin connector.
4. Remove the ignition coil attaching screws and remove the coil by pulling it straight up.

To install:

5. Inspect the coil-to-spark plug connection area for cracks or damage. If damage to the coil is found, replace the assembly.
6. Position the ignition coil over the spark plug and press it down firmly to ensure full engagement.
7. Align the mounting holes and install the coil attaching screws. Tighten the screws to 40–57 inch lbs. (4.5–6.4 Nm).
8. Attach the ignition coil 4-pin connector.
9. For the front bank of spark plugs, lubricate the sealing washers and install the charge air cooler. Tighten the attaching nuts to 12–16 ft. lbs. (16–22 Nm).
10. For the rear bank of spark plugs, install the solenoid bracket assembly.

1998 2.0L and 2.5L (except Millenia) Engines

▶ See Figures 23 and 24

1. Disconnect the negative battery cable.
2. As necessary for clearance, remove the air intake ducting.
3. Label and disconnect the spark plug wires from the coil pack.
4. Detach the electrical wire harness plug from the coil pack.
5. Remove the four coil pack-to-mounting bracket attaching bolts and remove the coil.

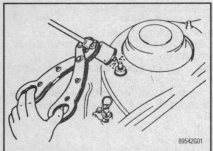

Fig. 16 To perform a spark test, hold the coil or spark plug wire 0.20–0.39 in. (5–10mm) from a ground and observe the spark

Fig. 17 View of the 2.0L engine coil pack terminal identification

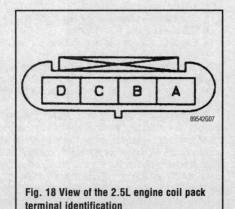

Fig. 18 View of the 2.5L engine coil pack terminal identification

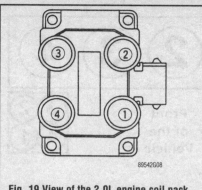

Fig. 19 View of the 2.0L engine coil pack spark plug terminal identification

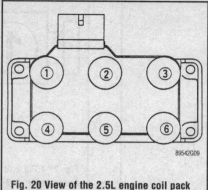

Fig. 20 View of the 2.5L engine coil pack spark plug terminal identification

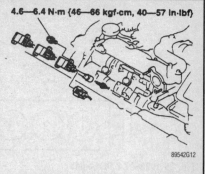

Fig. 21 Exploded view of the left-hand coil pack assemblies

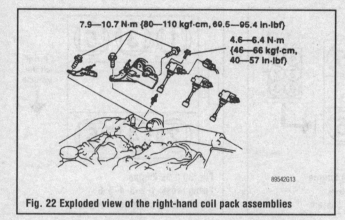

Fig. 22 Exploded view of the right-hand coil pack assemblies

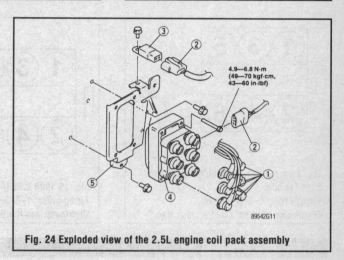

Fig. 24 Exploded view of the 2.5L engine coil pack assembly

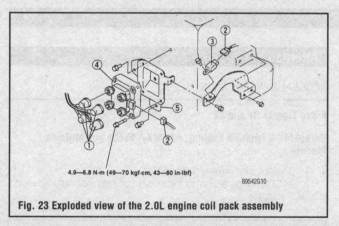

Fig. 23 Exploded view of the 2.0L engine coil pack assembly

6. Installation is the reverse of the removal procedure. Tighten the attaching bolts to 43–60 inch lbs. (5–7 Nm).

Ignition Module

The ignition module is integrated within the ignition coil itself, and the only repair possible is to replace the entire coil assembly.

➡ There are six ignition coils, therefore there are six ignition modules.

Crankshaft and Camshaft Position Sensors

Refer to Section 4, Driveability and Emission Controls, for service procedures.

FIRING ORDERS

♦ See Figures 25 thru 30

➡ To avoid confusion, remove and tag the spark plug wires one at a time, for replacement.

If a distributor is not keyed for installation with only one orientation, it could have been removed previously and rewired. The resultant wiring would hold the correct firing order, but could change the relative placement of the plug towers in relation to the engine. For this reason it is imperative that you label all wires before disconnecting any of them. Also, before removal, compare the current wiring with the accompanying illustrations. If the current wiring does not match, make notes in your book to reflect how your engine is wired.

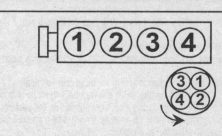

Fig. 25 1.5L, 1.6L, 1.8L (except K8) and 2.2L Engines
Firing order: 1–3–4–2
Distributor rotation: Counterclockwise

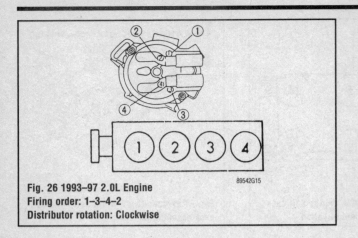

Fig. 26 1993–97 2.0L Engine
Firing order: 1–3–4–2
Distributor rotation: Clockwise

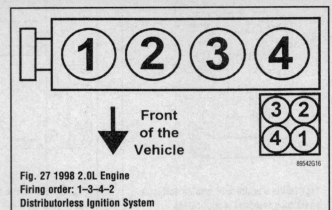

Fig. 27 1998 2.0L Engine
Firing order: 1–3–4–2
Distributorless Ignition System

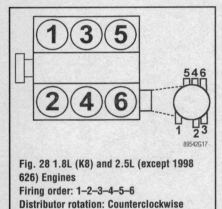

Fig. 28 1.8L (K8) and 2.5L (except 1998 626) Engines
Firing order: 1–2–3–4–5–6
Distributor rotation: Counterclockwise

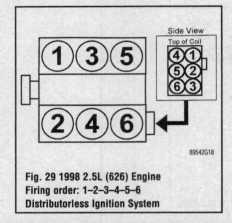

Fig. 29 1998 2.5L (626) Engine
Firing order: 1–2–3–4–5–6
Distributorless Ignition System

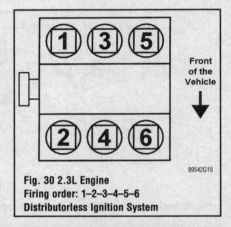

Fig. 30 2.3L Engine
Firing order: 1–2–3–4–5–6
Distributorless Ignition System

CHARGING SYSTEM

General Information

All Mazda vehicles use a small, high rpm, high performance type alternator with an integral regulator. The alternator also features a self check capability which monitors system operation and will illuminate a warning lamp should the system fail to operate within specifications.

Alternator Precautions

Several precautions must be observed with alternator equipped vehicles to avoid damage to the unit.

- If the battery is removed for any reason, make sure it is reconnected with the correct polarity. Reversing the battery connections may result in damage to the one-way rectifiers.
- When utilizing a booster battery as a starting aid, always connect the positive to positive terminals and the negative terminal from the booster battery to a good engine ground on the vehicle being started.
- Never use a fast charger as a booster to start vehicles.
- Disconnect the battery cables when charging the battery with a fast charger.
- Never attempt to polarize the alternator.
- Do not use test lights of more than 12 volts when checking diode continuity.
- Do not short across or ground any of the alternator terminals.
- The polarity of the battery, alternator and regulator must be matched and considered before making any electrical connections within the system.
- Never separate the alternator on an open circuit. Make sure all connections within the circuit are clean and tight.
- Disconnect the battery ground terminal when performing any service on electrical components.
- Disconnect the battery if arc welding is to be done on the vehicle.

Alternator

REMOVAL & INSTALLATION

♦ **See Figures 31 and 32**

Except MX-3 (with V6 Engine), 626/MX-6/Probe and Millenia Models

1. Disconnect the negative battery cable.
2. On 323/Protege, disconnect the vacuum hose and remove the solenoid bracket, if equipped.

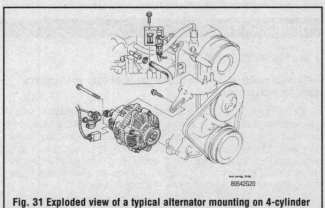

Fig. 31 Exploded view of a typical alternator mounting on 4-cylinder engines

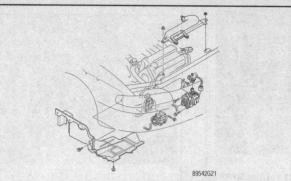

Fig. 32 Exploded view of a typical alternator mounting on 6-cylinder engines

3. On 1995–98 1.8L engines, remove the pressure pipe bracket and the EGR solenoid valve bracket.

4. Label and disconnect the electrical connectors from the alternator.

5. Remove the alternator drive belt.

6. On the 1995–98 1.8L engines, remove the alternator bracket.

7. Remove the alternator pivot and adjusting bar bolts and remove the alternator.

To install:

8. Install the alternator with the through–bolt.

9. On the 1995–98 1.8L engines, install the alternator bracket.

10. Connect the alternator electrical connectors.

11. Install the drive belt and upper mounting bolt. Adjust the belt tension. Tighten the lower through–bolt to 27–38 ft. lbs. (37–52 Nm) and the upper mounting bolt to 12–19 ft. lbs. (16–26 Nm).

12. On the 1995–98 1.8L engines, install the pressure pipe bracket and the EGR solenoid valve bracket.

13. Connect the negative battery cable.

4-Cylinder 626 and MX6 Models

▶ See Figures 33 thru 42

1. Disconnect the negative battery cable.

2. Remove the alternator upper mounting bolt.

3. Loosen the alternator adjusting bolt and remove the drive belt from the alternator pulley.

4. Raise and safely support the vehicle.

5. Remove the 6 bolts and remove the transverse member.

6. Disconnect the electrical connectors from the alternator.

7. Remove the front exhaust pipe as follows:

a. Support the exhaust system at the catalytic converter with a jack or by suspending it on a piece of wire.

b. Disconnect the oxygen sensor electrical connector and remove the sensor using a sensor wrench.

c. Remove the 3 exhaust manifold flange nuts and remove the clamp from the hold-down bracket.

d. Remove the exhaust pipe-to-converter nuts and pry the rubber hangers from the mounting hooks. Remove the pipe.

8. Remove the alternator lower through-bolt and remove the alternator.

To install:

9. Install the alternator with the through-bolt.

10. Install the exhaust pipe, using new gaskets. Tighten the pipe-to-converter nuts to 28–38 ft. lbs. (38–51 Nm) and the exhaust manifold flange nuts to 28–38 ft. lbs. (38–51 Nm). Tighten the exhaust clamp nuts to 14–18 ft. lbs. (19–25 Nm).

11. Install the oxygen sensor, using a sensor wrench, and tighten to 36 ft. lbs. (49 Nm). Connect the oxygen sensor electrical connector.

12. Connect the alternator electrical connectors.

13. Install the transverse member and tighten the bolts to 68–96 ft. lbs. (94–131 Nm). Lower the vehicle.

14. Install the drive belt and upper mounting bolt. Adjust the belt tension. Tighten the lower through-bolt to 24–33 ft. lbs. (32–46 Nm) and the upper mounting bolt to 12–16 ft. lbs. (16–22 Nm).

15. Connect the negative battery cable.

Fig. 33 To remove the alternator, first, remove the drive belt and upper mounting bolt. Next, remove the crossmember attaching bolts . . .

Fig. 34 . . . then remove the crossmember. Do not remove the transmission support member

Fig. 35 Unbolt the exhaust pipe from the engine manifold and also at the converter

Fig. 36 Disconnect the exhaust hangers (arrow) and separate the pipe from the converter.

Fig. 37 Support the catalytic converter either on a jackstand, or suspending it by length of mechanic's wire (arrow)

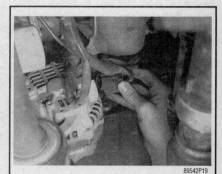

Fig. 38 Label and detach the wire harness plug (or plugs) from the alternator . . .

Fig. 39 . . . then, using the proper size socket, remove the battery positive terminal retaining nut (arrow)

Fig. 40 Remove the battery positive terminal wire from its attaching post on the alternator

Fig. 41 Remove the alternator lower through-bolt . . .

Fig. 42 . . . then remove the alternator by lowering through the access opening afforded by removing the crossmember and exhaust pipe

6-Cylinder MX3, 626 and MX6 Models

1. Disconnect the negative battery cable.
2. Remove the fresh air duct and radiator upper bracket.
3. If equipped, remove the condenser fan.
4. Disconnect the electrical connectors from the alternator.
5. Loosen the belt tensioner locknut and tension adjusting bolt. Remove the alternator upper mounting bolt.
6. Raise and safely support the vehicle.
7. Remove the right splash shield.
8. Remove the drive belt from the alternator pulley.
9. If necessary, remove the A/C compressor mounting bolts and support the compressor aside, leaving the refrigerant lines connected.
10. Remove the alternator through-bolt and the alternator.

To install:

11. Position the alternator and install the through-bolt. Tighten the alternator through-bolt to 24–33 ft. lbs. (32–46 Nm) on the 1.8L, and to 38 ft. lbs. (51 Nm) on the 2.5L engine.
12. If removed, install the mounting bolts and tighten the A/C compressor mounting bolts to 26 ft. lbs. (35 Nm).
13. Install the right splash shield, and lower the vehicle.
14. Install the drive belt and adjust the tension.
15. Install the alternator upper mounting bolt and tighten to 18 ft. lbs. (25 Nm).
16. Tighten the belt tensioner locknut and tension adjusting bolt.
17. Connect the electrical connectors from the alternator.
18. If removed, install the condenser fan.
19. Install the radiator upper bracket and fresh air duct.
20. Connect the negative battery cable.

Millenia

1. Disconnect the negative battery cable.
2. On models equipped with the 2.3L engine, remove the front charge air cooler, radiator upper seal board and the condenser fan assembly.
3. Disconnect the electrical connectors from the alternator.
4. Raise and safely support the vehicle.
5. Remove the right splash shield.
6. Remove the drive belt from the alternator pulley.
7. Remove the A/C compressor mounting bolts and support the compressor aside, leaving the refrigerant lines connected.
8. Remove the upper and lower alternator mounting bolts and the alternator.

To install:

9. Position the alternator and install the through-bolt. Tighten the alternator lower bolt to 24–33 ft. lbs. (32–46 Nm). Install the alternator upper mounting bolt and tighten to 12–16 ft. lbs. (16–22 Nm).
10. Install the mounting bolts and tighten the A/C compressor mounting bolts to 12–16 ft. lbs. (16–22 Nm).
11. Install the right splash shield, and lower the vehicle.
12. Install the drive belt.
13. Connect the electrical connectors to the alternator.
14. If removed, install the condenser fan assembly, radiator upper seal board and the front charge air cooler using new O-rings. Tighten the mounting bolts to 12–16 ft. lbs. (16–22 Nm).
15. Connect the negative battery cable.

TESTING

1. Verify that the battery if fully charged.
2. Ensure that the alternator drive belt is in good condition, and proper belt tension is maintained.
3. Turn off all electrical loads. Ensure that the cooling fan does not run.
4. Turn the ignition switch to **ON** and verify that the alternator warning light is on. If not, inspect the bulb and the wire harness between the alternator and the bulb.
5. Turn the ignition switch to **START** and verify that the alternator turns smoothly, without any noise while the engine is running.

✵ CAUTION

While the engine is running, keep yourself, loose clothing, long hair and any test equipment out of the path of rotating components. Severe injury or even death can occur.

6. Measure the voltage at the B + terminal of the alternator. The voltage should read 13.0–15.0 volts with the engine idling.
7. If the reading is not correct, check the charging system wiring harness. If the harness is OK, replace the alternator.

STARTING SYSTEM

General Information

♦ **See Figure 43**

Mazda uses three types of starters in their vehicles; conventional, reduction and direct drive.

Conventional starters use four individually wound magnets to produce a strong magnetic field. This field induces the armature to turn against these field. In addition to the magnetic field turning the armature, it also pulls down a lever, which in turn throws out the starter drive to engage into the flywheel teeth.

Reduction starters use a high speed electric motor to drive a gear-set. Some utilize a planetary gear-set while others use a standard small gear driving a larger gear. By using reduction gearing, a relatively weak electric motor can have its output turning power multiplied before it reaches the flywheel.

Direct drive starters, also use an electric motor, but their output speed and turning power is sent directly to the flywheel.

All starters utilize some sort of over-running clutch system, so that when the engine speed exceeds the starters, the unit will not be damaged.

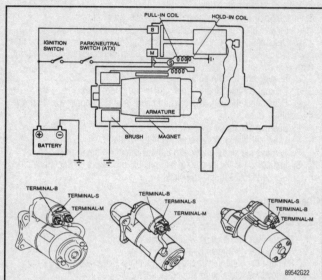

Fig. 43 Example of the various starter configurations and basic electrical system schematic

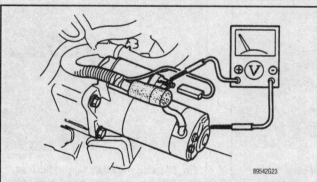

Fig. 44 Connect a voltmeter to the starter terminals and ground to check for battery voltage at the starter

Starter

TESTING

♦ **See Figures 43 and 44**

1. Ensure that the battery is fully charged.
2. Inspect the starter wire connections at the starter for looseness or corrosion.
3. Follow the positive battery cable to the starter and ensure that battery voltage is reaching the starter.
4. If battery voltage is found at the starter, continue with the test. If not, inspect or replace the battery cable.
5. If equipped with a manual transaxle, depress the clutch pedal.
6. Turn the ignition to **START** position and check for battery voltage at the S terminal of the starter.
7. If battery voltage is found at the S terminal, remove the starter and inspect the starter relay, field coil and armature. Replace as necessary.
8. If no battery voltage is found at the S terminal, inspect the ignition switch, wire harness and, if equipped, clutch pedal interlock switch (MTX) or transmission range sensor/neutral safety switch (ATX).

REMOVAL & INSTALLATION

♦ **See Figures 45, 46 and 47**

1995–98 Protege Models

1. Disconnect the negative battery cable.
2. Remove the air cleaner.
3. Raise and safely support the vehicle.
4. Disconnect the catalytic converter pipe from the front pipe.
5. Remove the intake manifold support bracket bolts and the bracket.
6. Disconnect the electrical connectors from the starter and solenoid.
7. Remove the starter mounting bolts, and remove the starter.

To install:

8. Position the starter and loosely tighten the lower starter mounting bolt.
9. Connect the electrical connectors to the starter solenoid and the starter.

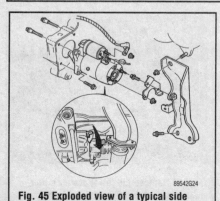

Fig. 45 Exploded view of a typical side mounted starter assembly

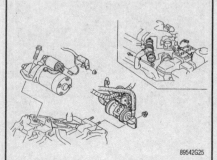

Fig. 46 Exploded view of a typical top mounted (mostly V6 engines with automatic transmissions) starter assembly

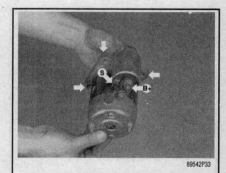

Fig. 47 View of the starter motor mounting bolt locations and electrical terminal identification

10. Install the intake manifold support bracket bolts and the bracket. Tighten the bolts to 28–38 ft. lbs. (38–51 Nm).

11. Install the upper starter mounting bolts. Tighten all starter mounting bolts to 24–33 ft. lbs. (32–46 Nm). The upper mounting bolts must be tightened first.

12. Connect the catalytic converter pipe to the front pipe. Tighten the bolts to 28–38 ft. lbs. (38–51 Nm).

13. Lower the vehicle.

14. Install the air cleaner.

15. Connect the negative battery cable.

MX-3 with 1.8L Engine

1. Disconnect the negative battery cable.
2. Remove the nuts and the upper strut bar from between the strut towers.
3. Remove the intake air hose from between the air cleaner and throttle body.
4. Label and disconnect the wiring from the starter.
5. Remove the mounting bolts and remove the starter.

To install:

6. Install the starter and install the mounting bolts. Tighten the bolts to 38 ft. lbs. (52 Nm).
7. Connect the wiring to the starter.
8. Install the intake air hose between the air cleaner and throttle body.
9. Install the upper strut bar to between the strut towers.
10. Connect the negative battery cable.

1993–98 626/MX-6/Probe Models

2.0L ENGINE

▶ See Figures 48 thru 53

1. Disconnect the negative battery cable.
2. Remove the fresh air duct and resonance chamber.
3. Label and disconnect the electrical connectors and remove the air cleaner assembly.

4. Remove the intake manifold bracket.
5. Label and disconnect the wiring at the starter.
6. Remove the starter mounting bolts and remove the starter.
7. Installation is the reverse of the removal procedure. Tighten the starter mounting bolts to 33 ft. lbs. (46 Nm) and the intake manifold bracket bolts to 38 ft. lbs. (51 Nm).

2.5L ENGINE

1. Disconnect the negative battery cable.
2. Remove the fresh air duct. Disconnect the electrical connector and remove the air cleaner assembly.
3. If equipped with automatic transaxle, proceed as follows:
    a. Relieve the fuel system pressure. Drain the cooling system.
    b. Disconnect the accelerator cable from the throttle body. Label and disconnect the electrical connectors, vacuum hoses and coolant hoses from the throttle body.
    c. Remove the throttle body.
    d. Disconnect and plug the fuel supply and return lines.
    e. Disconnect the transaxle selector cable from the transaxle and remove the cable bracket.
    f. Remove the starter bracket.
4. Label and disconnect the wiring at the starter.
5. Remove the starter mounting bolts and remove the starter.
6. Installation is the reverse of the removal procedure. Tighten the starter mounting bolts to 38 ft. lbs. (51 Nm).

Millenia Models

2.3L ENGINE

1. Disconnect the negative battery cable.
2. Remove the charge air cooler duct.
3. Remove the battery clamp, box, and battery. Remove the battery tray.
4. Remove the rear charge air cooler.
5. Remove the bolt from the pipe bracket and remove the bracket.

Fig. 48 To remove the starter motor, first remove any obstructing components, then loosen the upper starter motor attaching bolts

Fig. 49 Remove both upper bolts before going under the vehicle to finish the removal procedure

Fig. 50 Raise and safely support the front of the vehicle, then label and detach any plug-on wire connectors

Fig. 51 Using the proper size socket or wrench, remove the battery positive wire retaining nut . . .

Fig. 52 . . . and the wire terminal from the starter

Fig. 53 Remove the lower starter motor mounting bolt and carefully lower the starter and remove it from the vehicle

6. Remove the S-terminal wire from the starter solenoid.

7. Remove the nut and the B-terminal wire from the starter solenoid.

8. Remove the starter mounting bolts and remove the starter.

To install:

9. Position the starter and tighten the starter mounting bolts to 24–33 ft. lbs. (32–46 Nm).

10. Install the B-terminal wire and nut. Tighten the nut to 12–16 ft. lbs. (16–22 Nm).

11. Install the S-terminal wire to the solenoid.

12. Position the pipe bracket and install the bolt. Tighten the bolt to 14–18 ft. lbs. (19–25 Nm).

13. Install the rear charge air cooler, using new O-rings. Tighten the nuts to 14–18 ft. lbs. (19–25 Nm).

14. Install the battery tray. Install the battery, box, and clamp.

15. Install the charge air cooler duct.

16. Connect the negative battery cable.

2.5L ENGINE

1. Disconnect the negative battery cable.

2. Remove the battery clamp, box, and battery. Remove the battery tray.

3. Remove the shift cable from the selector lever using a screwdriver or suitable tool.

4. Squeeze the lock tabs on the shift cable and remove the cable from the bracket.

5. Disconnect the electrical connectors from the starter solenoid.

6. Position the wiring harness out of the way.

7. Remove the two selector cable bracket mounting bolts and the bracket.

8. Remove the two nuts and the bolt from the starter bracket and remove the bracket.

9. Remove the S-terminal wire from the starter solenoid.

10. Remove the nut and the B-terminal wire from the starter solenoid.

11. Remove the starter mounting bolts and remove the starter.

To install:

12. Position the starter and tighten the starter mounting bolts to 24–33 ft. lbs. (32–46 Nm).

13. Install the B-terminal wire and nut. Tighten the nut to 12–16 ft. lbs. (16–22 Nm).

14. Install the S-terminal wire to the solenoid.

15. Position the starter bracket and install the bolt and nuts.

16. Install the selector cable bracket and tighten the bolts to 5–7 ft. lbs. (7–9 Nm).

17. Connect the electrical connectors to the starter solenoid.

18. Install the shift cable into the cable bracket and into the selector lever.

19. Install the battery tray. Install the battery, box, and clamp.

20. Connect the negative battery cable.

Except MX-3 (w/1.8L), 1993–98 626/MX-6/Probe, 1995–98 Protege and Millenia

1. Disconnect the negative battery cable. On 323/Protege and MX-3 1.6L engine, disconnect the positive battery cable and remove the battery and battery tray.

2. Raise and safely support the vehicle. Remove the engine under cover.

3. On 323/Protege, MX-3 with 1.6L engine and MX-6/626 2.2L engine, remove the intake manifold bracket.

4. On 323 with 4WD, remove the differential lock assembly as follows:

   a. Remove the retaining bolt.

   b. Turn the differential lock shift rod 90 degrees clockwise with a flat-bladed tool.

   c. Remove the differential lock assembly.

5. Remove the starter bracket, if equipped.

6. Label and disconnect the wiring from the starter.

7. Remove the starter mounting bolts and remove the starter.

To install:

8. Install the starter and install the mounting bolts.

9. Tighten the starter mounting bolts to 34 ft. lbs. (46 Nm).

10. Connect the wiring to the starter and install the bracket, if equipped.

11. On 323 with 4WD install the differential lock assembly.

12. On 323/Protege, MX-3 with 1.6L engine and MX-6/626 2.2L engine, install the intake manifold bracket.

13. Install the engine under cover and lower the vehicle.

14. Install the battery, if removed. Connect the negative battery cable.

MAGNETIC SWITCH (SOLENOID) REPLACEMENT

▶ **See Figure 54**

1. Remove the starter according to the procedure in this Section.

2. Clamp the starter motor in a soft-jawed vise.

3. Remove the nut and disconnect the lead from the solenoid M-terminal.

4. Remove the solenoid retaining screws and remove the solenoid. If there are shims between the solenoid and the starter, save them as they are used to adjust the pinion depth clearance.

5. Install the replacement solenoid and tighten the retaining screws. Be sure to replace any shims that were removed during disassembly.

6. Proceed as follows:

   a. Leave the lead disconnected from the solenoid M-terminal.

   b. Connect the positive lead from a 12 volt battery to the S terminal of the solenoid and the negative lead to the starter motor body. When the battery is connected, the solenoid should engage and kick out the pinion.

➡ **Do not engage the solenoid for more than 20 seconds at a time. If this test must be repeated, wait at least 3 minutes between attempts to allow the solenoid to cool.**

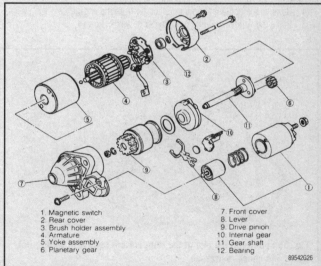

1. Magnetic switch
2. Rear cover
3. Brush holder assembly
4. Armature
5. Yoke assembly
6. Planetary gear
7. Front cover
8. Lever
9. Drive pinion
10. Internal gear
11. Gear shaft
12. Bearing

89542G26

Fig. 54 Exploded view of a typical starter assembly showing magnetic switch mounting details

   c. With the pinion extended, measure the clearance between the pinion and collar. The clearance should be 0.02–0.08 in. (0.5–2.0mm).

   d. If the gap measurement falls outside the specified range, add or remove shims between the solenoid and drive end housing until the pinion gap is within specification.

   e. Install the lead to the solenoid M-terminal and tighten the nut to 87–104 inch lbs. (10–12 Nm).

7. Install the starter according to the procedure in this section.

SENDING UNITS

→This section describes the operating principles of sending units, warning lights and gauges. Sensors which provide information to the Electronic Control Module (ECM) are covered in Section 4 of this manual.

Instrument panels contain a number of indicating devices (gauges and warning lights). These devices are composed of two separate components. One is the sending unit, mounted on the engine or other remote part of the vehicle, and the other is the actual gauge or light in the instrument panel.

Several types of sending units exist, however most can be characterized as being either a pressure type or a resistance type. Pressure type sending units convert liquid pressure into an electrical signal which is sent to the gauge. Resistance type sending units are most often used to measure temperature and use variable resistance to control the current flow back to the indicating device. Both types of sending units are connected in series by a wire to the battery (through the ignition switch). When the ignition is turned **ON**, current flows from the battery through the indicating device and on to the sending unit.

Coolant Temperature Sender

TESTING

▶ **See Figure 55**

1. Detach the single wire harness connector from the temperature sender.
2. Ground the connector to the engine block and verify that the gauge has gone to full HOT reading.
3. If the gauge is working, proceed with the test procedure. If not, inspect the wire harness between the sender and the gauge.
4. Remove the coolant temperature sender from the engine.
5. Place the sender unit into a container of water.

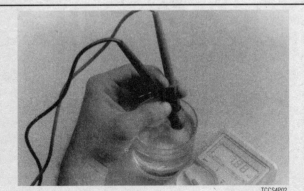

Fig. 55 Submerge the end of the temperature sender in cold or hot water and check resistance

6. Attach an ohmmeter to the coolant temperature sender connector and the sender body.
7. Heat the water to the temperature specified and read the meter.
- 1990–92 626 and MX-6 models: 49–58ohms at 176°F (80°C)
- 1995–98 Protege models: 153ohms at 129°F (54°C)
- All other models: 190–259ohms at 122°F (50°C)
8. If the meter does not read as specified, replace the sender.

REMOVAL & INSTALLATION

▶ **See Figures 56 and 57**

1. Drain and recycle the engine coolant.
2. Detach the single wire harness connector from the temperature sender.
3. Remove the sender from the engine by turning it counterclockwise.
4. Installation is the reverse of the removal procedure. When installing the sender, count three threads up the sender then apply sealant from the third thread to the head of the sender. Tighten the sender to 57–82 inch lbs. (6.4–9.3 Nm).

Oil Pressure Switch

TESTING

▶ **See Figure 58**

1. Detach the single wire harness connector from the oil pressure switch.
2. Turn the ignition switch **ON**. The oil pressure warning lamp should be off. If not, inspect the wire harness for shorts to ground.
3. Connect an ohmmeter to the pressure switch and a ground to check for continuity.
   a. With the engine **OFF**, the ohmmeter should read continuity.
   b. With the engine running, the ohmmeter should read no continuity.
4. If not as specified, perform an engine oil pressure test. Refer to Section 3.
5. If the oil pressure reads normal, replace the switch.

REMOVAL & INSTALLATION

▶ **See Figures 59 and 60**

1. Detach the single wire harness connector from the oil pressure switch.
2. Remove the switch from the engine by turning it counterclockwise.
3. Installation is the reverse of the removal procedure. When installing the switch, count three threads up the switch then apply sealant from the third thread to the head of the switch. Tighten the switch to 8.7–13 ft. lbs. (12–17 Nm).

Electric Fan Switch

The cooling fan on Mazda vehicles is controlled by the engine computer and the Engine Coolant Temperature (ECT) sensor. For sensor testing procedures, refer to Section 4.

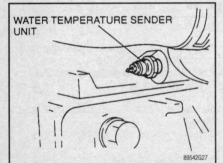

Fig. 56 The coolant temperature sender is a single wire unit, usually located near, or on, the water outlet or thermostat housing

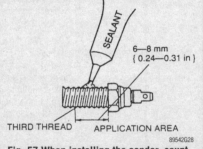

Fig. 57 When installing the sender, count three threads up the sender then apply sealant from the third thread to the head of the sender.

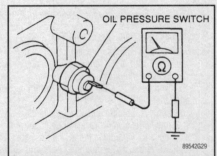

Fig. 58 Connect an ohmmeter between the oil pressure switch and ground to check for continuity; both with the engine off and running

Fig. 59 The oil pressure switch can usually be found near the oil filter

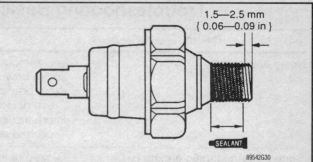

1.5—2.5 mm
{ 0.06—0.09 in }

SEALANT

89542G30

Fig. 60 When installing the switch, count three threads up the switch then apply sealant from the third thread to the head of the switch

Troubleshooting Basic Starting System Problems

Problem	Cause	Solution
Starter motor rotates engine slowly	• Battery charge low or battery defective	• Charge or replace battery
	• Defective circuit between battery and starter motor	• Clean and tighten, or replace cables
	• Low load current	• Bench-test starter motor. Inspect for worn brushes and weak brush springs.
	• High load current	• Bench-test starter motor. Check engine for friction, drag or coolant in cylinders. Check ring gear-to-pinion gear clearance.
Starter motor will not rotate engine	• Battery charge low or battery defective	• Charge or replace battery
	• Faulty solenoid	• Check solenoid ground. Repair or replace as necessary.
	• Damaged drive pinion gear or ring gear	• Replace damaged gear(s)
	• Starter motor engagement weak	• Bench-test starter motor
	• Starter motor rotates slowly with high load current	• Inspect drive yoke pull-down and point gap, check for worn end bushings, check ring gear clearance
	• Engine seized	• Repair engine
Starter motor drive will not engage (solenoid known to be good)	• Defective contact point assembly	• Repair or replace contact point assembly
	• Inadequate contact point assembly ground	• Repair connection at ground screw
	• Defective hold-in coil	• Replace field winding assembly
Starter motor drive will not disengage	• Starter motor loose on flywheel housing	• Tighten mounting bolts
	• Worn drive end busing	• Replace bushing
	• Damaged ring gear teeth	• Replace ring gear or driveplate
	• Drive yoke return spring broken or missing	• Replace spring
Starter motor drive disengages prematurely	• Weak drive assembly thrust spring	• Replace drive mechanism
	• Hold-in coil defective	• Replace field winding assembly
Low load current	• Worn brushes	• Replace brushes
	• Weak brush springs	• Replace springs

Troubleshooting Basic Charging System Problems

Problem	Cause	Solution
Noisy alternator	• Loose mountings • Loose drive pulley • Worn bearings • Brush noise • Internal circuits shorted (High pitched whine)	• Tighten mounting bolts • Tighten pulley • Replace alternator • Replace alternator • Replace alternator
Squeal when starting engine or accelerating	• Glazed or loose belt	• Replace or adjust belt
Indicator light remains on or ammeter indicates discharge (engine running)	• Broken belt • Broken or disconnected wires • Internal alternator problems • Defective voltage regulator	• Install belt • Repair or connect wiring • Replace alternator • Replace voltage regulator/alternator
Car light bulbs continually burn out—battery needs water continually	• Alternator/regulator overcharging	• Replace voltage regulator/alternator
Car lights flare on acceleration	• Battery low • Internal alternator/regulator problems	• Charge or replace battery • Replace alternator/regulator
Low voltage output (alternator light flickers continually or ammeter needle wanders)	• Loose or worn belt • Dirty or corroded connections • Internal alternator/regulator problems	• Replace or adjust belt • Clean or replace connections • Replace alternator/regulator

TCCS2C02

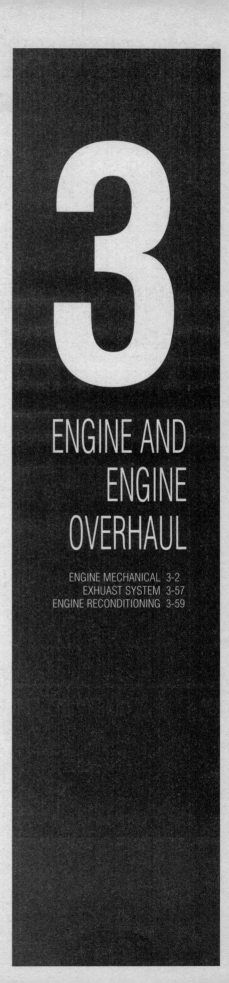

3

ENGINE AND ENGINE OVERHAUL

ENGINE MECHANICAL

1.5L (Z5) ENGINE SPECIFICATIONS

Description	English Specifications	Metric Specifications
Type	Gasoline, 4-cycle	
Cylinder arrangement and number	Inline, 4-cylinders	
Combustion chamber	Pentroof	
Valve system	Dual overhead camshaft, timing belt driven, 16 valves	
Displacement	90.83 cu. in.	1.5L (1489 cc)
Bore X stroke	2.96 x 3.29 in.	75.3 x 83.6 mm
Valve clearance (engine COLD)		
Intake	0.010-0.012 in.	0.25-0.31 mm
Exhaust	0.010-0.012 in.	0.25-0.31 mm
Compression ratio	9.4:1	
Compression pressure	195 psi @ 300 rpm	1,344 kPa @ 300 rpm
Cylinder head and valve train		
Cylinder head distortion (across gasket surface)	0.006 in. max.	0.15 mm max.
Cylinder head bolt length (maximum allowable)	3.957 in.	100.5 mm
Valves		
Margin thickness		
Intake	0.043 in.	1.1 mm
Exhaust	0.047 in.	1.2 mm
Stem diameter		
Intake		
Standard size	0.2154-0.2159 in.	5.470-5.485 mm
Minimum size	0.2134 in.	5.420 mm
Exhaust		
Standard size	0.2152-0.2157 in.	5.465-5.480 mm
Minimum size	0.2132 in.	5.415 mm
Valve guides		
Clearance		
Intake	0.0010-0.0023 in.	0.025-0.060 mm
Exhaust	0.0012-0.0025 in.	0.030-0.065 mm
Maximum allowable	0.008 in.	0.2 mm
Inner Diameter		
Intake	0.2170-0.2177 in.	5.51-5.53 mm
Exhaust	0.2174-0.2181 in.	5.52-5.54 mm
Height (above spring seat)	0.363-0.386 in.	9.22-9.82 mm
Valve seats		
Seat angle	45 degrees	
Seat width	0.032-0.055 in.	0.8-1.4 mm
Protruding length (from spring seat to valve tip)	1.323-1.342 in.	33.6-34.1 mm
Valve spring		
Test pressure	29-32 lbs. @ 1.24 in.	12.92-14.62 kgf @ 31.5 mm
Out-of-square	0.052 in. max.	1.33 mm max.
Runout	0.0012 in. max.	0.03 mm max.
Camshaft		
Lobe height		
Intake and exhaust		
Standard size	1.6102 in.	40.90 mm
Minimum size	1.6024 in.	40.70 mm
Journal diameter		
Standard size	1.0213-1.0222 in.	25.940-25.965 mm
Minimum size	1.0201 in.	25.910 mm
Oil clearance	0.0014-0.0033 in.	0.035-0.085 mm
End play		
Standard	0.0028-0.0074 in.	0.07-0.19 mm
Maximum	0.0079 in.	0.20 mm

89543C01

1.5L (Z5) ENGINE SPECIFICATIONS

Description	English Specifications	Metric Specifications
Cylinder block		
Cylinder block distortion (across head gasket surface)	0.006 in. max.	0.15 mm max.
Grinding limit	0.008 in. max.	0.20 mm max.
Height limit	8.72 in.	221.5 mm
Cylinder bore		
Standard size	2.9646-2.9653 in.	75.300-75.319 mm
Wear limit - taper and out-of-round	0.006 in.	0.15 mm
Oil jet (maximum air pressure)	25-32 psi	167-225 kPa
Piston and rings		
Standard size	2.9632-2.9638 in.	75.263-75.283 mm
Piston-to-bore clearance		
Standard	0.0012-0.0016 in.	0.030-0.043 mm
Maximum allowable	0.0039 in.	0.10 mm
Ring Clearance		
Side clearance		
Top	0.0014-0.0025 in.	0.035-0.065 mm
Second	0.0012-0.0025 in.	0.030-0.065 mm
Oil	0.003-0.006 in.	0.07-0.16 mm
Maximum allowable	0.006 in.	0.15 mm
End gap		
Top	0.006-0.011 in.	0.15-0.30 mm
Second	0.010-0.015 in.	0.25-0.40 mm
Oil	0.008-0.027 in.	0.20-0.70 mm
Maximum allowable	0.039 in.	1.0 mm
Piston pin		
Standard diameter	0.7864-0.7866 in.	19.974-19.980 mm
Piston pin bore	0.7870-0.7874 in.	19.988-20.000 mm
Clearance	0.0004-0.0010 in.	0.008-0.026 mm
Connecting rods		
Side clearance	0.0044-0.0103 in.	0.110-0.262 mm
Oil clearance (rod bearing-to-crankshaft)	0.0012-0.0039 in.	0.029-0.10 mm
Piston pin bushing diameter	0.7852-0.7858 in.	19.943-19.961 mm
Bend limit (maximum)	0.0073 in. within 1.97 in span	0.075 mm within 50 mm span
Twist limit (maximum)	0.0071 in. within 1.97 in span	0.180 mm within 50 mm span
Center-to-center distance	5.353-5.356	135.95-136.05 mm
Crankshaft		
Endplay	0.0032-0.0111 in.	0.080-0.282 mm
Runout	0.0016 in. max.	0.04 mm max.
Journal diameters		
Main journals		
Diameter	1.9661-1.9667 in.	49.938-49.956 mm
Minimum allowable	1.9647 in.	49.904 mm
Out-of-round	0.002 in. max.	0.05 mm max.
Rod journals		
Diameter	1.5725-1.5730 in.	39.940-39.956 mm
Minimum allowable	1.5712 in.	39.908 mm
Out-of-round	0.002 in. max.	0.05 mm max.
Main bearing oil clearance	0.0008-0.0040 in.	0.018-0.10 mm
Lubrication system		
Inner-to-outer rotor tooth tip clearance	0.0008-0.0079 in.	0.02-0.20 mm
Outer rotor-to-oil pump body clearance	0.0036-0.0087 in.	0.090-0.22 mm
Side clearance	0.0012-0.0055 in.	0.03-0.14 mm
Pressure relief spring		
Pressing force	14.1-15.4 lbs.	62.8-68.6 N
Height	1.394 in.	35.42 mm

89543C02

1.6L (B6) ENGINE SPECIFICATIONS

Description	English Specifications	Metric Specifications
Type	Gasoline, 4-cycle	
Cylinder arrangement and number	Inline, 4-cylinders	
Combustion chamber	Multi-spherical (8-valve) or Pentroof (16-valve)	
Valve system	Timing belt driven, SOHC 8 & 16 valve with rocker shafts, DOHC 16 valves	
Displacement	97.5 cu. in.	1.6L (1598cc)
Bore X stroke	3.07 x 3.29 in.	78.0 x 83.6 mm
Valve clearance		
Intake	Hydraulic	
Exhaust	Hydraulic	
Compression ratio		
SOHC - 8-valve	9.3:1	
SOHC - 16-valve	9.0:1	
DOHC	9.4:1	
Compression pressure	185 psi @ 300 rpm	1275 kPa @ 300 rpm
Cylinder head and valve train		
Cylinder head warpage	0.004-0.006 in.	0.10-0.15 mm
Valve guides		
Inside diameter		
SOHC - 8-valve	0.2760-0.2768 in.	7.01-7.03 mm
SOHC/DOHC - 16-valve	0.2366-0.2374 in.	6.01-6.03 mm
Valves		
Stem diameter		
SOHC - 8-valve		
Intake	0.2744-0.2750 in.	6.970-6.985 mm
Exhaust	0.2742-0.2748 in.	6.965-6.980 mm
SOHC/DOHC - 16-valve		
Intake	0.2350-0.2356 in.	5.970-5.985 mm
Exhaust	0.2348-0.2354 in.	5.965-5.980 mm
Stem-to-guide clearance		
Intake	0.0010-0.0024 in.	0.025-0.060 mm
Exhaust	0.0012-0.0026 in.	0.030-0.065 mm
Head minimum margin thickness		
SOHC - 8-valve		
Intake	0.031 in.	0.8 mm
Exhaust	0.043 in.	1.1 mm
SOHC/DOHC - 16-valve		
Intake	0.035 in.	0.9 mm
Exhaust	0.039 in.	1.0 mm
Valve spring		
Free length		
SOHC - 8-valve		
Intake	1.719 in.	43.66 mm
Exhaust	1.719 in.	43.66 mm
SOHC - 16-valve		
Intake	1.816 in.	46.12 mm
Exhaust	1.687 in.	42.86 mm
DOHC		
Intake	1.890 in.	48.01 mm
Exhaust	1.903 in.	48.34 mm
Out-of-square		
Intake	0.069-0.066 in.	1.50-1.68 mm
Exhaust	0.069-0.066 in.	1.50-1.68 mm

89543C03

1.6L (B6) ENGINE SPECIFICATIONS

Description	English Specifications	Metric Specifications
Camshaft		
Runout	0.0012 in. max	0.03 mm max
End-play	0.008 in. max	0.20 mm max
Journal diameter		
SOHC - 8-valve		
No. 1, 5	1.7102-1.7110 in.	43.440-43.460 mm
No. 2, 4	1.7099-1.7108 in.	43.430-43.445 mm
No. 3	1.7102-1.7110 in.	43.440-43.460 mm
SOHC - 16-valve		
No. 1, 5	1.7102-1.7110 in.	43.440-43.460 mm
No. 2, 4	1.7096-1.7106 in.	43.425-43.450 mm
No. 3	1.7091-1.7100 in.	43.410-43.435 mm
DOHC - all journals	1.3370-1.3386 in.	33.961-34.000 mm
Maximum oil clearance	0.006 in.	0.15 mm
Cam lobe height - wear limit		
SOHC - 8-valve		
Intake	1.4272 in.	36.251 mm
Exhaust	1.4272 in.	36.251 mm
SOHC - 16-valve		
Intake	1.4027 in.	35.629 mm
Exhaust	1.3960 in.	35.459 mm
DOHC - all journals		
Intake	1.6019 in.	40.688 mm
Exhaust	1.6018 in.	40.686 mm
Cylinder block		
Cylinder block distortion (across head surface)	0.006 in. max	0.15 max
Grinding limit	0.008 in. max	0.20 mm max
Cylinder bore		
Standard size	3.0711-3.0713 in.	78.006-78.013 mm
Wear limit - taper and out-of-round	0.0007 in. max	0.019 mm max
Piston and rings		
Piston diameter	3.0690-3.0698 in.	77.954-77.974 mm
Piston-to-cylinder wall clearance	0.0015-0.0020 in.	0.039-0.052 mm
Piston pin diameter	0.7864-0.7866 in.	19.974-19.980 mm
Interference in connecting rod	0.0005-0.0015 in.	0.013-0.037 mm
Piston ring side clearance		
Top ring	0.0012-0.0026 in.	0.030-0.065 mm
Second ring	0.0012-0.0028 in.	0.030-0.070 mm
Piston ring endgap		
Top ring	0.006-0.012 in.	0.15-0.30 mm
Second ring		
SOHC	0.006-0.012 in.	0.15-0.30 mm
DOHC	0.012-0.018 in.	0.30-0.45 mm
Oil ring	0.008-0.028 in.	0.20-0.70 mm
Connecting rods		
Length - center-to-center	5.2303-5.2342 in.	132.85-132.95 mm
Big end bore	1.8898-1.8904 in.	48.000-48.016 mm
Small end bore	0.7862-0.7869 in.	19.943-19.961 mm
Side clearance	0.012 in. max	0.30 mm max
Bending limit	0.003 in. over 1.97 in. span	0.075 mm over 50 mm span
Crankshaft		
Connecting rod journal diameter	1.7693-1.7699 in.	44.940-44.956 mm
Main journal diameter	1.9661-1.9668 in.	49.938-49.956 mm
Out-of-round and taper	0.002 in. max	0.05 mm max
Runout	0.0016 in. max	0.04 mm max
End-play	0.012 in. max	0.30 mm max

89543C04

1.8L (BP) ENGINE SPECIFICATIONS

Description	English Specifications	Metric Specifications
Type	Gasoline, 4-cycle	
Cylinder arrangement and number	Inline, 4-cylinders	
Combustion chamber	Pentroof	
Valve system	Timing belt driven, SOHC 16 valve with rocker shafts, DOHC 16 valves	
Displacement	112.2 cu. in.	1.8L (1839 cc)
Bore X stroke	3.27 x 3.35 in.	83.0 x 85.0 mm
Valve clearance		
1990-96		
Intake	Hydraulic	
Exhaust	Hydraulic	
1997-98		
Intake	0.008-0.009 in.	0.18-0.24 mm
Exhaust	0.012-0.013 in.	0.28-0.34 mm
Compression ratio		
SOHC	8.9:1	
DOHC	9.0:1	
Compression pressure	185 psi @ 300 rpm	1275 kPa @ 300 rpm
Cylinder head and valve train		
Cylinder head warpage	0.004-0.006 in.	0.10-0.15 mm
Valve guides		
Inside diameter	0.2366-0.2374 in.	6.01-6.03 mm
Valves		
Stem diameter		
Intake	0.2350-0.2356 in.	5.970-5.985 mm
Exhaust	0.2348-0.2354 in.	5.965-5.980 mm
Stem-to-guide clearance		
Intake	0.0010-0.0024 in.	0.025-0.060 mm
Exhaust	0.0012-0.0026 in.	0.030-0.065 mm
Head minimum margin thickness		
Intake	0.035 in.	0.9 mm
Exhaust	0.039 in.	1.0 mm
Valve spring		
Free length		
SOHC		
Intake	1.815 in.	46.1 mm
Exhaust	1.717 in.	43.6 mm
DOHC		
Intake	1.890 in.	48.01 mm
Exhaust	1.903 in.	48.34 mm
Out-of-square		
Intake	0.059-0.066 in.	1.50-1.68 mm
Exhaust	0.059-0.066 in.	1.50-1.68 mm

89543C05

1.8L (BP) ENGINE SPECIFICATIONS

Description	English Specifications	Metric Specifications
Camshaft		
Runout	0.0012 in. max	0.03 mm max
End-play	0.008 in. max	0.20 mm max
Journal diameter		
SOHC		
No. 1, 5	1.7102-1.7110 in.	43.440-43.460 mm
No. 2, 4	1.7096-1.7106 in.	43.425-43.450 mm
No. 3	1.7091-1.7100 in.	43.410-43.435 mm
DOHC - all journals	1.0213-1.0222 in.	25.940-25.965 mm
Maximum oil clearance	0.006 in.	0.15 mm
Cam lobe height + wear limit		
SOHC		
Intake	1.4092 in.	35.793 mm
Exhaust	1.4202 in.	36.073 mm
DOHC		
Intake	1.7281 in.	43.894 mm
Exhaust	1.7480 in.	44.400 mm
Cylinder block		
Cylinder block distortion (across head surface)	0.006 in. max	0.15 mm max
Grinding limit	0.008 in. max	0.20 mm max
Cylinder bore		
Standard size	3.2678-3.2684 in.	83.000-83.019 mm
Wear limit - taper and out-of-round	0.0007 in. max	0.019 mm max
Piston and rings		
Piston diameter	3.2659-3.2667 in.	82.954-82.974 mm
Piston-to-cylinder wall clearance	0.006 in. max	0.15 mm max
Piston pin diameter	0.7864-0.7866 in.	19.974-19.980 mm
Interference in connecting rod	0.0005-0.0015 in.	0.013-0.037 mm
Piston ring side clearance		
Top ring	0.0012-0.0026 in.	0.030-0.065 mm
Second ring	0.0012-0.0028 in.	0.030-0.070 mm
Piston ring endgap		
Top ring	0.006-0.012 in.	0.15-0.30 mm
Second ring	0.006-0.012 in.	0.15-0.30 mm
Oil ring	0.008-0.028 in.	0.20-0.70 mm
Connecting rods		
Length - center-to-center	5.2303-5.2342 in.	132.85-132.96 mm
Big end bore	1.8898-1.8904 in.	48.000-48.016 mm
Small end bore	0.7852-0.7859 in.	19.943-19.961 mm
Side clearance	0.012 in. max	0.30 mm max
Bending limit	0.003 in. over 1.97 in. span	0.075 mm over 50 mm span
Crankshaft		
Connecting rod journal diameter	1.7693-1.7699 in.	44.940-44.956 mm
Main journal diameter	1.9661-1.9668 in.	49.938-49.956 mm
Out-of-round and taper	0.002 in. max	0.05 mm max
Runout	0.0016 in. max	0.04 mm max
End-play	0.012 in. max	0.30 mm max

89543C06

2.0L (FS) ENGINE SPECIFICATIONS

Description	English Specifications	Metric Specifications
Type		
Cylinder arrangement and number	Gasoline, 4-cycle	
	Inline, 4-cylinders	
Combustion chamber	Pentroof	
Valve system	Timing belt driven, DOHC 16 valves	
Displacement	121.5 cu. in.	2.0L (1991 cc)
Bore X stroke	3.27 x 3.62 in.	83.0 x 92.0 mm
Valve clearance		
1990-97		
Intake	Hydraulic	
Exhaust	Hydraulic	
1998		
Intake	0.009-0.012 in.	0.225-0.295 mm
Exhaust	0.009-0.012 in.	0.225-0.295 mm
Compression ratio	9.0:1	
Compression pressure	171 psi @ 300 rpm	1,177 kPa @ 300 rpm
Cylinder head and valve train		
Cylinder head warpage	0.004-0.006 in.	0.10-0.15 mm
Valve guides		
Inside diameter	0.2366-0.2374 in.	6.01-6.03 mm
Valves		
Stem diameter		
Intake	0.2350-0.2356 in.	5.970-5.985 mm
Exhaust	0.2348-0.2354 in.	5.965-5.980 mm
Stem-to-guide clearance		
Intake	0.0010-0.0024 in.	0.025-0.060 mm
Exhaust	0.0012-0.0026 in.	0.030-0.065 mm
Head minimum margin thickness		
Intake	0.0433 in.	1.10 mm
Exhaust	0.0472 in.	1.20 mm
Valve spring		
Free length		
Intake	1.732 in.	44.0 mm
Exhaust	1.732 in.	44.0 mm
Out-of-square		
Intake	0.061 in. max	1.54 mm max
Exhaust	0.061 in. max	1.54 mm max
Camshaft		
Runout	0.0012 in. max	0.03 mm max
End-play	0.008 in. max	0.20 mm max
Journal diameter - all journals	1.0213-1.0222 in.	25.940-25.965 mm
Maximum oil clearance	0.006 in.	0.15 mm
Cam lobe height - wear limit		
Intake	1.6859 in.	42.823 mm
Exhaust	1.7003 in.	43.188 mm
Cylinder block		
Cylinder block distortion (across head surface)	0.002 in. max	0.05 mm max
Grinding limit	0.008 in. max	0.20 mm max
Cylinder bore		
Standard size	3.2678-3.2684 in.	83.000-83.019 mm
Wear limit - taper and out-of-round	0.0004 in. max	0.010 mm max

89543C07

2.0L (FS) ENGINE SPECIFICATIONS

Description	English Specifications	Metric Specifications
Piston and rings		
Piston diameter	3.2669-3.2667 in.	82.954-82.974 mm
Piston-to-cylinder wall clearance	0.006 in. max	0.15 mm max
Piston pin diameter	0.7470-0.7472 in.	18.974-18.980 mm
Interference in connecting rod	0.0005-0.0015 in.	0.013-0.037 mm
Piston ring side clearance		
Top ring	0.0014-0.0025 in.	0.035-0.065 mm
Second ring	0.0012-0.0025 in.	0.030-0.065 mm
Piston ring endgap		
Top ring	0.006-0.012 in.	0.15-0.30 mm
Second ring	0.006-0.012 in.	0.15-0.30 mm
Oil ring	0.008-0.028 in.	0.20-0.70 mm
Connecting rods		
Length - center-to-center	5.3209-5.3248 in.	135.15-135.25 mm
Big end bore	2.0079-2.0085 in.	51.000-51.015 mm
Small end bore	0.7458-0.7465 in.	18.945-18.961 mm
Side clearance	0.012 in. max	0.30 mm max
Bending limit	0.002 in. over 1.97 in. span	0.05 mm over 50 mm span
Crankshaft		
Connecting rod journal diameter	1.8874-1.8880 in.	47.940-47.955 mm
Main journal diameter	2.2022-2.2029 in.	55.937-55.955 mm
Out-of-round and taper	0.0002 in. max	0.006 mm max
Runout	0.0012 in. max	0.03 mm max
End-play	0.012 in. max	0.30 mm max

89543C08

2.2L (F2) ENGINE SPECIFICATIONS

Description	English Specifications	Metric Specifications
Type		
Cylinder arrangement and number	Gasoline, 4-cycle	
	Inline, 4-cylinders	
Combustion chamber	Multi-spherical (8-valve) or Pentroof (16-valve)	
Valve system	Over head cam, belt driven	
Displacement	133.2 cu. in.	2.2L (2184 cc)
Bore X stroke	3.39 x 3.70 in.	86.0 x 94.0 mm
Valve clearance		
Intake	Hydraulic	
Exhaust	Hydraulic	
Compression ratio		
Turbo	7.8:1	
Non-turbo	8.6:1	
Compression pressure		
Turbo	139 psi @ 260 rpm	960 kPa @ 260 rpm
Non-turbo	162 psi @ 270 rpm	1,120 @ 270 rpm
Cylinder head and valve train		
Cylinder head warpage	0.004-0.006 in.	0.10-0.15 mm
Valve guides		
Inside diameter	0.2760-0.2768 in.	7.01-7.03 mm
Valves		
Stem diameter		
Intake	0.2744-0.2750 in.	6.970-6.985 mm
Exhaust	0.2742-0.2748 in.	6.965-6.980 mm
Stem-to-guide clearance		
Intake	0.0010-0.0024 in.	0.025-0.060 mm
Exhaust	0.0012-0.0026 in.	0.030-0.065 mm
Head minimum margin thickness		
Intake	0.031 in.	0.8 mm
Exhaust	0.051 in.	1.3 mm
Valve spring		
Free length		
Intake	1.949 in.	49.5 mm
Exhaust	1.984 in.	50.4 mm
Out-of-square - maximum allowable	0.067 in.	1.7 mm
Camshaft		
Runout	0.0012 in. max	0.03 mm max
End-play	0.008 in. max	0.20 mm max
Journal diameter		
SOHC - 8-valve		
No. 1, 5	1.2575-1.2585 in.	31.940-31.965 mm
No. 2, 3 and 4	1.2563-1.2573 in.	31.910-31.935 mm
Maximum oil clearance	0.006 in.	0.15 mm
Cam lobe height - wear limit		
Intake	1.6197 in.	41.140 mm
Exhaust	1.6396 in.	41.647 mm
Cylinder block		
Cylinder block distortion (across head surface)	0.006 in. max	0.15 mm max
Grinding limit	0.008 in. max	0.20 mm max
Cylinder bore		
Standard size	3.3858-3.3866 in.	86.000-86.019 mm
Wear limit - taper and out-of-round	0.0007 in. max	0.019 mm max

89543C09

2.2L (F2) ENGINE SPECIFICATIONS

Description	English Specifications	Metric Specifications
Piston and rings		
Piston diameter	3.3836-3.3844 in.	85.944-85.964 mm
Piston-to-cylinder wall clearance	0.0014-0.0030 in.	0.036-0.075 mm
Piston pin diameter	0.8651-0.8654 in.	21.974-21.980 mm
Interference in connecting rod	0.0005-0.0015 in.	0.013-0.037 mm
Piston ring side clearance		
Top ring	0.0012-0.0028 in.	0.030-0.070 mm
Second ring	0.0012-0.0028 in.	0.030-0.070 mm
Piston ring endgap		
Top ring	0.008-0.0014 in.	0.20-0.35 mm
Second ring	0.006-0.012 in.	0.15-0.30 mm
Oil ring	0.008-0.028 in.	0.20-0.70 mm
Connecting rods		
Length - center-to-center	6.238-6.242 in.	158.45-158.55 mm
Big end bore	2.1261-2.1266 in.	54.002-54.017 mm
Small end bore	0.8640-0.8646 in.	21.943-21.961 mm
Side clearance	0.012 in. max	0.30 mm max
Bending limit	0.0094 in. max	0.24 mm max
Crankshaft		
Connecting rod journal diameter	2.0055-2.0061 in.	50.940-50.955 mm
Main journal diameter	2.3597-2.3604 in.	59.937-59.955 mm
Out-of-round and taper	0.002 in. max	0.05 mm max
Runout	0.0012 in. max	0.03 mm max
End-play	0.012 in. max	0.30 mm max

89543C10

1.8L (K8), 2.3L (KJ) and 2.5L (KL) ENGINE SPECIFICATIONS

Description	English Specifications	Metric Specifications
Type	Gasoline, 4-cycle	
Cylinder arrangement and number	60 degree V-configuration 6-cylinder	
Combustion chamber	Pentroof	
Valve system	DOHC, belt driven 24 valves	
Displacement		
K8	112.4 cu. in.	1.8L (1844 cc)
KJ	137.5 cu. in.	2.3L (2254 cc)
KL	152.2 cu. in.	2.5L (2495 cc)
Bore X stroke		
K8	2.95 x 2.74 in.	75 x 69.6 mm
KJ	3.16 x 2.92 in.	80.3 x 74.2 mm
KL	3.33 x 2.92 in.	84.5 x 74.2 mm
Valve clearance		
KJ - intake and exhaust	0.010-0.012 in.	0.245-0.315 mm
1998 KL - intake and exhaust	0.010-0.012 in.	0.245-0.315 mm
Compression ratio		
K8 and KL	9.2:1	
KJ	10.0:1	
Compression pressure		
K8 and KL	198 psi @ 300 rpm	1,334 kPa @ 300 rpm
KJ	185 psi @ 300 rpm	1,270 kPa @ 300 rpm
Cylinder head and valve train		
Cylinder head warpage	0.004 in.	0.10 mm
Valve guides		
Inside diameter	0.2367-0.2374 in.	6.01-6.03 mm
Valves		
Stem diameter		
Intake	0.2351-0.2356 in.	5.970-5.985 mm
Exhaust	0.2349-0.2354 in.	5.965-5.980 mm
Stem-to-guide clearance		
Intake	0.0010-0.0024 in.	0.025-0.060 mm
Exhaust	0.0012-0.0026 in.	0.030-0.065 mm
Head minimum margin thickness		
Intake	0.035 in.	0.9 mm
Exhaust	0.039 in.	1.0 mm
Valve spring		
Free length	1.847 in.	46.92 mm
Out-of-square	0.064 in. max	1.63 mm max
Camshaft		
Runout	0.0008 in. max	0.02 mm max
End-play	0.006 in. max	0.14 mm max
Journal diameter		
Journal No. 1		
RH cylinder head		
Intake cam	1.1802-1.1809 in.	29.975-29.995 mm
Exhaust cam	1.0213-1.0220 in.	25.940-25.960 mm
LH cylinder head		
Intake cam	1.0213-1.0220 in.	25.940-25.960 mm
Exhaust cam	1.1802-1.1809 in.	29.975-29.995 mm
Journal No. 2, 3 and 4	1.0201-1.0209 in.	25.910-25.930 mm
Journal No. 5	1.0213-1.0220 in.	25.940-25.960 mm
Maximum oil clearance	0.006 in.	0.15 mm

89543C11

1.8L (K8), 2.3L (KJ) and 2.5L (KL) ENGINE SPECIFICATIONS

Description	English Specifications	Metric Specifications
Cam lobe height - wear limit		
K8 engine		
Intake	1.6718 in.	42.465 mm
Exhaust	1.705 in.	43.318 mm
KJ engine		
Intake	1.7179 in	43.635 mm
Exhaust	1.6869 in.	42.847 mm
KL engine		
Intake	1.7067 in.	43.349 mm
Exhaust	1.7067 in.	43.349 mm
Cylinder block		
Cylinder block distortion (across head surface)	0.006 in. max	0.15 mm max
Grinding limit	0.008 in. max	0.20 mm max
Cylinder bore		
Standard size		
K8 engine	2.9528-2.9536 in.	75.000-75.022 mm
KJ engine	3.1615-3.1622 in.	80.300-80.322 mm
KL engine	3.3268-3.3276 in.	84.500-84.522 mm
Wear limit - taper and out-of-round	0.0008 in. max	0.022 mm max
Piston and rings		
Piston diameter		
K8 engine	2.9509-2.9521 in.	74.953-74.985 mm
KJ engine	3.1603-3.1615 in.	80.271-80.303 mm
KL engine	3.3250-3.3261 in.	84.453-84.485 mm
Piston-to-cylinder wall clearance	0.0015-0.0020 in.	0.039-0.052 mm
Piston ring side clearance		
Top ring	0.0012-0.0026 in.	0.030-0.065 mm
Second ring	0.0012-0.0026 in.	0.030-0.065 mm
Piston ring endgap		
Top ring	0.006-0.012 in.	0.15-0.30 mm
Second ring	0.010-0.015	0.25-0.40 mm
Oil ring	0.006-0.028 in.	0.20-0.70 mm
Connecting rods		
Length - center-to-center	5.4252-5.4291 in.	137.80-137.90 mm
Side clearance	0.016 in. max	0.40 mm max
Bending limit	0.002 in. over 1.97 in. span	0.05 mm over 50 mm span
Crankshaft		
Connecting rod journal diameter		
K8 engine	1.8874-1.8879 in.	47.940-47.955 mm
KJ and KL engines	2.0843-2.0848 in.	52.940-52.955 mm
Main journal diameter	2.4385-2.4391 in.	61.938-61.955 mm
Out-of-round and taper	0.0012 in. max	0.03 mm max
Runout	0.0006 in. max	0.015 mm max
End-play	0.012 in. max	0.30 mm max

89543C12

Engine

REMOVAL & INSTALLATION

♦ **See Figures 1 thru 6**

In the process of removing the engine, you will come across a number of steps which call for the removal of a separate component or system, such as "disconnect the exhaust system" or "remove the radiator." In most instances, a detailed removal procedure can be found elsewhere in this manual.

It is virtually impossible to list each individual wire and hose which must be disconnected, simply because so many different model and engine combinations have been manufactured. Careful observation and common sense are the best possible approaches to any repair procedure.

Removal and installation of the engine can be made easier if you follow these basic points:

• If you have to drain any of the fluids, use a suitable container.

• Always tag any wires or hoses and, if possible, the components they came from before disconnecting them.

• Because there are so many bolts and fasteners involved, store and label the retainers from components separately in muffin pans, jars or coffee cans. This will prevent confusion during installation.

• After unbolting the transmission or transaxle, always make sure it is properly supported.

• If it is necessary to disconnect the air conditioning system, have this service performed by a qualified technician using a recovery/recycling station. If the system does not have to be disconnected, unbolt the compressor and set it aside.

• When unbolting the engine mounts, always make sure the engine is properly supported. When removing the engine, make sure that any lifting devices are properly attached to the engine. It is recommended that if your engine is supplied with lifting hooks, your lifting apparatus be attached to them.

• Lift the engine from its compartment slowly, checking that no hoses, wires or other components are still connected.

• After the engine is clear of the compartment, place it on an engine stand or workbench.

• After the engine has been removed, you can perform a partial or full teardown of the engine using the procedures outlined in this manual.

✳✳ CAUTION

When draining the coolant, keep in mind that cats and dogs are attracted by the ethylene glycol antifreeze, and are quite likely to drink any that is left in an uncovered container or in puddles on the ground. This will prove fatal in sufficient quantity. Always drain the coolant into a sealable container. Coolant should be reused unless it is contaminated or several years old.

➡ The procedure for pulling the engine requires removing the transaxle along with it. As a result, when the half-shafts are pulled from the transaxle, a special plug/side gear holding tool is recommended.

✳✳ CAUTION

Observe all applicable safety precautions when working around fuel. Whenever servicing the fuel system, always work in a well ventilated area. Do not allow fuel spray or vapors to come in contact with a spark or open flame. Keep a dry chemical fire extinguisher near the work area. Always keep fuel in a container specifically designed for fuel storage; also, always properly seal fuel containers to avoid the possibility of fire or explosion.

1. Properly relieve the fuel system pressure. Raise and safely support the vehicle, as necessary.
2. Disconnect the battery cables and remove the battery and the battery tray.
3. Remove the hood.
4. Loosen the lug nuts on the front wheels.
5. Apply the parking brake, block the rear wheels, then raise and safely support the front of the vehicle securely on jackstands.
6. Remove the front wheels.
7. Remove the splash shield(s) from under the vehicle and drain the engine and transaxle oil as well as the coolant.

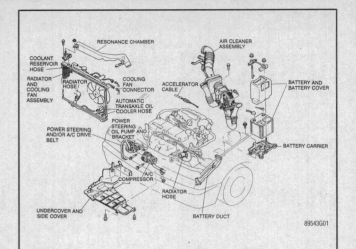

Fig. 1 View of typically removed external components for engine removal

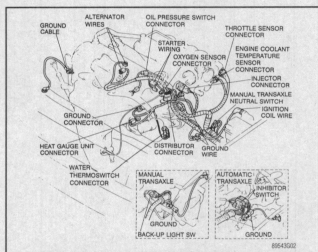

Fig. 2 View of the common electrical harness plug disconnection points for engine removal

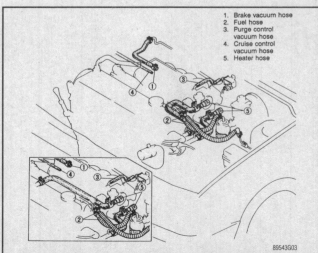

Fig. 3 Typical vacuum, fuel and water hose disconnect points for engine removal

※※ CAUTION

The EPA warns that prolonged contact with used engine oil may cause a number of skin disorders, including cancer! You should make every effort to minimize your exposure to used engine oil. Protective gloves should be worn when changing the oil. Wash your hands and any other exposed skin areas as soon as possible after exposure to used engine oil. Soap and water, or waterless hand cleaner should be used.

8. Remove the air cleaner assembly and resonance chamber, including the air flow meter and all of the ducting. Remove the oil dip stick.

9. On the Millienia with the 2.3L engine, remove the charge air cooler, front grille, upper seal board (panels that the grille mounts to) and coolant overflow tank.

10. Remove the radiator hoses. If equipped with automatic transaxle, disconnect the oil cooler lines from the radiator. Disconnect the cooling fan and, if equipped, radiator switch electrical connectors and remove the radiator/cooling fan assembly. On 4WD vehicles, remove the crossmember from the underside of the vehicle.

11. Disconnect the throttle and the speedometer cable.

12. Label and disconnect all vacuum hoses and wiring harnesses.

13. Disconnect the fuel supply and return hoses and the heater hoses.

14. Disconnect the exhaust pipe from the manifold. On 4WD vehicles, remove the exhaust manifold. If equipped, remove the water inlet pipe and gasket.

15. Remove the accessory drive belt or belts.

16. Without disconnecting the hydraulic hoses, remove the power steering pump and hang it from the body with wire.

17. Without disconnecting the refrigerant lines, remove the air conditioning compressor and hang it from the body with wire.

18. If equipped with manual transaxle, disconnect the clutch cable and shift control rod. If equipped with hydraulic clutch, remove the slave cylinder from the transaxle without disconnecting the hydraulic line.

19. If equipped with automatic transaxle, disconnect the shift control cable.

20. Remove the nuts and disconnect the tie rod ends from the steering knuckles. Disconnect the stabilizer bar from the lower control arms.

21. Attach an engine lifting chain to the engine lifting eyes. Attach the chain to a suitable engine hoist and raise the hoist until there is tension on the chain.

22. Remove the engine mount nuts and the engine mount member bolts and nuts and remove the engine mount member. On 4WD vehicles, remove the front transaxle mount.

➡ **Be careful so the engine does not fall when removing the engine mount member.**

23. Remove the pinch bolts from the steering knuckle and pry the control arm down to slip the lower ball joint out of the knuckle.

24. If equipped, remove the bolts from the right side intermediate shaft support and, using a suitable prybar, pry the intermediate shaft from the transaxle.

Insert a suitable prybar between the inner CV-joint and transaxle case and carefully pry the inner CV-joints out of the transaxle. Suspend the halfshafts with wire.

25. If equipped with 4WD, mark the position of the driveshaft on the transaxle and rear axle flanges. Remove the driveshaft, keeping all spacers, washers and bushings in order so they can be reinstalled in their original positions.

26. Remove the dynamic damper from the right side engine mount, if equipped. Remove the engine/transaxle mount nuts/bolts and right engine and, if equipped, left transaxle mounts. Carefully lift the engine/transaxle assembly from the vehicle.

27. Properly support the engine/transaxle assembly. Remove the intake manifold bracket, starter, torque converter nuts, stiffener, if equipped and No. 2 engine mount. Disconnect the throttle cable.

28. If equipped with 4WD, remove the center differential lock motor as follows:

   a. Remove the set bolt and lock sensor switch.

   b. Remove the plug from the end of the motor and use a small flat bladed tool to turn the shift rod ½ turn clockwise.

   c. Remove the retaining bolts and the center differential lock motor.

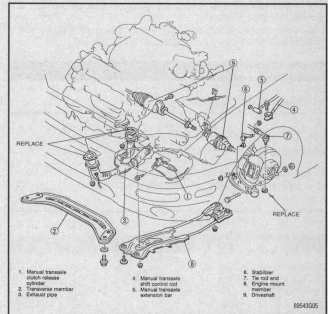

1. Manual transaxle clutch release cylinder
2. Transverse member
3. Exhaust pipe
4. Manual transaxle shift control rod
5. Manual transaxle extension bar
6. Stabilizer
7. Tie rod end
8. Engine mount member
9. Driveshaft

89543G05

Fig. 5 Typically removed 6-cylinder engine under vehicle components for engine removal

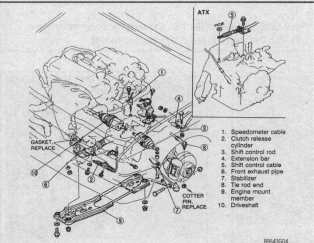

1. Speedometer cable
2. Clutch release cylinder
3. Shift control rod
4. Extension bar
5. Shift control cable
6. Front exhaust pipe
7. Stabilizer
8. Tie rod end
9. Engine mount member
10. Driveshaft

89543G04

Fig. 4 Typically removed 4-cylinder engine under vehicle components for engine removal

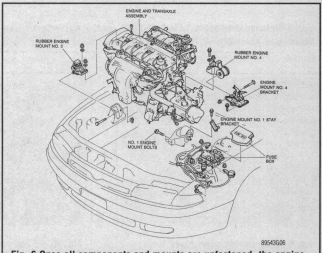

89543G06

Fig. 6 Once all components and mounts are unfastened, the engine is removed with the transaxle attached

29. Remove the transaxle mounting bolts and separate the transaxle from the engine.

To install:

30. Installation is the reverse of the removal procedure. Note the following important steps.

31. When possible, leave the engine mounting nuts/bolts loose (hand tight) until all mounts are aligned and bolted. This may help in aligning the engine and transmission assembly in the vehicle.

32. Install new circlips on the inner CV-joint stub shafts and, if equipped, intermediate shaft. Grease the shaft splines before installing the halfshaft/intermediate shaft into the transaxle.

33. Always install new gaskets and/or O-rings. Use new self-locking nuts, especially on the exhaust.

✳✳ WARNING

Operating the engine without the proper amount and type of engine oil will result in severe engine damage.

34. Fill the engine and the transaxle with the proper types and quantities of oil. Fill the cooling system.

35. Connect the negative battery cable, start the engine and check for leaks. Check the ignition timing and the idle speed. Check all fluid levels.

Rocker Arm (Valve) Cover

REMOVAL & INSTALLATION

1.6L, 1.8L SOHC (except K8) and 2.2L Engines

▶ **See Figure 7**

1. Disconnect the vent hose from the rocker arm cover.
2. Remove the PCV valve from the rocker arm cover.

3. Remove the spark plug wires from the wire clips.
4. Remove the rocker arm cover retaining bolts and remove the rocker arm cover and gasket.

To install:

5. Clean all old gasket material from the rocker arm cover and the cylinder head.

6. Install a new gasket onto the rocker arm cover.
7. Apply silicone sealer around the groove of the cover.
8. Install the rocker arm cover on the cylinder head with the retaining bolts. Tighten the bolts to 43–78 inch lbs. (5–9 Nm).

9. Install the spark plug wires to the retaining clips and install the PCV valve. Connect the vent hose to the rocker arm cover.

10. Start the engine and bring to normal operating temperature. Check for leaks.

1.5L, 1.8L DOHC (except K8) and 2.0L Engines

▶ **See Figures 8 thru 20**

1. As necessary, unbolt the power steering hose securing brackets from the valve cover. It may be necessary to remove the power steering pump in order to allow the hose enough range of motion to clear the valve cover.

2. Label and remove the spark plug wires from the plugs.
3. Disconnect the vent hose from the cover.
4. Disconnect the PCV hose from the cover.
5. Loosen the cover bolts evenly over three steps.
6. Remove the valve cover bolts, keeping them in order. Some bolts are longer than others and should be returned to their original locations.

7. Remove the cover from the engine.

To install:

8. Clean all old gasket material from the cover and the cylinder head.
9. Install a new gasket onto the cover.
10. Apply silicone sealer to the shaded area of the cylinder head as shown in the figure.

11. Install the cover on the cylinder head with the retaining bolts. Tighten the bolts in the order shown in fig39 to 52–69 inch lbs. (6–8 Nm).

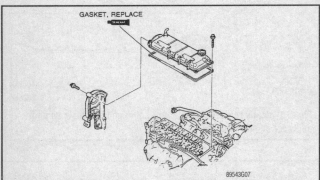

Fig. 7 Exploded view of the 1.6L, 1.8L SOHC (except K8) engine valve cover assembly—2.2L engine is similar

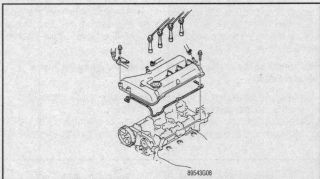

Fig. 8 Exploded view of the 1.5L engine valve cover assembly—1.8L DOHC (except K8) and 2.0L engine is similar

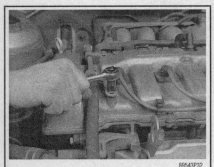

Fig. 9 To remove the valve cover, first unbolt any components which are attached to the valve cover . . .

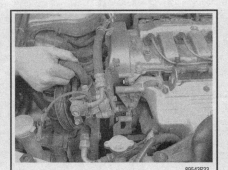

Fig. 10 . . . and ensure that any components which may obstruct cover removal are positioned aside

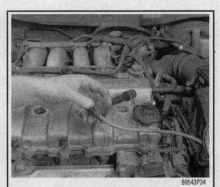

Fig. 11 Next, label and remove the spark plug wires from the plugs

Fig. 12 Also detach the PCV valve and vent hose (shown) from the valve cover

Fig. 13 Loosen the valve cover retaining bolts evenly, over three steps . . .

Fig. 14 . . . then remove them. Keep the bolts in order as some of them are of differing lengths and must be returned to their original hole

Fig. 15 Remove the valve cover. Some gentle tapping with a soft faced hammer may be necessary to break the seal

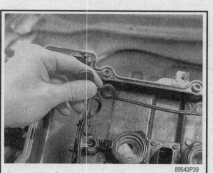

Fig. 16 Remove the old gasket from the valve cover and discard it. Clean all gasket mating surfaces thoroughly

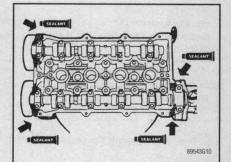

Fig. 17 Apply sealer to any point on the cylinder head mating surface where the gasket must arch over a cam cap

Fig. 18 Close up example of a cam cap arch where sealer should be placed

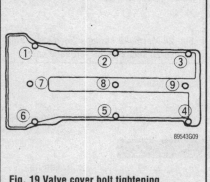

Fig. 19 Valve cover bolt tightening sequence for the 1.5L engine

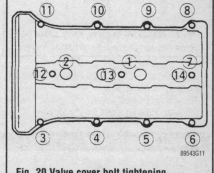

Fig. 20 Valve cover bolt tightening sequence for the 1.8L and 2.0L engines

12. Install the spark plug wires to the spark plugs. Connect the vent hose and the PCV hose to the cover.

13. Start the engine and bring to normal operating temperature. Check for leaks.

1.8L DOHC (K8), 2.3L and 2.5L Engine

▶ See Figures 21, 22, 23 and 24

1. Disconnect the negative battery cable.

2. On the 1.8L and 2.5L engines, remove the intake manifold stay bracket from the engine.

3. Disconnect the vent hoses from the intake manifold and from the cover assembly.

4. Remove the spark plug wires from the spark plugs, make a note of plug wire original location.

5. On 2.3L engines and for rear valve cover removal on the 1.8L and 2.5L engines perform the following:

a. Remove the intake manifold assembly from the engine.

6. Remove the ventilation pipe attaching bolts and disconnect the pipe from the front cover.

7. Remove the cover bolts and remove the cover assembly.

To install:

8. Clean all old gasket material from the rocker arm cover and the cylinder head.

9. Install a new gasket onto the cover.

10. Apply silicone sealer to the cylinder head perimeter.

11. Install the cover assembly and the bolts and tighten in the sequence shown over three steps to 43–78 inch lbs. (4.9–8.8 Nm).

12. Install the ventilation pipe to the front cover assembly and tighten the bolts to 69–95 inch lbs. (7.8–11 Nm).

13. If removed, install a new gasket to the intake manifold assembly and install it to the engine. Loosely tighten the bolts and nuts.

14. On the 1.8L and 2.5L engines, install the intake manifold stay and tighten the bolts to 14–19 ft. lbs. (19–25 Nm).

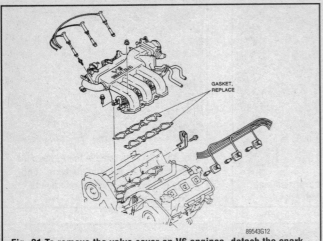

Fig. 21 To remove the valve cover on V6 engines, detach the spark plug wires from the plugs, and if necessary, remove the intake manifold

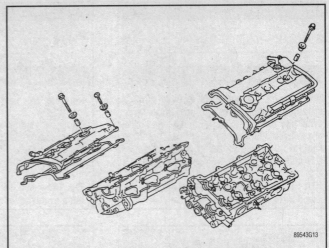

Fig. 22 Exploded view of the valve cover assemblies on the V6 engines

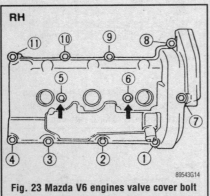

Fig. 23 Mazda V6 engines valve cover bolt tightening sequence for right-hand covers

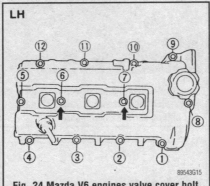

Fig. 24 Mazda V6 engines valve cover bolt tightening sequence for left-hand covers

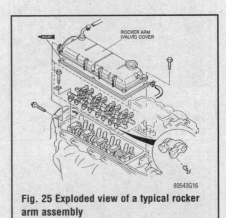

Fig. 25 Exploded view of a typical rocker arm assembly

15. If necessary, tighten the intake manifold nuts and bolts over three stages to the proper specification.

16. Connect the vent hoses and connect the negative battery cable.

17. Start the engine and inspect for leaks.

Rocker Arms/Shafts

REMOVAL & INSTALLATION

♦ See Figure 25

1.6L (B6 SOHC) AND 1.8L (BP SOHC) Engines

1. Remove the rocker arm (valve) cover.

2. Remove the rocker arm and shaft assembly mounting bolts. Start at the ends and work toward the center of the shafts, when removing the bolts.

3. If necessary, separate the rocker arms and springs from the shafts; be sure to keep the parts in order for reinstallation purposes.

4. Clean and inspect the shafts and rocker arms for wear. Measure the difference between the rocker arm shaft outside diameter and the rocker arm inside diameter; this is the oil clearance. If the oil clearance exceeds 0.004 in. (0.10mm), replace the shaft and/or the rocker arm(s).

To install:

5. If they were disassembled, coat the rocker arm shafts and rocker arms with engine oil and assemble them with the springs. When assembling and installing on the cylinder head, note the notches at the ends of the shafts; they are different on the intake and exhaust side and cannot be interchanged.

6. Install the rocker arm/shaft assemblies onto the cylinder head and torque the rocker arm shaft-to-cylinder head bolts, in sequence, to 16–21 ft. lbs. (22–28 Nm), in several steps.

7. Install the rocker arm (valve) cover.

2.2L Engine

1. Remove the rocker arm (valve) cover.

2. Remove the rocker arm and shaft assembly mounting bolts. Start at the ends and work toward the center of the shafts, when removing the bolts.

3. If necessary, separate the rocker arms and springs from the shafts; be sure to keep the parts in order for reinstallation purposes.

4. Clean and inspect the shafts and rocker arms for wear. Measure the difference between the rocker arm shaft outside diameter and the rocker arm inside diameter; this is the oil clearance. If the oil clearance exceeds 0.004 in. (0.10mm), replace the shaft and/or the rocker arm(s).

To install:

5. If they were disassembled, coat the rocker arm shafts and rocker arms with engine oil and assemble them with the springs. When assembling and installing on the cylinder head, note the notches at the ends of the shafts; they are different on the intake and exhaust side and cannot be interchanged.

6. Install the rocker arm/shaft assemblies onto the cylinder head and torque the rocker arm shaft-to-cylinder head bolts, in sequence, to 13–20 ft. lbs. (18–26 Nm), in 2 steps.

7. Install the rocker arm (valve) cover.

Thermostat

REMOVAL & INSTALLATION

✳✳ CAUTION

When draining the coolant, keep in mind that cats and dogs are attracted by the ethylene glycol antifreeze, and are quite likely to drink any that is left in an uncovered container or in puddles on the ground. This will prove fatal in sufficient quantity. Always drain the coolant into a sealable container. Coolant should be reused unless it is contaminated or several years old.

1.5L, 1.6L, 1.8L (except K8) and 2.2L Engines

▶ See Figures 26 and 27

1. Disconnect the negative battery cable. Drain the radiator to below the level of the thermostat.
2. If necessary, remove the air cleaner assembly.
3. If necessary, disconnect the coolant temperature switch at the thermostat housing.
4. Remove the upper radiator hose.
5. Remove the mounting nuts, thermostat housing, thermostat and gasket.

➡Do not pry the housing off.

To install:
6. Clean the thermostat housing and the cylinder head mating surfaces.
7. Insert the thermostat into the rear cylinder head housing with the jiggle pin at the top. The spring side of the thermostat should face the housing.
8. Position a new gasket onto the studs with the seal print side facing the rear cylinder housing.
9. Install the thermostat housing and 2 nuts. Tighten the nuts to 14–22 ft. lbs. (19–30 Nm).

10. Install the upper radiator hose.
11. If detached, connect the coolant temperature switch.
12. If removed, install the air cleaner housing.
13. Fill the cooling system. Connect the negative battery cable, start the engine and check for leaks. Check the coolant level and add coolant, as necessary.

2.0L Engine

▶ See Figures 28 thru 35

1. Disconnect the negative battery cable.
2. Drain the engine coolant from the radiator to below the level of the thermostat.
3. Disconnect the lower radiator hose from the engine.
4. Remove the housing bolts, thermostat housing, thermostat and gasket.

➡Do not pry the housing off.

To install:
5. Clean the thermostat housing and the cylinder head mating surfaces.
6. Make sure that the thermostat jiggle pin is aligned with the gasket projection.
7. Install the thermostat to the housing. Align the gasket projection with the opening in the housing. The spring side of the thermostat should face into the housing.
8. Install the thermostat housing cover and tighten both bolts to 14–19 ft. lbs. (19–25 Nm).
9. Fill the cooling system. Connect the negative battery cable, start the engine and check for leaks. Check the coolant level and add coolant, as necessary.

1.8L DOHC (K8) and 2.5L Engines

▶ See Figure 36

1. Disconnect the negative battery cable.
2. Drain the engine coolant from the radiator to below the level of the thermostat.

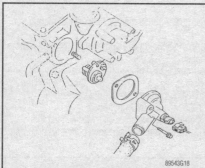

Fig. 26 Exploded view of the thermostat assembly for the 1.5L, 1.6L and 1.8L (except K8) engines

89543G18

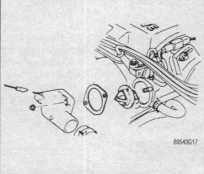

Fig. 27 Exploded view of the thermostat assembly for the 2.2L engine

89543G17

Fig. 28 To remove the thermostat, first drain the cooling system, then remove the radiator hose-to-thermostat housing cover clamp . . .

89543P57

Fig. 29 . . . by sliding back on the hose. Note the alignment marks on the hose and housing cover (arrows)

89543P58

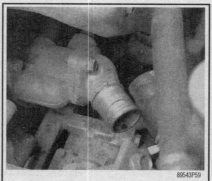

Fig. 30 Disconnect the hose from the thermostat housing cover

89543P59

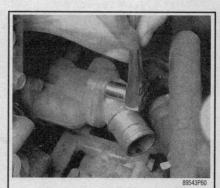

Fig. 31 Loosen the thermostat housing cover attaching bolts . . .

89543P60

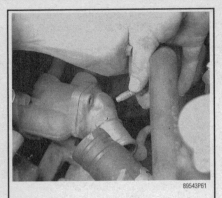

Fig. 32 . . . then remove them . . .

Fig. 33 . . . along with the housing cover/water outlet

Fig. 34 Remove the thermostat from the housing by simply pulling it outward

Fig. 35 When installing the new thermostat, note the tab (arrow) which seats into a notch in the housing. Jiggle pin must face straight up

Fig. 36 Exploded view of the thermostat assembly for the 1.8L (K8) and 2.5L engines

3. Remove the water outlet pipe mounting bolt and detach the pipe from the outlet housing. Remove and discard the O-ring.
4. Remove the engine harness bracket bolt and position the harness aside.
5. Remove the housing bolt, thermostat housing, thermostat and gasket.

➥Do not pry the housing off.

To install:
6. Clean the thermostat housing and the cylinder head mating surfaces.
7. Insert the thermostat into the housing with the jiggle pin at the top. The spring side of the thermostat should face the housing.
8. Position a new gasket with the projection facing the same direction as the thermostat jiggle pin.
9. Install the thermostat housing cover and loosely install the lower bolt. Install the engine harness bracket and loosely install the bolt. Tighten both bolts to 14–19 ft. lbs. (19–25 Nm).
10. Position a new O-ring onto the water pipe and wet the O-ring with fresh engine coolant.
11. Install the pipe to the outlet housing, using care to not rip or otherwise damage the O-ring, and install the mounting bolt. Tighten the mounting bolt to 14–19 ft. lbs. (19–25 Nm).
12. Fill the cooling system. Connect the negative battery cable, start the engine and check for leaks. Check the coolant level and add coolant, as necessary.

2.3L Engine

▶ **See Figure 37**

1. Disconnect the negative battery cable.
2. Drain the engine coolant from the radiator to below the level of the thermostat.
3. Remove the charge air cooler air duct.
4. Remove the air cleaner housing.
5. Remove the resonator.
6. Remove the two thermostat housing bolts, the housing and the thermostat.

To install:
7. Thoroughly clean the thermostat housing and cylinder head mating surfaces.
8. Position the thermostat on the housing and align the projection on the thermostat to the notch in the housing.
9. Position the housing/thermostat assembly to the cylinder head and install the two retaining bolts. Tighten the bolts to 14–18 ft. lbs. (19–25 Nm).
10. Install the resonator, air cleaner housing and air duct assemblies. Tighten all attaching bolts to 70–95 inch lbs. (8–11 Nm).
11. Fill the cooling system. Connect the negative battery cable, start engine and check for leaks. Check the coolant level and add coolant, as necessary.

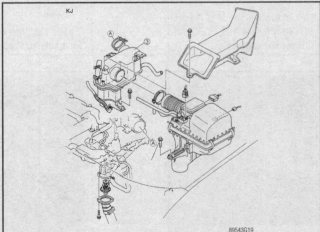

Fig. 37 Exploded view of the thermostat assembly for the 2.3L engine. Also shown are the removed components for thermostat access

Intake Manifold

REMOVAL & INSTALLATION

✳✳ CAUTION

When draining the coolant, keep in mind that cats and dogs are attracted by the ethylene glycol antifreeze, and are quite likely to drink any that is left in an uncovered container or in puddles on the ground. This will prove fatal in sufficient quantity. Always drain the coolant into a sealable container. Coolant should be reused unless it is contaminated or several years old.

2.0L and 1990–94 1.6L, 1.8L (except K8) and 2.2L Engines

▶ See Figures 38 thru 48

1. Properly relieve the fuel system pressure. Disconnect the negative battery cable and drain the cooling system.
2. Disconnect the air intake hose from the throttle body. Remove the hose, resonator(s) and air cleaner assembly.
3. Disconnect the accelerator and, if equipped, the cruise control cable. Disconnect and plug the fuel lines.
4. Label and disconnect all necessary vacuum hoses and electrical connectors. Disconnect the coolant hoses.
5. Disconnect the EGR tube, if equipped.
6. If necessary, remove the air valve and remove the fuel rail attaching bolts. Remove the fuel rail and injectors as an assembly.

Fig. 38 To remove the intake manifold, disconnect the throttle cable from the throttle body . . .

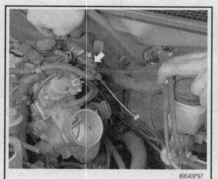

Fig. 39 . . . as well as the throttle cable housing (arrow) from its retaining bracket

Fig. 40 Next, disconnect the fuel lines (arrows), and label and detach all vacuum hose connections . . .

Fig. 41 . . . along with the electrical wire harness connections on the intake manifold

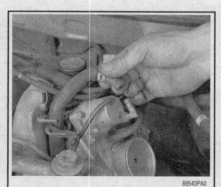

Fig. 42 Detach any throttle body pre-heat coolant hoses from the intake manifold

Fig. 43 Ensure that any coolant hoses connected to the intake are disconnected, as their can be quite a few of them (arrows)

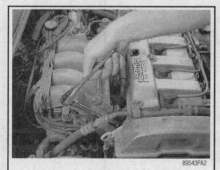

Fig. 44 From underneath, remove the intake manifold support, then remove the intake manifold attaching bolts and nuts

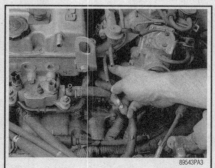

Fig. 45 Some bolts may prove difficult to reach. Switch to various wrenches and positions will help

Fig. 46 Once all fasteners and connections are removed, slide the intake backwards off its mounting studs then remove it from the vehicle

Fig. 47 Thoroughly clean the gasket mating surfaces of all traces of the old gasket

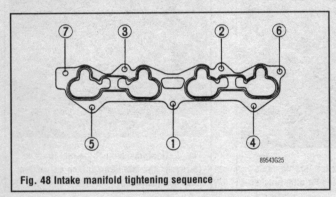

Fig. 48 Intake manifold tightening sequence

7. From below, remove the intake manifold support bracket.

8. If necessary, remove the bolt retaining the dipstick tube bracket to the intake manifold.

9. If necessary, unbolt the vacuum solenoid bracket from the manifold and position it aside. This will afford better access to the intake attaching nuts/bolts.

10. Remove the intake manifold-to-cylinder head bolts/nuts and remove the intake manifold assembly.

11. If necessary, remove the throttle body and separate the intake manifold upper and lower halves.

To install:

12. Clean all gasket mating surfaces.

13. If separated, connect the upper and lower intake manifolds using a new gasket. Tighten the nuts/bolts to 19 ft. lbs. (25 Nm). If removed, install the throttle body using a new gasket. Tighten the retaining nuts/bolts to 19 ft. lbs. (25 Nm).

14. Install the intake manifold assembly to the cylinder head using a new gasket. Tighten the nuts/bolts to 19 ft. lbs. (25 Nm) on all except 2.2L engine. On 2.2L engine, tighten to 22 ft. lbs. (30 Nm).

➡On all except the 2.2L engine, torque the intake manifold-to-cylinder head bolts in the proper sequence. On the 2.2L engine, tighten the bolts in the center of the manifold first and work outwards toward the ends.

15. If equipped, install the bolt retaining the dipstick tube to the intake manifold.

16. Install the intake manifold bracket. Tighten the attaching nuts/bolts to 38 ft. lbs. (52 Nm) for the 2.0L and 2.2L engine and 19 ft. lbs. (25 Nm) on the 1.6L and 1.8L engines.

17. If removed, install the fuel rail and injector assembly on the intake manifold using new insulators. Tighten the fuel rail mounting bolts to 19 ft. lbs. (25 Nm). Install the air valve and tighten the bolts to 57 inch lbs. (5.5 Nm).

18. Connect the EGR tube, if equipped. Connect the coolant and vacuum hoses, electrical connectors and fuel lines.

19. Connect the accelerator cable. Install the air cleaner assembly, if removed, and connect the air intake tube to the throttle body.

20. Connect the negative battery cable. Fill and bleed the cooling system.

21. Start the engine and bring to normal operating temperature. Check for leaks. Check the idle speed.

1995–98 1.5L and 1.8L (except K8) Engines

◆ See Figures 49 and 50

1. Relieve the fuel system pressure, and disconnect the negative battery cable. Drain the cooling system.

2. Disconnect the mass air flow sensor electrical connector. Remove the air ducts, air cleaner assembly, mass air flow sensor and resonance chamber.

3. Disconnect the throttle and accelerator cables. Disconnect and plug the fuel lines.

4. Remove the throttle body as follows:
   a. Disconnect the coolant hoses.
   b. Label and disconnect the electrical connectors for the idle air control valve and the throttle position sensor.
   c. Remove the mounting bolts/nuts from the throttle body, and remove the throttle body from the vehicle.

5. Label and disconnect the vacuum lines at the intake manifold.

6. Remove the dynamic chamber (upper intake manifold).

7. Disconnect and plug the fuel hoses from the fuel rail.

8. Label and disconnect the electrical connectors for the fuel injectors.

9. On some models you may need to remove the fuel rail with the injectors connected.

10. On the 1.5L engine, remove the EGR pipe from the intake manifold. Remove the EGR and pressure regulator control (PRC) solenoid valve brackets.

11. Remove the intake manifold support bracket.

12. Remove the bolts and nuts, and remove the intake manifold.

To install:

13. Clean all gasket mating surfaces.

14. Install the intake manifold, using a new gasket. Tighten the nuts and bolts to 14–18 ft. lbs. (19–25 Nm).

15. Attach the EGR pipe to the manifold and install the intake manifold support bracket. Tighten the support bracket bolts to 38 ft. lbs. (51 Nm).

16. If removed, install the EGR and pressure regulator control (PRC) solenoid valve brackets.

17. Install the fuel rail and injector assembly. Connect the electrical connectors to the injectors, and the fuel lines to the rail.

18. Install the upper intake manifold to the intake manifold using new gaskets. Tighten the nuts to 14–18 ft. lbs. (19–25 Nm).

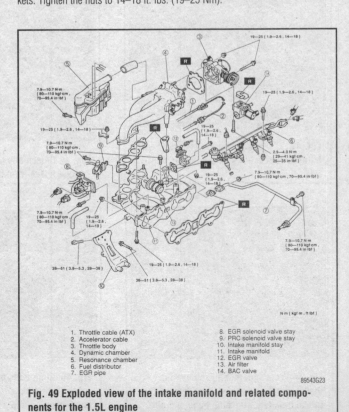

1. Throttle cable (ATX)
2. Accelerator cable
3. Throttle body
4. Dynamic chamber
5. Resonance chamber
6. Fuel distributor
7. EGR pipe
8. EGR solenoid valve stay
9. PRC solenoid valve stay
10. Intake manifold stay
11. Intake manifold
12. EGR valve
13. Air filter
14. BAC valve

Fig. 49 Exploded view of the intake manifold and related components for the 1.5L engine

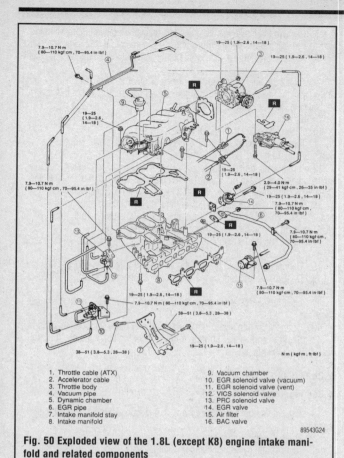

1. Throttle cable (ATX)
2. Accelerator cable
3. Throttle body
4. Vacuum pipe
5. Dynamic chamber
6. EGR pipe
7. Intake manifold stay
8. Intake manifold
9. Vacuum chamber
10. EGR solenoid valve (vacuum)
11. EGR solenoid valve (vent)
12. VICS solenoid valve
13. PRC solenoid valve
14. EGR valve
15. Air filter
16. BAC valve

89543G24

Fig. 50 Exploded view of the 1.8L (except K8) engine intake manifold and related components

19. Install the throttle body, using a new mounting gasket. Tighten the mounting bolts to 14–18 ft. lbs. (19–25 Nm).

20. Connect the electrical connectors for the idle air control valve and the throttle position sensor.

21. Connect the vacuum and coolant lines.

22. Connect and adjust the throttle and accelerator cables.

23. Connect the fuel lines.

24. Install the resonance chamber. Install the air cleaner assembly, mass air flow sensor and ducts. Connect the mass air flow sensor connector.

25. Connect the negative battery cable. Fill and bleed the cooling system. Run the engine and check for leaks.

1995 1.6L Engine

▶ **See Figure 51**

1. Relieve the fuel system pressure and disconnect the negative battery cable. Drain the cooling system.

2. Disconnect the mass air flow sensor electrical connector. Remove the air ducts, air cleaner assembly and resonance chamber.

3. Remove the fuel line mounting bracket and disconnect the throttle cable. Disconnect and plug the fuel lines.

4. Remove the throttle body as follows:

   a. Disconnect the coolant hoses.

   b. Label and disconnect the electrical connectors for the idle air control valve and the throttle position sensor.

   c. Remove the mounting bolts/nuts from the throttle body, and remove the throttle body from the vehicle.

5. Label and disconnect the vacuum lines at the intake manifold.

6. Remove the bypass air control (BAC) valve, variable inertia charging system (VICS) solenoid valve, pressure regulator control (PRC) solenoid valves, and the EGR solenoid vent and vacuum valves from the intake manifold.

7. Disconnect and plug the fuel hoses from the fuel rail.

8. Label and disconnect the electrical connectors for the fuel injectors.

9. Remove the fuel rail with the injectors connected.

10. Remove the intake manifold support bracket and remove the EGR pipe from the intake manifold.

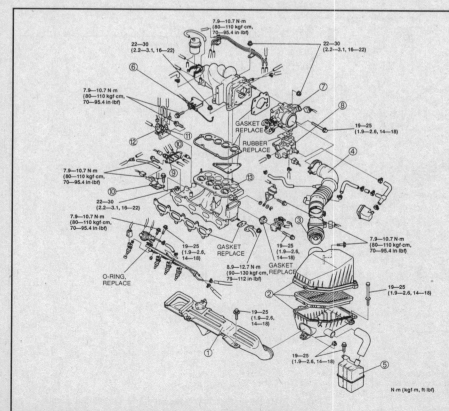

1. Air duct
2. Air cleaner
3. Mass air flow sensor
4. Air hose
5. Resonance chamber
6. Accelerator pedal/cable
7. Throttle body
8. BAC valve
9. VICS solenoid valve
10. PRC solenoid valve and PRC solenoid valve No.2
11. EGR solenoid valve (vacuum)
12. EGR solenoid valve (vent)
13. Intake manifold

89543G22

Fig. 51 Exploded view of the intake manifold for the 1995 1.6L engine

11. Lower the vehicle. Remove the bolts and nuts, and remove the intake manifold.

To install:

12. Clean all gasket mating surfaces.

13. Install the intake manifold, using a new gasket. Tighten the nuts and bolts to 16–22 ft. lbs. (22–30 Nm).

14. Raise and safely support the vehicle.

15. Attach the EGR pipe to the manifold and install the intake manifold support bracket. Tighten the support bracket bolts to 38 ft. lbs. (51 Nm).

16. Install the fuel rail and injector assembly. Connect the electrical connectors to the injectors, and the fuel lines to the rail.

17. Install the bypass air control (BAC) valve, variable inertia charging system (VICS) solenoid valve, pressure regulator control (PRC) solenoid valves, and the EGR solenoid vent and vacuum valves to the intake manifold.

18. Install the throttle body, using a new mounting gasket. Tighten the mounting bolts to 14–18 ft. lbs. (19–25 Nm).

19. Connect the electrical connectors, vacuum lines and coolant lines.

20. Connect the throttle cable and the fuel lines. Install the fuel line mounting bracket and tighten the bolt to 97 inch lbs. (11 Nm).

21. Install the resonance chamber. Install the air cleaner assembly and ducts. Connect the mass air flow sensor connector.

22. Connect the negative battery cable. Fill and bleed the cooling system. Run the engine and check for leaks.

1.8L (K8) and 2.5L Engines

▶ See Figure 52

1. Properly relieve the fuel system pressure. (See Chapter 5).
2. Disconnect the negative battery cable and drain the cooling system.
3. On MX-3, remove the upper strut bar.
4. Remove the air cleaner assembly and ducts.
5. Disconnect the accelerator cable. Label and disconnect the necessary electrical connectors and vacuum hoses.
6. Disconnect and plug the fuel lines. Disconnect the coolant hose from the air bypass valve.

7. Remove the intake manifold support bracket. Remove the intake manifold-to-cylinder head bolts and remove the intake manifold.

8. If necessary, remove the throttle body and air intake pipe from the manifold.

9. Check the intake manifold for cracks or other damage. Check the surface of the cylinder heads and intake manifold for warpage using a straightedge. Replace the intake manifold, as necessary.

To install:

10. Clean all gasket mating surfaces.

11. If removed, install the throttle body using new gaskets. Tighten the nuts/bolts to 19 ft. lbs. (25 Nm).

12. If removed, apply clean engine oil to new O-rings and install the air intake pipe to the intake manifold. Tighten the bolts to 95 inch lbs. (10.8 Nm). On 1.8L engine, the bolts must be tightened in the proper sequence.

13. Position new gaskets and install the intake manifold to the cylinder head. Install the mounting bolts and tighten, in 2–3 steps, to 19 ft. lbs. (25 Nm), working from the center toward the ends of the manifold.

14. Install the intake manifold bracket and tighten the bolts to 19 ft. lbs. (25 Nm).

15. Connect the coolant hose to the air bypass valve. Connect the fuel lines.

16. Connect the vacuum hoses and electrical connectors. Connect the accelerator cable.

17. Install the air cleaner assembly and ducts. On MX-3, install the upper strut bar.

18. Connect the negative battery cable. Fill and bleed the cooling system.

19. Start the engine and bring to normal operating temperature. Check for leaks. Check the idle speed.

2.3L Engine

▶ See Figures 53, 54 and 55

1. Relieve the fuel system pressure, and disconnect the negative battery cable.
2. Drain the cooling system.
3. Remove the dynamic chamber cover.

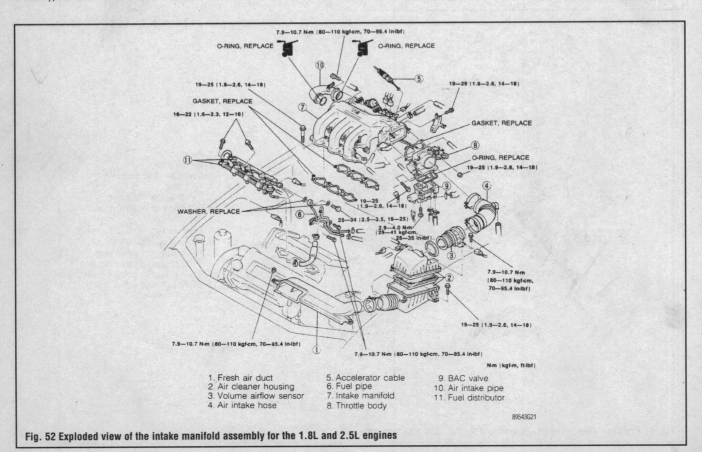

1. Fresh air duct
2. Air cleaner housing
3. Volume airflow sensor
4. Air intake hose
5. Accelerator cable
6. Fuel pipe
7. Intake manifold
8. Throttle body
9. BAC valve
10. Air intake pipe
11. Fuel distributor

Fig. 52 Exploded view of the intake manifold assembly for the 1.8L and 2.5L engines

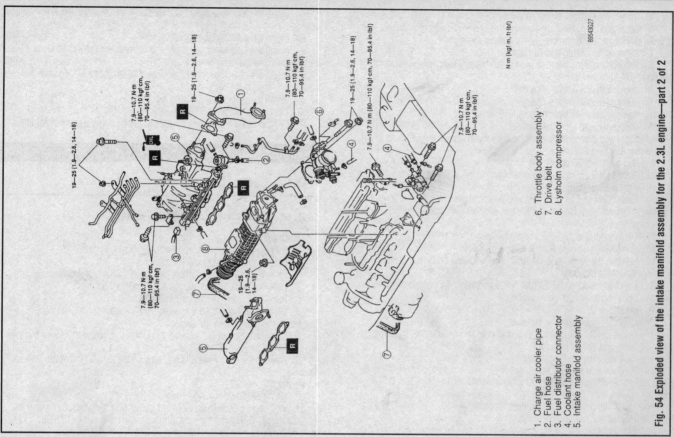

Fig. 54 Exploded view of the intake manifold assembly for the 2.3L engine—part 2 of 2

1. Charge air cooler pipe
2. Fuel hose
3. Fuel distributor connector
4. Coolant hose
5. Intake manifold assembly
6. Throttle body assembly
7. Drive belt
8. Lysholm compressor

N·m (kgf·m, ft·lbf)

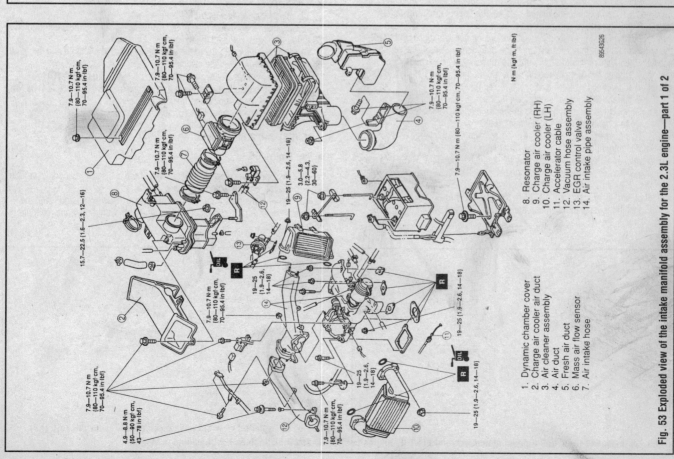

Fig. 53 Exploded view of the intake manifold assembly for the 2.3L engine—part 1 of 2

1. Dynamic chamber cover
2. Charge air cooler air duct
3. Air cleaner assembly
4. Air duct
5. Fresh air duct
6. Mass air flow sensor
7. Air intake hose
8. Resonator
9. Charge air cooler (RH)
10. Charge air cooler (LH)
11. Accelerator cable
12. Vacuum hose assembly
13. EGR control valve
14. Air intake pipe assembly

N·m (kgf·m, ft·lbf)

4. Remove the charge air cooler air duct.

5. Label and disconnect the vacuum hoses and electrical connectors from the air cleaner housing. Remove the air cleaner assembly.

6. Remove the air and fresh air ducts.

7. Remove the mass air flow sensor and the air intake hose from the throttle body.

8. Remove the resonator.

9. Remove the right-hand charge air cooler.

10. Remove the left-hand charge air cooler.

11. Disconnect the accelerator cable.

12. Label and disconnect the necessary vacuum hoses from the rear of the intake manifold and EGR valve.

13. Remove the EGR valve.

14. Remove the air intake pipe assembly.

15. Remove the charge air cooler pipe.

16. Disconnect and plug the fuel supply line at the fuel rails and discard the copper crush washers. Disconnect the fuel and vacuum lines from the fuel pressure regulator.

17. Disconnect and plug the coolant hoses.

18. Remove the harness from the intake manifold.

19. Remove the intake manifold mounting nuts and bolts in 2–3 steps, then remove the intake manifold.

20. Label and disconnect the fuel hoses and electrical connectors from the throttle body. Remove the throttle body.

To install:

21. Clean all gasket mating surfaces.

22. Install the throttle body. Tighten the nuts and bolts to 14–18 ft. lbs. (19–25 Nm), and connect the fuel

hoses and electrical connectors.

23. Position new gaskets and install the intake manifold. Tighten the nuts and bolts in 2–3 steps, from the center to the ends, to 14–18 ft. lbs. (19–25 Nm).

24. Install the harness onto the intake manifold.

25. Unplug and connect the coolant hoses.

26. Connect the fuel and vacuum lines to the fuel pressure regulator. Connect the fuel supply line to the fuel rail, using new copper crush washers.

27. Install the charge air cooler pipe.

28. Position the air intake pipe assembly using new gaskets. Hand tighten the nuts and bolts in the order shown in the graphic until the air intake pipe contacts the intake manifold. Verify that the rubber gaskets are not twisted or distorted. Tighten the bolts marked **A** to 70–95 inch lbs. (8–11 Nm), and all others, in sequence, to 14–18 ft. lbs. (19–25 Nm).

29. Install the EGR valve using a new gasket.

30. Connect the vacuum hoses to the intake manifold and EGR valve.

31. Connect and adjust the accelerator cable.

32. Using new gaskets, position the left and right-hand charge air coolers. Hand tighten the nuts and bolts in the order shown in the graphic until the air intake pipes and charge air coolers contact the intake manifold. Verify that the rubber gaskets are not twisted or distorted. Tighten the bolts marked **A** to 44–78 inch lbs. (5–9 Nm). Tighten the bolts marked **B** to 70–95 inch lbs. (8–11 Nm), and all others, in sequence, to 14–18 ft. lbs. (19–25 Nm).

33. Install the resonator. Tighten the nuts and bolts to 12–16 ft. lbs. (16–22 Nm)

34. Install the air intake hose onto the throttle body. Install the mass air flow sensor.

35. Install the fresh air and air ducts.

36. Install the air cleaner assembly and connect the vacuum hoses and electrical connectors to the air cleaner housing.

37. Install the charge air cooler air duct. Tighten the mounting bolts to 70–95 inch lbs. (8–11 Nm).

38. Install the dynamic chamber cover.

39. Connect the negative battery cable.

40. Fill and bleed the cooling system. Run the engine and check for leaks.

Exhaust Manifold

REMOVAL & INSTALLATION

1995–98 1.5L and 1.8L (except K8) Engines

1. Disconnect the negative battery cable.

2. Remove the air cleaner, and disconnect the air hose.

3. Remove the water bypass pipe bolt.

4. Remove the exhaust manifold heat shield bolts and the heat shield.

5. Disconnect the oxygen sensor electrical connector.

6. Raise and safely support the vehicle.

7. Remove and discard the exhaust pipe-to-exhaust manifold nuts. Suspend the exhaust system with wire.

8. Disconnect the EGR pipe from the exhaust manifold and lower the vehicle.

9. Remove the nuts and bolts and remove the exhaust manifold. Discard the nuts.

To install:

10. Clean all gasket mating surfaces.

11. Position a new exhaust manifold gasket over the studs and install the exhaust manifold. Tighten the mounting nuts and bolts to 14–16 ft. lbs. (19–22 Nm) on the 1.5L, and for the 1.8L to 29–34 ft. lbs. (39–47 Nm).

12. Raise and safely support the vehicle.

13. Connect the exhaust pipe to the manifold. Install new nuts and tighten to 38 ft. lbs. (52 Nm). Connect the oxygen sensor connector.

14. Connect the EGR pipe to the back of the exhaust manifold and tighten to 34 ft. lbs. (47 Nm). Lower the vehicle.

15. Install the heat shield and tighten the bolts to 88 inch lbs. (10 Nm).

16. Install the water bypass pipe bolt, and tighten to 48–65 ft. lbs. (64–89 Nm).

17. Connect the air hose, and install the air cleaner.

18. Connect the negative battery cable.

1.8L (K8) and 2.5L Engines

▶ **See Figure 56**

1. Disconnect the negative battery cable. Raise and safely support the vehicle.

2. Disconnect the oxygen sensor connectors.

3. Remove the nuts from the front and rear exhaust pipes and lower the exhaust system. Both pipes must be disconnected, even if only one manifold is to be removed.

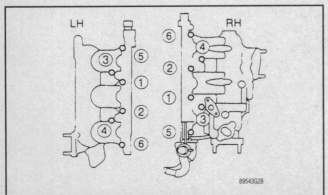

Fig. 55 Intake manifold bolt tightening sequence for the 2.3L engine

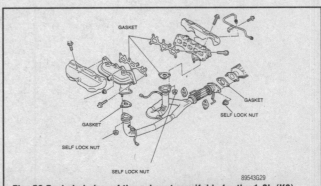

Fig. 56 Exploded view of the exhaust manifolds for the 1.8L (K8) and 2.5L engines—2.3L engine is similar

4. If removing the rear (right side) manifold, disconnect the EGR pipe.

5. Remove the 3 heat shield bolts and remove the heat shield.

6. Remove the 2 nuts and 5 bolts and remove the exhaust manifold.

To install:

7. Clean all gasket mating surfaces.

8. Install the exhaust manifold, using a new gasket, and tighten the nuts to 15–20 ft. lbs. (20–28 Nm), and the bolts to 12–16 ft. lbs. (16–22 Nm).

9. Install the heat shield and tighten the bolts to 88 inch lbs. (10 Nm).

10. If installing the rear (right side) manifold, connect the EGR pipe.

11. Connect the exhaust pipes to the manifolds, using new gaskets and nuts, and tighten the nuts to 38 ft. lbs. (51 Nm).

12. Connect the oxygen sensor connectors and lower the vehicle.

13. Connect the negative battery cable.

2.3L Engine

▶ See Figure 56

1. Disconnect the negative battery cable.

2. Raise and safely support the vehicle.

3. Remove the nuts from the front and rear exhaust pipes and lower the exhaust system. Both pipes must be disconnected, even if only one manifold is to be removed.

4. If removing the rear (right side) manifold, disconnect the EGR pipe.

5. If removing the front (left side) manifold, remove the charge air cooler and the coolant/condenser fans.

6. Disconnect the front and rear oxygen sensor connectors.

7. Remove the three heat shield bolts and remove the heat shield.

8. Remove the 2 nuts and 5 bolts and remove the exhaust manifold.

To install:

9. Clean all gasket mating surfaces.

10. Install the exhaust manifold, using a new gasket, and tighten the nuts and bolts to 12–16 ft. lbs. (16–22 Nm).

11. Install the heat shield and tighten the bolts to 70–95 inch lbs. (8–11 Nm).

12. Connect the oxygen sensor connectors.

13. If installing the front (left side) manifold, install the coolant/condenser fans and the charge air cooler. Tighten the charge air cooler mounting bolts to 14–18 ft. lbs. (19–25 Nm)

14. If installing the rear (right side) manifold, connect the EGR pipe.

15. Connect the exhaust pipes to the manifolds, using new gaskets and nuts, and tighten the nuts to 28–38 ft. lbs. (38–51 Nm).

16. Lower the vehicle.

17. Connect the negative battery cable.

Except 1.5L, 1.8L (K8), 2.3L, 2.5L and 1995–98 1.8L (except K8) Engines

▶ See Figures 57 thru 68

1. Disconnect the negative battery cable.

2. Remove the retaining bolts and remove the exhaust manifold insulator.

3. Disconnect the oxygen sensor electrical connector. Remove the oxygen sensor, if necessary, if it is installed in the manifold.

4. Disconnect the EGR pipe, if equipped.

5. Raise and safely support the vehicle. Remove the nuts from the exhaust pipe flange and disconnect the exhaust pipe from the manifold or turbocharger, if equipped.

6. Lower the vehicle.

7. If equipped with turbocharger, proceed as follows:

   a. Drain the cooling system.

   b. Disconnect the air hose and coolant hoses from the turbocharger.

   c. Disconnect the oil feed and return lines.

8. Remove the mounting nuts/bolts and remove the exhaust manifold. On turbocharged vehicles, the manifold and turbocharger are removed as an assembly.

9. Installation is the reverse of the removal procedure. Make sure all gasket mating surfaces are clean prior to assembly.

10. Use new gaskets and tighten the exhaust manifold-to-cylinder head nuts/bolts to 17 ft. lbs. (23 Nm) on 1.6L and 1.8L SOHC engines, 34 ft. lbs. (46 Nm) on 1.6L and 1.8L DOHC 4-cylinder engines and 2.2L engine. On 2.0L

Fig. 57 To remove the exhaust manifold, first raise the vehicle and loosen the exhaust pipe-to-engine block support bracket bolts . . .

Fig. 58 . . . then remove them. Detach the oxygen sensor (arrow) wire harness connection

Fig. 59 Remove the exhaust pipe-to-manifold attaching nuts . . .

Fig. 60 . . . then pull the pipe down to detach it from the manifold

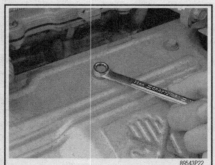

Fig. 61 Lower the vehicle and remove the exhaust manifold heat shield retaining bolts . . .

Fig. 62 . . . and remove the shield from the manifold. Some models may need the power steering pump to be removed for better access

Fig. 63 If equipped, loosen and remove the EGR pipe retaining bolt

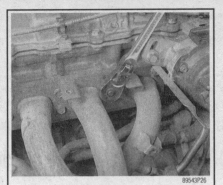

Fig. 64 Loosen the exhaust manifold-to-head attaching nuts/bolts . . .

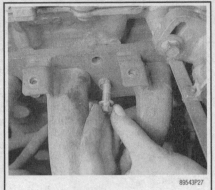

Fig. 65 . . .and remove them

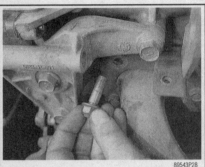

Fig. 66 Don't be alarmed if some of the studs have come out of the head. The stud should thread back in as if it were a bolt

Fig. 67 Pull the manifold backwards off of the mounting studs and remove it from the vehicle

Fig. 68 Remove and discard the old gaskets and clean the mating surfaces thoroughly

engine, tighten the nuts to 20 ft. lbs. (26 Nm) and the bolts to 16 ft. lbs. (22 Nm).

11. Use a new gasket and tighten the exhaust pipe flange-to-exhaust manifold nuts to 34 ft. lbs. (46 Nm).

Supercharger

REMOVAL AND INSTALLATION

2.3L Engine

▶ See Figures 65 and 69

✳✳ CAUTION

Fuel injection systems remain under pressure after the engine has been turned OFF. Properly relieve fuel pressure before disconnecting any fuel lines. Failure to do so may result in fire or personal injury.

1. Relieve the fuel system pressure, and disconnect the negative battery cable.
2. Drain the cooling system.
3. Remove the dynamic chamber cover.
4. Remove the charge air cooler air duct.
5. Label and disconnect the vacuum hoses and electrical connectors from the air cleaner housing. Remove the air cleaner assembly.
6. Remove the air and fresh air ducts.
7. Remove the mass air flow sensor and the air intake hose from the throttle body.
8. Remove the resonator.
9. Remove the right-hand charge air cooler.
10. Remove the left-hand charge air cooler.
11. Disconnect the accelerator cable.

12. Label and disconnect the necessary vacuum hoses from the rear of the intake manifold and EGR valve.
13. Remove the EGR valve.
14. Remove the air intake pipe assembly.
15. Remove the charge air cooler pipe.
16. Disconnect and plug the fuel supply line at the fuel rails and discard the copper crush washers. Disconnect the fuel and vacuum lines from the fuel pressure regulator.

✳✳ CAUTION

Do not allow fuel spray or fuel vapors to come in contact with a spark or open flame. Keep a dry chemical fire extinguisher nearby. Never store fuel in an open container due to risk of fire or explosion.

17. Disconnect and plug the coolant hoses.
18. Remove the harness from the intake manifold.
19. Remove the intake manifold mounting nuts and bolts in 2–3 steps, then remove the intake manifold.
20. Label and disconnect the fuel hoses and electrical connectors from the throttle body. Remove the throttle body.
21. Remove the drive belt from the Lysholm compressor (supercharger).
22. Remove the mounting bolts from the Lysholm compressor, and remove the compressor from the vehicle.
To install:
23. Clean all gasket mating surfaces.
24. Position the rubber shield for the Lysholm compressor onto the compressor using double sided adhesive tape. Place the compressor onto the mounting studs and tighten the mounting nuts to 14–18 ft. lbs. (19–25 Nm).
25. Install and adjust the drive belt.
26. Install the throttle body. Tighten the nuts and bolts to 14–18 ft. lbs. (19–25 Nm), and connect the fuel hoses and electrical connectors.
27. Position new gaskets and install the intake manifold. Tighten the nuts and bolts in 2–3 steps, from the center to the ends, to 14–18 ft. lbs. (19–25 Nm).

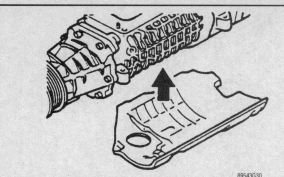

Fig. 69 When installing the compressor, ensure that the rubber insulating pad is temporarily affixed to the compressor

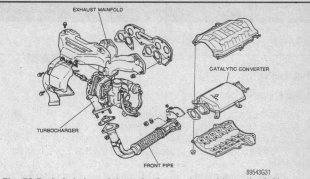

Fig. 70 Exploded view of the turbocharger assembly on the 2.2L engine

28. Install the harness onto the intake manifold.

29. Unplug and connect the coolant hoses.

30. Connect the fuel and vacuum lines to the fuel pressure regulator. Connect the fuel supply line to the fuel rail, using new copper crush washers.

31. Install the charge air cooler pipe.

32. Position the air intake pipe assembly using new gaskets. Hand tighten the nuts and bolts in the order shown in the graphic until the air intake pipe contacts the intake manifold. Verify that the rubber gaskets are not twisted or distorted. Tighten the bolts marked **A** to 70–95 inch lbs. (8–11 Nm), and all others, in sequence, to 14–18 ft. lbs. (19–25 Nm).

33. Install the EGR valve using a new gasket.

34. Connect the vacuum hoses to the intake manifold and EGR valve.

35. Connect and adjust the accelerator cable.

36. Using new gaskets, position the left and right-hand charge air coolers. Hand tighten the nuts and bolts in the order shown in the graphic until the air intake pipes and charge air coolers contact the intake manifold. Verify that the rubber gaskets are not twisted or distorted. Tighten the bolts marked **A** to 44–78 inch lbs. (5–9 Nm). Tighten the bolts marked **B** to 70–95 inch lbs. (8–11 Nm), and all others, in sequence, to 14–18 ft. lbs. (19–25 Nm).

37. Install the resonator. Tighten the nuts and bolts to 12–16 ft. lbs. (16–22 Nm)

38. Install the air intake hose onto the throttle body. Install the mass air flow sensor.

39. Install the fresh air and air ducts.

40. Install the air cleaner assembly and connect the vacuum hoses and electrical connectors to the air cleaner housing.

41. Install the charge air cooler air duct. Tighten the mounting bolts to 70–95 inch lbs. (8–11 Nm).

42. Install the dynamic chamber cover.

43. Connect the negative battery cable.

44. Fill and bleed the cooling system. Run the engine and check for leaks.

Turbocharger

REMOVAL & INSTALLATION

2.2L Engine

▶ **See Figure 70**

Before starting the following procedure, clean the area around the turbocharger assembly with a non-caustic solution. After the turbocharger is removed, cover the openings to prevent the entry of foreign material while it is off the engine.

During removal, be careful not to bend, nick, or in any way damage the compressor wheel blades. Damage may result in rotating assembly imbalance, and bearing and oil seal failure. Any time a turbocharger assembly has been removed, gently spin the turbine wheel before reassembly to ensure the rotating assembly does not bind.

Any time an engine bearing (main bearing, connecting rod bearing, camshaft bearing) has been damaged in a turbocharged engine, the oil and filter should be changed and the turbocharger flushed with clean engine oil to reduce the possibility of contamination.

1. Disconnect the negative battery cable.

2. Raise and safely support the vehicle. Remove the engine undercover and drain the cooling system.

3. Remove the inlet and outlet hoses from the turbocharger. Cover the turbocharger openings with clean rags to prevent the entry of dirt or foreign material.

4. Remove the retaining bolts and remove the insulator covers from the exhaust manifold and turbocharger.

5. Disconnect the coolant hoses.

6. Disconnect the oil feed and return lines. Cover the openings in the turbocharger to prevent the entry of dirt or foreign material.

7. Disconnect the oxygen sensor connector. Disconnect the EGR pipe from the exhaust manifold.

8. Remove the nuts and disconnect the exhaust pipe from the turbocharger. Remove the bolt from the turbocharger support bracket.

9. Remove the exhaust manifold-to-cylinder head nuts while supporting the manifold/turbocharger assembly.

10. Remove the exhaust manifold and turbocharger as an assembly.

11. Remove the nuts and separate the manifold from the turbocharger.

➡**Do not carry the turbocharger by the actuator rod. Be careful not to bend the actuator mounting or rod.**

12. Clean all gasket mating surfaces of sealant and old gasket material.

To install:

13. Assemble the exhaust manifold to the turbocharger, using a new gasket. Tighten the nuts to 34 ft. lbs. (46 Nm).

14. Pour approximately 0.85 oz. (25 ml) of clean engine oil into the turbocharger oil inlet.

15. Install the turbocharger/exhaust manifold assembly to the cylinder head, using a new gasket. Tighten the nuts to 34 ft. lbs. (46 Nm).

16. Connect the support bracket to the turbocharger. Tighten the bolt to 30 ft. lbs. (41 Nm).

17. Connect the exhaust pipe to the turbocharger, using a new gasket. Tighten the nuts to 34 ft. lbs. (46 Nm).

18. Connect the EGR pipe to the exhaust manifold. Connect the oxygen sensor connector.

19. Connect the oil feed and return lines. Connect the coolant hoses.

20. Install the insulators on the exhaust manifold and turbocharger and secure with the bolts.

21. Install the turbocharger inlet and outlet hoses.

22. Check the engine oil level and add, as necessary. Change the oil and filter if the oil is dirty.

23. Install the engine undercover and lower the vehicle.

24. On 323, disconnect the connector from the ignition coil negative terminal. Disconnect the connector from the igniter.

25. Connect the negative battery cable and crank the engine for at least 20 seconds.

26. Reconnect the electrical connector. Fill and bleed the cooling system.

27. Start the engine and run at idle for 30 seconds.

28. Stop the engine and disconnect the negative battery cable. Depress the brake pedal for at least 5 seconds to cancel the malfunction code.

Intercooler

REMOVAL & INSTALLATION

2.2L Engine

▶ **See Figure 71**

1. Remove the front fascia from the vehicle.
2. Remove the front bumper assembly. Refer to Section 10.
3. Remove all mounting nuts from the intercooler housing.
4. Loosen the clamps and remove the inlet and outlet air hoses from the intercooler.
5. Remove the intercooler.
6. Installation is the reverse of the removal procedure.

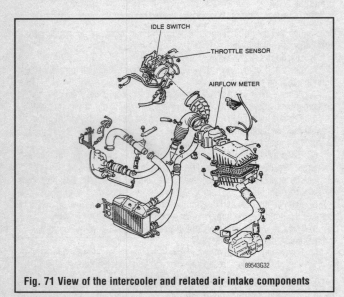

Fig. 71 View of the intercooler and related air intake components

Radiator

REMOVAL & INSTALLATION

▶ **See Figure 72**

1995–98 1.5L and 1.8L (except K8) Engines

1. Disconnect the negative battery cable.
2. Drain the cooling system.
3. Remove the upper seal board and radiator grille.
4. Remove the hood safety lever.
5. Disconnect the coolant reservoir and upper and lower radiator hoses. If equipped with automatic transaxle, disconnect the oil cooler lines and plug the hoses.
6. Disconnect the electric cooling fan connector.
7. Remove the cooling fan/shroud assembly from the radiator. Move the assembly to the side of the engine to gain clearance space.
8. Remove the radiator brackets.
9. Lift and remove the radiator from the vehicle.
To install:
10. Install the radiator, making sure the lower tank engages the insulators.
11. Install the radiator brackets. Tighten the mounting bolts to 70–95 inch lbs. (8–11 Nm).
12. Install the fan and shroud assembly. Tighten the mounting bolts to 70–95 inch lbs. (8–11 Nm).
13. Unplug and connect the cooler lines, if required.
14. Reattach the wiring harness to the routing clips, and install the upper and lower radiator hoses to the radiator.

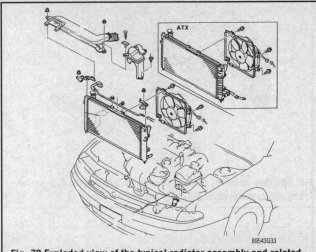

Fig. 72 Exploded view of the typical radiator assembly and related components

15. Connect the overflow tube to the radiator, and connect the cooling fan wiring connector.
16. Install the hood safety lever. Tighten the mounting bolts to 70–95 inch lbs. (8–11 Nm).
17. Install the radiator grille and upper seal board.
18. Close the radiator drain valve and fill the system with coolant. Install the pressure cap to the first stop only.
19. Connect the negative battery cable. Start the engine and run it at fast idle until the upper radiator hose feels warm, indicating the thermostat has opened and coolant is flowing throughout the system.
20. Stop the engine. Carefully remove the radiator cap and top off the radiator with coolant, if required.
21. Install the radiator cap securely and fill the coolant reservoir to the FULL mark.
22. Run the engine and check for leaks.

2.3L Engine

1. Disconnect the negative battery cable.
2. Drain the cooling system.
3. If equipped, remove the right-hand splash shield.
4. If necessary, remove the charge air cooler.
5. If necessary, remove the radiator grill.
6. Remove the upper seal board.
7. Disconnect the coolant reservoir hose. Remove the coolant reservoir.
8. Disconnect the cooling fan electrical connector.
9. Remove the cooling and condenser fan assembly shroud (cowling) mounting bolts, and remove the shrouds from the radiator.
10. Disconnect the upper and lower radiator hoses.
11. Disconnect the oil cooler lines and plug the hoses.
12. Remove the upper radiator mounting brackets.
13. Remove the radiator from the vehicle.
To install:
14. Install the radiator, making sure the lower tank engages the insulators.
15. Install the upper radiator mounting brackets, and tighten the retaining bolts to 70–95 inch lbs. (8–11 Nm).
16. Unplug and connect the cooler lines.
17. Install the upper and lower radiator hoses to the radiator.
18. Install the coolant and condenser fan assemblies onto the radiator.
19. Connect the cooling fan electrical connector.
20. Install the coolant reservoir. Connect the coolant reservoir hose.
21. If removed, install the radiator grill.
22. If removed, install the charge air cooler.
23. Install the right-hand splash shield, if equipped.
24. Install the upper seal board.
25. Properly fill the cooling system.
26. Connect the negative battery cable.

Except 2.3L and 1995–98 1.5L, 1.8L (except K8) Engines

▶ See Figures 73 thru 86

1. Disconnect the negative battery cable.
2. Remove the engine under cover, if equipped and drain the cooling system.
3. Remove the necessary air ducts.
4. Disconnect the electric cooling fan connector and, if equipped, temperature sensor connector.
5. Disconnect the coolant reservoir and upper and lower radiator hoses. If equipped with automatic transaxle, disconnect the oil cooler lines from the radiator and plug the hoses.
6. Unattach any line from the radiator or fan assembly.
7. On all except MX-3, remove the upper radiator mounting brackets. On MX-3, remove the upper shroud panel.
8. Lift the radiator/cooling fan(s) assembly from the vehicle.
9. If necessary, remove the cooling fan(s)/shroud assembly from the radiator.

To install:

10. If removed, install the fan and shroud assembly. Tighten the mounting bolts to 61–87 inch lbs. (7–10 Nm).
11. Install the radiator, making sure the lower tank engages the insulators.
12. Install the upper radiator insulators and tighten the retaining bolts to 69–95 inch lbs. (8–11 Nm).
13. Unplug and connect the cooler lines, if required.
14. Reattach the wiring harness to the routing clips and install the upper and lower radiator hoses to the radiator.
15. Connect the overflow tube to the radiator and connect the cooling fan wiring connectors.
16. Close the radiator drain valve and fill the system with coolant. Install the pressure cap to the first stop only.
17. Connect the negative battery cable. Start the engine and run it at fast idle until the upper radiator hose feels warm, indicating the thermostat has opened and coolant is flowing throughout the system.

Fig. 73 To remove the radiator, first drain the cooling system, then remove the air duct-to-vehicle attaching nuts . . .

Fig. 74 . . . as well as any components-to-air duct fasteners

Fig. 75 Remove the air duct-to-hose retaining clamp . . .

Fig. 76 . . . then remove the air duct from the vehicle

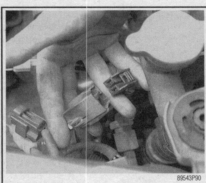

Fig. 77 Detach the electric cooling fan wire harness connectors

Fig. 78 Disconnect the coolant overflow/reservoir hose from the radiator

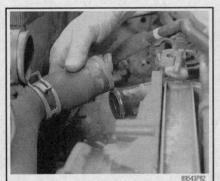

Fig. 79 Disconnect the upper and lower radiator hoses

Fig. 80 If equipped, detach the ATX fluid cooler lines from the radiator by removing the attaching bolt

Fig. 81 When removing the cooler line bolts, make sure to discard the old copper sealing washers and install new ones on installation

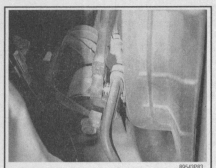

Fig. 82 Also remove any lines which are attached to the cooling fan by removing its retaining bracket attaching bolt or screw

Fig. 83 Remove the radiator-to-vehicle retaining bracket bolts . . .

Fig. 84 . . . then remove them by disengaging the rubber bushing from the mounting post on the radiator

Fig. 85 Lift the radiator up and remove it from the vehicle

Fig. 86 Sometimes the lower mounting bushings stick to the radiator, remove them . . .

Fig. 87 . . . and install them back into their mounting holes in the vehicle frame (arrow)

18. Stop the engine. Carefully remove the radiator cap and top off the radiator with coolant, if required.

19. Install the radiator cap securely and fill the coolant reservoir to the FULL mark.

20. Run the engine and check for leaks.

Electric Cooling Fan

REMOVAL & INSTALLATION

▶ See Figure 87

1995–98 1.5L and 1.8L (except K8) Engines

1. Disconnect the negative battery cable.
2. Drain the cooling system.

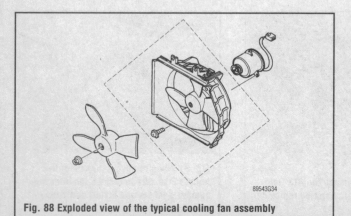

Fig. 88 Exploded view of the typical cooling fan assembly

3. Remove the upper seal board and radiator grille.
4. Remove the hood safety lever.
5. Disconnect the coolant reservoir and upper and lower radiator hoses. If equipped with automatic transaxle, disconnect the oil cooler lines and plug the hoses.
6. Disconnect the electric cooling fan connector.
7. Remove the shroud (cowling) mounting bolts, and remove the shroud from the radiator. Move the assembly to the side of the engine to gain clearance space.
8. Remove the radiator brackets.
9. Lift and remove the radiator from the vehicle.
10. Remove the cooling fan from the vehicle. Remove the mounting nut, and remove the fan blade from the fan motor.
11. Remove the mounting bolts, and remove the fan motor from the shroud.
To install:
12. Position the fan motor on the shroud and install the mounting bolts.
13. Install the fan blade onto the fan motor. Apply a locking compound on the mounting nut, and install the mounting nut.
14. Install the radiator, making sure the lower tank engages the insulators.
15. Install the radiator brackets. Tighten the mounting bolts to 70–95 inch lbs. (8–11 Nm).
16. Install the fan and shroud assembly. Tighten the mounting bolts to 70–95 inch lbs. (8–11 Nm).
17. Unplug and connect the cooler lines, if required.
18. Reattach the wiring harness to the routing clips, and install the upper and lower radiator hoses to the radiator.
19. Connect the overflow tube to the radiator, and connect the cooling fan wiring connector.
20. Install the hood safety lever. Tighten the mounting bolts to 70–95 inch lbs. (8–11 Nm).
21. Install the radiator grille and upper seal board.
22. Close the radiator drain valve and fill the system with coolant. Install the pressure cap to the first stop only.
23. Connect the negative battery cable. Start the engine and run it at fast idle until the upper radiator hose feels warm, indicating the thermostat has opened and coolant is flowing throughout the system.

24. Stop the engine. Carefully remove the radiator cap and top off the radiator with coolant, if required.

25. Install the radiator cap securely and fill the coolant reservoir to the FULL mark.

26. Run the engine and check for leaks.

2.3L Engine

1. Disconnect the negative battery cable.
2. Drain the cooling system.
3. If equipped, remove the right-hand splash shield.
4. If necessary, remove the charge air cooler.
5. If necessary, remove the radiator grill.
6. Remove the upper seal board.
7. Disconnect the coolant reservoir hose. Remove the coolant reservoir.
8. Disconnect the cooling fan electrical connector.
9. Remove the shroud (cowling) mounting bolts and remove the shroud from the radiator.
10. Remove the mounting nut and remove the fan from the fan motor.
11. Remove the mounting bolts and remove the fan motor from the shroud.

To install:

12. Position the fan motor on the shroud and install the mounting bolts.
13. Install the fan onto the fan motor. Apply a locking compound on the mounting nut, and install the mounting nut.
14. Install the shroud onto the radiator.
15. Connect the cooling fan electrical connector.
16. Install the coolant reservoir. Connect the coolant reservoir hose.
17. Install the upper seal board.
18. If removed, install the radiator grill.
19. If removed, install the charge air cooler.
20. If equipped, install the right-hand splash shield.
21. Properly fill the cooling system.
22. Connect the negative battery cable.

Except 1.5L, 2.3L and 1995–98 1.8L Engines

1. Disconnect the negative battery cable and drain the cooling system.
2. Remove the radiator.
3. Remove the shroud mounting bolts and remove the shroud from the radiator.
4. Remove the mounting nut and remove the fan from the fan motor.
5. Remove the mounting bolts and remove the fan motor from the shroud.
6. Installation is the reverse of the removal procedure.

TESTING

▶ **See Figures 88 and 89**

1. Detach the cooling fan wire harness connector.
2. On two wire connectors (single speed fans), apply battery voltage to one of the terminals on the fan connector and ground the other one.
3. On four wire connectors (two speed fans), apply battery voltage to two terminals and ground the other two. This will check the high speed mode of the fan, to check the low speed connect the wires the same as two wire models.
4. Attach an ammeter inline on the positive wire.

5. The fan should operate, if not, replace the fan assembly.
6. If the fan operates when battery voltage is applied, but not when connected to the vehicle, check the cooling fan relay and/or the engine coolant temperature sensor.
7. While the fan is operating, the current draw should be as follows:
   a. Single speed fan: 2.6—7.6 Amps
   b. Two speed fan (low): 8.0—14.0 Amps
   c. Two speed fan (high): 11.5—17.5 Amps

Water Pump

REMOVAL & INSTALLATION

1.5L, 1.6L and 1.8L (except K8) Engines

▶ **See Figure 90**

1. Disconnect the negative battery cable. Drain the cooling system.
2. Remove the timing belt covers, and remove the timing belt.
3. Disconnect the coolant inlet pipe and gasket.
4. Remove the timing belt idler pulleys still attached to the water pump.
5. Remove the water pump mounting bolts, and remove the water pump.

To install:

6. Clean all gasket mating surfaces.
7. Install a new rubber seal on the water pump.
8. Using a new gasket, install the water pump on the engine. Tighten the mounting bolts to 14–18 ft. lbs. (19–25 Nm). Tighten the bolt from the water pump to the alternator bracket to 28–38 ft. lbs. (38–51 Nm).
9. Install the timing belt idler pulleys that were removed.
10. Install the coolant inlet pipe, using a new gasket. Tighten the bolts to 14–18 ft. lbs. (19–25 Nm).
11. Install the timing belt and the timing belt covers.
12. Fill and bleed the cooling system. Connect the negative battery cable, start the engine and bring to normal operating temperature. Check for leaks.

2.0L Engines

▶ **See Figures 91 thru 102**

1. Disconnect the negative battery cable. Drain the cooling system.
2. Remove the timing belt.
3. Remove the power steering oil pump adjuster.
4. Remove the 5 water pump mounting bolts and remove the water pump.

To install:

5. Clean all gasket mating surfaces.
6. Install a NEW gasket on the water pump and install the water pump on the engine. Install the mounting bolts and tighten to 14–18 ft. lbs. (19–25 Nm).
7. Install the power steering oil pump adjuster, torque the mounting bolts to 12–16 ft. lbs. (16–22 Nm).
8. Install the timing belt.
9. Connect the negative battery cable. Fill and bleed the cooling system.
10. Start the engine and bring to normal operating temperature. Check for leaks.

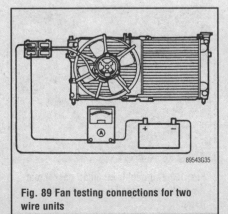

89543G35

Fig. 89 Fan testing connections for two wire units

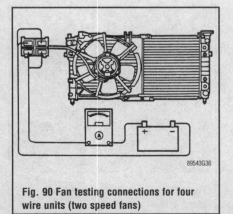

89543G36

Fig. 90 Fan testing connections for four wire units (two speed fans)

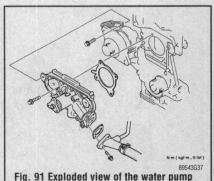

89543G37

Fig. 91 Exploded view of the water pump assembly for the 1.5L, 1.6L and 1.8L (except K8) engines

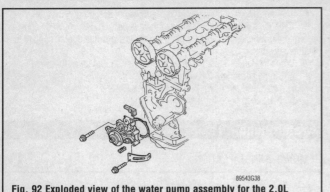

Fig. 92 Exploded view of the water pump assembly for the 2.0L engine

Fig. 93 To remove the water pump, first drain the cooling system, then loosen the water pump pulley attaching bolts

Fig. 94 Remove the accessory drive belts, then remove the water pump pulley

Fig. 95 Remove the engine timing belt . . .

Fig. 96 . . . and the belt idler pulley which is attached to the water pump

Fig. 97 Remove the water pump attaching bolts . . .

Fig. 98 . . . as well as the mounting bolts . . .

Fig. 99 . . . for the lower power steering adjuster bracket

Fig. 100 Remove the water pump from the engine . . .

Fig. 101 . . . as well as the old water pump gasket

Fig. 102 Thoroughly clean all gasket mating surfaces before installing the water pump

1.8L (K8) and 2.5L Engines

▶ **See Figure 103**

1. Disconnect the negative battery cable. Drain the cooling system.
2. Remove the timing belt.
3. Remove the No.3 engine mount bracket.
4. Position a drain pan under the water pump.
5. Remove the 5 water pump mounting bolts, and remove the water pump.

To install:

6. Clean the mating surfaces of the water pump and the engine block.
7. Install a NEW rubber seal onto the water pump.
8. Install the water pump and torque the bolts 14–18 ft. lbs. (19–25 Nm).
9. Install the engine mount bracket, and tighten the mounting bolt to 32–44 ft. lbs. (44–60 Nm).
10. Install the timing belt.
11. Connect the negative battery cable. Fill and bleed the cooling system.
12. Start the engine and bring to normal operating temperature. Check for leaks.

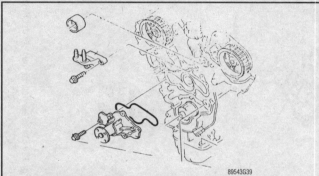

Fig. 103 Exploded view of the water pump assembly for the 1.8L (K8) and 2.5L engines—2.3L engine is similar

2.3L Engine

▶ **See Figure 103**

1. Disconnect the negative battery cable. Drain the cooling system.
2. Remove the timing belt covers and the timing belt.
3. Use a pulley removal tool to hold the water pump pulley and remove the bolts. Remove the water pump pulley.
4. Position a drain pan under the water pump.
5. Remove the water pump mounting bolts, and remove the water pump.

To install:

6. Clean the mating surfaces of the water pump and the engine block.
7. Install a new O-ring onto the water pump.
8. Install the water pump and torque the bolts 18 ft. lbs. (25 Nm).
9. Install the water pump pulley with the bolts. Hold the pulley with the tool and tighten the bolts to 88 inch lbs. (10 Nm).

10. Install the timing belt and timing covers.
11. Connect the negative battery cable. Fill and bleed the cooling system.
12. Start the engine and bring to normal operating temperature. Check for leaks.

Cylinder Head

REMOVAL & INSTALLATION

▶ **See Figures 104, 105 and 106**

✳✳ CAUTION

When draining the coolant, keep in mind that cats and dogs are attracted by the ethylene glycol antifreeze, and are quite likely to drink any that is left in an uncovered container or in puddles on the ground. This will prove fatal in sufficient quantity. Always drain the coolant into a sealable container. Coolant should be reused unless it is contaminated or several years old.

➡Before installing the cylinder head, thoroughly clean and inspect it, especially if the head needed to be removed to replace a blown gasket. Refer to the Engine Reconditioning procedures, later in this section.

1990–94 1.6L and 1.8L (except K8) Engines

▶ **See Figures 107 and 108**

1. Disconnect the negative battery cable and remove the engine undercover.
2. Remove the air ducts from the air cleaner and throttle body.
3. Tag and disconnect the spark plug wires from the spark plugs. Remove the spark plugs and the distributor cap and wires assembly. Remove the distributor.
4. Drain the cooling system and disconnect the radiator and heater hoses.
5. Disconnect the exhaust pipe and remove the exhaust manifold.
6. On DOHC engines, remove the coolant bypass pipe.
7. Disconnect the accelerator cable.
8. Label and disconnect all necessary electrical connections and vacuum hoses. Disconnect the fuel lines.
9. Remove the intake manifold bracket and the intake manifold.
10. Remove the cylinder head cover bolts and the cylinder head cover.
11. Remove the timing belt cover(s). Rotate the crankshaft, in the normal direction of rotation, until the No. 1 cylinder piston is at TDC on the compression stroke. Make sure the timing marks on the crankshaft and camshaft sprocket(s) are properly aligned and mark the direction of rotation of the belt.
12. Loosen the timing belt tensioner and remove the belt. Do not rotate the crankshaft until the timing belt is reinstalled.
13. When everything is disconnected, loosen the cylinder head bolts in the reverse of the tightening sequence. Remove the bolts and lift the head off the engine.

To install:

14. Thoroughly, clean the cylinder head and the block contact surfaces. Examine the head gasket and check the cylinder head for cracks. Check the

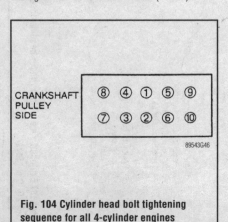

Fig. 104 Cylinder head bolt tightening sequence for all 4-cylinder engines

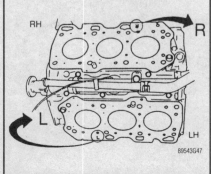

Fig. 105 Cylinder head gasket positioning for the 6-cylinder engines

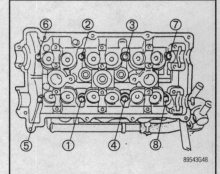

Fig. 106 Cylinder head bolt tightening sequence for the 6-cylinder engines

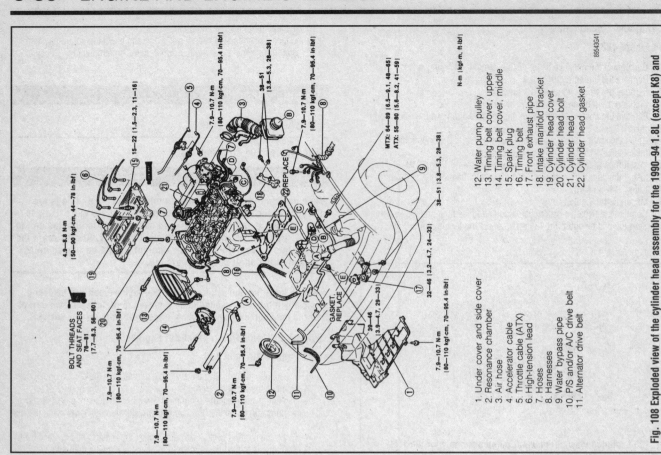

89543G41

1. Under cover and side cover
2. Resonance chamber
3. Air hose
4. Accelerator cable
5. Throttle cable (ATX)
6. High-tension lead
7. Hoses
8. Harnesses
9. Water bypass pipe
10. P/S and/or A/C drive belt
11. Alternator drive belt
12. Water pump pulley
13. Timing belt cover, upper
14. Timing belt cover, middle
15. Spark plug
16. Timing belt
17. Front exhaust pipe
18. Intake manifold bracket
19. Cylinder head cover
20. Cylinder head bolt
21. Cylinder head
22. Cylinder head gasket

Fig. 108 Exploded view of the cylinder head assembly for the 1990–94 1.8L (except K8) and 1995 1.6L DOHC engines

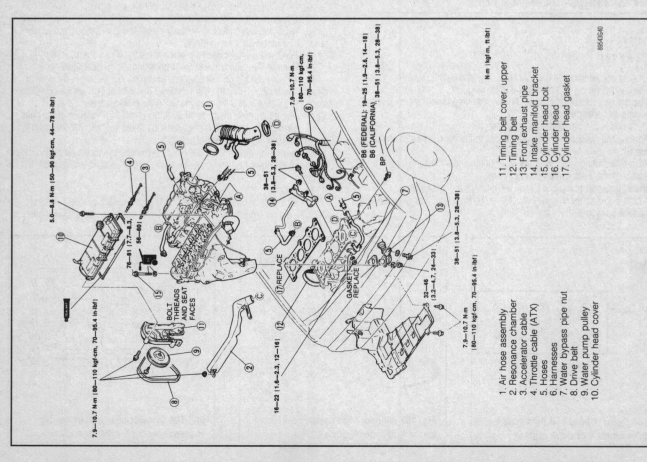

89543G40

1. Air hose assembly
2. Resonance chamber
3. Accelerator cable
4. Throttle cable (ATX)
5. Hoses
6. Harnesses
7. Water bypass pipe nut
8. Drive belt
9. Water pump pulley
10. Cylinder head cover
11. Timing belt cover, upper
12. Timing belt
13. Front exhaust pipe
14. Intake manifold bracket
15. Cylinder head bolt
16. Cylinder head
17. Cylinder head gasket

Fig. 107 Exploded view of the cylinder head assembly for the 1990–94 1.6L and 1.8L (except K8) SOHC engines

cylinder head for warpage using a feeler gauge and straightedge. The maximum allowable distortion is 0.004 in. (0.10mm) on 1.8L engine.

15. Clean the cylinder head bolts and the threads in the block. Make sure the bolts turn freely in the block.

16. Install a new head gasket on the engine block. Make sure the camshaft sprocket timing marks are still aligned, as set during the removal procedure. Install the cylinder head.

17. Lubricate the bolt threads and seat surfaces with clean engine oil and install them. Torque the bolts in 2–3 steps to 56–60 ft. lbs. (75–81 Nm) in the proper sequence.

18. Make sure the crankshaft and camshaft sprocket timing marks are aligned, install the timing belt and set the tension. Carefully rotate the crankshaft 2 turns to make sure the timing marks still line up.

19. Apply a thin bead of sealant to the cylinder head cover and install the new gasket. Install the cover and torque the cover bolts to 78 inch lbs. (9 Nm).

20. Install the timing belt cover(s) and tighten the bolts to 95 inch lbs. (11 Nm).

21. Use new gaskets and install the manifolds. Torque the intake manifold bolts/nuts to 19 ft. lbs. (25 Nm) and install the intake manifold bracket. Torque the exhaust manifold nuts to 34 ft. lbs. (46 Nm).

22. Use a new gasket to connect the exhaust pipe and torque the nuts to 34 ft. lbs. (46 Nm).

23. If removed, install the radiator and connect all cooling system hoses. On DOHC engines, install the coolant bypass pipe.

24. Install the distributor, spark plugs, distributor cap and wires.

25. Connect all vacuum and fuel system hoses and connect all wiring.

26. Connect the accelerator cable and install the air ducts and engine undercover.

27. Connect the negative battery cable. Fill and bleed the cooling system. Change the engine oil.

28. Start the engine and bring to normal operating temperature. Check for leaks. Check the ignition timing and idle speed.

1995 1.6L Engines

▶ See Figure 108

1. Relieve the fuel system pressure and disconnect the negative battery cable. Drain the cooling system.

2. Remove the splash shield, fresh air duct and air cleaner assembly.

3. Disconnect the accelerator and throttle cables.

4. Tag and disconnect the spark plug wires from the spark plugs. Remove the spark plugs and the distributor cap and wires assembly. Remove the distributor.

5. Disconnect the following hoses: Heater, brake vacuum, purge, fuel, water and upper radiator.

6. Label and disconnect the distributor/coil connectors, engine coolant temperature sensor connector, cooling fan coolant
temperature sensor connector and temperature gauge sensor connector.

7. Remove the coolant bypass pipe.

8. Remove the accessory drive belts. Remove the power steering pump bolts and secure the pump aside with mechanics wire, leaving the hoses attached.

9. Remove the water pump pulley.

10. Remove the alternator bracket nut and bolt and position the bracket aside.

11. Disconnect the hoses from the cylinder head cover and loosen the cover bolts in 5–6 step sequences. Remove the cylinder head cover.

12. Remove the timing belt cover(s). Rotate the crankshaft, in the normal direction of rotation, until the No. 1 cylinder piston is at TDC on the compression stroke. Make sure the timing marks on the crankshaft and camshaft sprocket(s) are properly aligned and mark the direction of rotation of the belt.

13. Loosen the timing belt tensioner and remove the belt. Do not rotate the crankshaft until the timing belt is reinstalled.

14. Remove the camshaft sprockets and the camshaft.

15. Remove the hydraulic lifters. Identify each lifter as it is removed so it can be reinstalled in the same position. If the lifters are to be reused, store them upside down in an oil-filled sealed container.

16. Disconnect the exhaust pipe and remove the exhaust manifold.

17. Remove the intake manifold bracket and the intake manifold.

18. Loosen the cylinder head bolts, in 2–3 steps, in sequence. Remove the bolts and the cylinder head.

To install:

19. Thoroughly, clean the cylinder head and the block contact surfaces. Examine the head gasket and check the cylinder head for cracks. Check the cylinder head for warpage using a feeler gauge and straightedge. The maximum allowable distortion is 0.004 in. (0.10mm).

20. Clean the cylinder head bolts and the threads in the block. Make sure the bolts turn freely in the block.

21. Install a new head gasket on the engine block. Make sure the camshaft sprocket timing marks are still aligned, as set during the removal procedure. Install the cylinder head.

22. Lubricate the bolt threads and seat surfaces with clean engine oil and install them. Torque the bolts in 2–3 steps to 56–60 ft. lbs. (75–81 Nm) in the proper sequence.

23. Use new gaskets and install the manifolds. Torque the intake manifold bolts/nuts to 19 ft. lbs. (25 Nm) and install the intake manifold bracket. Torque the exhaust manifold nuts to 34 ft. lbs. (46 Nm).

24. Use a new gasket to connect the exhaust pipe and torque the nuts to 34 ft. lbs. (46 Nm).

25. Apply clean engine oil to the hydraulic lifters and install them in their original positions. Make sure they move freely in the bores.

26. Install the camshaft and sprockets.

27. Make sure the crankshaft and camshaft sprocket timing marks are aligned, install the timing belt and set the tension. Carefully rotate the crankshaft 2 turns to make sure the timing marks still line up.

28. Apply a thin bead of sealant to the cylinder head cover and install the new gasket. Install the cover and torque the cover bolts to 78 inch lbs. (9 Nm).

29. Install the timing belt cover(s) and tighten the bolts to 95 inch lbs. (11 Nm).

30. Install the alternator bracket. Tighten the bracket nut and bolt to 19 ft. lbs. (25 Nm).

31. Install the water pump pulley.

32. Install the alternator belt and adjust the tension.

33. Loosely install the power steering pump through and lockbolts. Connect the pump pressure switch connector.

34. Install the power steering pump belt and adjust the tension. Tighten the pump through-bolt to 45 ft. lbs. (61 Nm) and the lockbolt to 34 ft. lbs. (46 Nm).

35. Install the power steering pump belt shield and tighten the bolts to 86 inch lbs. (9 Nm). Install the power steering hose brackets to the cylinder head cover, and tighten the bolts to 88 inch lbs. (10 Nm).

36. Install the coolant bypass pipe.

37. Connect the electrical engine harness connectors.

38. Connect the heater, brake vacuum, purge, fuel, water and upper radiator hoses.

39. Install the distributor, spark plugs, distributor cap and wires.

40. Connect and adjust the accelerator and throttle cables.

41. Install the air ducts, cleaner and splash shield.

42. Connect the negative battery cable. Fill and bleed the cooling system. Change the engine oil.

43. Adjust the ignition timing.

44. Start the engine and bring to normal operating temperature. Check for leaks. Check the ignition timing and idle speed.

1.5L and 1995–98 1.8L (except K8) Engines

▶ See Figures 109 and 110

1. Relieve the fuel system pressure and disconnect the negative battery cable. Drain the cooling system.

2. Raise and safely support the vehicle.

3. Remove the right front wheel and splash shield.

4. Loosen the water pump pulley attaching bolts.

5. Remove the power steering belt shield. Loosen the power steering adjusting bolt, lockbolt and through-bolt and remove the power steering belt.

6. Loosen the alternator adjusting bolt and upper mounting bolt. Remove the alternator belt.

7. Remove the water pump pulley.

8. Using a holder tool, hold the crankshaft pulley and remove the pulley bolt. Use a suitable puller to remove the pulley, then remove the guide plate.

9. Remove the power steering hose brackets from the cylinder head cover. Label and disconnect the spark plug wires and wire clips.

10. Disconnect the breather tube and PCV valve from the cylinder head cover. Remove the bolts, in 2 steps, in the reverse order of the tightening sequence. Remove the cylinder head cover.

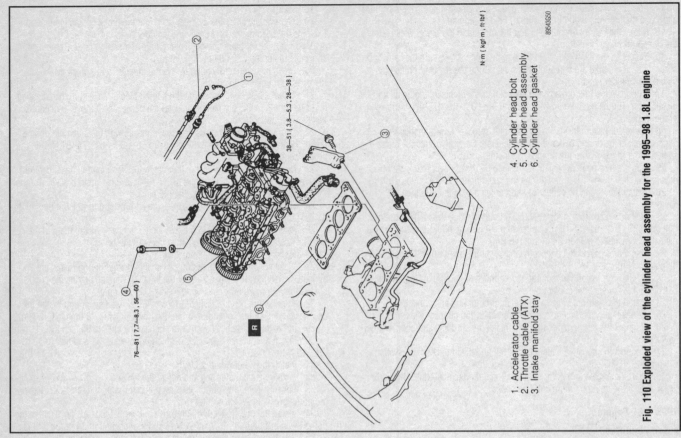

N·m (kgf·m , ft·lbf)

1. Accelerator cable
2. Throttle cable (ATX)
3. Intake manifold stay

4. Cylinder head bolt
5. Cylinder head assembly
6. Cylinder head gasket

Fig. 110 Exploded view of the cylinder head assembly for the 1995–98 1.8L engine

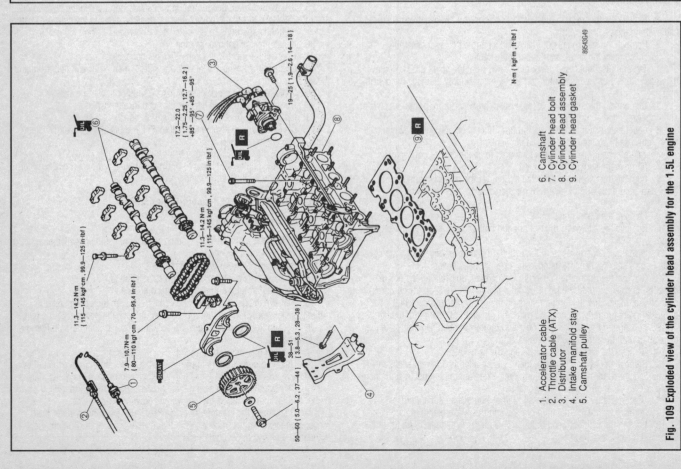

N·m (kgf·m , ft·lbf)

1. Accelerator cable
2. Throttle cable (ATX)
3. Distributor
4. Intake manifold stay
5. Camshaft pulley

6. Camshaft
7. Cylinder head bolt
8. Cylinder head assembly
9. Cylinder head gasket

Fig. 109 Exploded view of the cylinder head assembly for the 1.5L engine

11. Remove the oil dipstick and bracket.

12. Remove the timing belt upper cover.

13. Use a suitable engine support tool, and remove the number three engine mount bracket.

14. Remove the timing belt middle and lower covers.

15. Rotate the crankshaft, in the normal direction of rotation, until the No. 1 cylinder piston is at TDC on the compression stroke. Make sure the timing marks on the crankshaft and camshaft sprocket(s) are properly aligned and mark the direction of rotation of the belt.

16. Loosen the timing belt tensioner and remove the belt. Do not rotate the crankshaft until the timing belt is reinstalled.

17. Remove air cleaner assembly and front pipe.

18. Remove the exhaust manifold.

19. Disconnect the accelerator and throttle cables.

20. Tag and disconnect the spark plug wires from the spark plugs. Remove the spark plugs and the distributor cap and wires assembly. Remove the distributor.

21. Disconnect the following hoses: Heater, brake vacuum, purge, fuel, water and upper radiator.

22. Label and disconnect the distributor/coil connectors, engine coolant temperature sensor connector, cooling fan coolant temperature sensor connector, and temperature gauge sensor connector.

23. Remove the camshaft sprockets and the camshaft.

24. On the 1.5L engine, remove the tappets. Identify each tappet as it is removed so it can be reinstalled in the same position.

25. On the 1.8L engine, remove the hydraulic lifters. Identify each lifter as it is removed so it can be reinstalled in the same position. If the lifters are to be reused, store them upside down in an oil-filled sealed container.

26. Remove the intake manifold bracket and the intake manifold.

27. Loosen the cylinder head bolts, in 2–3 steps, in sequence. Remove the bolts and the cylinder head.

To install:

28. Thoroughly, clean the cylinder head and the block contact surfaces. Examine the head gasket and check the cylinder head for cracks. Check the cylinder head for warpage using a feeler gauge and straightedge. The maximum allowable distortion is 0.004 in. (0.10mm).

29. Clean the cylinder head bolts and the threads in the block. Make sure the bolts turn freely in the block.

30. Install a new head gasket on the engine block. Make sure the camshaft sprocket timing marks are still aligned, as set during the removal procedure. Install the cylinder head.

31. Lubricate the bolt threads and seat surfaces with clean engine oil and install them as follows;

    a. On the 1.5L (Z5D) engines, torque the bolts in 2–3 steps to 13–16 ft. lbs. (17–22 Nm) in the proper sequence. Paint a reference mark on each bolt head and turn the bolts, in sequence, 90°, and then an additional 90°.

    b. On the 1.8L (BPD) engines, torque the bolts in 2–3 steps to 56–60 ft. lbs. (75–81 Nm) in the proper sequence.

32. Use new gaskets and install the manifolds. Torque the intake manifold bolts/nuts to 19 ft. lbs. (25 Nm) and install the intake manifold bracket. Torque the exhaust manifold nuts to 34 ft. lbs. (46 Nm).

33. Use a new gasket to connect the exhaust pipe and torque the nuts to 34 ft. lbs. (46 Nm).

34. Apply clean engine oil to the tappets and install them in their original positions.

35. Install the camshaft and sprockets.

36. Make sure the crankshaft and camshaft sprocket timing marks are aligned, install the timing belt and set the tension. Carefully rotate the crankshaft 2 turns to make sure the timing marks still line up.

37. Install the timing belt middle and lower covers, and tighten the bolts to 70–95 inch lbs. (8–11 Nm).

38. Install the number three engine mount bracket. Tighten the nut to 70–95 inch lbs. (8–11 Nm), and the bolt to 14–16 ft. lbs. (19–22 Nm). Remove the engine support tool.

39. Install the upper timing belt cover and tighten the bolts to 70–95 inch lbs. (8–11 Nm).

40. Install the oil dipstick and bracket.

41. Apply silicone sealant to the cylinder surface in the area adjacent to the front camshaft bearing caps. Apply sealant to a new gasket and install it on the cylinder head cover.

42. Install the cylinder head cover and tighten the bolts in 5–6 steps, in sequence, to 61–95 inch lbs. (7–11 Nm) on the 1.5 (Z5D) engines and 44–78 inch lbs. (5–9 Nm) on the 1.8L (BPD) engines.

43. Install the power steering hose brackets and tighten the bolts to 70–95 inch lbs. (7–11 Nm). Connect the spark plug wires and wire clips. Connect the breather tube and PCV valve.

44. Install the guide plate, crankshaft pulley and pulley bolt. Hold the pulley with the holder tool and tighten the bolt to 116–122 ft. lbs. (157–166 Nm).

45. Install the water pump pulley.

46. Install the alternator belt and adjust the tension.

47. Install the power steering belt and adjust the tension. Tighten the through-bolt to 32–44 ft. lbs. (44–60 Nm) and the lockbolt to 24–33 ft. lbs. (32–46 Nm). Install the power steering belt shield and tighten the bolts to 86 inch lbs. (9 Nm).

48. Install the splash shield and wheel. Lower the vehicle.

49. Connect the electrical engine harness connectors.

50. Connect the heater, brake vacuum, purge, fuel, water and upper radiator hoses.

51. Install the distributor, spark plugs, distributor cap and wires.

52. Connect and adjust the accelerator and throttle cables.

53. Install the cleaner.

54. Connect the negative battery cable. Fill and bleed the cooling system. Change the engine oil.

55. Adjust the ignition timing.

56. Start the engine and bring to normal operating temperature. Check for leaks. Check the ignition timing and idle speed.

2.0L Engines

▶ See Figures 111 thru 122

1. Relieve the fuel system pressure and disconnect the negative battery cable. Drain the cooling system.

2. Remove the splash shield, fresh air duct and air cleaner assembly.

3. Disconnect the accelerator cable.

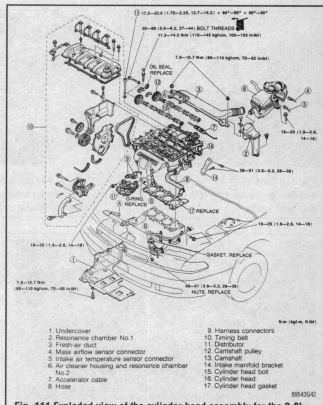

1. Undercover
2. Resonance chamber No.1
3. Fresh-air duct
4. Mass airflow sensor connector
5. Intake air temperature sensor connector
6. Air cleaner housing and resonance chamber No.2
7. Accelerator cable
8. Hose
9. Harness connectors
10. Timing belt
11. Distributor
12. Camshaft pulley
13. Camshaft
14. Intake manifold bracket
15. Cylinder head bolt
16. Cylinder head
17. Cylinder head gasket

Fig. 111 Exploded view of the cylinder head assembly for the 2.0L engine

Fig. 112 To remove the cylinder head, first drain the coolant, then remove the air intake ducting, valve cover, distributor and radiator hose

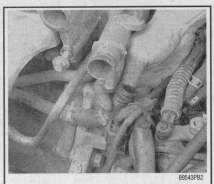

Fig. 113 Also disconnect the water bypass hose . . .

Fig. 114 . . . as well as the engine wire harness, fuel lines (arrows) and heater hoses

Fig. 115 If necessary, unbolt the EGR pipe securing bracket from the engine block

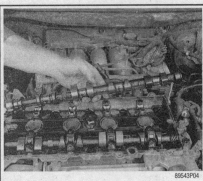

Fig. 116 Remove the timing belt and camshafts from the cylinder head

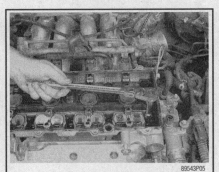

Fig. 117 Loosen the cylinder head bolts evenly in 2–3 steps following the sequence

Fig. 118 Once all of the cylinder head bolts are loosened remove them along with their washers

Fig. 119 With the help of an assistant, lift the cylinder head off of the engine, complete with intake and exhaust manifolds

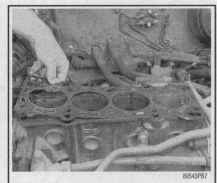

Fig. 120 Remove the old cylinder head gasket . . .

Fig. 121 . . . and, after stuffing rags in the cylinder bores, thoroughly clean the gasket mating surfaces

4. Disconnect the following hoses: heater, brake vacuum, purge, fuel, water and upper radiator.

5. Remove the accessory drive belts. Remove the power steering pump bolts and secure the pump aside with mechanics wire, leaving the hoses attached.

6. Remove the alternator bracket nut and bolt and position the bracket aside. Detach the exhaust pipe from the manifold.

7. Label and disconnect the spark plug wires. Remove the power steering hose brackets from the cylinder head cover.

8. Label and detach the distributor/coil connectors, engine coolant temperature sensor connector, cooling fan coolant temperature sensor connector and temperature gauge sensor connector.

9. Disconnect the hoses from the cylinder head cover and loosen the cover bolts in 5–6 steps, in the reverse order of the tightening sequence. Remove the cylinder head cover.

10. Remove the timing belt cover and the timing belt.

Fig. 122 When installing the head, tighten the head bolts in sequence to the proper specifications

11. Remove the coolant temperature sensor housing from the cylinder head. Remove the distributor.

12. Remove the camshaft sprockets and the camshaft.

13. Remove the hydraulic lifters. Identify each lifter as it is removed so it can be reinstalled in the same position. If the lifters are to be reused, store them upside down in an oil-filled sealed container.

14. Loosen the cylinder head bolts, in 2–3 steps, in sequence. Remove the bolts and the cylinder head.

15. Clean all gasket mating surfaces. Inspect the cylinder head for damage, cracks, and water and oil leakage. Check the head gasket surface for distortion using a straight-edge and feeler gauge. Maximum allowable distortion is 0.004 inch (0.10mm).

To install:

16. Position a new cylinder head gasket on the cylinder block, and install the cylinder head.

17. Apply clean engine oil to the bolt threads and seating faces. Install new cylinder head bolts and tighten in 2–3 steps, in sequence, to 13–16 ft. lbs. (17–22 Nm).

18. Paint a mark on the edge of each cylinder head bolt to use as a reference. Turn each bolt, in sequence, 90 degrees. Again, turn each bolt, in sequence, an additional 90 degrees.

19. Apply clean engine oil to the hydraulic lifters and install them in their original positions. Make sure they move freely in the bores.

20. Install the camshafts and sprockets. Install the distributor and connect the distributor/coil connectors.

21. Install the timing belt and cover.

22. Install a new cylinder head cover gasket on the cylinder head cover. Apply sealant to the cylinder head surface in the area adjacent to the front camshaft caps, then install the cover. Tighten the bolts in 5–6 steps, in sequence, to 61–95 inch lbs. (7–11 Nm).

23. Connect the hoses to the cylinder head cover. Connect the spark plug wires.

24. Install the exhaust manifold and the alternator bracket. Tighten the bracket nut and bolt to 19 ft. lbs. (25 Nm).

25. Install the alternator belt and adjust the tension.

26. Loosely install the power steering pump through and lockbolts. Connect the pump pressure switch connector.

27. Install the power steering pump belt and adjust the tension. Tighten the pump through-bolt to 45 ft. lbs. (61 Nm) and the lockbolt to 34 ft. lbs. (46 Nm).

28. Install the power steering pump belt shield and tighten the bolts to 86 inch lbs. (9 Nm). Install the power steering hose brackets to the cylinder head cover, and tighten the bolts to 88 inch lbs. (10 Nm).

29. Install the coolant temperature sensor housing with a new gasket. Tighten the bolts to 19 ft. lbs. (25 Nm). Connect the electrical connectors at the housing.

30. Connect and adjust the accelerator cable.

31. Connect the heater, brake vacuum, purge, fuel, water and upper radiator hoses.

32. Install the air cleaner assembly, fresh air duct and splash shield.

33. Connect the negative battery cable. Fill and bleed the cooling system. Run the engine and check for proper operation.

2.2L Engine

♦ **See Figure 123**

1. Properly relieve the fuel system pressure.

2. Disconnect the negative battery cable and drain the cooling system.

3. Disconnect the spark plug wires and remove the spark plugs and the distributor.

4. Disconnect the accelerator cable and if equipped, throttle valve cable.

5. Disconnect the air intake hose from the throttle body. Disconnect and plug the fuel lines.

6. Remove the upper radiator hose, water bypass hose, heater hose, oil cooler hose and brake vacuum hose. If equipped with turbocharger, disconnect the oil cooler hose.

7. Remove the 3-way solenoid and EGR solenoid valve assemblies.

8. Label and disconnect the wiring and vacuum hoses.

9. Remove the vacuum chamber and exhaust manifold shield.

10. Remove the EGR pipe, turbocharger oil pipe, if equipped, and exhaust pipe.

11. Remove the exhaust manifold. On turbocharged engines, remove the manifold and turbocharger as an assembly.

12. Remove the intake manifold bracket and the intake manifold.

13. Remove the air conditioning compressor and bracket and position the compressor aside, without disconnecting the refrigerant lines.

14. Remove the upper timing belt cover.

15. To remove the timing belt, perform the following:

a. Rotate the crankshaft so the **1** on the camshaft sprocket is aligned with the timing mark on the front housing.

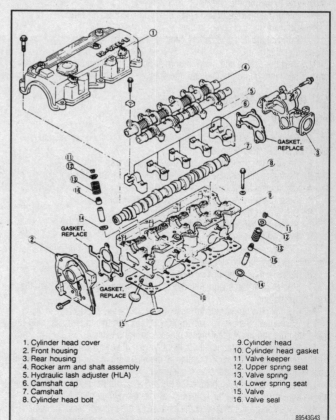

1. Cylinder head cover
2. Front housing
3. Rear housing
4. Rocker arm and shaft assembly
5. Hydraulic lash adjuster (HLA)
6. Camshaft cap
7. Camshaft
8. Cylinder head bolt
9. Cylinder head
10. Cylinder head gasket
11. Valve keeper
12. Upper spring seat
13. Valve spring
14. Lower spring seat
15. Valve
16. Valve seal

Fig. 123 Exploded view of the cylinder head assembly for the 2.2L engine

b. When timing marks are aligned, loosen the timing belt tensioner lock bolt. Pull the tensioner outward as far as possible and temporarily tighten the lock bolt.

c. Lift the timing belt from the camshaft pulley and position it aside.

16. Remove the cylinder head cover and gasket.

17. Loosen the cylinder head bolts in the reverse of the tightening sequence, and remove the cylinder head and head gasket.

18. Thoroughly clean all gasket mating surfaces. Check the cylinder head for cracks or other damage. Check the cylinder head for warpage using a feeler gauge and straightedge. The maximum allowable distortion is 0.006 in. (0.15mm). 19.

Inspect the cylinder head bolts for damaged threads and make sure they turn freely in the threads in the block.

To install:

19. Position a new cylinder head gasket on the engine block and install the cylinder head.

20. Lubricate the bolt threads and seat surfaces with clean engine oil and install them. Torque the bolts in 2–3 steps to 59–64 ft. lbs. (80–86 Nm), in the proper sequence.

21. Apply sealant to the 4 corners of the cylinder head and install the cover with a new gasket. Torque the cover bolts to 69 inch lbs. (8 Nm).

22. Make sure the camshaft sprocket and front housing timing marks are aligned and install the timing belt. Set the tension and carefully rotate the crankshaft 2 turns to make sure the timing marks still line up. Install the timing belt cover.

23. Use a new gasket and install the intake manifold. Torque the nuts/bolts to 22 ft. lbs. (30 Nm). Install the intake manifold bracket.

24. Use new gaskets and install the exhaust manifold. Torque the nuts to 36 ft. lbs. (49 Nm). On turbocharged engines, connect the turbocharger oil line.

25. Connect the exhaust pipe with a new gasket and torque the nuts to 34 ft. lbs. (46 Nm).

26. Install the EGR pipe, exhaust manifold shield and vacuum chamber. Install the EGR solenoid and 3-way solenoid.

27. Connect all the coolant, vacuum and fuel system hoses. Connect the air intake hose to the throttle body.

28. Install the distributor and spark plugs and connect all wiring

29. Connect the accelerator cable.

30. Connect the negative battery cable. Fill and bleed the cooling system. Change the engine oil.

31. Start the engine and bring to normal operating temperature. Check for leaks. Check the ignition timing and idle speed.

1.8L (K8) and 2.5L Engines

▶ **See Figure 124**

1. Relieve the fuel system pressure and disconnect the negative battery cable. Drain the cooling system.

2. Remove the fresh air duct and the air cleaner assembly.

3. If additional clearance space is needed, remove the battery.

4. Disconnect the accelerator cable.

5. Disconnect the wiring harness from the cylinder heads.

6. Disconnect the fuel, heater and vacuum hoses.

7. Remove the intake manifold.

8. Remove the distributor.

9. Disconnect the ventilation pipe from the left cylinder head cover, remove the bolts and remove the cylinder head covers.

10. Remove the timing belt covers and the timing belt.

11. Remove the camshafts. Remove the 3 bolts and the seal plate from the front of the engine.

12. Remove the upper radiator hose. Raise and safely support the vehicle.

13. Disconnect the oxygen sensor connectors. Remove the exhaust pipe-to-manifold nuts and lower the exhaust pipes. Lower the vehicle.

14. Remove the hydraulic lifters. Identify each lifter as it is removed so it can be reinstalled in the same position. If the lifters are to be reused, store them upside down in an oil-filled, sealed container.

15. Loosen the cylinder head bolts, in 2–3 steps, in the reverse order of the torque sequence. Remove the bolts and remove the cylinder heads.

16. Clean all gasket mating surfaces. Inspect the cylinder head for damage, cracks, and water and oil leakage. Check the head gasket surface for distortion using a straight-edge and feeler gauge. Maximum allowable distortion is 0.004 in. (0.10mm).

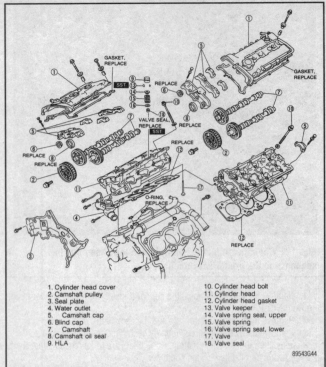

1. Cylinder head cover
2. Camshaft pulley
3. Seal plate
4. Water outlet
5. Camshaft cap
6. Blind cap
7. Camshaft
8. Camshaft oil seal
9. HLA
10. Cylinder head bolt
11. Cylinder head
12. Cylinder head gasket
13. Valve keeper
14. Valve spring seat, upper
15. Valve spring
16. Valve spring seat, lower
17. Valve
18. Valve seal

89543G44

Fig. 124 Exploded view of the cylinder head assemblies for the 1.8L (K8) and 2.5L engines

To install:

17. Position NEW head gaskets on the cylinder block. The gaskets cannot be interchanged between sides and are marked R and L for right and left side.

18. Install the cylinder heads. Apply clean engine oil to the threads of new cylinder head bolts and install. Tighten the cylinder head bolts in 2–3 steps, in sequence, to 17–19 ft. lbs. (23–26 Nm).

19. Paint a mark on the edge of each cylinder head bolt to use as a reference. Turn each bolt, in sequence, 90 degrees. Again, turn each bolt, in sequence, an additional 90 degrees.

20. Apply clean engine oil to the hydraulic lifters and install them in their original positions. Make sure they move freely in the bores.

21. Install the camshafts. Raise and safely support the vehicle.

22. Connect the exhaust pipes to the manifolds and tighten the nuts to 41 ft. lbs. (55 Nm). Connect the oxygen sensor connectors. Lower the vehicle.

23. Install the timing belt and timing belt covers.

24. Apply sealant to the cylinder head surface in the area of the front and rear camshaft caps. Install new gaskets and install the cylinder head covers. Tighten the bolts in 5–6 steps, in sequence, to 44–78 inch lbs. (5–9 Nm).

25. Install the intake manifold using new gaskets. Tighten the mounting bolts to 14–18 ft. lbs. (19–25 Nm).

26. Install the distributor:

a. Apply clean engine oil to a new O-ring, and position it on the distributor.

b. Apply clean engine oil to the drive blade. Install the distributor with the blade fit into the camshaft groove.

c. Hand tighten the mounting bolts.

27. Connect the vacuum, heater and fuel hoses.

28. Connect the wiring harness to the cylinder heads.

29. Connect and adjust the accelerator cable.

30. If removed, install the battery.

31. Install the air cleaner assembly and the fresh air duct.

32. Connect the negative battery cable. Fill and bleed the cooling system. Adjust the ignition timing and idle speed. Run the engine and check for proper operation.

2.3L Engines

▶ See Figure 125

1. Relieve the fuel system pressure. Disconnect the negative battery cable.
2. Drain the engine coolant.
3. Raise and safely support the vehicle.
4. Disconnect the oxygen sensor connectors. Remove the exhaust pipe-to-manifold nuts and lower the exhaust pipes.
5. Remove the right-hand three-way catalytic converter. Lower the vehicle.
6. Remove the Lysholm compressor (supercharger).
7. Remove the intake manifold.
8. Remove the timing belt covers and timing belt.
9. Remove the spacer and O-ring from the front of the camshaft.
10. Remove the ignition coils.
11. Remove the cylinder head cover mounting bolts, in 5–6 steps, using the reverse of the tightening sequence. Remove the cylinder head cover.
12. Remove the camshaft sprockets.
13. Turn the camshafts so the knock pins are aligned with the marks on the camshaft caps. This will reduce the pressure on the adjustment shims.
14. Note the markings on the camshaft caps prior to removal, so they can be reinstalled in the same positions. The right hand (rear) caps are marked with numbers and the left hand (front) caps are marked with letters.
15. Loosen the front camshaft cap bolts in sequence, in 5–6 steps. Remove the front camshaft caps.
16. Remove the remaining camshaft cap bolts in the proper sequence. Remove the caps, being sure to remove the thrust caps last. Do not damage the cylinder head thrust bearing support.
17. Remove the camshafts and oil seals.
18. Remove the lifters and adjustment shims. Identify and mark each lifter as it is removed so it can be reinstalled in the same position.
19. Remove the lower radiator hose and water inlet pipe.
20. Remove the Lysholm compressor bracket.
21. Remove the alternator bracket bolt to gain additional clearance.
22. Remove the rubber insulator from the left-hand cylinder head.
23. Temporarily install the number three engine mount, which was removed with the timing belt, to support the engine. Remove the engine support device.
24. Loosen the cylinder head bolts, in 2–3 steps, in the reverse order of the torque sequence. Remove the bolts and remove the cylinder heads.

25. Remove the oil control plug O-rings.
26. Clean all gasket mating surfaces. Inspect the cylinder head for damage, cracks, and water and oil leakage. Check the head gasket surface for distortion using a straight-edge and feeler gauge. Maximum allowable distortion is 0.004 inch (0.10mm).

To install:

27. Apply clean engine oil to the O-rings, and install them onto the oil control plugs.
28. Position new head gaskets on the cylinder block. The gaskets cannot be interchanged between sides and are marked **R** and **L** for right and left side.
29. Install the cylinder heads. Apply clean engine oil to the threads of new cylinder head bolts and install. Tighten the cylinder head bolts in 2–3 steps, in sequence, to 17–19 ft. lbs. (23–26 Nm).
30. Paint a mark on the edge of each cylinder head bolt to use as a reference. Turn each bolt, in sequence, 90 degrees. Again, turn each bolt, in sequence, an additional 90 degrees.
31. Install the rubber insulator onto the left-hand cylinder head.
32. Fit the knock sensor harness into the drill hole on the cylinder block. Pass the harness under the rubber insulator.
33. Install an engine support device, and remove the number three engine mount.
34. Install the alternator bracket bolt. Tighten the mounting bolt to 12–16 ft. lbs. (16–22 Nm).
35. Install the Lysholm compressor bracket. Tighten the mounting bolts to 14–18 ft. lbs. (19–25 Nm).
36. Install the water inlet pipe. Tighten the mounting bolts to 14–18 ft. lbs. (19–25 Nm). Install the lower radiator hose.
37. Apply clean engine oil to the lifters, then install them in their original positions. Verify that they move smoothly in their bore.
38. Install new oil seals on the camshafts. Apply clean engine oil to the camshaft lobes, journals and supports.
39. Install the camshafts so the gear marks align.
40. Remove all oil and dirt from the mating surfaces between the front camshaft cap and the cylinder head.
41. Install the thrust caps. Tighten the thrust cap bolts, in 5–6 steps, until the caps are fully seated on the cylinder head.
42. Apply silicone sealant, at a thickness of 0.06–0.09 inch (1.5–2.5mm), to the cylinder head surface in the area forward of the camshaft gear cavity.
43. Install the remaining camshaft caps in their original positions. Tighten the caps, in sequence, in five equal steps, with the final step being 100–125 inch lbs. (11–14 Nm).
44. Apply clean engine oil to the lip of the new camshaft oil seal. Push the seal in lightly by hand. Tap the seal in evenly with a seal installer (49 F401 337A or equivalent) with a final protrusion of 0–0.02 inch (0–0.5mm). Tap in a new blind cap.
45. Install the camshaft sprockets. Tighten the mounting bolts to 91–103 ft. lbs. (123–140 Nm).
46. Measure and adjust valve clearances.
47. Remove any sealant and gasket material from the cylinder head cover contact surfaces.
48. Apply silicone sealant to the cylinder head in the area adjacent to the front and rear camshaft caps. Install a new gasket on the cylinder head.
49. Install the cylinder head cover. Tighten the bolts in 5–6 steps, in sequence, to 44–78 inch lbs. (5–9 Nm).
50. Using a new O-ring, install the distributor.
51. Install the ignition coils.
52. Install the spacer, using a new O-ring. Tighten the mounting bolt to 14–18 ft. lbs. (19–25 Nm).
53. Install the timing belt and timing belt cover.
54. Install the intake manifold.
55. Install the Lysholm compressor (supercharger).
56. Raise and safely support the vehicle.
57. Install the right-hand three-way catalytic converter.
58. Connect the exhaust pipes to the manifolds and tighten the nuts to 28–38 ft. lbs. (38–51 Nm). Connect the oxygen sensor connectors. Lower the vehicle.
59. Connect the negative battery cable.
60. Fill and bleed the coolant system.
61. Run the engine and check for leaks.

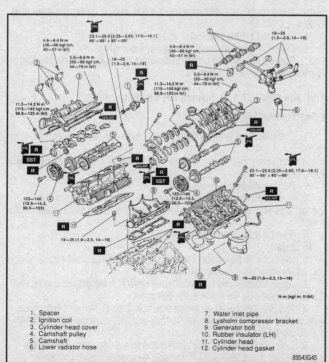

1. Spacer
2. Ignition coil
3. Cylinder head cover
4. Camshaft pulley
5. Camshaft
6. Lower radiator hose
7. Water inlet pipe
8. Lysholm compressor bracket
9. Generator bolt
10. Rubber insulator (LH)
11. Cylinder head
12. Cylinder head gasket

89543G45

Fig. 125 Exploded view of the cylinder head assemblies and related components for the 2.3L engine

Oil Pan

REMOVAL & INSTALLATION

1990–94 1.6L and 1.8L (except K8) Engines

▶ **See Figures 126 and 127**

1. Disconnect the negative battery cable. Raise and safely support the vehicle.

2. Remove the engine undercover, if equipped. Position a suitable container under the oil pan. Remove the drain plug and drain the oil.

3. Remove the exhaust pipe from the exhaust manifold and from the catalytic converter. If necessary, remove the exhaust pipe bracket from the engine block.

4. On 1993–94 323 1.6L (B6E) and 1994 Protege 1.8L (BPD) engines, remove the integrated stiffener from the engine block and transaxle.

5. 1993–94 Protege 1.8L (BPE) and 1994 MX3 1.8L (BPD) engines, remove the main bearing support/stiffener plate that is installed between the oil pan and engine block.

6. Remove the bolts and remove the oil pan. It may be necessary to pry the pan away from the engine; be careful not to damage the gasket contact surfaces.

7. If necessary remove the oil strainer.

8. Remove the main bearing support/stiffener plate that is installed between the oil pan and engine block.

To install:

9. Clean all oil, dirt, old gasket material and sealer from the oil pan, support/stiffener plate, oil pan bolts and all gasket mating surfaces. If removed, clean the oil strainer.

10. If equipped with the main bearing support/stiffener plate, run a bead of silicone sealer around the perimeter of the plate, going inside the bolt holes. Install the plate and tighten the bolts.

➡**Make sure all old sealer is removed from the bolts prior to installation. Installing a bolt coated with old sealer could result in cracking of the bolt holes.**

11. If removed, install the oil strainer using a new gasket. Tighten the bolts.

12. If used, apply silicone sealer to new rubber end gaskets and press them into place on the engine.

13. Apply a bead of silicone to the perimeter of the oil pan, going around the inside of the bolt holes and install the pan to the engine. Install the oil pan bolts finger tight.

14. Tighten the oil pan bolts.

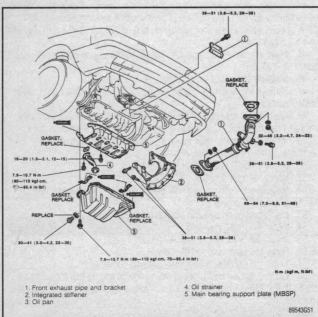

1. Front exhaust pipe and bracket
2. Integrated stiffener
3. Oil pan
4. Oil strainer
5. Main bearing support plate (MBSP)

89543G51

Fig. 126 Exploded view of the oil pan and related components for the 1990–94 1.6L engine—2.2L engine is similar

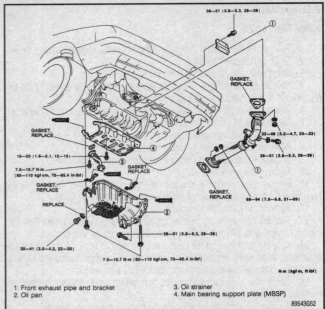

1. Front exhaust pipe and bracket
2. Oil pan
3. Oil strainer
4. Main bearing support plate (MBSP)

89543G52

Fig. 127 Exploded view of the oil pan and related components for the 1.8L engine

➡**Make sure all old sealer is removed from the bolts prior to installation. Installing a bolt coated with old sealer could result in cracking of the bolt holes.**

15. On 1990–94 323 1.6L (B6E) and 1994 Protege 1.8L (BPD) engines, install the integrated stiffener to the engine block and transaxle. Tighten the bolts to 38 ft. lbs. (52 Nm).

16. 1990–94 Protege 1.8L (BPE) and 1994 MX3 1.8L (BPD) engines, install the transverse member. Tighten the bolts to 93 ft. lbs. (126 Nm).

17. Install the front exhaust pipe bracket, if equipped. Install the front exhaust pipe, using new gaskets. Tighten the exhaust manifold flange nuts to 34 ft. lbs. (46 Nm).

18. Install the oil pan drain plug using a new gasket. Tighten the drain plug to 30 ft. lbs. (41 Nm).

19. Install the engine undercover and lower the vehicle.

20. Fill the engine with the proper type and quantity of oil.

21. Connect the negative battery cable. Start the engine and bring to normal operating temperature. Check for leaks.

1.5L and 1995–97 1.8L (except K8) Engines

▶ **See Figures 127 and 128**

1. Disconnect the negative battery cable. Raise and safely support the vehicle.

2. Remove the right-hand splash shield. Drain the engine oil into a suitable container.

3. Remove the transverse member.

4. Disconnect the oxygen sensor connector. Remove and discard the exhaust pipe-to-manifold nuts. Move the exhaust pipe aside and support it with a jack.

5. Remove the oil pan bolts and the oil pan.

To install:

6. Clean the oil pan. Clean all dirt, oil, gasket and old sealant from the oil pan and cylinder block contact surfaces.

7. Apply a continuous bead of silicone sealant on the gaskets and around the oil pan, going on the inside of the bolt holes.

8. Position the gaskets on the oil pan. Install the oil pan, and tighten the vertical bolts to 70–95 inch lbs. (8–11 Nm), and the horizontal bolts to 28–38 ft. lbs. (38–51 Nm).

9. Connect the exhaust pipe to the manifold with new nuts. Tighten the nuts to 28–38 ft. lbs. (38–51 Nm). Connect the oxygen sensor connector.

10. Install the transverse member, and tighten the mounting bolts to 69–97 ft. lbs. (94–131 Nm).

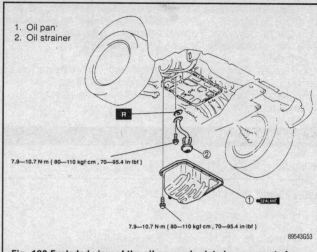

Fig. 128 Exploded view of the oil pan and related components for the 1.5L engine—2.0L engine is similar

11. Install the right-hand splash shield and tighten the mounting bolts to 70–95 inch lbs. (8–11 Nm). Lower the vehicle.

12. Fill the engine with the proper type and quantity of engine oil. Connect the negative battery, run the engine and check for leaks.

2.2L Engine

▶ See Figure 127

1. Disconnect the negative battery cable. Raise and safely support the vehicle.

2. Remove the engine under cover, if equipped. Position a suitable container under the oil pan. Remove the drain plug and drain the oil.

3. Remove the exhaust pipe from the exhaust manifold and from the catalytic converter. If necessary, remove the exhaust pipe bracket from the engine block.

4. Remove the gusset plates and the clutch housing cover.

5. Remove the bolts and remove the oil pan. It may be necessary to pry the pan away from the engine; be careful not to damage the gasket contact surfaces.

6. If necessary remove the oil strainer.

7. Remove the main bearing support/stiffener plate that is installed between the oil pan and engine block.

To install:

8. Clean all oil, dirt, old gasket material and sealer from the oil pan, support/stiffener plate, oil pan bolts and all gasket mating surfaces. If removed, clean the oil strainer.

9. On the main bearing support/stiffener plate, run a bead of silicone sealer around the perimeter of the plate, going inside the bolt holes. Install the plate and tighten the bolts to 104 inch lbs. (12 Nm).

➡**Make sure all old sealer is removed from the bolts prior to installation. Installing a bolt coated with old sealer could result in cracking of the bolts holes.**

10. If removed, install the oil strainer using a new gasket. Tighten the bolts to 95 inch lbs. (11 Nm).

11. If used, apply silicone sealer to new rubber end gaskets and press them into place on the engine.

12. Apply a bead of silicone to the perimeter of the oil pan, going around the inside of the bolt holes and install the pan to the engine. Install the oil pan bolts finger tight.

13. Tighten the oil pan bolts to 95 inch lbs. (11 Nm).

➡**Make sure all old sealer is removed from the bolts prior to installation. Installing a bolt coated with old sealer could result in cracking of the bolts holes.**

14. Install the clutch housing cover and tighten the bolts to 95 inch lbs. (11 Nm). Install the gusset plates and tighten the bolts to 38 ft. lbs. (52 Nm).

15. Install the front exhaust pipe bracket, if equipped. Install the front exhaust pipe, using new gaskets. Tighten the exhaust manifold flange nuts to 34 ft. lbs. (46 Nm).

16. Install the oil pan drain plug using a new gasket. Tighten the drain plug to 15 ft. lbs. (20 Nm).

17. Install the engine under cover and lower the vehicle.

18. Fill the engine with the proper type and quantity of oil.

19. Connect the negative battery cable. Start the engine and bring to normal operating temperature. Check for leaks.

1.8L (K8), 2.0L, 2.3L and 2.5L Engines

▶ See Figures 128 and 129

1. Disconnect the negative battery cable. Raise and safely support the vehicle.

2. Remove the passenger side splash shield. Drain the engine oil into a suitable container.

3. Disconnect the oxygen sensor connector. Remove the front exhaust pipe.

4. Remove the oil pan bolts and the oil pan.

To install:

5. Clean the oil pan. Clean all dirt, oil and old sealant from the oil pan and cylinder block contact surfaces.

6. Apply a continuous bead of silicone sealant around the oil pan, going on the inside of the bolt holes.

7. Install the oil pan and tighten the bolts to 14–18 ft. lbs. (19–25 Nm).

8. Install the front pipe. Tighten the nuts to 28–38 ft. lbs. (38–51 Nm). Connect the oxygen sensor connector.

9. Install the splash shield and tighten the mounting bolts to 70–95 inch lbs. (8–11 Nm). Lower the vehicle.

10. Fill the engine with the proper type and quantity of engine oil. Connect the negative battery, run the engine and check for leaks.

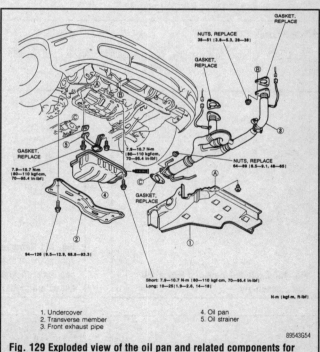

1. Undercover
2. Transverse member
3. Front exhaust pipe
4. Oil pan
5. Oil strainer

Fig. 129 Exploded view of the oil pan and related components for the 1.8L (K8), 2.3L and 2.5L engines

Oil Pump and Front Seal

REMOVAL & INSTALLATION

▶ See Figure 130

➡**Due to space constraints, the 2.3L engine must be removed from the vehicle in order to service the oil pump assembly. Refer to the Engine Removal & Installation procedure earlier in this section.**

1. Disconnect the negative battery cable. Raise and safely support the vehicle.
2. Remove the timing belt. Remove the crankshaft damper retaining bolt, the damper and the timing belt sprocket. Drain the engine oil and remove the oil pan.
3. Remove the oil pump pickup tube-to-oil pump bolts, the tube and gasket.

➡ **When removing the pump housing from the front of the block, some engines have an additional engine block support structure which the bottom surface of the pump seals against. This may make it difficult to remove the pump. Try not to pry between gasket mating surfaces and always pull the pump outward from the engine, not up.**

4. Remove the oil pump housing-to-cylinder block bolts, the pump and, if equipped, the gasket.
5. If necessary, pry the oil seal from the pump and clean the seal bore.
6. Thoroughly clean all of the gasket mounting surfaces. Inspect the pump and gears for wear.

To install:

7. Apply a continuous bead of silicone sealer to the oil pump gasket surface.

➡ **Do not allow the sealer to squeeze into the pump's outlet hole in the pump or cylinder block.**

8. Install a new O-ring into the pump body.
9. Install the oil pump to the cylinder block; be careful not to cut the oil seal lip. Tighten the oil pump-to-cylinder block bolts to specifications.
10. Install the oil pump pickup tube using a new gasket.
11. Install the oil pan and the crankshaft sprocket. Tighten the crankshaft sprocket bolt to specifications.
12. Connect the negative battery cable and refill the crankcase. Start the engine and check for leaks.

FRONT SEAL REMOVAL & INSTALLATION

▶ **See Figures 131 and 132**

1. Disconnect the negative battery cable. Raise and safely support the vehicle.

2. Remove the timing belt. Remove the crankshaft damper retaining bolt, the damper and the timing belt sprocket. Remove the sprocket key from the crankshaft.
3. Using a small prybar, pry the oil seal from the engine block; be careful not to score the crankshaft or the seal seat. Clean the seal bore.

To install:

4. Using an oil seal installation tool or equivalent, lubricate the seal lip with clean engine oil and drive the new seal into the engine until it seats.
5. The rest of the installation is the reverse of the removal procedure. Tighten all bolts to the proper specification.

Crankshaft Damper

REMOVAL & INSTALLATION

▶ **See Figures 133, 134, 135 and 136**

1. Remove the accessory drive belts.
2. Raise and safely support the vehicle.
3. Remove the right front wheel and tire assembly.
4. Remove the right inner fender panel.
5. Examine the damper attaching bolts.
6. If the damper has one bolt in the center, with no perimeter bolts, proceed as follows:

   a. The damper will have two or more open, threaded bolt holes. Install the proper size metric bolt into these holes and thread them in by hand. Ensure that you have at least ⅜ inch (9.5 mm) of engagement on the bolt.

   b. Position a breaker bar and socket assembly onto the center bolt head and place a prybar between the installed bolts to keep the damper from rotating while loosening the center bolt.

   c. Loosen the center bolt while holding the prybar, however, watch the installed bolts carefully. Any excessive flexing or bending is unacceptable, and the bolts may break off in the damper.

   d. Once the center bolt is loose, remove the installed bolts, then the center bolt.

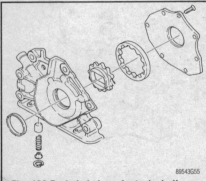

Fig. 130 Exploded view of a typical oil pump assembly

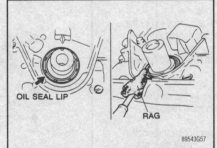

Fig. 131 Remove the front engine seal by cutting the seal lip then, so as not to damage the crankshaft, carefully pry the seal out with a prybar

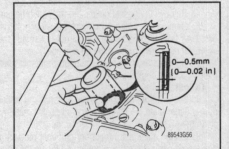

Fig. 132 Install the seal using an appropriate driver, which fits over the crankshaft snout and presses on the outside edge of the seal

Fig. 133 To remove the crankshaft, first loosen the center bolt while keeping the crankshaft from turning

Fig. 134 Remove the center crankshaft bolt or, if equipped, the perimeter bolts . . .

Fig. 135 . . . then pull the damper from the end of the crankshaft snout. Some models may require a puller to remove it

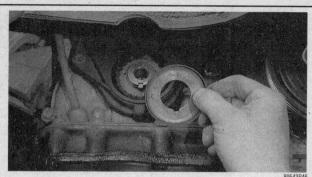

Fig. 136 Finally, remove the timing belt baffle plate to complete the removal procedure

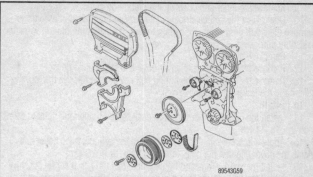

Fig. 138 Exploded view of the 1.8L DOHC timing belt cover assembly

7. If the damper has one bolt in the center, with additional perimeter bolts, proceed as follows:

    a. Remove all of the perimeter bolts.

    b. Remove the crankshaft pulley from the engine.

    c. If the center bolt must also be removed, install the proper size metric bolt into the perimeter bolt holes and thread them in by hand. Ensure that you have at least ⅜ inch (9.5 mm) of engagement on the bolt.

    d. Position a breaker bar and socket assembly onto the center bolt head and place a prybar between the installed bolts to keep the damper from rotating while loosening the center bolt.

    e. Loosen the center bolt while holding the prybar, however, watch the installed bolts carefully. Any excessive flexing or bending is unacceptable, and the bolts may break off in the damper.

    f. Once the center bolt is loose, remove the installed bolts, then the center bolt.

8. Remove the damper and, if necessary, the baffle plate.

9. Inspect the damper for damage and replace, as necessary.

To install:

10. Installation is the reverse of the removal procedure. When installing the baffle, ensure that the curved lip faces outward. Tighten all bolts to specification.

Timing Belt Cover

REMOVAL & INSTALLATION

1990–94 1.6L and 1.8L (except K8) Engines

▶ See Figures 137 and 138

1. Disconnect the negative battery cable.
2. Remove the engine under splash shield.
3. Remove the accessory drive belts. Refer to Section 1.
4. Remove the crankshaft pulley.
5. Remove the inner and outer timing belt guide plates.

6. Remove the 2 bolts and remove the upper timing belt cover assembly.

7. Remove the 1 bolt and remove the lower timing belt cover assembly and gasket.

To install:

8. Install the lower cover gasket and the lower cover. Tighten the bolt to 69–95 inch lbs. (8–11 Nm).

9. Install the upper cover gasket and the upper cover. Tighten the bolts to 69–95 inch lbs. (8–11 Nm).

10. Install the timing belt inner and outer guide plates. Make sure that the inner guide plate is installed in the proper direction.

11. Install the crankshaft pulley. Tighten the bolts to 109–152 inch lbs. (12–17 Nm).

12. Install the accessory drive belts. Refer to Section 1.

13. Install the under engine splash shield.

14. Connect the negative battery cable.

1.5L and 1995 1.6L DOHC Engines

▶ See Figure 139

1. Disconnect the negative battery cable.
2. Remove the engine under splash shield.
3. Drain the cooling system.
4. Remove the air intake pipe.
5. Disconnect the upper radiator hose and the 2 lower coolant hoses from the thermostat housing.
6. Remove the power steering, air conditioning and alternator drive belts. Refer to Section 1.
7. Remove the retaining bolts and remove the water pump pulley.
8. Remove the crankshaft pulley bolts and remove the crankshaft pulley.

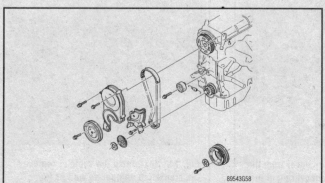

Fig. 137 Exploded view of the 1990–94 1.6L and 1.8L SOHC timing belt cover assembly

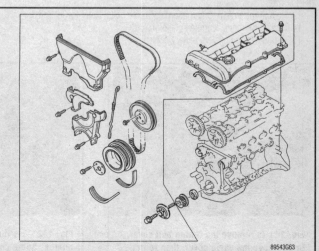

Fig. 139 Exploded view of the timing cover assembly for the 1.5L and 1995 1.6L engines—1995–98 1.8L engine is similar

9. Remove the inner and outer timing belt guide plates.

10. Disconnect the coil electrical connectors and remove coil assembly. Remove the spark plug wires. Be certain to record positioning of plug wires for assembly purposes.

11. Remove the spark plugs.

12. Remove the cylinder head cover bolts and remove the cover.

·13. Remove the bolts from the timing belt covers and remove the top, the center and the lower timing belt covers.

To install:

14. Install the timing belt covers with gaskets and tighten the bolts to 69–95 inch lbs. (8–11 Nm).

15. Apply silicone sealant to the corners of the cylinder head cover and install the cover. Tighten the bolts to 43–78 inch lbs. (5–9 Nm).

16. Install the spark plugs and tighten them to 11–17 ft. lbs. (15–23 Nm).

17. Install the coil assembly and connect the electrical connectors and the spark plug wires.

18. Install the inner and outer timing belt guide plates.

19. Install the crankshaft pulley and tighten the bolts to 109–152 inch lbs.(12–17 Nm).

20. Install the water pump pulley and tighten the bolts to 69–95 inch lbs. (8–11 Nm).

21. Install the power steering, air conditioning and alternator drive belts. Refer to Section 1.

22. Install the coolant and radiator hoses and refill the coolant to the proper level.

23. Install the air intake pipe and connect the negative battery cable.

1995–98 1.8L (except K8) DOHC Engines

▶ **See Figure 139**

1. Disconnect the negative battery cable.

2. Remove the engine under splash shield.

3. Remove the power steering, air conditioning and alternator drive belts. Refer to Section 1.

4. Remove the retaining bolts and remove the water pump pulley.

5. Remove the crankshaft pulley bolts and remove the crankshaft pulley.

6. Remove the inner and outer timing belt guide plates.

7. Remove the bolt and remove the upper timing belt cover assembly.

8. Remove the bolts from the middle and lower timing belt cover assembly and remove the covers and the gaskets.

To install:

9. Install the upper, the center and the lower timing belt covers. Tighten the bolts to 69–95 inch lbs. (8–11 Nm).

10. Install the timing belt inner and outer guide plates. Make sure that the inner guide plate is installed in the proper direction.

11. Install the crankshaft pulley. Tighten the bolts to 109–152 inch lbs. (12–17 Nm).

12. Install the water pump pulley and tighten the bolts to 69–95 inch lbs. (8–11 Nm).

13. Install the P/S, A/C and alternator drive belts. Refer to Section 1.

14. Install the under engine splash shield.

15. Connect the negative battery cable.

2.0L Engine

▶ **See Figures 140, 141, 142, 143 and 144**

1. Disconnect the negative battery cable.

2. Raise and safely support the vehicle. Remove the right front wheel.

3. Remove the engine under splash shield.

4. Remove the accessory drive belts. Refer to Section 1.

5. Remove the power steering pump pulley shield.

6. Remove the power steering pump, leaving the hoses attached and position the pump out of the way.

7. Remove the retaining bolts and remove the water pump pulley.

8. Remove the crankshaft pulley bolt and remove the pulley using a steering wheel puller.

9. Remove the spark plug wires, noting the original location of the wires for installation purposes. Disconnect the power steering hose from the cylinder head cover.

10. Remove the spark plugs and remove the cylinder head cover bolts. Remove the cylinder head cover with the gasket in place.

11. Remove the oil level dipstick bolt and remove the oil dipstick and plug the hole.

12. Remove the timing belt cover bolts and remove the upper and lower covers and the gaskets.

To install:

13. Install the timing covers with the gaskets in place. Install the timing cover bolts and tighten to 69–95 inch lbs. (8–11 Nm).

14. Install the bolt that secures the oil level dipstick and tighten the bolt to 69–95 inch lbs. (8–11 Nm).

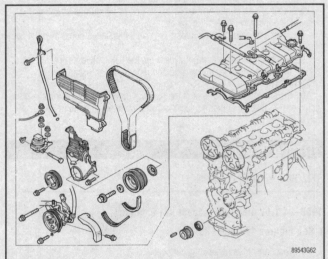

Fig. 140 Exploded view of the timing belt cover for the 2.0L engine

Fig. 141 To remove the timing belt cover, first remove the valve cover, then remove the upper belt cover attaching screws . . .

Fig. 142 . . . then pull the cover from the engine. Some careful maneuvering of the cover is required

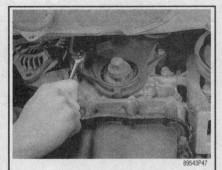

Fig. 143 Next, raise the vehicle, remove the crankshaft damper as well as the lower belt cover attaching screws . . .

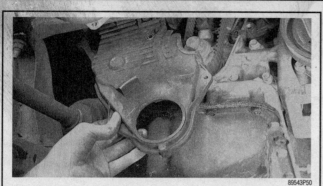

Fig. 144 . . . then pull the cover outward and down to remove it from the vehicle

15. Apply silicone sealant to the corners of the cylinder head cover and install the cylinder head cover to the engine and tighten the cylinder head bolts to 69–95 inch lbs. (8–11 Nm).

16. Install the spark plugs to the engine and connect the spark plug wires.

17. Install the crankshaft pulley, with the guide plate in place behind the pulley. Hold the pulley in place with special tool 49 E011 1A1 or equivalent and tighten the bolt to 116–123 ft. lbs. (157–167 Nm).

18. Install the water pump pulley and tighten the bolts to 69–95 inch lbs. (8–11 Nm).

19. Install the power steering pump. Tighten the upper bolt to 32–44 ft. lbs. (44–66 Nm) and the lower bolt to 24–33 ft. lbs. (32–46 Nm).

20. Install the power steering pump pulley shield and tighten the bolt to 60–87 inch lbs. (7–10 Nm).

21. Install the accessory belts and adjust as necessary. Refer to section One.

22. Install the under engine splash shield and install the right front wheel.

23. Lower the vehicle and connect the negative battery cable.

2.2L Engine

♦ See Figure 145

1. Disconnect the negative battery cable.
2. Remove the bolts and remove the engine side cover.
3. Remove the accessory drive belts, refer to section 1.
4. Remove the crankshaft pulley bolts and remove the crankshaft pulley.
5. Remove the timing cover bolts and remove the upper and lower covers.

To install:

6. Install the upper and lower timing belt covers with the gaskets. Tighten the bolts to 61–87 inch lbs. (7–10 Nm).

7. Install the crankshaft pulley and tighten the bolts to 109–153 inch lbs. (12–17 Nm).

8. Install the accessory drive belts, refer to section 1.

9. Install the engine side cover and connect the negative battery cable.

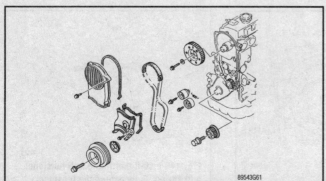

Fig. 145 Exploded view of the 2.2L engines timing belt cover assembly

1.8L (K8) and 2.5L Engines

♦ See Figure 146

1. Disconnect the negative battery cable.
2. Remove the engine under splash shield.
3. Remove the accessory drive belts. Refer to Section 1.
4. Remove the retaining bolts and remove the water pump pulley.
5. Remove the idler pulley bracket bolt and remove the idler pulley bracket.
6. Remove the power steering pump bolts and the pump as shown in section 8 (if necessary).
7. Remove the crankshaft pulley bolts and remove the pulley using a steering wheel puller.
8. Disconnect the crank angle sensor electrical connector and remove the clip from the oil dipstick tube. Remove the oil dipstick and plug the hole.
9. Remove the bolt from the knock sensor harness bracket.
10. Remove the 2 bolts that secure the engine harness to the timing cover.
11. Remove the remaining timing belt cover bolts and remove the covers and the gaskets.

To install:

12. Install the timing covers with the gaskets in place. Install the timing cover bolts and tighten to 69–95 inch lbs. (8–11 Nm).

13. Install the 2 bolts that secure the engine harness to the timing cover and tighten the bolts to 69–95 inch lbs. (8–11 Nm).

14. Install the knock sensor harness bracket to the timing cover and tighten the bolt to 69–95 inch lbs. (8–11 Nm).

15. Install the oil dipstick tube complete with a new O-ring. Install the crank angle sensor harness clip to the dipstick tube and connect the electrical connector.

16. Install the crankshaft pulley and loosely tighten the bolt. Hold the pulley in place with special tool 49 E011 1A1 or equivalent and tighten the bolt to 116–123 ft. lbs. (157–167 Nm).

17. Install the power steering fluid pump assembly and tighten the upper bolts to 23–34 ft. lbs. (31–46 Nm) and the lower bolt to 14–19 ft. lbs. (19–25 Nm).

18. Install the power steering pump pulley nut and tighten to 46–69 ft. lbs. (63–93 Nm). Connect the power steering fluid line bracket to the engine and tighten the bolts to 69–95 inch lbs. (7.8–11 Nm).

19. Connect the power steering pressure switch electrical connector and install the power steering oil reservoir and the engine ground.

20. Install the water pump pulley and the power steering idler pulley. Install the belts and tighten the pulley bolts to 69–95 inch lbs. (8–11 Nm).

21. Install the A/C belt and adjust as necessary. Refer to section One.

22. Install the under engine splash shield and connect the negative battery cable.

2.3L Engine

♦ See Figure 146

1. Disconnect the negative battery cable.

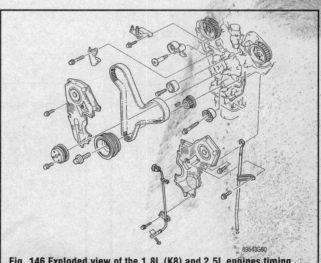

Fig. 146 Exploded view of the 1.8L (K8) and 2.5L engines timing belt cover assembly—2.3L engine is similar

✳✳ CAUTION

Never open, service or drain the radiator or cooling system when hot; serious burns can occur from the steam and hot coolant. Also, when draining engine coolant, keep in mind that cats and dogs are attracted to ethylene glycol antifreeze and could drink any that is left in an uncovered container or in puddles on the ground. This will prove fatal in sufficient quantities. Always drain coolant into a sealable container. Coolant should be reused unless it is contaminated or is several years old.

2. Drain the cooling system.
3. Loosen the lug nuts on the right front wheel.
4. Apply the parking brake, block the rear wheels, then raise and safely support the front of the vehicle securely on jackstands.
5. Remove the right front wheel.
6. Remove the engine under splash shield.
7. Remove the right-hand dust cover.
8. Loosen the water pump and power steering pump pulley attaching bolts.
9. Remove the accessory drive belts.
10. Remove the crankshaft pulley.
11. Unbolt and remove the power steering pump pulley.
12. Remove the water pump pulley attaching bolts and the pulley.
13. Remove the alternator belt auto tensioner pulley assembly.
14. Remove the camshaft position sensor.
15. Unbolt the engine oil dipstick tube and remove it from the engine. Plug the hole to keep debris from falling into the engine.
16. Unbolt and remove the vacuum pipe.
17. Remove the upper radiator hose.
18. Support the engine from underneath and remove the No. 3 (front) engine mount.
19. Remove the timing belt cover attaching bolts and remove the covers.

To install:
20. Inspect the dust seals on the belt covers and replace them as necessary.
21. Position the timing belt covers and install the attaching bolts. Tighten the bolts to 70–95 inch lbs. (8–11 Nm).
22. The remainder of the installation is the reverse of the removal procedure. Tighten all fasteners to specification.

Timing Belt and Sprockets

The timing belt should be replaced every 60,000 miles. Failure to replace the belt may result in damage to the engine.

REMOVAL & INSTALLATION

1990–94 1.6L and 1.8L (except K8) Engines

SOHC ENGINES

▶ See Figures 147, 148, 149, 150 and 151

1. Disconnect the negative battery cable. Remove the engine undercover.
2. Remove the accessory drive belts.

3. Remove the water pump pulley.
4. Remove the crankshaft pulley bolts and remove the crankshaft pulley and baffle plate. Using a suitable tool to hold the crankshaft pulley and remove the pulley lockbolt. Remove the crankshaft pulley boss.
5. Remove the upper and lower timing belt covers.
6. Tag and disconnect the spark plug wires. Remove the spark plugs.

➡Spark plugs are removed to make it easier to rotate the engine.

7. Temporarily reinstall the crankshaft pulley boss and lockbolt.
8. Turn the crankshaft, using the bolt, until the camshaft sprocket and crankshaft sprocket timing marks are aligned. Mark the direction of rotation on the timing belt.
9. Remove the belt tensioner lockbolt, the tensioner wheel and the spring. Remove the timing belt.

➡Do not rotate the engine after the timing belt has been removed.

10. Inspect the belt for wear, peeling, cracking, hardening or signs of oil contamination. Inspect the tensioner for free and smooth rotation. Check the tensioner spring free length; it should not exceed 2.520 in. (64mm). Inspect the sprocket teeth for wear or damage. Replace parts, as necessary.
11. If necessary to remove the sprockets:
    a. Insert a small prybar through one of the camshaft sprocket holes to keep it from turning.
    b. Remove the sprocket bolt and the sprocket from the camshaft.

To install:
12. Align the dowel on the camshaft with the dowel pin facing straight up. The dowel pin on the camshaft should also be facing upward.
13. Install the camshaft sprocket bolt. Hold the sprocket with the prybar and tighten the bolt(s) to 36–45 ft. lbs. (49–61 Nm).
14. Make sure the timing marks on the sprockets are properly aligned.
15. Install the timing belt tensioner and spring. Temporarily tighten the bolt with the spring fully extended.
16. Install the timing belt so there is no looseness on the tension side. If reusing the old timing belt, make sure it is reinstalled in the same direction of rotation.
17. Turn the crankshaft 2 turns clockwise and check the timing mark alignment. If the marks are not aligned, repeat Steps 11–14.
18. Loosen the tensioner lockbolt to set the tension, then torque the bolt to 19 ft. lbs. (25 Nm).
19. Turn the crankshaft 2 turns clockwise and check the alignment of the timing marks. If they are not aligned, repeat Steps 11–16.
20. Apply approximately 22 lbs. pressure to the timing belt on the side opposite the tensioner, at a point midway between the sprockets. The belt should deflect 0.43–0.51 in. (11–13mm). If the tension is not as specified, repeat Steps 14–17 or, if necessary, replace the tensioner spring.
21. Install the spark plugs and connect the spark plug wires.
22. Install the upper and lower timing belt covers. Tighten the bolts to 95 inch lbs. (11 Nm).
23. Install the crankshaft pulley boss and tighten the lockbolt to 123 ft. lbs. (167 Nm), while holding the pulley boss with a suitable tool.
24. Install the crankshaft pulley and baffle plate.
25. Install the undercover or side cover. Connect the negative battery cable.
26. Start the engine and check for proper operation. Check the ignition timing.

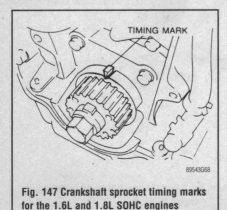

Fig. 147 Crankshaft sprocket timing marks for the 1.6L and 1.8L SOHC engines

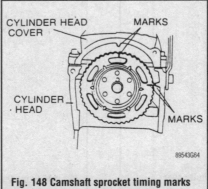

Fig. 148 Camshaft sprocket timing marks for the 1.6L and 1.8L SOHC engines

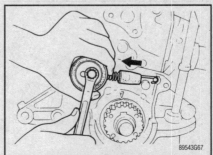

Fig. 149 Install the timing belt tensioner and spring. Fully extend the tensioner spring then tighten the bolt to hold the tensioner pulley

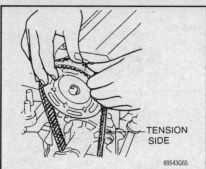

Fig. 150 When installing the belt, ensure that there is no looseness on the tension side of the belt

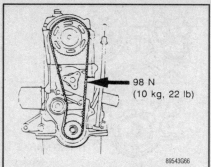

Fig. 151 Check timing belt deflection by applying pressure at the point shown, and measuring the deflection

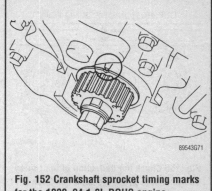

Fig. 152 Crankshaft sprocket timing marks for the 1990–94 1.8L DOHC engine

DOHC ENGINES

▶ **See Figures 152, 153, 154, 155 and 156**

1. Disconnect the negative battery cable. Remove the engine undercover.
2. Remove the accessory drive belts.
3. Remove the crankshaft pulley bolts and remove the crankshaft pulley.
4. Remove the outer timing belt guide plate. Remove the inner timing belt guide plate if so equipped.
5. Tag and disconnect the spark plug wires. Remove the spark plugs.

➡ **Spark plugs are removed to make it easier to rotate the engine.**

6. Remove the engine oil dipstick.
7. Remove the upper, middle and lower timing belt covers.
8. Turn the crankshaft until the timing marks on the crankshaft and camshaft sprockets are aligned. On 1993–94 vehicles, the pin on the pulley boss must face upward.
9. On 1993–94 vehicles, hold the crankshaft pulley boss with a suitable tool and remove the pulley lockbolt, being careful not to rotate the crankshaft. Remove the crankshaft pulley boss.
10. Mark the direction of rotation on the timing belt. Loosen the tensioner lockbolt and pry the tensioner outward. Tighten the lockbolt with the tensioner spring fully extended. Remove the timing belt.

➡ **Protect the tensioner with a shop towel before prying on it. Do not rotate the crankshaft after the timing belt has been removed.**

11. Remove the tensioner and spring. If necessary, remove the idler pulley.
12. Inspect the belt for wear, peeling, cracking, hardening or signs of oil contamination. Inspect the tensioner for free and smooth rotation. Check the tensioner spring free length; it should not exceed 2.315 in. (58.8mm). Inspect the sprocket teeth for wear or damage. Replace parts, as necessary.

To install:

13. If removed, install the idler pulley and tighten the bolt to 38 ft. lbs. (52 Nm).
14. Install the tensioner and tensioner spring. Pry the tensioner outward and temporarily tighten the tensioner lockbolt with the tensioner spring fully extended.

15. Make sure the crankshaft sprocket timing mark is aligned with the mark on the oil pump housing and the camshaft sprocket timing marks are aligned with the marks on the seal plate.
16. Install the timing belt so there is no looseness at the idler pulley side or between the camshaft sprockets. If reusing the old belt, make sure it is installed in the same direction of rotation.
17. On 1993–94 vehicles, temporarily install the pulley boss and lockbolt.
18. Turn the crankshaft 2 turns clockwise and align the crankshaft sprocket timing mark. On 1993–94 vehicles, face the pin on the pulley boss upright. Make sure the camshaft sprocket timing marks are aligned. If they are not, repeat Steps 15–19.
19. Turn the crankshaft 1⅚ turns clockwise and align the crankshaft sprocket timing mark with the tension set mark for proper belt tension adjustment. On 1992–94 vehicles, remove the lockbolt and pulley boss.
20. Make sure the crankshaft sprocket timing mark is aligned with the tension set mark. Loosen the tensioner lockbolt and allow the spring to apply tension to the belt. Tighten the tensioner lockbolt to 38 ft. lbs. (52 Nm).
21. On 1993–94 vehicles, install the pulley boss and lockbolt.
22. Turn the crankshaft 2⅙ turns clockwise and make sure the timing marks are correctly aligned.
23. Apply approximately 22 lbs. pressure to the timing belt at a point midway between the camshaft sprockets. The belt should deflect 0.35–0.45 in. (9.0–11.5mm). If the deflection is not correct, repeat Steps 21–24.
24. On 1993–94 vehicles, hold the pulley boss with a suitable tool and tighten the lockbolt to 123 ft. lbs. (167 Nm).
25. Install the timing belt covers and tighten the bolts to 95 inch lbs. (11 Nm). Install the engine oil dipstick.
26. Install the spark plugs and connect the spark plug wires.
27. Install the timing belt inner guide plate, if equipped. Make sure the dished side of the plate faces away from the timing belt. Install the outer guide plate, if equipped.
28. Install the crankshaft pulley and tighten the bolts to 13 ft. lbs. (17 Nm).
29. Install the water pump pulley and the accessory drive belts. Adjust the belt tension.

Fig. 153 Camshaft sprocket timing marks for the 1990–94 1.8L DOHC engine

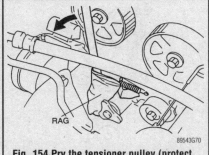

Fig. 154 Pry the tensioner pulley (protect it with a rag) outward to fully extend the spring, then tighten the bolt to hold it in position

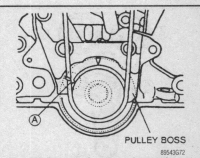

Fig. 155 To properly set tension on the belt, turn the crankshaft 1⅚ turns and align the tension set mark with the crankshaft sprocket

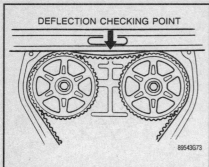

Fig. 156 Check the deflection of the timing belt to ensure proper tension has been set on the belt

Fig. 157 Cam and crankshaft sprocket alignment marks for the 1995 1.6L and 1995–98 1.8L (except K8) DOHC engines

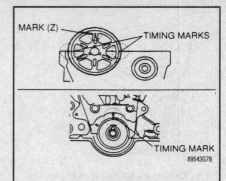

Fig. 158 Cam and crankshaft sprocket alignment marks for the 1.5L engine

30. Install the engine side or undercover, as necessary. Connect the negative battery cable.

31. Start the engine and check for proper operation. Check the ignition timing.

1995 1.6L, 1995–98 1.5L and 1.8L (except K8) DOHC Engines

♦ See Figures 155, 157 thru 162

1. Disconnect the negative battery cable.
2. Remove the timing belt covers.
3. Turn the crankshaft until the timing mark on the crankshaft sprocket aligns with the timing mark on the oil pump.
4. On the 1.5L engine, ensure that the **Z** mark on the camshaft sprocket is pointing straight up and the two notches are even with the valve cover gasket surface.
5. On the 1.6 and 1.8L engines, align the **E** and the **I** marks on the camshaft sprockets are aligned with the marks on the backing plate (they should point down and towards each other at approximately a 45° angle).

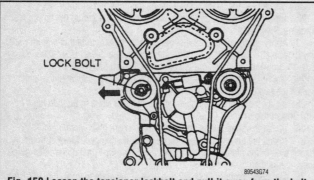

Fig. 159 Loosen the tensioner lockbolt and pull it away from the belt to reduce the tension on it

6. Remove the crankshaft pulley lockbolt and pulley boss.
7. Lower the vehicle. Insert a camshaft sprocket holding tool between the camshaft sprockets.
8. Loosen the tensioner pulley lockbolt. Pull the tensioner pulley away from the center of the engine to reduce the tension on the timing belt.
9. If the timing belt is to be reused, mark the direction of rotation on the timing belt. Remove the timing belt.
10. To remove the tensioner, unhook the tensioner spring, and remove the pulley lockbolt and tensioner.
11. If necessary to remove the sprockets:
   a. Hold the camshaft by using a wrench on the cast hexagon, and loosen the sprocket mounting bolt.
   b. Remove the sprocket bolt and the sprocket from the camshaft.
   c. If equipped with a manual transaxle, place the shift lever in **4th** gear and apply the parking brake. If equipped with an automatic transaxle, remove the flywheel dust cover and install a flywheel locking tool to hold the flywheel.
   d. Remove the crankshaft sprocket bolt, sprocket and key.

To install:

12. On the 1.5L engine, install the camshaft sprocket, aligning the dowel with the letter **Z** mark.
13. On the 1.6L and 1.8L engine, install the camshaft sprocket, aligning the dowel (which should be pointing straight up) with the letter **I** mark on the intake side, and the letter **E** mark on the exhaust side.
14. Install the camshaft sprocket bolt. Hold the camshaft, on the cast hexagon, with the wrench and tighten the bolt to 37–44 ft. lbs. (50–60 Nm).
15. Install the crankshaft sprocket and key. Align the keyway with the timing mark on the oil pump housing.
16. Install the crankshaft sprocket bolt. Install the flywheel locking tool, if equipped with automatic transaxle, or place the shift lever in **4th** gear and apply the parking brake, if equipped with manual transaxle. Tighten the bolt to 116–122 ft. lbs. (157–166 Nm).
17. Make sure the timing marks on the camshaft and crankshaft sprockets are still aligned.

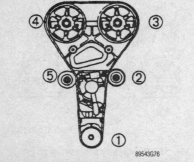

Fig. 160 Install the timing belt onto the sprockets following the numbered sequence for 1995 1.6L and 1995–98 1.8L engines

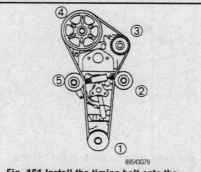

Fig. 161 Install the timing belt onto the sprockets following the numbered sequence for the 1.5L engine

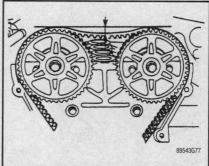

Fig. 162 Measure the timing belt deflection to determine if the proper tension has been set

18. If removed, position the tensioner with the spring fully extended, and install the lockbolt tightening the mounting bolt to 28–38 ft. lbs. (38–51 Nm).

19. Install the timing belt. If reusing the original timing belt, make sure it is installed in the same direction of rotation.

20. Rotate the crankshaft clockwise 1 ⅝ turns and align the timing marks. Make sure all marks are still correctly aligned.

21. Loosen the tensioner lockbolt to apply tension to the timing belt. Tighten the tensioner lockbolt to 28–38 ft. lbs. (38–51 Nm). Remove the holding tool from between the camshaft sprockets.

22. Rotate the crankshaft clockwise 2 ⅛ turns and make sure all marks are still correctly aligned.

23. Raise and safely support the vehicle. Install the crankshaft pulley lockbolt and boss. Tighten the bolt to 116–122 ft. lbs. (157–166 Nm).

24. Install the timing belt covers.

25. Connect the negative battery cable.

2.0L Engine

♦ See Figures 163 thru 175

1. Disconnect the negative battery cable.

2. Remove the timing belt covers. Temporarily reinstall the crankshaft pulley bolt.

3. Remove the front engine mount by supporting the engine then remove the mount attaching bolts and the mount.

4. Turn the crankshaft until the timing mark on the crankshaft sprocket aligns with the timing mark on the oil pump and the camshaft sprocket timing marks, **E** and **I**, line up on the camshaft sprockets.

5. Insert a camshaft sprocket holding tool between the camshaft sprockets.

6. Turn the timing belt tensioner with an Allen wrench and remove the tensioner spring from the hook pin.

7. If the timing belt is to be reused, mark the direction of rotation on the timing belt. Remove the timing belt.

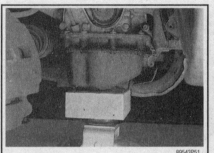

Fig. 163 To remove the timing belt, first remove the timing belt cover then, using a jack and block of wood, support the engine

Fig. 164 Next, loosen and remove the engine mount-to-engine block attaching bolts . . .

Fig. 165 . . . as well as the mount-to-body through-bolt . . .

Fig. 166 . . . and remove the engine mount

Fig. 167 Mark the direction of rotation on the timing belt in case you need to re-install the original belt

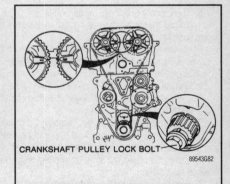

CRANKSHAFT PULLEY LOCK BOLT

Fig. 168 Cam and crankshaft sprocket alignment positions for the 2.0L engine

Fig. 169 Rotate the crankshaft until the timing marks (arrows) on the camshaft sprockets align with each other

Fig. 170 Loosen the lockbolt on the timing belt tensioner

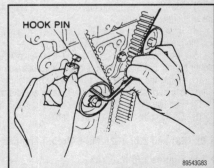

HOOK PIN

Fig. 171 Turn the timing belt tensioner with an Allen wrench and remove the tensioner spring from the hook pin

Fig. 172 Space may be limited when trying to turn the tensioner with the Allen wrench (arrow) . . .

Fig. 173 . . . or when trying to detach the tensioner spring from the hook pin (arrow)

Fig. 174 Remove the timing belt from the sprockets and examine it. Refer to Section 1 for examples

Fig. 175 If necessary, or in case of high mileage, remove the tensioner pulley by removing the lockbolt

8. If necessary to remove the sprockets:

a. Hold the camshaft by using a wrench on the cast hexagon, and loosen the sprocket mounting bolt.

b. Remove the sprocket bolt and the sprocket from the camshaft.

c. If equipped with a manual transaxle, place the shift lever in **4th** gear and apply the parking brake. If equipped with an automatic transaxle, remove the flywheel dust cover and install a flywheel locking tool to hold the flywheel.

d. Remove the crankshaft sprocket bolt, sprocket and key.

To install:

9. Install the camshaft sprocket, aligning the dowel with the number **1** mark.

10. Install the camshaft sprocket bolt. Hold the camshaft, on the cast hexagon, with the wrench and tighten the bolt to 35–48 ft. lbs. (47–65 Nm).

11. Install the crankshaft sprocket and key. Align the keyway with the timing mark on the oil pump housing.

12. Install the crankshaft sprocket bolt. Install the flywheel locking tool, if equipped with automatic transaxle, or place the shift lever in **4th** gear and apply the parking brake, if equipped with manual transaxle. Tighten the bolt to 108–116 ft. lbs. (147–157 Nm).

13. Make sure the timing marks on the camshaft and crankshaft sprockets are still aligned.

14. Install the timing belt. If reusing the original timing belt, make sure it is installed in the same direction of rotation.

15. Turn the tensioner clockwise with an Allen wrench and install the tensioner spring. Remove the holding tool from between the camshaft sprockets.

16. Rotate the crankshaft 2 turns in the normal direction of rotation and align the timing marks. Make sure all marks are still correctly aligned.

17. Remove the crankshaft pulley bolt and install the timing belt covers.

18. Connect the negative battery cable.

1.8L (K8) and 2.5L (626/MX-6/Probe) Engines

▶ See Figures 176 thru 185

1. Disconnect the negative battery cable.

2. Support the engine, and remove the nuts and through-bolt from the right side engine mount Remove the mount.

3. Remove the timing belt covers. Temporarily reinstall the crankshaft pulley bolt.

4. Turn the crankshaft until the timing mark on the crankshaft sprocket aligns with the timing mark on the oil pump and the camshaft sprocket timing marks align with the marks on the cylinder head. The number one piston should be at TDC of the compression stroke.

5. Remove the 2 bolts from the automatic tensioner, removing the lower one first. Keep the bolt holes aligned by holding the tensioner to reduce the chance of stripping the threads on the bolts.

6. If the timing belt is to be reused, mark the direction of rotation on the timing belt.

7. Remove the number one idler pulley. Remove the timing belt.

8. If necessary, remove the sprockets as follows:

a. Insert a proper tool through one of the camshaft sprocket holes to keep it from turning.

b. Remove the sprocket bolt and the sprocket from the camshaft.

c. If equipped with a manual transaxle, place the shift lever in **4th** gear and apply the parking brake. If equipped with an automatic transaxle, remove the flywheel dust cover and install a flywheel locking tool to hold the flywheel.

d. Remove the crankshaft sprocket bolt, sprocket and key.

To install:

9. Install the camshaft sprockets (which are marked (R) Right and (L) Left), aligning the dowel on the camshaft with the slot on the sprocket.

10. Install the camshaft sprocket bolt. Hold the sprocket with a suitable tool and tighten the bolt to 35–48 ft. lbs. (47–65 Nm).

11. Install the crankshaft sprocket and key. Align the keyway with the timing mark on the oil pump housing.

12. Install the crankshaft sprocket bolt. Install the flywheel locking tool, if equipped with automatic transaxle, or place the shift lever in **4th** gear and apply the parking brake, if equipped with manual transaxle. Tighten the bolt to 116–122 ft. lbs. (157–166 Nm).

13. Position the automatic tensioner in a suitable press. Set a flat washer under the tensioner body to prevent damage to the body plug.

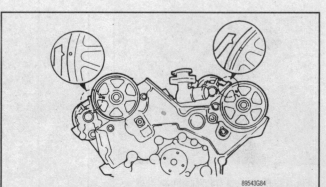

Fig. 176 Camshaft sprocket alignment marks for the 1.8L (K8) and 2.5L engines

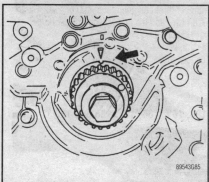

Fig. 177 Crankshaft sprocket alignment marks for the 1.8L (K8) and 2.5L engines

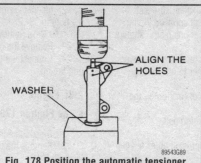

Fig. 178 Position the automatic tensioner in a press and set a flat washer under the tensioner body to prevent damage to the body plug

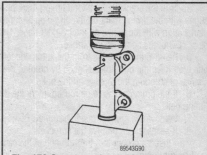

Fig. 179 Compress the tensioner until the hole in the piston is aligned with the 2nd hole in the case. Insert a pin to keep it compressed

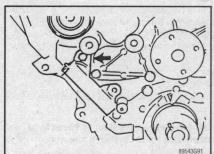

Fig. 180 Install the tensioner to the engine and snugly tighten the upper bolt. This will reduce belt tension when installing the upper idler

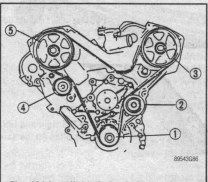

Fig. 181 Install the timing belt onto the sprockets in the sequence shown

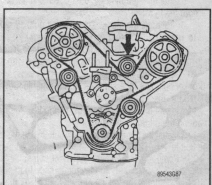

Fig. 182 Then install the upper idler pulley while pushing downward on the belt

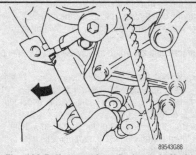

Fig. 183 Pull outward on the lower half of the tensioner and install the lower mounting bolt. Tighten both bolts to specification

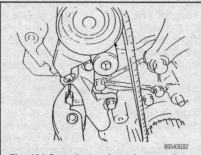

Fig. 184 Once the tensioner is properly tightened, remove the pin which is holding the piston compressed in the tensioner case

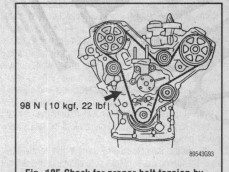

Fig. 185 Check for proper belt tension by measuring the belt deflection at the point indicated

14. Compress the tensioner until the hole in the piston is aligned with the 2nd hole in the tensioner case. Insert a 0.063 in. (1.6mm) diameter wire or pin through the 2nd hole to keep the piston compressed.

15. Make sure the camshaft sprocket timing marks are still aligned. Turn the crankshaft counterclockwise until the timing sprocket is offset from TDC by 1 tooth.

16. With the number one idler pulley removed, install the timing belt. If the original belt is being reused, make sure it is installed in the same direction of rotation. The order of installation is: timing belt (crankshaft) sprocket, number two idler pulley, LH camshaft sprocket, tensioner pulley and RH camshaft sprocket.

17. Install the number one idler pulley while applying pressure on the timing belt. Tighten the bolt to 28–38 ft. lbs. (38–51 Nm).

18. Install the automatic belt tensioner and tighten the bolts to 14–18 ft. lbs. (19–25 Nm). Remove the wire or pin from the tensioner.

19. Rotate the crankshaft 2 turns in the normal direction of rotation and align the timing marks. Make sure all marks are still correctly aligned.

20. Inspect the timing belt deflection, 0.24–0.31 ft. lbs. (6–8mm), between the crankshaft sprocket and the tensioner pulley. If it is out of specification, replace the auto tensioner.

21. Remove the crankshaft damper bolt and install the timing belt covers.

22. Install the right side engine mount. Tighten the nuts to 55–77 ft. lbs. (75–104 Nm) and the through-bolt to 63–86 ft. lbs. (86–116 Nm). Remove the engine support.

23. Connect the negative battery cable.

2.5L (Millenia) Engine

▶ See Figures 176 thru 185

1. Disconnect the negative battery cable.

2. Remove the timing belt covers. Temporarily reinstall the crankshaft pulley bolt.

3. Support the engine, and remove the nuts and through-bolt from the right side (number three) engine mount sub bracket. Remove the sub bracket.

4. Turn the crankshaft until the timing mark on the crankshaft sprocket aligns with the timing mark on the oil pump and the camshaft sprocket timing marks align with the marks on the cylinder head. The number one piston should be at TDC of the compression stroke.

5. Remove the two bolts from the automatic tensioner, removing the lower one first. Keep the bolt holes aligned by holding the tensioner to reduce the chance of stripping the threads on the bolts.

6. If the timing belt is to be reused, mark the direction of rotation on the timing belt.

7. Remove the number one idler pulley. Remove the timing belt.

8. If necessary to remove the sprockets:

a. Insert a proper tool through one of the camshaft sprocket holes to keep it from turning.

➡**The right and left camshaft sprockets are different and need to be installed on the same camshaft from which they were removed.**

b. Remove the sprocket bolt and the sprocket from the camshaft.

c. Remove the flywheel dust cover and install a flywheel locking tool to hold the flywheel.

d. Remove the crankshaft sprocket bolt, sprocket and key.

To install:

9. Install the camshaft sprocket so that the **R** (on right-hand) and **L** (on left-hand) face out, and align the timing marks with the knock/dowel pin.

10. Apply clean engine oil to the bolt threads, and install the camshaft sprocket bolt. Hold the sprocket with a suitable tool and tighten the bolt to 91–103 ft. lbs. (123–140 Nm).

11. Install the crankshaft sprocket and key. Align the keyway with the timing mark on the oil pump housing.

12. Install the crankshaft sprocket bolt. Install the flywheel locking tool. Tighten the bolt to 116–122 ft. lbs. (157–166 Nm). remove the flywheel locking tool.

13. Position the automatic tensioner in a suitable press. Set a flat washer under the tensioner body to prevent damage to the body plug.

14. Compress the tensioner until the hole in the piston is aligned with the 2nd hole in the tensioner case. Insert a 0.060 in. (1.6 mm) diameter wire or pin through the 2nd hole to keep the piston compressed.

15. Make sure the camshaft sprocket timing marks are still aligned. Turn the crankshaft counterclockwise until the timing sprocket is aligned.

16. With the number one idler pulley removed, install the timing belt. If the original belt is being reused, make sure it is installed in the same direction of rotation. The order of installation is: timing belt (crankshaft) sprocket, number two idler pulley, LH camshaft sprocket, tensioner pulley and RH camshaft sprocket.

17. Install the number one idler pulley while applying pressure on the timing belt. Tighten the bolt to 28–38 ft. lbs. (38–51 Nm).

18. Install the automatic belt tensioner and tighten the bolts to 14–18 ft. lbs. (19–25 Nm). Remove the wire or pin from the tensioner.

19. Turn the crankshaft clockwise, until the crankshaft sprocket timing mark is again at TDC. This should place all of the belt slack in the automatic tensioner portion of the belt.

20. Rotate the crankshaft 2 turns in the normal direction of rotation and align the timing marks. Make sure all marks are still correctly aligned.

21. Inspect the timing belt deflection, 0.24–0.31 in. (6–8 mm), between the crankshaft sprocket and the tensioner pulley. If it is out of specification, replace the auto tensioner.

22. Install the right side (number three) engine mount sub bracket. Tighten the nuts to 55–77 ft. lbs. (75–104 Nm) and the through-bolt to 63–86 ft. lbs. (86–116 Nm). Remove the engine support.

23. Remove the crankshaft damper bolt and install the timing belt covers.

24. Connect the negative battery cable. Start the engine, and check the ignition timing.

2.3L Engine

⬥ See Figures 178, 179, 180, 184, 186, 187, 188 and 189

1. Disconnect the negative battery cable.

2. Remove the timing belt covers. Temporarily reinstall the crankshaft pulley bolt.

3. Remove the power steering auto tensioner and pulley.

4. Turn the crankshaft until the timing mark on the crankshaft sprocket aligns with the timing mark on the oil pump and the camshaft sprocket timing marks align with the marks on the cylinder head. The number one piston should be at TDC of the compression stroke.

5. Remove the two bolts from the automatic tensioner, removing the lower one first. Keep the bolt holes aligned by holding the tensioner to reduce the chance of stripping the threads on the bolts.

6. If the timing belt is to be reused, mark the direction of rotation on the timing belt.

7. Remove the timing belt.

8. If necessary to remove the sprockets:

a. Insert a proper tool through one of the camshaft sprocket holes to keep it from turning.

➡**The right and left camshaft sprockets are different and need to be installed on the same camshaft from which they were removed.**

b. Remove the sprocket bolt and the sprocket from the camshaft.

c. Remove the flywheel dust cover and install a flywheel locking tool to hold the flywheel.

d. Remove the crankshaft sprocket bolt, sprocket and key.

To install:

9. Install the camshaft sprocket so that the **R** (on right-hand) and **L** (on left-hand) face out, and align the timing marks with the knock/dowel pin.

10. Apply clean engine oil to the bolt threads, and install the camshaft sprocket bolt. Hold the sprocket with a suitable tool and tighten the bolt to 91–103 ft. lbs. (123–140 Nm).

11. Install the crankshaft sprocket and key. Align the keyway with the timing mark on the oil pump housing.

12. Install the crankshaft sprocket bolt. Install the flywheel locking tool. Tighten the bolt to 116–122 ft. lbs. (157–166 Nm). remove the flywheel locking tool.

13. Position the automatic tensioner in a press. Set a flat washer under the tensioner body to prevent damage to the body plug.

14. Compress the tensioner until the hole in the piston is aligned with the 2nd hole in the tensioner case. Insert a 0.063 inch (1.6 mm) diameter wire or pin through the 2nd hole to keep the piston compressed.

15. Make sure the camshaft sprocket timing marks are still aligned. Turn the crankshaft clockwise until the timing sprocket is aligned.

16. Install the timing belt. If the original belt is being reused, make sure it is installed in the same direction of rotation. The order of installation is: timing

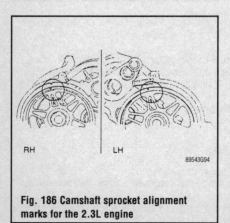

Fig. 186 Camshaft sprocket alignment marks for the 2.3L engine

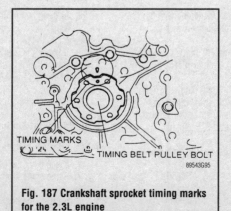

Fig. 187 Crankshaft sprocket timing marks for the 2.3L engine

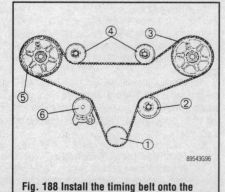

Fig. 188 Install the timing belt onto the sprockets in the sequence shown

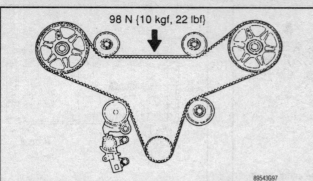

98 N {10 kgf, 22 lbf}

89543G97

Fig. 189 Inspect the timing belt tension by measuring the deflection at the point shown

belt (crankshaft) sprocket, number two idler pulley, LH camshaft sprocket, both number one idler pulleys, RH camshaft sprocket and the tensioner pulley.

17. Install the automatic belt tensioner and tighten the bolts to 14–18 ft. lbs. (19–25 Nm). Remove the wire or pin from the tensioner.

18. Turn the crankshaft clockwise, until the crankshaft sprocket timing mark is again at TDC. This should place all of the belt slack in the automatic tensioner portion of the belt.

19. Rotate the crankshaft two turns in the normal direction of rotation and align the timing marks. Make sure all marks are still correctly aligned.

20. Inspect the timing belt deflection, 0.24–0.31 inches (6–8 mm), between the crankshaft sprocket and the tensioner pulley. If it is out of specification, replace the auto tensioner.

21. Install the power steering auto tensioner and tighten the bolts to 14–18 ft. lbs. (19–25 Nm). Install the pulley, and tighten the bolt to 29–34 ft. lbs. (40–47 Nm).

22. Remove the crankshaft damper bolt and install the timing belt covers.

23. Connect the negative battery cable. Start the engine, and check the ignition timing.

Camshaft

REMOVAL & INSTALLATION

Camshaft

1.5L ENGINE

▶ **See Figures 190 thru 195**

1. Disconnect the negative battery cable.
2. Remove the power steering hose brackets from the cylinder head cover.
3. Label and disconnect the spark plug wires and spark plug wire clips.
4. Disconnect the breather tube and PCV valve from the cylinder head cover. Loosen the cylinder head cover in 2–3 steps. Remove the cylinder head cover.
5. Remove the accessory drive belts, water pump pulley, timing belt covers and timing belt.
6. Remove the distributor.
7. Hold the camshaft with a wrench on the cast hexagon, and loosen the camshaft sprocket mounting bolt. Remove the camshaft sprockets.
8. Remove the seal plate.
9. Rotate the camshafts clockwise so the cams don't press on the tappets.
10. Loosen the front camshaft cap bolts in 5–6 steps, starting on the two outside bolts and finishing on the two inside bolts. Remove the front camshaft bolts and caps.

➡**Note the location of the numbers on top of the camshaft caps, so the caps can be reinstalled in their original positions.**

11. Loosen the camshaft cap bolts in 5–6 steps, in the reverse order of removal. Remove the camshaft caps.
12. Remove the camshafts. Remove the chain and oil seals from the camshafts.

To install:

13. Insert the chain adjuster between the camshafts.

14. Lubricate the camshaft lobes and journals with clean engine oil and install the camshafts on the cylinder head. Make sure none of the lobes are located directly on the tappets. Align the marks on the camshaft gear and the timing chain.

15. Apply silicone sealant to the cylinder head on the front camshaft caps mating surface. Do not get sealant on the camshaft journals.

16. Install the camshaft bearing caps in their original locations. Hand tighten the camshaft cap bolts numbered: 5, 7, 2, and 4. Install all the bolts and tighten, in sequence, in 5–6 steps with a final torque of 100–125 inch lbs. (11–14 Nm).

17. Apply clean engine oil to the lips of new camshafts seals. Install the seals using a suitable seal installer flush with the edge of the camshaft cap.

18. Install the seal plate.

19. Install the camshaft sprockets, timing belt and timing belt covers. Install the water pump pulley and accessory drive belts. Adjust the tension.

20. Apply silicone sealant to a new cylinder head cover gasket, and install the gasket on the cylinder head cover.

21. Apply silicone sealant to the cylinder head in the area adjacent to the front camshaft caps.

22. Install the distributor.

23. Install the cylinder head cover. Tighten the bolts in 2 steps, in reverse of the loosening sequence, to 61–95 inch lbs. (7–11 Nm).

24. Install the power steering hose brackets and tighten the bolts to 88 inch lbs. (10 Nm). Connect the spark plug wires and clips.

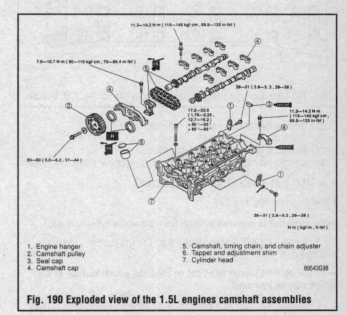

1. Engine hanger
2. Camshaft pulley
3. Seal cap
4. Camshaft cap
5. Camshaft, timing chain, and chain adjuster
6. Tappet and adjustment shim
7. Cylinder head

89543G98

Fig. 190 Exploded view of the 1.5L engines camshaft assemblies

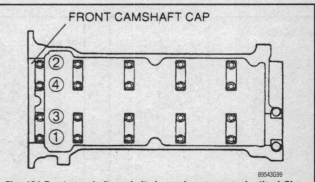

FRONT CAMSHAFT CAP

89543G99

Fig. 191 Front camshaft cap bolts loosening sequence for the 1.5L engine

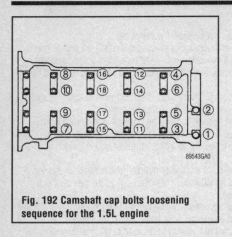

Fig. 192 Camshaft cap bolts loosening sequence for the 1.5L engine

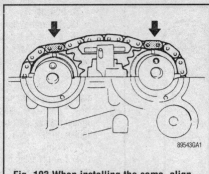

Fig. 193 When installing the cams, align the marks on the camshaft gears with the colored/marked links of the chain

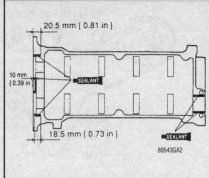

Fig. 194 Apply sealant in the positions shown before installing the cam caps

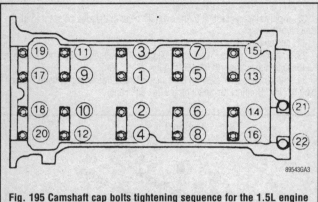

Fig. 195 Camshaft cap bolts tightening sequence for the 1.5L engine

25. Connect the breather hose and PCV valve.
26. Adjust the valve clearance.
27. Adjust the ignition timing and idle speed.
28. Connect the negative battery cable, run the engine and check for leaks.

1.6L AND 1.8L (EXCEPT K8) SOHC ENGINES

▶ **See Figures 196 and 197**

➡**The camshaft is removed through the front of the cylinder head.**

1. Remove the cylinder head from the vehicle and position in a suitable holding fixture.

➡**Do not lay the cylinder head flat on the head gasket surface as the valves may be damaged.**

2. Hold the camshaft with a wrench on the hexagon cast into the front of the camshaft.

3. Remove the sprocket bolt and the sprocket.
4. Loosen the rocker arm shaft bolts in 2–3 steps, in the reverse of the torque sequence. Remove the rocker arm and shaft assemblies.
5. Pry out the camshaft seal using a small prybar, being careful not to damage the camshaft or seal bore.
6. Remove the thrust plate at the rear of the cylinder head.
7. Carefully slide the camshaft from the cylinder head, being careful not to damage the cylinder head bearing surfaces.

To install:

8. Lubricate the camshaft lobes and journals and the cylinder head bearing surfaces with clean engine oil.
9. Carefully slide the camshaft into the cylinder head, being careful not to damage the bearing surfaces.
10. Install the camshaft thrust plate. On the 1.6L 8-valve engine, tighten the thrust retaining bolt to 95 in. lbs. (11 Nm). On the 1.6L and 1.8L 16-valve engines, the thrust plate is held in place by the rocker arm and shaft assembly.
11. Lubricate the lip of a new camshaft seal with clean engine oil and install in the cylinder head, using a seal installer.
12. Lubricate the rocker arms and valve stem tips with clean engine oil. Install the rocker arm and shaft assemblies and tighten the bolts, in 2–3 steps, in the proper sequence. The final torque should be 21 ft. lbs. (28 Nm) on the 1.6L and 1.8L engines.
13. Install the camshaft sprocket and retaining bolt. Hold the camshaft with the wrench on the hexagon and tighten the bolt to 45 ft. lbs. (61 Nm).
14. Install the cylinder head and the remaining components in the reverse order of removal.

1.6L, 1.8L AND 2.0L DOHC ENGINES

▶ **See Figures 198 thru 206**

1. Disconnect the negative battery cable.
2. Label and disconnect the spark plug wires and remove the spark plugs.
3. Disconnect the hoses from the cylinder head cover, if equipped.

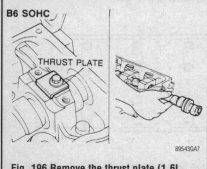

Fig. 196 Remove the thrust plate (1.6L SOHC engine) then slide the camshaft out of the cylinder head

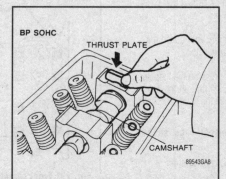

Fig. 197 Thrust plate removal for the 1.8L SOHC engine

Fig. 198 To remove the camshafts, first remove the timing belt, then while holding the cam on the cast hexagon, loosen the cam sprocket bolt

Fig. 199 Remove the camshaft sprocket bolt and sprocket

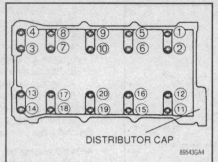

Fig. 200 Camshaft cap bolts loosening sequence for the 1.6L, 1.8L and 2.0L DOHC engines

Fig. 201 Loosen the camshaft cap bolts gradually in 2–3 steps in sequence

Fig. 202 Once the cap bolts are loose, remove them. Keep the caps in order and do not mix up intake and exhaust sides

Fig. 203 Also remove the camshaft seals and discard them. Always install new seals whenever the camshafts are removed

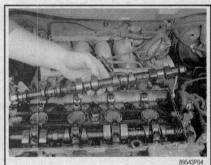

Fig. 204 Remove the camshafts from the cylinder head. Again, do not mix up exhaust and intake sides

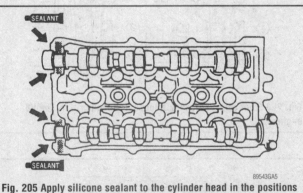

Fig. 205 Apply silicone sealant to the cylinder head in the positions shown

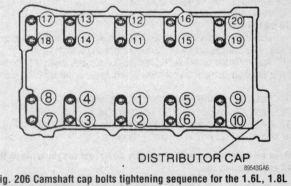

Fig. 206 Camshaft cap bolts tightening sequence for the 1.6L, 1.8L and 2.0L DOHC engine

4. Remove the cylinder head cover bolts and remove the cylinder head cover. On 2.0L engine, loosen the bolts in 2–3 steps in the reverse of the torque sequence.

5. Remove the timing belt and the distributor.

6. Hold the camshaft with a wrench on the hexagon cast into the camshaft. Remove the sprocket bolts and remove the sprockets.

7. Label the caps so they can be reinstalled in their original positions. Loosen the camshaft cap bolts in 2–3 steps in the reverse of the torque sequence, then remove the camshaft caps.

8. Remove the camshafts. Remove the camshaft oil seals from the camshafts.

To install:

9. Lubricate the camshaft journals and lobes with clean engine oil. Install the camshafts in the cylinder head.

10. Apply silicone sealant to the cylinder head on the front camshaft cap mating surfaces. Do not allow any sealant on the camshaft journals.

11. Install the camshaft caps in their original positions. Loosely install the cap bolts.

12. Tighten the camshaft cap bolts in 2–3 steps to 125 inch lbs. (14 Nm) in the proper sequence.

13. Apply clean engine oil to the lip of a new camshaft seal. Push the seal slightly in by hand. Tap the seal into position, using a seal installer, until it is flush with the edge of the camshaft cap.

14. Turn the camshafts until the dowel pins face straight up. Install the camshaft sprockets and the sprocket bolts.

15. Hold the camshaft with the wrench on the cast hexagon and tighten the sprocket bolts to 44 ft. lbs. (60 Nm).

16. Install the remaining components in the reverse order of removal.

2.2L ENGINE

▶ See Figure 207

1. Disconnect the negative battery cable.

2. Disconnect the spark plug wires and hoses from the cylinder head cover and remove the cylinder head cover.

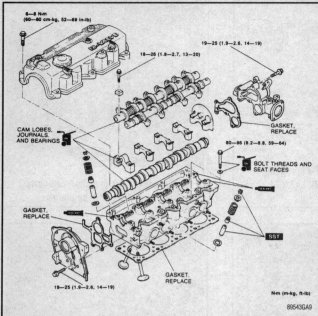

Fig. 207 Exploded view of the 2.2L engine camshaft assembly and related components

3. Remove the timing belt and the distributor.

4. Insert a suitable tool through one of the camshaft sprocket holes to keep the camshaft from turning. Remove the sprocket bolt and remove the sprocket.

5. Remove the front and rear housings from the cylinder head.

6. Loosen the rocker arm shaft bolts, in 2–3 steps, in the reverse of the torque sequence. Remove the rocker arm and shaft assemblies with the bolts.

7. Remove the camshaft caps. Label their position prior to removal so they can be reinstalled in their original locations.

8. Remove the camshaft.

To install:

9. Lubricate the camshaft journals and lobes with clean engine oil and position in the cylinder head with the dowel pin facing straight up.

10. Apply silicone sealant the cylinder head in the area adjacent to the front and rear camshaft journals. Do not allow sealant to get on the camshaft journals.

11. Install the camshaft caps in their original locations.

12. Apply clean engine oil to the valve stem tips and rocker arms.

13. Install the rocker arm and shaft assemblies. Tighten the bolts in 2–3 steps to 20 ft. lbs. (26 Nm) in the proper sequence.

➡ **Make sure the rocker arms or spacers do not get caught between the shaft and camshaft cap.**

14. Pry the old oil seal from the front housing. Apply engine oil to the front housing and a new oil seal and press the seal into the housing.

15. Install the front housing using a new gasket. Tighten the bolt and nut to 19 ft. lbs. (25 Nm).

16. Install the rear housing using a new gasket. Tighten the bolts/nuts to 19 ft. lbs. (25 Nm).

17. Apply silicone sealant at the front and rear corners of the cylinder head and install the cylinder head cover. Tighten the bolts to 69 inch lbs. (8 Nm). Connect the hoses and spark plug wires.

18. Install the camshaft sprocket on the camshaft with the sprocket bolt. Hold the camshaft sprocket using a suitable tool inserted through a sprocket hole and tighten the bolt to 48 ft. lbs. (65 Nm).

19. Install the timing belt and the remaining components in the reverse order of removal.

1.8L (K8) AND 2.5L ENGINES

♦ **See Figures 208 thru 213**

1. Properly relieve the fuel system pressure. Disconnect the negative battery cable and drain the cooling system.

2. Remove the timing belt.

3. Disconnect the accelerator cable. On 1.8L engine, disconnect the throttle cable.

4. Label and disconnect the spark plug wires.

5. Label and disconnect the necessary wiring and hoses.

6. Remove the intake manifold and the cylinder head covers.

7. Remove the distributor.

8. Hold the camshaft with a wrench on the hexagon cast into the camshaft. Remove the sprocket bolt and remove the sprocket.

9. Turn the camshaft, using a wrench on the cast hexagon, until the camshaft knock pin is aligned with the cylinder head marks.

➡ **Do not remove the camshaft caps when the camshaft lobe is pressing on a lifter, as the thrust journal support may become damaged.**

10. Loosen the front camshaft cap bolts in 5–6 steps, in the proper sequence. Bolt **A** is only on the right cylinder head. Remove the front camshaft cap.

11. Mark the position of the camshaft caps so they can be reinstalled in their original locations. Loosen the remaining camshaft cap bolts in 5–6 steps, in the proper sequence, then remove the caps.

12. Remove the camshafts.

To install:

13. Lubricate the camshaft journals, lobes and gears with clean engine oil. Align the intake and exhaust camshaft timing marks and install the camshafts.

➡ **The thrust plate positions for the right and left cylinder head camshafts are different.**

14. Make sure the camshaft cap and cylinder head surfaces are clean. Apply a small amount of sealant to the mating surface of the front camshaft cap on

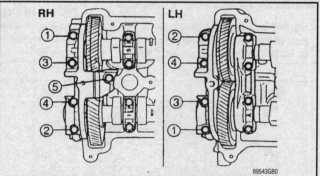

Fig. 208 Front camshaft cap bolt loosening sequence for the V6 engines

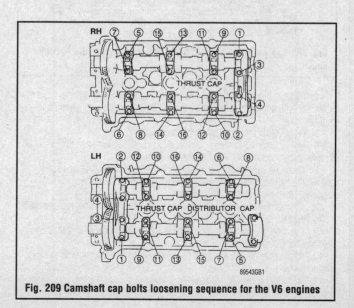

Fig. 209 Camshaft cap bolts loosening sequence for the V6 engines

Fig. 210 When installing the camshafts, ensure that the marks on the cam gears are aligned

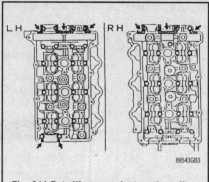

Fig. 211 Put silicone sealant on the cylinder head at the positions shown

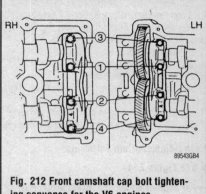

Fig. 212 Front camshaft cap bolt tightening sequence for the V6 engines

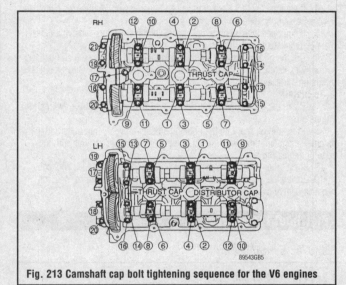

Fig. 213 Camshaft cap bolt tightening sequence for the V6 engines

both cylinder heads and the rear exhaust camshaft cap on the left cylinder head. Do not get any sealant on the camshaft rotating surfaces.

15. Install the front camshaft caps and thrust plate caps and tighten the bolts until the cap seats fully to the cylinder head. Install the remaining camshaft caps in their original locations and loosely tighten the bolts.

16. Tighten the camshaft cap bolts in 5–6 steps to 126 inch lbs. (14 Nm), in the proper sequence.

17. Apply clean engine oil to a new oil seal and the cylinder head. Install the seal, using a suitable installer. Apply sealant to a new blind cap and install, using a plastic hammer.

18. Install the camshaft sprockets. On the right cylinder head, install the sprocket so the **R** mark can be seen and the timing mark aligns with the camshaft knock pin. On the left cylinder head, install the sprocket so the **L** mark can be seen and the timing mark aligns with the camshaft knock pin.

19. Apply clean engine oil to the camshaft sprocket bolt threads and install. Hold the camshaft with a wrench on the cast hexagon and tighten the sprocket bolt to 103 ft. lbs. (140 Nm).

20. Coat a new gasket with sealant and install onto the cylinder head cover. Install the cover and tighten the bolts, in sequence, in 2–3 steps, to 78 inch lbs. (8.8 Nm). Install the ventilation pipe to the left cover.

21. Apply clean engine oil to a new O-ring and install on the distributor. Install the distributor with the blade fitting into the camshaft groove and loosely tighten the retaining bolt.

22. Install the intake manifold using a new gasket. Loosely install the bolts and nuts. Install the intake manifold stay and tighten the bolts to 19 ft. lbs. (25 Nm), then tighten the intake manifold bolts/nuts, in 2–3 steps, to 19 ft. lbs. (25 Nm).

23. Connect the wiring, hoses, and the fuel lines.

24. Connect the accelerator and, if equipped, throttle valve cables.

25. Install the timing belt.

26. Connect the negative battery cable. Fill and bleed the cooling system.

27. Start the engine and bring to normal operating temperature. Check for leaks. Check the ignition timing and idle speed.

2.3L ENGINE

▶ See Figures 208 thru 213

1. Relieve the fuel system pressure. Disconnect the negative battery cable.

2. Remove the timing belt covers and timing belt.

3. Remove the spacer and O-ring from the front of the camshaft.

4. Remove the ignition coils.

5. Remove the intake manifold.

6. Remove the bolts, in 5–6 steps, using the reverse of the tightening sequence. Remove the cylinder head cover.

7. Remove the camshaft sprockets.

8. Turn the camshafts so the knock pins are aligned with the marks on the camshaft caps. This will reduce the pressure on the adjustment shims.

9. Note the markings on the camshaft caps prior to removal, so they can be reinstalled in the same positions. The right hand (rear) caps are marked with numbers and the left hand (front) caps are marked with letters.

10. Loosen the front camshaft cap bolts in the reverse of the torque sequence, in 5–6 steps. Remove the front camshaft caps.

11. Remove the remaining camshaft cap bolts in the proper sequence. Remove the caps, being sure to remove the thrust caps last. Do not damage the cylinder head thrust bearing support.

12. Remove the camshafts and oil seals.

13. If necessary, remove the lifters and adjustment shims. Identify and mark each lifter as it is removed so it can be reinstalled in the same position.

To install:

14. Apply clean engine oil to the lifters, then install them in their original positions. Verify that they move smoothly in their bore.

15. Install new oil seals on the camshafts. Apply clean engine oil to the camshaft lobes, journals and supports.

16. Install the camshafts so the gear marks align.

17. Remove all oil and dirt from the mating surfaces between the front camshaft cap and the cylinder head.

18. Install the thrust caps. Tighten the thrust cap bolts, in 5–6 steps, until the caps are fully seated on the cylinder head.

19. Apply silicone sealant, at a thickness of 0.06–0.09 inch (1.5–2.5mm), to the cylinder head surface in the area forward of the camshaft gear cavity.

20. Install the remaining camshaft caps in their original positions. Tighten the caps, in sequence, in five equal steps, with the final step being 100–125 inch lbs. (11–14 Nm).

21. Apply clean engine oil to the lip of the new camshaft oil seal. Push the seal in lightly by hand. Tap the seal in evenly with a seal installer (49 F401 337A or equivalent) with a final protrusion of 0–0.02 inch (0–0.5mm). Tap in a new blind cap.

22. Install the camshaft sprockets. Tighten the mounting bolts to 91–103 ft. lbs. (123–140 Nm).

23. Measure and adjust valve clearances.

24. Remove any sealant and gasket material from the cylinder head cover contact surfaces.

25. Apply silicone sealant to the cylinder head in the area adjacent to the front and rear camshaft caps. Install a new gasket on the cylinder head.

26. Install the cylinder head cover. Tighten the bolts in 5–6 steps, in sequence, to 44–78 inch lbs. (5–9 Nm).

27. Using a new O-ring, install the distributor.

28. Install the ignition coils.

29. Install the intake manifold.

30. Install the spacer, using a new O-ring. Tighten the mounting bolt to 14–18 ft. lbs. (19–25 Nm).

31. Install the timing belt and timing belt cover.

32. Connect the negative battery cable. Run the engine and check for leaks.

Lash Adjusters/Cam Followers

◆ See Figure 214

➡ **For engines which use rocker arms, refer to the Rocker Arm Removal & Installation procedures earlier in this section.**

1. Remove the camshaft(s)

2. As a precaution, to avoid mix-ups, wipe the oil off the top of all the lash adjuster/cam followers and, using a permanent type marker, label or number them. On DOHC engines, also designate whether the adjuster/follower is on the intake or exhaust side.

3. Use a magnet and pull the lash adjuster/cam follower from its bore.

➡ **On non-hydraulic cam followers, the adjustment shim may come out of the follower before the follower is removed from its bore. If this happens, remove the shim from the magnet and repeat the removal procedure until the follower is removed. Place the shim back onto the follower.**

4. Arrange the adjusters/followers, on a clean work surface, in the order that they are removed.

5. Installation is the reverse of the removal procedure.

INSPECTION

Camshaft

1. Clean the camshaft in solvent and allow to dry.

2. Inspect the camshaft for obvious signs of wear: scores, nicks or pits on the journals or lobes. Light scuffs or nicks can be removed with an oil stone.

3. Using a micrometer, measure the diameter of the journals and compare to specifications. Replace the camshaft if any journals are not within specification.

4. Measure the camshaft lobes across their maximum lobe height dimensions, using a micrometer. Compare your measurements with the lobe height specifications. Replace the camshaft if any lobe heights are not within specification.

5. Mount the camshaft in V-blocks with the front and rear journals riding on the blocks. Check if the camshaft is bent using a dial indicator on the center bearing journal. The limit at the center journal is 0.0012 in. (0.03mm). Replace the camshaft if runout is excessive.

6. Check the camshaft endplay with the camshaft laying in the cylinder head on the lower bearing journals. Mount a dial indicator to the front of the cylinder head with the indicator foot resting on the end of the camshaft. Move the camshaft back and forth and observe the indicator. Compare the reading with the specification. If endplay is excessive, replace the camshaft or the cylinder head.

Lash Adjusters/Cam Followers

1. Inspect each adjuster/follower for wear, pitting and scuffing.

2. Ensure that the adjuster/follower-to-camshaft contact surface is not convex or excessively worn.

Rear Main Seal

REMOVAL & INSTALLATION

1. Disconnect the negative battery cable.

2. Raise and safely support the vehicle.

3. Remove the transaxle/transmission assembly. Refer to Section 7.

4. If equipped with a manual transaxle/transmission, remove the clutch and flywheel assembly. Refer to Section 7.

5. If equipped with an automatic transaxle/transmission, remove the flexplate-to-crankshaft bolts, the flexplate and shim plates.

6. Cut the oil seal lip with a knife. Install a rag to the housing and using a screwdriver, carefully pry the oil seal from the oil seal housing. Clean the gasket mounting surfaces.

To install:

7. Clean the oil seal housing. Coat the oil seal and the housing with clean engine oil.

8. Press the oil seal into the housing and tap it evenly into place with a hammer and a large diameter piece of pipe. The seal must be flush with the edge of the rear cover.

9. Install the clutch and flywheel assembly or the flexplate, as applicable.

10. Install the transaxle/transmission, lower the vehicle and connect the negative battery cable.

Flywheel/Flexplate

REMOVAL & INSTALLATION

◆ See Figures 215 and 216

1. Disconnect the negative battery cable.

2. Raise and safely support the vehicle.

3. Remove the transaxle assembly. Refer to Section 7.

4. If equipped with a manual transaxle, remove the clutch assembly. Refer to Section 7.

5. If equipped with manual transaxle, remove the flywheel-to-crankshaft bolts and the flywheel.

6. If equipped with automatic transaxle, remove the flexplate-to-crankshaft bolts, the flexplate and, if equipped, the flexplate shims.

7. Installation is the reverse of the removal procedure. Tighten the flywheel/flexplate bolts to specification.

Fig. 214 With the camshafts removed, simply pull the followers from their bores using a magnet

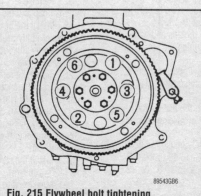

Fig. 215 Flywheel bolt tightening sequence for 6-bolt flywheels

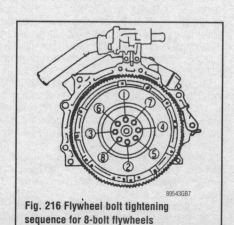

Fig. 216 Flywheel bolt tightening sequence for 8-bolt flywheels

EXHAUST SYSTEM

Inspection

♦ See Figures 217 thru 223

➡ Safety glasses should be worn at all times when working on or near the exhaust system. Older exhaust systems will almost always be covered with loose rust particles which will shower you when disturbed. These particles are more than a nuisance and could injure your eye.

❊ CAUTION

DO NOT perform exhaust repairs or inspection with the engine or exhaust hot. Allow the system to cool completely before attempting any work. Exhaust systems are noted for sharp edges, flaking metal and rusted bolts. Gloves and eye protection are required. A healthy supply of penetrating oil and rags is highly recommended.

Your vehicle must be raised and supported safely to inspect the exhaust system properly. By placing 4 safety stands under the vehicle for support should provide enough room for you to slide under the vehicle and inspect the system completely. Start the inspection at the exhaust manifold or turbocharger pipe where the header pipe is attached and work your way to the back of the vehicle. On dual exhaust systems, remember to inspect both sides of the vehicle. Check the complete exhaust system for open seams, holes loose connections, or other deterioration which could permit exhaust fumes to seep into the passenger compartment. Inspect all mounting brackets and hangers for deterioration, some models may have rubber O-rings that can be overstretched and non-supportive. These components will need to be replaced if found. It has always been a practice to use a pointed tool to poke up into the exhaust system where the deterioration spots are to see whether or not they crumble. Some models may have heat shield covering certain parts of the exhaust system , it will be necessary to remove these shields to have the exhaust visible for inspection also.

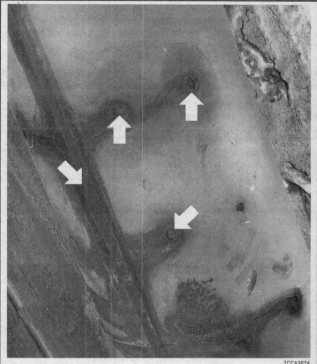

TCCA3P74

Fig. 217 Check the muffler for rotted spot welds and seams

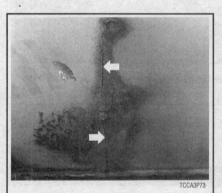

TCCA3P73

Fig. 218 Cracks in the muffler are a guaranteed leak

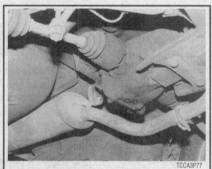

TCCA3P77

Fig. 219 Make sure the exhaust components are not contacting the body or suspension

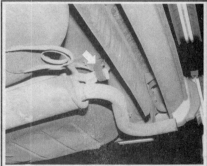

TCCA3P78

Fig. 220 Check for overstretched or torn exhaust hangers

TCCA3P75

Fig. 221 Example of a badly deteriorated exhaust pipe

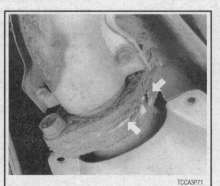

TCCA3P71

Fig. 222 Inspect flanges for gaskets that have deteriorated and need replacement

TCCA3P76

Fig. 223 Some systems, like this one, use large O-rings (donuts) in between the flanges

REPLACEMENT

▶ **See Figures 224, 225, 226 and 227**

There are basically two types of exhaust systems. One is the flange type where the component ends are attached with bolts and a gasket in-between. The other exhaust system is the slip joint type. These components slip into one another using clamps to retain them together.

❄ CAUTION

Allow the exhaust system to cool sufficiently before spraying a solvent exhaust fasteners. Some solvents are highly flammable and could ignite when sprayed on hot exhaust components.

Before removing any component of the exhaust system, ALWAYS squirt a liquid rust dissolving agent onto the fasteners for ease of removal. A lot of knuckle skin will be saved by following this rule. It may even be wise to spray the fasteners and allow them to sit overnight.

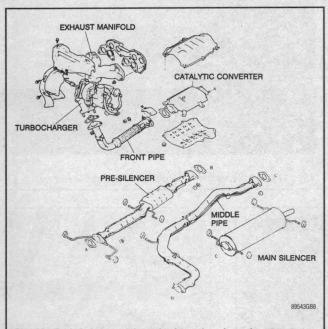

Fig. 224 Exploded view of the turbocharged engine exhaust system

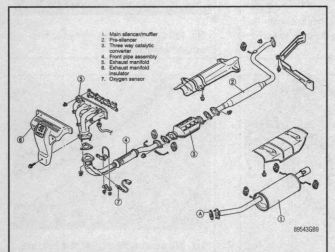

Fig. 225 Exploded view of the typical 4-cylinder engines exhaust system

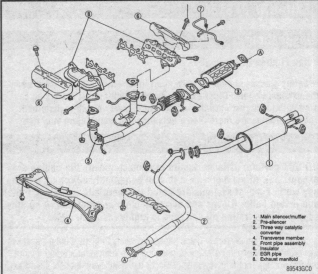

Fig. 226 Exploded view of the typical 6-cylinder engines exhaust system

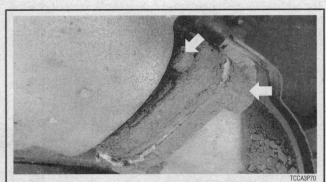

Fig. 227 Nuts and bolts will be extremely difficult to remove when deteriorated with rust

Flange Type

▶ **See Figure 228**

❄ CAUTION

Do NOT perform exhaust repairs or inspection with the engine or exhaust hot. Allow the system to cool completely before attempting any work. Exhaust systems are noted for sharp edges, flaking metal and rusted bolts. Gloves and eye protection are required. A healthy supply of penetrating oil and rags is highly recommended. Never spray liquid rust dissolving agent onto a hot exhaust component.

Before removing any component on a flange type system, ALWAYS squirt a liquid rust dissolving agent onto the fasteners for ease of removal. Start by unbolting the exhaust piece at both ends (if required). When unbolting the headpipe from the manifold, make sure that the bolts are free before trying to remove them. if you snap a stud in the exhaust manifold, the stud will have to be removed with a bolt extractor, which often means removal of the manifold itself. Next, disconnect the component from the mounting; slight twisting and turning may be required to remove the component completely from the vehicle. You may need to tap on the component with a rubber mallet to loosen the component. If all else fails, use a hacksaw to separate the parts. An oxy-acetylene cutting torch may be faster but the sparks are DANGEROUS near the fuel tank, and at the very least, accidents could happen, resulting in damage to the undercar parts, not to mention yourself.

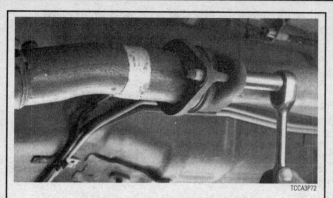

Fig. 228 Example of a flange type exhaust system joint

Fig. 229 Example of a common slip joint type system

Slip Joint Type

▶ See Figure 229

Before removing any component on the slip joint type exhaust system, ALWAYS squirt a liquid rust dissolving agent onto the fasteners for ease of removal. Start by unbolting the exhaust piece at both ends (if required). When unbolting the headpipe from the manifold, make sure that the bolts are free before trying to remove them. if you snap a stud in the exhaust manifold, the stud will have to be removed with a bolt extractor, which often means removal of the manifold itself. Next, remove the mounting U-bolts from around the exhaust pipe you are extracting from the vehicle. Don't be surprised if the U-bolts break while removing the nuts. Loosen the exhaust pipe from any mounting brackets retaining it to the floor pan and separate the components.

ENGINE RECONDITIONING

Determining Engine Condition

Anything that generates heat and/or friction will eventually burn or wear out (i.e. a light bulb generates heat, therefore its life span is limited). With this in mind, a running engine generates tremendous amounts of both; friction is encountered by the moving and rotating parts inside the engine and heat is created by friction and combustion of the fuel. However, the engine has systems designed to help reduce the effects of heat and friction and provide added longevity. The oiling system reduces the amount of friction encountered by the moving parts inside the engine, while the cooling system reduces heat created by friction and combustion. If either system is not maintained, a break-down will be inevitable. Therefore, you can see how regular maintenance can affect the service life of your vehicle. If you do not drain, flush and refill your cooling system at the proper intervals, deposits will begin to accumulate in the radiator, thereby reducing the amount of heat it can extract from the coolant. The same applies to your oil and filter; if it is not changed often enough it becomes laden with contaminates and is unable to properly lubricate the engine. This increases friction and wear.

There are a number of methods for evaluating the condition of your engine. A compression test can reveal the condition of your pistons, piston rings, cylinder bores, head gasket(s), valves and valve seats. An oil pressure test can warn you of possible engine bearing, or oil pump failures. Excessive oil consumption, evidence of oil in the engine air intake area and/or bluish smoke from the tail pipe may indicate worn piston rings, worn valve guides and/or valve seals. As a general rule, an engine that uses no more than one quart of oil every 1000 miles is in good condition. Engines that use one quart of oil or more in less than 1000 miles should first be checked for oil leaks. If any oil leaks are present, have them fixed before determining how much oil is consumed by the engine, especially if blue smoke is not visible at the tail pipe.

COMPRESSION TEST

▶ See Figure 230

A noticeable lack of engine power, excessive oil consumption and/or poor fuel mileage measured over an extended period are all indicators of internal engine wear. Worn piston rings, scored or worn cylinder bores, blown head gaskets, sticking or burnt valves, and worn valve seats are all possible culprits. A check of each cylinder's compression will help locate the problem.

➡A screw-in type compression gauge is more accurate than the type you simply hold against the spark plug hole. Although it takes slightly longer to use, it's worth the effort to obtain a more accurate reading.

1. Make sure that the proper amount and viscosity of engine oil is in the crankcase, then ensure the battery is fully charged.
2. Warm-up the engine to normal operating temperature, then shut the engine **OFF**.
3. Disable the ignition system.
4. Label and disconnect all of the spark plug wires from the plugs.
5. Thoroughly clean the cylinder head area around the spark plug ports, then remove the spark plugs.
6. Set the throttle plate to the fully open (wide-open throttle) position. You can block the accelerator linkage open for this, or you can have an assistant fully depress the accelerator pedal.
7. Install a screw-in type compression gauge into the No. 1 spark plug hole until the fitting is snug.

❊❊ WARNING

Be careful not to crossthread the spark plug hole.

8. According to the tool manufacturer's instructions, connect a remote starting switch to the starting circuit.
9. With the ignition switch in the **OFF** position, use the remote starting switch to crank the engine through at least five compression strokes (approximately 5 seconds of cranking) and record the highest reading on the gauge.
10. Repeat the test on each cylinder, cranking the engine approximately the same number of compression strokes and/or time as the first.

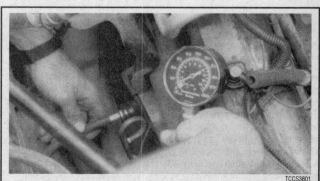

Fig. 230 A screw-in type compression gauge is more accurate and easier to use without an assistant

11. Compare the highest readings from each cylinder to that of the others. The indicated compression pressures are considered within specifications if the lowest reading cylinder is within 75 percent of the pressure recorded for the highest reading cylinder. For example, if your highest reading cylinder pressure was 150 psi (1034 kPa), then 75 percent of that would be 113 psi (779 kPa). So the lowest reading cylinder should be no less than 113 psi (779 kPa).

12. If a cylinder exhibits an unusually low compression reading, pour a tablespoon of clean engine oil into the cylinder through the spark plug hole and repeat the compression test. If the compression rises after adding oil, it means that the cylinder's piston rings and/or cylinder bore are damaged or worn. If the pressure remains low, the valves may not be seating properly (a valve job is needed), or the head gasket may be blown near that cylinder. If compression in any two adjacent cylinders is low, and if the addition of oil doesn't help raise compression, there is leakage past the head gasket. Oil and coolant in the combustion chamber, combined with blue or constant white smoke from the tail pipe, are symptoms of this problem. However, don't be alarmed by the normal white smoke emitted from the tail pipe during engine warm-up or from cold weather driving. There may be evidence of water droplets on the engine dipstick and/or oil droplets in the cooling system if a head gasket is blown.

OIL PRESSURE TEST

Check for proper oil pressure at the sending unit passage with an externally mounted mechanical oil pressure gauge (as opposed to relying on a factory installed dash-mounted gauge). A tachometer may also be needed, as some specifications may require running the engine at a specific rpm.

1. With the engine cold, locate and remove the oil pressure sending unit.
2. Following the manufacturer's instructions, connect a mechanical oil pressure gauge and, if necessary, a tachometer to the engine.
3. Start the engine and allow it to idle.
4. Check the oil pressure reading when cold and record the number. You may need to run the engine at a specified rpm, so check the specifications chart located earlier in this section.
5. Run the engine until normal operating temperature is reached (upper radiator hose will feel warm).
6. Check the oil pressure reading again with the engine hot and record the number. Turn the engine **OFF**.
7. Compare your hot oil pressure reading to that given in the chart. If the reading is low, check the cold pressure reading against the chart. If the cold pressure is well above the specification, and the hot reading was lower than the specification, you may have the wrong viscosity oil in the engine. Change the oil, making sure to use the proper grade and quantity, then repeat the test.

Low oil pressure readings could be attributed to internal component wear, pump related problems, a low oil level, or oil viscosity that is too low. High oil pressure readings could be caused by an overfilled crankcase, too high of an oil viscosity or a faulty pressure relief valve.

Buy or Rebuild?

Now that you have determined that your engine is worn out, you must make some decisions. The question of whether or not an engine is worth rebuilding is largely a subjective matter and one of personal worth. Is the engine a popular one, or is it an obsolete model? Are parts available? Will it get acceptable gas mileage once it is rebuilt? Is the car it's being put into worth keeping? Would it be less expensive to buy a new engine, have your engine rebuilt by a pro, rebuild it yourself or buy a used engine from a salvage yard? Or would it be simpler and less expensive to buy another car? If you have considered all these matters and more, and have still decided to rebuild the engine, then it is time to decide how you will rebuild it.

➥**The editors at Chilton feel that most engine machining should be performed by a professional machine shop. Don't think of it as wasting money, rather, as an assurance that the job has been done right the first time. There are many expensive and specialized tools required to perform such tasks as boring and honing an engine block or having a valve job done on a cylinder head. Even inspecting the parts requires expensive micrometers and gauges to properly measure wear and clearances. Also, a machine shop can deliver to you clean, and ready to assemble parts, saving you time and aggravation. Your maximum savings will come from performing the removal, disassembly, assembly and installation of the engine and purchasing or renting only the tools required to**

perform the above tasks. Depending on the particular circumstances, you may save 40 to 60 percent of the cost doing these yourself.

A complete rebuild or overhaul of an engine involves replacing all of the moving parts (pistons, rods, crankshaft, camshaft, etc.) with new ones and machining the non-moving wearing surfaces of the block and heads. Unfortunately, this may not be cost effective. For instance, your crankshaft may have been damaged or worn, but it can be machined undersize for a minimal fee.

So, as you can see, you can replace everything inside the engine, but, it is wiser to replace only those parts which are really needed, and, if possible, repair the more expensive ones. Later in this section, we will break the engine down into its two main components: the cylinder head and the engine block. We will discuss each component, and the recommended parts to replace during a rebuild on each.

Engine Overhaul Tips

Most engine overhaul procedures are fairly standard. In addition to specific parts replacement procedures and specifications for your individual engine, this section is also a guide to acceptable rebuilding procedures. Examples of standard rebuilding practice are given and should be used along with specific details concerning your particular engine.

Competent and accurate machine shop services will ensure maximum performance, reliability and engine life. In most instances it is more profitable for the do-it-yourself mechanic to remove, clean and inspect the component, buy the necessary parts and deliver these to a shop for actual machine work.

Much of the assembly work (crankshaft, bearings, piston rods, and other components) is well within the scope of the do-it-yourself mechanic's tools and abilities. You will have to decide for yourself the depth of involvement you desire in an engine repair or rebuild.

TOOLS

The tools required for an engine overhaul or parts replacement will depend on the depth of your involvement. With a few exceptions, they will be the tools found in a mechanic's tool kit (see Section 1 of this manual). More in-depth work will require some or all of the following:

- A dial indicator (reading in thousandths) mounted on a universal base
- Micrometers and telescope gauges
- Jaw and screw-type pullers
- Scraper
- Valve spring compressor
- Ring groove cleaner
- Piston ring expander and compressor
- Ridge reamer
- Cylinder hone or glaze breaker
- Plastigage®
- Engine stand

The use of most of these tools is illustrated in this section. Many can be rented for a one-time use from a local parts jobber or tool supply house specializing in automotive work.

Occasionally, the use of special tools is called for. See the information on Special Tools and the Safety Notice in the front of this book before substituting another tool.

OVERHAUL TIPS

Aluminum has become extremely popular for use in engines, due to its low weight. Observe the following precautions when handling aluminum parts:
- Never hot tank aluminum parts (the caustic hot tank solution will eat the aluminum.
- Remove all aluminum parts (identification tag, etc.) from engine parts prior to the tanking.
- Always coat threads lightly with engine oil or anti-seize compounds before installation, to prevent seizure.
- Never overtighten bolts or spark plugs especially in aluminum threads.

When assembling the engine, any parts that will be exposed to frictional contact must be prelubed to provide lubrication at initial start-up. Any product specifically formulated for this purpose can be used, but engine oil is not recommended as a prelube in most cases.

When semi-permanent (locked, but removable) installation of bolts or nuts is desired, threads should be cleaned and coated with Loctite® or another similar, commercial non-hardening sealant.

CLEANING

▶ **See Figures 231, 232, 233 and 234**

Before the engine and its components are inspected, they must be thoroughly cleaned. You will need to remove any engine varnish, oil sludge and/or carbon deposits from all of the components to insure an accurate inspection. A crack in the engine block or cylinder head can easily become overlooked if hidden by a layer of sludge or carbon.

Most of the cleaning process can be carried out with common hand tools and readily available solvents or solutions. Carbon deposits can be chipped away using a hammer and a hard wooden chisel. Old gasket material and varnish or sludge can usually be removed using a scraper and/or cleaning solvent. Extremely stubborn deposits may require the use of a power drill with a wire brush. If using a wire brush, use extreme care around any critical machined surfaces (such as the gasket surfaces, bearing saddles, cylinder bores, etc.). Use of a wire brush is NOT RECOMMENDED on any aluminum components. Always follow any safety recommendations given by the manufacturer of the tool and/or solvent. You should always wear eye protection during any cleaning process involving scraping, chipping or spraying of solvents.

An alternative to the mess and hassle of cleaning the parts yourself is to drop them off at a local garage or machine shop. They will, more than likely, have the necessary equipment to properly clean all of the parts for a nominal fee.

✳✳ CAUTION

Always wear eye protection during any cleaning process involving scraping, chipping or spraying of solvents.

Remove any oil galley plugs, freeze plugs and/or pressed-in bearings and carefully wash and degrease all of the engine components including the fasteners and bolts. Small parts such as the valves, springs, etc., should be placed in a metal basket and allowed to soak. Use pipe cleaner type brushes, and clean all passageways in the components. Use a ring expander and remove the rings from the pistons. Clean the piston ring grooves with a special tool or a piece of broken ring. Scrape the carbon off of the top of the piston. You should never use a wire brush on the pistons. After preparing all of the piston assemblies in this manner, wash and degrease them again.

✳✳ WARNING

Use extreme care when cleaning around the cylinder head valve seats. A mistake or slip may cost you a new seat.

When cleaning the cylinder head, remove carbon from the combustion chamber with the valves installed. This will avoid damaging the valve seats.

REPAIRING DAMAGED THREADS

▶ **See Figures 235, 236, 237, 238 and 239**

Several methods of repairing damaged threads are available. Heli-Coil® (shown here), Keenserts® and Microdot® are among the most widely used. All involve basically the same principle—drilling out stripped threads, tapping the hole and installing a prewound insert—making welding, plugging and oversize fasteners unnecessary.

Two types of thread repair inserts are usually supplied: a standard type for most inch coarse, inch fine, metric course and metric fine thread sizes and a spark lug type to fit most spark plug port sizes. Consult the individual tool manufacturer's catalog to determine exact applications. Typical thread repair kits will contain a selection of prewound threaded inserts, a tap (corresponding to the outside diameter threads of the insert) and an installation tool. Spark plug inserts usually differ because they require a tap equipped with pilot threads and a combined reamer/tap section. Most manufacturers also supply blister-packed thread repair inserts separately in addition to a master kit containing a variety of taps and inserts plus installation tools.

TCCS3132

Fig. 231 Use a gasket scraper to remove the old gasket material from the mating surfaces

TCCS3211

Fig. 232 Use a ring expander tool to remove the piston rings

TCCS3208

Fig. 233 Clean the piston ring grooves using a ring groove cleaner tool, or . . .

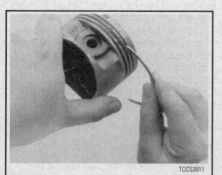

TCCS3911

Fig. 234 . . . use a piece of an old ring to clean the grooves. Be careful, the ring can be quite sharp

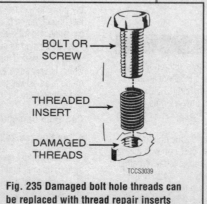

BOLT OR SCREW →

THREADED INSERT →

DAMAGED THREADS →

TCCS3039

Fig. 235 Damaged bolt hole threads can be replaced with thread repair inserts

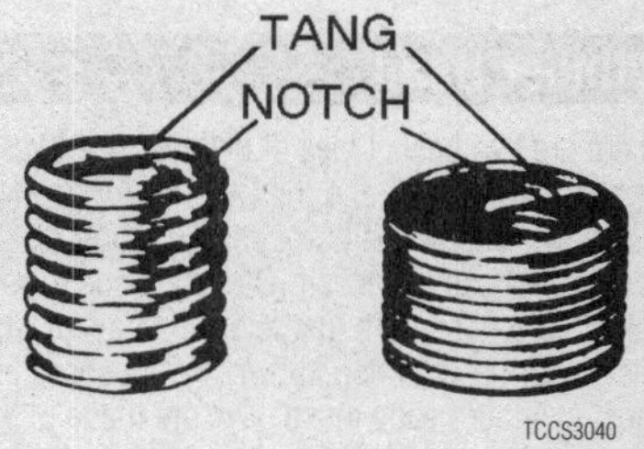

TANG

NOTCH

TCCS3040

Fig. 236 Standard thread repair insert (left), and spark plug thread insert

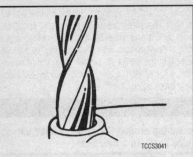

Fig. 237 Drill out the damaged threads with the specified size bit. Be sure to drill completely through the hole or to the bottom of a blind hole

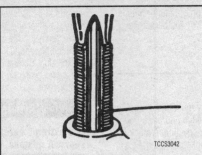

Fig. 238 Using the kit, tap the hole in order to receive the thread insert. Keep the tap well oiled and back it out frequently to avoid clogging the threads

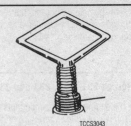

Fig. 239 Screw the insert onto the installer tool until the tang engages the slot. Thread the insert into the hole until it is ¼–½ turn below the top surface, then remove the tool and break off the tang using a punch

Before attempting to repair a threaded hole, remove any snapped, broken or damaged bolts or studs. Penetrating oil can be used to free frozen threads. The offending item can usually be removed with locking pliers or using a screw/stud extractor. After the hole is clear, the thread can be repaired, as shown in the series of accompanying illustrations and in the kit manufacturer's instructions.

Engine Preparation

To properly rebuild an engine, you must first remove it from the vehicle, then disassemble and diagnose it. Ideally you should place your engine on an engine stand. This affords you the best access to the engine components. Follow the manufacturer's directions for using the stand with your particular engine. Remove the flywheel or flexplate before installing the engine to the stand.

Now that you have the engine on a stand, and assuming that you have drained the oil and coolant from the engine, it's time to strip it of all but the necessary components. Before you start disassembling the engine, you may want to take a moment to draw some pictures, or fabricate some labels or containers to mark the locations of various components and the bolts and/or studs which fasten them. Modern day engines use a lot of little brackets and clips which hold wiring harnesses and such, and these holders are often mounted on studs and/or bolts that can be easily mixed up. The manufacturer spent a lot of time and money designing your vehicle, and they wouldn't have wasted any of it by haphazardly placing brackets, clips or fasteners on the vehicle. If it's present when you disassemble it, put it back when you assemble, you will regret not remembering that little bracket which holds a wire harness out of the path of a rotating part.

You should begin by unbolting any accessories still attached to the engine, such as the water pump, power steering pump, alternator, etc. Then, unfasten any manifolds (intake or exhaust) which were not removed during the engine removal procedure. Finally, remove any covers remaining on the engine such as the rocker arm, front or timing cover and oil pan. Some front covers may require the vibration damper and/or crank pulley to be removed beforehand. The idea is to reduce the engine to the bare necessities (cylinder head(s), valve train, engine block, crankshaft, pistons and connecting rods), plus any other `in block' components such as oil pumps, balance shafts and auxiliary shafts.

Finally, remove the cylinder head(s) from the engine block and carefully place on a bench. Disassembly instructions for each component follow later in this section.

Cylinder Head

There are two basic types of cylinder heads used on today's automobiles: the Overhead Valve (OHV) and the Overhead Camshaft (OHC). The latter can also be broken down into two subgroups: the Single Overhead Camshaft (SOHC) and the Dual Overhead Camshaft (DOHC). Generally, if there is only a single camshaft on a head, it is just referred to as an OHC head. Also, an engine with a OHV cylinder head is also known as a pushrod engine.

Most cylinder heads these days are made of an aluminum alloy due to its light weight, durability and heat transfer qualities. However, cast iron was the material of choice in the past, and is still used on many vehicles today. Whether made from aluminum or iron, all cylinder heads have valves and seats. Some use two valves per cylinder, while the more hi-tech engines will utilize a multi-valve configuration using 3, 4 and even 5 valves per cylinder. When the valve contacts the seat, it does so on precision machined surfaces, which seals the combustion chamber. All cylinder heads have a valve guide for each valve. The guide centers the valve to the seat and allows it to move up and down within it. The clearance between the valve and guide can be critical. Too much clearance and the engine may consume oil, lose vacuum and/or damage the seat. Too little, and the valve can stick in the guide causing the engine to run poorly if at all, and possibly causing severe damage. The last component all cylinder heads have are valve springs. The spring holds the valve against its seat. It also returns the valve to this position when the valve has been opened by the valve train or camshaft. The spring is fastened to the valve by a retainer and valve locks (sometimes called keepers). Aluminum heads will also have a valve spring shim to keep the spring from wearing away the aluminum.

An ideal method of rebuilding the cylinder head would involve replacing all of the valves, guides, seats, springs, etc. with new ones. However, depending on how the engine was maintained, often this is not necessary. A major cause of valve, guide and seat wear is an improperly tuned engine. An engine that is running too rich, will often wash the lubricating oil out of the guide with gasoline, causing it to wear rapidly. Conversely, an engine which is running too lean will place higher combustion temperatures on the valves and seats allowing them to wear or even burn. Springs fall victim to the driving habits of the individual. A driver who often runs the engine rpm to the redline will wear out or break the springs faster then one that stays well below it. Unfortunately, mileage takes it toll on all of the parts. Generally, the valves, guides, springs and seats in a cylinder head can be machined and re-used, saving you money. However, if a valve is burnt, it may be wise to replace all of the valves, since they were all operating in the same environment. The same goes for any other component on the cylinder head. Think of it as an insurance policy against future problems related to that component.

Unfortunately, the only way to find out which components need replacing, is to disassemble and carefully check each piece. After the cylinder head(s) are disassembled, thoroughly clean all of the components.

DISASSEMBLY

▶ See Figures 240 and 241

Whether it is a single or dual overhead camshaft cylinder head, the disassembly procedure is relatively unchanged. One aspect to pay attention to is careful labeling of the parts on the dual camshaft cylinder head. There will be an intake camshaft and followers as well as an exhaust camshaft and followers and they must be labeled as such. In some cases, the components are identical and could easily be installed incorrectly. DO NOT MIX THEM UP! Determining which is which is very simple; the intake camshaft and components are on the same side of the head as was the intake manifold. Conversely, the exhaust camshaft and components are on the same side of the head as was the exhaust manifold.

Cup Type Camshaft Followers

▶ See Figures 242, 243 and 244

Most cylinder heads with cup type camshaft followers will have the valve spring, retainer and locks recessed within the follower's bore. You will need a C-clamp style valve spring compressor tool, an OHC spring removal tool (or equivalent) and a small magnet to disassemble the head.

Fig. 240 Exploded view of a valve, seal, spring, retainer and locks from an OHC cylinder head

Fig. 241 Example of a multi-valve cylinder head. Note how it has 2 intake and 2 exhaust valve ports

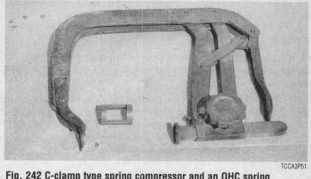

Fig. 242 C-clamp type spring compressor and an OHC spring removal tool (center) for cup type followers

Fig. 243 Most cup type follower cylinder heads retain the camshaft using bolt-on bearing caps

Fig. 244 Position the OHC spring tool in the follower bore, then compress the spring with a C-clamp type tool

1. If not already removed, remove the camshaft(s) and/or followers. Mark their positions for assembly.

2. Position the cylinder head to allow use of a C-clamp style valve spring compressor tool.

➡ **It is preferred to position the cylinder head gasket surface facing you with the valve springs facing the opposite direction and the head laying horizontal.**

3. With the OHC spring removal adapter tool positioned inside of the follower bore, compress the valve spring using the C-clamp style valve spring compressor.

4. Remove the valve locks. A small magnetic tool or screwdriver will aid in removal.

5. Release the compressor tool and remove the spring assembly.

6. Withdraw the valve from the cylinder head.

7. If equipped, remove the valve seal.

➡ **Special valve seal removal tools are available. Regular or needle nose type pliers, if used with care, will work just as well. If using ordinary pliers, be sure not to damage the follower bore. The follower and its bore are machined to close tolerances and any damage to the bore will effect this relationship.**

8. If equipped, remove the valve spring shim. A small magnetic tool or screwdriver will aid in removal.

9. Repeat Steps 3 through 8 until all of the valves have been removed.

Rocker Arm Type Camshaft Followers

▶ **See Figures 245 thru 253**

Most cylinder heads with rocker arm-type camshaft followers are easily disassembled using a standard valve spring compressor. However, certain models may not have enough open space around the spring for the standard tool and may require you to use a C-clamp style compressor tool instead.

1. If not already removed, remove the rocker arms and/or shafts and the camshaft. If applicable, also remove the hydraulic lash adjusters. Mark their positions for assembly.

2. Position the cylinder head to allow access to the valve spring.

3. Use a valve spring compressor tool to relieve the spring tension from the retainer.

➡ **Due to engine varnish, the retainer may stick to the valve locks. A gentle tap with a hammer may help to break it loose.**

4. Remove the valve locks from the valve tip and/or retainer. A small magnet may help in removing the small locks.

5. Lift the valve spring, tool and all, off of the valve stem.

6. If equipped, remove the valve seal. If the seal is difficult to remove with the valve in place, try removing the valve first, then the seal. Follow the steps below for valve removal.

7. Position the head to allow access for withdrawing the valve.

➡ **Cylinder heads that have seen a lot of miles and/or abuse may have mushroomed the valve lock grove and/or tip, causing difficulty in removal of the valve. If this has happened, use a metal file to carefully remove the high spots around the lock grooves and/or tip. Only file it enough to allow removal.**

8. Remove the valve from the cylinder head.

9. If equipped, remove the valve spring shim. A small magnetic tool or screwdriver will aid in removal.

10. Repeat Steps 3 though 9 until all of the valves have been removed.

INSPECTION

Now that all of the cylinder head components are clean, it's time to inspect them for wear and/or damage. To accurately inspect them, you will need some specialized tools:

- A 0–1 inch micrometer for the valves
- A dial indicator or inside diameter gauge for the valve guides
- A spring pressure test gauge

If you do not have access to the proper tools, you may want to bring the components to a shop that does.

Fig. 245 Example of the shaft mounted rocker arms on some OHC heads

Fig. 246 Another example of the rocker arm type OHC head. This model uses a follower under the camshaft

Fig. 247 Before the camshaft can be removed, all of the followers must first be removed . . .

Fig. 248 . . . then the camshaft can be removed by sliding it out (shown), or unbolting a bearing cap (not shown)

Fig. 249 Compress the valve spring . . .

Fig. 250 . . . then remove the valve locks from the valve stem and spring retainer

Fig. 251 Remove the valve spring and retainer from the cylinder head

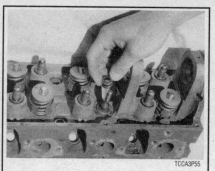

Fig. 252 Remove the valve seal from the guide. Some gentle prying or pliers may help to remove stubborn ones

Fig. 253 All aluminum and some cast iron heads will have these valve spring shims. Remove all of them as well

Valves

▶ See Figures 254 and 255

The first thing to inspect are the valve heads. Look closely at the head, margin and face for any cracks, excessive wear or burning. The margin is the best place to look for burning. It should have a squared edge with an even width all around the diameter. When a valve burns, the margin will look melted and the edges rounded. Also inspect the valve head for any signs of tulipping. This will show as a lifting of the edges or dishing in the center of the head and will usually not occur to all of the valves. All of the heads should look the same, any that seem dished more than others are probably bad. Next, inspect the valve lock grooves and valve tips. Check for any burrs around the lock grooves, especially if you had to file them to remove the valve. Valve tips should appear flat, although slight rounding with high mileage engines is normal. Slightly worn valve tips will need to be machined flat. Last, measure the valve stem diameter with the micrometer. Measure the area that rides within the guide, especially towards the tip where most of the wear occurs. Take several measurements along its length and com-

pare them to each other. Wear should be even along the length with little to no taper. If no minimum diameter is given in the specifications, then the stem should not read more than 0.001 in. (0.025mm) below the unworn portion of the stem. Any valves that fail these inspections should be replaced.

Springs, Retainers and Valve Locks

▶ See Figures 256 and 257

The first thing to check is the most obvious, broken springs. Next check the free length and squareness of each spring. If applicable, insure to distinguish between intake and exhaust springs. Use a ruler and/or carpenters square to measure the length. A carpenters square should be used to check the springs for squareness. If a spring pressure test gauge is available, check each springs rating and compare to the specifications chart. Check the readings against the specifications given. Any springs that fail these inspections should be replaced.

The spring retainers rarely need replacing, however they should still be checked as a precaution. Inspect the spring mating surface and the valve lock retention area for any signs of excessive wear. Also check for any signs of cracking. Replace any retainers that are questionable.

Valve locks should be inspected for excessive wear on the outside contact area as well as on the inner notched surface. Any locks which appear worn or broken and its respective valve should be replaced.

Cylinder Head

There are several things to check on the cylinder head: valve guides, seats, cylinder head surface flatness, cracks and physical damage.

VALVE GUIDES

▶ See Figure 258

Now that you know the valves are good, you can use them to check the guides, although a new valve, if available, is preferred. Before you measure anything, look at the guides carefully and inspect them for any cracks, chips or breakage. Also if the guide is a removable style (as in most aluminum heads),

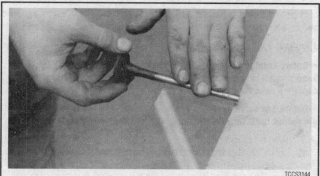

Fig. 254 Valve stems may be rolled on a flat surface to check for bends

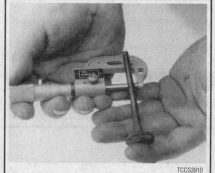

Fig. 255 Use a micrometer to check the valve stem diameter

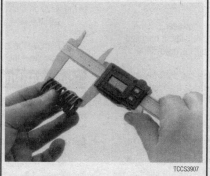

Fig. 256 Use a caliper to check the valve spring free-length

Fig. 257 Check the valve spring for squareness on a flat surface; a carpenter's square can be used

Fig. 258 A dial gauge may be used to check valve stem-to-guide clearance; read the gauge while moving the valve stem

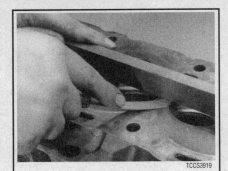

Fig. 259 Check the head for flatness across the center of the head surface using a straightedge and feeler gauge

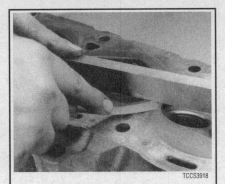

Fig. 260 Checks should also be made along both diagonals of the head surface

check them for any looseness or evidence of movement. All of the guides should appear to be at the same height from the spring seat. If any seem lower (or higher) from another, the guide has moved. Mount a dial indicator onto the spring side of the cylinder head. Lightly oil the valve stem and insert it into the cylinder head. Position the dial indicator against the valve stem near the tip and zero the gauge. Grasp the valve stem and wiggle towards and away from the dial indicator and observe the readings. Mount the dial indicator 90 degrees from the initial point and zero the gauge and again take a reading. Compare the two readings for a out of round condition. Check the readings against the specifications given. An Inside Diameter (I.D.) gauge designed for valve guides will give you an accurate valve guide bore measurement. If the I.D. gauge is used, compare the readings with the specifications given. Any guides that fail these inspections should be replaced or machined.

VALVE SEATS

A visual inspection of the valve seats should show a slightly worn and pitted surface where the valve face contacts the seat. Inspect the seat carefully for severe pitting or cracks. Also, a seat that is badly worn will be recessed into the cylinder head. A severely worn or recessed seat may need to be replaced. All cracked seats must be replaced. A seat concentricity gauge, if available, should be used to check the seat run-out. If run-out exceeds specifications the seat must be machined (if no specification is given use 0.002 in. or 0.051mm).

CYLINDER HEAD SURFACE FLATNESS

▶ See Figures 259 and 260

After you have cleaned the gasket surface of the cylinder head of any old gasket material, check the head for flatness.

Place a straightedge across the gasket surface. Using feeler gauges, determine the clearance at the center of the straightedge and across the cylinder head at several points. Check along the centerline and diagonally on the head surface. If the warpage exceeds 0.003 in. (0.076mm) within a 6.0 in. (15.2cm) span, or 0.006 in. (0.152mm) over the total length of the head, the cylinder head must be resurfaced. After resurfacing the heads of a V-type engine, the intake manifold flange surface should be checked, and if necessary, milled proportionally to allow for the change in its mounting position.

CRACKS AND PHYSICAL DAMAGE

Generally, cracks are limited to the combustion chamber, however, it is not uncommon for the head to crack in a spark plug hole, port, outside of the head or in the valve spring/rocker arm area. The first area to inspect is always the hottest: the exhaust seat/port area.

A visual inspection should be performed, but just because you don't see a crack does not mean it is not there. Some more reliable methods for inspecting for cracks include Magnaflux®, a magnetic process or Zyglo®, a dye penetrant. Magnaflux® is used only on ferrous metal (cast iron) heads. Zyglo® uses a spray on fluorescent mixture along with a black light to reveal the cracks. It is strongly recommended to have your cylinder head checked professionally for cracks, especially if the engine was known to have overheated and/or leaked or consumed coolant. Contact a local shop for availability and pricing of these services.

Physical damage is usually very evident. For example, a broken mounting ear from dropping the head or a bent or broken stud and/or bolt. All of these defects should be fixed or, if irrepairable, the head should be replaced.

Camshaft and Followers

Inspect the camshaft(s) and followers as described earlier in this section.

REFINISHING & REPAIRING

Many of the procedures given for refinishing and repairing the cylinder head components must be performed by a machine shop. Certain steps, if the inspected part is not worn, can be performed yourself inexpensively. However, you spent a lot of time and effort so far, why risk trying to save a couple bucks if you might have to do it all over again?

Valves

Any valves that were not replaced should be refaced and the tips ground flat. Unless you have access to a valve grinding machine, this should be done by a machine shop. If the valves are in extremely good condition, as well as the valve seats and guides, they may be lapped in without performing machine work.

It is a recommended practice to lap the valves even after machine work has been performed and/or new valves have been purchased. This insures a positive seal between the valve and seat.

LAPPING THE VALVES

➥Before lapping the valves to the seats, read the rest of the cylinder head section to insure that any related parts are in acceptable enough condition to continue.

➥Before any valve seat machining and/or lapping can be performed, the guides must be within factory recommended specifications.

1. Invert the cylinder head.
2. Lightly lubricate the valve stems and insert them into the cylinder head in their numbered order.
3. Raise the valve from the seat and apply a small amount of fine lapping compound to the seat.
4. Moisten the suction head of a hand-lapping tool and attach it to the head of the valve.
5. Rotate the tool between the palms of both hands, changing the position of the valve on the valve seat and lifting the tool often to prevent grooving.
6. Lap the valve until a smooth, polished circle is evident on the valve and seat.
7. Remove the tool and the valve. Wipe away all traces of the grinding compound and store the valve to maintain its lapped location.

✳✳ WARNING

Do not get the valves out of order after they have been lapped. They must be put back with the same valve seat they were lapped with.

Springs, Retainers and Valve Locks

There is no repair or refinishing possible with the springs, retainers and valve locks. If they are found to be worn or defective, they must be replaced with new (or known good) parts.

Cylinder Head

Most refinishing procedures dealing with the cylinder head must be performed by a machine shop. Read the sections below and review your inspection data to determine whether or not machining is necessary.

VALVE GUIDE

➡ If any machining or replacements are made to the valve guides, the seats must be machined.

Unless the valve guides need machining or replacing, the only service to perform is to thoroughly clean them of any dirt or oil residue.

There are only two types of valve guides used on automobile engines: the replaceable-type (all aluminum heads) and the cast-in integral-type (most cast iron heads). There are four recommended methods for repairing worn guides.

- Knurling
- Inserts
- Reaming oversize
- Replacing

Knurling is a process in which metal is displaced and raised, thereby reducing clearance, giving a true center, and providing oil control. It is the least expensive way of repairing the valve guides. However, it is not necessarily the best, and in some cases, a knurled valve guide will not stand up for more than a short time. It requires a special knurlizer and precision reaming tools to obtain proper clearances. It would not be cost effective to purchase these tools, unless you plan on rebuilding several of the same cylinder head.

Installing a guide insert involves machining the guide to accept a bronze insert. One style is the coil-type which is installed into a threaded guide. Another is the thin-walled insert where the guide is reamed oversize to accept a split-sleeve insert. After the insert is installed, a special tool is then run through the guide to expand the insert, locking it to the guide. The insert is then reamed to the standard size for proper valve clearance.

Reaming for oversize valves restores normal clearances and provides a true valve seat. Most cast-in type guides can be reamed to accept an valve with an oversize stem. The cost factor for this can become quite high as you will need to purchase the reamer and new, oversize stem valves for all guides which were reamed. Oversizes are generally 0.003 to 0.030 in. (0.076 to 0.762mm), with 0.015 in. (0.381mm) being the most common.

To replace cast-in type valve guides, they must be drilled out, then reamed to accept replacement guides. This must be done on a fixture which will allow centering and leveling off of the original valve seat or guide, otherwise a serious guide-to-seat misalignment may occur making it impossible to properly machine the seat.

Replaceable-type guides are pressed into the cylinder head. A hammer and a stepped drift or punch may be used to install and remove the guides. Before removing the guides, measure the protrusion on the spring side of the head and record it for installation. Use the stepped drift to hammer out the old guide from the combustion chamber side of the head. When installing, determine whether or not the guide also seals a water jacket in the head, and if it does, use the recommended sealing agent. If there is no water jacket, grease the valve guide and its bore. Use the stepped drift, and hammer the new guide into the cylinder head from the spring side of the cylinder head. A stack of washers the same thickness as the measured protrusion may help the installation process.

VALVE SEATS

➡ Before any valve seat machining can be performed, the guides must be within factory recommended specifications.

➡ If any machining or replacements were made to the valve guides, the seats must be machined.

If the seats are in good condition, the valves can be lapped to the seats, and the cylinder head assembled. See the valves section for instructions on lapping.

If the valve seats are worn, cracked or damaged, they must be serviced by a machine shop. The valve seat must be perfectly centered to the valve guide, which requires very accurate machining.

CYLINDER HEAD SURFACE

If the cylinder head is warped, it must be machined flat. If the warpage is extremely severe, the head may need to be replaced. In some instances, it may be possible to straighten a warped head enough to allow machining. In either case, contact a professional machine shop for service.

➡ Any OHC cylinder head that shows excessive warpage should have the camshaft bearing journals align bored after the cylinder head has been resurfaced.

✳✳ WARNING

Failure to align bore the camshaft bearing journals could result in severe engine damage including but not limited to: valve and piston damage, connecting rod damage, camshaft and/or crankshaft breakage.

CRACKS AND PHYSICAL DAMAGE

Certain cracks can be repaired in both cast iron and aluminum heads. For cast iron, a tapered threaded insert is installed along the length of the crack. Aluminum can also use the tapered inserts, however welding is the preferred method. Some physical damage can be repaired through brazing or welding. Contact a machine shop to get expert advice for your particular dilemma.

ASSEMBLY

▶ See Figure 261

The first step for any assembly job is to have a clean area in which to work. Next, thoroughly clean all of the parts and components that are to be assembled. Finally, place all of the components onto a suitable work space and, if necessary, arrange the parts to their respective positions.

Cup Type Camshaft Followers

To install the springs, retainers and valve locks on heads which have these components recessed into the camshaft follower's bore, you will need a small screwdriver-type tool, some clean white grease and a lot of patience. You will also need the C-clamp style spring compressor and the OHC tool used to disassemble the head.

1. Lightly lubricate the valve stems and insert all of the valves into the cylinder head. If possible, maintain their original locations.
2. If equipped, install any valve spring shims which were removed.
3. If equipped, install the new valve seals, keeping the following in mind:
- If the valve seal presses over the guide, lightly lubricate the outer guide surfaces.
- If the seal is an O-ring type, it is installed just after compressing the spring but before the valve locks.
4. Place the valve spring and retainer over the stem.
5. Position the spring compressor and the OHC tool, then compress the spring.
6. Using a small screwdriver as a spatula, fill the valve stem side of the lock with white grease. Use the excess grease on the screwdriver to fasten the lock to the driver.
7. Carefully install the valve lock, which is stuck to the end of the screwdriver, to the valve stem then press on it with the screwdriver until the grease squeezes out. The valve lock should now be stuck to the stem.
8. Repeat Steps 6 and 7 for the remaining valve lock.

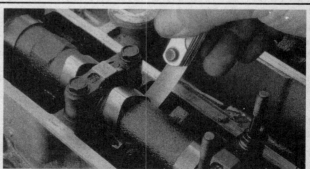

TCCA3P64

Fig. 261 Once assembled, check the valve clearance and correct as needed

9. Relieve the spring pressure slowly and insure that neither valve lock becomes dislodged by the retainer.

10. Remove the spring compressor tool.

11. Repeat Steps 2 through 10 until all of the springs have been installed.

12. Install the followers, camshaft(s) and any other components that were removed for disassembly.

Rocker Arm Type Camshaft Followers

1. Lightly lubricate the valve stems and insert all of the valves into the cylinder head. If possible, maintain their original locations.

2. If equipped, install any valve spring shims which were removed.

3. If equipped, install the new valve seals, keeping the following in mind:

• If the valve seal presses over the guide, lightly lubricate the outer guide surfaces.

• If the seal is an O-ring type, it is installed just after compressing the spring but before the valve locks.

4. Place the valve spring and retainer over the stem.

5. Position the spring compressor tool and compress the spring.

6. Assemble the valve locks to the stem.

7. Relieve the spring pressure slowly and insure that neither valve lock becomes dislodged by the retainer.

8. Remove the spring compressor tool.

9. Repeat Steps 2 through 8 until all of the springs have been installed.

10. Install the camshaft(s), rockers, shafts and any other components that were removed for disassembly.

Engine Block

GENERAL INFORMATION

A thorough overhaul or rebuild of an engine block would include replacing the pistons, rings, bearings, timing belt/chain assembly and oil pump. For OHV engines also include a new camshaft and lifters. The block would then have the cylinders bored and honed oversize (or if using removable cylinder sleeves, new sleeves installed) and the crankshaft would be cut undersize to provide new wearing surfaces and perfect clearances. However, your particular engine may not have everything worn out. What if only the piston rings have worn out and the clearances on everything else are still within factory specifications? Well, you could just replace the rings and put it back together, but this would be a very rare example. Chances are, if one component in your engine is worn, other components are sure to follow, and soon. At the very least, you should always replace the rings, bearings and oil pump. This is what is commonly called a "freshen up".

Cylinder Ridge Removal

Because the top piston ring does not travel to the very top of the cylinder, a ridge is built up between the end of the travel and the top of the cylinder bore.

Pushing the piston and connecting rod assembly past the ridge can be difficult, and damage to the piston ring lands could occur. If the ridge is not removed before installing a new piston or not removed at all, piston ring breakage and piston damage may occur.

➡ It is always recommended that you remove any cylinder ridges before removing the piston and connecting rod assemblies. If you know that new pistons are going to be installed and the engine block will be bored oversize, you may be able to forego this step. However, some ridges may actually prevent the assemblies from being removed, necessitating its removal.

There are several different types of ridge reamers on the market, none of which are inexpensive. Unless a great deal of engine rebuilding is anticipated, borrow or rent a reamer.

1. Turn the crankshaft until the piston is at the bottom of its travel.

2. Cover the head of the piston with a rag.

3. Follow the tool manufacturers instructions and cut away the ridge, exercising extreme care to avoid cutting too deeply.

4. Remove the ridge reamer, the rag and as many of the cuttings as possible. Continue until all of the cylinder ridges have been removed.

DISASSEMBLY

▶ **See Figures 262 and 263**

The engine disassembly instructions following assume that you have the engine mounted on an engine stand. If not, it is easiest to disassemble the engine on a bench or the floor with it resting on the bellhousing or transmission mounting surface. You must be able to access the connecting rod fasteners and turn the crankshaft during disassembly. Also, all engine covers (timing, front, side, oil pan, whatever) should have already been removed. Engines which are seized or locked up may not be able to be completely disassembled, and a core (salvage yard) engine should be purchased.

➡ In addition to an oil pan, Mazda engines utilize a lower block strengthening component, which is sandwiched between the pan and the block. Some additional fasteners retain this structure to the block and main caps, and it may be necessary to remove it in order to access the connecting rod fasteners.

TCCS3803

Fig. 262 Place rubber hose over the connecting rod studs to protect the crankshaft and cylinder bores from damage

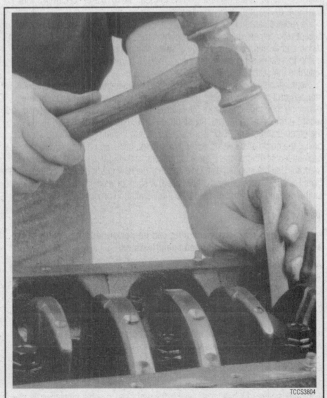

TCCS3804

Fig. 263 Carefully tap the piston out of the bore using a wooden dowel

If not done during the cylinder head removal, remove the timing chain/belt and/or gear/sprocket assembly. Remove the oil pick-up and pump assembly and, if necessary, the pump drive. If equipped, remove any balance or auxiliary shafts. If necessary, remove the cylinder ridge from the top of the bore. See the cylinder ridge removal procedure earlier in this section.

Rotate the engine over so that the crankshaft is exposed. Use a number punch or scribe and mark each connecting rod with its respective cylinder number. The cylinder closest to the front of the engine is always number 1. However, depending on the engine placement, the front of the engine could either be the flywheel or damper/pulley end. Generally the front of the engine faces the front of the vehicle. Use a number punch or scribe and also mark the main bearing caps from front to rear with the front most cap being number 1 (if there are five caps, mark them 1 through 5, front to rear).

※※ WARNING

Take special care when pushing the connecting rod up from the crankshaft because the sharp threads of the rod bolts/studs will score the crankshaft journal. Insure that special plastic caps are installed over them, or cut two pieces of rubber hose to do the same.

Again, rotate the engine, this time to position the number one cylinder bore (head surface) up. Turn the crankshaft until the number one piston is at the bottom of its travel, this should allow the maximum access to its connecting rod. Remove the number one connecting rods fasteners and cap and place two lengths of rubber hose over the rod bolts/studs to protect the crankshaft from damage. Using a sturdy wooden dowel and a hammer, push the connecting rod up about 1 in. (25mm) from the crankshaft and remove the upper bearing insert. Continue pushing or tapping the connecting rod up until the piston rings are out of the cylinder bore. Remove the piston and rod by hand, put the upper half of the bearing insert back into the rod, install the cap with its bearing insert installed, and hand-tighten the cap fasteners. If the parts are kept in order in this manner, they will not get lost and you will be able to tell which bearings came form what cylinder if any problems are discovered and diagnosis is necessary. Remove all the other piston assemblies in the same manner. On V-style engines, remove all of the pistons from one bank, then reposition the engine with the other cylinder bank head surface up, and remove that banks piston assemblies.

The only remaining component in the engine block should now be the crankshaft.

➡The V6 Mazda engines are a split block design. The lower half of the block is integral with the main caps. Follow the 6-cylinder procedures for these engines.

4-Cylinder Engines

Loosen the main bearing caps evenly until the fasteners can be turned by hand, then remove them and the caps. Remove the crankshaft from the engine block. Thoroughly clean all of the components.

6-Cylinder Engines

Loosen the lower cylinder block bolts and the crankshaft cap bolts in 3 steps in the order shown in the figure. DO NOT mix up the bolts. Label and mark each bolt to the hole it was removed from. Separate the lower half of the cylinder block from the upper half by inserting prytool in the locations shown, and gently prying upwards. Gently tapping on the lower portion of the cylinder block with a plastic hammer may help to break the gasket seal.

Remove the lower half of the engine block. Remove the crankshaft from the upper half of the cylinder block. Thoroughly clean all of the components.

INSPECTION

Now that the engine block and all of its components are clean, it's time to inspect them for wear and/or damage. To accurately inspect them, you will need some specialized tools:

- Two or three separate micrometers to measure the pistons and crankshaft journals
- A dial indicator
- Telescoping gauges for the cylinder bores
- A rod alignment fixture to check for bent connecting rods

If you do not have access to the proper tools, you may want to bring the components to a shop that does.

Generally, you shouldn't expect cracks in the engine block or its components unless it was known to leak, consume or mix engine fluids, it was severely overheated, or there was evidence of bad bearings and/or crankshaft damage. A visual inspection should be performed on all of the components, but just because you don't see a crack does not mean it is not there. Some more reliable methods for inspecting for cracks include Magnaflux®, a magnetic process or Zyglo®, a dye penetrant. Magnaflux® is used only on ferrous metal (cast iron). Zyglo® uses a spray on fluorescent mixture along with a black light to reveal the cracks. It is strongly recommended to have your engine block checked professionally for cracks, especially if the engine was known to have overheated and/or leaked or consumed coolant. Contact a local shop for availability and pricing of these services.

Engine Block

ENGINE BLOCK BEARING ALIGNMENT

Remove the main bearing caps and, if still installed, the main bearing inserts. Inspect all of the main bearing saddles and caps for damage, burrs or high spots. If damage is found, and it is caused from a spun main bearing, the block will need to be align-bored or, if severe enough, replacement. Any burrs or high spots should be carefully removed with a metal file.

Place a straightedge on the bearing saddles, in the engine block, along the centerline of the crankshaft. If any clearance exists between the straightedge and the saddles, the block must be align-bored.

Align-boring consists of machining the main bearing saddles and caps by means of a flycutter that runs through the bearing saddles.

DECK FLATNESS

The top of the engine block where the cylinder head mounts is called the deck. Insure that the deck surface is clean of dirt, carbon deposits and old gasket material. Place a straightedge across the surface of the deck along its centerline and, using feeler gauges, check the clearance along several points. Repeat the checking procedure with the straightedge placed along both diagonals of the deck surface. If the reading exceeds 0.003 in. (0.076mm) within a 6.0 in. (15.2cm) span, or 0.006 in. (0.152mm) over the total length of the deck, it must be machined.

CYLINDER BORES

♦ See Figure 264

The cylinder bores house the pistons and are slightly larger than the pistons themselves. A common piston-to-bore clearance is 0.0015–0.0025 in. (0.0381mm–0.0635mm). Inspect and measure the cylinder bores. The bore should be checked for out-of-roundness, taper and size. The results of this inspection will determine whether the cylinder can be used in its existing size

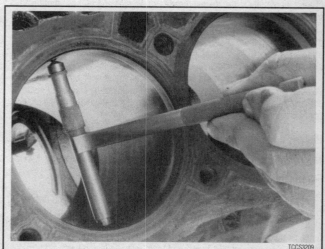

TCCS3209

Fig. 264 Use a telescoping gauge to measure the cylinder bore diameter—take several readings within the same bore

and condition, or a rebore to the next oversize is required (or in the case of removable sleeves, have replacements installed).

The amount of cylinder wall wear is always greater at the top of the cylinder than at the bottom. This wear is known as taper. Any cylinder that has a taper of 0.0012 in. (0.305mm) or more, must be rebored. Measurements are taken at a number of positions in each cylinder: at the top, middle and bottom and at two points at each position; that is, at a point 90 degrees from the crankshaft center-line, as well as a point parallel to the crankshaft centerline. The measurements are made with either a special dial indicator or a telescopic gauge and micrometer. If the necessary precision tools to check the bore are not available, take the block to a machine shop and have them mike it. Also if you don't have the tools to check the cylinder bores, chances are you will not have the necessary devices to check the pistons, connecting rods and crankshaft. Take these components with you and save yourself an extra trip.

For our procedures, we will use a telescopic gauge and a micrometer. You will need one of each, with a measuring range which covers your cylinder bore size.

1. Position the telescopic gauge in the cylinder bore, loosen the gauges lock and allow it to expand.

➡**Your first two readings will be at the top of the cylinder bore, then proceed to the middle and finally the bottom, making a total of six measurements.**

2. Hold the gauge square in the bore, 90 degrees from the crankshaft center-line, and gently tighten the lock. Tilt the gauge back to remove it from the bore.
3. Measure the gauge with the micrometer and record the reading.
4. Again, hold the gauge square in the bore, this time parallel to the crank-shaft centerline, and gently tighten the lock. Again, you will tilt the gauge back to remove it from the bore.
5. Measure the gauge with the micrometer and record this reading. The difference between these two readings is the out-of-round measurement of the cylinder.
6. Repeat steps 1 through 5, each time going to the next lower position, until you reach the bottom of the cylinder. Then go to the next cylinder, and continue until all of the cylinders have been measured.

The difference between these measurements will tell you all about the wear in your cylinders. The measurements which were taken 90 degrees from the crank-shaft centerline will always reflect the most wear. That is because at this position is where the engine power presses the piston against the cylinder bore the hardest. This is known as thrust wear. Take your top, 90 degree measurement and compare it to your bottom, 90 degree measurement. The difference between them is the taper. When you measure your pistons, you will compare these readings to your piston sizes and determine piston-to-wall clearance.

Crankshaft

Inspect the crankshaft for visible signs of wear or damage. All of the journals should be perfectly round and smooth. Slight scores are normal for a used crankshaft, but you should hardly feel them with your fingernail. When measuring the crankshaft with a micrometer, you will take readings at the front and rear of each journal, then turn the micrometer 90 degrees and take two more readings, front and rear. The difference between the front-to-rear readings is the journal taper and the first-to-90 degree reading is the out-of-round measurement. Generally, there should be no taper or out-of-roundness found, however, up to 0.0005 in. (0.0127mm) for either can be overlooked. Also, the readings should fall within the factory specifications for journal diameters.

If the crankshaft journals fall within specifications, it is recommended that it be polished before being returned to service. Polishing the crankshaft insures that any minor burrs or high spots are smoothed, thereby reducing the chance of scoring the new bearings.

Pistons and Connecting Rods

PISTONS

▶ **See Figure 265**

The piston should be visually inspected for any signs of cracking or burning (caused by hot spots or detonation), and scuffing or excessive wear on the skirts. The wristpin attaches the piston to the connecting rod. The piston should move freely on the wrist pin, both sliding and pivoting. Grasp the connecting rod securely, or mount it in a vise, and try to rock the piston back and forth along the centerline of the wristpin. There should not be any excessive play evident between the piston and the pin. If there are C-clips retaining the pin in the piston then you have wrist pin bushings in the rods. There should not be any

TCCS3210
Fig. 265 Measure the piston's outer diameter, perpendicular to the wrist pin, with a micrometer

excessive play between the wrist pin and the rod bushing. Normal clearance for the wrist pin is approx. 0.001–0.002 in. (0.025mm–0.051mm).

Use a micrometer and measure the diameter of the piston, perpendicular to the wrist pin, on the skirt. Compare the reading to its original cylinder measurement obtained earlier. The difference between the two readings is the piston-to-wall clearance. If the clearance is within specifications, the piston may be used as is. If the piston is out of specification, but the bore is not, you will need a new piston. If both are out of specification, you will need the cylinder rebored and oversize pistons installed. Generally if two or more pistons/bores are out of specification, it is best to rebore the entire block and purchase a complete set of oversize pistons.

CONNECTING ROD

You should have the connecting rod checked for straightness at a machine shop. If the connecting rod is bent, it will unevenly wear the bearing and piston, as well as place greater stress on these components. Any bent or twisted connecting rods must be replaced. If the rods are straight and the wrist pin clearance is within specifications, then only the bearing end of the rod need be checked. Place the connecting rod into a vice, with the bearing inserts in place, install the cap to the rod and torque the fasteners to specifications. Use a telescoping gauge and carefully measure the inside diameter of the bearings. Compare this reading to the rods original crankshaft journal diameter measurement. The difference is the oil clearance. If the oil clearance is not within specifications, install new bearings in the rod and take another measurement. If the clearance is still out of specifications, and the crankshaft is not, the rod will need to be reconditioned by a machine shop.

➡**You can also use Plastigage® to check the bearing clearances. The assembling section has complete instructions on its use.**

Camshaft

Inspect the camshaft and lifters/followers as described earlier in this section.

Bearings

All of the engine bearings should be visually inspected for wear and/or damage. The bearing should look evenly worn all around with no deep scores or pits. If the bearing is severely worn, scored, pitted or heat blued, then the bearing, and the components that use it, should be brought to a machine shop for inspection. Full-circle bearings (used on most camshafts, auxiliary shafts, balance shafts, etc.) require specialized tools for removal and installation, and should be brought to a machine shop for service.

Oil Pump

➡**The oil pump is responsible for providing constant lubrication to the whole engine and so it is recommended that a new oil pump be installed when rebuilding the engine.**

Completely disassemble the oil pump and thoroughly clean all of the components. Inspect the oil pump gears and housing for wear and/or damage. Insure that the pressure relief valve operates properly and there is no binding or sticking due to varnish or debris. If all of the parts are in proper working condition, lubricate the gears and relief valve, and assemble the pump.

REFINISHING

▶ **See Figure 266**

Almost all engine block refinishing must be performed by a machine shop. If the cylinders are not to be rebored, then the cylinder glaze can be removed with a ball hone. When removing cylinder glaze with a ball hone, use a light or penetrating type oil to lubricate the hone. Do not allow the hone to run dry as this may cause excessive scoring of the cylinder bores and wear on the hone. If new pistons are required, they will need to be installed to the connecting rods. This should be performed by a machine shop as the pistons must be installed in the correct relationship to the rod or engine damage can occur.

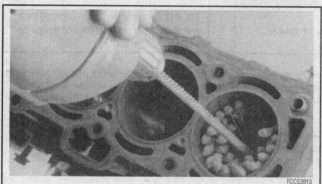

Fig. 266 Use a ball type cylinder hone to remove any glaze and provide a new surface for seating the piston rings

Pistons and Connecting Rods

▶ **See Figure 267**

Only pistons with the wrist pin retained by C-clips are serviceable by the home-mechanic. Press fit pistons require special presses and/or heaters to remove/install the connecting rod and should only be performed by a machine shop.

All pistons will have a mark indicating the direction to the front of the engine and the must be installed into the engine in that manner. Usually it is a notch or arrow on the top of the piston, or it may be the letter F cast or stamped into the piston.

Fig. 267 Most pistons are marked to indicate positioning in the engine (usually a mark means the side facing the front)

C-CLIP TYPE PISTONS

1. Note the location of the forward mark on the piston and mark the connecting rod in relation.
2. Remove the C-clips from the piston and withdraw the wrist pin.

➡**Varnish build-up or C-clip groove burrs may increase the difficulty of removing the wrist pin. If necessary, use a punch or drift to carefully tap the wrist pin out.**

3. Insure that the wrist pin bushing in the connecting rod is usable, and lubricate it with assembly lube.

4. Remove the wrist pin from the new piston and lubricate the pin bores on the piston.
5. Align the forward marks on the piston and the connecting rod and install the wrist pin.
6. The new C-clips will have a flat and a rounded side to them. Install both C-clips with the flat side facing out.
7. Repeat all of the steps for each piston being replaced.

ASSEMBLY

Before you begin assembling the engine, first give yourself a clean, dirt free work area. Next, clean every engine component again. The key to a good assembly is cleanliness.

Mount the engine block into the engine stand and wash it one last time using water and detergent (dishwashing detergent works well). While washing it, scrub the cylinder bores with a soft bristle brush and thoroughly clean all of the oil passages. Completely dry the engine and spray the entire assembly down with an anti-rust solution such as WD-40® or similar product. Take a clean lint-free rag and wipe up any excess anti-rust solution from the bores, bearing saddles, etc. Repeat the final cleaning process on the crankshaft. Replace any freeze or oil galley plugs which were removed during disassembly.

Crankshaft

▶ **See Figures 268 and 269**

1. Remove the main bearing inserts from the block and bearing caps.
2. If the crankshaft main bearing journals have been refinished to a definite undersize, install the correct undersize bearing. Be sure that the bearing inserts and bearing bores are clean. Foreign material under inserts will distort bearing and cause failure.
3. Place the upper main bearing inserts in bores with tang in slot.

➡**The oil holes in the bearing inserts must be aligned with the oil holes in the cylinder block.**

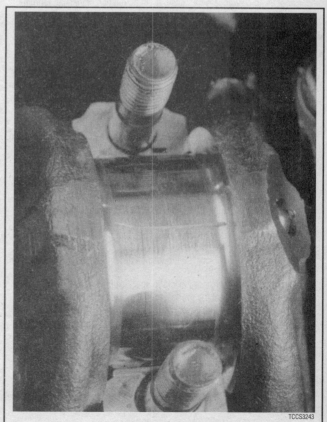

Fig. 268 Apply a strip of gauging material to the bearing journal, then install and torque the cap

Fig. 269 After the cap is removed again, use the scale supplied with the gauging material to check the clearance

Fig. 270 A dial gauge may be used to check crankshaft end-play

Fig. 271 Carefully pry the crankshaft back and forth while reading the dial gauge for end-play

4. Install the lower main bearing inserts in bearing caps.

5. Clean the mating surfaces of block and rear main bearing cap.

6. Carefully lower the crankshaft into place. Be careful not to damage bearing surfaces.

7. Check the clearance of each main bearing by using the following procedure:

    a. Place a piece of Plastigage® or its equivalent, on bearing surface across full width of bearing cap and about ¼ in. off center.

    b. Install cap and tighten bolts to specifications. Do not turn crankshaft while Plastigage® is in place.

    c. Remove the cap. Using the supplied Plastigage® scale, check width of Plastigage® at widest point to get maximum clearance. Difference between readings is taper of journal.

    d. If clearance exceeds specified limits, try a 0.001 in. or 0.002 in. undersize bearing in combination with the standard bearing. Bearing clearance must be within specified limits. If standard and 0.002 in. undersize bearing does not bring clearance within desired limits, refinish crankshaft journal, then install undersize bearings.

4-CYLINDER ENGINES

▶ See Figures 270 and 271

1. After the bearings have been fitted, apply a light coat of engine oil to the journals and bearings. Install all bearing caps except the thrust bearing cap. Be sure that main bearing caps are installed in original locations. Tighten the bearing cap bolts to specifications.

2. Install the thrust bearing cap with bolts finger-tight.

3. Pry the crankshaft forward against the thrust surface of upper half of bearing.

4. Hold the crankshaft forward and pry the thrust bearing cap to the rear. This aligns the thrust surfaces of both halves of the bearing.

5. Retain the forward pressure on the crankshaft. Tighten the cap bolts to specifications.

6. Measure the crankshaft end-play as follows:

    a. Mount a dial gauge to the engine block and position the tip of the gauge to read from the crankshaft end.

    b. Carefully pry the crankshaft toward the rear of the engine and hold it there while you zero the gauge.

    c. Carefully pry the crankshaft toward the front of the engine and read the gauge.

    d. Confirm that the reading is within specifications. If not, install a new thrust bearing and repeat the procedure. If the reading is still out of specifications with a new bearing, have a machine shop inspect the thrust surfaces of the crankshaft, and if possible, repair it.

7. Install the rear main seal.

8. Rotate the crankshaft so as to position the first rod journal to the bottom of its stroke.

6-CYLINDER ENGINES

1. After the bearings have been fitted, apply a light coat of engine oil to the journals and bearings.

2. Install the crankshaft into the cylinder block.

3. Apply silicone sealant to the contact surfaces as shown. Bead thickness should be 0.10–0.13 inches (2.5–3.5 mm).

➥The main bearing cap/block half must be installed within 5 minutes of applying the silicone sealant. If this time limit is exceeded, all of the silicone must be cleaned off and a fresh bead applied.

4. Lower the bearing cap/block half assembly into position.

➥Refer to the illustrations to determine proper bolt placement and tightening sequences. Also, the bolts will be referred to as A, B and C bolts. Note the following:

- Bolts A are marked with the number "4" on the head.
- Bolts B are marked with the number "1" or "I" on the head.
- Bolts C have no markings on the head.

5. Apply clean engine oil to the threads and seat faces of the lower cylinder block bolts and install them hand-tight.

6. Tighten the bolts marked A and B to 17–19 ft. lbs. (23–26 Nm) in the sequence shown.

7. Tighten the bolts marked C to 13.5–15.5 ft. lbs. (18–21 Nm) in the sequence shown.

8. Put a paint mark on the lower cylinder block half next to the A, B and C bolt flange marks as shown.

9. Using the marks as a reference, further tighten the bolts A and B in sequence, and bolts C in sequence, until the second mark on the bolt flanges aligns with the paint marks.

10. The distance between the marks is as follows:

    a. Bolt A: 75–85°

    b. Bolt B: 65–75°

    c. Bolt C: 55–65°

11. Further tighten the bolts by performing the above steps again.

12. Install and tighten the eight remaining outer bolts (marked D in the illustration) to 14–18 ft. lbs. (19–25 Nm).

13. Install the rear main seal.

14. Rotate the crankshaft so as to position the first rod journal to the bottom of its stroke.

Pistons and Connecting Rods

▶ See Figures 272, 273, 274 and 275

1. Before installing the piston/connecting rod assembly, oil the pistons, piston rings and the cylinder walls with light engine oil. Install connecting rod bolt protectors or rubber hose onto the connecting rod bolts/studs. Also perform the following:

    a. Select the proper ring set for the size cylinder bore.

    b. Position the ring in the bore in which it is going to be used.

    c. Push the ring down into the bore area where normal ring wear is not encountered.

    d. Use the head of the piston to position the ring in the bore so that the ring is square with the cylinder wall. Use caution to avoid damage to the ring or cylinder bore.

    e. Measure the gap between the ends of the ring with a feeler gauge. Ring gap in a worn cylinder is normally greater than specification. If the ring gap is greater than the specified limits, try an oversize ring set.

    f. Check the ring side clearance of the compression rings with a feeler gauge inserted between the ring and its lower land according to specification.

The gauge should slide freely around the entire ring circumference without binding. Any wear that occurs will form a step at the inner portion of the lower land. If the lower lands have high steps, the piston should be replaced.

2. Unless new pistons are installed, be sure to install the pistons in the cylinders from which they were removed. The numbers on the connecting rod and bearing cap must be on the same side when installed in the cylinder bore. If a connecting rod is ever transposed from one engine or cylinder to another, new bearings should be fitted and the connecting rod should be numbered to correspond with the new cylinder number. The notch on the piston head goes toward the front of the engine.

3. Install all of the rod bearing inserts into the rods and caps.

4. Install the rings to the pistons. Install the oil control ring first, then the second compression ring and finally the top compression ring. Use a piston ring expander tool to aid in installation and to help reduce the chance of breakage.

5. Make sure the ring gaps are properly spaced around the circumference of the piston. Fit a piston ring compressor around the piston and slide the piston and connecting rod assembly down into the cylinder bore, pushing it in with the wooden hammer handle. Push the piston down until it is only slightly below the top of the cylinder bore. Guide the connecting rod onto the crankshaft bearing journal carefully, to avoid damaging the crankshaft.

6. Check the bearing clearance of all the rod bearings, fitting them to the crankshaft bearing journals. Follow the procedure in the crankshaft installation above.

7. After the bearings have been fitted, apply a light coating of assembly oil to the journals and bearings.

8. Turn the crankshaft until the appropriate bearing journal is at the bottom of its stroke, then push the piston assembly all the way down until the connecting rod bearing seats on the crankshaft journal. Be careful not to allow the bearing cap screws to strike the crankshaft bearing journals and damage them.

9. After the piston and connecting rod assemblies have been installed, check the connecting rod side clearance on each crankshaft journal.

Fig. 272 Checking the piston ring-to-ring groove side clearance using the ring and a feeler gauge

10. Prime and install the oil pump and the oil pump intake tube.
11. Install the cylinder head(s) using new gaskets.
12. Install the timing sprockets/gears and the belt/chain assemblies.

Install the timing cover(s) and oil pan. Refer to your notes and drawings made prior to disassembly and install all of the components that were removed. Install the engine into the vehicle.

Engine Start-up and Break-in

STARTING THE ENGINE

Now that the engine is installed and every wire and hose is properly connected, go back and double check that all coolant and vacuum hoses are connected. Check that you oil drain plug is installed and properly tightened. If not already done, install a new oil filter onto the engine. Fill the crankcase with the proper amount and grade of engine oil. Fill the cooling system with a 50/50 mixture of coolant/water.

1. Connect the vehicle battery.
2. Start the engine. Keep your eye on your oil pressure indicator; if it does not indicate oil pressure within 10 seconds of starting, turn the vehicle off.

✷✷ WARNING

Damage to the engine can result if it is allowed to run with no oil pressure. Check the engine oil level to make sure that it is full. Check for any leaks and if found, repair the leaks before continuing. If there is still no indication of oil pressure, you may need to prime the system.

3. Confirm that there are no fluid leaks (oil or other).
4. Allow the engine to reach normal operating temperature (the upper radiator hose will be hot to the touch).
5. If necessary, set the ignition timing.
6. Install any remaining components such as the air cleaner (if removed for ignition timing) or body panels which were removed.

BREAKING IT IN

Make the first miles on the new engine, easy ones. Vary the speed but do not accelerate hard. Most importantly, do not lug the engine, and avoid sustained high speeds until at least 100 miles. Check the engine oil and coolant levels frequently. Expect the engine to use a little oil until the rings seat. Change the oil and filter at 500 miles, 1500 miles, then every 3000 miles past that.

KEEP IT MAINTAINED

Now that you have just gone through all of that hard work, keep yourself from doing it all over again by thoroughly maintaining it. Not that you may not have maintained it before, heck you could have had one to two hundred thousand miles on it before doing this. However, you may have bought the vehicle used, and the previous owner did not keep up on maintenance. Which is why you just went through all of that hard work. See?

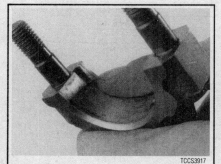

Fig. 273 The notch on the side of the bearing cap matches the tang on the bearing insert

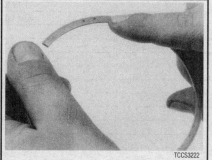

Fig. 274 Most rings are marked to show which side of the ring should face up when installed to the piston

Fig. 275 Install the piston and rod assembly into the block using a ring compressor and the handle of a hammer

1.5L (Z5) ENGINE TORQUE SPECIFICATIONS

Component	English	Metric
Camshaft cap bolts	125 inch lbs.	14 Nm
Camshaft sprocket bolt	44 ft. lbs.	60 Nm
Connecting rod bolts	22-25 ft. lbs.	30-34 Nm
Crankshaft sprocket bolt	116-123 ft. lbs.	158-167 Nm
Cylinder head bolts*		
Step 1:	12.7-16.2 ft. lbs.	17.2-22.0 Nm
Step 2:	+85-95 degrees turn	+85-95 degrees turn
Step 3:	+85-95 degrees turn	+85-95 degrees turn
Cylinder head cover bolts	61-95.4 inch lbs.	6.9-10.7 Nm
Exhaust manifold nuts/bolts	12-17 ft. lbs.	17-23 Nm
Exhaust pipe flange nuts	28-38 ft. lbs.	38-51 Nm
Flywheel bolts	71-76 ft. lbs.	97-103 Nm
Intake manifold bolts	14-19 ft. lbs.	19-25 Nm
Main bearing cap bolts	40-43 ft. lbs.	55-58 Nm
Oil pan bolts*		
Pan-to-engine support	95 inch lbs.	11 Nm
Engine support-to-block	12-15 ft. lbs.	16-20 Nm
Oil pump bolts	14-18 ft. lbs.	19-25 Nm
Spark plugs	11-16 ft. lbs.	15-21 Nm
Timing belt cover bolts	95 inch lbs.	11 Nm
Water pump nuts/bolts	14-18 ft. lbs.	19-25 Nm

* See text for sequence

89543C13

1.6L (B6) ENGINE TORQUE SPECIFICATIONS

Component	English	Metric
Camshaft cap bolts	100-125 inch lbs.	11.3-14.2 Nm
Camshaft sprocket bolt	37-44 ft. lbs.	50-60 Nm
Connecting rod bolts		
SOHC engine		
323	35-38 ft. lbs.	48-51 Nm
MX-3	35-36 ft. lbs.	48-50 Nm
DOHC engine		
323	37-38 ft. lbs.	50-51 Nm
MX-3	35-36 ft. lbs.	48-50 Nm
Crankshaft sprocket bolt		
1990-91	80-87 ft. lbs.	109-118 Nm
1992-95	116-123 ft. lbs.	158-167 Nm
Cylinder head bolts	56-60 ft. lbs.	75-81 Nm
Cylinder head cover bolts	44-78 inch lbs.	5-9 Nm
Exhaust manifold nuts/bolts		
SOHC engine	12-17 ft. lbs.	17-23 Nm
DOHC engine	29-42 ft. lbs.	40-57 Nm
Exhaust pipe flange nuts	34 ft. lbs.	46 Nm
Flywheel bolts	71-76 ft. lbs.	97-103 Nm
Intake manifold bolts	14-19 ft. lbs.	19-25 Nm
Main bearing cap bolts	40-43 ft. lbs.	55-58 Nm
Oil pan bolts		
323	95 inch lbs.	11 Nm
MX-3		
Bolts A*	95 inch lbs.	11 Nm
Bolts B*	38 ft. lbs.	52 Nm
Oil pump bolts	19 ft. lbs.	25 Nm
Rocker arm shaft bolts		
SOHC engines	21 ft. lbs.	28 Nm
Spark plugs	11-16 ft. lbs.	15-21 Nm
Timing belt cover bolts	95 inch lbs.	11 Nm
Water pump nuts/bolts	19 ft. lbs.	25 Nm

* See text for sequence

89543C14

1.8L (BP) ENGINE TORQUE SPECIFICATIONS

Component	English	Metric
Camshaft cap bolts	125 inch lbs.	14 Nm
Camshaft sprocket bolt		
SOHC engine	45 ft. lbs.	61 Nm
DOHC engine	44 ft. lbs.	60 Nm
Connecting rod bolts		
SOHC engine	36-38 ft. lbs.	49-51 Nm
DOHC engine	35-37 ft. lbs.	48-50 Nm
Crankshaft sprocket bolt		
1990-91	80-87 ft. lbs.	109-118 Nm
1992-98	116-123 ft. lbs.	158-167 Nm
Cylinder head bolts	56-60 ft. lbs.	75-81 Nm
Cylinder head cover bolts	78 inch lbs.	9 Nm
Exhaust manifold nuts/bolts		
SOHC engine	12-17 ft. lbs.	17-23 Nm
DOHC engines	28-34 ft. lbs.	38-46 Nm
Exhaust pipe flange nuts	34 ft. lbs.	46 Nm
Flywheel bolts	71-76 ft. lbs.	97-103 Nm
Intake manifold bolts	14-19 ft. lbs.	19-25 Nm
Main bearing cap bolts	40-43 ft. lbs.	55-58 Nm
Oil pan bolts		
Bolts A*	95 inch lbs.	11 Nm
Bolts B*	38 ft. lbs.	52 Nm
Oil pump bolts	19 ft. lbs.	25 Nm
Rocker arm shaft bolts		
SOHC engines	21 ft. lbs.	28 Nm
Spark plugs	11-16 ft. lbs.	15-21 Nm
Timing belt cover bolts	95 inch lbs.	11 Nm
Water pump nuts/bolts	19 ft. lbs.	25 Nm

    * See text for sequence

89543C15

2.0L ENGINE TORQUE SPECIFICATIONS

Component	English	Metric
Camshaft cap bolts	125 inch lbs.	14 Nm
Camshaft sprocket bolt	44 ft. lbs.	60 Nm
Connecting rod bolts		
Step 1:	19 ft. lbs.	26 Nm
Step 2:	+ 90 degrees turn	+ 90 degrees turn
Crankshaft sprocket bolt	116-123 ft. lbs.	158-167 Nm
Cylinder head bolts		
Step 1:	16 ft. lbs.	22 Nm
Step 2:	+ 90 degrees turn	+ 90 degrees turn
Step 3:	+ 90 degrees turn	+ 90 degrees turn
Cylinder head cover bolts	69 inch lbs.	8 Nm
Exhaust manifold nuts/bolts		
Nuts	15-20 ft. lbs.	21-27 Nm
Bolts	12-16 ft. lbs.	17-21 Nm
Exhaust pipe flange nuts	34 ft. lbs.	46 Nm
Flywheel bolts	71-76 ft. lbs.	97-103 Nm
Intake manifold bolts	14-18 ft. lbs.	19-24 Nm
Main bearing cap bolts		
Step 1:	16 ft. lbs.	22 Nm
Step 2:	+ 90 degrees turn	+ 90 degrees turn
Oil pan bolts	18 ft. lbs.	25 Nm
Oil pump bolts	19 ft. lbs.	25 Nm
Spark plugs	11-16 ft. lbs.	15-21 Nm
Timing belt cover bolts	95 inch lbs.	11 Nm
Water pump nuts/bolts	19 ft. lbs.	25 Nm

    * See text for sequence

89543C16

2.2L (FS) ENGINE TORQUE SPECIFICATIONS

Component	English	Metric
Camshaft sprocket bolt	48 ft. lbs.	65 Nm
Connecting rod bolts	48-51 ft. lbs.	66-69 Nm
Crankshaft sprocket bolt	116-123 ft. lbs.	158-167 Nm
Cylinder head bolts	59-64 ft. lbs.	80-86 Nm
Cylinder head cover bolts	69 inch lbs.	8 Nm
Exhaust manifold nuts/bolts	25-36 ft. lbs.	34-49 Nm
Exhaust pipe flange nuts	34 ft. lbs.	46 Nm
Flywheel bolts	71-76 ft. lbs.	97-103 Nm
Intake manifold bolts	14-22 ft. lbs.	19-30 Nm
Main bearing cap bolts	61-65 ft. lbs.	83-88 Nm
Oil pan bolts	95 inch lbs.	11 Nm
Oil pump bolts		
8mm bolts	19 ft. lbs.	25 Nm
10mm bolts	38 ft. lbs.	52 Nm
Rocker arm shaft bolts	20 ft. lbs.	26 Nm
Spark plugs	11-16 ft. lbs.	15-21 Nm
Timing belt cover bolts	87 inch lbs.	10 Nm
Water pump nuts/bolts	19 ft. lbs.	25 Nm

* See text for sequence

89543C17

1.8L (K8) & 2.5L (KL) ENGINE TORQUE SPECIFICATIONS

Component	English	Metric
Camshaft cap bolts	125 inch lbs.	14 Nm
Camshaft sprocket bolt	103 ft. lbs.	140 Nm
Connecting rod bolts		
Step 1:	19 ft. lbs.	26 Nm
Step 2:	+ 90 degrees turn	+ 90 degrees turn
Crankshaft sprocket bolt	116-123 ft. lbs.	158-167 Nm
Cylinder head bolts		
Step 1:	19 ft. lbs.	26 Nm
Step 2:	+ 90 degrees turn	+ 90 degrees turn
Step 3:	+ 90 degrees turn	+ 90 degrees turn
Cylinder head cover bolts	78 inch lbs.	9 Nm
Exhaust manifold nuts/bolts	14-18 ft. lbs.	19-24 Nm
Exhaust pipe flange nuts	34 ft. lbs.	46 Nm
Flywheel bolts	45-49 ft. lbs.	62-66 Nm
Intake manifold bolts	14-18 ft. lbs.	19-24 Nm
Main bearing cap bolts		
Step 1:		
Inner bolts	18 ft. lbs.	24 Nm
Outer bolts	15 ft. lbs.	20 Nm
Step 2:		
Inner bolts		
Nos. 1 2 & 3	+ 70 degrees turn	+ 70 degrees turn
No. 4	+ 80 degrees turn	+ 80 degrees turn
Outer bolts	+ 60 degrees turn	+ 60 degrees turn
Step 3:		
Inner bolts		
Nos. 1 2 & 3	+ 70 degrees turn	+ 70 degrees turn
No. 4	+ 80 degrees turn	+ 80 degrees turn
Outer bolts	+ 60 degrees turn	+ 60 degrees turn
Oil pan bolts		
Bolts A*	95 inch lbs.	11 Nm
Bolts B*	18 ft. lbs.	25 Nm
Oil pump bolts	19 ft. lbs.	25 Nm
Spark plugs	11-16 ft. lbs.	15-21 Nm
Timing belt cover bolts	95 inch lbs.	11 Nm
Water pump nuts/bolts	19 ft. lbs.	25 Nm

* See text for sequence

89543C18

2.3L (KJ) ENGINE TORQUE SPECIFICATIONS

Component	English	Metric
Camshaft cap bolts	125 inch lbs.	14 Nm
Camshaft sprocket bolt	103 ft. lbs.	140 Nm
Connecting rod bolts		
Step 1:	19 ft. lbs.	26 Nm
Step 2:	+ 90 degrees turn	+ 90 degrees turn
Crankshaft sprocket bolt	116-123 ft. lbs.	158-167 Nm
Cylinder head bolts		
Step 1:	19 ft. lbs.	26 Nm
Step 2:	+ 90 degrees turn	+ 90 degrees turn
Step 3:	+ 90 degrees turn	+ 90 degrees turn
Cylinder head cover bolts	78 inch lbs.	9 Nm
Exhaust manifold nuts/bolts	12-16 ft. lbs.	16-22 Nm
Exhaust pipe flange nuts	34 ft. lbs.	46 Nm
Flywheel bolts	45-49 ft. lbs.	62-66 Nm
Intake manifolds-to-cylinder head bolts	14-18 ft. lbs.	19-24 Nm
Lysholm compressor-to-mounting bracket nuts	16-22 ft. lbs.	22-30 Nm
Main bearing cap bolts*		
Step 1:		
Inner bolts	18 ft. lbs.	24 Nm
Outer bolts	15 ft. lbs.	20 Nm
Step 2:		
Inner bolts		
Nos. 1 2 & 3	+ 70 degrees turn	+ 70 degrees turn
No. 4	+ 80 degrees turn	+ 80 degrees turn
Outer bolts	+ 60 degrees turn	+ 60 degrees turn
Step 3:		
Inner bolts		
Nos. 1 2 & 3	+ 70 degrees turn	+ 70 degrees turn
No. 4	+ 80 degrees turn	+ 80 degrees turn
Outer bolts	+ 60 degrees turn	+ 60 degrees turn
Oil pan bolts		
Bolts A*	95 inch lbs.	11 Nm
Bolts B*	18 ft. lbs.	25 Nm
Oil pump bolts	14-18 ft. lbs.	19-25Nm
Spark plugs	11-16 ft. lbs.	15-21 Nm
Timing belt cover bolts	95 inch lbs.	11 Nm
Water pump nuts/bolts	14-18 ft. lbs.	19-25Nm

* See text for sequence

89543C20

Troubleshooting Engine Mechanical Problems

Problem	Cause	Solution
External oil leaks	• Cylinder head cover RTV sealant broken or improperly seated	• Replace sealant; inspect cylinder head cover sealant flange and cylinder head sealant surface for distortion and cracks
	• Oil filler cap leaking or missing	• Replace cap
	• Oil filter gasket broken or improperly seated	• Replace oil filter
	• Oil pan side gasket broken, improperly seated or opening in RTV sealant	• Replace gasket or repair opening in sealant; inspect oil pan gasket flange for distortion
	• Oil pan front oil seal broken or improperly seated	• Replace seal; inspect timing case cover and oil pan seal flange for distortion
	• Oil pan rear oil seal broken or improperly seated	• Replace seal; inspect oil pan rear oil seal flange; inspect rear main bearing cap for cracks, plugged oil return channels, or distortion in seal groove
	• Timing case cover oil seal broken or improperly seated	• Replace seal
	• Excess oil pressure because of restricted PCV valve	• Replace PCV valve
	• Oil pan drain plug loose or has stripped threads	• Repair as necessary and tighten
	• Rear oil gallery plug loose	• Use appropriate sealant on gallery plug and tighten
	• Rear camshaft plug loose or improperly seated	• Seat camshaft plug or replace and seal, as necessary
Excessive oil consumption	• Oil level too high	• Drain oil to specified level
	• Oil with wrong viscosity being used	• Replace with specified oil
	• PCV valve stuck closed	• Replace PCV valve
	• Valve stem oil deflectors (or seals) are damaged, missing, or incorrect type	• Replace valve stem oil deflectors
	• Valve stems or valve guides worn	• Measure stem-to-guide clearance and repair as necessary
	• Poorly fitted or missing valve cover baffles	• Replace valve cover
	• Piston rings broken or missing	• Replace broken or missing rings
	• Scuffed piston	• Replace piston
	• Incorrect piston ring gap	• Measure ring gap, repair as necessary
	• Piston rings sticking or excessively loose in grooves	• Measure ring side clearance, repair as necessary
	• Compression rings installed upside down	• Repair as necessary
	• Cylinder walls worn, scored, or glazed	• Repair as necessary

TCCS3202

USING A VACUUM GAUGE

The vacuum gauge is one of the most useful and easy-to-use diagnostic tools. It is inexpensive, easy to hook up, and provides valuable information about the condition of your engine.

White needle = steady needle   **Dark needle = drifting needle**

Indication: Normal engine in good condition

Gauge reading: Steady, from 17–22 in.Hg.

Indication: Late ignition or valve timing, low compression, stuck throttle valve, leaking carburetor or manifold gasket.

Gauge reading: Low (15–20 in.Hg.) but steady

Indication: Weak valve springs, worn valve stem guides, or leaky cylinder head gasket (vibrating excessively at all speeds).

NOTE: A plugged catalytic converter may also cause this reading.

Gauge reading: Needle fluctuates as engine speed increases

Indication: Choked muffler or obstruction in system. Speed up the engine. Choked muffler will exhibit a slow drop of vacuum to zero.

Gauge reading: Gradual drop in reading at idle

Indication: Sticking valve or ignition miss

Gauge reading: Needle fluctuates from 15–20 in.Hg. at idle

Indication: Improper carburetor adjustment, or minor intake leak at carburetor or manifold

NOTE: Bad fuel injector O-rings may also cause this reading.

Gauge reading: Drifting needle

Indication: Burnt valve or improper valve clearance. The needle will drop when the defective valve operates.

Gauge reading: Steady needle, but drops regularly

Indication: Worn valve guides

Gauge reading: Needle vibrates excessively at idle, but steadies as engine speed increases

TCCS3201

Troubleshooting Engine Mechanical Problems

Problem	Cause	Solution
Excessive oil consumption (cont.)	Piston ring gaps not properly staggered	Repair as necessary
	Excessive main or connecting rod bearing clearance	Measure bearing clearance, repair as necessary
No oil pressure	Low oil level	Add oil to correct level
	Oil pressure gauge, warning lamp or sending unit inaccurate	Replace oil pressure gauge or warning lamp
	Oil pump malfunction	Replace oil pump
	Oil pressure relief valve sticking	Remove and inspect oil pressure relief valve assembly
	Oil passages on pressure side of pump obstructed	Inspect oil passages for obstruction
	Oil pickup screen or tube obstructed	Inspect oil pickup for obstruction
	Loose oil inlet tube	Tighten or seal inlet tube
Low oil pressure	Low oil level	Add oil to correct level
	Inaccurate gauge, warning lamp or sending unit	Replace oil pressure gauge or warning lamp
	Oil excessively thin because of dilution, poor quality, or improper grade	Drain and refill crankcase with recommended oil
	Excessive oil temperature	Correct cause of overheating engine
	Oil pressure relief spring weak or sticking	Remove and inspect oil pressure relief valve assembly
	Oil inlet tube and screen assembly has restriction or air leak	Remove and inspect oil inlet tube and screen assembly. (Fill inlet tube with lacquer thinner to locate leaks.)
	Excessive oil pump clearance	Measure clearances
	Excessive main, rod, or camshaft bearing clearance	Measure bearing clearances, repair as necessary
High oil pressure	Improper oil viscosity	Drain and refill crankcase with correct viscosity oil
	Oil pressure gauge or sending unit inaccurate	Replace oil pressure gauge
	Oil pressure relief valve sticking closed	Remove and inspect oil pressure relief valve assembly
Main bearing noise	Insufficient oil supply	Inspect for low oil level and low oil pressure
	Main bearing clearance excessive	Measure main bearing clearance, repair as necessary
	Bearing insert missing	Replace missing insert
	Crankshaft end-play excessive	Measure end-play, repair as necessary
	Improperly tightened main bearing cap bolts	Tighten bolts with specified torque
	Loose flywheel or drive plate	Tighten flywheel or drive plate attaching bolts
	Loose or damaged vibration damper	Repair as necessary

TCCS3C03

Troubleshooting Engine Mechanical Problems

Problem	Cause	Solution
Connecting rod bearing noise	Insufficient oil supply	Inspect for low oil level and low oil pressure
	Carbon build-up on piston	Remove carbon from piston crown
	Bearing clearance excessive or bearing missing	Measure clearance, repair as necessary
	Crankshaft connecting rod journal out-of-round	Measure journal dimensions, repair or replace as necessary
	Misaligned connecting rod or cap	Repair as necessary
	Connecting rod bolts tightened improperly	Tighten bolts with specified torque
Piston noise	Piston-to-cylinder wall clearance excessive (scuffed piston)	Measure clearance and examine piston
	Cylinder walls excessively tapered or out-of-round	Measure cylinder wall dimensions, rebore cylinder
	Piston ring broken	Replace all rings on piston
	Loose or seized piston pin	Measure piston-to-pin clearance, repair as necessary
	Connecting rods misaligned	Measure rod alignment, straighten or replace
	Piston ring side clearance excessively loose or tight	Measure ring side clearance, repair as necessary
	Carbon build-up on piston is excessive	Remove carbon from piston
Valve actuating component noise	Insufficient oil supply	Check for: (a) Low oil level (b) Low oil pressure (c) Wrong hydraulic tappets (d) Restricted oil gallery (e) Excessive tappet to bore clearance
	Rocker arms or pivots worn	Replace worn rocker arms or pivots
	Foreign objects or chips in hydraulic tappets	Clean tappets
	Excessive tappet leak-down	Replace valve tappet
	Tappet face worn	Replace tappet; inspect corresponding cam lobe for wear
	Broken or cocked valve springs	Properly seat cocked springs; replace broken springs
	Stem-to-guide clearance excessive	Measure stem-to-guide clearance, repair as required
	Valve bent	Replace valve
	Loose rocker arms	Check and repair as necessary
	Valve seat runout excessive	Regrind valve seat/valves
	Missing valve lock	Install valve lock
	Excessive engine oil	Correct oil level

TCCS3C04

Troubleshooting Engine Performance

Problem	Cause	Solution
Hard starting (engine cranks normally)	• Faulty engine control system component	• Repair or replace as necessary
	• Faulty fuel pump	• Replace fuel pump
	• Faulty fuel system component	• Repair or replace as necessary
	• Faulty ignition coil	• Test and replace as necessary
	• Improper spark plug gap	• Adjust gap
	• Incorrect ignition timing	• Adjust timing
	• Incorrect valve timing	• Check valve timing; repair as necessary
Rough idle or stalling	• Incorrect curb or fast idle speed	• Adjust curb or fast idle speed (If possible)
	• Incorrect ignition timing	• Adjust timing to specification
	• Improper feedback system operation	• Refer to Chapter 4
	• Faulty EGR valve operation	• Test EGR system and replace as necessary
	• Faulty PCV valve air flow	• Test PCV valve and replace as necessary
	• Faulty TAC vacuum motor or valve	• Repair as necessary
	• Air leak into manifold vacuum	• Inspect manifold vacuum connections and repair as necessary
	• Faulty distributor rotor or cap	• Replace rotor or cap (Distributor systems only)
	• Improperly seated valves	• Test cylinder compression, repair as necessary
	• Incorrect ignition wiring	• Inspect wiring and correct as necessary
	• Faulty ignition coil	• Test coil and replace as necessary
	• Restricted air vent or idle passages	• Clean passages
	• Restricted air cleaner	• Clean or replace air cleaner filter element
Faulty low-speed operation	• Restricted idle air vents and passages	• Clean air vents and passages
	• Restricted air cleaner	• Clean or replace air cleaner filter element
	• Faulty spark plugs	• Clean or replace spark plugs
	• Dirty, corroded, or loose ignition secondary circuit wire connections	• Clean or tighten secondary circuit wire connections
	• Improper feedback system operation	• Refer to Chapter 4
	• Faulty ignition coil high voltage wire	• Replace ignition coil high voltage wire (Distributor systems only)
	• Faulty distributor cap	• Replace cap (Distributor systems only)
Faulty acceleration	• Incorrect ignition timing	• Adjust timing
	• Faulty fuel system component	• Repair or replace as necessary
	• Faulty spark plug(s)	• Clean or replace spark plug(s)
	• Improperly seated valves	• Test cylinder compression, repair as necessary
	• Faulty ignition coil	• Test coil and replace as necessary

TCCS3G05

Troubleshooting Engine Performance

Problem	Cause	Solution
Faulty acceleration (cont.)	• Improper feedback system operation	• Refer to Chapter 4
Faulty high speed operation	• Incorrect ignition timing	• Adjust timing (if possible)
	• Faulty advance mechanism	• Check advance mechanism and repair as necessary (Distributor systems only)
	• Low fuel pump volume	• Replace fuel pump
	• Wrong spark plug air gap or wrong plug	• Adjust air gap or install correct plug
	• Partially restricted exhaust manifold, exhaust pipe, catalytic converter, muffler, or tailpipe	• Eliminate restriction
	• Restricted vacuum passages	• Clean passages
	• Restricted air cleaner	• Cleaner or replace filter element as necessary
	• Faulty distributor rotor or cap	• Replace rotor or cap (Distributor systems only)
	• Faulty ignition coil	• Test coil and replace as necessary
	• Improperly seated valve(s)	• Test cylinder compression, repair as necessary
	• Faulty valve spring(s)	• Inspect and test valve spring tension, replace as necessary
	• Incorrect valve timing	• Check valve timing and repair as necessary
	• Intake manifold restricted	• Remove restriction or replace manifold
	• Worn distributor shaft	• Replace shaft (Distributor systems only)
	• Improper feedback system operation	• Refer to Chapter 4
Misfire at all speeds	• Faulty spark plug(s)	• Clean or relace spark plug(s)
	• Faulty spark plug wire(s)	• Replace as necessary
	• Faulty distributor cap or rotor	• Replace cap or rotor (Distributor systems only)
	• Faulty ignition coil	• Test coil and replace as necessary
	• Primary ignition circuit shorted or open intermittently	• Troubleshoot primary circuit and repair as necessary
	• Improperly seated valve(s)	• Test cylinder compression, repair as necessary
	• Faulty hydraulic tappet(s)	• Clean or replace tappet(s)
	• Improper feedback system operation	• Refer to Chapter 4
	• Faulty valve spring(s)	• Inspect and test valve spring tension, repair as necessary
	• Worn camshaft lobes	• Replace camshaft
	• Air leak into manifold	• Check manifold vacuum and repair as necessary
	• Fuel pump volume or pressure low	• Replace fuel pump
	• Blown cylinder head gasket	• Replace gasket
	• Intake or exhaust manifold passage(s) restricted	• Pass chain through passage(s) and repair as necessary
Power not up to normal	• Incorrect ignition timing	• Adjust timing
	• Faulty distributor rotor	• Replace rotor (Distributor systems only)

TCCS3G06

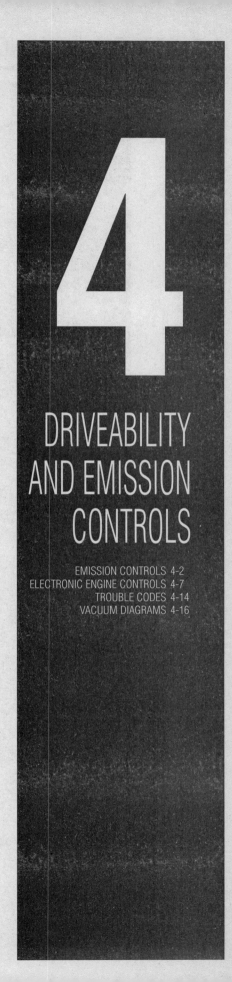

4

DRIVEABILITY AND EMISSION CONTROLS

EMISSION CONTROLS

EMISSION COMPONENT LOCATIONS

1. EVAP and EGR vacuum solenoids
2. PCV valve
3. EGR modulator
4. Camshaft position sensor
5. PCV breather hose
6. Idle speed control valve
7. Engine coolant temperature sensor
8. Mass airflow sensor
9. Intake air temperature sensor
10. EVAP charcoal canister

Crankcase Ventilation System

OPERATION

▶ **See Figure 1**

All Mazda engines are equipped with the Positive Crankcase Ventilation (PCV) system. The PCV system vents crankcase gases into the engine air intake where they are burned with the fuel and air mixture. The PCV system keeps pollutants from being released into the atmosphere, and also helps to keep the engine oil clean, by ridding the crankcase of moisture and corrosive fumes. The PCV system consists of the rocker arm cover mounted PCV valve, the nipple in the air intake and the connecting hoses.

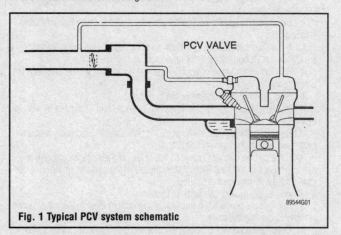

Fig. 1 Typical PCV system schematic

The PCV valve regulates the amount of ventilating air and blow-by gas to the intake manifold. It also prevents backfire from traveling into the crankcase, avoiding the explosion of crankcase gases.

TESTING

▶ **See Figure 2**

1. Visually inspect the PCV valve hose and the fresh air supply hose and their attaching nipples or grommets for splits, cuts, damage, clogging, or restrictions. Repair or replace, as necessary.
2. If the hoses pass inspection, remove the PCV valve from the rocker arm cover. Shake the PCV valve and listen or feel for the rattle of the valve plunger within the valve body. If the valve plunger does not rattle, the PCV valve should be cleaned or replaced.
3. Start the engine and bring it to normal operating temperature.
4. Unplug the PCV valve and check for vacuum at the valve. If no vacuum is felt check the hose for clogging.
5. Plug the valve back in. Remove the fresh air supply hose from the throttle body air hose nipple, and plug or cap the nipple immediately to keep the engine from stalling. Check for vacuum at the end of the supply hose using a stiff piece of paper. If the paper is retained by vacuum at the end of the hose, the PCV system is okay.
6. If the paper is not held by vacuum, check the fresh air and PCV hoses for leaks or loose connections. Also check for a loose fitting oil fill cap or loose dipstick. Correct as required until vacuum can be felt at the end of the supply hose.

➡**If air pressure and oil or sludge is present at the end of the fresh air supply hose, the engine has excessive blow-by and cylinder bore or piston ring wear.**

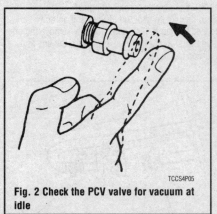

Fig. 2 Check the PCV valve for vacuum at idle

Fig. 3 To remove the PCV valve, first detach the vacuum hose connected to the valve . . .

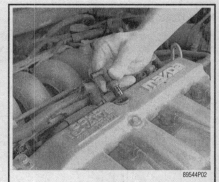

Fig. 4 . . . then pull the valve out of its retaining grommet

REMOVAL & INSTALLATION

▶ **See Figures 3 and 4**

1. Remove the PCV valve from the mounting grommet in the valve cover.
2. Disconnect the valve from the PCV hose and remove the valve from the vehicle.
3. Installation is the reverse of the removal procedure.

Evaporative Emission Control System

OPERATION

▶ **See Figure 5**

The evaporative emission control system prevents the escape of fuel vapors to the atmosphere under hot soak and engine off conditions by storing the vapors in a carbon canister. Then, with the engine warm and running, the system controls the purging of stored vapors from the canister to the engine, where

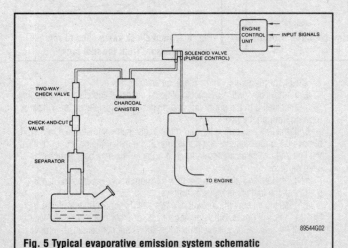

Fig. 5 Typical evaporative emission system schematic

they are efficiently burned. Evaporative emission control components consist of the fuel vapor valve, check valve, purge control solenoid valve(s), charcoal canister and input devices.

Charcoal Canister

▶ See Figure 6

The fuel vapors from the fuel tank are stored in the charcoal canister until the vehicle is operated, at which time, the vapors will purge from the canister into the engine for consumption. The charcoal canister contains activated carbon, which absorbs the fuel vapor. The canister is located in the engine compartment.

Purge Control Solenoid Valves

▶ See Figure 7

The purge control solenoid valves control the flow of fuel vapor from the carbon canister to the engine. The solenoid valves are electronically controlled. Purging occurs when the engine is at operating temperature and off idle.

Check Valve

▶ See Figure 8

The check valve releases excessive pressure or vacuum in the fuel tank to atmosphere. The valve is connected in-line with the evaporative hose and rollover/vent valve. On all engines, the valve is a 2-way check valve.

Fuel Vapor Valve

The fuel vapor valve prevents fuel vapors from flowing from the fuel tank at all times through the fuel tank hose. The valve is located in the fuel tank.

TESTING

▶ See Figure 9

1. Visually inspect the vapor and vacuum lines and connections for looseness, pinching, leakage, or other damage. If fuel line, vacuum line, or orifice

blockage is suspected as the obvious cause of a malfunction, correct the cause before proceeding further.

2. Check the wiring and connectors to the solenoid, vane air flow meter, speed sensor and ECM for looseness, corrosion, damage or other problems. This must be done with the engine fully warmed so as to activate the purging controls.

3. If all checks are okay, proceed with the testing.

4. Check the canister purge solenoid as follows:

    a. Detach the vacuum hoses and the electrical connector from the solenoid valve.

    b. Attach a clean test hose to port A.

    c. Blow air through the solenoid from port A and confirm that no air exits from port B.

    d. Apply 12 volts to one terminal of the solenoid connector and ground the other terminal.

    e. Blow air through the solenoid from port A and confirm that air exits from port B.

    f. If the solenoid does not function as specified, it must be replaced.

5. Check the carbon canister for liquid fuel as follows:

    a. Run the engine long enough to warm it up and purge any fuel from the carbon canister.

    b. Stop the engine and remove the canister.

    c. Inspect the canister for the presence of liquid fuel, indicated by odor or by excessive weight.

    d. Blow into the air vent in the bottom of the canister and verify that air exits readily from the fuel vapor inlet.

    e. If the carbon canister is free of liquid fuel and air passes through it easily, proceed to the next Step. If there is fuel in the canister or air does not pass through it, replace the canister.

6. Check for purge line blockage as follows:

    a. Remove the purge lines (including any orifice) leading from the carbon canister to the engine intake.

    b. Check each line for blockage by blowing through it. If air flows slowly, the line may contain an orifice that may be partially plugged.

    c. If the line allows air to flow freely, proceed to Step 8. If air flows very slow through the line, proceed to Step 7. If air does not flow, remove the orifice, clean it thoroughly and install it in a new line, or replace the line and orifice as an assembly; proceed to Step 8.

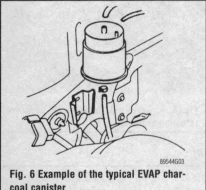

Fig. 6 Example of the typical EVAP charcoal canister

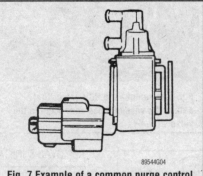

Fig. 7 Example of a common purge control valve or solenoid

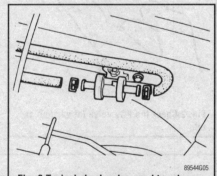

Fig. 8 Typical check valve used to release excess pressure from the fuel tank

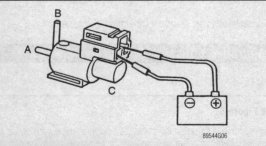

Fig. 9 By applying voltage to the solenoid valve, air flow between the ports should change

7. Check for purge line orifice blockage as follows:

    a. Remove any orifice suspected of being restricted and clean it thoroughly.

    b. Reinstall it in the purge line and recheck it for resistance to air flow by blowing through the line.

    c. If the line and orifice flow air more freely than when checked in Step 6, remove the orifice, replace the purge line, and reinstall the orifice, or replace the line and orifice as an assembly. The original line may contain accumulated particles.

    d. If the line and orifice do not flow air more freely, proceed to Step 8.

8. Check the fuel vapor valve as follows:

    a. Visually inspect the fuel vapor valve and its connections with the fuel tank for pinched hoses, blockage, looseness, or other mechanical damage.

    b. If the fuel vapor valve and its connections are not damaged, remove the valve from the fuel tank.

c. Holding the valve in an upright position, with the tank end pointing down, blow air into the valve exhaust hose connection. Air should flow freely.

d. Holding the valve in the reverse position, with the tank end pointing upward, blow air into the vapor exhaust hose connection, air should not flow.

e. If the valve does not operate properly, replace it.

9. Check the 2-way check valve function as follows:

a. Visually inspect the check valve and its connections for hose pinching, blockage, looseness, or for evidence of other damage or leakage.

b. Remove the 2-way check valve.

c. Blow air through the valve from A to B and then from B to A. Verify that air passes easily in either direction.

d. If there is no evidence of leakage, and air passes easily in either direction, the check valve is okay; system testing is completed. If the valve leaks or air will not pass easily, replace the 2-way check valve.

REMOVAL & INSTALLATION

▶ **See Figure 10**

Charcoal Canister

1. Disconnect the negative battery cable.
2. Tag and disconnect the vapor hoses from the canister.
3. Remove the canister fasteners and remove the canister.
4. Installation is the reverse of the removal procedure.

Fuel Vapor Valve

1. Disconnect the negative battery cable.
2. Relieve the fuel system pressure and drain the fuel tank.
3. Remove the fuel tank from the vehicle.
4. Remove the fuel vapor valve from the top of the fuel tank.
5. Installation is the reverse of the removal procedure.

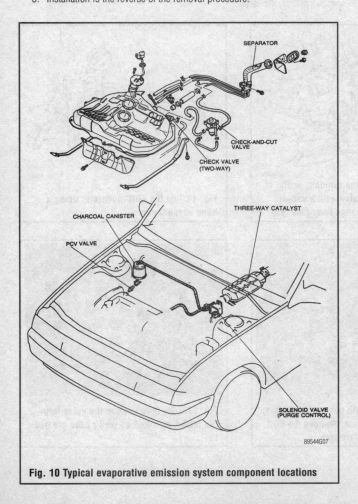

Fig. 10 Typical evaporative emission system component locations

Purge Control Solenoid Valve

1. Disconnect the negative battery cable.
2. Tag and disconnect the hoses from the valve.
3. If equipped, detach the electrical connector from the valve.
4. Remove the valve from its mounting and remove it from the vehicle.
5. Installation is the reverse of the removal procedure.

Check Valve

1. Disconnect the negative battery cable.
2. Raise and safely support the vehicle.
3. Tag and disconnect the vapor hoses from the check valve.
4. Remove the check valve mounting screw and the check valve from the underside of the vehicle.
5. Installation is the reverse of the removal procedure.

Exhaust Gas Recirculation System

OPERATION

▶ **See Figure 11**

The Exhaust Gas Recirculation (EGR) System introduces exhaust gas into the intake manifold which reduces the NOx content in the exhaust gas. The system utilizes a control valve, a modulator valve, the engine control unit, a solenoid valve, throttle sensor and a water thermosensor.

TESTING

EGR System

1. Start the engine.
2. Accelerate the engine and verify that the EGR control valve diaphragm does not move upon acceleration with the engine cold.
3. Continue to run the engine until it reaches the normal operating temperature.
4. Accelerate the engine and verify that the EGR control valve diaphragm moves upward upon acceleration with the engine warm.

EGR Valve

▶ **See Figures 12 and 13**

1. Manually operate the valve by pushing on the diaphragm with a finger.
2. There should be spring resistance felt and the diaphragm should not stick or bind.
3. Start the engine and allow it to reach normal operating temperature.
4. Attach a vacuum pump to the valve and apply vacuum.
5. The engine should begin to run rough or stall as the vacuum increases.
6. If there is no change in the engine speed, turn the engine **OFF**.
7. Apply at least 5.91 in.Hg (150mmHg) of vacuum to the valve to check for a bad diaphragm. The vacuum should stay at the same reading. If it does not, or you are not able to achieve a vacuum, replace the EGR valve.

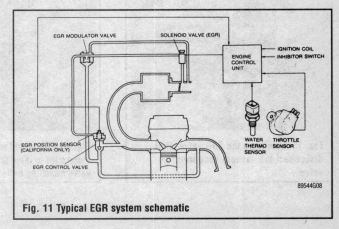

Fig. 11 Typical EGR system schematic

8. If the vacuum did not bleed off, remove the valve and check the passages for blockage. Clean as necessary.

EGR Modulator Valve

▶ **See Figure 14**

1. Remove the EGR modulator valve assembly.
2. Plug the number 1 port and attach a vacuum gauge to the number 3 port as shown.
3. Blow air into the exhaust port and operate the vacuum pump. Make sure that vacuum is held.
4. Release the plug from the exhaust port and make sure that the vacuum pressure is released.
5. If vacuum pressure is not held or released as required, replace the EGR modulator valve assembly.

EGR Solenoid Valve

DUAL PORT VALVE

1. Label and disconnect the vacuum hoses from the solenoid valve.
2. Detach the solenoid valve electrical connector.
3. As shown, blow air through the solenoid valve from vacuum port A and make sure that air flows out of port B.
4. Apply 12 volts and a ground to the valve at the electrical connector point.
5. Blow through the vent hose and make sure that the air flows.
6. Replace the solenoid valve if the valve is not as specified.

THREE PORT VALVE

Vent Side
1. Label and disconnect the vacuum hoses.
2. Blow through the vent hose and make sure the air flows.
3. Detach the solenoid valve electrical connector.

4. Apply 12 volts and a ground to the valve at the electrical connector point.
5. Blow through the vent hose and make sure that the air does not flow.
6. Replace the solenoid valve if the valve is not as specified.

Vacuum Side
7. Disconnect the vacuum hoses.
8. Blow through the vent hose and make sure the air does not flow.
9. Detach the solenoid valve electrical connector.
10. Apply 12 volts and a ground to the valve at the electrical connector point.
11. Blow through the vent hose and make sure that the air flows.
12. Replace the solenoid valve if the valve is not as specified.

REMOVAL AND INSTALLATION

▶ **See Figures 15, 16 and 17**

1. Disconnect the negative battery cable.
2. If necessary, remove the air cleaner assembly.
3. If equipped with an EGR position sensor, detach the wire harness connector from the sensor.
4. Some models use a cooling system preheat on the EGR valve, if so equipped, disconnect and plug the water hoses.
5. Disconnect the EGR valve vacuum line. If equipped with more than one hose, label their positions before disconnecting them.
6. If equipped, loosen the exhaust feed pipe retaining nut at the EGR valve and disconnect the pipe. Additional clearance can be gained by also loosening the retaining nut at the exhaust manifold, as well as any pipe retaining clamp bolts.
7. Remove the EGR valve mounting bolts or nuts and remove the valve.
8. Thoroughly clean the gasket mating surfaces.
9. Installation is the reverse of the removal procedure. Use a new gasket when installing the valve.

Fig. 12 Press on the underside of the EGR valve diaphragm to check for proper movement and resistance

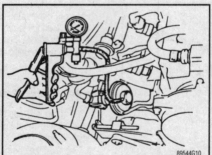

Fig. 13 With the engine running, apply vacuum to the EGR valve with a vacuum pump and verify a change in engine rpm

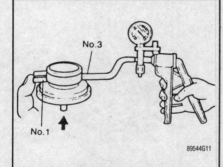

Fig. 14 Test the EGR modulator using a hand vacuum pump

Fig. 15 To remove the EGR valve, first disconnect the vacuum hose from the valve

Fig. 16 If equipped with two vacuum hoses, make sure to label them. Remove the EGR valve attaching bolts (arrows) . . .

Fig. 17 . . . then remove the valve from the intake manifold as well as the old gasket

ELECTRONIC ENGINE CONTROLS

Engine Control Unit (ECU)

OPERATION

The Engine Control Unit (ECU) does exactly what its name suggests; it controls the engine. By reading input signals from various sensors, it interprets the signal, then makes adjustments by controlling various output devices, such as the fuel injectors or an EGR solenoid. In this manner, the ECU can monitor and control the air/fuel ratio, ignition timing, idle speed, engine temperature, etc. By doing so, the ECU is able to run the engine at an optimal level at all times, giving fuel economy, power and stringent emission control.

REMOVAL AND INSTALLATION

▶ See Figure 18

✳✳ WARNING

Whenever working on or around the ECU, ensure that the negative battery cable has been disconnected. The ECU is a sensitive microcomputer and susceptible to electrical shock damage.

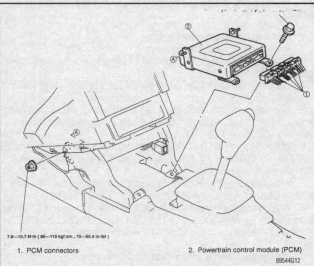

7.9—10.7 N·m (80—110 kgf·cm , 70—95.4 in·lbf)

1. PCM connectors
2. Powertrain control module (PCM)

89544G12

Fig. 18 The ECU is mounted under the center console. Typical ECU mounting shown

1. Disconnect the negative battery cable.
2. On all models except the 1993–98 626/MX-6/Probe models, proceed as follows:
    a. If necessary, remove the driver side under dash cover.
    b. Remove the passenger and driver side cover walls from the center console unit. On 1995–98 Protege, this includes the front center console cover as well.
    c. If applicable, detach the rear heater ducts behind the side covers to gain access to the ECU electrical connectors.
3. On 1993–98 626/MX-6/Probe models, remove the center console trim plate around the gear select lever.
4. Remove the ECU mounting bolts/nuts and detach the ECU electrical connectors.
5. Installation is the reverse of the removal procedure.

Oxygen Sensor

OPERATION

▶ See Figure 19

The oxygen sensor reacts with the oxygen in the exhaust gases and sends a voltage signal to the ECU based on this reaction. A low voltage signal indicates too much oxygen or a lean condition while a high voltage signal indicates not enough oxygen or a rich condition. The ECU uses this information along with other sensor inputs to calculate air/fuel ratio.

The oxygen sensor is threaded into the exhaust manifold and/or pipes on all engines except turbocharged engines. On turbocharged engines, the sensor is screwed into the turbocharger itself.

Some Mazda engines utilize more than one oxygen sensor, often having a front and rear sensor (as in V6 engines) and/or pre- and post catalytic converter sensors (which enables the ECU to measure catalytic converter efficiency).

TESTING

Sensor Output Voltage

▶ See Figures 20, 21 and 22

➡**If equipped with a heated element oxygen sensor (more than one wire connection), perform the Heater Element Resistance test first, as it requires a specific temperature. Performing the output voltage test first will require you to wait for the engine to almost completely cool down.**

1. Start the engine and bring to normal operating temperature.
2. Detach the oxygen sensor connector.
3. On single wire connectors, measure the voltage between the oxygen sensor wire and ground.

89544P21

Fig. 19 The O₂ sensor (A) is threaded into the exhaust so that the element (B) is in the exhaust gas stream

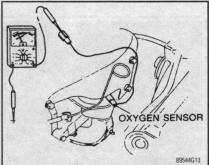

OXYGEN SENSOR

89544G13

Fig. 20 Measure the single wire sensors by grounding one terminal of the voltmeter and reading the sensor terminal with the engine running

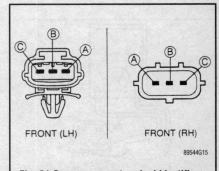

FRONT (LH)   FRONT (RH)

89544G15

Fig. 21 Oxygen sensor terminal identification for 3-wire sensors. If only one three wire sensor is used, the FRONT (LH) diagram should be used

4. On three wire connectors, measure the voltage between the oxygen sensor wire terminal A and ground.

5. On four wire connectors, measure the voltage between the oxygen sensor wire terminal A and terminal B.

6. When the engine speed is increased, the voltage should be 0.5–1.0 volts. When decreasing engine speed, the voltage should drop to 0–0.4 volts.

➡**Voltage that remains above 0.55 volts indicates a continuously rich condition while below 0.55 volts indicates a continuously lean condition. Rich or lean conditions could be an indication of another problem.**

7. If the voltage readings are not as specified, replace the oxygen sensor.

Heater Element Resistance

♦ **See Figures 21 and 22**

➡**This procedure does not apply to single wire sensors.**

1. Detach the oxygen sensor connector.
2. On three wire connectors, measure the resistance between terminals B and C.
3. On four wire connectors, measure the resistance between terminals C and D.
4. On all sensors except four wire front sensors, the resistance should read approximately 6 ohms at 68°F (20°C).
5. On four wire front sensors, the resistance should read approximately 13 ohms at 68°F (20°C).

➡**If the sensor readings are out of range, double check the temperature of the sensor. If the temperature is too hot or cold, it may influence an inaccurate reading. If possible, adjust the temperature of the sensor to the proper specification and re-check it.**

6. If the readings are not within range, replace the oxygen sensor.

REMOVAL AND INSTALLATION

Except Turbocharged Engines

♦ **See Figures 23, 24, 25 and 26**

1. If necessary, remove the under vehicle splash shield.
2. Detach the oxygen sensor electrical connector.
3. On some California models equipped with a V6 engine, it may be necessary to remove the exhaust manifold due to space limitations.
4. Remove the oxygen sensor from the exhaust manifold or pipe.
5. Installation is the reverse of the removal procedure. Tighten the oxygen sensor to 22–36 ft. lbs. (29–49 Nm).

Turbocharged Engines

1. Disconnect the negative battery cable.
2. Detach the sensor electrical connector.
3. Remove the wiring harness from the spark plug wire retaining bracket and the retaining bracket on the turbocharger heat shield.
4. Remove the sensor from the turbocharger.
5. Installation is the reverse of the removal procedure.

Mass Airflow Meter/Sensor

OPERATION

The mass airflow meter or sensor, measures the amount of air which passes through it. The ECU uses this information to determine the operating condition of the engine, to control fuel delivery. A large quantity of air indicates acceleration, while a small quantity indicates deceleration or idle. Mazda used two types of meters in their vehicles.

One style uses a mechanical door or cone system connected to a variable resistor. The door/cone is pushed open by the incoming air, which in turn changes the resistance. The wider the door/cone is open, the larger the amount of air flow. This style is generally called a Mass Air Flow (MAF) meter.

The second style functions on a hot wire principle. A wire is heated to a certain temperature. The amount of voltage necessary to keep the wire at that temperature with air flowing over it is used to calculate airflow. The more air that flows over the wire, the cooler it will become and the more voltage will be required to heat it. This style is generally called a Mass Airflow Sensor (MAS).

TESTING

♦ **See Figures 27, 28 and 29**

MX-3 (except 1.6L DOHC and 1.8L V6 Engine), 1990–94 323 and Protege

1. Disconnect the negative battery cable.
2. Remove the airflow meter assembly.
3. Inspect the meter body for cracks and for smooth operation of the measuring plate.
4. Using a suitable ohmmeter, check the resistance between the terminals of the airflow meter plate.
5. When measuring the resistance between terminals E1 and FC (fuel pump switch), the reading should be infinity with the plate fully closed and 0 ohms when fully opened.
6. When measuring the resistance between terminals E2 and VS, the reading should be 200–600 ohms with the measuring plate fully closed and 20–1000 ohms when fully opened.
7. When measuring the resistance between terminals E2 and VC, the reading should be 200–400 ohms with the metering plate in any position.
8. When measuring the resistance between terminals E2 and THA (intake air thermosensor), the reading should be 13.6–18.4 kohms at -4°F; 2.21–2.69 kohms at 68°F and 493–667 ohms at 140°F with the metering plate in any position.
9. If not as specified, the airflow meter must be replaced.

1990–92 626 and MX-6

1. Disconnect the negative battery cable.
2. Remove the airflow meter assembly.

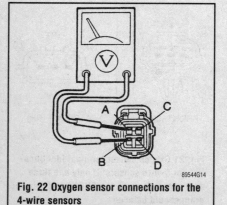

Fig. 22 Oxygen sensor connections for the 4-wire sensors

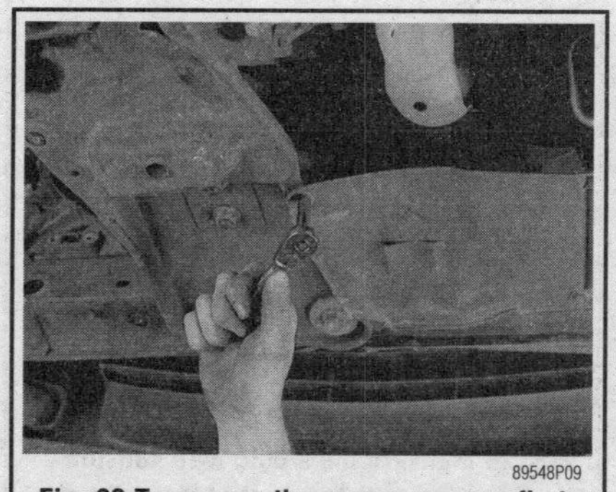

Fig. 23 To remove the oxygen sensor, first remove any splash shielding from the underside of the vehicle as required

Fig. 24 Detach the oxygen sesnor wire connection . . .

Fig. 25 . . . then loosen the sensor . . .

Fig. 26 . . . and remove it from the exhaust pipe or manifold

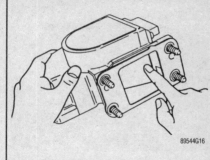

Fig. 27 On plate or cone type airflow meters, verify that the plate or cone moves freely

3. Inspect the meter body for cracks and for smooth operation of the measuring plate.

4. Using an ohmmeter, check the resistance between the terminals of the airflow meter plate.

5. When measuring the resistance between terminals E1 and FC (fuel pump switch), the reading should be infinity with the plate fully closed and 0 ohms when fully opened.

6. When measuring the resistance between terminals E2 and VS, the reading should be 200–400 ohms with the measuring plate fully closed and 20–1000 ohms when fully opened.

7. When measuring the resistance between terminals E2 and VC, the reading should be 100–400 ohms with the metering plate in any position.

8. When measuring the resistance between terminals E2 and VB, the reading should be 200–400 ohms with the metering plate in any position.

9. When measuring the resistance between terminals E2 and THA (intake air thermosensor), the reading should be 13.6–18.4 kohms at -4°F; 2.21–2.69 kohms at 68°F and 493–667 ohms at 140°F with the metering plate in any position.

10. If not as specified, the airflow meter must be replaced.

1994–95 MX-3 with 1.6L DOHC Engine, 1995–98 Protege

1. Disconnect the negative battery cable.
2. Remove the airflow meter assembly.
3. Inspect the meter body for cracks or damage.
4. Using an ohmmeter, measure the resistance between terminals C and D on the sensor.
5. The reading should be 2.21–2.69 kohms at 68°F (20°C).
6. If not as specified, replace the mass air flow sensor.

MX-3 (1.8L), 1993–98 626/MX-6/Probe (2.5L) with V6 Engines

1. Disconnect the negative battery cable.
2. Remove the airflow meter assembly.

3. Inspect the meter body for cracks and for smooth operation of the measuring cone.

4. Using an ohmmeter, check the resistance between the terminals of the airflow meter cone.

5. When measuring the resistance between terminals E2 and VS, the reading should be 200–1000 ohms with the measuring cone fully closed and 20–800 ohms when fully opened.

6. When measuring the resistance between terminals E2 and VC, the reading should be 200–400 ohms with the metering cone in any position.

7. When measuring the resistance between terminals E2 and THA (intake air thermosensor), the reading should be 2000–3000 ohms at 68°F (20°C) and 400–700 ohms at 140°F (60°C) with the metering cone in any position.

8. If not as specified, the airflow meter must be replaced.

626/MX-6/Probe with 2.0L Engine and Millenia

1. Back probe terminal B (center wire) of the air flow sensor electrical connector using a high impedance volt meter.
2. Connect the other termianl of the meter to ground.
3. Turn the ignition switch to the **ON** position.
4. The meter should read 1.0–1.5 volts.
5. Start the engine and allow to idle.
6. The volt meter should read 1.5–2.5 volts.
7. If the readings are not as specified, replace the sensor.

REMOVAL AND INSTALLATION

▶ **See Figures 30, 31, 32 and 33**

1. Disconnect the negative battery cable.
2. Loosen the hose band and remove the intake hose.
3. Remove the airflow meter attaching bolts and detach the wire harness connector.
4. Remove the airflow meter from the air cleaner housing.
5. Installation is the reverse order of the removal procedure.

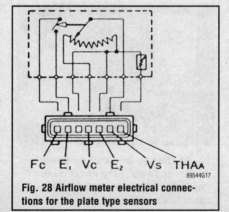

Fig. 28 Airflow meter electrical connections for the plate type sensors

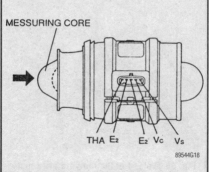

Fig. 29 Airflow meter electrical connections for the cone type sensors

Fig. 30 To remove the mass air flow sensor, first detach its wire harness connection

Fig. 31 Next, remove the sensor-to-air cleaner housing retaining bolts and loosen the air intake pipe clamp

Fig. 32 Pull the sensor out of the air cleaner housing

Fig. 33 Inspect the air flow sensor sealing ring and replace as needed

Water Thermosensor (Coolant Temperature Sensor)

OPERATION

The coolant temperature sensor is a variable resistor that is influenced by temperature. Which means, as the temperature changes, so does the resistance inside the sensor. The computer reads this change in resistance to determine the operating temperature of the engine. It uses this reading to determine proper air/fuel mixture and ignition timing settings.

TESTING

♦ See Figures 34 and 35

➡ This test can also be performed with the sensor still installed in the motor, provided the engine is at the same temperatures as given for the specifications.

1. Remove the thermosensor.
2. Place the sensor in water with a thermometer and heat the water gradually.
3. Measure the resistance of the sensor and compare to the following values:
- -4°F (-20°C)—14.6–17.8 kohms
- 68°F (20°C)—2.2–2.7 kohms
- 104°F (40°C)—1.0–1.3 kohms
- 140°F (60°C)—0.50–0.65 kohms
- 176°F (80°C)—0.29–0.35 kohms

REMOVAL & INSTALLATION

1. Drain the engine coolant.
2. Remove the thermosensor from the rear of the engine or intake manifold.
To install:
3. Install a new sealing washer to the thermosensor.
4. Torque the sensor to 18–22 ft. lbs. (25–29 Nm).

Intake Air Temperature (IAT) Sensor

OPERATION

The intake air temperature sensor is a variable resistor that is influenced by temperature. Which means, as the temperature changes, so does the resistance inside the sensor. The computer reads this change in resistance to determine the temperature of the incoming air. It uses this reading to determine proper air/fuel mixture and ignition timing settings.

TESTING

♦ See Figure 36

➡ Vehicles which use a plate or cone type mass air flow meter have the IAT sensor built into the meter. Refer to the air flow meter testing earlier in this section.

1. Disconnect the negative battery cable.
2. Detach the IAT sensor connector.
3. Connect an ohmmeter across the sensor connectors.
4. Measure the resistance of the sensor and compare to the following values:
- 77°F (25°C)—29.7–36.3 kohms
- 185°F (85°C)—3.3–3.7 kohms
5. If not as specified, replace the sensor.

REMOVAL & INSTALLATION

♦ See Figure 37

1. Disconnect the negative battery cable.
2. Remove the IAT sensor from the air cleaner housing or intake air pipe.
To install:
3. Install a new sealing washer to the thermosensor.

Fig. 34 To test the sensor while still installed in the engine, verify the temperature of the sensor then take the resistance reading

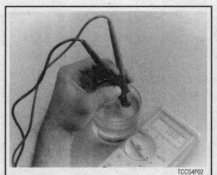

Fig. 35 The end of the temperature sensor can be submerged in cold or hot water to check the resistance

Fig. 36 Measure the sensor resistance by connecting an ohmmeter across the two terminals. This sensor reads infinte indicating it is bad

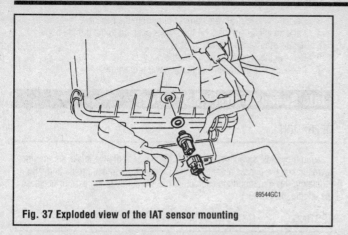

Fig. 37 Exploded view of the IAT sensor mounting

Throttle Position Sensor

OPERATION

The throttle position sensor is a variable resistor. As the accelerator pedal is depressed and released, the resistance inside the sensor changes. The computer uses this reading to determine proper air/fuel mixture and ignition timing settings.

TESTING

▶ **See Figures 38, 39 and 40**

MX-3 with 1.6L SOHC Engine, 323 and Protege

MANUAL TRANSAXLE

1. Detach the connector from the throttle position sensor.
2. Connect an ohmmeter between terminals IDL and E.
3. Insert a 0.004 in. (0.1mm) feeler gauge between the throttle stop screw and stop lever.
4. Verify there is continuity between terminals IDL and E.
5. Then replace the feeler gauge with a 0.039 in. (1.0mm) feeler gauge, verify there is no continuity between terminals **IDL** and **E**.
6. Then open the throttle wide and verify there is no continuity again between terminals IDL and E.
7. Next, connect the ohmmeter between terminals POW and E.
8. Insert a 0.004 in. (0.1mm) feeler gauge between the throttle stop screw and stop lever.
9. Verify there is no continuity between terminals POW and E.
10. Then replace the feeler gauge with 0.039 in. (1.0mm), verify there is no continuity between terminals POW and E.
11. Then open the throttle wide and verify there is continuity between terminals POW and E.
12. If not as specified, adjust or replace the throttle sensor.

AUTOMATIC TRANSAXLE

1. Detach the connector from the throttle position sensor.
2. Connect an ohmmeter between terminals IDL and E.
3. Insert a 0.004 in. (0.1mm) feeler gauge between the throttle stop screw and stop lever.
4. Verify there is continuity between terminals IDL and E.
5. Insert a 0.024 in. (0.6mm) feeler gauge between the throttle stop screw and stop lever.
6. Verify there is continuity no between terminals IDL and E.
7. Connect an ohmmeter to the throttle sensor terminals Vt and E.
8. Verify that resistance increases as throttle valve opening increase.
9. With throttle valve fully closed the resistance should be below 1 kilohm and as throttle valve is fully opened resistance should increase to approximately 5 kohms.
10. If not as specified, adjust or replace the throttle sensor.

626 and MX-6 with 2.2L Engine

1. Remove the air hose from the throttle body.
2. Detach the 3-pin throttle sensor connector.
3. Connect the 49-G018-901 testing harness or equivalent, between the throttle sensor and the wiring harness.
4. Turn the ignition switch **ON**.
5. Verify the throttle valve is fully closed.
6. Measure the voltage at the black and the red wires of the testing harness using a precision voltmeter with a scale of 0.01 volts, the voltage at the black wire should be approximately 0 volts and the voltage at the red wire should be 4.5–5.5 volts.
7. If the voltage reading is not as specified, check the battery voltage and wiring harness, if these are okay, replace the engine control unit.
8. Record the red wire voltage.
9. Measure the voltage of the blue wire, verify that the blue wire voltage is within specification according to the red wire voltage. For example; if the red wire voltage reading is 4.50–4.59 volts, then the blue wire voltage reading would have to be within 0.37–0.54 volts.
10. Hold the throttle valve fully open.
11. Measure the blue wire voltage, verify that the blue wire voltage is within specification according to that of the red wire voltage. For example; if the red wire voltage reading is 4.50–4.59 volts, then the blue wire voltage reading would have to be within 3.58–4.23 volts.
12. Check that blue wire voltage increases smoothly when opening the throttle valve from closed to fully open.
13. If the throttle sensor does not perform as specified, adjust or replace the sensor.
14. Turn the ignition **OFF**.
15. Detach the testing harness and reattach the throttle sensor connector.
16. Disconnect the negative battery terminal and depress the brake pedal for at least 5 seconds to eliminate the control unit malfunction memory.

MX-3 with 1.6L DOHC and 626/MX-6/Probe with 2.0L Engine

MANUAL TRANSAXLE

1. Detach the connector from the throttle position sensor.
2. Connect an ohmmeter between terminals IDL and E.

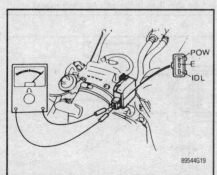

Fig. 38 Throttle position sensor test connections for 3-wire sensors

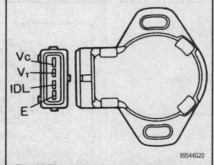

Fig. 39 Throttle position sensor test connections for 4-wire sensors

Fig. 40 When measuring the resistance (arrow), open and close the throttle and check for smooth changes in resistance

3. Insert a 0.004 in. (0.1mm) feeler gauge between the throttle stop screw and stop lever.

4. Verify there is continuity between terminals IDL and E.

5. Then replace the feeler gauge with a 0.027 in. (0.7mm) feeler gauge, verify there is no continuity between terminals IDL and E

6. Then open the throttle wide and verify there is no continuity again between terminals IDL and E.

7. Next, connect the ohmmeter between terminals POW and E.

8. Insert a 0.004 in. (0.1mm) feeler gauge between the throttle stop screw and stop lever.

9. Verify there is no continuity between terminals POW and E.

10. Then replace the feeler gauge with 0.027 in (0.7mm), verify there is no continuity between terminals POW and E.

11. Then open the throttle wide and verify there is continuity between terminals POW and E.

12. If not as specified, adjust or replace the throttle

AUTOMATIC TRANSAXLE

1. Detach the connector from the throttle position sensor.

2. Connect an ohmmeter between the terminals IDL and E.

3. Insert a 0.004 in. (0.1mm) feeler gauge between the throttle stop screw and stop lever.

4. Verify there is continuity between terminals IDL and E.

5. Insert a 0.024 in. (0.6mm) feeler gauge between the throttle stop screw and stop lever.

6. Verify there is no continuity between terminals IDL and E.

7. Connect an ohmmeter to the throttle sensor terminals Vt and E.

8. Verify that resistance increases as throttle valve opening increase.

9. With throttle valve fully closed the resistance should be below 1 kilohm and as throttle valve is fully opened resistance should increase to approximately 5 kohms.

10. If not as specified, adjust or replace the throttle sensor.

Millenia, MX-3 with 1.8L (K8) and 626/MX-6/Probe with 2.5L Engines

1. Detach the connector from the throttle position sensor.

2. Connect an ohmmeter between terminals IDL and GND.

3. Detach the electrical wire harness plug from the sensor.

4. Paint an alignment mark on the sensor housing to the throttle body.

5. Remove the sensor attaching bolts.

6. Remove the sensor from the throttle body.

7. Installation is the reverse of the removal procedure.

Idle Speed Control (ISC) Valve

OPERATION

To improve idle smoothness, the ISC system controls the intake air amount by regulating the bypass air amount that passes through the throttle body. By regulating this air amount, the computer has the ability to increase or decrease the engine idle speed.

TESTING

▶ **See Figures 42, 43 and 44**

1. Detach the ISC valve connector when the engine is cold and idling.

2. Note the engine rpm and reconnect the connector.

3. Warm the engine to normal operating temperature and detach the connector again.

4. Verify the engine rpm is lower with the ISC detached when the engine is warm.

5. Check the resistance of the valve using an ohmmeter.

6. The resistance should be approximately:
- 1990–92 626 and MX-6: 6.3–9.9 ohms at normal operating temperature.
- 1993–98 626/MX-6/Probe: 7.7–9.3 ohms at 73°F (23°C).
- 1990–94 323 and Protege: 11–13 ohms at 68°F (20°C).
- 1995–98 Protege: 7.7–9.3 ohms at 73°F (23°C).
- MX-3 and Millenia: 10.7–12.3 ohms at 68°F (20°C).

7. If not as specified, remove the valve from the throttle body.

8. Blow air through the valve port A and verify that no air comes out of port B when the valve is at normal operating temperature.

9. Allow the valve to cool. Watch the movement of the valve as it cools, it should open.

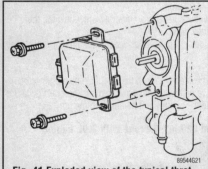

Fig. 41 Exploded view of the typical throttle position sensor-to-throttle body mounting

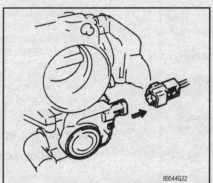

Fig. 42 To test the ISC valve, disconnect the IAC valve electrical plug

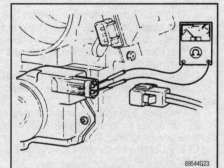

Fig. 43 Measure the resistance across both terminals of the ISC valve, at the temperature specified in the text for each model

3. Rotate the throttle linkage by hand. With the throttle valve fully closed, the ohmmeter should read 0.1–1.1 volts.

4. With the throttle valve fully open, the ohmmeter should read 3.1–4.4 volts.

5. If not as specified, adjust or replace the throttle position sensor.

REMOVAL & INSTALLATION

▶ **See Figure 41**

1. Disconnect the negative battery cable.

2. Remove the necessary air intake components to access the throttle position sensor.

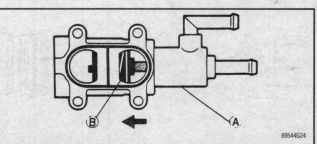

Fig. 44 With the valve removed, cool it down at point A and watch the valve movement at B

10. Blow air through the valve port A and verify air comes out of port B when the valve is cold.
11. If not as specified, replace the valve.

REMOVAL & INSTALLATION

▶ **See Figure 45**

1. Disconnect the negative battery cable.
2. If necessary for access, remove the air intake piping to the throttle body.
3. Detach the electrical harness connection from the valve, or valve pigtail.
4. Disconnect any hoses from the ISC valve. Some valves will also have engine coolant hoses connected to them. Plug the engine coolant hoses to minimize coolant leakage.
5. Remove the ISC valve attaching bolts.
6. Remove the ISC valve from the throttle body or intake manifold.
7. Thoroughly clean the gasket mating surfaces.
8. Installation is the reverse of the removal procedure.

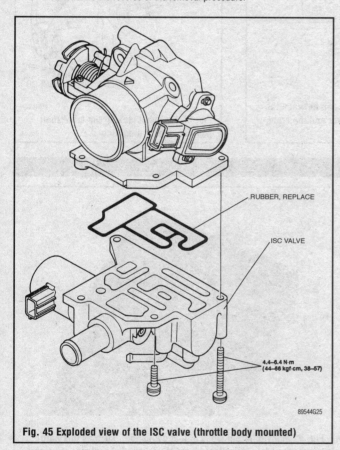

RUBBER, REPLACE

ISC VALVE

4.4—6.4 N·m
(44—66 kgf·cm, 38—57)

89544G25

Fig. 45 Exploded view of the ISC valve (throttle body mounted)

Camshaft Position Sensor

OPERATION

The camshaft position sensor reads the rotation of the camshaft which the computer translates to determine engine timing sequences. The computer uses these readings to determine engine rpm and proper fuel injection and ignition timing.

TESTING

▶ **See Figures 46 and 47**

➡ **The camshaft position sensor requires a scan tool in order to properly test the component.**

TCCS4P08

Fig. 46 When using a scan tool, make sure to follow all of the manufacturers instructions carefully to ensure proper diagnosis

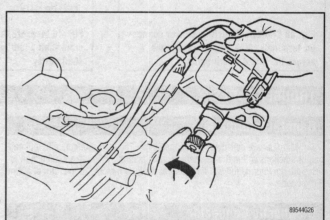

89544G26

Fig. 47 To test the camshaft position sensor, remove the distributor, connect a scan tool then rotate the distributor drive by hand

1. Connect a scan tool to the diagnostic link.
2. Detach the fuel injector wire harness connectors. This will ensure that the engine does not try to start and run while performing the test.
3. Remove the distributor from the engine.
4. Detach the 3-wire connector from the distributor.
5. Enable the scan tool to record the camshaft position sensor output.
6. Rotate the distributor drive by hand and verify that there were four 5 volt pulses within one revolution of the distributor drive.
7. If not as specified, replace the distributor assembly.

REMOVAL & INSTALLATION

The camshaft position sensor is an integral part of the distributor and not serviceable. The entire distributor assembly must be replaced. Refer to Section 2 for procedures involving the distributor.

Crankshaft Position Sensor

OPERATION

The crankshaft position sensor reads the rotation of the crankshaft which the computer translates to determine engine timing sequences. The computer uses this reading, in conjunction with the camshaft position sensor, to determine proper fuel injection and ignition timing.

TESTING

♦ **See Figures 48 and 49**

1. Disconnect the crankshaft position sensor wire harness plug.
2. Connect an ohmmeter to the sensor terminals A and B and measure the resistance.
3. The reading should be 520–580 ohms at 68°F (20°C).
4. If not as specified, replace the sensor.
5. Measure the air gap of the sensor between the crankshaft pulley and the sensor.
6. Proper air gap should be 0.040–0.080 in. (1–2 mm).

7. If not as specified, inspect the crankshaft pulley and/or replace the sensor.

REMOVAL & INSTALLATION

♦ **See Figure 50**

1. Disconnect the negative battery cable.
2. Remove the necessary accessory drive belts to access the sensor.
3. If necessary, remove the engine oil dipstick tube.
4. Remove the sensor attaching bolt, then withdraw the sensor from the engine.
5. Installation is the reverse of the removal procedure.

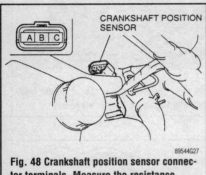

Fig. 48 Crankshaft position sensor connector terminals. Measure the resistance across the A and B terminals

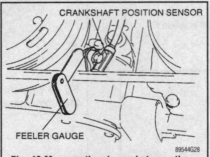

Fig. 49 Measure the air gap between the crankshaft position sensor and the crankshaft pulley

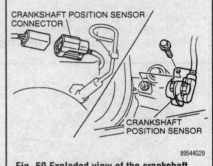

Fig. 50 Exploded view of the crankshaft position sensor mounting

TROUBLE CODES

General Information

All Mazdas have self-diagnostic capabilities. The ECU monitors all input and output functions within the electronic engine control system. If a malfunction is detected, the information will be stored in the ECU memory in the form of a 2 or 3 digit code.

Diagnostic Connector

The diagnostic connector (called the data link connector) on all models is located under the hood, on the driver side. On 1995 Protege and Millenia and all 1996–98 models, a second diagnostic connector (called data link connector-2) is located just under the drivers side of the dashboard, near the center console.

Models equipped with the data link connector-2, must use an OBD II compliant scanner or test equipment.

Reading Codes

♦ **See Figure 51**

If the check engine light comes on while the vehicle is running or driving, it indicates that the computer has detected a malfunction with one or more engine components, sensors or harness wiring, and a code has been set.

In order to retrieve the trouble code(s), you must have the Mazda system selector 49 B019 9A0 and self diagnosis checker (a digital readout tool) 49 H018 9A1 or an equivalent OBD I compliant scan tool for 1990–95 (except 1994–95 626 with ATX and 1995 Protege and Millenia) models. For 1994–95 626 with ATX, 1995 Protege and Millenia and all 1996–98 Models, you must have an OBD I (1994–95 626 with ATX only) or OBD II compliant scan tool.

1994–95 626 with ATX transmission, 1995 Protege and Millenia and 1996–98 Models

1. Ensure that the ignition switch is in the **OFF** position.
2. Attach an OBD II compliant scan tool to the data link connector-2, located beneath the drivers side of the dash panel, as instructed by the tool manufacturers directions.

Fig. 51 Many different types of test equipment, such as this Auto Xray® scan tool, is available through aftermarket tool manufacturers

3. Follow the manufacturers instructions for initializing the scan tool and performing the appropriate test procedures (key on engine off, key on engine running, output control test, etc.).
4. Read the trouble code, or codes, on the scan tool and record them.

Except 1994–95 626 with ATX transmission, 1995 Protege and Millenia and 1996–98 Models

1. Ensure that the ignition switch is in the **OFF** position.
2. Attach the Mazda system selector and self diagnosis tools or equivalent scan tool to the data link connector as instructed by the tool manufacturers directions.
3. Turn the ignition switch to the **ON** position.
4. Read the trouble code, or codes, on the scan tool and record them.

Clearing Codes

➧ See Figures 52, 53, 54 and 55

1994–95 626 with ATX transmission, 1995 Protege and Millenia and 1996–98 Models

1. Ensure that the ignition switch is in the **OFF** position.
2. Attach an OBD II compliant scan tool to the data link connector-2, located beneath the drivers side of the dash panel, as instructed by the tool manufacturers directions.
3. Follow the manufacturers instructions for initializing the scan tool and select the Clear Codes function.

CODE NO.	LOCATION OF MALFUNCTION	OUTPUT SIGNAL PATTERN	SELF-DIAGNOSIS	FAIL-SAFE
02	Ne-signal	ON / OFF	No Ne-signal	—
03	G-signal (DOHC and California B6)	ON / OFF	No G-signal	Cancels 2-group (DOHC) or sequential (California B6) injection
06	Vehicle speed sensor	ON / OFF	No input signal from vehicle speed sensor	Shifting performed normally
08	Volume airflow sensor	ON / OFF	Open or short circuit	Basic fuel injection amount fixed as for two driving modes (1) Idle switch ON (2) Idle switch OFF
09	Engine coolant temperature sensor	ON / OFF		Maintains constant 20°C (68°F) command
10	Intake air temperature sensor	ON / OFF		Maintains constant 20°C (68°F) command
12	Throttle position sensor	ON / OFF		Throttle opening judged as full stroke lockup not provided
14	Barometric absolute pressure sensor (in PCME (PCM))	ON / OFF		Maintains constant command of sea level pressure
15	Oxygen sensor (Inactivation)	ON / OFF	Sensor output continues less than 0.55V 95 sec. after engine starts (1500 rpm)	Cancels engine feedback operation
17	Oxygen sensor (Inversion)	ON / OFF	Sensor output continues uncharged 50 sec. after engine exceeds 1500 rpm	Cancels engine feedback operation
25	Solenoid valve (pressure regulator)	ON / OFF	Open or short circuit	–

89544GD0

Fig. 52 Diagnostic trouble code chart for OBD-1 vehicles—Part 1 of 2

CODE NO.	LOCATION OF MALFUNCTION	OUTPUT SIGNAL PATTERN	SELF-DIAGNOSIS	FAIL-SAFE
26	Solenoid valve (purge control)	ON / OFF	Open or short circuit	–
34	IAC valve	ON / OFF		–
41	Solenoid valve (VICS) [DOHC]	ON / OFF		–
55	Vehicle speed pulse generator	ON / OFF	No input signal from vehicle speed pulse generator	Shifting performed in accordance with signals from vehicle speed sensor
60	1-2 shift solenoid valve	ON / OFF	Open or short circuit	Solenoid valve(s) performs the shifting with as little interference as possible with driving performance Lockup not provided
61	2-3 shift solenoid valve	ON / OFF		
62	3-4 shift solenoid valve	ON / OFF		
63	Lockup solenoid valve	ON 1.6 sec. 4 sec. / OFF 1.2 sec. 0.4 sec. 0.4 sec.		Shifting performed normally Lockup not provided

89544GD1

Fig. 53 Diagnostic trouble code chart for OBD-1 vehicles—Part 2 of 2

Code No.	Display on the NGS	Condition
P0100	MAF/VAF—CIRCUIT MALFUNCTION	Mass air flow circuit malfunction
P0110	IAT—CIRCUIT MALFUNCTION	Intake air temperature circuit malfunction
P0115	ECT—CIRCUIT MALFUNCTION	Engine coolant temperature circuit malfunction
P0120	TP—CIRCUIT MALFUNCTION	Throttle position circuit malfunction
P0125	EXCESSIVE TIME TO ENTER CLOSED LOOP	Excessive time to enter closed loop fuel control
P0130	O2S 11—CIRCUIT MALFUNCTION	O_2 sensor circuit malfunction
P0134	O2S 11—CIRCUIT NO ACTIVITY DETECTED	O_2 sensor circuit no activity detected
P0135	O2S 11—HEATER CIRCUIT MALFUNCTION	O_2 sensor heater circuit malfunction
P0140	O2S 12—CIRCUIT NO ACTIVITY DETECTED	O_2 sensor circuit no activity detected
P0170	BANK1—FUEL TRIM MALFUNCTION	Fuel trim malfunction
P0300	RANDOM MISFIRE DETECTED	Random misfire detected
P0301	CYLINDER 1 MISFIRE DETECTED	Cylinder 1 misfire detected
P0302	CYLINDER 2 MISFIRE DETECTED	Cylinder 2 misfire detected
P0303	CYLINDER 3 MISFIRE DETECTED	Cylinder 3 misfire detected
P0304	CYLINDER 4 MISFIRE DETECTED	Cylinder 4 misfire detected
P0335	CRANKSHAFT POS SENSOR—CKT MALFUNCTION	Crankshaft position sensor circuit malfunction
P0340	CAMSHAFT POS SENSOR—CKT MALFUNCTION	Camshaft position sensor circuit malfunction
P0400	EGR—FLOW MALFUNCTION	Exhaust gas recirculation flow malfunction
P0420	BANK 1 CAT EFFICIENCY BELOW LIMIT	Catalyst system effciency below threshold

89544GD2

Fig. 54 Diagnostic trouble code chart for OBD-2 vehicles—Part 1 of 2

Code No.	Display on the NGS	Condition
P0440	EVAP SYSTEM—MALFUNCTION	Evaporative emission control system malfunction
P0443	EVAP SYSTEM—PURGE CTRL VALVE CKT MALF	Evaporative emission control system purge control valve circuit malfunction
P0500	VEHICLE SPEED SENSOR—MALFUNCTION	Vehicle speed sensor malfunction
P0505	IDLE CONTROL SYSTEM MALFUNCTION	Idle air control system malfunction
P0510	CLOSED THROTTLE POS SWITCH —MALFUNCTION	Closed throttle position switch malfunction
P0703	TORQUE CONV/BRAKE SW—MALFUNCTION	Brake switch input malfunction
P1000	MORE DRIVING NEEDED TO COMPLETE TEST	Check of all OBD-II systems is not complete since last memory order
P1170	HO2S 11—INVERSION	Heated oxygen sensor (Front) (Stuck)
P1195	EGRBS—OPEN OR SHORT	EGR boost sensor open or short
P1250	PRC—OPEN OR SHORT	PRC solenoid valve open or short
P1345	SGC SIGNAL—NO SGC SIGNAL	No SGC signal
P1402	EGRS—OPEN OR SHORT	EGR valve position sensor open or short
P1485	EGR (VACUUM)—OPEN OR SHORT	EGR solenoid valve (vacuum) open or short
P1486	EGR (VENT)—OPEN OR SHORT	EGR solenoid valve (vent) open or short
P1487	EGRCHK SOL—OPEN OR SHORT	EGR boost sensor solenoid valve
P1608	PCME (CPU)—MALFUNCTION	ECM malfunction
P1794	BAT—BAT OR CIRCUIT FAIL	Battery or circuit malfunction
P1797	PNS—OPEN OR SHORT	Neutral/clutch switch open or short

89544GD3

Fig. 55 Diagnostic trouble code chart for OBD-2 vehicles—Part 2 of 2

4. After clearing the code, perform the code retrieval procedure again to ensure there are no remaining or newly set codes present.

Except 1994–95 626 with ATX transmission, 1995 Protege and Millenia and 1996–98 Models

Codes stored within the ECM memory must be erased when repairs are completed. Also, erasing codes during diagnosis can separate hard faults from intermittents. To erase stored codes:

1. Disconnect the negative battery cable.
2. Depress the brake pedal for at least 5 seconds.

➡**Not all Mazdas covered by this book require that the brake pedal be depressed to reset a code, however, as a precaution, we've added it as a necessary step for all models. If your model does not require it, this action will be ignored by the ECU.**

3. Wait an additional 10 seconds, then reconnect the battery cable.
4. After clearing the code, perform the code retrieval procedure again to ensure there are no remaining or newly set codes present.

VACUUM DIAGRAMS

Following are vacuum diagrams for most of the engine and emissions package combinations covered by this manual. Because vacuum circuits will vary based on various engine and vehicle options, always refer first to the vehicle emission control information label, if present. Should the label be missing, or should vehicle be equipped with a different engine from the vehi-

cle's original equipment, refer to the diagrams below for the same or similar configuration.

If you wish to obtain a replacement emissions label, most manufacturers make the labels available for purchase. The labels can usually be ordered from a local dealer.

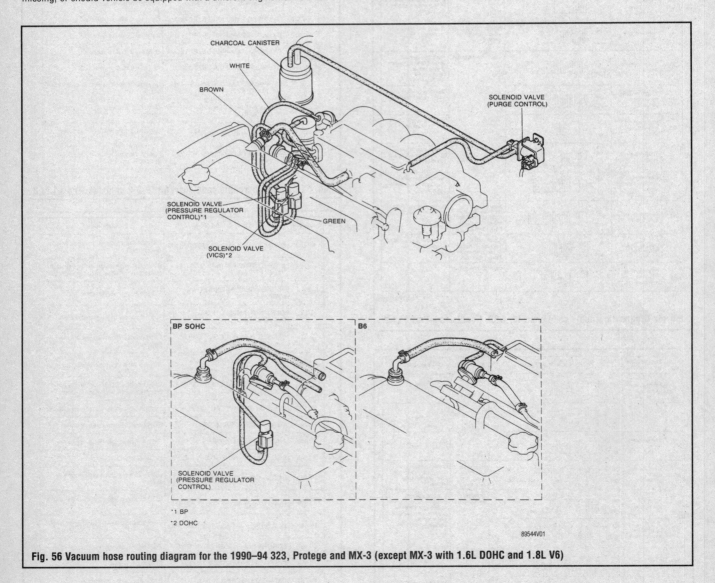

Fig. 56 Vacuum hose routing diagram for the 1990–94 323, Protege and MX-3 (except MX-3 with 1.6L DOHC and 1.8L V6)

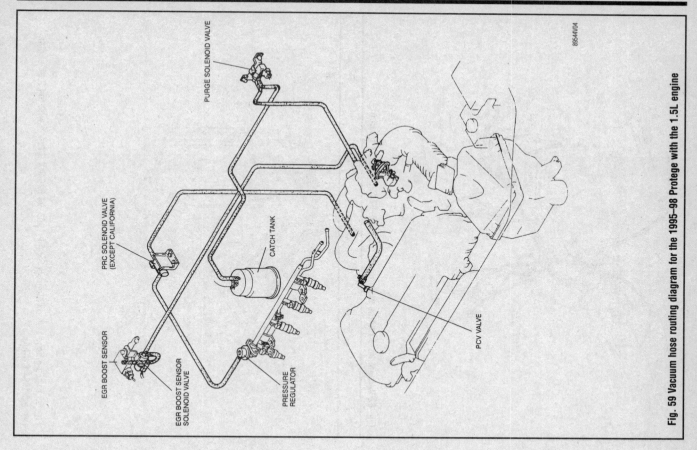

Fig. 59 Vacuum hose routing diagram for the 1995–98 Protege with the 1.5L engine

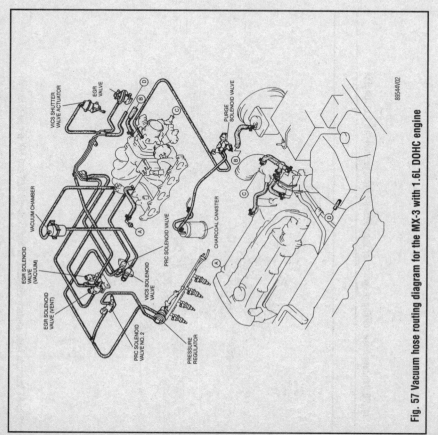

Fig. 57 Vacuum hose routing diagram for the MX-3 with 1.6L DOHC engine

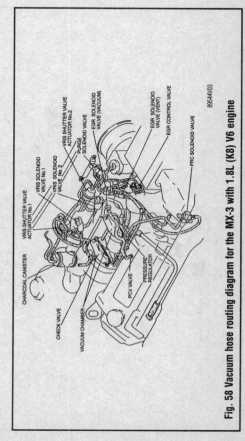

Fig. 58 Vacuum hose routing diagram for the MX-3 with 1.8L (K8) V6 engine

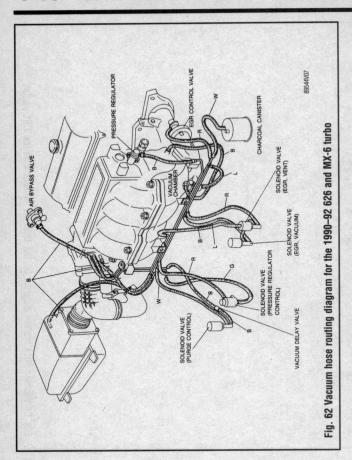

Fig. 62 Vacuum hose routing diagram for the 1990–92 626 and MX-6 turbo

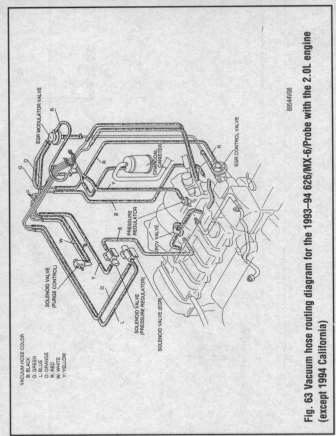

Fig. 63 Vacuum hose routing diagram for the 1993–94 626/MX-6/Probe with the 2.0L engine (except 1994 California)

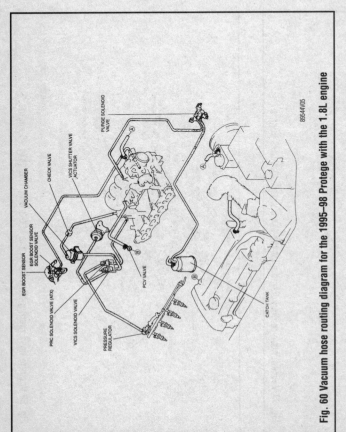

Fig. 60 Vacuum hose routing diagram for the 1995–98 Protege with the 1.8L engine

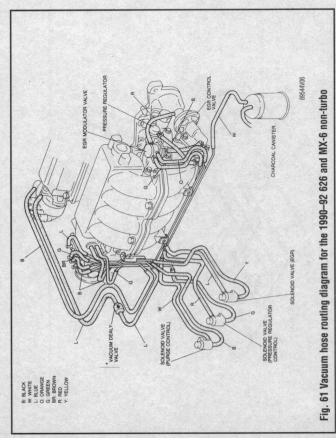

Fig. 61 Vacuum hose routing diagram for the 1990–92 626 and MX-6 non-turbo

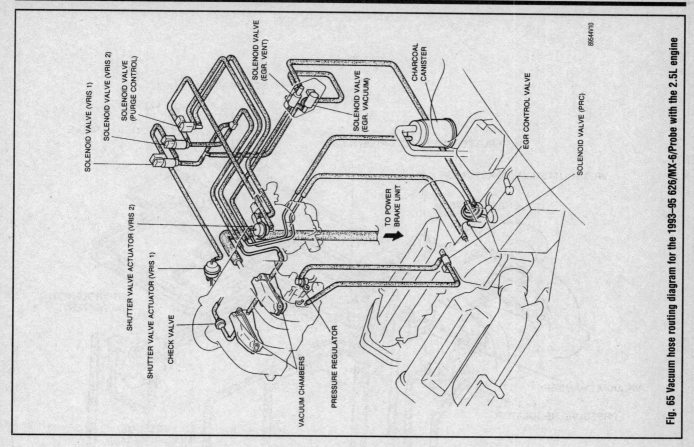

SOLENOID VALVE (VRIS 1)

SOLENOID VALVE (VRIS 2)

SOLENOID VALVE (PURGE CONTROL)

SOLENOID VALVE (EGR. VENT)

SOLENOID VALVE (EGR. VACUUM)

CHARCOAL CANISTER

EGR CONTROL VALVE

SOLENOID VALVE (PRC)

SHUTTER VALVE ACTUATOR (VRIS 2)

SHUTTER VALVE ACTUATOR (VRIS 1)

CHECK VALVE

TO POWER BRAKE UNIT

VACUUM CHAMBERS

PRESSURE REGULATOR

89544V10

Fig. 65 Vacuum hose routing diagram for the 1993–95 626/MX-6/Probe with the 2.5L engine

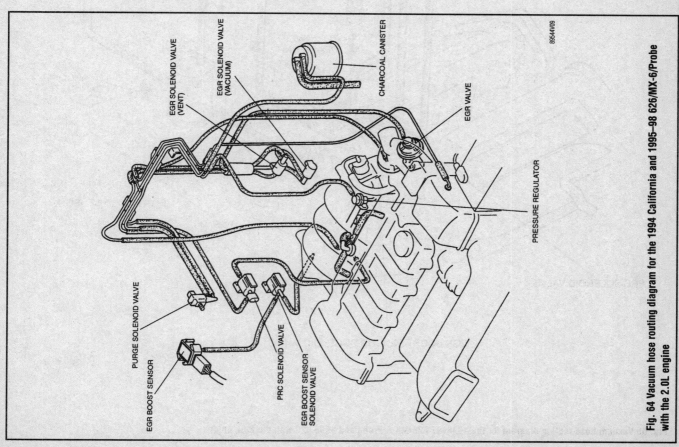

EGR SOLENOID VALVE (VENT)

EGR SOLENOID VALVE (VACUUM)

CHARCOAL CANISTER

EGR VALVE

PRESSURE REGULATOR

PURGE SOLENOID VALVE

EGR BOOST SENSOR

PRC SOLENOID VALVE

EGR BOOST SENSOR SOLENOID VALVE

89544V09

Fig. 64 Vacuum hose routing diagram for the 1994 California and 1995–98 626/MX-6/Probe with the 2.0L engine

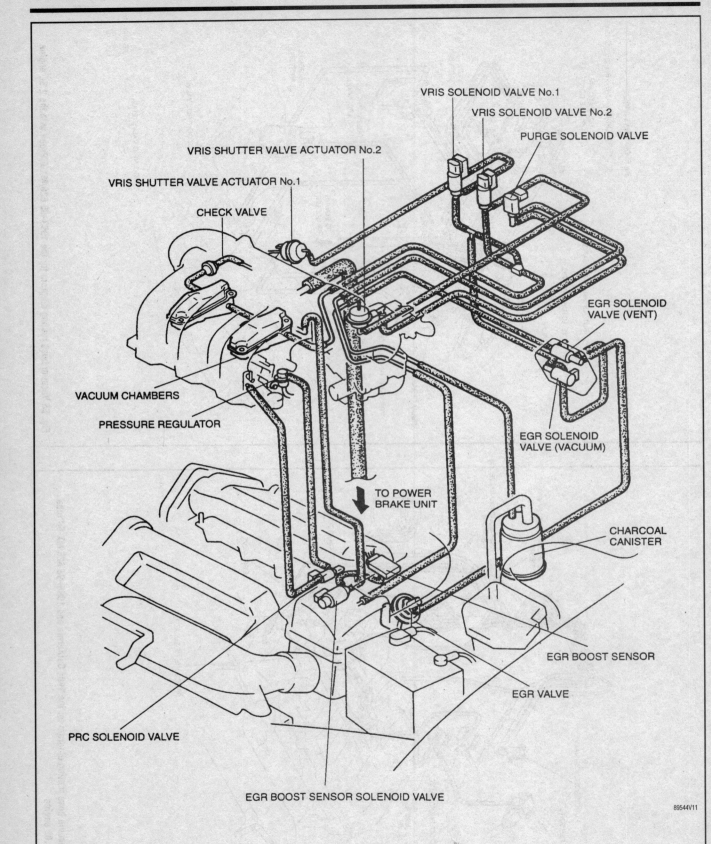

Fig. 66 Vacuum hose routing diagram for the 1996–97 626/MX-6/Probe and 1998 626 with the 2.5L engine

89544V11

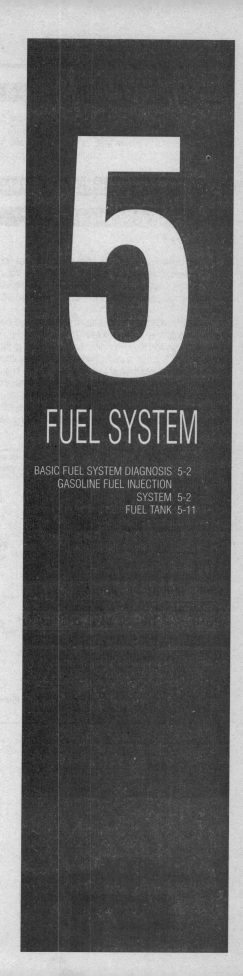

5

FUEL SYSTEM

BASIC FUEL SYSTEM DIAGNOSIS

When there is a problem starting or driving a vehicle, two of the most important checks involve the ignition and the fuel systems. The questions most mechanics attempt to answer first, "is there spark?" and "is there fuel?" will often lead to solving most basic problems. For ignition system diagnosis and testing, please refer to the information on engine electrical components and ignition systems found earlier in this manual. If the ignition system checks out (there is spark), then you must determine if the fuel system is operating properly (is there fuel?).

GASOLINE FUEL INJECTION SYSTEM

Description of System

▶ See Figure 1

The electronic fuel injection system on your Mazda consists of two subsystems, the fuel delivery system and the electronic control system. The fuel delivery system supplies fuel to the fuel injectors at a specified pressure. The electronic control system regulates the flow of fuel from the injectors into the engine.

The fuel delivery system consists of an electric fuel pump, fuel filters, fuel pressure regulator and fuel injectors. The electric fuel pump, mounted in the fuel tank, draws fuel through a filter screen attached to the fuel pump/sending unit assembly. The fuel is then pumped to the engine compartment, through another filter, and into the fuel injection distributor. The fuel injection distributor supplies fuel directly to the injectors. Constant fuel pressure is maintained by the fuel pressure regulator. The pressure regulator is mounted at the end of the fuel injection distributor, downstream from the fuel injectors. Excess fuel supplied by the fuel pump is relieved by the regulator and returned to the fuel tank through the fuel return line. The fuel injectors spray a metered quantity of fuel into the intake air stream when they are energized. The quantity of fuel is determined by the electronic control system.

The electronic control system consists of the Electronic Control Unit (ECU) and the engine sensors and switches that provide input to the ECU. The Vane Air Flow (VAF) meter monitors the amount of air flow into the engine, measures air temperature, controls the electric fuel pump and supplies this information to the ECU. Information is also supplied to the ECU regarding engine coolant temperature, engine speed, and exhaust gas oxygen content. Based on the input information, the ECU computes the required fuel flow rate and determines the needed injector pulse width, then outputs a command to the fuel injector to meter the exact quantity of fuel.

On turbocharged engines, exhaust gas energy is used to pressurize the intake air, thereby providing more than the normal amount of air into the combustion chamber. This engine has sensors and provides input to the ECU exclusive to this type of induction, otherwise the fuel injection system on the turbocharged engine operates the same as the normally aspirated engines.

Relieving Fuel System Pressure

FUEL PRESSURE

323, Protege and MX-3

▶ See Figure 2

1. Remove the rear seat cushion and locate the fuel pump connector.
2. Start the engine.
3. Detach the fuel pump connector.
4. After the engine stalls, turn the ignition switch **OFF** and reconnect the fuel pump connector.
5. Install the rear seat cushion.

626/MX-6/Probe

2.0L AND 2.5L ENGINES

▶ See Figures 3, 4 and 5

1. Start the engine.
2. Remove the fuel pump relay from the relay box, located in the left side of the engine compartment.
3. After the engine stalls, turn the ignition switch **OFF** and reinstall the relay.

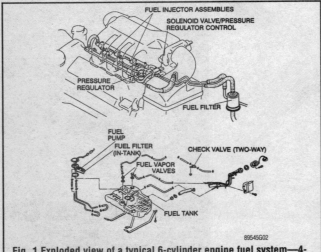

Fig. 1 Exploded view of a typical 6-cylinder engine fuel system—4-cylinder engines are similar

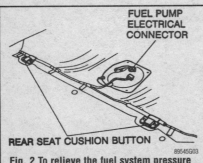

Fig. 2 To relieve the fuel system pressure on 323, Protege and MX-3 models, disconnect the fuel pump wires with the engine running

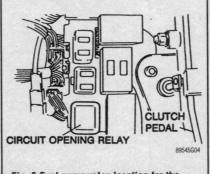

Fig. 3 Fuel pump relay location for the 2.0L and 2.5L engines

Fig. 4 To relieve the fuel system pressure on the 626/MX-6/Probe models with 2.0L or 2.5L engines, remove the underhood fuse box cover . . .

Fig. 5 . . . and remove the fuel pump relay while the engine is running. Once the engine stalls, the fuel pressure is relieved

Fig. 6 On 2.2L engines, remove the pump relay (under the dashboard) with the engine running to relieve the system pressure

Fig. 7 Detach the fuel hoses and electrical connections from the fuel pump, then remove the attaching screws and the pump

2.2L ENGINE

♦ See Figure 6

1. Start the engine.
2. Detach the circuit opening relay connector, located under the left side of the instrument panel.
3. After the engine stalls, turn the ignition switch **OFF** and reconnect the circuit opening relay.

Millenia

2.3L ENGINES

1. Remove the cruise actuator mounting nuts, and move the cruise actuator to the side.
2. Start the engine.
3. Remove the fuel pump relay from the relay box, located in the right side of the engine compartment.
4. After the engine stalls, turn the ignition switch to **OFF** and reinstall the relay connector.
5. Position and install the cruise actuator.

2.5L ENGINES

To relieve the fuel system pressure on the 2.5L engine, refer to the 626/MX-6/Probe procedure for the 2.0L and 2.5L engines.

Electric Fuel Pump

REMOVAL & INSTALLATION

323, Protege, 1990–92 626 and MX-6 and 1992–94 MX-3 Models

♦ See Figures 7 and 8

1. Relieve the fuel pressure and disconnect the negative battery cable.
2. If not already removed, depress the clips on each end of the rear seat cushion and remove the cushion.
3. If not already done, detach the electrical connector from the fuel pump/sending unit.
4. Remove the attaching screws from the fuel pump/sending unit access cover and remove the cover.
5. Disconnect the fuel supply and return hoses from the fuel pump/sending unit.
6. Remove the attaching screws and the fuel pump/sending unit from the fuel tank.
7. Detach the sending unit electrical connector, remove the sending unit attaching nuts and remove the sending unit from the fuel pump assembly.
   To install:
8. Attach the sending unit to the fuel pump assembly and install the nuts. attach the sending unit electrical connector.
9. Install the fuel pump/sending unit into the fuel tank with a new gasket and install the mounting screws.

Fig. 8 Exploded view of the fuel pump assembly for the 323, Protege, 1990–92 626, MX-6 and 1992–94 MX-3

10. Connect the fuel supply and return lines.
11. Install the access cover and the mounting screws.
12. Attach the sending unit electrical connector.
13. Position the rear seat cushion over the floor, making sure to align the retaining pins with the clips. Push down firmly until the two retaining pins are locked into the rear seat retaining clips.
14. Connect the negative battery cable, start the engine and check for proper system operation and for fuel leaks.

1995 MX3 Models

✳✳ CAUTION

Do not allow fuel spray or vapors to come in contact with a spark or an open flame. Keep a dry chemical fire extinguisher nearby. Never store fuel in an open container due to risk of fire or explosion.

1. Relieve the fuel system pressure.
2. Disconnect the negative battery cable.
3. Remove the rear seat cushion from the vehicle.
4. Remove any dirt that has accumulated around the fuel pump cover so it will not enter the tank during pump removal and installation.
5. Remove the fuel pump cover.
6. Detach the fuel gauge connector, hoses, and the gauge.
7. Unplug the fuel pump electrical connector.
8. Remove the fuel pump from the bracket assembly. Remove and discard the seal ring.
   To install:
9. Clean the fuel pump mounting flange, fuel tank mounting surface and seal ring groove.
10. Apply a light coating of grease on a new seal ring to hold it in place during assembly and install in the seal ring groove.
11. Install the fuel pump to the bracket assembly carefully to ensure the filter is not damaged. Make sure the seal ring remains in the groove.

12. Hold the pump assembly in place, and pull the fuel pump down so that it is tight against the bracket.

13. Attach the fuel pump electrical connector.

14. Install the fuel gauge, hoses, and gauge connector.

15. Install the fuel pump cover.

16. Install the rear seat cushion.

17. Connect the negative battery cable, start the engine and check for proper system operation and for fuel leaks.

Millenia and 1993–98 626/MX-6/Probe Models

▶ See Figures 9, 10, 11 and 12

1. Relieve the fuel system pressure and disconnect the negative battery cable.

2. Drain and remove the fuel tank.

3. Disconnect all fuel hoses from the fuel pump unit.

4. Turn the fuel pump ring counterclockwise and remove it.

5. Remove the fuel pump and gaskets from the fuel tank.

To install:

6. Install the fuel pump with a new gasket. Turn the fuel pump ring clockwise to tighten it until the flange hits the stopper.

7. Connect the fuel hoses to the fuel pump.

8. Install the fuel tank, add a minimum of 10 gallons and check for leaks.

9. Lower the vehicle and connect the negative battery cable.

TESTING

▶ See Figures 13 and 14

1. Relieve the pressure in the fuel system and disconnect the negative battery cable.

2. Install a suitable fuel pressure gauge between the fuel filter and the fuel distributor.

3. Connect a jumper wire between the **F/P** and **GRND** terminals of the fuel pump test connector.

4. Connect the negative battery cable, turn the ignition key **ON** and check the fuel pump pressure. The pressure should be within specifications given in the Tune up specifications chart.

5. If there is no fuel pressure, remove the fuel tank cap and try to hear if the fuel pump is operating. If the pump sounds like it's running, check for a restriction in the fuel line. If the pump is not running, check for power to the pump and check the pump motor ground. If there is no power to the pump, check all electrical connections and check the fuel pump relay.

6. If fuel pressure is low, check for a restriction in the fuel line or clogged fuel filters.

7. Remove the jumper wire, relieve the fuel system pressure and disconnect the negative battery cable.

8. Remove the fuel pressure gauge and reconnect the fuel line.

9. Connect the negative battery cable.

Throttle Body

REMOVAL & INSTALLATION

▶ See Figures 15 and 16

323 and Protege Models

1. Disconnect the negative battery cable.

2. Remove the air cleaner intake duct.

3. Remove the air cleaner and the air cleaner element.

4. Detach the air flow meter connector and remove the top of the air cleaner assembly.

5. Remove the resonance chamber.

6. Remove the air hose from the throttle body.

7. Tag and remove the hoses and electrical connectors from the throttle body. Disconnect the accelerator cable.

8. Remove the throttle body attaching bolts and remove the assembly with the gasket.

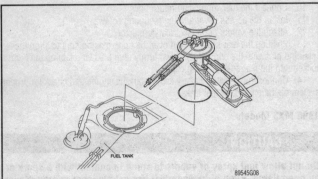

Fig. 9 Exploded view of the 1993–98 626/MX-6/Probe fuel pump assembly

89545G08

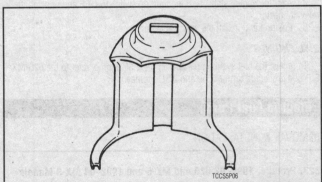

Fig. 10 A special tool is usually available to remove or install the fuel pump locking cam

TCCS5P06

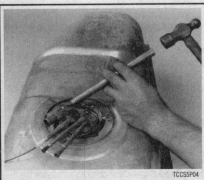

Fig. 11 A brass drift and a hammer can be used to loosen the fuel pump locking cam

TCCS5P04

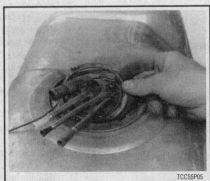

Fig. 12 Once the locking cam is released it can be removed to free the fuel pump

TCCS5P05

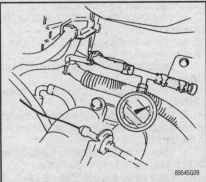

Fig. 13 To test the fuel system pressure, connect a fuel gauge to the filter outlet . . .

89545G09

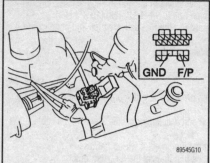

Fig. 14 . . . then jumper the diagnostic link terminals GND and F/P to run the fuel pump

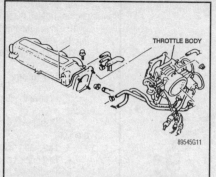

Fig. 15 Exploded view of the typical 4-cylinder engine throttle body assembly

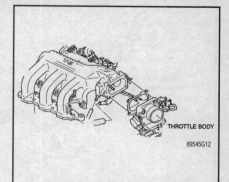

Fig. 16 Exploded view of the typical 6-cylinder engine throttle body assembly

To install:

9. Replace the throttle body assembly and the gasket. Tighten the bolts to 14–19 ft. lbs. (19–25 Nm).

10. Attach the accelerator cable to the throttle body and adjust as is necessary.

11. Connect the air hose to the throttle body.

12. Install the resonance chamber and attach the airflow meter connector.

13. Install the air cleaner base and install the air cleaner.

14. Install the air cleaner duct and connect the negative battery cable.

MX-3 Models

1. Disconnect the negative battery cable. Disconnect the air intake hose from the throttle body.

2. Tag and remove the hoses and electrical connectors from the throttle body. Disconnect the accelerator cable.

3. Remove the throttle body attaching bolts and remove the throttle body assembly.

4. Installation is the reverse of the removal procedure. Tighten the mounting nuts to 14–19 ft. lbs. (19–25 Nm).

626/MX-6/Probe and Millenia Models

▶ **See Figures 17, 18, 19 and 20**

1. Disconnect the negative battery cable.

2. On Millenia models with 2.3L engines, remove the charge air cooler air duct.

3. Disconnect the air intake hose from the throttle body. If necessary, remove the air cleaner housing.

4. Tag and remove the hoses and electrical connectors from the throttle body. Disconnect the accelerator cable.

5. Remove the throttle body attaching bolts and remove the throttle body assembly.

6. Installation is the reverse of the removal procedure. Tighten the mounting nuts to 14–19 ft. lbs. (19–25 Nm).

Fig. 17 To remove the throttle body, first label and detach all vacuum, coolant lines and electrical connections to the throttle body

Fuel Injectors

REMOVAL & INSTALLATION

▶ **See Figures 21 and 22**

MX-3 with 4-Cylinder Engine and 1990–94 323, Protege

1. Relieve the fuel system pressure.

2. Disconnect the negative battery cable.

Fig. 18 Then, remove the throttle body attaching nuts and bolts . . .

Fig. 19 . . . and remove the throttle body from the intake manifold. Shown with manifold removed from engine for clarity, but not necessary

Fig. 20 Thoroughly clean the gasket mating surfaces before installing and always use a new gasket

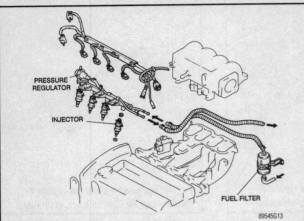

Fig. 21 Exploded view of the typical 4-cylinder engine fuel injector and distributor assembly

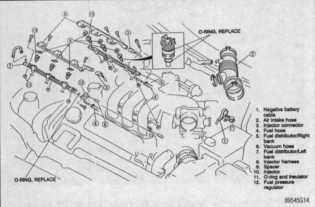

Fig. 22 Exploded view of the typical 6-cylinder engine fuel injector and distributor assemblies

3. Detach the electrical connectors at the injectors.
4. Remove the fuel injector harness from the fuel delivery pipe.
5. Remove the delivery pipe bolt(s) and remove the delivery pipe with the injectors and the pressure regulator.
6. Separate the injectors, grommets and the insulators from the delivery pipe assembly.

To install:

7. Replace the fuel injector O-rings and apply a small amount of clean engine oil to the O-rings before installation.
8. Replace the fuel injector insulator seals.

9. Install the injectors to the delivery pipe and install the assembly to the engine. Tighten the delivery pipe bolt to 14–18 ft. lbs. (19–25 Nm).
10. Install the injector harness to the fuel delivery pipe and connect the injector wiring.
11. Connect the negative battery cable.

1995–97 Protege

1. Relieve the fuel system pressure, and disconnect the negative battery cable.
2. Disconnect the throttle and accelerator cables. Remove the cable bracket.
3. Label and disconnect the fuel injector wiring harness.
4. Disconnect and plug the fuel lines at the fuel distributor.
5. Disconnect the vacuum hose from the fuel pressure regulator.
6. Remove the fuel line mounting bracket bolt.
7. Remove the fuel distributor mounting bolts, spacers, insulators and the fuel distributor, with the injectors attached.
8. Remove the fuel injectors, grommets and O-rings from the fuel distributor. Remove the O-rings from the fuel injectors.

To install:

9. Apply a small amount of clean engine oil to new O-rings and install them and the grommets on the fuel injectors.
10. Install the insulators and injectors on the intake manifold.
11. Install the grommets and the fuel distributor onto the injectors.
12. Install the fuel distributor attaching bolts and tighten to 14–18 ft. lbs. (19–25 Nm).
13. Connect the vacuum hose to the fuel pressure regulator and the fuel lines to the fuel distributor.
14. Install the fuel line mounting bracket, and tighten the bolt to 70–95 inch lbs. (8–11 Nm).
15. Connect the fuel injector wiring harness.
16. Install the cable bracket, and tighten the bolt to 70–95 inch lbs. (8–11 Nm). Connect and adjust the throttle and accelerator cables.
17. Connect the negative battery cable and turn the ignition switch **ON** to pressurize the fuel system. Check for leaks and correct as necessary, before starting the engine.

626/MX-6/Probe with 4-Cylinder Engines

2.0L ENGINE

♦ **See Figures 23 thru 32**

1. Properly relieve the fuel system pressure.
2. Disconnect the negative battery cable.
3. If necessary, remove the air intake piping near the throttle body.
4. Detach the electrical connectors from the injectors and remove the wiring harness.
5. Disconnect the vacuum hose from the pressure regulator.
6. Disconnect the fuel lines from the fuel distributor and remove the fuel line attaching bolt on the side of the intake manifold.
7. Remove the bolts from the fuel distributor and remove the it with injectors attached.

Fig. 23 To remove the fuel injectors, first label and detach the injector wire harness connectors

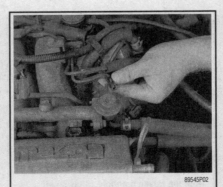

Fig. 24 Remove the vacuum line from the fuel pressure regulator . . .

Fig. 25 . . . then disconnect the fuel lines. Also, remove the fuel line retaining clamp bolt from the side of the intake manifold

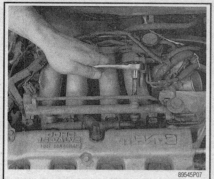

Fig. 26 Loosen the fuel distributor attaching bolts evenly . . .

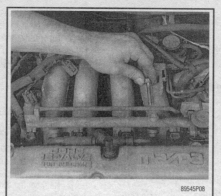

Fig. 27 . . . then remove them

Fig. 28 Lift the complete fuel distributor/injector assembly from the engine. The spacers (arrows) may remain on the intake . . .

Fig. 29 . . . or stick to the fuel distributor. Ensure that you have both of them and do not lose them

Fig. 30 Remove the old insulators from the injectors and discard them

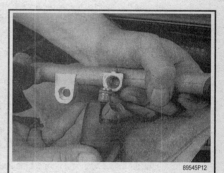

Fig. 31 Remove the injector from the fuel distributor by pulling outward while slightly twisting the injector

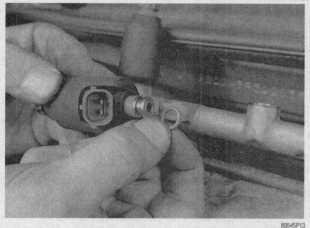

Fig. 32 Also remove the old injector-to-fuel distributor O-ring seal and discard them. Always install new insulators and O-rings when installing

8. Remove the injectors complete with the O-rings and the insulators from the fuel distributor.

To install:

9. Replace the fuel injector O-rings and apply a small amount of clean engine oil to the O-rings before installation.

10. Replace the injector insulators and install the injectors to the fuel distributor. Make sure that the injectors are properly seated and that the electrical connector points are facing upward.

11. Install the fuel distributor to the intake manifold, making sure that the injectors are properly seated. Tighten the top bolts to 14–18 ft. lbs. (19–25 Nm) and the side bolt to 70–95 inch lbs. (8–11 Nm).

12. Connect the fuel lines to the fuel distributor and to the pressure regulator.

13. Connect the electrical harness to the injectors.

14. If removed, install the air intake piping around the throttle body.

15. Connect the negative battery cable.

2.2L ENGINE

1. Properly relieve the fuel system pressure.

2. Disconnect the negative battery cable.

3. Remove the wiring harness bracket from the end of the engine.

4. Remove the EGR modulator valve and remove the bracket.

5. Disconnect the vacuum pipe mounting bolts.

6. Remove the intake air hose from the throttle body.

7. Remove the side engine lift hook assembly.

8. Remove the dynamic chamber mounting bolts and nuts and lift the dynamic chamber away from the engine.

9. Disconnect the fuel return pipe bracket from the intake manifold.

10. Detach the fuel injector electrical connectors.

11. Remove the fuel delivery pipe with the pressure regulator and pulsation damper intact.

12. Separate the fuel injectors from the delivery pipe. Remove the grommets and the insulators.

To install:

13. Position the insulators and fuel injectors into the intake manifold. Position the grommets and new O-rings onto the fuel injectors. Apply a small amount of engine oil to the O-rings during installation.

14. Position the spacers and the fuel distributor on the injectors. Install the attaching bolts to the fuel distributor and tighten to 14–19 ft. lbs. (19–25 Nm).

15. Attach the electrical connectors to the fuel injectors.

16. Install the fuel return line bracket onto the intake manifold and install the return fuel line at the bracket. Secure with the clamp.

17. Connect the fuel return pipe bracket to the intake manifold.

18. Lower the dynamic chamber into place and tighten the mounting bolts to 14–19 ft. lbs. (19–25 Nm).

19. Install the side engine lift hook assembly and tighten the bolts to 14–19 ft. lbs. (19–25 Nm).

20. Install the intake air hose to the throttle body.
21. Install the vacuum pipe mounting bolts.
22. Install the EGR modulator valve and bracket.
23. Install the wiring harness bracket at the end of the intake manifold.
24. Connect the negative battery cable.

MX-3, 626/MX-6/Probe and Millenia with V6 Engines

▶ See Figures 33 and 34

1.8L (K8) AND 2.5L ENGINES

1. Relieve the fuel system pressure.
2. Disconnect the negative battery cable.
3. Remove the air intake hose assembly.
4. Detach the injector electrical connectors from the injector harness.
5. Disconnect the fuel hoses from the end of the fuel distributor.
6. Remove the fuel distributor attaching screws and remove the fuel distributor.
7. Remove the fuel injector harnesses from the fuel distributor.
8. Separate the injectors from the distributor and remove the O-ring and spacer.

To install:

9. Replace the fuel injector O-rings and apply a small amount of clean engine oil to the O-rings before installation.
10. Install the injectors to the fuel distributor. Turn until the injector is fully seated, aligning the tab on the injector with the notch in the fuel distributor.
11. Install the injector harness on the fuel distributor and install the assembly to the engine.
12. Tighten the fuel distributor screws to 22–31 inch lbs. (2.5–3.5 Nm).
13. Connect the fuel hoses to the fuel distributor and attach the electrical connectors to the injector harness.
14. Install the air intake hose and connect the negative battery cable.

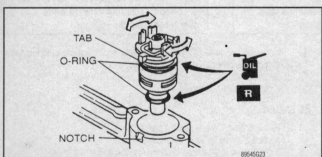

Fig. 33 When installing the injector on V6 engines, replace the O-rings and lightly oil them with engine oil

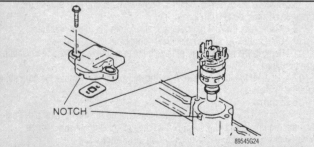

Fig. 34 Align the tab on the injector with the notches on the fuel distributor and wire harness connector

2.3L ENGINE

▶ See Figure 35

1. Relieve the fuel system pressure, and disconnect the negative battery cable.
2. Remove the charge air cooler air duct.
3. Remove the air cleaner assembly.

4. Remove the resonator.
5. Remove the left and right-hand charge air coolers.
6. Disconnect the accelerator cable.
7. Remove the air intake pipe assembly.
8. Remove the vacuum hose assembly.
9. Label and detach the fuel injector electrical connectors.
10. Disconnect and plug the fuel supply and return lines. Discard the copper crush washers.
11. Remove the fuel distributor mounting bolts and the fuel distributors.
12. Remove the six insulators.
13. Remove the distribution harness (accumulated connector) attaching screws, and remove the distribution harness from the fuel distributors.
14. Remove and discard the spacer from the top of each fuel injector. Remove the fuel injectors from the fuel distributors by rotating back and forth.
15. Remove the fuel pressure regulator mounting bolts and the fuel pressure regulator.

To install:

16. Install the fuel pressure regulator and tighten the bolts to 61–86 inch lbs. (7–10 Nm).
17. Apply clean engine oil to new O-rings and install them on the injectors. Install the injectors into the fuel distributors.
18. Install new spacers on the injectors, then install the distribution harness with the screws. Tighten the screws to 22–31 inch lbs. (2.5–3.5 Nm).
19. Install the 6 insulators and the fuel distributors. Install the fuel distributor mounting bolts and tighten to 14–18 ft. lbs. (19–25 Nm).
20. Using new copper crush washers, connect the fuel supply and return lines.
21. Attach the fuel injector electrical connectors.
22. Install the vacuum hose assembly. Tighten the mounting nuts to 70–95 inch lbs. (8–11 Nm).
23. Install the air intake pipe assembly. Tighten the mounting nuts to 70–95 inch lbs. (8–11 Nm), and the mounting bolts to 44–78 inch lbs. (5–9 Nm).
24. Connect and adjust the accelerator cable. Tighten the mounting bolt to 70–95 inch lbs. (8–11 Nm).
25. Install the left and right-hand charge air coolers. Install new O-rings, and tighten the bolts to 14–18 ft. lbs. (19–25 Nm).
26. Install the resonator. Tighten the mounting nuts to 70–95 inch lbs. (8–11 Nm).
27. Install the air cleaner assembly. Tighten the mounting nuts to 70–95 inch lbs. (8–11 Nm).
28. Install the charge air cooler air duct. Tighten the mounting nuts to 70–95 inch lbs. (8–11 Nm).
29. Connect the negative battery cable. Turn the ignition switch **ON** to pressurize the fuel system. Check for fuel leaks and correct as necessary before starting the engine.

TESTING

▶ See Figures 36 and 37

1. Start the engine and warm it up to normal operating temperature. Allow the engine to run at idle.
2. Hold a long screwdriver against the injector and place an ear down close to the screwdriver handle. Listen for injector operation noise.
3. If no sound is heard, proceed as follows:
   a. Disconnect the injector harness from the injector.
   b. Measure the resistance of the injector with an ohmmeter.
   c. The resistance should be between 12–16 ohms.
   d. If the resistance is not as specified, replace the injector.
   e. If the injector resistance is as specified, inspect the wiring to the injectors and to the control unit terminals.

Fuel Pressure Regulator

REMOVAL & INSTALLATION

▶ See Figures 38 and 39

MX-3 with 4-Cylinder Engine, 323 and Protege

1. Properly relieve the fuel system pressure.
2. Disconnect the vacuum hose from the pressure regulator.

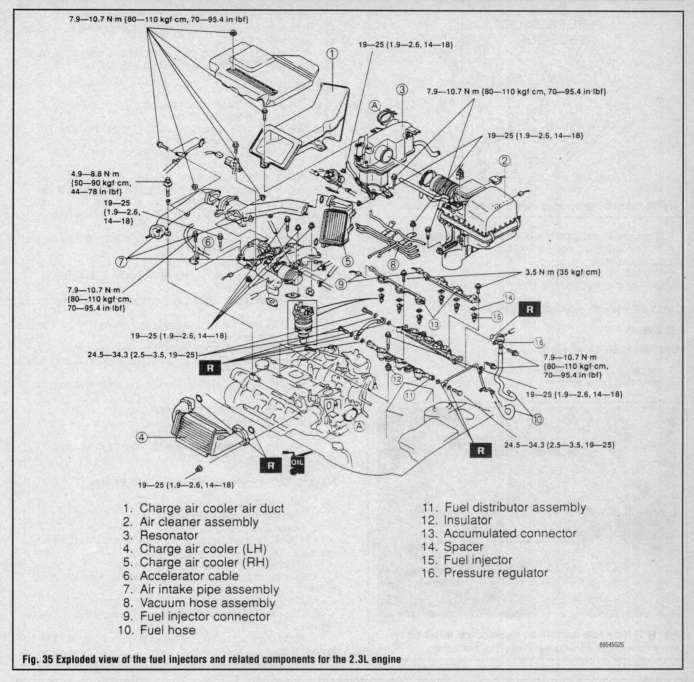

7.9—10.7 N·m {80—110 kgf·cm, 70—95.4 in·lbf}

19—25 {1.9—2.6, 14—18}

7.9—10.7 N·m {80—110 kgf·cm, 70—95.4 in·lbf}

19—25 {1.9—2.6, 14—18}

4.9—8.8 N·m {50—90 kgf·cm, 44—78 in·lbf}

19—25 {1.9—2.6, 14—18}

7.9—10.7 N·m {80—110 kgf·cm, 70—95.4 in·lbf}

3.5 N·m {35 kgf·cm}

19—25 {1.9—2.6, 14—18}

24.5—34.3 {2.5—3.5, 19—25}

7.9—10.7 N·m {80—110 kgf·cm, 70—95.4 in·lbf}

19—25 {1.9—2.6, 14—18}

24.5—34.3 {2.5—3.5, 19—25}

19—25 {1.9—2.6, 14—18}

1. Charge air cooler air duct
2. Air cleaner assembly
3. Resonator
4. Charge air cooler (LH)
5. Charge air cooler (RH)
6. Accelerator cable
7. Air intake pipe assembly
8. Vacuum hose assembly
9. Fuel injector connector
10. Fuel hose
11. Fuel distributor assembly
12. Insulator
13. Accumulated connector
14. Spacer
15. Fuel injector
16. Pressure regulator

89545G25

Fig. 35 Exploded view of the fuel injectors and related components for the 2.3L engine

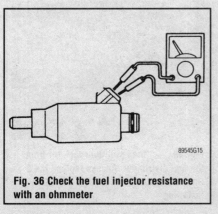

89545G15

Fig. 36 Check the fuel injector resistance with an ohmmeter

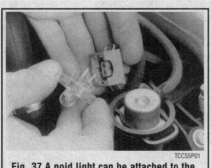

TCCS5P01

Fig. 37 A noid light can be attached to the fuel injector harness in order to test for injector pulse

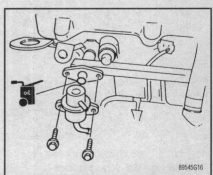

89545G16

Fig. 38 Exploded view of a typical 4-cylinder engine fuel pressure regulator

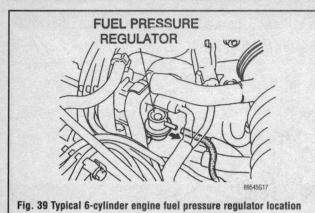

Fig. 39 Typical 6-cylinder engine fuel pressure regulator location

3. Disconnect the fuel return hose from the pressure regulator.

4. Remove the pressure regulator attaching bolts and remove the fuel pressure regulator assembly.

5. Installation is the reverse of the removal procedure. Replace the O-ring and tighten the attaching bolts to 69–95 inch lbs. (8–11 Nm).

626/MX-6/Probe with 4-Cylinder Engines

2.0L ENGINE

▶ See Figures 40, 41, 42 and 43

1. Properly relieve the fuel system pressure.
2. Disconnect the vacuum hose from the pressure regulator.

Fig. 40 To remove the fuel pressure regulator, first relieve the system pressure, then slide the fuel hose clamp backwards . . .

3. Disconnect the fuel return hose from the pressure regulator.

4. Remove the pressure regulator attaching bolts and remove the fuel pressure regulator assembly.

5. Installation is the reverse of the removal procedure. Replace the O-ring and tighten the attaching bolts to 70–95 inch lbs. (7.8–10.7 Nm.)

2.2L ENGINE

1. Properly relieve the fuel system pressure.
2. Disconnect the negative battery cable.
3. Remove the wiring harness bracket from the end of the engine.
4. Remove the EGR modulator valve and remove the bracket.
5. Disconnect the vacuum pipe mounting bolts.
6. Remove the intake air hose from the throttle body.
7. Remove the side engine lift hook assembly.
8. Remove the dynamic chamber mounting bolts and nuts and lift the dynamic chamber away from the engine.
9. Disconnect the fuel return pipe bracket from the intake manifold.
10. Disconnect the vacuum hose and the fuel return hose.
11. Remove the pressure regulator attaching bolts and remove the fuel pressure regulator.

To install:

12. Install the fuel pressure regulator and tighten the attaching bolts to 69–95 inch lbs. (7.8–11 Nm).

13. Connect the vacuum hose and the fuel return hose to the fuel pressure regulator.

14. Install the fuel return line bracket onto the intake manifold and install the return fuel line at the bracket. Secure with the clamp.

15. Connect the fuel return pipe bracket to the intake manifold.

16. Lower the dynamic chamber into place and tighten the mounting bolts to 14–19 ft. lbs. (19–25 Nm).

17. Install the side engine lift hook assembly and tighten the bolts to 14–19 ft. lbs. (19–25 Nm).

18. Install the intake air hose to the throttle body.
19. Install the vacuum pipe mounting bolts.
20. Install the EGR modulator valve and bracket.
21. Install the wiring harness bracket at the end of the intake manifold.
22. Connect the negative battery cable.

MX-3, 626/MX-6/Probe and Millenia with V6 Engines

1. Relieve the fuel system pressure.
2. Disconnect the negative battery cable.
3. Remove the air cleaner assembly.
4. If necessary, detach the injector electrical connectors from the injector harness.
5. Disconnect the fuel hoses from the fuel distributor.
6. Remove the fuel distributor attaching screws and remove the fuel distributor.
7. Remove the injector harnesses from the fuel distributor.
8. Disconnect the vacuum hose and the fuel return hose from the pressure regulator.
9. Remove the attaching bolts and remove the pressure regulator from the fuel distributor.

Fig. 41 . . . and disconnect the fuel hose from the regulator. A rag positioned beneath the hose will catch any spilled fuel

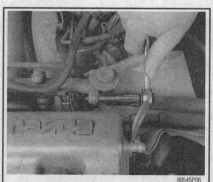

Fig. 42 Remove the fuel pressure regulator attaching bolts . . .

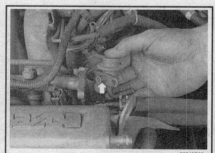

Fig. 43 . . . then pull the regulator from the fuel distributor. Always replace the O-ring seal (arrow) on the regulator when installing

To install:

10. Install the fuel pressure regulator to the fuel distributor and tighten the bolts to 61–87 inch lbs. (7–10 Nm).

11. Connect the vacuum hose and the fuel return line to the fuel pressure regulator.

12. Align the fuel injector tabs with the distributor and install the distributor assemblies.

13. Tighten the fuel distributor screws to 22–31 inch lbs. (2.5–3.5 Nm).

14. Connect the fuel hose to the fuel distributor and, if removed, attach the electrical connectors to the injector harness.

15. Install the air cleaner assembly and connect the negative battery cable.

FUEL TANK

Tank

REMOVAL & INSTALLATION

323 and Protege—Except 4WD

▶ **See Figure 44**

1. Properly relieve the fuel system pressure.

2. Disconnect the negative battery cable.

3. Depress the clips on each end of the rear seat cushion and remove the cushion.

4. Detach the sending unit electrical connector, remove the 4 attaching screws and the sending unit access cover.

5. Raise and safely support the vehicle.

6. Disconnect the fuel hoses and the evaporative hoses from the sending unit and from the fuel tank itself.

7. Position a suitable container under the fuel tank and drain the fuel tank.

8. Remove the attaching screws and the fuel tank insulator from the front of the fuel tank.

9. Support the fuel tank and remove the 2 fuel tank straps.

10. Remove the fuel tank.

11. Position the fuel tank in place and install the 2 tank straps. Tighten the bolts to 27–38 ft. lbs. (37–52 Nm).

12. Install the fuel tank insulator and tighten the bolts to 69–95 inch lbs. (8–11 Nm).

13. Connect the evaporative and fuel hoses. Push the hoses on at least 1.4 inches (35mm).

14. Attach the sending unit electrical connector and install the cover.

15. Install the rear seat and connect the negative battery cable.

1.	Fuel pump cover
2.	Fuel pump connector
3.	Fuel hoses
4.	Evaporative hoses
5.	Insulator
6.	Fuel tank straps
7.	Fuel tank
8.	Separator
9.	Check valve (two way)
10.	Check and cut valve

89545G18

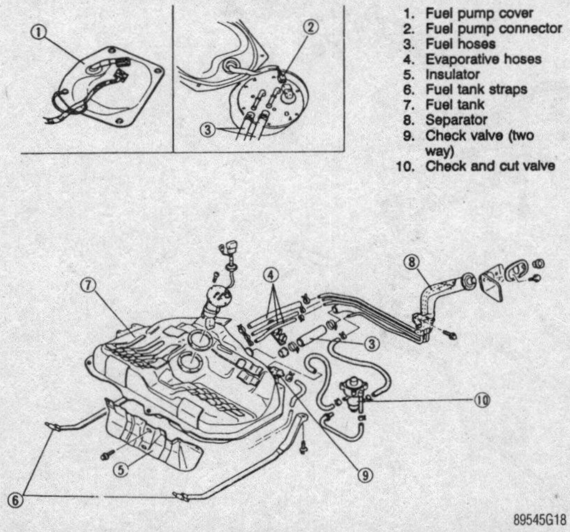

Fig. 44 Exploded view of the 323 and Protege (Except 4WD) fuel tank assembly

Pressure Regulator Control Solenoid Valve

REMOVAL & INSTALLATION

➡ **This applies to California emissions equipped vehicles only.**

1. Disconnect the negative battery cable.

2. Detach the vacuum hose and the electrical connector from the pressure regulator control solenoid valve.

3. Disconnect the pressure regulator control solenoid valve from the intake manifold.

4. Installation is the reverse of the removal procedure.

4WD 323 and Protege

1. Properly relieve the fuel system pressure.

2. Disconnect the negative battery cable.

3. Depress the clips on each end of the rear seat cushion and remove the cushion.

4. Remove both fuel pump covers and detach the sending unit electrical connectors.

5. Disconnect the fuel hoses and the evaporative hoses from the sending unit/fuel pumps.

6. Raise and safely support the vehicle.

7. Position a suitable container under the fuel tank and drain the fuel tank.

8. Remove the exhaust system intermediate pipe and muffler from below the fuel tank.

9. Remove the driveshaft.

10. Disconnect the fuel hoses from the fuel tank.

11. Support the fuel tank and remove the 2 fuel tank straps.

12. Remove the fuel tank.

13. Position the fuel tank in place and install the 2 tank straps. Tighten the bolts to 32–45 ft. lbs. (43–61 Nm).

14. Connect the hoses to the fuel tank.

15. Install the driveshaft. Tighten the shaft end nuts to 20–22 ft. lbs. (27–30 Nm) and the center shaft support nuts to 27–38 ft. lbs. (37–51 Nm).

16. Install the exhaust intermediate pipe/muffler with new gaskets and tighten the nuts to 30–41 ft. lbs. (40–55 Nm).

17. Attach the hoses and electrical connectors to the fuel sending unit/pump assemblies. Push the hoses on at least 1.4 inches (35mm).

18. Install the fuel pump cover assemblies and install the rear seat.

19. Connect the negative battery cable.

MX-3

▶ **See Figure 45**

1. Properly relieve the fuel system pressure.

2. Disconnect the negative battery cable.

3. Depress the clips on each end of the rear seat cushion and remove the cushion.

4. Detach the sending unit electrical connector, remove the 4 attaching screws and the sending unit access cover.

5. Raise and safely support the vehicle.

6. Disconnect the fuel hoses and the evaporative hoses from the sending unit and from the fuel tank itself.

7. Position a suitable container under the fuel tank and drain the fuel tank.

8. Remove the attaching screws and the fuel tank insulator from the front of the fuel tank.

9. Support the fuel tank and remove the 2 fuel tank straps.

10. Remove the fuel tank.

11. Position the fuel tank in place and install the 2 tank straps. Tighten the bolts to 32–45 ft. lbs. (43–62 Nm).

12. Install the fuel tank insulator and tighten the bolts to 69–95 inch lbs. (8–11 Nm).

13. Connect the evaporative and fuel hoses. Push the hoses on at least 1.4 inches (35mm).

14. Attach the sending unit electrical connector and install the cover.

15. Install the rear seat and connect the negative battery cable.

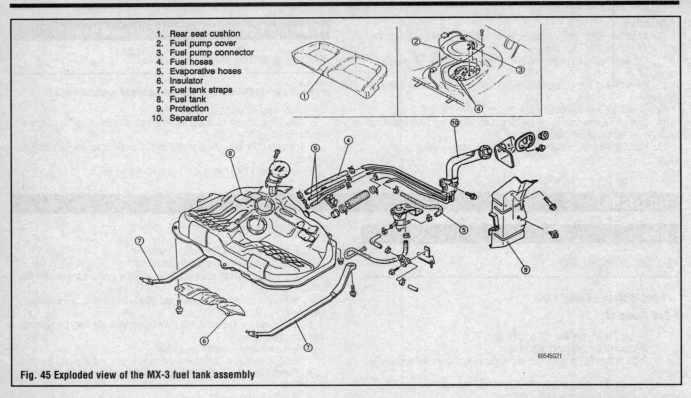

1. Rear seat cushion
2. Fuel pump cover
3. Fuel pump connector
4. Fuel hoses
5. Evaporative hoses
6. Insulator
7. Fuel tank straps
8. Fuel tank
9. Protection
10. Separator

Fig. 45 Exploded view of the MX-3 fuel tank assembly

1990–92 626 and MX-6

▶ **See Figure 46**

1. Properly relieve the fuel system pressure.
2. Disconnect the negative battery cable.
3. Depress the clips on each end of the rear seat cushion and remove the cushion.

4. Detach the sending unit electrical connector, remove the 4 attaching screws and the sending unit access cover. Disconnect the fuel hoses from the sending unit.
5. Raise and safely support the vehicle.
6. Disconnect the fuel hoses and the evaporative hoses from the fuel tank itself.
7. Position a suitable container under the fuel tank and remove the drain plug to drain the fuel tank.

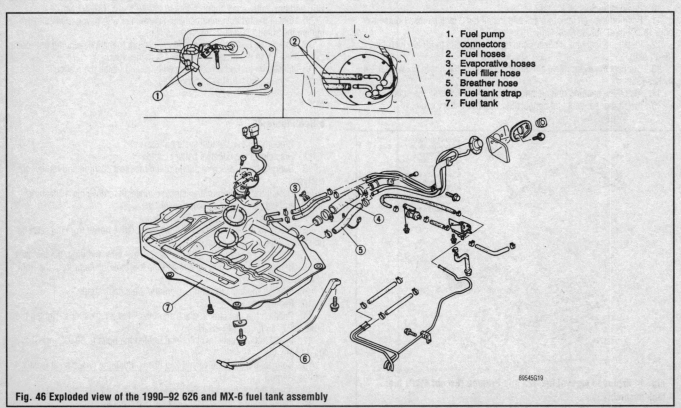

1. Fuel pump connectors
2. Fuel hoses
3. Evaporative hoses
4. Fuel filler hose
5. Breather hose
6. Fuel tank strap
7. Fuel tank

Fig. 46 Exploded view of the 1990–92 626 and MX-6 fuel tank assembly

8. Support the fuel tank.

9. Remove the 2 fuel tank straps and the corner mounting bolts.

10. Remove the fuel tank.

11. Position the fuel tank in place and install the 2 tank straps. Tighten the bolts to 32–45 ft. lbs. (43–61 Nm).

12. Install the corner mounting bolts and tighten them to 16–22 ft. lbs. (22–30 Nm).

13. Connect the evaporative and fuel hoses. Push the hoses on at least 1.4 inches (35mm).

14. Lower the vehicle and attach the sending unit electrical connector and hoses. Install the cover.

15. Install the rear seat and connect the negative battery cable.

1993–98 626/MX-6/Probe

▶ **See Figure 47**

1. Properly relieve the fuel system pressure.

2. Drain the fuel tank and disconnect the negative battery cable.

3. Raise and safely support the vehicle.

4. Remove the pre-silencer exhaust pipe.

5. Remove the exhaust pipe insulator assembly.

6. Detach the electrical connectors from the top of the fuel tank.

7. Disconnect the fuel and evaporative hoses from the fuel tank.

8. While having an assistant support the fuel tank, remove the fuel tank support straps and lower the fuel tank from the vehicle.

To install:

9. Lift the fuel tank into place and install the fuel tank straps. Tighten the bolts to 32–45 ft. lbs. (43–61 Nm).

10. Connect the fuel and evaporative hoses to the fuel tank, making sure to push the hose on at least 1.4 inches (35mm).

11. Attach the electrical connector to the top of the fuel tank.

12. Install the exhaust pipe insulator assembly and tighten the nut to 70–95 inch lbs. (7.9–10.7 Nm).

13. Install the pre-silencer exhaust pipe with new gaskets and tighten the rear nuts to 28–38 ft. lbs. (38–51 Nm). Tighten the front nuts to 48–65 ft. lbs. (64–89 Nm).

14. Lower the vehicle and connect the negative battery cable.

Millenia

1. Properly relieve the fuel system pressure.

2. Disconnect the negative battery cable.

3. Remove the rear seat cushion.

4. Detach the fuel pump connector, located beneath the rear seat cushion.

5. Drain the fuel tank.

6. Raise and safely support the vehicle.

7. Disconnect the fuel lines at the tank.

8. Disconnect the fuel filler hose from the tank.

9. Disconnect the fuel tank vapor and breather hoses.

10. Properly support the fuel tank and remove the tank retaining straps.

11. Lower the fuel tank and remove it from the vehicle.

To install:

12. Raise the fuel into position and install the tank retaining straps. Tighten the bolts to 32–44 ft. lbs. (44–60 Nm).

13. Connect the fuel vapor, breather and filler hoses to the tank.

14. Connect the fuel lines to the tank.

15. From inside the vehicle, attach the fuel pump electrical connector.

16. Fill the tank with fuel.

17. Connect the negative battery cable.

18. Cycle the ignition switch **ON** and **OFF** several times to pressurize the fuel system.

19. Check all hose connections for leaks. Repair any leaks which are found (loose hose clamps, worn or damaged hoses, etc.).

20. Lower the vehicle and install the rear seat cushion.

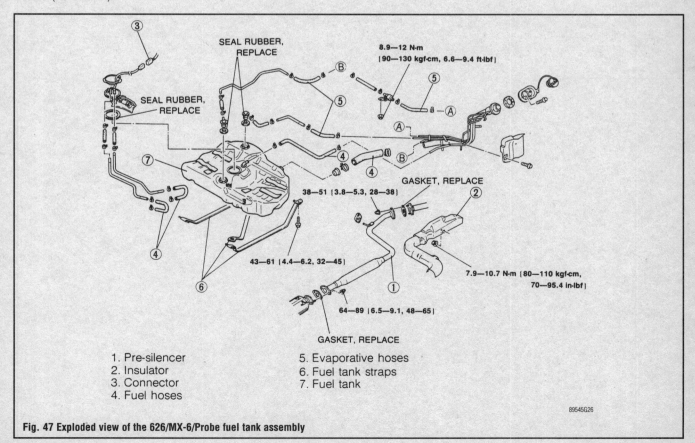

1. Pre-silencer
2. Insulator
3. Connector
4. Fuel hoses
5. Evaporative hoses
6. Fuel tank straps
7. Fuel tank

89545G26

Fig. 47 Exploded view of the 626/MX-6/Probe fuel tank assembly

SENDING UNIT REPLACEMENT

MX-3, 323, Protege and 1990–92 626 and MX-6

1. Relieve the fuel pressure and disconnect the negative battery cable.
2. Depress the clips on each end of the rear seat cushion and remove the cushion.
3. Detach the electrical connector from the fuel pump/sending unit.
4. Remove the attaching screws from the fuel pump/sending unit access cover and remove the cover.
5. Disconnect the fuel supply and return hoses from the fuel pump/sending unit.
6. Remove the attaching screws and the fuel pump/sending unit from the fuel tank.
7. Detach the sending unit electrical connector, remove the sending unit attaching nuts and remove the sending unit from the fuel pump assembly.

To install:

8. Attach the sending unit to the fuel pump assembly and install the nuts. attach the sending unit electrical connector.
9. Install the fuel pump/sending unit into the fuel tank and install the mounting screws.
10. Connect the fuel supply and return lines.
11. Install the access cover and the mounting screws.
12. Attach the sending unit electrical connector.
13. Position the rear seat cushion over the floor, making sure to align the retaining pins with the clips. Push down firmly until the 2 retaining pins are locked into the rear seat retaining clips.
14. Connect the negative battery cable, start the engine and check for proper system operation and for fuel leaks.

1993–98 626/MX-6/Probe

1. Relieve the fuel system pressure and disconnect the negative battery cable. Drain the fuel tank and remove the fuel tank from the vehicle as follows.
2. Raise and safely support the vehicle.
3. Remove the pre-silencer exhaust pipe and the heat shield.
4. Detach the electrical connectors from the top of the fuel tank.
5. Disconnect the fuel and evaporative hoses from the fuel tank.
6. While having an assistant support the fuel tank, remove the fuel tank support straps and lower the fuel tank from the vehicle.
7. Disconnect all fuel hoses from the fuel pump unit.
8. Turn the fuel pump ring counterclockwise and remove it.
9. Remove the fuel pump/sending unit assembly and gaskets from the fuel tank. Separate the sending unit from the fuel tank.

To install:

10. Connect the sending unit to the fuel pump. Install the fuel pump with a new gasket. Turn the fuel pump ring clockwise to tighten it until the flange hits the stopper.
11. Attach the fuel hoses to the fuel pump.
12. Install the fuel tank to the vehicle as follows:
    a. Have an assistant support the fuel tank in place and install the fuel tank straps. Tighten the strap bolts to 32–45 ft. lbs. (43–61 Nm).
    b. Connect the fuel and evaporative hoses, making sure to push the hoses on at least 1.4 inches (35 mm).
    c. Attach the fuel pump electrical connector.
    d. Install the exhaust pre-silencer pipe heat shield. Tighten the bolt to 70–90 inch lbs. (7.9–10 Nm).
    e. Install the exhaust pre-silencer pipe with new gaskets intact. Tighten the front nuts to 28–38 ft. lbs. (38–51 Nm). Tighten the rear bolts to 48–65 ft. lbs. (64–89 Nm).
13. Lower the vehicle and connect the negative battery cable.

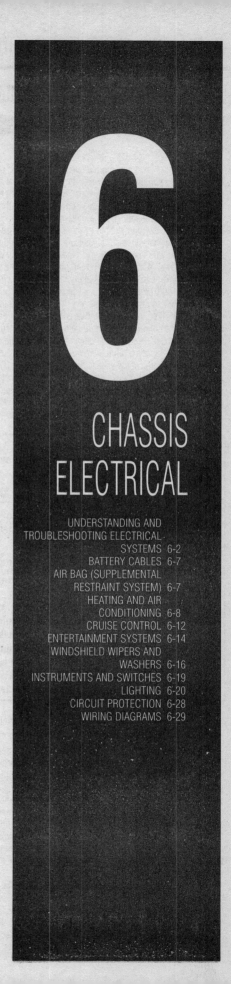

6

CHASSIS ELECTRICAL

UNDERSTANDING AND TROUBLESHOOTING ELECTRICAL SYSTEMS

Basic Electrical Theory

▶ See Figure 1

For any 12 volt, negative ground, electrical system to operate, the electricity must travel in a complete circuit. This simply means that current (power) from the positive (+) terminal of the battery must eventually return to the negative (-) terminal of the battery. Along the way, this current will travel through wires, fuses, switches and components. If, for any reason, the flow of current through the circuit is interrupted, the component fed by that circuit will cease to function properly.

Perhaps the easiest way to visualize a circuit is to think of connecting a light bulb (with two wires attached to it) to the battery—one wire attached to the negative (-) terminal of the battery and the other wire to the positive (+) terminal. With the two wires touching the battery terminals, the circuit would be complete and the light bulb would illuminate. Electricity would follow a path from the battery to the bulb and back to the battery. It's easy to see that with longer wires on our light bulb, it could be mounted anywhere. Further, one wire could be fitted with a switch so that the light could be turned on and off.

The normal automotive circuit differs from this simple example in two ways. First, instead of having a return wire from the bulb to the battery, the current travels through the frame of the vehicle. Since the negative (-) battery cable is attached to the frame (made of electrically conductive metal), the frame of the vehicle can serve as a ground wire to complete the circuit. Secondly, most automotive circuits contain multiple components which receive power from a single circuit. This lessens the amount of wire needed to power components on the vehicle.

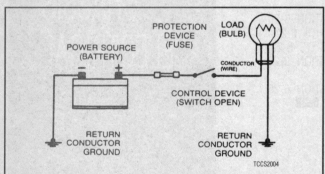

Fig. 1 This example illustrates a simple circuit. When the switch is closed, power from the positive (+) battery terminal flows through the fuse and the switch, and then to the light bulb. The light illuminates and the circuit is completed through the ground wire back to the negative (-) battery terminal. In reality, the two ground points shown in the illustration are attached to the metal frame of the vehicle, which completes the circuit back to the battery

HOW DOES ELECTRICITY WORK: THE WATER ANALOGY

Electricity is the flow of electrons—the subatomic particles that constitute the outer shell of an atom. Electrons spin in an orbit around the center core of an atom. The center core is comprised of protons (positive charge) and neutrons (neutral charge). Electrons have a negative charge and balance out the positive charge of the protons. When an outside force causes the number of electrons to unbalance the charge of the protons, the electrons will split off the atom and look for another atom to balance out. If this imbalance is kept up, electrons will continue to move and an electrical flow will exist.

Many people have been taught electrical theory using an analogy with water. In a comparison with water flowing through a pipe, the electrons would be the water and the wire is the pipe.

The flow of electricity can be measured much like the flow of water through a pipe. The unit of measurement used is amperes, frequently abbreviated as amps (a). You can compare amperage to the volume of water flowing through a pipe. When connected to a circuit, an ammeter will measure the actual amount of current flowing through the circuit. When relatively few electrons flow through a circuit, the amperage is low. When many electrons flow, the amperage is high.

Water pressure is measured in units such as pounds per square inch (psi); The electrical pressure is measured in units called volts (v). When a voltmeter is connected to a circuit, it is measuring the electrical pressure.

The actual flow of electricity depends not only on voltage and amperage, but also on the resistance of the circuit. The higher the resistance, the higher the force necessary to push the current through the circuit. The standard unit for measuring resistance is an ohm. Resistance in a circuit varies depending on the amount and type of components used in the circuit. The main factors which determine resistance are:

• Material—some materials have more resistance than others. Those with high resistance are said to be insulators. Rubber materials (or rubber-like plastics) are some of the most common insulators used in vehicles as they have a very high resistance to electricity. Very low resistance materials are said to be conductors. Copper wire is among the best conductors. Silver is actually a superior conductor to copper and is used in some relay contacts, but its high cost prohibits its use as common wiring. Most automotive wiring is made of copper.

• Size—the larger the wire size being used, the less resistance the wire will have. This is why components which use large amounts of electricity usually have large wires supplying current to them.

• Length—for a given thickness of wire, the longer the wire, the greater the resistance. The shorter the wire, the less the resistance. When determining the proper wire for a circuit, both size and length must be considered to design a circuit that can handle the current needs of the component.

• Temperature—with many materials, the higher the temperature, the greater the resistance (positive temperature coefficient). Some materials exhibit the opposite trait of lower resistance with higher temperatures (negative temperature coefficient). These principles are used in many of the sensors on the engine.

OHM'S LAW

There is a direct relationship between current, voltage and resistance. The relationship between current, voltage and resistance can be summed up by a statement known as Ohm's law.

Voltage (E) is equal to amperage (I) times resistance (R): $E = I \times R$
Other forms of the formula are $R = E/I$ and $I = E/R$

In each of these formulas, E is the voltage in volts, I is the current in amps and R is the resistance in ohms. The basic point to remember is that as the resistance of a circuit goes up, the amount of current that flows in the circuit will go down, if voltage remains the same.

The amount of work that the electricity can perform is expressed as power. The unit of power is the watt (w). The relationship between power, voltage and current is expressed as:

Power (w) is equal to amperage (I) times voltage (E): $W = I \times E$

This is only true for direct current (DC) circuits; The alternating current formula is a tad different, but since the electrical circuits in most vehicles are DC type, we need not get into AC circuit theory.

Electrical Components

POWER SOURCE

Power is supplied to the vehicle by two devices: The battery and the alternator. The battery supplies electrical power during starting or during periods when the current demand of the vehicle's electrical system exceeds the output capacity of the alternator. The alternator supplies electrical current when the engine is running. Just not does the alternator supply the current needs of the vehicle, but it recharges the battery.

The Battery

In most modern vehicles, the battery is a lead/acid electrochemical device consisting of six 2 volt subsections (cells) connected in series, so that the unit is capable of producing approximately 12 volts of electrical pressure. Each subsection consists of a series of positive and negative plates held a short distance apart in a solution of sulfuric acid and water.

The two types of plates are of dissimilar metals. This sets up a chemical reaction, and it is this reaction which produces current flow from the battery when its positive and negative terminals are connected to an electrical load . The power removed from the battery is replaced by the alternator, restoring the battery to its original chemical state.

The Alternator

On some vehicles there isn't an alternator, but a generator. The difference is that an alternator supplies alternating current which is then changed to direct current for use on the vehicle, while a generator produces direct current. Alternators tend to be more efficient and that is why they are used.

Alternators and generators are devices that consist of coils of wires wound together making big electromagnets. One group of coils spins within another set and the interaction of the magnetic fields causes a current to flow. This current is then drawn off the coils and fed into the vehicles electrical system.

GROUND

Two types of grounds are used in automotive electric circuits. Direct ground components are grounded to the frame through their mounting points. All other components use some sort of ground wire which is attached to the frame or chassis of the vehicle. The electrical current runs through the chassis of the vehicle and returns to the battery through the ground (-) cable; if you look, you'll see that the battery ground cable connects between the battery and the frame or chassis of the vehicle.

➡**It should be noted that a good percentage of electrical problems can be traced to bad grounds.**

PROTECTIVE DEVICES

▶ **See Figure 2**

It is possible for large surges of current to pass through the electrical system of your vehicle. If this surge of current were to reach the load in the circuit, the surge could burn it out or severely damage it. It can also overload the wiring, causing the harness to get hot and melt the insulation. To prevent this, fuses, circuit breakers and/or fusible links are connected into the supply wires of the electrical system. These items are nothing more than a built-in weak spot in the system. When an abnormal amount of current flows through the system, these protective devices work as follows to protect the circuit:

• Fuse—when an excessive electrical current passes through a fuse, the fuse "blows" (the conductor melts) and opens the circuit, preventing the passage of current.

• Circuit Breaker—a circuit breaker is basically a self-repairing fuse. It will open the circuit in the same fashion as a fuse, but when the surge subsides, the circuit breaker can be reset and does not need replacement.

• Fusible Link—a fusible link (fuse link or main link) is a short length of special, high temperature insulated wire that acts as a fuse. When an excessive electrical current passes through a fusible link, the thin gauge wire inside the link melts, creating an intentional open to protect the circuit. To repair the circuit, the link must be replaced. Some newer type fusible links are housed in plug-in modules, which are simply replaced like a fuse, while older type fusible links must be cut and spliced if they melt. Since this link is very early in the electrical path, it's the first place to look if nothing on the vehicle works, yet the battery seems to be charged and is properly connected.

✷✷ CAUTION

Always replace fuses, circuit breakers and fusible links with identically rated components. Under no circumstances should a component of higher or lower amperage rating be substituted.

SWITCHES & RELAYS

▶ **See Figures 3 and 4**

Switches are used in electrical circuits to control the passage of current. The most common use is to open and close circuits between the battery and the various electric devices in the system. Switches are rated according to the amount of amperage they can handle. If a sufficient amperage rated switch is not used in a circuit, the switch could overload and cause damage.

Some electrical components which require a large amount of current to operate use a special switch called a relay. Since these circuits carry a large amount of current, the thickness of the wire in the circuit is also greater. If this large wire were connected from the load to the control switch, the switch would have to carry the high amperage load and the fairing or dash would be twice as large to accommodate the increased size of the wiring harness. To prevent these problems, a relay is used.

Relays are composed of a coil and a set of contacts. When the coil has a current passed though it, a magnetic field is formed and this field causes the contacts to move together, completing the circuit. Most relays are normally open, preventing current from passing through the circuit, but they can take any electrical form depending on the job they are intended to do. Relays can be considered "remote control switches." They allow a smaller current to operate devices that require higher amperages. When a small current operates the coil, a larger current is allowed to pass by the contacts. Some common circuits which may use relays are the horn, headlights, starter, electric fuel pump and other high draw circuits.

LOAD

Every electrical circuit must include a "load" (something to use the electricity coming from the source). Without this load, the battery would attempt to deliver its entire power supply from one pole to another. This is called a "short circuit." All

Fig. 2 Most vehicles use one or more fuse panels. This one is located on the driver's side kick panel

TCCA6P01

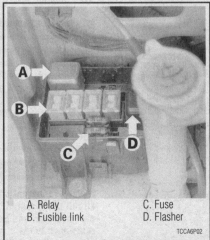

A. Relay   C. Fuse
B. Fusible link   D. Flasher

TCCA6P02

Fig. 3 The underhood fuse and relay panel usually contains fuses, relays, flashers and fusible links

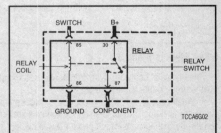

TCCA6G02

Fig. 4 Relays are composed of a coil and a switch. These two components are linked together so that when one operates, the other operates at the same time. The large wires in the circuit are connected from the battery to one side of the relay switch (B+) and from the opposite side of the relay switch to the load (component). Smaller wires are connected from the relay coil to the control switch for the circuit and from the opposite side of the relay coil to ground

this electricity would take a short cut to ground and cause a great amount of damage to other components in the circuit by developing a tremendous amount of heat. This condition could develop sufficient heat to melt the insulation on all the surrounding wires and reduce a multiple wire cable to a lump of plastic and copper.

WIRING & HARNESSES

The average vehicle contains meters and meters of wiring, with hundreds of individual connections. To protect the many wires from damage and to keep them from becoming a confusing tangle, they are organized into bundles, enclosed in plastic or taped together and called wiring harnesses. Different harnesses serve different parts of the vehicle. Individual wires are color coded to help trace them through a harness where sections are hidden from view.

Automotive wiring or circuit conductors can be either single strand wire, multi-strand wire or printed circuitry. Single strand wire has a solid metal core and is usually used inside such components as alternators, motors, relays and other devices. Multi-strand wire has a core made of many small strands of wire twisted together into a single conductor. Most of the wiring in an automotive electrical system is made up of multi-strand wire, either as a single conductor or grouped together in a harness. All wiring is color coded on the insulator, either as a solid color or as a colored wire with an identification stripe. A printed circuit is a thin film of copper or other conductor that is printed on an insulator backing. Occasionally, a printed circuit is sandwiched between two sheets of plastic for more protection and flexibility. A complete printed circuit, consisting of conductors, insulating material and connectors for lamps or other components is called a printed circuit board. Printed circuitry is used in place of individual wires or harnesses in places where space is limited, such as behind instrument panels.

Since automotive electrical systems are very sensitive to changes in resistance, the selection of properly sized wires is critical when systems are repaired. A loose or corroded connection or a replacement wire that is too small for the circuit will add extra resistance and an additional voltage drop to the circuit.

The wire gauge number is an expression of the cross-section area of the conductor. Vehicles from countries that use the metric system will typically describe the wire size as its cross-sectional area in square millimeters. In this method, the larger the wire, the greater the number. Another common system for expressing wire size is the American Wire Gauge (AWG) system. As gauge number increases, area decreases and the wire becomes smaller. An 18 gauge wire is smaller than a 4 gauge wire. A wire with a higher gauge number will carry less current than a wire with a lower gauge number. Gauge wire size refers to the size of the strands of the conductor, not the size of the complete wire with insulator. It is possible, therefore, to have two wires of the same gauge with different diameters because one may have thicker insulation than the other.

It is essential to understand how a circuit works before trying to figure out why it doesn't. An electrical schematic shows the electrical current paths when a circuit is operating properly. Schematics break the entire electrical system down into individual circuits. In a schematic, usually no attempt is made to represent wiring and components as they physically appear on the vehicle; switches and other components are shown as simply as possible. Face views of harness connectors show the cavity or terminal locations in all multi-pin connectors to help locate test points.

CONNECTORS

▶ **See Figures 5 and 6**

Three types of connectors are commonly used in automotive applications—weatherproof, molded and hard shell.

• Weatherproof—these connectors are most commonly used where the connector is exposed to the elements. Terminals are protected against moisture and dirt by sealing rings which provide a weathertight seal. All repairs require the use of a special terminal and the tool required to service it. Unlike standard blade type terminals, these weatherproof terminals cannot be straightened once they are bent. Make certain that the connectors are properly seated and all of the sealing rings are in place when connecting leads.

• Molded—these connectors require complete replacement of the connector if found to be defective. This means splicing a new connector assembly into the harness. All splices should be soldered to insure proper contact. Use care when probing the connections or replacing terminals in them, as it is possible to create a short circuit between opposite terminals. If this happens to the wrong terminal pair, it is possible to damage certain components. Always use jumper wires between connectors for circuit checking and NEVER probe through weatherproof seals.

Fig. 5 Hard shell (left) and weatherproof (right) connectors have replaceable terminals

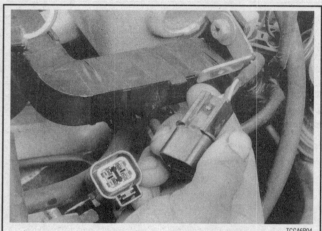

Fig. 6 Weatherproof connectors are most commonly used in the engine compartment or where the connector is exposed to the elements

• Hard Shell—unlike molded connectors, the terminal contacts in hard-shell connectors can be replaced. Replacement usually involves the use of a special terminal removal tool that depresses the locking tangs (barbs) on the connector terminal and allows the connector to be removed from the rear of the shell. The connector shell should be replaced if it shows any evidence of burning, melting, cracks, or breaks. Replace individual terminals that are burnt, corroded, distorted or loose.

Test Equipment

Pinpointing the exact cause of trouble in an electrical circuit is most times accomplished by the use of special test equipment. The following describes different types of commonly used test equipment and briefly explains how to use them in diagnosis. In addition to the information covered below, the tool manufacturer's instructions booklet (provided with the tester) should be read and clearly understood before attempting any test procedures.

JUMPER WIRES

❈ CAUTION

Never use jumper wires made from a thinner gauge wire than the circuit being tested. If the jumper wire is of too small a gauge, it may overheat and possibly melt. Never use jumpers to bypass high resistance loads in a circuit. Bypassing resistances, in effect, creates a short circuit. This may, in turn, cause damage and fire. Jumper wires should only be used to bypass lengths of wire or to simulate switches.

Jumper wires are simple, yet extremely valuable, pieces of test equipment. They are basically test wires which are used to bypass sections of a circuit. Although jumper wires can be purchased, they are usually fabricated from lengths of standard automotive wire and whatever type of connector (alligator clip, spade connector or pin connector) that is required for the particular application being tested. In cramped, hard-to-reach areas, it is advisable to have insulated boots over the jumper wire terminals in order to prevent accidental grounding. It is also advisable to include a standard automotive fuse in any jumper wire. This is commonly referred to as a "fused jumper". By inserting an in-line fuse holder between a set of test leads, a fused jumper wire can be used for bypassing open circuits. Use a 5 amp fuse to provide protection against voltage spikes.

Jumper wires are used primarily to locate open electrical circuits, on either the ground (-) side of the circuit or on the power (+) side. If an electrical component fails to operate, connect the jumper wire between the component and a good ground. If the component operates only with the jumper installed, the ground circuit is open. If the ground circuit is good, but the component does not operate, the circuit between the power feed and component may be open. By moving the jumper wire successively back from the component toward the power source, you can isolate the area of the circuit where the open is located. When the component stops functioning, or the power is cut off, the open is in the segment of wire between the jumper and the point previously tested.

You can sometimes connect the jumper wire directly from the battery to the "hot" terminal of the component, but first make sure the component uses 12 volts in operation. Some electrical components, such as fuel injectors or sensors, are designed to operate on about 4 to 5 volts, and running 12 volts directly to these components will cause damage.

TEST LIGHTS

▶ See Figure 7

The test light is used to check circuits and components while electrical current is flowing through them. It is used for voltage and ground tests. To use a 12 volt test light, connect the ground clip to a good ground and probe wherever necessary with the pick. The test light will illuminate when voltage is detected. This does not necessarily mean that 12 volts (or any particular amount of voltage) is present; it only means that some voltage is present. It is advisable before using the test light to touch its ground clip and probe across the battery posts or terminals to make sure the light is operating properly.

✳✳ WARNING

Do not use a test light to probe electronic ignition, spark plug or coil wires. Never use a pick-type test light to probe wiring on computer controlled systems unless specifically instructed to do so. Any wire insulation that is pierced by the test light probe should be taped and sealed with silicone after testing.

Like the jumper wire, the 12 volt test light is used to isolate opens in circuits. But, whereas the jumper wire is used to bypass the open to operate the load, the 12 volt test light is used to locate the presence of voltage in a circuit. If the test light illuminates, there is power up to that point in the circuit; if the test light does

not illuminate, there is an open circuit (no power). Move the test light in successive steps back toward the power source until the light in the handle illuminates. The open is between the probe and a point which was previously probed.

The self-powered test light is similar in design to the 12 volt test light, but contains a 1.5 volt penlight battery in the handle. It is most often used in place of a multimeter to check for open or short circuits when power is isolated from the circuit (continuity test).

The battery in a self-powered test light does not provide much current. A weak battery may not provide enough power to illuminate the test light even when a complete circuit is made (especially if there is high resistance in the circuit). Always make sure that the test battery is strong. To check the battery, briefly touch the ground clip to the probe; if the light glows brightly, the battery is strong enough for testing.

➡ **A self-powered test light should not be used on any computer controlled system or component. The small amount of electricity transmitted by the test light is enough to damage many electronic automotive components.**

MULTIMETERS

Multimeters are an extremely useful tool for troubleshooting electrical problems. They can be purchased in either analog or digital form and have a price range to suit any budget. A multimeter is a voltmeter, ammeter and ohmmeter (along with other features) combined into one instrument. It is often used when testing solid state circuits because of its high input impedance (usually 10 megaohms or more). A brief description of the multimeter main test functions follows:

• Voltmeter—the voltmeter is used to measure voltage at any point in a circuit, or to measure the voltage drop across any part of a circuit. Voltmeters usually have various scales and a selector switch to allow the reading of different voltage ranges. The voltmeter has a positive and a negative lead. To avoid damage to the meter, always connect the negative lead to the negative (-) side of the circuit (to ground or nearest the ground side of the circuit) and connect the positive lead to the positive (+) side of the circuit (to the power source or the nearest power source). Note that the negative voltmeter lead will always be black and that the positive voltmeter will always be some color other than black (usually red).

• Ohmmeter—the ohmmeter is designed to read resistance (measured in ohms) in a circuit or component. Most ohmmeters will have a selector switch which permits the measurement of different ranges of resistance (usually the selector switch allows the multiplication of the meter reading by 10, 100, 1,000 and 10,000). Some ohmmeters are "auto-ranging" which means the meter itself will determine which scale to use. Since the meters are powered by an internal battery, the ohmmeter can be used like a self-powered test light. When the ohmmeter is connected, current from the ohmmeter flows through the circuit or component being tested. Since the ohmmeter's internal resistance and voltage are known values, the amount of current flow through the meter depends on the resistance of the circuit or component being tested. The ohmmeter can also be used to perform a continuity test for suspected open circuits. In using the meter for making continuity checks, do not be concerned with the actual resistance readings. Zero resistance, or any ohm reading, indicates continuity in the circuit. Infinite resistance indicates an opening in the circuit. A high resistance reading where there should be none indicates a problem in the circuit. Checks for short circuits are made in the same manner as checks for open circuits, except that the circuit must be isolated from both power and normal ground. Infinite resistance indicates no continuity, while zero resistance indicates a dead short.

✳✳ WARNING

Never use an ohmmeter to check the resistance of a component or wire while there is voltage applied to the circuit.

• Ammeter—an ammeter measures the amount of current flowing through a circuit in units called amperes or amps. At normal operating voltage, most circuits have a characteristic amount of amperes, called "current draw" which can be measured using an ammeter. By referring to a specified current draw rating, then measuring the amperes and comparing the two values, one can determine what is happening within the circuit to aid in diagnosis. An open circuit, for example, will not allow any current to flow, so the ammeter reading will be zero. A damaged component or circuit will have an increased current draw, so the reading will be high. The ammeter is always connected in series with the circuit being tested. All of the current that normally flows through the circuit must also flow through the ammeter; if there is any other path for the current to follow, the ammeter reading

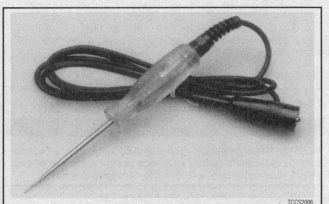

TCCS2006

Fig. 7 A 12 volt test light is used to detect the presence of voltage in a circuit

will not be accurate. The ammeter itself has very little resistance to current flow and, therefore, will not affect the circuit, but it will measure current draw only when the circuit is closed and electricity is flowing. Excessive current draw can blow fuses and drain the battery, while a reduced current draw can cause motors to run slowly, lights to dim and other components to not operate properly.

Troubleshooting Electrical Systems

When diagnosing a specific problem, organized troubleshooting is a must: The complexity of a modern automotive vehicle demands that you approach any problem in a logical, organized manner. There are certain troubleshooting techniques, however, which are standard:

• Establish when the problem occurs. Does the problem appear only under certain conditions? Were there any noises, odors or other unusual symptoms? Isolate the problem area. To do this, make some simple tests and observations, then eliminate the systems that are working properly. Check for obvious problems, such as broken wires and loose or dirty connections. Always check the obvious before assuming something complicated is the cause.

• Test for problems systematically to determine the cause once the problem area is isolated. Are all the components functioning properly? Is there power going to electrical switches and motors. Performing careful, systematic checks will often turn up most causes on the first inspection, without wasting time checking components that have little or no relationship to the problem.

• Test all repairs after the work is done to make sure that the problem is fixed. Some causes can be traced to more than one component, so a careful verification of repair work is important in order to pick up additional malfunctions that may cause a problem to reappear or a different problem to arise. A blown fuse, for example, is a simple problem that may require more than another fuse to repair. If you don't look for a problem that caused a fuse to blow, a shorted wire (for example) may go undetected.

Experience has shown that most problems tend to be the result of a fairly simple and obvious cause, such as loose or corroded connectors, bad grounds or damaged wire insulation which causes a short. This makes careful visual inspection of components during testing essential to quick and accurate troubleshooting.

Testing

OPEN CIRCUITS

▶ **See Figure 8**

This test already assumes the existence of an open in the circuit and it is used to help locate the open portion.
1. Isolate the circuit from power and ground.
2. Connect the self-powered test light or ohmmeter ground clip to the ground side of the circuit and probe sections of the circuit sequentially.
3. If the light is out or there is infinite resistance, the open is between the probe and the circuit ground.

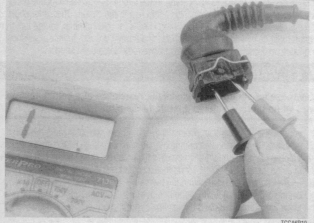

TCCA6P10

Fig. 8 The infinite reading on this multimeter indicates that the circuit is open

4. If the light is on or the meter shows continuity, the open is between the probe and the end of the circuit toward the power source.

SHORT CIRCUITS

➡**Never use a self-powered test light to perform checks for opens or shorts when power is applied to the circuit under test. The test light can be damaged by outside power.**

1. Isolate the circuit from power and ground.
2. Connect the self-powered test light or ohmmeter ground clip to a good ground and probe any easy-to-reach point in the circuit.
3. If the light comes on or there is continuity, there is a short somewhere in the circuit.
4. To isolate the short, probe a test point at either end of the isolated circuit (the light should be on or the meter should indicate continuity).
5. Leave the test light probe engaged and sequentially open connectors or switches, remove parts, etc. until the light goes out or continuity is broken.
6. When the light goes out, the short is between the last two circuit components which were opened.

VOLTAGE

This test determines voltage available from the battery and should be the first step in any electrical troubleshooting procedure after visual inspection. Many electrical problems, especially on computer controlled systems, can be caused by a low state of charge in the battery. Excessive corrosion at the battery cable terminals can cause poor contact that will prevent proper charging and full battery current flow.

1. Set the voltmeter selector switch to the 20V position.
2. Connect the multimeter negative lead to the battery's negative (-) post or terminal and the positive lead to the battery's positive (+) post or terminal.
3. Turn the ignition switch **ON** to provide a load.
4. A well charged battery should register over 12 volts. If the meter reads below 11.5 volts, the battery power may be insufficient to operate the electrical system properly.

VOLTAGE DROP

▶ **See Figure 9**

When current flows through a load, the voltage beyond the load drops. This voltage drop is due to the resistance created by the load and also by small resistances created by corrosion at the connectors and damaged insulation on the wires. The maximum allowable voltage drop under load is critical, especially if there is more than one load in the circuit, since all voltage drops are cumulative.

1. Set the voltmeter selector switch to the 20 volt position.
2. Connect the multimeter negative lead to a good ground.
3. Operate the circuit and check the voltage prior to the first component (load).
4. There should be little or no voltage drop in the circuit prior to the first component. If a voltage drop exists, the wire or connectors in the circuit are suspect.
5. While operating the first component in the circuit, probe the ground side of the component with the positive meter lead and observe the voltage readings. A small voltage drop should be noticed. This voltage drop is caused by the resistance of the component.
6. Repeat the test for each component (load) down the circuit.
7. If a large voltage drop is noticed, the preceding component, wire or connector is suspect.

RESISTANCE

▶ **See Figures 10 and 11**

✳✳ WARNING

Never use an ohmmeter with power applied to the circuit. The ohmmeter is designed to operate on its own power supply. The normal 12 volt electrical system voltage could damage the meter!

1. Isolate the circuit from the vehicle's power source.
2. Ensure that the ignition key is **OFF** when disconnecting any components or the battery.

Fig. 9 This voltage drop test revealed high resistance (low voltage) in the circuit

Fig. 10 Checking the resistance of a coolant temperature sensor with an ohmmeter. Reading is 1.04 kilohms

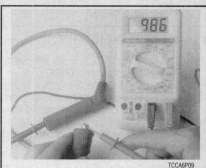

Fig. 11 Spark plug wires can be checked for excessive resistance using an ohmmeter

3. Where necessary, also isolate at least one side of the circuit to be checked, in order to avoid reading parallel resistances. Parallel circuit resistances will always give a lower reading than the actual resistance of either of the branches.

4. Connect the meter leads to both sides of the circuit (wire or component) and read the actual measured ohms on the meter scale. Make sure the selector switch is set to the proper ohm scale for the circuit being tested, to avoid misreading the ohmmeter test value.

Wire and Connector Repair

Almost anyone can replace damaged wires, as long as the proper tools and parts are available. Wire and terminals are available to fit almost any need. Even the specialized weatherproof, molded and hard shell connectors are now available from aftermarket suppliers.

Be sure the ends of all the wires are fitted with the proper terminal hardware and connectors. Wrapping a wire around a stud is never a permanent solution and will only cause trouble later. Replace wires one at a time to avoid confusion. Always route wires exactly the same as the factory.

➡**If connector repair is necessary, only attempt it if you have the proper tools. Weatherproof and hard shell connectors require special tools to release the pins inside the connector. Attempting to repair these connectors with conventional hand tools will damage them.**

BATTERY CABLES

Disconnecting the Cables

When working on any electrical component on the vehicle, it is always a good idea to disconnect the negative (-) battery cable. This will prevent potential damage to many sensitive electrical components such as the Engine Control Module (ECM), radio, alternator, etc.

➡**Any time you disengage the battery cables, it is recommended that you disconnect the negative (-) battery cable first. This will prevent your accidentally grounding the positive (+) terminal to the body of the vehicle when disconnecting it, thereby preventing damage to the above mentioned components.**

Before you disconnect the cable(s), first turn the ignition to the **OFF** position. This will prevent a draw on the battery which could cause arcing (electricity trying to ground itself to the body of a vehicle, just like a spark plug jumping the gap) and, of course, damaging some components such as the alternator diodes.

When the battery cable(s) are reconnected (negative cable last), be sure to check that your lights, windshield wipers and other electrically operated safety components are all working correctly. If your vehicle contains an Electronically Tuned Radio (ETR), don't forget to also reset your radio stations. Ditto for the clock.

AIR BAG (SUPPLEMENTAL RESTRAINT SYSTEM)

General Information

SYSTEM OPERATION

There are 3 crash sensors mounted in the front of the vehicle. There is another sensor mounted in the passenger compartment of the vehicle which monitors the deceleration rate of the vehicle upon collision. When any of the crash sensors and the deceleration sensor are simultaneously activated, the air bag will be deployed. The air bag system does contain a warning lamp which will illuminate and stay lit if there is a problem within the system. The complete air bag system is controlled by the diagnostic module unit. The module unit contains a diagnostic feature which will display a coded warning lamp display when trouble does exist.

SYSTEM PRECAUTIONS

1. Before replacing any air bag component, disconnect the negative battery cable and disconnect the orange and blue clockspring electrical connector, located below the steering wheel.

2. The air bag components are not intended to be disassembled. They should be replaced if they are defective.

3. The air bag wiring harness should never be repaired, if it is defective it must be replaced.

4. Never use an ohmmeter to test the air bag module. Doing so could accidentally deploy the air bag.

5. When carrying a live undeployed air bag module, carry it so that the trim cover is pointing away from your body at all times.

6. When placing a live undeployed air bag on a flat surface, make certain to face the trim cover upward at all times.

7. In the event that the air bag has been deployed, always wear gloves and safety glasses to handle the air bag assembly. The air bag may contain caustic material deposits.

8. Because of the content of the air bag assembly, a deployed unit must be properly disposed of.

9. The position of the crash sensors in the front end is very important, if the front end ever suffers any damage of any type, the sensors must be inspected.

10. If the steering wheel is ever removed, the air bag clockspring connector must be adjusted.

DISARMING THE SYSTEM

▶ **See Figures 12 thru 17**

1. If equipped, deactivate the audio anti-theft system.
2. Turn the ignition switch to **LOCK**.
3. Disconnect the negative battery cable and wait for more than one minute to allow the backup power supply to deplete its stored power.
4. Remove the driver side undercover and lower dash panel. Disconnect the orange and blue clock spring connectors for the drivers side air bag.
5. Remove the glove compartment and disconnect the orange and blue passenger side air bag module connectors.

ARMING THE SYSTEM

1. If equipped, deactivate the audio anti-theft system.
2. Turn the ignition switch to **LOCK**.

3. Disconnect the negative battery cable.
4. If not already done, remove the driver side undercover and lower dash panel.
5. Connect the orange and blue clock spring connectors for the drivers side air bag.
6. If not already done, remove the glove compartment.
7. Connect the orange and blue passenger side air bag module connectors.
8. Install the glove compartment and the driver's side undercover and lower dash panels.
9. Ensure that no one is sitting in the vehicle, especially in front of an air bag module.
10. Connect the negative battery cable.

Fig. 12 To disable the air bag system, first disconnect the negative battery cable, then loosen the hood latch pull knob retaining nut . . .

Fig. 13 . . . and disengage the knob from the lower driver's side undercover

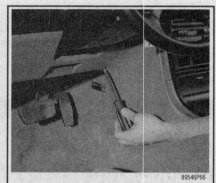

Fig. 14 Remove the lower driver's side undercover retaining screws . . .

Fig. 15 . . . then pull the cover down and, if equipped, detach the A/C vent hose from it

Fig. 16 Locate and disconnect the orange and blue air bag clockspring electrical harness plugs

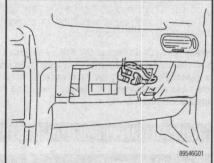

Fig. 17 Passenger's side air bag connectors are located behind the glove compartment

HEATING AND AIR CONDITIONING

Blower Motor

REMOVAL & INSTALLATION

MX-3, 1990–94 323 and Protege

▶ **See Figures 18 and 19**

1. Disconnect the negative battery cable.
2. Open the glove box and remove the glove box retaining screws. Remove the glove box assembly.
3. Remove the inner glove box assembly screws and remove the inner glove box.

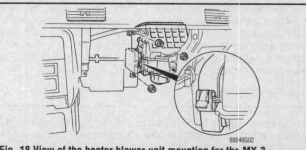

Fig. 18 View of the heater blower unit mounting for the MX-3, 1990–94 323 and Protege

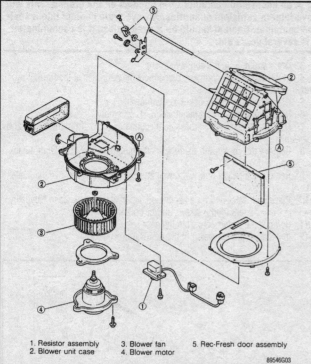

1. Resistor assembly   3. Blower fan   5. Rec-Fresh door assembly
2. Blower unit case   4. Blower motor

89546G03

Fig. 19 Exploded view of the MX-3, 1990–94 323 and Protege heater blower unit. The 1990–92 626 and MX-6 use a similar mounting

4. Unclip and remove the heater blower seal plate.
5. Remove the 3 heater blower mounting nuts and remove the blower unit case.
6. Remove the screws and separate the two halves of the blower unit case.
7. Remove the blower fan from the blower motor. Remove the mounting screws and separate the blower motor from the case.

To install:
8. Install the blower motor to the case and install the screws.
9. Install the blower fan to the blower motor.
10. Connect the 2 halves of the blower unit case and install the screws.
11. Install the heater blower unit case to the vehicle and tighten the mounting nuts.
12. Install the heater blower seal plate.
13. Install the inner glove box assembly.
14. Install the glove box door.
15. Connect the negative battery cable.

1990–92 626 and MX-6

♦ **See Figure 19**

1. Disconnect the negative battery cable.
2. Remove the glove box and the underdash cover.
3. Detach the electrical connectors from the blower unit.
4. Remove the blower unit-to-fire wall attaching bolts and remove the blower unit assembly.
5. Remove the blower motor fan-to-motor fastener.
6. Remove the blower motor-to-unit attaching bolts, then remove the motor.
7. Installation is the reverse of the removal procedure.

1993–98 626/MX-6/Probe, 1995–98 Protege and Millenia

♦ **See Figure 20**

➡ **The blower motor is located on the right side of the vehicle underneath the dashboard.**

1. Disconnect the negative battery cable.
2. If necessary, remove the sound deadening panel from the passenger side.
3. Remove the glove box assembly and, if equipped, the brace.

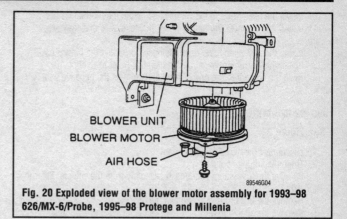

BLOWER UNIT
BLOWER MOTOR
AIR HOSE

89546G04

Fig. 20 Exploded view of the blower motor assembly for 1993–98 626/MX-6/Probe, 1995–98 Protege and Millenia

4. Remove the cooling air hose from the blower motor assembly.
5. Detach the electrical connector from the blower motor.
6. Remove the 3 blower motor-to-blower motor housing screws and blower motor.
7. If necessary, remove the blower wheel-to-blower motor clip and the wheel.
8. To install, reverse the removal procedure and check the blower motor operation.

Heater Core

REMOVAL & INSTALLATION

MX-3, 1990–94 323 and Protege

♦ **See Figure 21**

1. Disconnect the negative battery cable.
2. Drain the engine coolant.
3. Remove the instrument panel/dash assembly from the vehicle. Refer to Section 10.
4. Remove the seal plate from between the heater unit and the blower unit.
5. Unlock the heater hose connector at the heater core side and disconnect the hose(s).
6. Remove the heater hose(s) and cap the hose(s).
7. Remove the attaching nuts and remove the heater unit assembly.
8. Remove the heater core attaching screw and remove the heater core.

To install:
9. Install the heater core to the heater case and install the mounting screws.

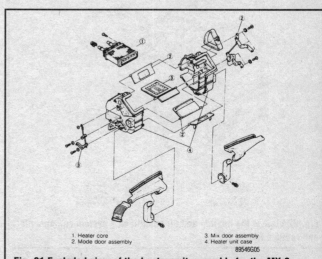

1. Heater core   3. Mix door assembly
2. Mode door assembly   4. Heater unit case

89546G05

Fig. 21 Exploded view of the heater unit assembly for the MX-3, 1990–94 323 and Protege

10. Install the heater unit to the vehicle and install the mounting nuts.
11. Install and connect the heater hose(s). Make sure that they are secure.
12. Install the seal plate to between the heater case and the blower case.
13. Install the instrument panel/dash assembly. Refer to Section 10.
14. Refill the coolant to the proper level and connect the negative battery cable.

1990–92 626/MX-6

▶ See Figure 21

1. Disconnect the negative battery cable.
2. Drain the engine coolant.
3. Remove the instrument panel/dash assembly from the vehicle. Refer to Section 10.
4. Remove the heater hose(s) and cap the hose(s).
5. Remove the attaching nuts and remove the heater unit assembly.
6. Remove the heater core attaching screw and remove the heater core.

To install:

7. Install the heater core to the heater case and install the mounting screws.
8. Install the heater unit to the vehicle and install the mounting nuts.
9. Install and connect the heater hose(s). Make sure that they are secure.
10. Install the instrument panel/dash assembly. Refer to section 10.
11. Refill the coolant to the proper level and connect the negative battery cable.

1993–98 626/MX-6/Probe, 1995–98 Protege and Millenia

▶ See Figures 22, 23, 24 and 25

➡The A/C system must be discharged and the evaporator removed in order to service the heater core on these models. It is illegal for anyone to vent A/C refrigerant into the atmosphere. Refer to Section 1 for information on the A/C system.

1. Take the vehicle to a EPA certified repair facility and have the A/C system refrigerant recovered.
2. Disconnect the negative battery cable.

✳✳ CAUTION

Never open, service or drain the radiator or cooling system when hot; serious burns can occur from the steam and hot coolant. Also, when draining engine coolant, keep in mind that cats and dogs are attracted to ethylene glycol antifreeze and could drink any that is

left in an uncovered container or in puddles on the ground. This will prove fatal in sufficient quantities. Always drain coolant into a sealable container. Coolant should be reused unless it is contaminated or is several years old.

3. Drain and recycle the engine coolant.
4. In the engine compartment, disconnect the A/C lines at the firewall by removing the fitting fasteners.
5. Disconnect the heater hoses at the firewall as well.
6. Remove the instrument panel and dash assembly.
7. Detach any electrical harness connections or cables from the heater and cooler units.
8. Remove the cooler unit-to-firewall attaching nuts and pull the unit backwards and remove it.
9. Remove the heater unit-to-firewall attaching nuts and remove the heater unit.
10. Place the heater unit on a bench and separate the heater case halves by removing the fasteners (clips, screws and/or bolts).
11. Remove the heater core from the case half.
12. Installation is the reverse of the removal procedure.

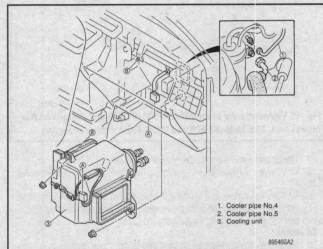

1. Cooler pipe No.4
2. Cooler pipe No.5
3. Cooling unit

89546GA2

Fig. 23 Before the heater core can be removed, you must first remove the cooler (A/C) unit from the firewall

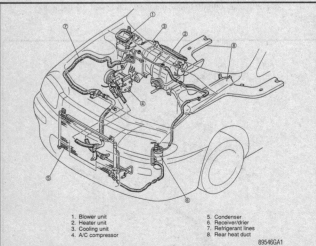

1. Blower unit
2. Heater unit
3. Cooling unit
4. A/C compressor
5. Condenser
6. Receiver/drier
7. Refrigerant lines
8. Rear heat duct

89546GA1

Fig. 22 View of the heating and air conditioning system components and relative locations

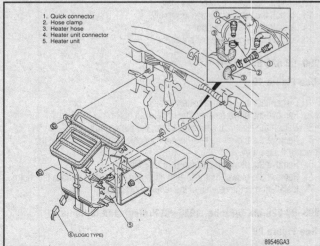

1. Quick connector
2. Hose clamp
3. Heater hose
4. Heater unit connector
5. Heater unit

④(LOGIC TYPE)

89546GA3

Fig. 24 View of the heater unit mounting and hose/electrical connections

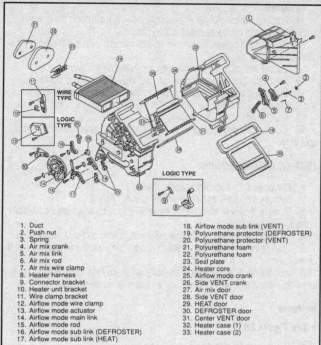

1. Duct
2. Push nut
3. Spring
4. Air mix crank
5. Air mix link
6. Air mix rod
7. Air mix wire clamp
8. Heater harness
9. Connector bracket
10. Heater unit bracket
11. Wire clamp bracket
12. Airflow mode wire clamp
13. Airflow mode actuator
14. Airflow mode main link
15. Airflow mode rod
16. Airflow mode sub link (DEFROSTER)
17. Airflow mode sub link (HEAT)
18. Airflow mode sub link (VENT)
19. Polyurethane protector (DEFROSTER)
20. Polyurethane protector (VENT)
21. Polyurethane foam
22. Polyurethane foam
23. Seal plate
24. Heater core
25. Airflow mode crank
26. Side VENT crank
27. Air mix door
28. Side VENT door
29. HEAT door
30. DEFROSTER door
31. Center VENT door
32. Heater case (1)
33. Heater case (2)

89546GA4

Fig. 25 Exploded view of the typical heater unit and core assembly. When disassembling, only remove the case half fasteners

Air Conditioning Components

REMOVAL & INSTALLATION

Repair or service of air conditioning components is not covered by this manual, because of the risk of personal injury or death, and because of the legal ramifications of servicing these components without the proper EPA certification and experience. Cost, personal injury or death, environmental damage, and legal considerations (such as the fact that it is a federal crime to vent refrigerant into the atmosphere), dictate that the A/C components on your vehicle should be serviced only by a Motor Vehicle Air Conditioning (MVAC) trained, and EPA certified automotive technician.

➡**If your vehicle's A/C system uses R-12 refrigerant and is in need of recharging, the A/C system can be converted over to R-134a refrigerant (less environmentally harmful and expensive). Refer to Section 1 for additional information on R-12 to R-134a conversions, and for additional considerations dealing with your vehicle's A/C system.**

Control Cables

REMOVAL & INSTALLATION

♦ **See Figure 26**

These procedures apply only to MX-3, 1990–92 626, MX-6, 1990–94 323 and Protege models. Other models are not equipped with cable controls. Note that some 1990–92 626 and MX-6 models are not equipped with cable controls.
1. Disconnect the negative battery cable.
2. Remove the control panel assembly. Refer to the procedure in this Section.
3. Remove the applicable housing brace and remove the cable.
To install:
4. Insert the cable end into the hole of the control lever.
5. Position the cable housing into its seat.
6. Install the cable housing brace.
7. Install the control panel assembly.
8. Check the operation of the control cable.

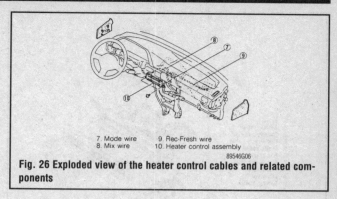

7. Mode wire   9. Rec-Fresh wire
8. Mix wire   10. Heater control assembly

89546G06

Fig. 26 Exploded view of the heater control cables and related components

ADJUSTMENT

Airflow Mode Cable

MX-3, 1990–94 323 AND PROTEGE

1. Position the mode lever to the **DEFROST** position.
2. From under the dash at the control linkage on the heater unit side, remove the cable from the retaining clip.
3. Align the set pin hole with the matching hole of the heater unit and insert a pin in the holes to hold in place.
4. Make certain that the mode lever is in the **DEFROST** position.
5. Connect the mode cable to the retaining clip. Keep tension on the wire when installing the clip.
6. Check the function of the mode lever. If the lever functions properly, remove the set pin.

1990–92 626 AND MX-6

1. Position the mode control lever to the **DEFROST** position.
2. At the control linkage, located on the side of the heater assembly, adjust the shutter lever so that it is as close as can be to the heater unit. Clamp the wire tight at that point.
3. Check the mode control lever for proper operation.

Mix/Temperature Blend Cable

MX-3, 1990–94 323 AND PROTEGE

1. At the heater assembly, disconnect the mix cable from the heater unit.
2. Set the mix lever to the **COLD** position.
3. Set the door to the **COLD** position and tighten the clamp to the cable in place.
4. Check the operation of the mix lever.

REC/FRESH Control Cable

MX-3, 1990–94 323 AND PROTEGE

1. Position the REC/FRESH control lever in the fresh air position.
2. Remove the passenger's side sound deadening panel.
3. Remove the cable located on the left side of the blower case from the cable housing brace.
4. Installation is the reverse of the removal procedure. With the cable end on the door lever pin, push the door lever forward to its extreme stop.
5. Secure the cable into the cable housing brace.
6. Check the air door control lever for proper operation.
7. Install the passenger's side sound deadening panel.

Control Panel

REMOVAL & INSTALLATION

♦ **See Figure 27**

MX-3, 1990–94 323 and Protege

1. Disconnect the negative battery cable.

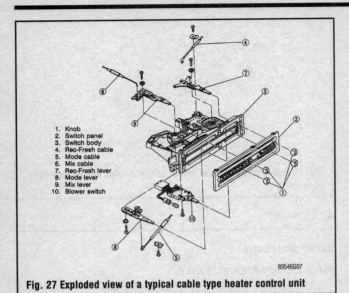

1. Knob
2. Switch panel
3. Switch body
4. Rec-Fresh cable
5. Mode cable
6. Mix cable
7. Rec-Fresh lever
8. Mode lever
9. Mix lever
10. Blower switch

89546G07

Fig. 27 Exploded view of a typical cable type heater control unit

2. From the right side of the dash, remove the side trim panel.
3. From directly below the glovebox, remove the trim panel.
4. Remove the center trim panel.
5. Remove the upper and lower instrument cluster assemblies. Disconnect the electrical connectors from the top assembly.
6. Remove the glove box and the inside glove box lining.
7. Remove the control panel retaining screws and disconnect the control cable wires from the control panel. Remove the control panel from the vehicle.

To install:

8. Connect the control cable wires to the control panel and install the panel assembly.
9. Install the glove box and the inside glove box lining.
10. Install the instrument cluster upper and lower assemblies. Make sure to connect all of the electrical connectors.
11. Install the center trim panel assembly.
12. Install the trim panel below the glovebox and install the side trim panel.
13. Connect the negative battery cable.

1990–92 626/MX-6

1. Disconnect the negative battery cable.
2. Remove the bezel cover from the control assembly face.
3. Remove the 4 attaching screws from the control assembly housing.
4. Remove the passenger and driver side sound deadening panels.
5. Remove the REC/FRESH control cable at the REC/FRESH selector door assembly.
6. Disconnect the blower switch electrical connector and the control assembly illumination electrical connector.
7. Remove the temperature control cable from the temperature blend door assembly at the right-hand side of the heater case.
8. Remove the function selector cable from the function control door assembly at the left-hand side of the heater case.
9. Remove the control assembly and control cables as an assembly.

➡While removing the control panel assembly, notice how the cables are routed for proper installation

To install:

10. Position the control panel assembly into the instrument panel while routing the control cables as noted during removal.
11. Connect the blower switch and control assembly illumination electrical connectors.
12. Secure the control assembly with the 4 attaching screws.
13. Install the plastic bezel cover onto the face of the control assembly.
14. Install and adjust all control cables to their respective control and selector door assemblies and adjust the cables. Refer to the procedures in this Section.
15. Install both sound deadening panels.
16. Connect the negative battery cable. Check for proper control assembly operation.

1993–98 626/MX-6/Probe

1. Disconnect the negative battery cable.
2. Remove the upper and lower steering wheel panels.
3. Remove the lower dash panel. Make sure to disconnect the switch connectors.
4. Remove the heater control unit mounting screws and pull the unit out.
5. Disconnect the electrical connectors from the control unit and remove the control unit.
6. Installation is the reverse of the removal procedure. Make sure to connect all of the electrical connectors and test all accessories when done.

Millenia

▶ See Figure 28

1. Disconnect the negative battery cable.
2. Remove the upper and lower steering wheel panels.
3. Remove the hazard warning switch as follows:
   a. Remove the instrument cluster trim panel.
   b. Detach the hazard warning switch electrical connector.
   c. Remove the switch-to-trim panel retaining screw and remove the switch from the panel.
4. Detach the electrical wire connectors from the back of the heater control unit.
5. Remove the heater control-to-trim panel retaining screws and remove the control unit from the panel.
6. Installation is the reverse of the removal procedure. Use care when tightening the control unit and hazard switch retaining screws so as not to damage the plastic trim panel.

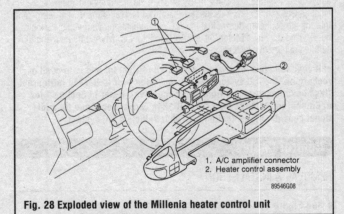

1. A/C amplifier connector
2. Heater control assembly

89546G08

Fig. 28 Exploded view of the Millenia heater control unit

CRUISE CONTROL

▶ See Figures 29, 30 and 31

Mazda vehicles used both vacuum actuated and electric stepper motor type cruise control systems. The actuator, located in the engine compartment, will have a vacuum line and electrical wires connected to it if it is a vacuum model. Electric stepper motor type units will have no vacuum line connected to the actuator.

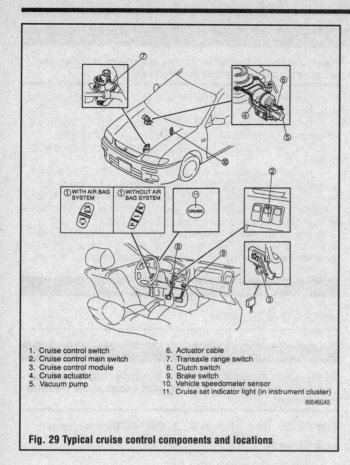

Fig. 29 Typical cruise control components and locations

1. Cruise control switch
2. Cruise control main switch
3. Cruise control module
4. Cruise actuator
5. Vacuum pump
6. Actuator cable
7. Transaxle range switch
8. Clutch switch
9. Brake switch
10. Vehicle speedometer sensor
11. Cruise set indicator light (in instrument cluster)

89546GA5

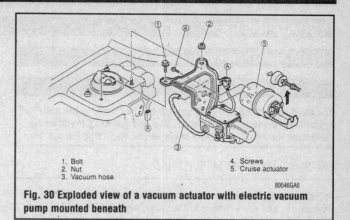

1. Bolt
2. Nut
3. Vacuum hose
4. Screws
5. Cruise actuator

89546GA6

Fig. 30 Exploded view of a vacuum actuator with electric vacuum pump mounted beneath

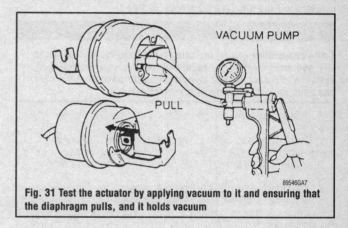

89546GA7

Fig. 31 Test the actuator by applying vacuum to it and ensuring that the diaphragm pulls, and it holds vacuum

CRUISE CONTROL TROUBLESHOOTING

Problem	Possible Cause
Will not hold proper speed	Incorrect cable adjustment
	Binding throttle linkage
	Leaking vacuum servo diaphragm
	Leaking vacuum tank
	Faulty vacuum or vent valve
	Faulty stepper motor
	Faulty transducer
	Faulty speed sensor
	Faulty cruise control module
Cruise intermittently cuts out	Clutch or brake switch adjustment too tight
	Short or open in the cruise control circuit
	Faulty transducer
	Faulty cruise control module
Vehicle surges	Kinked speedometer cable or casing
	Binding throttle linkage
	Faulty speed sensor
	Faulty cruise control module
Cruise control inoperative	Blown fuse
	Short or open in the cruise control circuit
	Faulty brake or clutch switch
	Leaking vacuum circuit
	Faulty cruise control switch
	Faulty stepper motor
	Faulty transducer
	Faulty speed sensor
	Faulty cruise control module

Note: Use this chart as a guide. Not all systems will use the components listed.

TCCA6C01

ENTERTAINMENT SYSTEMS

Radio Anti-Theft System (RATS)

❊❊ WARNING

You must disarm the anti-theft system before removing the anti-theft radio, tape or compact disc player. You will say RATS if you've disconnected the negative battery cable before disarming the system.

DISARMING THE ANTI-THEFT SYSTEM

➡ Perform Steps 1–3 within 10 seconds or the disarming procedure will be canceled and you will have to start over. Also, Step 4 must be completed within 10 seconds of completing Steps 3 or the procedure will be canceled and you will have to start over at Step 1.

❊❊ WARNING

Three consecutive errors, including turning the ignition switch to OFF and disconnecting the audio unit, will activate the anti-theft system and render the unit completely inoperative. If this occurs, you must contact your vehicle manufacturer.

1. Turn the ignition switch to the accessory (ACC) position and turn off the audio unit.
2. Press and hold the SCAN and AUTO-M buttons simultaneously for approximately 1.5 seconds until the word CODE appears on the display.
3. Press the SCAN and AUTO-M buttons again until bars (–) appear on the display.
4. Use channel buttons 1–4 to input the current code number. Press button 1 for the first digit, 2 for the second, etc. (if your code were 2321, you would press button 1 three times to display, 0, 1, then 2 followed by pressing button 2 four times to display 0, 1, 2 then 3 and so on). If at any point during the input of the code the display is deleted, you must start over at Step 1.
5. With the code number displayed, press and hold the SCAN and AUTO-M buttons for approximately 1.5 seconds until a beep is heard. The word CODE will be displayed for about 5 seconds. After it disappears, the code number is canceled.

ARMING THE ANTI-THEFT SYSTEM

Use the following procedure to input a new code number into the audio unit when the previous code has been canceled. As with disarming the unit, these steps are under a 10 second time limit. When inputting a new code into the system, make sure to record it and keep it in a safe place. Also, an old code can be reentered, or reused.

❊❊ WARNING

Three consecutive errors, including turning the ignition switch to OFF and disconnecting the audio unit, will activate the anti-theft

system and render the unit completely inoperative. If this occurs, you must contact your vehicle manufacturer.

1. Turn the ignition switch to the accessory (ACC) position and turn off the audio unit.
2. Press and hold the SCAN and AUTO-M buttons simultaneously for approximately 1.5 seconds until the word CODE appears on the display.
3. Press the SCAN and AUTO-M buttons again until bars (–) appear on the display.
4. Use channel buttons 1–4 to input the new code number. Press button 1 for the first digit, 2 for the second, etc. (if your code were 2321, you would press button 1 three times to display, 0, 1, then 2 followed by pressing button 2 four times to display 0, 1, 2 then 3 and so on). If at any point during the input of the code the display is deleted, you must start over at Step 1.
5. With the code number displayed, press and hold the SCAN and AUTO-M buttons for approximately 1.5 seconds until a beep is heard. The word CODE will be displayed for about 5 seconds. After it disappears, the code number has been set.

Radio, Tape and Compact Disc Player

REMOVAL & INSTALLATION

❊❊ WARNING

On any vehicle equipped with an anti-theft radio, tape or compact disc player, you must disarm the anti-theft system before removing the audio unit.

1990–92 626, MX-6, 1992–93 MX-3, 1990–94 323 and Protege

▶ See Figure 32

1. Disconnect the negative battery cable.
2. On 626 and MX-6 models, remove the center storage pocket from below the radio.
3. Remove the trim panel from around the radio. Be careful not to break the trim panel clips.
4. Remove the radio mounting screws and remove the radio. Unplug the connectors at the back of the radio.
5. Installation is the reverse of the removal procedure.

1994–95 MX-3, 1993–98 626/MX-6/Probe, 1995–98 Protege and Millenia

▶ See Figures 33, 34, 35 and 36

1. Using a protected prytool, pry out the hole covers on the radio unit.
2. Use Mazda special radio puller tools 49 UN01 050, or equivalent, and pull the radio out.

➡ Two sets of tools will be required if the radio unit also includes the CD changer controller.

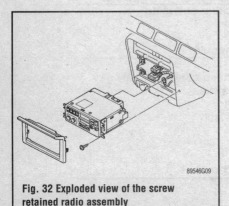

Fig. 32 Exploded view of the screw retained radio assembly

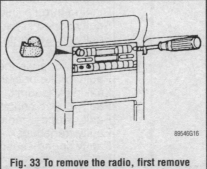

Fig. 33 To remove the radio, first remove the rubber protective hole covers by prying them out

Fig. 34 Then insert the special radio removal tools (arrows) into the uncovered holes to release the inner spring clip retainers

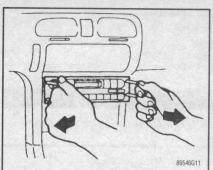

Fig. 35 While maintaining side pressure on the tools, pull the radio straight out of the dash assembly

Fig. 36 Detach the electrical and antenna wire connections (arrows) from the back of the radio

Fig. 37 To remove the front speaker, first remove the door trim, then loosen and remove the speaker attaching screws . . .

3. Detach the antenna and electrical connectors from the back of the unit.

4. Installation is the reverse of the removal procedure. The anti-theft code must be entered to the radio to reset it once the power has been disconnected from the radio. Consult with the original owners manual for this code.

Speakers

REMOVAL & INSTALLATION

Front Door Speakers

▶ See Figures 37, 38 and 39

1. Disconnect the negative battery cable.
2. Remove the inner door trim panel. Refer to the procedure in Section 10.

3. Remove the speaker retaining screws.
4. Pull out the speaker and unplug the electrical connector.
5. Remove the speaker.

✱✱ WARNING

Handle the speaker carefully to avoid damaging the cone during removal and installation.

6. Installation is the reverse of the removal procedure.

Rear Speakers

REAR SHELF MOUNTED SPEAKERS

▶ See Figures 40, 41, 42 and 43

1. Disconnect the negative battery cable.

Fig. 38 . . . and carefully pull the speaker from the door

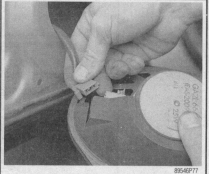

Fig. 39 Finally, detach the wire harness plug from the speaker

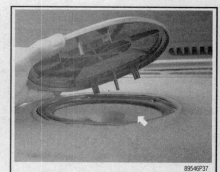

Fig. 40 Remove the speaker cover from the rear shelf. Use care around the exposed speaker element (arrow)

Fig. 41 Remove the speaker attaching screws . . .

Fig. 42 . . . and carefully lift the speaker up to access the wire harness plug

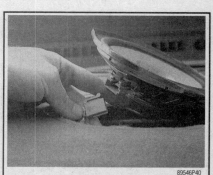

Fig. 43 Finally, detach the wire harness plug from the speaker and remove the speaker from the vehicle

2. On 1990–92 626, MX-6, 1990–94 323 and Protege, remove the rear package trim panel. Refer to the procedure in Section 10.

3. On all other models, remove the speaker cover by carefully prying it off.

4. Remove the speaker retaining screws.

5. Unplug the electrical connector.

6. Remove the speaker.

❋❋ WARNING

Handle the speaker carefully to avoid damaging the cone during removal and installation.

7. Installation is the reverse of the removal procedure.

WINDSHIELD WIPERS AND WASHERS

▸ **See Figure 44**

Windshield Wiper Blade and Arm

REMOVAL & INSTALLATION

Front Wiper Arms

▸ **See Figures 45, 46, 47 and 48**

1. If equipped, lift the cover on the wiper arm.

2. Unscrew the retaining nut and remove the arm and blade assembly from the pivot shaft.

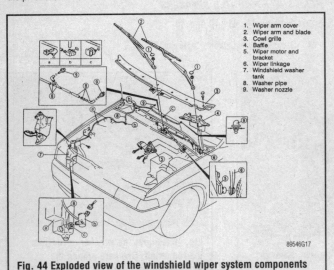

1. Wiper arm cover
2. Wiper arm and blade
3. Cowl grille
4. Baffle
5. Wiper motor and bracket
6. Wiper linkage
7. Windshield washer tank
8. Washer pipe
9. Washer nozzle

89546G17

Fig. 44 Exploded view of the windshield wiper system components

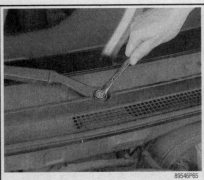

89546P65

Fig. 46 . . . then loosen and remove the wiper arm retaining nut

REAR QUARTER MOUNTED SPEAKERS

1. Disconnect the negative battery cable.

2. Remove the speaker cover.

3. Remove the speaker retaining screws.

4. Unplug the electrical connector.

5. Remove the speaker.

❋❋ WARNING

Handle the speaker carefully to avoid damaging the cone during removal and installation.

6. Installation is the reverse of the removal procedure.

3. Remove the wiper blade from the wiper arm. Refer to Section 1.

To install:

4. Install the wiper blade on the wiper arm.

5. Turn the wiper switch **ON** and allow the motor to move the pivot shafts through 3–4 cycles. Turn the wiper switch **OFF**.

6. Install the arm and blade assembly so the tip of the wiper blade is 0.79–1.18 in. (20–30mm) from the bottom of the windshield.

7. Install the retaining nut and tighten to 7–10 ft. lbs. (10–14 Nm).

8. Cycle the wipers several times and retorque the retaining nut.

➥**Make sure the windshield wiper arm is horizontal to the pivot shaft so the pivot shaft splines are fully seated in the wiper arm.**

Rear Wiper Arm

1. Lift the cover and remove the retaining nut.

2. Remove the arm and blade assembly.

3. Remove the wiper blade from the wiper arm. Refer to Section 1.

To install:

4. Install the wiper blade on the wiper arm.

5. Turn the wiper switch **ON** and allow the motor to move the pivot shafts through 3–4 cycles. Turn the wiper switch **OFF**.

89546P48

Fig. 45 To remove the windshield wiper arm, first remove the arm retaining nut cover . . .

89546P49

Fig. 47 Before removing the wiper arm, make a matchmark across the arm and shaft to ease installation

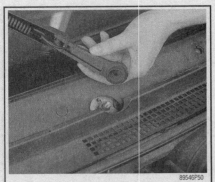

89546P50

Fig. 48 Pull the wiper arm assembly from the shaft

6. Install the arm and blade assembly so the tip of the wiper blade is 0.79–1.18 in. (20–30mm) from the bottom of the rear window.

7. Install and tighten the retaining nut.

Windshield Wiper Motor

REMOVAL & INSTALLATION

Except Millenia

FRONT WIPER MOTOR

♦ **See Figures 49 thru 57**

1. Disconnect the negative battery cable.
2. Remove the wiper arm nut covers, the wiper arm nuts and the wiper arms.

3. Remove the cowl grille screw caps, the screws, and the cowl grille assembly.

4. If equipped, remove the baffle.

5. Make an alignment mark on the wiper motor bracket which shows the orientation of the wiper arm to the motor.

6. Detach the electrical connector and remove the wiper link from the wiper motor arm.

7. Remove the three wiper motor mounting bolts and remove the wiper motor from the vehicle.

To install:

8. Install the wiper arm to the wiper motor with the nut and aligning the mark made earlier. Torque the nut to 95–156 in. lbs. (11–18 Nm).

9. Reinstall the wiper link to the wiper motor and mount the wiper motor with the three bolts. Torque the mounting bolts to 61–87 in. lbs. (6.9–9.8 Nm).

10. Attach the electrical connector.

11. If removed, install the baffle.

Fig. 49 Remove the cowl grille screw caps . . .

Fig. 50 . . . then remove the grille retaining screws

Fig. 51 Carefully remove the cowl from the vehicle

Fig. 52 Detach the electrical harness plug from the wiper motor

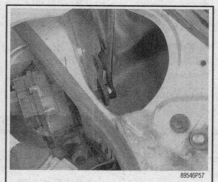

Fig. 53 Remove the linkage-to-motor shaft retaining nut . . .

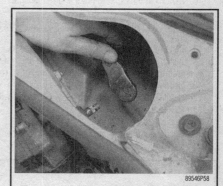

Fig. 54 . . . then disengage the linkage from the motor shaft

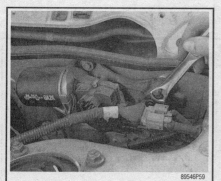

Fig. 55 Remove the wiper motor attaching screws . . .

Fig. 56 . . . paying attention to any ground wire attaching points (arrow) . . .

Fig. 57 . . . and pull the motor assembly from the vehicle

12. Reinstall the cowl grille assembly with the mounting screws and install the screw caps.

13. Reconnect the negative battery cable.

14. Turn the wiper motor on to operate the motor. Turn the wiper switch off to set the automatic park position. Install the wiper arms and set to the correct height. Install and torque the wiper arm nuts to 87–122 in. lbs. (9.8–14 Nm). Reinstall the wiper arm nut caps.

REAR WIPER MOTOR

1. Disconnect the negative battery cable.
2. Remove the wiper arm cover, remove the nut, and remove the wiper arm.
3. Remove the seal cap and bushing.
4. Remove the rear hatch lower trim.
5. Unplug the wiper motor electrical connector and remove the wiper motor mounting bolts and the motor.

To install:

6. Install the wiper motor with its mounting bolts. Torque the mounting bolts to 61–87 in. lbs. (6.9–9.8 Nm). Reconnect the electrical connector.

7. Install the outer bushing and the seal cap.

8. Reconnect the negative battery cable. Set the wiper motor shaft to the park position by turning the rear wiper switch from on to off. Install the rear wiper arm and adjust to the correct height.

9. Install the rear wiper arm nut and torque the nut to 52–87 in. lbs. (5.9–9.8 Nm). Replace the wiper arm cover.

10. Reinstall the rear hatch lower trim panel.

Millenia

▶ **See Figure 58**

1. Disconnect the negative battery cable.
2. Remove the cowl grille and remove the wiper arm mounting nuts and the wiper arm assemblies.
3. Unplug the wiper motor electrical connector.
4. Remove the wiper frame mounting bolts and wiper frame and link.
5. Remove the nut and the wiper arm bell crank.
6. Remove the mounting bolts and remove the motor.

To install:

7. Install the wiper motor to the wiper frame and link assembly. Torque the mounting bolts to 61–88 inch lbs. (7–10 Nm).

8. Install the wiper motor bell crank with the lock washer and the nut.

9. Install the wiper frame and link assembly to the cowl with the mounting bolts and torque the bolts to 61–88 inch lbs. (7–10 Nm).

10. Reconnect the wiper motor connector.

11. Reinstall the wiper arms to the wiper pivots with the nuts. Torque the nuts to 12–14 ft. lbs. (16–20 Nm).

12. Replace the cowl grille.

13. Reconnect the negative battery cable and check for proper operation.

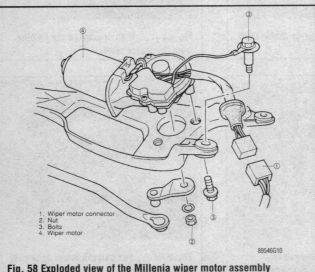

1. Wiper motor connector
2. Nut
3. Bolts
4. Wiper motor

89546G10

Fig. 58 Exploded view of the Millenia wiper motor assembly

Windshield Washer Fluid Reservoir

REMOVAL & INSTALLATION

▶ **See Figure 59**

Front Washer Fluid Reservoir

1. Disconnect the negative battery cable.
2. If necessary, remove the radiator coolant reservoir.
3. Remove the washer reservoir retaining bolts.
4. Disconnect the electrical connector and the hose from the washer reservoir.
5. Remove the washer reservoir assembly.
6. Installation is the reverse of the removal procedure.

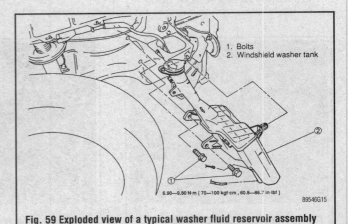

1. Bolts
2. Windshield washer tank

6.90–9.80 N·m [70–100 kgf·cm , 60.8–86.7 in·lbf]

89546G15

Fig. 59 Exploded view of a typical washer fluid reservoir assembly

Rear Washer Fluid Reservoir

1. Disconnect the negative battery cable.
2. Remove the left-hand lower trunk side trim panel. Refer to Section 10.
3. Remove the refill cap and disengage the support. Remove the support from the refill hose.
4. Disconnect the electrical connector and remove the hose.
5. Remove the rear washer reservoir.
6. Installation is the reverse of the removal procedure.

Windshield Washer Motor

REMOVAL & INSTALLATION

▶ **See Figure 60**

Front Washer Fluid Motor

1. Disconnect the negative battery cable.
2. Remove the windshield washer fluid reservoir, as previously described.

WINDSHIELD WASHER MOTOR

89546G12

Fig. 60 Exploded view of a common washer fluid pump-to-reservoir mounting

3. Pry off the washer motor and pump assembly.
4. Installation is the reverse of the removal procedure.

Rear Washer Fluid Motor

1. Disconnect the negative battery cable.
2. Remove the rear window washer reservoir, as previously described.

3. Remove the motor and pump assembly.
4. Installation is the reverse of the removal procedure.

INSTRUMENTS AND SWITCHES

Instrument Cluster

REMOVAL & INSTALLATION

MX-3, 323 and Protege

▶ See Figure 61

1. Disconnect the negative battery cable.
2. Remove the steering wheel. Refer to Section 8.
3. Remove the 2 column cover screws and remove the cover.
4. Remove the meter hood assembly and remove the instrument cluster screws.
5. Carefully pull the cluster module outward and disconnect the electrical connectors and the speedometer cable connector from the instrument cluster.
6. Remove the instrument cluster.
7. Installation is the reverse of the removal procedure. Check all gauges for proper operation.

626, MX6 and Millenia

▶ See Figures 62 thru 67

1. Disconnect the negative battery cable.
2. Remove the steering column shrouds and instrument cluster cover.

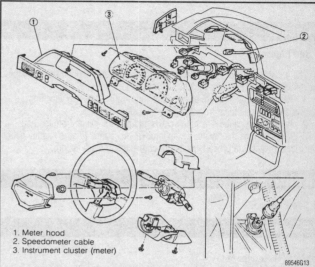

1. Meter hood
2. Speedometer cable
3. Instrument cluster (meter)

89546G13

Fig. 61 Exploded view of the 1990–94 323 and Protege instrument cluster assembly. Other models are similar

89546P78

Fig. 62 To remove the instrument cluster, first remove the meter hood retaining screws . . .

89546P80

Fig. 63 Disengage the retention clips and lift the lower edge up and over the dash . . .

89546P81

Fig. 64 . . . then carefully pull the top edge down and remove the hood

89546P82

Fig. 65 Remove the instrument cluster attaching screws . . .

89546P83

Fig. 66 . . . and pull the cluster outward

89546P84

Fig. 67 Slip your hand behind the cluster and detach the wiring harness connectors from it

3. If necessary, lower the steering column and/or remove the steering wheel.

4. Remove the meter hood assembly. On Millenia models, this will require removing the panel light control switch (to the left of the steering column) and a hole cover (to the right of the column) to access the two meter hood retaining screws.

5. Remove the instrument cluster retaining screws.

6. Carefully pull the cluster module outward and disconnect the electrical connectors and, if equipped, the speedometer cable connector from the instrument cluster.

7. Remove the instrument cluster.

8. Installation is the reverse of the removal procedure. Check all gauges for proper operation.

Gauges

▶ See Figure 68

The individual gauges can be removed from the instrument cluster once the cluster is removed from the vehicle.

1. Remove the instrument cluster lens and/or outer housing attaching screws and separate them from the gauge housing.

2. Remove the gauge attaching screws and pull the gauge from the housing.

3. Installation is the reverse of the removal procedure. Ensure that the gauge electrical contacts are properly seated or connected to the housing.

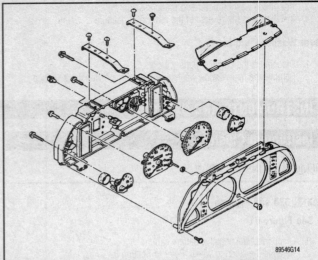

Fig. 68 Exploded view of a typical instrument cluster assembly

89546G14

LIGHTING

▶ See Figure 69

Headlights

REMOVAL & INSTALLATION

▶ See Figures 70, 71, 72 and 73

✷✷ CAUTION

The halogen headlight contains pressurized gas. It may shatter if the glass envelope is scratched or dropped. Handle the headlight carefully. Keep the headlight out of the reach of children.

1. Disconnect the negative battery cable.

2. Turn the plastic surrounding ring, or cover, located in the back of the headlight lens assembly and slide it backwards (ring) or remove it (cover).

3. If necessary, unfasten the bulb clasp.

4. Remove the bulb from the headlight housing.

5. Unplug the bulb from the electrical connector.

To install:

6. Engage the electrical connector to the headlight bulb, caution should be taken not to touch the bulb, as oil from skin can cause the bulb to burn out prematurely.

7. Install the bulb into the headlight assembly.

8. If necessary, fasten the bulb retaining clasp.

9. Install the retaining collar or cover and securely tighten it.

10. Connect the negative battery cable.

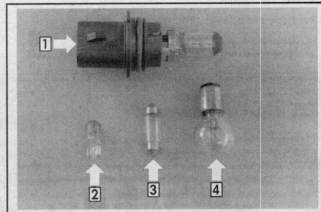

1. Halogen headlight bulb
2. Side marker light bulb
3. Dome light bulb
4. Turn signal/brake light bulb

TCCA6P11

Fig. 69 Examples of various types of automotive light bulbs

Fig. 70 To change a headlight bulb, first remove the bulb cover. Headlight lens assembly shown removed for clarity

89546P10

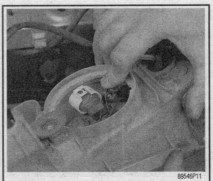

Fig. 71 Disengage the bulb retaining clasp . . .

89546P11

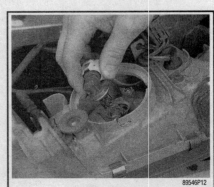

Fig. 72 . . . and pull the bulb from the lens assembly

89546P12

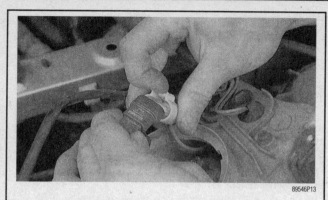

Fig. 73 Disengage the wire harness connector from the bulb

AIMING THE HEADLIGHTS

◆ See Figures 74, 75, 76, 77 and 78

The headlights must be properly aimed to provide the best, safest road illumination. The lights should be checked for proper aim and adjusted as necessary. Certain state and local authorities have requirements for headlight aiming; these should be checked before adjustment is made.

✳✳ CAUTION

About once a year, when the headlights are replaced or any time front end work is performed on your vehicle, the headlight should be accurately aimed by a reputable repair shop using the proper equipment. Headlights not properly aimed can make it virtually impossible to see and may blind other drivers on the road, possibly causing an accident. Note that the following procedure is a temporary fix, until you can take your vehicle to a repair shop for a proper adjustment.

Headlight adjustment may be temporarily made using a wall, as described below, or on the rear of another vehicle. When adjusted, the lights should not glare in oncoming car or truck windshields, nor should they illuminate the passenger compartment of vehicles driving in front of you. These adjustments are rough and should always be fine-tuned by a repair shop which is equipped with headlight aiming tools. Improper adjustments may be both dangerous and illegal.

For most of the vehicles covered by this manual, horizontal and vertical aiming of each sealed beam unit is provided by two adjusting screws which move the retaining ring and adjusting plate against the tension of a coil spring. There is no adjustment for focus; this is done during headlight manufacturing.

➡**Because the composite headlight assembly is bolted into position, no adjustment should be necessary or possible. Some applications, however, may be bolted to an adjuster plate or may be retained by adjusting screws. If so, follow this procedure when adjusting the lights, BUT always have the adjustment checked by a reputable shop.**

Before removing the headlight bulb or disturbing the headlamp in any way, note the current settings in order to ease headlight adjustment upon reassembly. If the high or low beam setting of the old lamp still works, this can be done using the wall of a garage or a building:

1. Park the vehicle on a level surface, with the fuel tank about ½ full and with the vehicle empty of all extra cargo (unless normally carried). The vehicle should be facing a wall which is no less than 6 feet (1.8m) high and 12 feet (3.7m) wide. The front of the vehicle should be about 25 feet from the wall.

2. If aiming is to be performed outdoors, it is advisable to wait until dusk in order to properly see the headlight beams on the wall. If done in a garage, darken the area around the wall as much as possible by closing shades or hanging cloth over the windows.

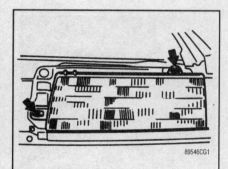

Fig. 74 Most models have two adjusting screws. One for vertical and one for horizontal aiming

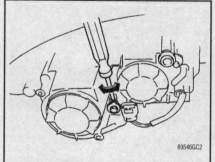

Fig. 75 Other models, such as the Millenia, are adjusted using gear assemblies located at the back of the headlamp

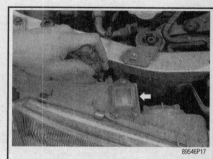

Fig. 76 Mazda vehicles also have a built in level (arrow) on the headlight assembly. Adjust until the bubble is within 2 lines from center

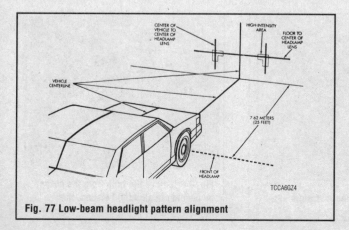

Fig. 77 Low-beam headlight pattern alignment

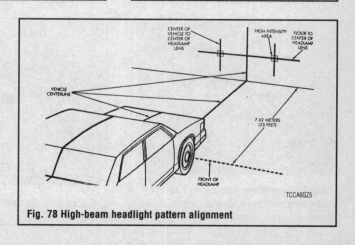

Fig. 78 High-beam headlight pattern alignment

3. Turn the headlights **ON** and mark the wall at the center of each light's low beam, then switch on the brights and mark the center of each light's high beam. A short length of masking tape which is visible from the front of the vehicle may be used. Although marking all four positions is advisable, marking one position from each light should be sufficient.

4. If neither beam on one side is working, and if another like-sized vehicle is available, park the second one in the exact spot where the vehicle was and mark the beams using the same-side light. Then switch the vehicles so the one to be aimed is back in the original spot. It must be parked no closer to or farther away from the wall than the second vehicle.

5. Perform any necessary repairs, but make sure the vehicle is not moved, or is returned to the exact spot from which the lights were marked. Turn the headlights **ON** and adjust the beams to match the marks on the wall.

6. Have the headlight adjustment checked as soon as possible by a reputable repair shop.

Signal and Marker Lights

REMOVAL & INSTALLATION

Front Turn Signal and Parking Lights

▶ See Figures 79 thru 84

1. If equipped with two-piece headlight/signal lens, remove the attaching screw(s) and partially remove the front parking light lens.
2. If equipped with a one-piece headlight/signal lens, remove the headlight lens assembly to access the bulb socket.
3. Remove the bulb socket and rubber gasket from the lens assembly by turning it in a counterclockwise direction.
4. Remove the bulb from the socket by carefully pushing it in to clear the socket slots and twisting it counterclockwise.
5. Installation is the reverse of the removal procedure.

Side Marker Lights

▶ See Figures 85, 86, 87 and 88

1. If visible, remove the attaching screws and partially remove the front side marker light lens.
2. If no screw head is visible, carefully pry the lens assembly from the vehicle body.
3. Remove the bulb socket and rubber gasket from the lens by turning it in a clockwise direction.
4. Remove the bulb from the socket by pulling it straight outwards.
5. Installation is the reverse of the removal procedure.

Rear Turn Signal, Brake and Parking Lights

▶ See Figures 89 thru 95

1. If necessary, remove the plastic fasteners securing the trunk end trim panel and remove the panel. Remove the right side upper trunk side garnish to gain access to the far right side bulb.
2. If access to the bulb sockets cannot be gained through the trunk, remove the rear lens assembly. Usually retained by one or more screws and clips.
3. Carefully remove the desired socket wiring from its respective retaining clip and turn it counterclockwise to remove the socket.
4. Carefully push the bulb in far enough to clear the socket slots, turn it counterclockwise and remove.
5. Installation is the reverse of the removal procedure.

High Mount (Third) Brake Light

EXTERNALLY MOUNTED

1. If mounted on the rear liftgate, remove the retaining screw covers.
2. Remove the high mount brake light lens attaching screws.
3. Pull the lens assembly outward to gain access to the wire/socket assembly.
4. Turn the socket counterclockwise and remove the bulb/socket assembly.

Fig. 79 To change a front signal bulb on one-piece lens assemblies, you must first remove the assembly attaching screws . . .

Fig. 80 . . . ensuring that all fasteners, front, top and side or rear are removed

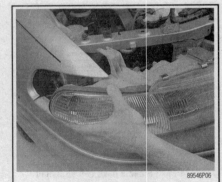

Fig. 81 Pull the lens assembly out far enough to access the signal bulb socket

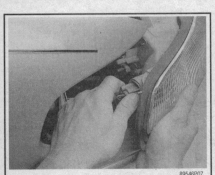

Fig. 82 Remove the bulb socket from the lens assembly by twisting it counter clockwise . . .

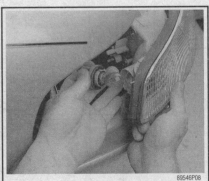

Fig. 83 . . . then pulling it straight outward

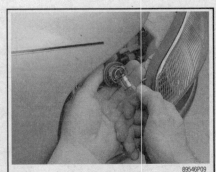

Fig. 84 Remove the bulb from the socket by pushing in slightly, twisting, then pulling outward

Fig. 85 To change a side marker bulb with no attaching screw, protect the body with a rag and gently pry the lens assembly outward . . .

89546P18

Fig. 86 . . . until the entire assembly is free of the body and access to the bulb socket is achieved

89546P19

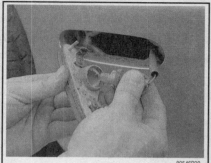

Fig. 87 Remove the bulb socket and rubber gasket from the lens by turning it in a clockwise direction

89546P20

Fig. 88 Remove the bulb from the socket by pulling it straight outwards

89546P21

Fig. 89 To change a rear tail/brake bulb, first, if so equipped, remove the lens retaining screws . . .

89546P25

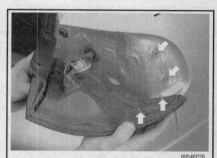

Fig. 90 . . . then disengage the lens from the body. Note the retaining pins on the lens which lock into the body grommets (arrows)

89546P26

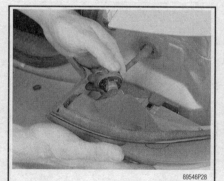

Fig. 91 Pull the bulb socket from the lens . . .

89546P28

Fig. 92 . . . and carefully push the bulb in far enough to clear the socket slots, turn it counterclockwise and remove it

89546P27

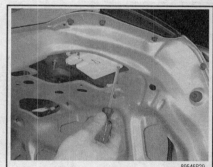

Fig. 93 If equipped with trunk mounted rear lights, remove the bulb retaining assembly screws . . .

89546P29

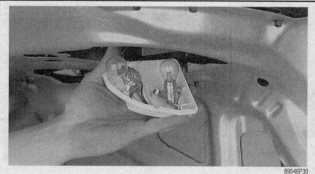

Fig. 94 . . . and pull the assembly from the trunk lid to access the bulbs

89546P30

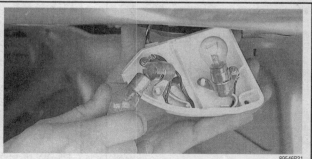

Fig. 95 Remove the bulbs by carefully pushing the bulb in far enough to clear the socket slots, turn it counterclockwise and pull outward

89546P31

5. Remove the bulb from the socket by pulling it straight out.
6. Installation is the reverse of the removal procedure.

INTERNALLY (REAR PACKAGE TRAY) MOUNTED

▶ See Figures 96, 97, 98 and 99

1. If equipped, remove the high mount brake light cover retaining fasteners.
2. Remove the cover by disengaging the locktabs and sliding it backwards.
3. Turn the socket counterclockwise and remove the bulb/socket assembly.
4. Remove the bulb from the socket by pulling it straight out.
5. Installation is the reverse of the removal procedure.

Dome and Interior Lights

▶ See Figures 100 thru 106

1. Disconnect the negative battery cable.
2. Grasp the dome or interior light lens and pull down until the lens is removed.

3. Carefully pull the bulb from its holder. If the bulb is difficult to remove, carefully pry it out with a small piece of wood or equivalent.
4. Check the bulb holder for bent tangs and adjust them, if necessary.
To install:
5. Push the bulb into its holder until it is firmly secured.
6. Position the dome or interior light lens into the holder, then push up on the lens until it snaps into position.
7. Connect the negative battery cable.

License Plate Lights

▶ See Figures 107, 108 and 109

1. Loosen, but do not completely remove the attaching screws on the light lens. Remove the license plate lens assembly.
2. If necessary for working clearance, pull the entire assembly out from the body.
3. Remove the bulb by pulling it straight down and away from the socket.
4. Installation is the reverse of the removal procedure.

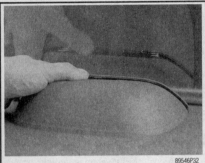
Fig. 96 To change a third brake light bulb, first remove the light assemblies cover by pushing on the center and sides . . .

Fig. 97 . . . to disengage the locktabs, then slide it backwards and remove it from the assembly

Fig. 98 Turn the socket counterclockwise and remove the bulb/socket assembly

Fig. 99 Remove the bulb from the socket by pulling it straight out

Fig. 100 To change the dome light bulb, carefully pry the dome light lens

Fig. 101 Then remove the lens from the dome light assembly

Fig. 102 Pull the bulb from the assembly, using care not to bend or damage the bulb holders/electrical contacts

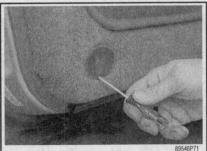
Fig. 103 As with the dome light, other interior bulbs can be changed by following the same steps. Pry the lens interior light lens . . .

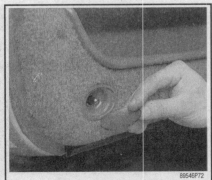
Fig. 104 . . . and remove it from the assembly

89546P73

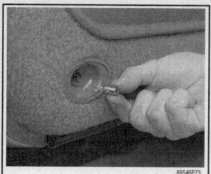

Fig. 105 Then simply pull the bulb from the light housing

89546P85

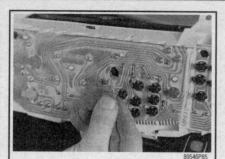

Fig. 106 Instrument cluster lights can be changed by removing the cluster, then twist and pull out the individual bulb sockets from the back

89546P22

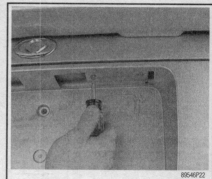

Fig. 107 To change a license plate light bulb, loosen the lens attaching screws . . .

89546P23

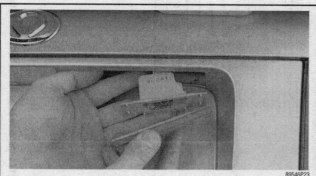

Fig. 108 . . . and, if necessary for clearance, pull the entire assembly from the vehicle body. Remove the lens . . .

89546P24

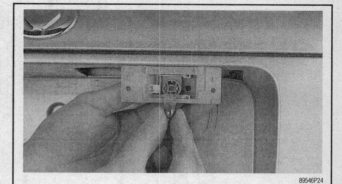

Fig. 109 . . . and pull the bulb from the light housing/socket

Fog Lights

REMOVAL & INSTALLATION

1. Disconnect the negative battery cable.
2. Remove the mounting nut from the fog light mounting bracket.
3. Remove the fog light housing and bracket as an assembly through the front fascia of the vehicle.
4. Remove the attaching screws from the fog light lens retaining brackets at the housing. Carefully remove the lens assembly from the housing, then disconnect the electrical connectors.
5. Remove the wire retaining rubber grommet from the housing and remove the wire harness from the housing.
6. Remove the mounting nut from the mounting bracket and remove the bracket from the fog light housing.
7. Remove the bulb as follows:
   a. Carefully remove the rubber grommet from the lens assembly.
   b. Release the bulb retaining bracket by pushing in on the release tabs and pulling up.
   c. Remove the bulb assembly from the housing by pulling it straight out of the lens.
8. Installation is the reverse of the removal procedure. Make sure the bulb is correctly piloted into the lens assembly.

CAUTION

The halogen fog light bulb contains gas under pressure. The bulb may shatter if the glass envelope is scratched or the bulb is dropped. Handle the bulb carefully. Grasp the bulb only by its base. Avoid touching the glass envelope. Keep the bulb out of the reach of children.

Headlight	65/45W × 2 (9004)
Front turn and hazard warning / Parking light	27/8W × 2 (1157)
Front side marker light	3.8W × 2 (194)
Stop/Taillight	27/8W × 4 (1157)
High-mount stoplight	18.4W × 3 (921)
Rear turn and hazard warning light	27W × 2 (1156)
Back-up light	27W × 2 (1156)
Rear side marker light	3.8W × 2 (194)
License plate light	5W × 2 (168)

89546G22

Fig. 110 Light bulb chart for the MX-3

Item		Specification (W) (Bulb Trade number)
Exterior lamps	Headlight	65/45 (9004)
	Front turn signal/Parking light	27/8 (1157)
	Stop/Taillight	27/8 (1157)
	High mount stoplight	18.4 (1141)
	Rear turn single light	27 (1156)
	Back-up light	27 (1156)
	Rear side marker light (Sedan)	3.8 (194)
	License plate light	7.5 (89) [Sedan], 5 (168) [3HB]
Interior lamps	Interior and spot lamp — Interior	10
	Interior and spot lamp — Spot	10
	Interior lamp	10
	Spot lamp (in overhead console)	8 (67)
	Cargo room lamp	5 (168)
	Turnk room lamp	5 (168)
Indicator and warning lamps	High beam	3.4
	Turn light	3.4
	Brake	3
	Hold	3 (158)
	Charge	3 (158)
	Oil pressure	3 (158)
	Washer	3 (158)
	Seat belt	3 (158)
	Malfunction	3 (158)
	Fuel	3 (158)
	Illumination	3.4

89546618

Fig. 111 Light bulb chart for the 1990–94 323 and Protege

	Item		Specification (W) × number
LIGHTING SYSTEMS			
Exterior lights	Headlight		60/55 × 2
	Front combination light (front turn light/parking light)		27/8 × 2
	Rear turn light		27 × 2
	Brake light/taillight		27/8 × 2
	Back-up light		21 × 2
	High-mount brake light	Without rear spoiler	18.4 × 1
		With rear spoiler	5.8 × 1
	Licence plate light		5 × 2
Interior lights	Interior and spot light	Interior light	8 × 1
		Spot light	5 × 2
	Interior light		8 × 1
	Spot light		5 × 2
	Trunk compartment light		5 × 1
	Instrument cluster illumination	Without tachometer	3.4 × 2, 2.2 × 1
		With tachometer	3.4 × 2, 2.2 × 1, 1.4 × 1
INSTRUMENTATION/DRIVER INFO.			
Warning and indicator lights	High beam indicator light		1.4 × 1
	Rear window defroster indicator light		1.4 × 1
	Air bag system warning light		1.4 × 1
	Oil pressure warning light		1.4 × 1
	ABS warning light		1.4 × 1
	Generator warning light		1.4 × 1
	Brake system warning light		1.4 × 1
	Cruise set indicator light		1.4 × 1
	Door ajar warning light		1.4 × 1
	MIL		1.4 × 1
	Washer fluid-level warning light	Canada only	1.4 × 1
	Turn indicator light		1.4 × 2

89546621

Fig. 112 Light bulb chart for the 1995–98 Protege

626

Item	Bulb	Wattage (W)	Trade number
Headlight	High beam	65 × 2	9005
	High/low beam	55 × 2	9006
Front turn and hazard warning light/parking light		27/8 × 2	1157 NA
Front side marker light		3.8 × 2	194
Front fog light		35 × 2	—
Rear combination light	Brake light/taillight	27/8 × 2	1157
	Rear turn light	27 × 2	1156 NA
Inboard combination light	Brake light/taillight	27/8 × 2	1157
	Back-up light	27 × 2	1156
Rear side marker light		3.8 × 2	194
Licence plate light		5 × 2	—
High-mount brake light		18.4 × 1	921

MX-6

Item	Bulb	Wattage (W)	Trade number
Headlight	High/low beam	65/45 × 2	9004
Front turn and hazard warning light/parking light		27/8 × 2	1157 NA
Front side marker light		3.8 × 2	194
Front fog light		35 × 2	—
Rear combination light	Brake light/taillight	27/8 × 4	1157
	Rear turn light	27 × 2	1156
Rear side marker light		3.8 × 2	194
Licence plate light		4.9 × 2	168
High-mount brake light	Without rear spoiler	18.4 × 1	921
	With rear spoiler	8.1 × 1	—

89546619

Fig. 113 Light bulb chart for the 626 and MX-6

Item			Specification (W) × number
LIGHTING SYSTEMS			
Exterior lights	Headlight	High beam	60 × 2
		Low beam*	51 × 2
	Front side marker light		3.8 × 2
	Parking light		5 × 2
	Front turn light		27 × 2
	Front fog light		55 × 2
	Brake light and taillight		27/8 × 2
	Rear turn light		27 × 2
	Back-up light		27 × 2
	License plate light		5 × 2
	High-mount brake light	(CANADA only)	18.4 × 2
		(Except CANADA)	21 × 1
Interior lights	Interior and spot light		8 × 3
	•Rear personal light		5 × 2
	Courtesy light		3.4 × 4
	Trunk compartment light		5 × 1
	Glove compartment light		3 × 1
	Vanity mirror illumination		1.8 × 2 or 4
INSTRUMENTATION/DRIVE INFO.			
Warning and indicator lights	Cruise set indicator light		1.4 × 1
	Washer fluid-level warning light		1.4 × 1
	TCS indicator light		1.4 × 1
	Brake system warning light		1.4 × 1
	Malfunction indicator lamp		1.4 × 1
	TCS OFF light		1.4 × 1
	Generator warning light		3.0 × 1
	Oil pressure warning light		1.4 × 1
	ABS warning light		1.4 × 1
	Seat belt warning light		1.4 × 1
	Air bag system warning light		1.4 × 1
	Door ajar warning light		1.4 × 1
	High beam indicator light		3.0 × 1
	Fuel-level warning light		3.0 × 1
	Turn indicator light		3.4 × 2
	HOLD indicator light		1.4 × 1
	Instrument cluster illumination		3.4 × 3, 1.4 × 1

* : Low beam, however also remains illuminated when high beam turned on.

89546620

Fig. 114 Light bulb chart for the Millenia

CIRCUIT PROTECTION

Fuses

The main fuse block is located inside the left side of the engine compartment near the battery. There is also an interior fuse panel located just above the left side kick panel.

REPLACEMENT

❉❉ CAUTION

Never replace a blown fuse with one of a higher rating. Severe damage to the vehicle, electrical harness and components, as well as personal injury or even death could occur.

Main Fuse Block

▶ **See Figure 115**

1. Disconnect the negative battery cable.
2. Unhook the lock tab from the main fuse block cover and open the cover.
3. Pull the fuse from the main fuse holder.
4. Installation is the reverse of the removal procedure.

Interior Fuse Panel

The interior fuses simply unplug from the fuse panel. Use the fuse puller tool provided with your car to remove fuses from the panel. The tool is located on the back of the interior fuse panel cover.

Circuit Breaker

A bimetal circuit breaker is located in the joint box, which is just above the interior fuse panel. This circuit breaker protects the rear window defrost circuit and is the plug-in type.

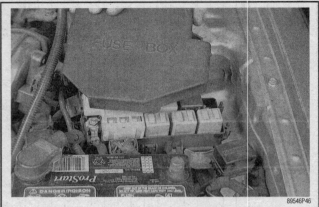

Fig. 115 Remove the fuse box cover, located in the engine compartment, to access the main fuses for the vehicle

89546P46

Relays

The main relay box is located on the upper left-hand side of the firewall (bulkhead). There is also a relay box mounted inside the vehicle under the left side of the instrument panel.

REPLACEMENT

1. Disconnect the negative battery cable.
2. If replacing a relay at the main relay box, disconnect the electrical connector and slide the relay from its mounting bracket.
3. If replacing a relay at the interior relay box, simply unplug the relay.
4. Installation is the reverse of the removal procedure.

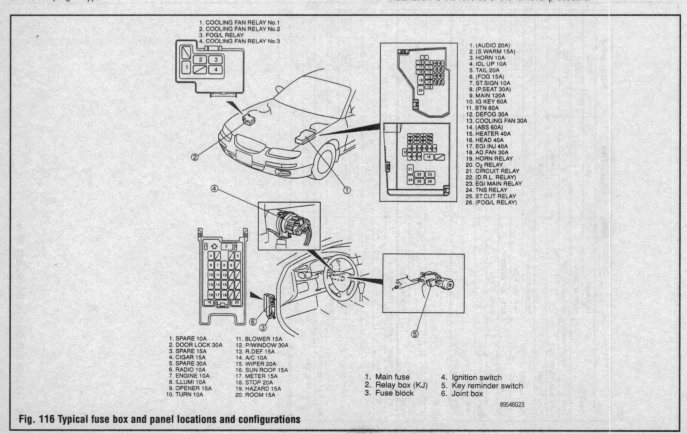

1. COOLING FAN RELAY No.1
2. COOLING FAN RELAY No.2
3. FOG/L RELAY
4. COOLING FAN RELAY No.3

1. (AUDIO 20A)
2. (S.WARM 15A)
3. HORN 10A
4. IDL UP 10A
5. TAIL 20A
6. (FOG 15A)
7. ST.SIGN 10A
8. (P.SEAT 30A)
9. MAIN 120A
10. IG KEY 60A
11. BTN 60A
12. DEFOG 30A
13. COOLING FAN 30A
14. (ABS 60A)
15. HEATER 40A
16. HEAD 40A
17. EGI INJ 40A
18. AD.FAN 30A
19. HORN RELAY
20. O₂ RELAY
21. CIRCUIT RELAY
22. (D.R.L. RELAY)
23. EGI MAIN RELAY
24. TNS RELAY
25. ST.CUT RELAY
26. (FOG/L RELAY)

1. SPARE 10A
2. DOOR LOCK 30A
3. SPARE 15A
4. CIGAR 15A
5. SPARE 30A
6. RADIO 10A
7. ENGINE 10A
8. ILLUMI 10A
9. OPENER 15A
10. TURN 10A
11. BLOWER 15A
12. P/WINDOW 30A
13. R.DEF 15A
14. A/C 10A
15. WIPER 20A
16. SUN ROOF 15A
17. METER 15A
18. STOP 20A
19. HAZARD 15A
20. ROOM 15A

1. Main fuse
2. Relay box (KJ)
3. Fuse block
4. Ignition switch
5. Key reminder switch
6. Joint box

89546G23

Fig. 116 Typical fuse box and panel locations and configurations

INDEX OF WIRING DIAGRAMS

DIAGRAM 1 SAMPLE DIAGRAM: HOW TO READ & INTERPRET WIRING DIAGRAMS
DIAGRAM 2 WIRING DIAGRAM SYMBOLS
DIAGRAM 3 1997-98 MILLENIA (2.3L) ENGINE SCHEMATIC
DIAGRAM 4 1995-96 MILLENIA (2.3L) ENGINE SCHEMATIC
DIAGRAM 5 1995-96 MILLENIA (2.5L) ENGINE SCHEMATIC
DIAGRAM 6 1997-98 MILLENIA (2.5L) ENGINE SCHEMATIC
DIAGRAM 7 1996- 626/MX-6/PROBE (2.5L) ENGINE SCHEMATIC
DIAGRAM 8 1993-95 626/MX-6/PROBE (2.5L) ENGINE SCHEMATIC
DIAGRAM 9 1990-91 323/PROTEGE ENGINE SCHEMATIC
DIAGRAM 10 1996 626/MX-6/PROBE (2.0L M/T) ENGINE SCHEMATIC
DIAGRAM 11 1993-95 626/MX-6/PROBE (2.0L M/T) ENGINE SCHEMATIC
DIAGRAM 12 1996 626/MX-6/PROBE (2.0L A/T) ENGINE SCHEMATIC
DIAGRAM 13 1994-95 626/MX-6/PROBE (2.0L A/T) ENGINE SCHEMATIC
DIAGRAM 14 1993 626/MX-6/PROBE (2.0L A/T) ENGINE SCHEMATIC
DIAGRAM 15 1990-92 626/MX-6 (Turbo) ENGINE SCHEMATIC
DIAGRAM 16 1990-92 626/MX-6 (Non-Turbo M/T) ENGINE SCHEMATIC
DIAGRAM 17 1990-92 626/MX-6 (Non-Turbo W/EC-A/T) ENGINE SCHEMATIC
DIAGRAM 18 1995-98 323/PROTEGE (1.5L & 1.8L) ENGINE SCHEMATIC
DIAGRAM 19 1993-94 323/PROTEGE (Except Calif.) & 1992 323/PROTEGE ENGINE SCHEMATIC
DIAGRAM 20 1993-94 323/PROTEGE (Calif.) 1992 323/PROTEGE ENGINE SCHEMATIC
DIAGRAM 21 1994-95 MX-3 (1.6L) ENGINE SCHEMATIC
DIAGRAM 22 1992-93 MX-3 (1.6L M/T) ENGINE SCHEMATIC
DIAGRAM 23 1992 MX-3 (1.6L Federal A/T) & 1993 MX-3 (1.6L A/T) ENGINE SCHEMATIC
DIAGRAM 24 1992 MX-3 (1.6L Calif A/T) ENGINE SCHEMATIC
DIAGRAM 25 1992-95 MX-3 (1.8L) ENGINE SCHEMATIC
DIAGRAM 26 1990-94 323/PROTEGE STARTING, CHARGING, COOLING FAN, TURBO 1991 CHASSIS SCHEMATICS
DIAGRAM 27 1990-94 323/PROTEGE FUEL PUMP, 1995-98 STARTING, CHARGING, COOLING FAN, FUEL CHASSIS SCHEMATICS
DIAGRAM 28 1990-98 323/PROTEGE BACK UP LIGHTS, STOP LIGHTS, 1990-96 TURN CHASSIS SCHEMATICS
DIAGRAM 29 1995-98 323/PROTEGE MARKER LIGHTS CHASSIS SCHEMATICS
DIAGRAM 30 1990-94 323/PROTEGE MARKER LIGHTS CHASSIS SCHEMATICS
DIAGRAM 31 1990-94 323/PROTEGE HEADLIGHTS CHASSIS SCHEMATICS
DIAGRAM 32 1995-98 323/PROTEGE HEADLIGHTS, 1997-98 TURN/HAZARD, 1992-95 MX-3 TURN/HAZARD CHASSIS SCHEMATICS
DIAGRAM 33 1991-92 626/MX-6 CHARGING, 1991-92 STARTING, 1993 STARTING W/O THEFT DETERRENT CHASSIS SCHEMATICS
DIAGRAM 34 1994-96 626/MX-6 STARTING, 1993 STARTING W/THEFT DETERRENT CHASSIS SCHEMATICS
DIAGRAM 35 1991-94 626/MX-6 & 1993-94 PROBE FUEL, 1990-92/1994-96 BACKUP LIGHTS CHASSIS SCHEMATICS
DIAGRAM 36 1995-96 626-MX-6/PROBE FUEL CHASSIS SCHEMATICS
DIAGRAM 37 1990-96 626/MX-6 & 1993-96 PROBE COOLING FAN CHASSIS SCHEMATICS
DIAGRAM 38 1994-96 626/MX-6/PROBE HEADLIGHT CHASSIS SCHEMATICS
DIAGRAM 39 1993 626/MX-6/PROBE HEADLIGHT CHASSIS SCHEMATICS
DIAGRAM 40 1990-96 626/MX-6 & 1994-96 PROBE STOP LIGHTS, TURN CHASSIS SCHEMATICS
DIAGRAM 41 1993 626/MX-6/PROBE STOP LIGHTS, TURN, BACKUP CHASSIS SCHEMATICS
DIAGRAM 42 1990-92 626/MX-6 TURN, 1992-96 MX-3 BACKUP/STOP CHASSIS SCHEMATICS
DIAGRAM 43 1990-93 626/MX-6 & 1993 PROBE PARKING/MARKER LIGHTS CHASSIS SCHEMATICS
DIAGRAM 44 1992-95 MX-3 STARTING, CHARGING, COOLING FAN CHASSIS SCHEMATICS
DIAGRAM 45 1992-95 MX-3 FUEL, PARKING/MARKER LIGHTS, 1995-98 MILLENIA FUEL CHASSIS SCHEMATICS
DIAGRAM 46 1992-95 MX-3 HEADLIGHTS, 1995-98 MILLENIA FUEL 2.3L CHASSIS SCHEMATIC
DIAGRAM 47 1995-98 MILLENIA START, CHARGE, COOLING FAN 2.5L CHASSIS SCHEMATICS
DIAGRAM 48 1995-98 MILLENIA HEADLIGHTS/DRL, COOLING FAN 2.3L, BACKUP LIGHTS CHASSIS SCHEMATICS
DIAGRAM 49 1995-98 MILLENIA TURN, BRAKE & PARKING LIGHTS CHASSIS SCHEMATICS

89546W00

WIRING DIAGRAM SYMBOLS

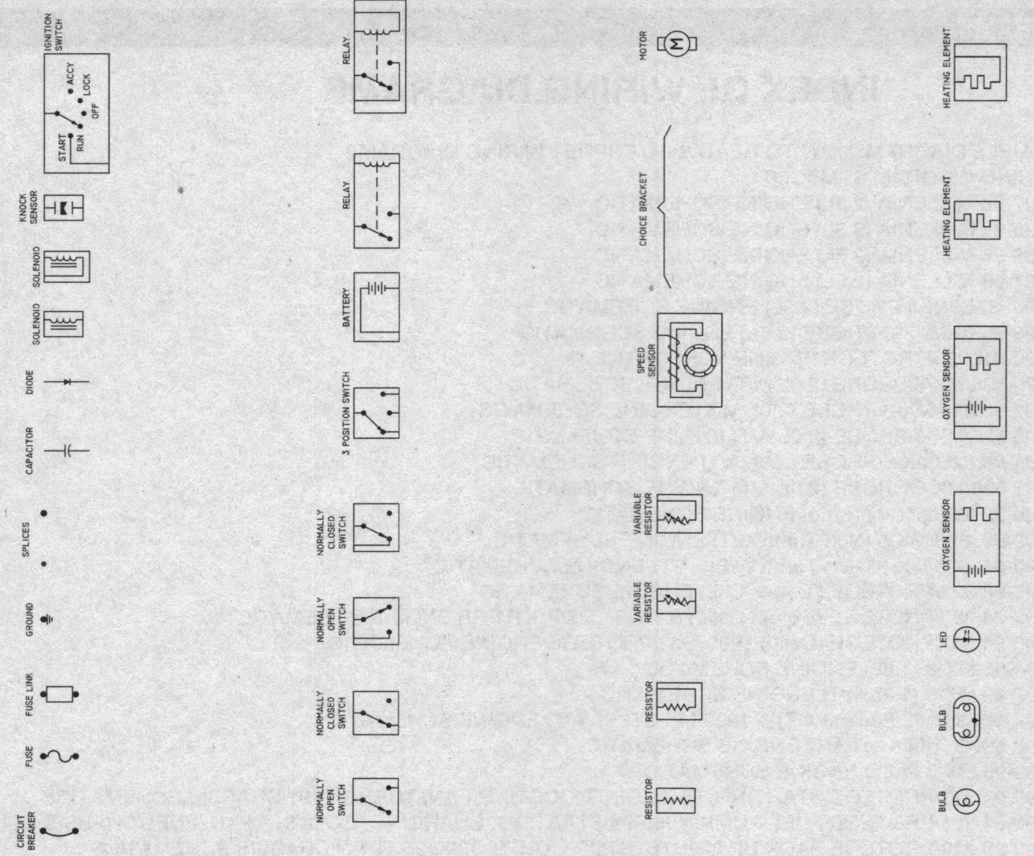

IGNITION SWITCH

START · ACCY
RUN · LOCK
OFF

KNOCK SENSOR

SOLENOID

SOLENOID

DIODE

CAPACITOR

SPLICES

GROUND

FUSE LINK

FUSE

CIRCUIT BREAKER

RELAY

RELAY

BATTERY

3 POSITION SWITCH

NORMALLY CLOSED SWITCH

NORMALLY OPEN SWITCH

NORMALLY CLOSED SWITCH

NORMALLY OPEN SWITCH

MOTOR

SPEED SENSOR

CHOICE BRACKET

VARIABLE RESISTOR

VARIABLE RESISTOR

RESISTOR

RESISTOR

LED

BULB

BULB

HEATING ELEMENT

HEATING ELEMENT

OXYGEN SENSOR

OXYGEN SENSOR

DIAGRAM 2

TCCA6W02

SAMPLE DIAGRAM: HOW TO READ & INTERPRET WIRING DIAGRAMS

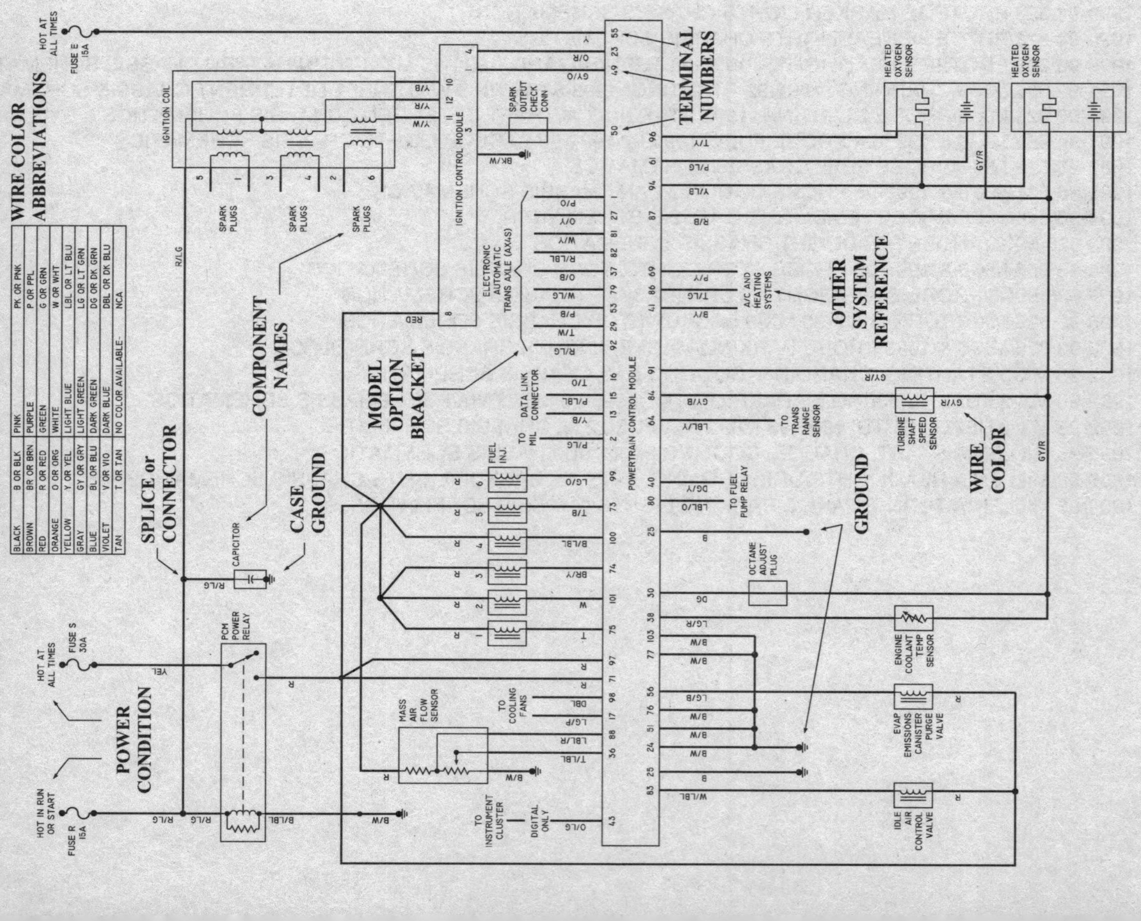

WIRE COLOR ABBREVIATIONS

BLACK	B OR BLK	PINK
BROWN	BN OR BRN	PURPLE
RED	R OR RED	GREEN
ORANGE	O OR ORG	WHITE
YELLOW	Y OR YEL	LIGHT BLUE
GRAY	GY OR GRY	LIGHT GREEN
BLUE	BL OR BLU	DARK GREEN
VIOLET	V OR VIO	DARK BLUE
TAN	T OR TAN	NO COLOR AVAILABLE

PK OR PNK
P OR PPL
G OR GRN
W OR WHT
LBL OR LT BLU
LG OR LT GRN
DG OR DK GRN
DBL OR DK BLU
NCA

POWER CONDITION

COMPONENT NAMES

SPLICE or CONNECTOR

CASE GROUND

MODEL OPTION BRACKET

GROUND

WIRE COLOR

TERMINAL NUMBERS

OTHER SYSTEM REFERENCE

IGNITION COIL

SPARK OUTPUT CHECK CONN

IGNITION CONTROL MODULE

ELECTRONIC AUTOMATIC TRANS AXLE (AXAS)

POWERTRAIN CONTROL MODULE

TO DATA LINK CONNECTOR

TO MIL

FUEL INJ.

MASS AIR FLOW SENSOR

TO COOLING FANS

TO INSTRUMENT CLUSTER

DIGITAL ONLY

OCTANE ADJUST PLUG

TO TRANS RANGE SENSOR

TO FUEL PUMP RELAY

TURBINE SHAFT SENSOR

ENGINE COOLANT TEMP SENSOR

EVAP EMISSIONS CANISTER PURGE VALVE

IDLE AIR CONTROL VALVE

A/C AND HEATING SYSTEMS

HEATED OXYGEN SENSOR

HEATED OXYGEN SENSOR

HOT AT ALL TIMES

FUSE E 15A

FUSE S 30A

PCM POWER RELAY

FUSE R 15A

HOT IN RUN OR START

HOT AT ALL TIMES

DIAGRAM 1

TCCA6W01

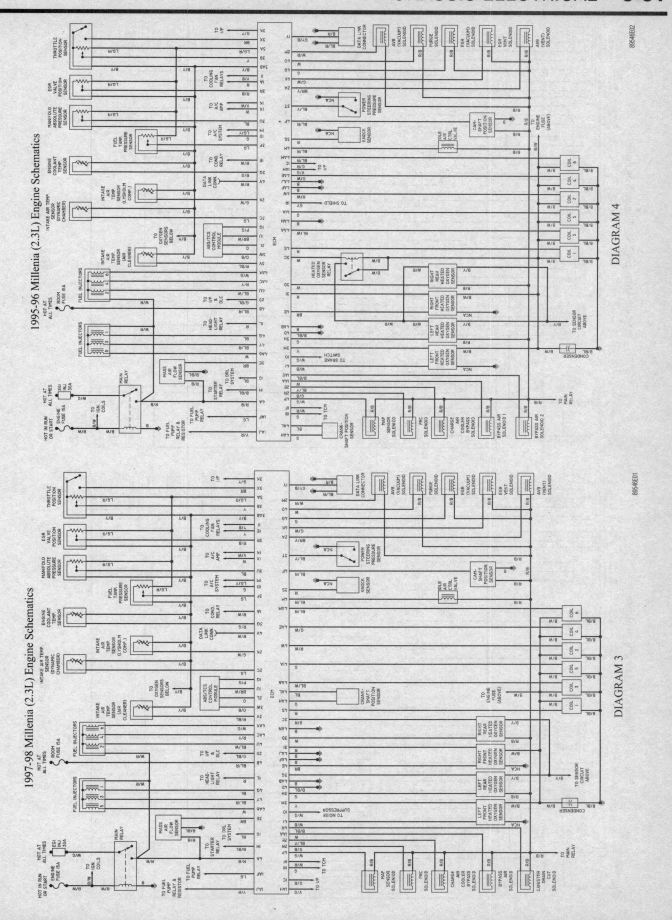

1995-96 Millenia (2.3L) Engine Schematics

DIAGRAM 4

1997-98 Millenia (2.3L) Engine Schematics

DIAGRAM 3

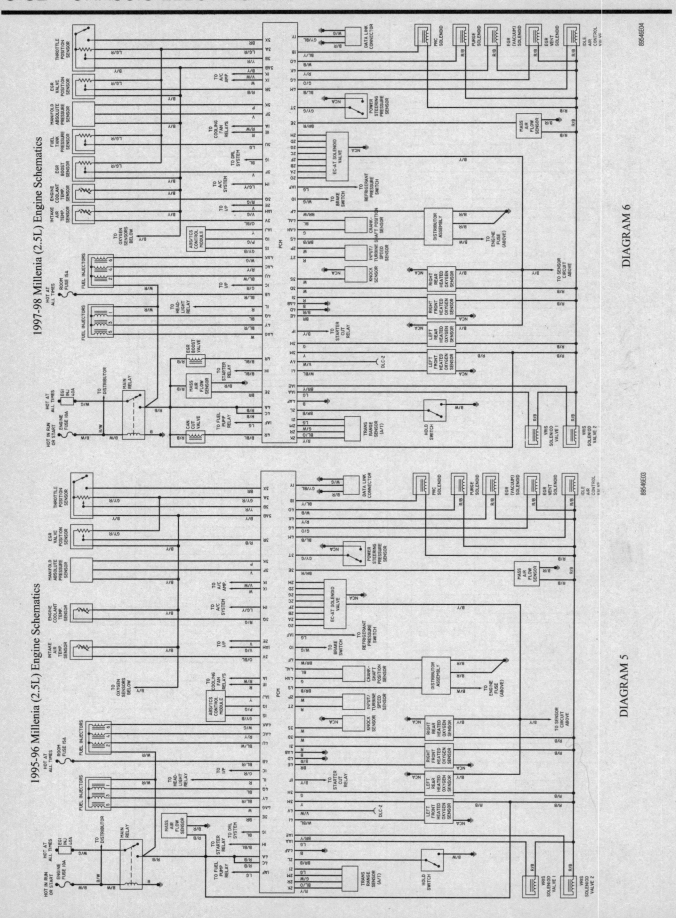

1997-98 Millenia (2.5L) Engine Schematics

DIAGRAM 6

1995-96 Millenia (2.5L) Engine Schematics

DIAGRAM 5

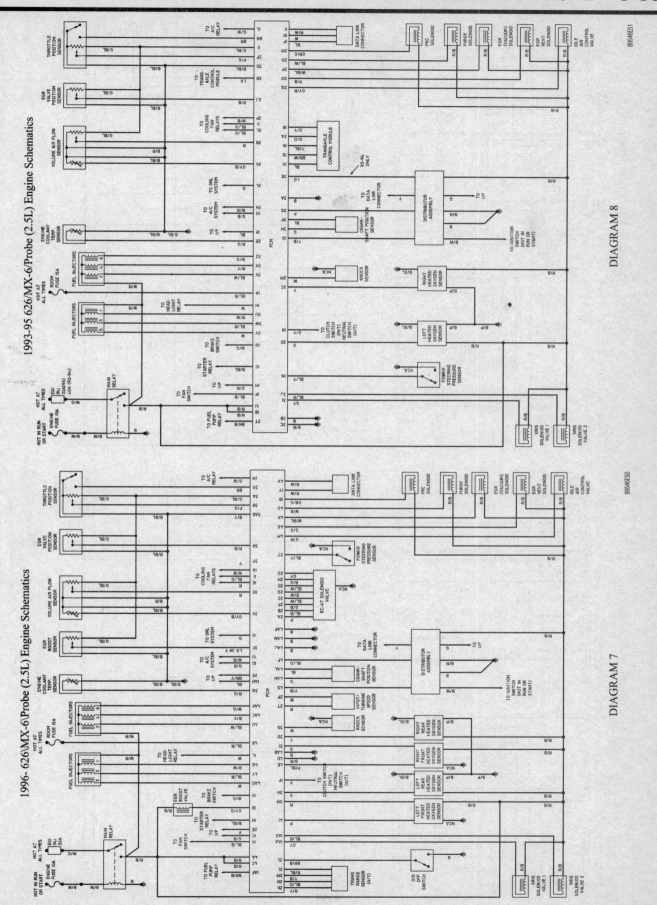

1993-95 626/MX-6/Probe (2.5L) Engine Schematics

DIAGRAM 8

1996- 626\MX-6\Probe (2.5L) Engine Schematics

DIAGRAM 7

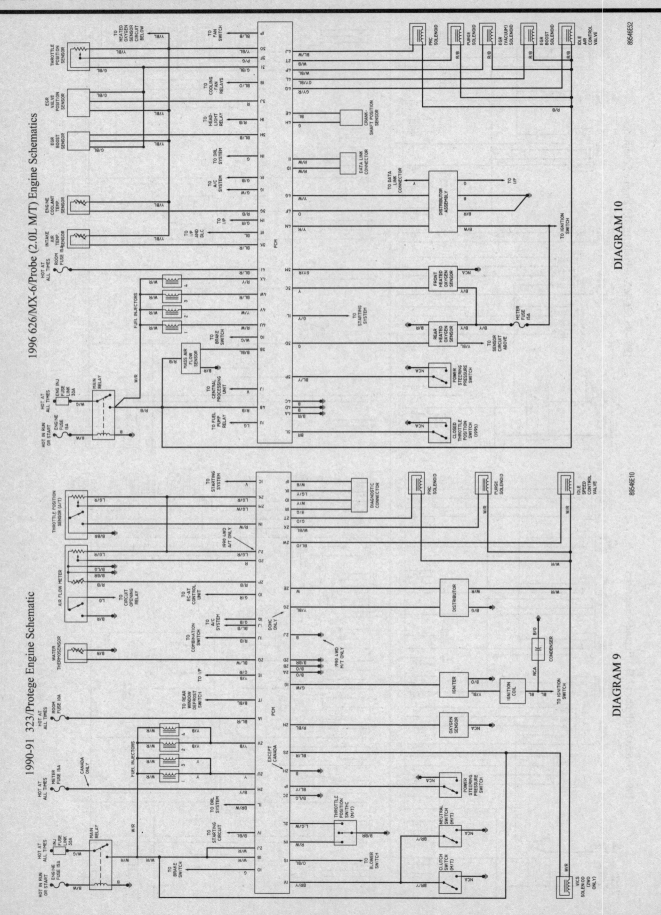

1996 626/MX-6/Probe (2.0L M/T) Engine Schematics

DIAGRAM 10

1990-91 323/Protege Engine Schematic

DIAGRAM 9

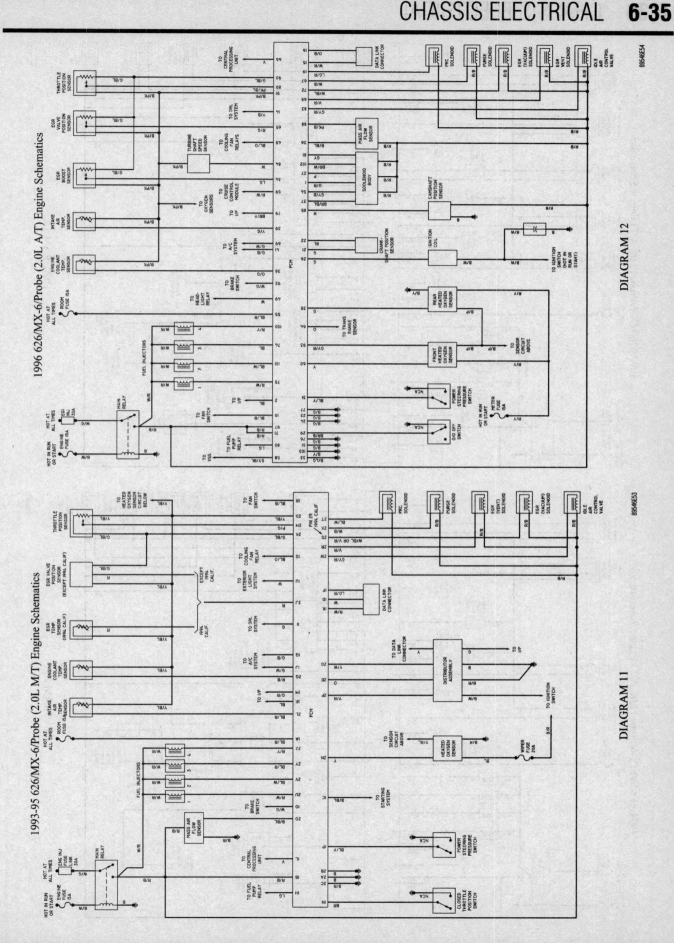

1996 626/MX-6/Probe (2.0L A/T) Engine Schematics

DIAGRAM 12

1993-95 626/MX-6/Probe (2.0L M/T) Engine Schematics

DIAGRAM 11

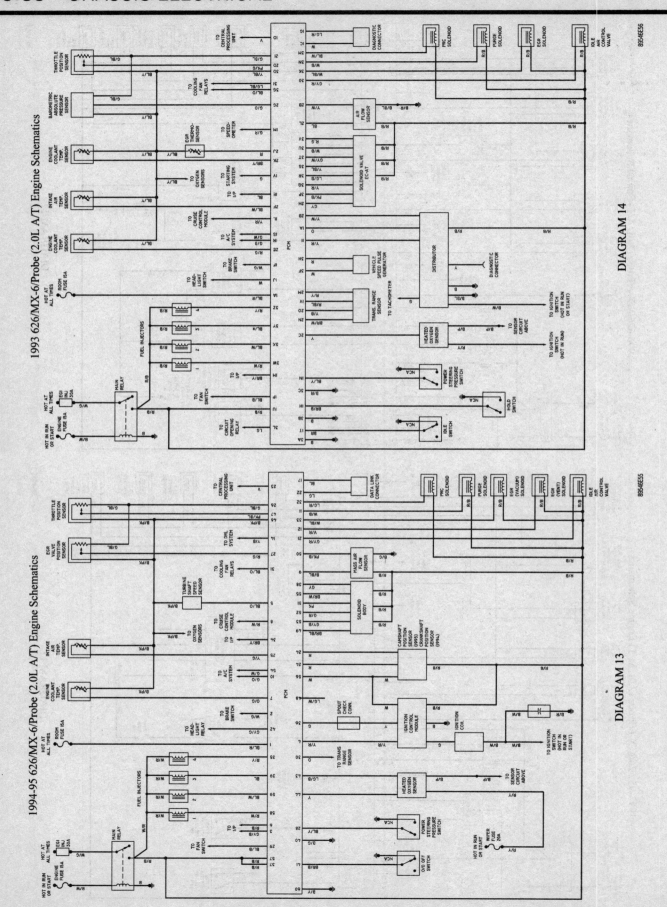

1993 626/MX-6/Probe (2.0L A/T) Engine Schematics

DIAGRAM 14

1994-95 626/MX-6/Probe (2.0L A/T) Engine Schematics

DIAGRAM 13

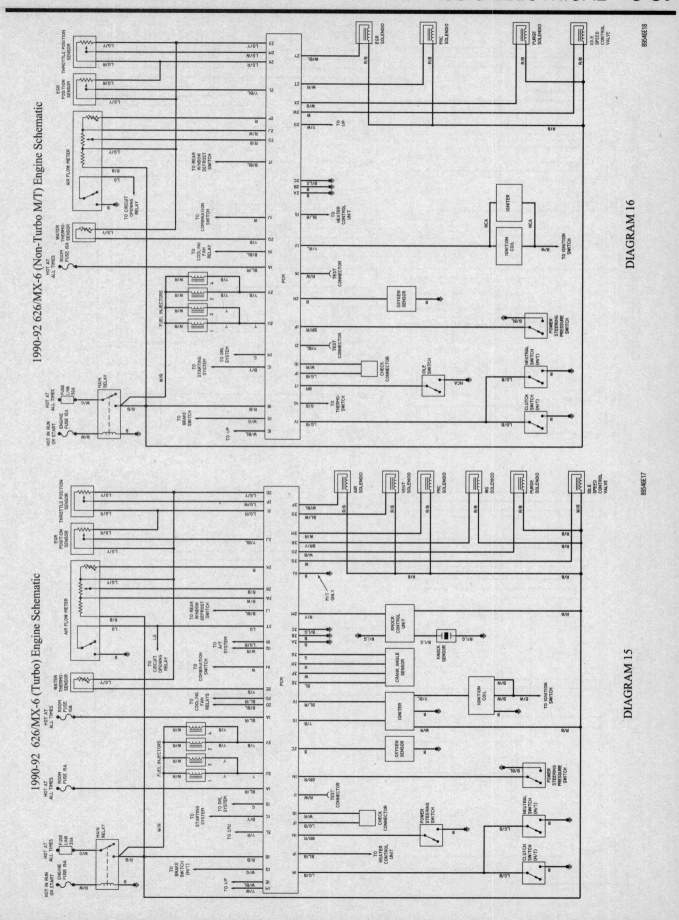

1990-92 626/MX-6 (Non-Turbo M/T) Engine Schematic

DIAGRAM 16

1990-92 626/MX-6 (Turbo) Engine Schematic

DIAGRAM 15

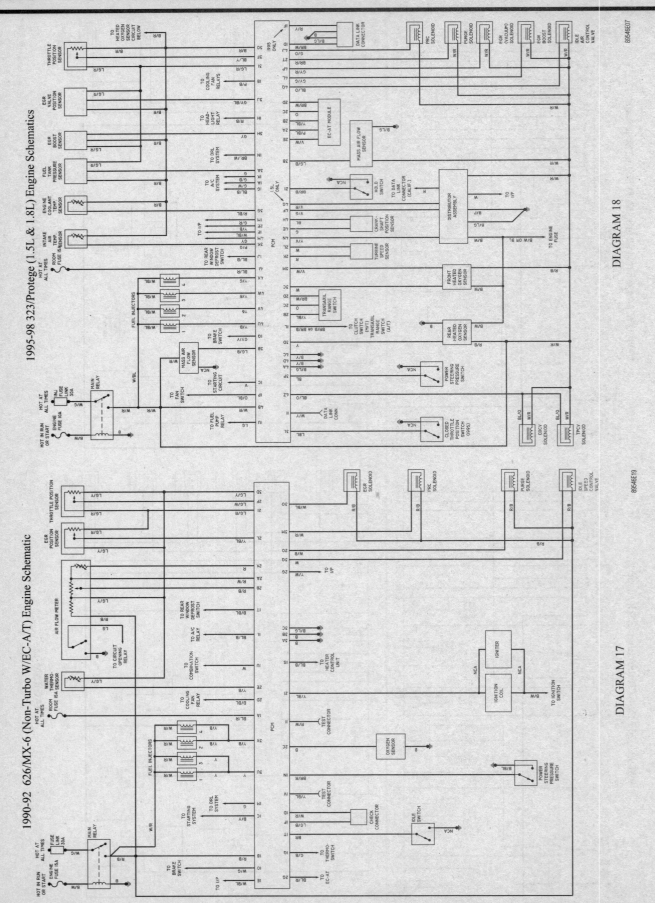

1995-98 323/Protege (1.5L & 1.8L) Engine Schematics

DIAGRAM 18

1990-92 626/MX-6 (Non-Turbo W/EC-A/T) Engine Schematic

DIAGRAM 17

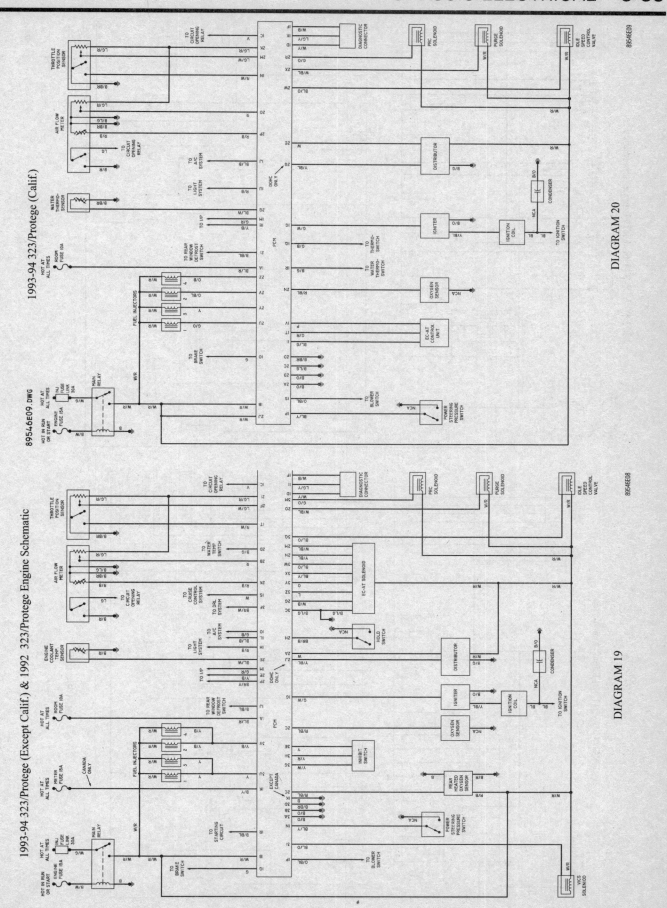

1993-94 323/Protege (Calif.)

89546E09.DWG

DIAGRAM 20

1993-94 323/Protege (Except Calif.) & 1992 323/Protege Engine Schematic

DIAGRAM 19

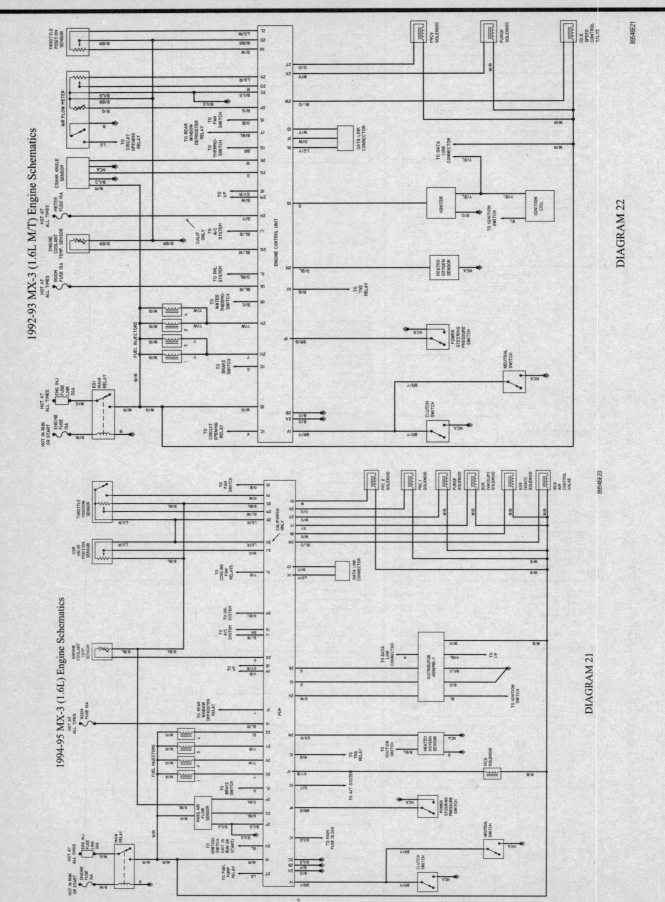

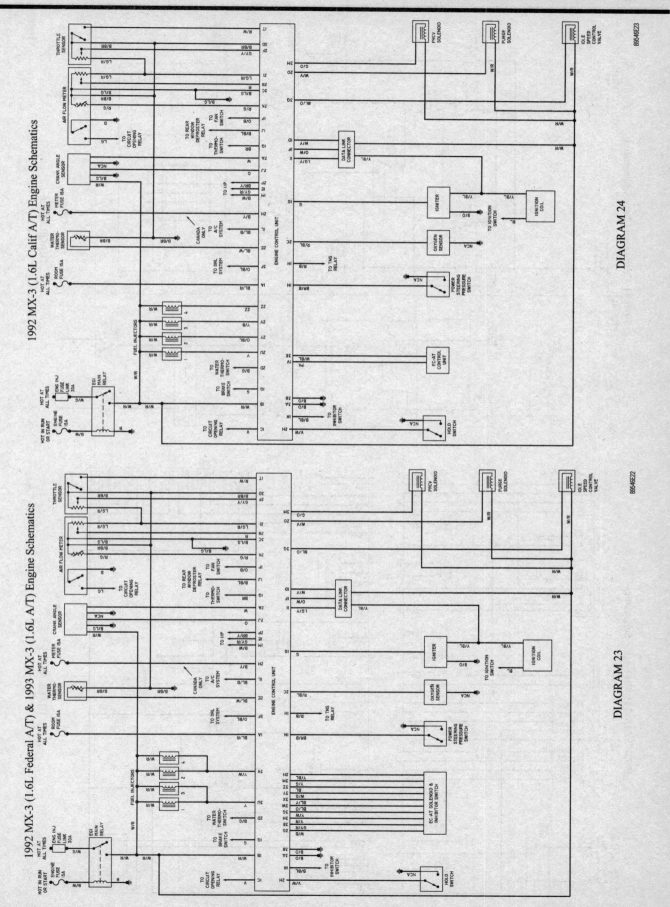

1992 MX-3 (1.6L Calif A/T) Engine Schematics

DIAGRAM 24

1992 MX-3 (1.6L Federal A/T) & 1993 MX-3 (1.6L A/T) Engine Schematics

DIAGRAM 23

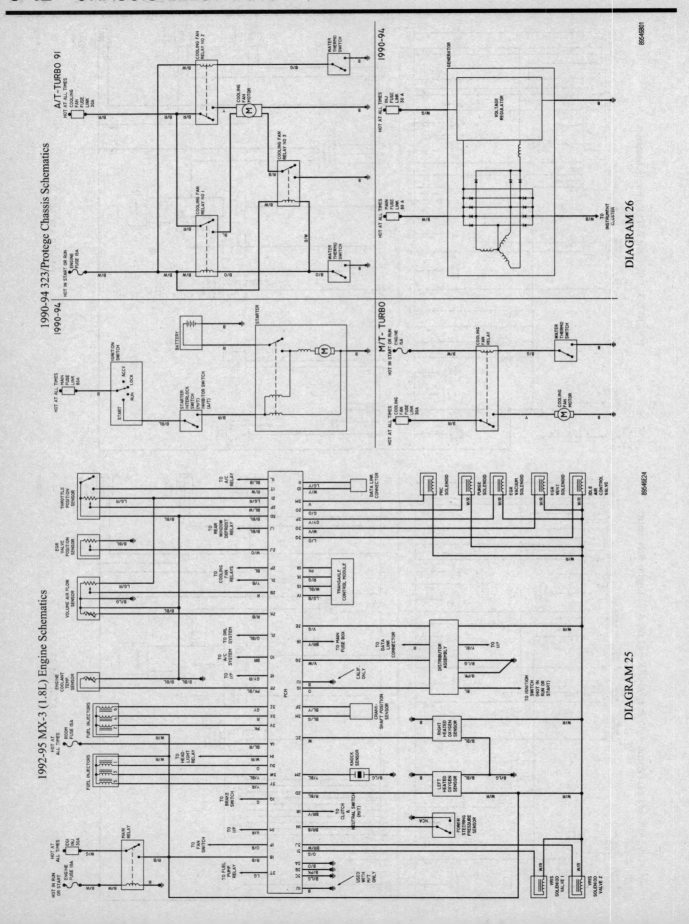

DIAGRAM 26

DIAGRAM 25

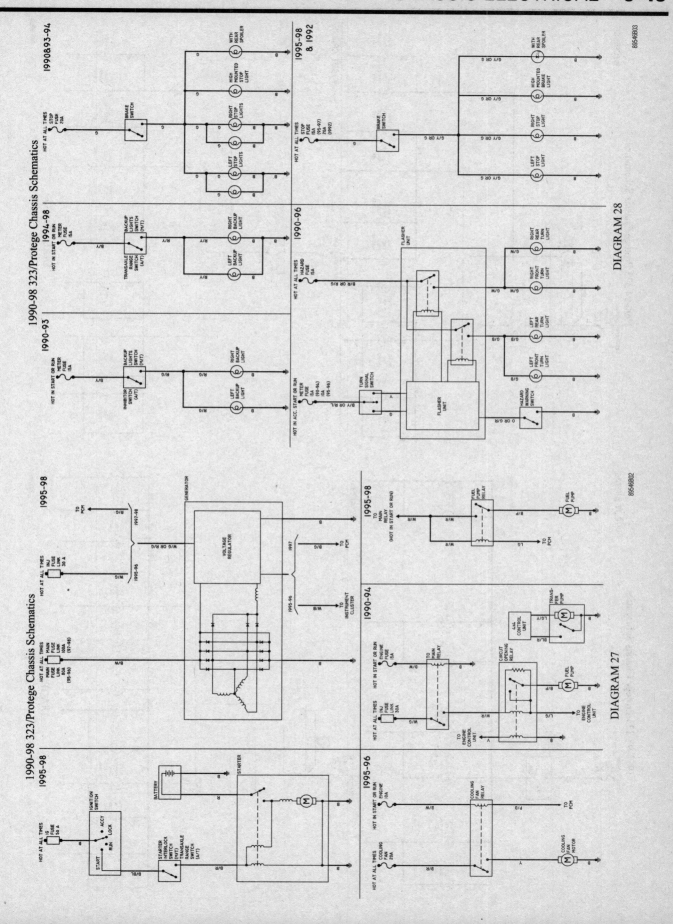

DIAGRAM 28

DIAGRAM 27

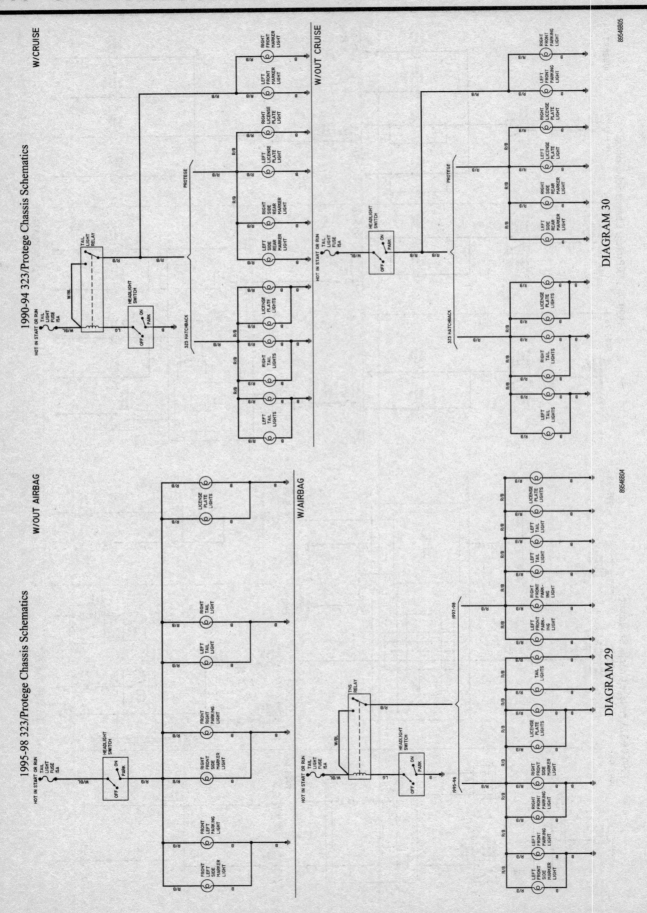

1990-94 323/Protege Chassis Schematics

1995-98 323/Protege Chassis Schematics

DIAGRAM 30

DIAGRAM 29

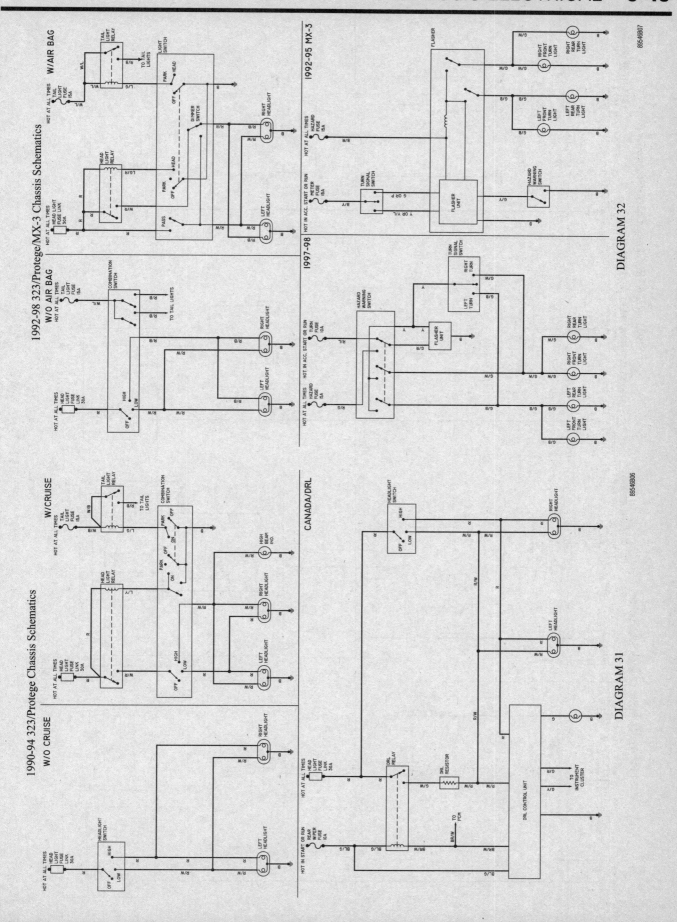

DIAGRAM 32

DIAGRAM 31

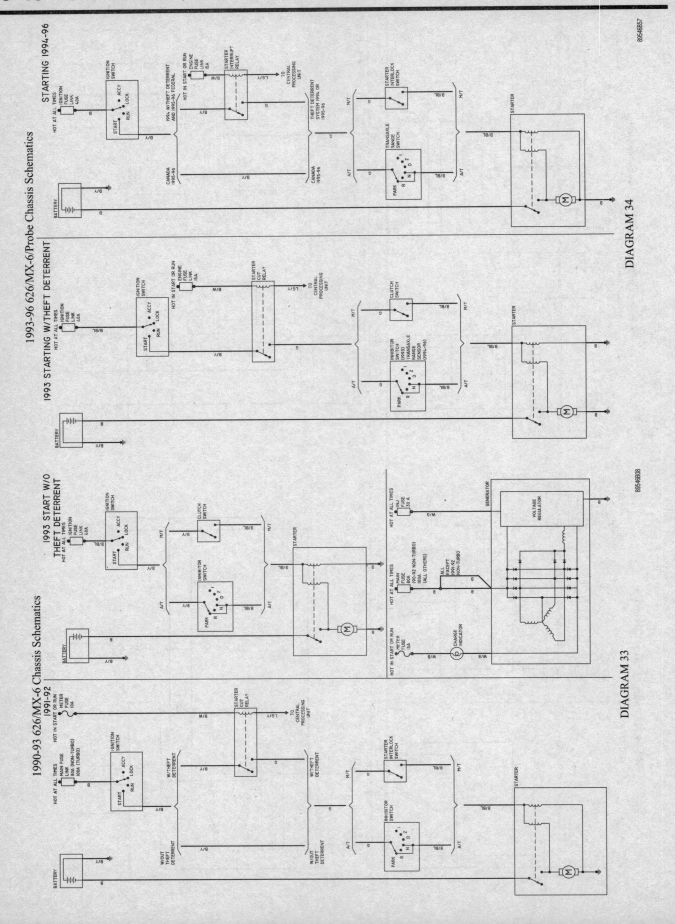

DIAGRAM 34

DIAGRAM 33

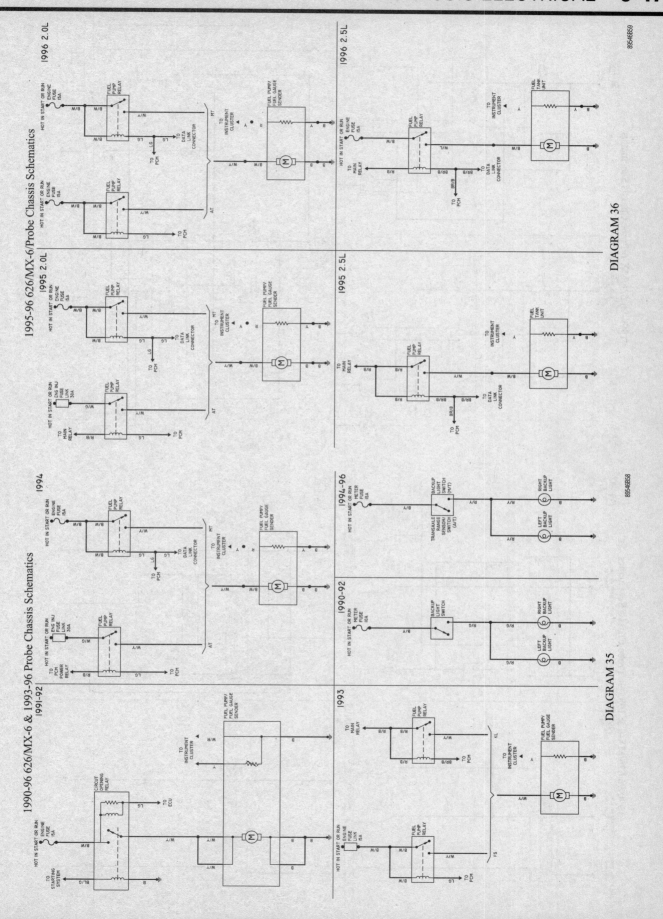

DIAGRAM 36

DIAGRAM 35

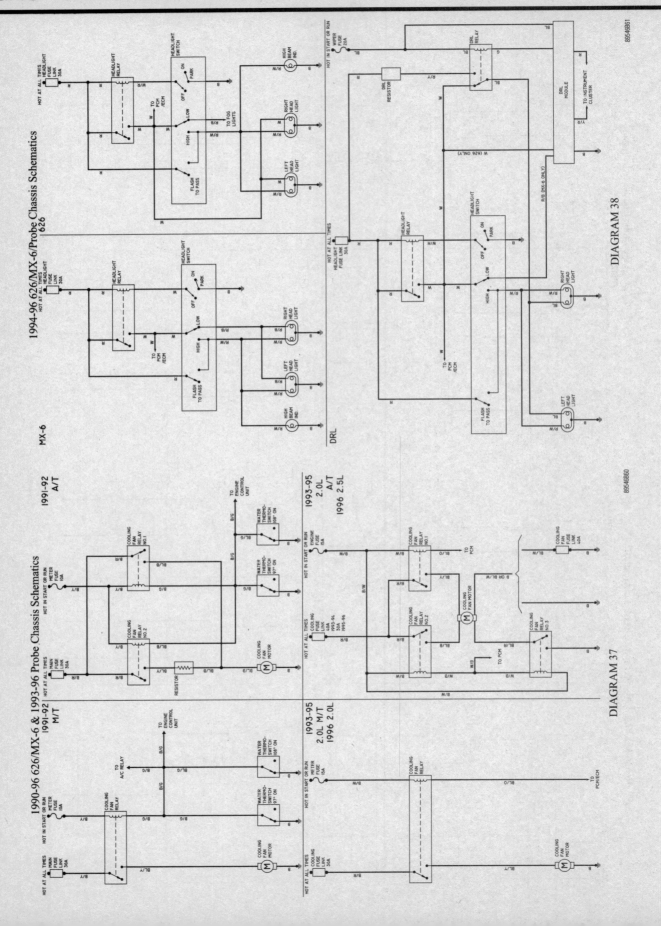

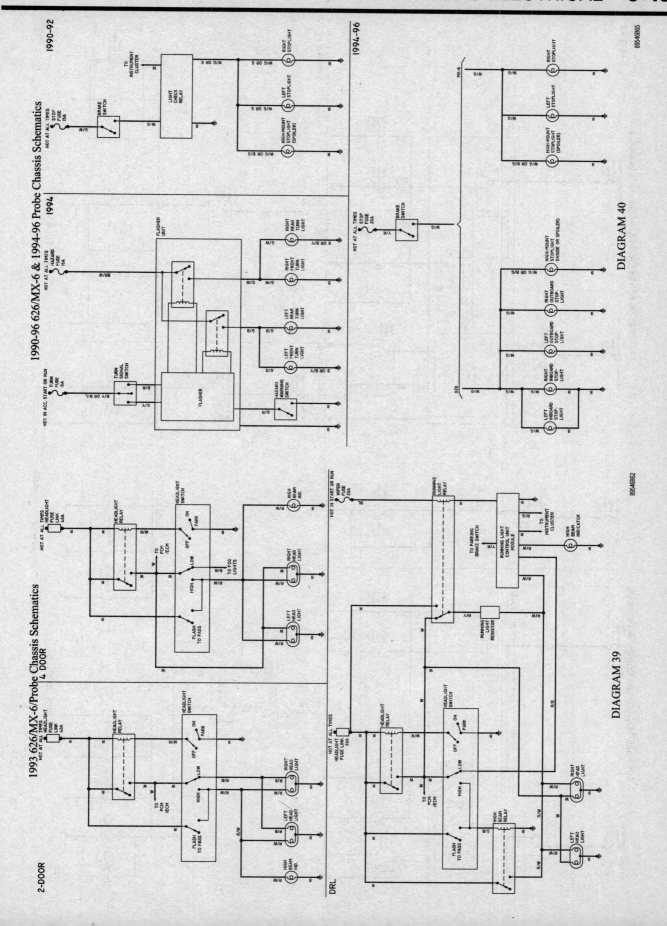

1990-96 626/MX-6 & 1994-96 Probe Chassis Schematics

1993 626/MX-6/Probe Chassis Schematics

DIAGRAM 40

DIAGRAM 39

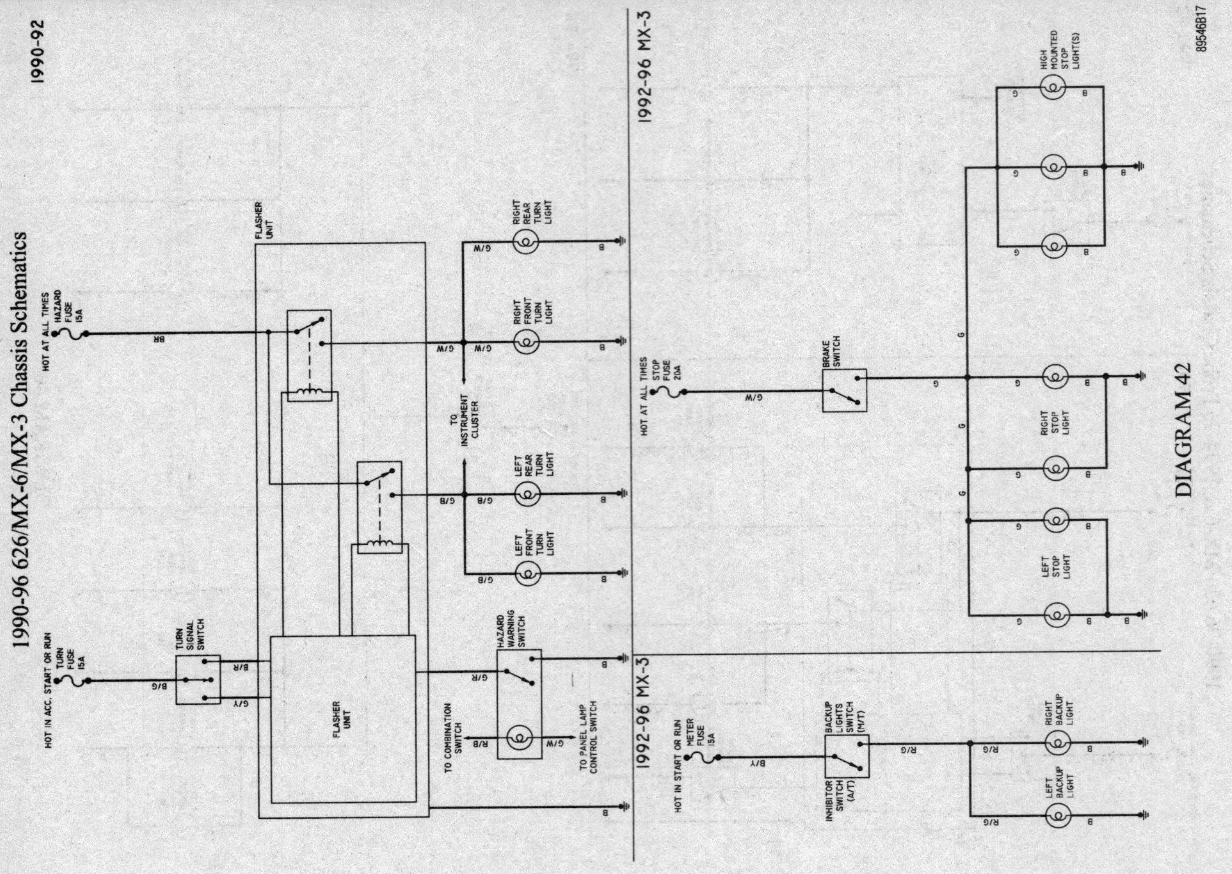

1990-92

1990-96 626/MX-6/MX-3 Chassis Schematics

DIAGRAM 42

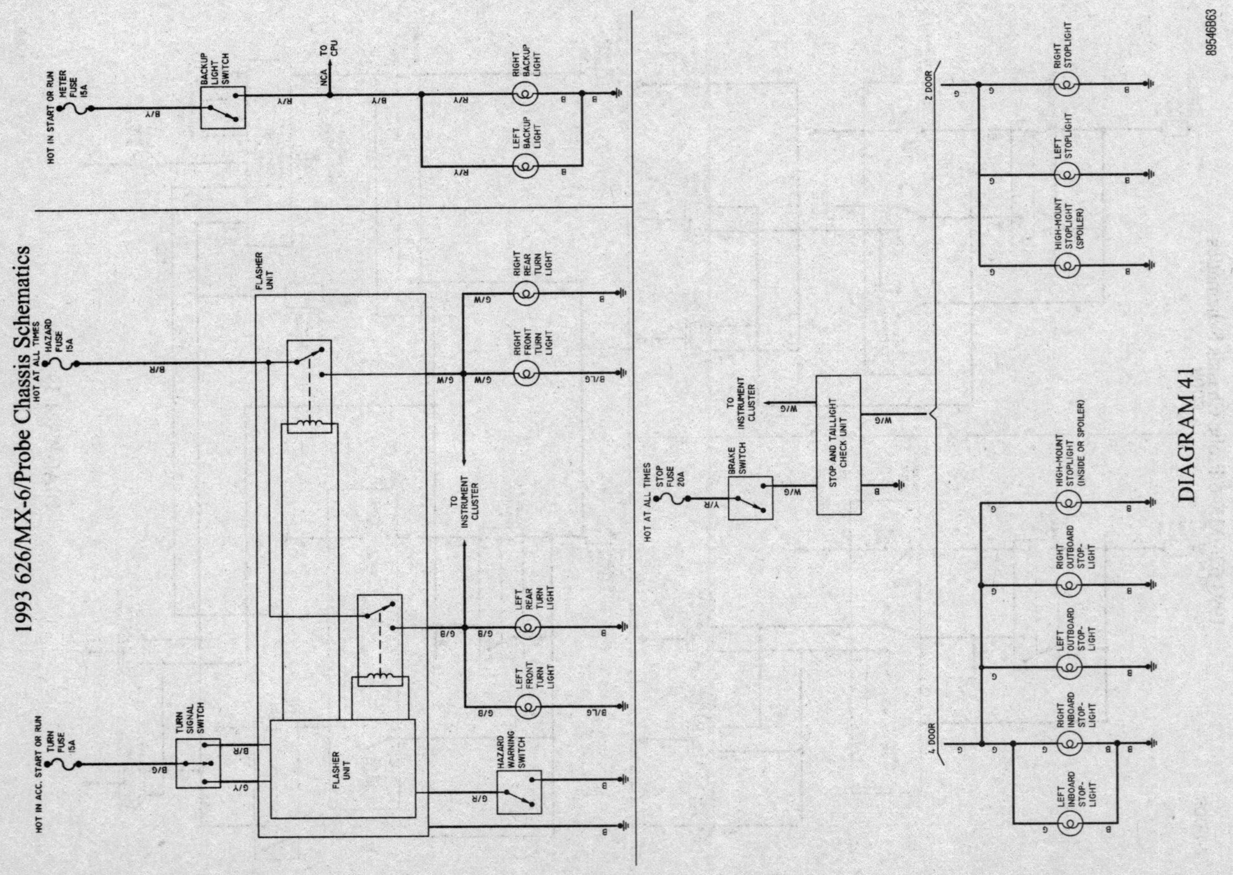

1992-96 MX-3

1992-96 MX-3

89546B17

1993 626/MX-6/Probe Chassis Schematics

DIAGRAM 41

89546663

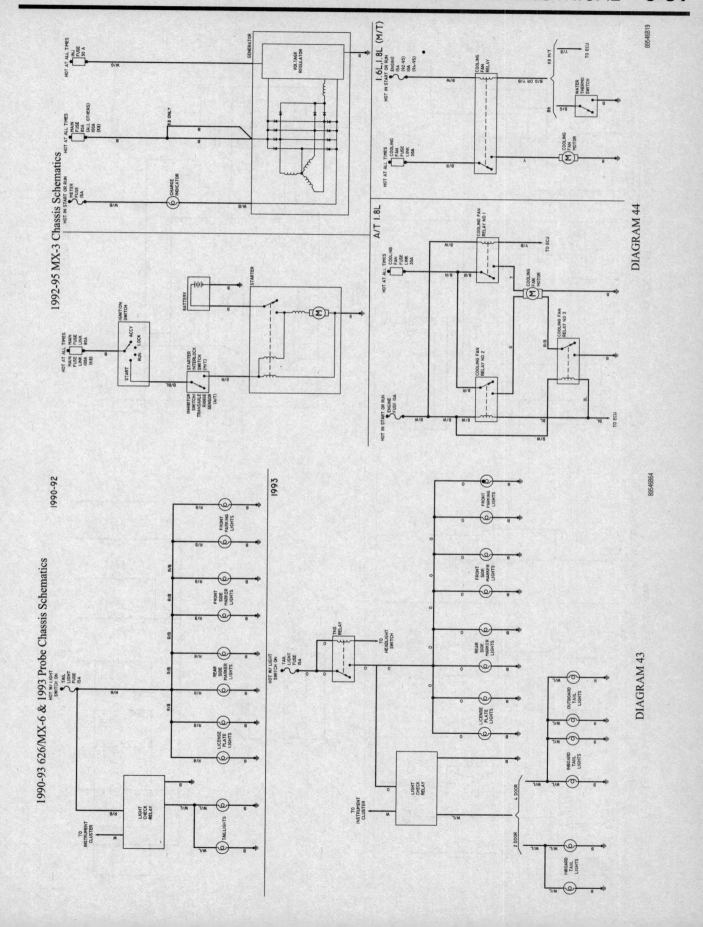

1992-95 MX-3 Chassis Schematics

1.6L, 1.8L (M/T)

A/T 1.8L

DIAGRAM 44

89546819

1990-93 626/MX-6 & 1993 Probe Chassis Schematics

1990-92

1993

DIAGRAM 43

89546864

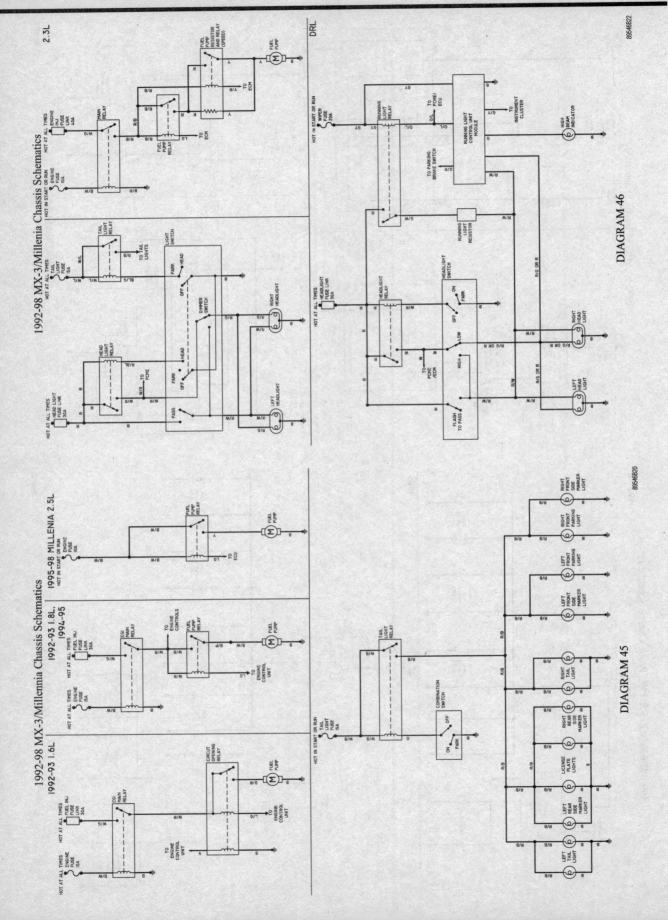

DIAGRAM 46

DIAGRAM 45

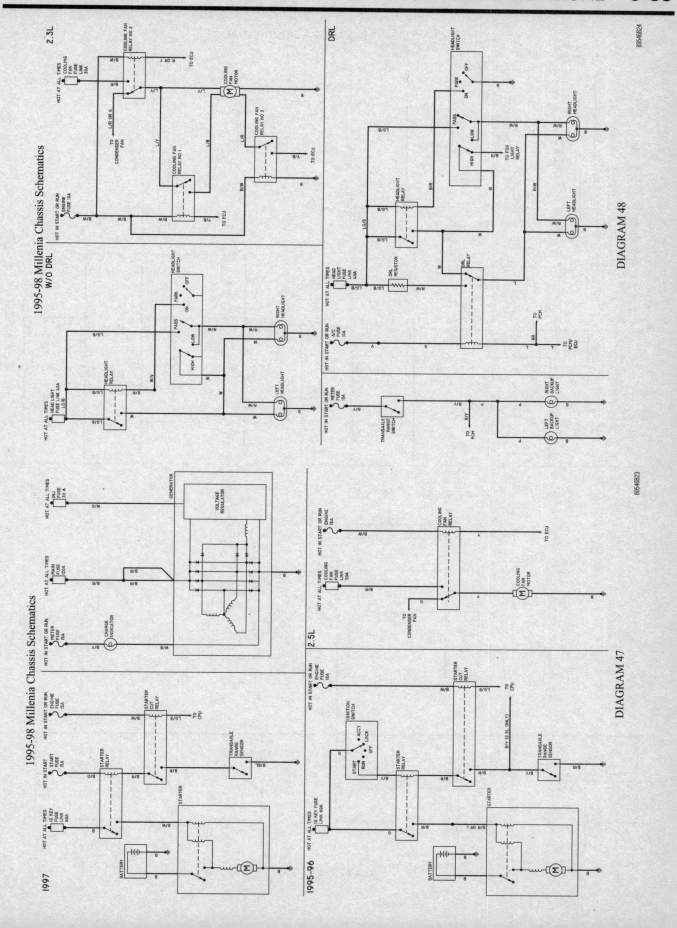

1995-98 Millenia Chassis Schematics W/O DRL

1995-98 Millenia Chassis Schematics

DIAGRAM 48

DIAGRAM 47

1995-98 Millenia Chassis Schematics

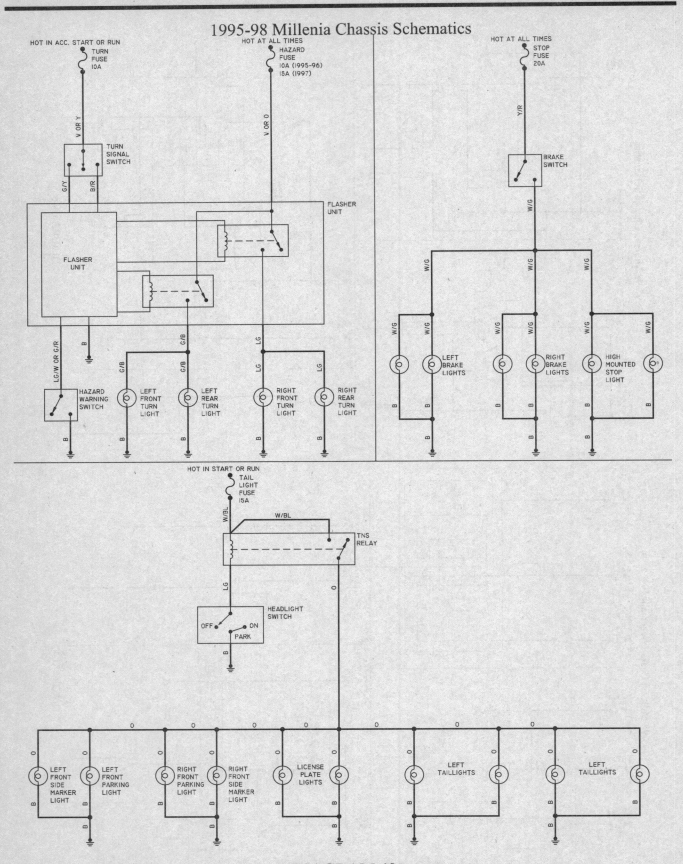

DIAGRAM 49

89546B25

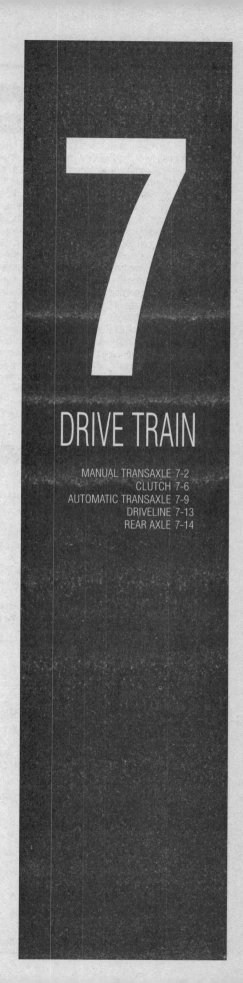

7

DRIVE TRAIN

MANUAL TRANSAXLE

Understanding the Manual Transaxle

Because of the way an internal combustion engine breathes, it can produce torque, or twisting force, only within a narrow speed range. Most modern, overhead valve pushrod engines must turn at about 2500 rpm to produce their peak torque. By 4500 rpm they are producing so little torque that continued increases in engine speed produce no power increases. The torque peak on overhead camshaft engines is generally much higher, but much narrower.

The manual transaxle and clutch are employed to vary the relationship between engine speed and the speed of the wheels so that adequate engine power can be produced under all circumstances. The clutch allows engine torque to be applied to the transaxle input shaft gradually, due to mechanical slippage. Consequently, the vehicle may be started smoothly from a full stop. The transaxle changes the ratio between the rotating speeds of the engine and the wheels by the use of gears. The gear ratios allow full engine power to be applied to the wheels during acceleration at low speeds and at highway/passing speeds.

In a front wheel drive transaxle, power is usually transmitted from the input shaft to a mainshaft or output shaft located slightly beneath and to the side of the input shaft. The gears of the mainshaft mesh with gears on the input shaft, allowing power to be carried from one to the other. All forward gears are in constant mesh and are free from rotating with the shaft unless the synchronizer and clutch is engaged. Shifting from one gear to the next causes one of the gears to be freed from rotating with the shaft and locks another to it. Gears are locked and unlocked by internal dog clutches which slide between the center of the gear and the shaft. The forward gears employ synchronizers; friction members which smoothly bring gear and shaft to the same speed before the toothed dog clutches are engaged.

Back-up Light Switch

REMOVAL & INSTALLATION

▶ **See Figure 1**

The back-up light switch is threaded into the transaxle case.
1. Remove the wire clamp from the transaxle case that secures the switch wire.
2. Detach the electrical wiring multi-connector.
3. Loosen and remove the switch from the transaxle case.
4. Remove the metal gasket from the switch and discard.
To install:
5. Install a new metal gasket sealing washer to the switch.
6. Thread the back-up light switch into the transaxle case and tighten just enough to crush the gasket.
7. Connect the wiring, install the wire clamp and check that the switch operates properly.

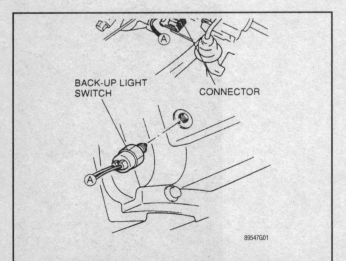

BACK-UP LIGHT SWITCH   CONNECTOR

89547G01

Fig. 1 View of the back-up light switch and harness connection

Manual Transaxle Assembly

REMOVAL & INSTALLATION

▶ **See Figure 2**

1. Disconnect the negative battery cable. Remove the air cleaner. Loosen the front wheel lug nuts.
2. Disconnect the speedometer cable or sensor wires from the transaxle.
3. On 4WD models, detach the neutral safety switch, back-up lamp switch, differential lock sensor switch and differential lock motor electrical connectors. Disconnect the transaxle shift and select control cables from the transaxle by removing the pins and cable retaining clips. Route the cables off to the side and out of the way.
4. Remove the clutch release (slave) cylinder from the transaxle.
5. Remove the water, secondary air, and EGR pipe brackets.
6. Remove the wire harness clip. Disconnect the coupler for the neutral switch and back-up lamp switch. Detach the body ground connector.
7. Remove the two upper transaxle mounting bolts. Mount an engine support tool, 49–ER301–025A or equivalent, to the engine hanger.
8. Raise and support the vehicle safely. Drain the transaxle oil into a suitable container and remove the front wheels.
9. If necessary, remove the intake manifold support bracket.
10. Remove the engine under cover and side covers.
11. On 4WD models, remove the propeller shaft and crossmember. Remove the oil filter and differential lock assembly (the differential lock assembly is fastened with three bolts).
12. Remove the halfshafts.
13. Insert differential side gear holder 49–B027–001 or its equivalent to hold the side gears in place and prevent misalignment.
14. Remove the transaxle crossmember. Separate the gear shift control rod from the transaxle. Remove the extension bar from the transaxle. Remove the wiring and the starter motor.
15. On 4WD models, remove the end plate bolts and connect a suitable hoist and lifting strap to the transaxle. Lift the transaxle and transfer carrier assembly out of the engine compartment.
16. On 2WD models, proceed as follows:
    a. Remove the end plates. Lean the engine toward the transaxle side to lower the transaxle by loosening the engine support hook bolt. Support the transaxle with a suitable transaxle jack.
    b. Remove the necessary engine brackets. Remove the remaining transaxle mounting bolt and engine brackets. Lower the jack and slide the transaxle out from under the vehicle.
To install:
17. Before installing the transaxle, lightly coat the splines of the primary shaft gear with molybdenum disulfide grease.
18. On 4WD models, connect a suitable hoist and lifting strap to the transaxle. Lower the transaxle and transfer carrier assembly into the engine compartment. Align the transaxle assembly to the engine.
19. On 2WD models, attach a thick rope to two places on the transaxle. Place a board on the jack and lower the transaxle onto the board. Using the jack, lift the transaxle into position and throw the end of the rope over the support fixture bar. Tension the rope to guide the transaxle onto its mounts while lifting the transaxle with the jack.
20. Once the transaxle is in place, have an assistant install and tighten all the transaxle-to-engine mounting bolts.
21. The remainder of the installation is the reverse of the removal procedure. Tighten all fasteners to specifications. Fill the transaxle with the proper amount and grade of fluid. Adjust any clutch and/or shifter linkages as necessary.

Halfshafts

REMOVAL & INSTALLATION

▶ **See Figures 3 thru 14**

1. Raise and safely support the vehicle. Remove the wheel and tire assemblies.

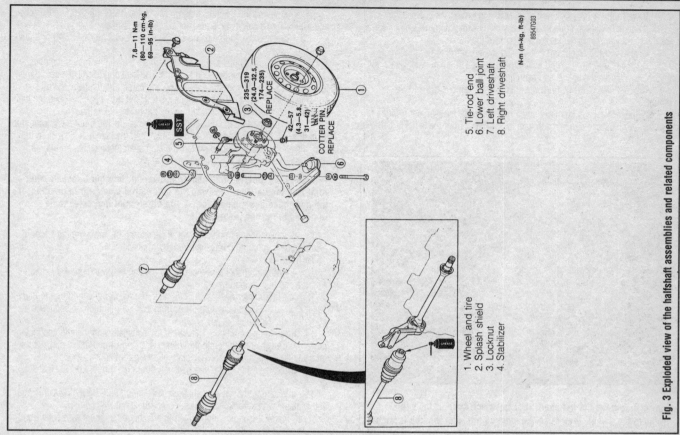

7.8—11 N·m
(80—110 cm-kg,
69—95 in-lb)

235—319
(24.0—32.5,
174—235)
REPLACE

42—57
(4.3—5.8,
31—42)

COTTER PIN.
REPLACE

N·m (m-kg, ft-lb)

1. Wheel and tire
2. Splash shield
3. Locknut
4. Stabilizer

5. Tie-rod end
6. Lower ball joint
7. Left driveshaft
8. Right driveshaft

Fig. 3 Exploded view of the halfshaft assemblies and related components

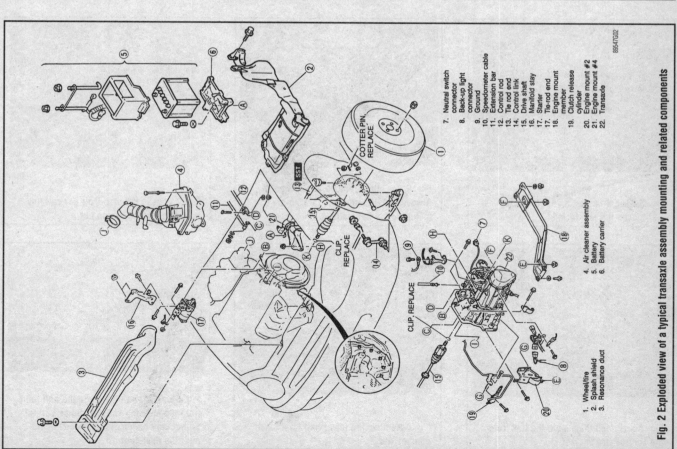

COTTER PIN.
REPLACE

CLIP.
REPLACE

CLIP. REPLACE

1. Wheel/tire
2. Splash shield
3. Resonance duct
4. Air cleaner assembly
5. Battery
6. Battery carrier
7. Neutral switch connector
8. Back-up light connector
9. Ground
10. Speedometer cable
11. Extension bar
12. Control rod
13. Tie rod end
14. Control link
15. Drive shaft
16. Manifold stay
17. Starter
17. Tie-rod end
18. Engine mount
18. Engine mount member
19. Clutch release cylinder
20. Engine mount #2
21. Engine mount #4
22. Transaxle

Fig. 2 Exploded view of a typical transaxle assembly mounting and related components

2. Remove the splash shield, if equipped, and drain the transaxle.

3. Raise the staked portion of the hub locknut with a hammer and chisel. Lock the hub by applying the brakes and remove the nut.

4. Disconnect the stabilizer bar from the lower control arm.

5. Remove the cotter pin and nut from the tie rod end ball stud. Use a suitable tool to separate the tie rod end from the knuckle.

6. On 1993–98 626/MX-6/Probe and Millenia, remove the transverse member.

7. Remove the lower ball joint pinch bolt and nut. Use a prybar to pry down the lower control arm and separate the ball joint from the knuckle.

Fig. 4 To remove the halfshaft, first raise and support the vehicle. Remove the wheel, then raise the staked portion of the hub locknut

8. If removing the left side shaft on MX-3 and 1993–98 626/MX-6/Probe and Millenia with automatic transaxle, proceed as follows:

a. Suspend the engine using engine support tool 49 G017 5A0 or equivalent.

b. Remove the bolts and nuts and remove the engine mount member.

9. Position a prybar between the inner CV-joint and transaxle case. Carefully pry the halfshaft from the transaxle being careful not damage the oil seal. If equipped with a right side intermediate shaft, insert the prybar between the halfshaft and intermediate shaft and tap on the bar to uncouple the shaft.

10. Pull outward on the hub/knuckle assembly, push the outer CV-joint stub shaft through the hub, and remove the halfshaft. If the halfshaft is stuck in the hub, install the old hub nut to protect the stub shaft threads. Tap on the nut, using only a soft mallet, to remove the halfshaft.

➡**Install plug tool 49 G030 455 or equivalent, into the transaxle after removing the halfshaft, to keep the differential side gear in position. If the gear becomes mispositioned, the differential may have to be removed to realign the gear.**

11. Remove the intermediate shaft, if necessary, by removing the support bearing bolts and pulling the shaft from the transaxle.

To install:

12. If removed, install a new circlip on the end of the intermediate shaft, with the end gap facing upward.

13. Install the intermediate shaft in the transaxle, being careful not to damage the oil seals. Install the support bearing bolts and tighten, in sequence, to 45 ft. lbs. (61 Nm).

14. Install a new circlip on the end of the halfshaft, with the end gap facing upward. Insert the halfshaft into the transaxle, being careful not to damage the oil seal. If equipped, push the halfshaft into the intermediate shaft.

15. Insert the other end of the halfshaft through the hub. Loosely install a new locknut.

16. If installing the left side shaft on MX-3 and 1993–98 626/MX-6/Probe and Millenia with automatic transaxle, proceed as follows:

a. Install the engine mount member. Tighten the mount member-to-body nuts and bolts to 66 ft. lbs. (89 Nm).

Fig. 5 Have an assistant apply the brakes and loosen the hub locknut . . .

Fig. 6 . . . then remove and discard it. Always install a new hub locking nut when installing the halfshaft

Fig. 7 Loosen the stabilizer bar end link-to-control arm retaining nut . . .

Fig. 8 . . . and disengage the link from the control arm bracket

Fig. 9 Remove the lower ball joint pinch bolt and nut . . .

Fig. 10 . . . and disengage the ball joint from the steering knuckle. Some careful prying may be necessary, but use care near the dust boot

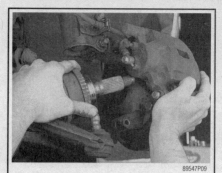

Fig. 11 Pull outward on the knuckle assembly and withdraw the splined axle-shaft from the wheel hub

89547P09

Fig. 12 If the axleshaft end seems stuck in the wheel hub, gently tap it with a soft faced hammer to break it loose

89547P04

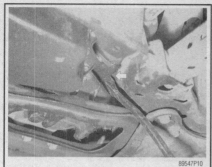

Fig. 13 With the outer end of the halfshaft free, use a prybar and remove the inner end from the transaxle case . . .

89547P10

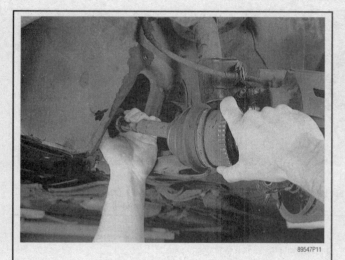

Fig. 14 . . . then remove the entire axleshaft from the vehicle

89547P11

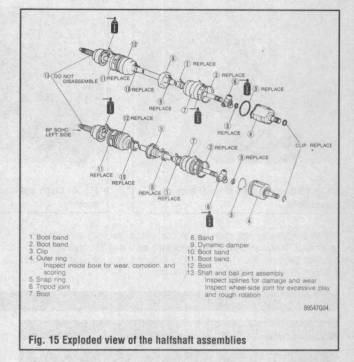

1. Boot band
2. Boot band
3. Clip
4. Outer ring
   Inspect inside bore for wear, corrosion, and scoring
5. Snap ring
6. Tripod joint
7. Boot
8. Band
9. Dynamic damper
10. Boot band
11. Boot band
12. Boot
13. Shaft and ball joint assembly
   Inspect splines for damage and wear
   Inspect wheel-side joint for excessive play and rough rotation

89547G04

Fig. 15 Exploded view of the halfshaft assemblies

b. On MX-3, tighten the mount-to-mount member nuts to 38 ft. lbs. (52 Nm).

c. On 1993–98 626/MX-6/Probe and Millenia, tighten the front mount-to-mount member nuts to 77 ft. lbs. (104 Nm) and the side mount bolts to 44 ft. lbs. (60 Nm).

d. Remove the engine support tool.

17. Install the lower ball joint into the knuckle. Install the pinch bolt and nut and tighten to 40 ft. lbs. (54 Nm).

18. On 1993–98 626/MX-6/Probe and Millenia, install the transverse member and tighten the bolts to 96 ft. lbs. (132 Nm).

19. Connect the tie rod end to the steering knuckle and tighten the nut to 42 ft. lbs. (57 Nm) on all except 1993–98 626/MX-6/Probe and Millenia, where the torque is 32 ft. lbs. (44 Nm). Install a new cotter pin. Tighten the nut, if necessary, to align the ball stud hole with the nut castellation.

20. Connect the stabilizer bar to the lower control arm.

21. Install the splash shield and the wheel and tire assemblies. Lower the vehicle.

22. Lock the hub with the brakes. Tighten the new hub nut to 174–235 ft. lbs. (235–318 Nm). After tightening, stake the locknut using a hammer and dull bladed chisel.

23. Fill the transaxle with the proper type and quantity of fluid.

CV-JOINT OVERHAUL

◆ **See Figures 15 thru 22**

Disassemble the driveshaft as shown in the exploded view. The clip (3) should be removed with a prytool, while the snapring (5) should be removed with snapring pliers or a similar tool.

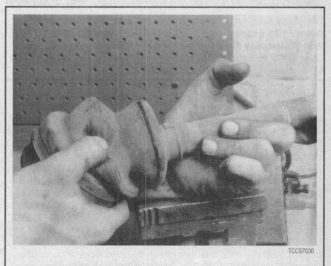

Fig. 16 Check the CV-boot for wear

TCCS7030

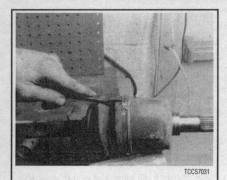

Fig. 17 Remove the outer band from the CV-boot . . .

Fig. 18 . . . then remove the inner band

Fig. 19 Clean the CV-joint housing prior to removing boot

Fig. 20 Removing the CV-joint housing assembly

Fig. 21 Clean and inspect the CV-joint housing

Fig. 22 Remove the CV-joint outer snapring, then remove the joint tripod

Pull the ball bearings, inner ring and cage out of the shaft while still assembled. Then insert a prytool between the inner ring and cage to gently pry each ball out. Finally, matchmark the cage and inner ring and then turn the cage 30 degrees and pull it off the inner ring.

Assemble in reverse order, being careful to repack bearings in the grease supplied with the kit in a thorough manner.

CLUTCH

Understanding the Clutch

The purpose of the clutch is to disconnect and connect engine power at the transaxle. A vehicle at rest requires a lot of engine torque to get all that weight moving. An internal combustion engine does not develop a high starting torque (unlike steam engines) so it must be allowed to operate without any load until it builds up enough torque to move the vehicle. Torque increases with engine rpm. The clutch allows the engine to build up torque by physically disconnecting the engine from the transaxle, relieving the engine of any load or resistance.

The transfer of engine power to the transaxle (the load) must be smooth and gradual; if it weren't, drive line components would wear out or break quickly. This gradual power transfer is made possible by gradually releasing the clutch pedal. The clutch disc and pressure plate are the connecting link between the engine and transaxle. When the clutch pedal is released, the disc and plate contact each other (the clutch is engaged) physically joining the engine and transaxle. When the pedal is pushed inward, the disc and plate separate (the clutch is disengaged) disconnecting the engine from the transaxle.

Most clutches utilize a single plate, dry friction disc with a diaphragm-style spring pressure plate. The clutch disc has a splined hub which attaches the disc to the input shaft. The disc has friction material where it contacts the flywheel and pressure plate. Torsion springs on the disc help absorb engine torque pulses. The pressure plate applies pressure to the clutch disc, holding it tight against the surface of the flywheel. The clutch operating mechanism consists of a release bearing, fork and cylinder assembly.

The release fork and actuating linkage transfer pedal motion to the release bearing. In the engaged position (pedal released) the diaphragm spring holds the pressure plate against the clutch disc, so engine torque is transmitted to the input shaft. When the clutch pedal is depressed, the release bearing pushes the diaphragm spring center toward the flywheel. The diaphragm spring pivots the fulcrum, relieving the load on the pressure plate. Steel spring straps riveted to the clutch cover lift the pressure plate from the clutch disc, disengaging the engine drive from the transaxle and enabling the gears to be changed.

The clutch is operating properly if:

1. It will stall the engine when released with the vehicle held stationary.

2. The shift lever can be moved freely between 1st and reverse gears when the vehicle is stationary and the clutch disengaged.

Driven Disc and Pressure Plate

REMOVAL & INSTALLATION

◆ See Figures 23 thru 33

1. Disconnect the negative battery cable. Raise and safely support the vehicle.

2. Remove the transaxle.

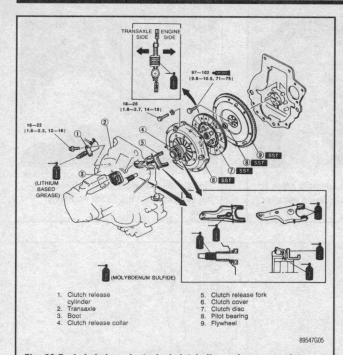

Fig. 23 Exploded view of a typical clutch disc and pressure plate assembly with related components

1. Clutch release cylinder
2. Transaxle
3. Boot
4. Clutch release collar
5. Clutch release fork
6. Clutch cover
7. Clutch disc
8. Pilot bearing
9. Flywheel

3. Gradually loosen the clutch pressure plate bolts, in a criss-cross pattern. Support the pressure plate and remove the bolts. Remove the pressure plate and clutch disc.

4. Inspect the pilot bearing. If it is worn or damaged and does not turn easily by hand, remove it using a puller/slide hammer.

5. Check the flywheel surface for scoring, cracks or burning and machine or replace, as necessary.

6. Install holder tool 49 E011 1A0 or equivalent, to keep the flywheel from turning. Loosen the flywheel bolts evenly and gradually in a criss-cross pattern. Remove the flywheel.

7. Install holder tool 49 F011 101 or equivalent, to keep the flywheel from turning. Remove the locknut. Remove the flywheel, using a suitable puller and remove the key from the eccentric shaft.

8. Inspect the clutch release bearing for wear. Replace it if it sticks or does not turn easily.

9. Inspect the release fork for wear or damage and replace as necessary.

To install:

10. Lubricate the release fork fingers and pivot with molybdenum grease and install in the release fork boot.

11. Install the clutch release bearing on the release fork.

12. If removed, install a new pilot bearing in the flywheel, using a suitable installation tool.

13. Make sure the flywheel mounting surface and the crankshaft or eccentric shaft mounting surfaces are clean. Remove any old sealant from the flywheel bolt hole threads and the flywheel bolts.

14. Install the flywheel.

15. Apply sealant to the flywheel bolt threads and install them hand tight. Install the flywheel holding tool. Tighten the bolts, in a criss-cross pattern, to specification.

16. Apply a small amount of molybdenum grease to the clutch disc splines

Fig. 24 Loosen and remove the clutch and pressure plate bolts evenly, a little at a time . . .

Fig. 25 . . . then carefully remove the clutch and pressure plate assembly from the flywheel

Fig. 26 Check across the flywheel surface, it should be flat

Fig. 27 If necessary, lock the flywheel in place and remove the retaining bolts . . .

Fig. 28 . . . then remove the flywheel from the crankshaft in order replace it or have it machined

Fig. 29 Upon installation, it is usually a good idea to apply a threadlocking compound to the flywheel bolts

Fig. 30 Be sure that the flywheel surface is clean, before installing the clutch

Fig. 31 Install a clutch alignment arbor, to align the clutch assembly during installation

Fig. 32 You may want to use a threadlocking compound on the clutch assembly bolts

Fig. 33 Be sure to use a torque wrench to tighten all bolts

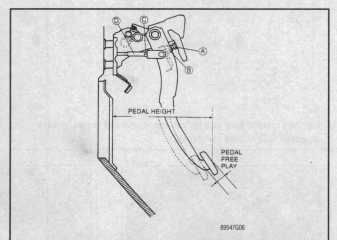

Fig. 34 Clutch pedal measurement and adjustment points. (A) and (B) are for adjusting the pedal height, while (C) and (D) are for the free-play adjustment

and install the clutch disc on the flywheel, spring side toward the transaxle. Install a suitable alignment tool in the pilot bearing to position the clutch disc.

17. Install the clutch pressure plate, aligning the dowel holes with the flywheel dowels. Install the pressure plate bolts and gradually tighten, in a crisscross pattern to 20 ft. lbs. (26 Nm). Remove the alignment tool.

18. Install the transaxle and lower the vehicle.

ADJUSTMENTS

▶ See Figure 34

Pedal Height

1. Measure the distance from the upper surface of the pedal pad to the carpet.
2. The distance should be as follows:
- MX-3 and 1990–94 323/Protege: 7.72–8.03 in. (196–204mm)
- 1995–98 Protege: 8.35–8.45 in. (212–217 mm)
- 1990–92 MX-6/626: 6.73–7.13 in. (171–181mm)
- 1993–98 626/MX-6/Probe: 7.32–8.31 in. (186–211mm)
3. If the distance is not as specified, loosen the locknut on the stopper bolt or switch.
4. Turn the switch or bolt until the distance is correct, then tighten the locknut.

Free-Play

1. Depress the clutch pedal by hand until resistance is felt. The free-play should be 0.03–0.13 in. (0.7–3.4mm).

2. If the free-play is not correct, loosen the clutch master cylinder pushrod locknut and turn the pushrod to adjust.

Clutch Master Cylinder

REMOVAL & INSTALLATION

▶ See Figure 35

1. Disconnect the negative battery cable.
2. On MX-3 and 1990–94 323/Protege, remove the battery and the diagnostic connector.
3. On 1993–98 626/MX-6/Probe, remove the evaporative canister.
4. If so equipped, disconnect the hose from the brake master cylinder reservoir and plug the reservoir port.
5. Remove the hydraulic line from the master cylinder using a tubing wrench.
6. Remove the mounting nuts and remove the master cylinder and gasket.
To install:
7. Install the master cylinder with a new gasket. Tighten the nuts to 18 ft. lbs. (25 Nm) on all except MX-3. On MX-3, tighten the nuts to 8.7 ft. lbs. (12 Nm).
8. Attach the hydraulic line and tighten the fitting with the tubing wrench.
9. If equipped, remove the plug from the brake master cylinder reservoir and connect the hose.
10. Install the remaining components in the reverse of removal. Bleed the air from the system.

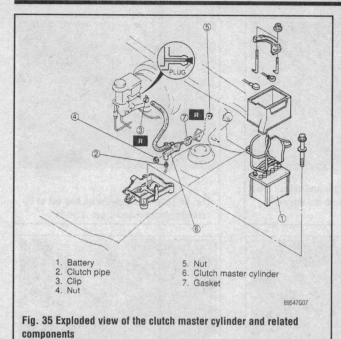

1. Battery
2. Clutch pipe
3. Clip
4. Nut
5. Nut
6. Clutch master cylinder
7. Gasket

89547G07

Fig. 35 Exploded view of the clutch master cylinder and related components

Clutch Release (Slave) Cylinder

REMOVAL & INSTALLATION

▶ **See Figure 36**

1. Disconnect the negative battery cable.
2. If equipped with a flexible hydraulic line connecting the slave cylinder, loosen the fitting at the hose-to-tube junction and remove the clip from the bracket. Remove the hose from the slave cylinder using a tubing wrench and plug the hydraulic line.
3. On all other vehicles, loosen the hydraulic line fitting at the slave cylinder. Disconnect and plug the line.

AUTOMATIC TRANSAXLE

Understanding the Automatic Transaxle

The automatic transaxle allows engine torque and power to be transmitted to the front wheels within a narrow range of engine operating speeds. It will allow the engine to turn fast enough to produce plenty of power and torque at very low speeds, while keeping it at a sensible rpm at high vehicle speeds (and it does this job without driver assistance). The transaxle uses a light fluid as the medium for the transmission of power. This fluid also works in the operation of various hydraulic control circuits and as a lubricant. Because the transaxle fluid performs all of these functions, trouble within the unit can easily travel from one part to another.

Park/Neutral Safety Switch

The park/neutral safety switch also functions as the reverse light switch.

REMOVAL AND INSTALLATION

▶ **See Figures 37 thru 48**

1. Disconnect the negative battery cable.
2. Block the wheels and apply the parking brake. Place the gear shift in NEUTRAL.

4. Remove the slave cylinder mounting bolts and remove the slave cylinder.
To install:
5. Install the slave cylinder and tighten the bolts to 16 ft. lbs. (22 Nm).
6. Connect the hydraulic line and tighten with a tubing wrench.
7. If equipped with a flexible hose, connect the hose and tighten with a tubing wrench. Attach the hose to the bracket and install the clip. Connect the hydraulic line and tighten the fitting with a tubing wrench.
8. Bleed the air from the system.

HYDRAULIC SYSTEM BLEEDING

1. Remove the rubber cap from the bleeder screw on the release cylinder.
2. Place a bleeder tube over the end of the bleeder screw.
3. Submerge the other end of the tube in a jar half filled with hydraulic brake fluid.
4. Slowly pump the clutch pedal fully and allow it to return slowly, several times.
5. While pressing the clutch pedal to the floor, loosen the bleeder screw until the fluid starts to run out. Then close the bleeder screw. Keep repeating this Step, while watching the hydraulic fluid in the jar. As soon as the air bubbles disappear, close the bleeder screw.
6. During the bleeding procedure the reservoir must be kept at least ¾ full.

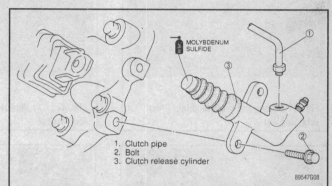

MOLYBDENUM SULFIDE

1. Clutch pipe
2. Bolt
3. Clutch release cylinder

89547G08

Fig. 36 Exploded view of the clutch release (slave) cylinder assembly

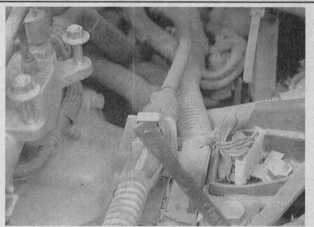

89547P14

Fig. 37 To remove the park/neutral safety switch, first gain access to it, then pry up on . . .

Fig. 38 . . . and remove the gear select cable-to-transaxle bracket retaining clip

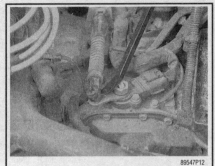

Fig. 39 Use a small prybar and detach the gear select cable end from the transaxle manual select lever

Fig. 40 Then lift the cable up and out of its retaining bracket and move it aside

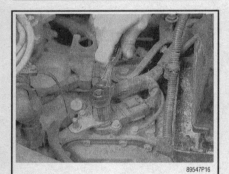

Fig. 41 Loosen the manual select lever retaining nut . . .

Fig. 42 . . . then remove it along with its lockwasher

Fig. 43 Ensure that the lever is still in the neutral position and matchmark the shaft, lever and switch housing

Fig. 44 Remove the manual select lever . . .

Fig. 45 . . . then loosen the switch attaching screws . . .

Fig. 46 . . . and remove the attaching screws

3. As necessary for access, remove the resonance chamber, fresh air duct and air cleaner assembly.

4. Remove the spring pin and clip and disconnect the shift cable or rod at the transaxle and the switch manual lever.

5. Remove the manual shaft nut, lockwasher and lever.

➠**As a precaution, make a matchmark on the shaft, manual lever and the switch assembly.**

6. Remove the switch mounting bolts and the switch.

7. Disconnect the neutral safety switch connector.

To install:

8. Rotate the manual shaft to **N**.

9. Turn the neutral safety switch so the neutral mark is in line with the flat, straight surfaces on either side of the manual shaft.

10. Loosely tighten the switch bolts and adjust the switch. Tighten the bolts to 70–95 inch lbs. (8–11 Nm).

11. Install the manual shaft nut, lockwasher and lever. Torque to 24–33 ft. lbs. (32–46 Nm).

12. Connect the neutral safety switch electrical connector.

13. Connect the shift cable at the transaxle. Install the spring pin and clip.

14. If removed, install the resonance chamber, fresh air duct and air cleaner assembly.

15. Connect the negative battery cable.

ADJUSTMENT

◆ **See Figure 49**

1. Place the transaxle selector lever in the neutral position.

2. Loosen the switch mounting bolts.

3. Remove the screw on the switch body and move the switch so that

Fig. 47 Lift the park/neutral switch assembly from the shaft . . .

Fig. 48 . . . and detach the electrical wire harness connector from it

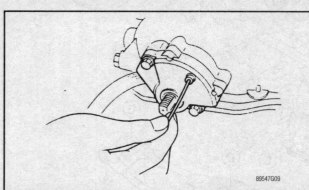

Fig. 49 With the switch in the neutral position, insert the proper size pin into the adjustment hole and tighten the attaching screws

the screw hole is aligned with the small hole inside of the switch. Check the alignment by inserting a small pin (0.079 in. or 2mm for all models except Millenia, which uses a 0.157 in. or 4mm pin) in the hole.

4. Tighten the mounting bolts and remove the pin.
5. Install the screw to the switch body and tighten.
6. Check the adjustment by trying to start the engine in all gears. It should only start in Park and Neutral.

Automatic Transaxle Assembly

REMOVAL & INSTALLATION

▶ **See Figure 50**

1. Raise and safely support the vehicle and remove the front wheels. Remove the battery and battery box and the air cleaner and ducting.
2. Remove the splash shield and drain the transaxle oil.
3. Disconnect the speedometer cable, throttle cable, shift cable and the wiring from the transaxle.
4. If necessary, properly relieve the fuel system pressure and disconnect the fuel lines.
5. If the fuel filter is mounted to the transaxle, unbolt its mounting bracket and position it aside.
6. Unbolt any exhaust crossover, coolant, vacuum or EGR pipe mounting brackets from the transaxle.
7. On 2.0L engines, remove the intake manifold support bracket.
8. Disconnect the wiring and remove the starter.
9. On 4WD models, matchmark the flanges and remove the driveshaft.
10. Disconnect the exhaust pipe from the manifold and the catalytic converter and remove the pipe.
11. Disconnect the tie rod ends and lower ball joints and remove the halfshafts. Use special tool 49 G030 455 or equivalent to hold the differential side gears in place when the halfshafts are removed.
12. On 4WD models, to remove the differential lock motor, remove the sensor switch. Insert a small screwdriver into the hole and turn the rod ½ turn counterclockwise. Remove the bolts and remove the motor.
13. Remove the torque converter–to–flywheel nuts and/or bolts.
14. Disconnect the oil cooler hoses and plug them to prevent leakage.
15. Install the necessary lifting equipment and support the engine from above. Remove the lower mounting frame and support the transaxle from below with a jack.
16. Remove the front and left rear mounts and allow the engine/transaxle to tilt towards the left.
17. Remove the bolts and slide the transaxle away from the engine to lower it out of the vehicle. Do not let the torque converter fall out.
To install:
18. Make sure the torque converter is properly placed and carefully guide the transaxle into place. Start all the transaxle–to–engine bolts, then tighten them to specifications.
19. The remainder of the installation is the reverse of the removal procedure.

Halfshafts

Halfshaft removal, installation and overhaul procedures for automatic transaxles are the same for manual transaxles described earlier in this section.

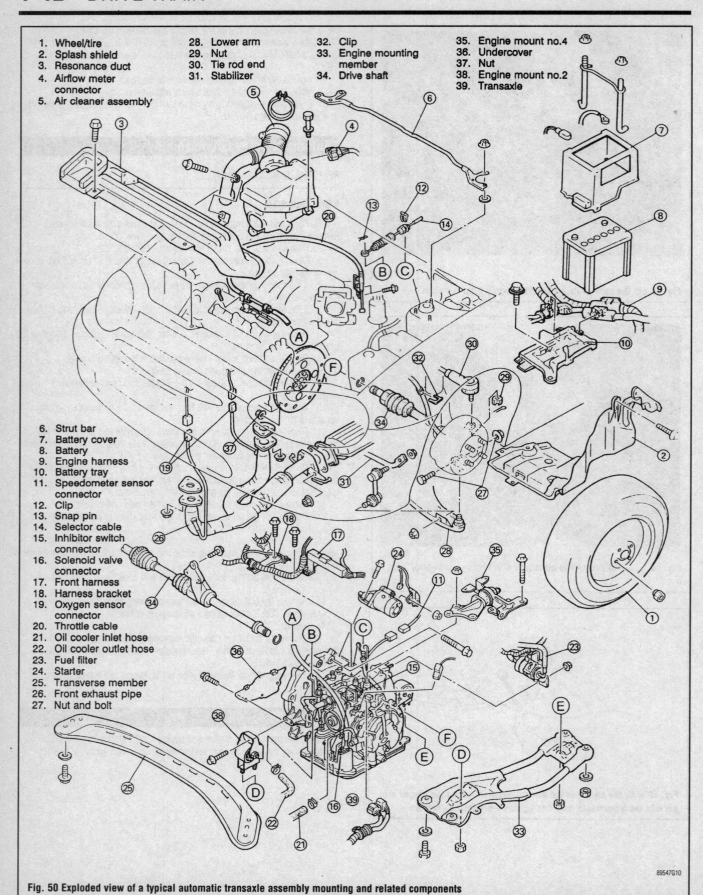

1. Wheel/tire
2. Splash shield
3. Resonance duct
4. Airflow meter connector
5. Air cleaner assembly
6. Strut bar
7. Battery cover
8. Battery
9. Engine harness
10. Battery tray
11. Speedometer sensor connector
12. Clip
13. Snap pin
14. Selector cable
15. Inhibitor switch connector
16. Solenoid valve connector
17. Front harness
18. Harness bracket
19. Oxygen sensor connector
20. Throttle cable
21. Oil cooler inlet hose
22. Oil cooler outlet hose
23. Fuel filter
24. Starter
25. Transverse member
26. Front exhaust pipe
27. Nut and bolt
28. Lower arm
29. Nut
30. Tie rod end
31. Stabilizer
32. Clip
33. Engine mounting member
34. Drive shaft
35. Engine mount no.4
36. Undercover
37. Nut
38. Engine mount no.2
39. Transaxle

Fig. 50 Exploded view of a typical automatic transaxle assembly mounting and related components

89547G10

DRIVELINE

Rear Driveshaft and U-Joints

REMOVAL & INSTALLATION

➡**This procedure applies to 4-wheel drive models only.**

1. Matchmark the front and rear U-joint with the companion flanges. Remove the bolts attaching the driveshaft to the rear companion flange.
2. Remove the center support bearing bracket nuts, spacers and washers from the underbody.
3. Make sure to mark each set of spacers and washers in relation to their original positions.
4. Remove the bolts attaching the driveshaft to the front companion flange.
5. Pull the driveshaft rearward and away from the transaxle.
6. Installation is the reverse of removal. Make sure that you align the matchmarks. Tighten the driveshaft flange bolts to 22 ft. lbs. (30 Nm) and the center support bracket nuts to 27–38 ft. lbs. (37–51 Nm).

U-JOINT OVERHAUL

▸ **See Figure 51**

Perform this procedure with the driveshaft removed from the car.
1. Matchmark both the yoke and the driveshaft so that they can be returned to their original balancing position during assembly.
2. Remove the bearing snaprings from the yoke.
3. Use a hammer and a brass drift to drive in one of the bearing cups. Remove the cup which is protruding from the other side of the yoke.
4. Remove the other bearing cups by pressing them from the spider.
5. Withdraw the spider from the yoke.
6. Examine the spider journals for rusting or wear. Check the bearing for smoothness or pitting.

➡**The spider and bearing are replace as a complete assembly only.**

7. Check the seals and rollers for wear or damage.
To assemble:
8. Pack the bearing cups with grease.
9. Fit the rollers into the cups and install the dust seals.
10. Place the spider in the yoke and them fit one of the bearing cups into its bore in the yoke.
11. Press the bearing cup home, while guiding the spider into it, so that a snapring can be installed.
12. Press-fit the other bearings into the yoke.
13. Select a snapring to obtain minimum end-play of the spider. Use snaprings of the same thickness on both sides to center the spider.

➡**When assembled, the U-joint should have a slight drag but should not bind. If it does bind, use different thickness snaprings. Selective fit snaprings are available in sizes ranging from 1.2mm to 1.4mm.**

14. Install the spider/yoke assembly and bearings into the driveshaft in the same manner as the spider was assembled to the yoke.
15. Test the operation of the U-joint assembly. The spider should move freely with no binding.

Center Bearing

➡**This procedure applies to 4-wheel drive models only.**

REPLACEMENT

▸ **See Figure 51**

The center support bearing is a sealed unit which requires no periodic maintenance. The following procedure should be used if it becomes neces-

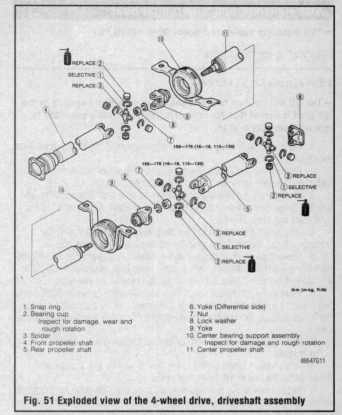

1. Snap ring
2. Bearing cup
   Inspect for damage, wear and rough rotation
3. Spider
4. Front propeller shaft
5. Rear propeller shaft
6. Yoke (Differential side)
7. Nut
8. Lock washer
9. Yoke
10. Center bearing support assembly
    Inspect for damage and rough rotation
11. Center propeller shaft

156—176 (16—18, 115—130)

N·m (m-kg, ft-lb)

89547G11

Fig. 51 Exploded view of the 4-wheel drive, driveshaft assembly

sary to replace the bearing. You will need a pair of snapring pliers for this job.
1. Remove the driveshaft assembly.
2. To maintain driveline balance, matchmark the rear driveshaft, the center yoke and the front driveshaft so that they may be installed in their original positions.
3. Remove the center universal joint from the center yoke, leaving it attached to the rear driveshaft. See the following section for the correct procedure.
4. Remove the nut and washer securing the center yoke to the front driveshaft.
5. Slide the center yoke off the splines. The rear oil seal should slide off with it.
6. If the oil has remained on top of the snapring, remove and discard the seal. Remove the snapring from its groove. Remove the bearing.
7. Slide the center support and front oil seal from the front driveshaft. Discard the seal.
8. Install the new bearing into the center support. Secure it with the snapring.
9. Apply a coat of grease to the lips of the new oil seals, and install them into the center support on either side of the bearing.
10. Coat the splines of the front driveshaft with grease. Install the center support assembly and the center yoke onto the front driveshaft, being sure to match up the marks made during disassembly.
11. Install the washer and nut. Torque the nut to 116-130 ft. lbs.
12. Check that the center support assembly rotates smoothly around the driveshaft.
13. Align the mating marks on the center yoke and the rear driveshaft, and assemble the center universal joint.
14. Install the driveshaft. Be sure that the rear yoke and the axle flange are aligned properly.

REAR AXLE

Axle Halfshaft and Differential Seal

➡This procedure applies to 4-wheel drive models only.

REMOVAL & INSTALLATION

▶ **See Figures 52, 53 and 54**

➡The left and the right rear axle shafts are not interchangeable as the left shaft is shorter than the right. It is, therefore, not a good idea to remove them both at once.

1. Raise and safely support the rear of the vehicle. Drain the lubricant from the differential.
2. Remove the rear wheels. Raise the tab on the wheel hub locknut, and then have someone apply the brakes as you loosen the nut.
3. Clearly mark the relationship between the axle shaft flange and the differential flange. Remove the nuts and washers that attach the axle shaft to the differential and separate them.
4. Disconnect the lateral link from the rear axle hub by removing the through bolt and washer. Disconnect the trailing link in the same manner.
5. Lower the axle shaft flange from the differential and pull the splined end from the wheel hub. If the axle shaft is stuck in the hub, use special hub puller 49–0839–425C to withdraw the hub so you can remove the axle shaft.
6. Remove the differential flange from the differential carrier by positioning two prybars on either side of the flange, between it and the carrier and prying the flange outward. Remove the circlip from the differential flange shaft and discard it.
7. Remove the oil seal from the differential by prying it out as well.

To install:

8. Apply lithium based grease to the new oil seal lip and, using a seal driver, install the seal to the differential carrier.
9. Install a new circlip to the differential flange shaft, insert the flange into the differential carrier and seat it by lightly tapping it with a hammer. Ensure that the circlip is engaged into the internal groove by attempting to pull it out by hand.
10. Attach the knuckle assembly to the shock absorber support and torque the retaining bolts to 58–86 ft. lbs.

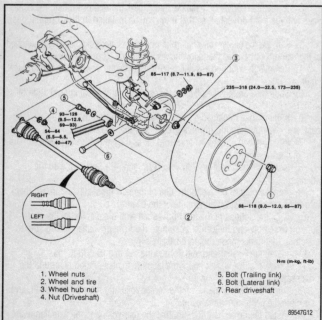

1. Wheel nuts
2. Wheel and tire
3. Wheel hub nut
4. Nut (Driveshaft)
5. Bolt (Trailing link)
6. Bolt (Lateral link)
7. Rear driveshaft

89547G12

Fig. 52 Exploded view of the rear axle halfshaft assemblies and related components

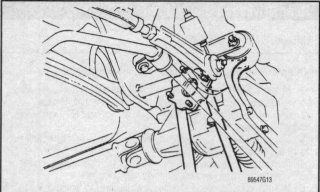

89547G13

Fig. 53 Use two prybars to remove the flanges from the differential

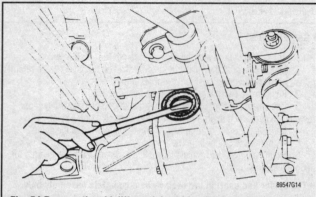

89547G14

Fig. 54 Remove the old differential seal by simply prying it out

11. Insert the splined end of the axle shaft into the wheel hub and connect the trailing and lateral links. Torque the trailing link bolt to 58–56 ft. lbs. and the lateral link bolt to 46–55 ft. lbs.
12. Attach the axle shaft to the differential flange by aligning the matchmarks. Torque the flange nuts to 39–47 ft. lbs. (53–63 Nm).
13. Install a new locknut and torque it to 174–235 ft. lbs. (235–318 Nm). Stake the locknut tab into the groove of the spindle using a small cold chisel.
14. Install the rear wheels and lower the vehicle.

Differential Carrier

➡This procedure applies to 4-wheel drive models only.

REMOVAL & INSTALLATION

▶ **See Figures 55 and 56**

1. Drain the differential fluid into a suitable drain pan.
2. Remove the driveshaft.
3. Raise the rear of the vehicle and support safely.
4. Mark the relationship between the driveshaft and output flanges and separate the driveshaft from the differential.
5. Have an assistant apply the brakes and remove the axle nut.
6. Disconnect the stabilizer from the crossmember.
7. Disconnect the lateral and trailing links.
8. Grasp the wheel hub by the rotor disc and pull it out until the driveshaft can be disconnected from the spline.
9. Support the differential with a jack and remove the mounting hardware from the front and rear attachment points. Lower the differential to the floor.

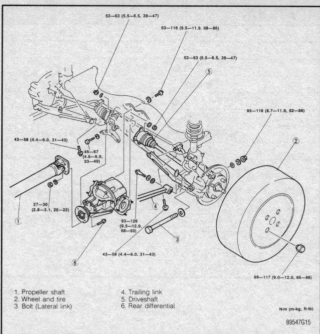

1. Propeller shaft
2. Wheel and tire
3. Bolt (Lateral link)
4. Trailing link
5. Driveshaft
6. Rear differential

N·m (m-kg, ft-lb)

89547G15

Fig. 55 Exploded view of the rear differential mounting, including related components

To install:

10. Raise the differential up into the frame and install the front and rear fasteners. Torque the front fasteners to 33–49 ft. lbs. (45–67 Nm) and the rear fasteners to 68–86 ft. lbs. (93–116 Nm).

11. Insert the driveshaft spline into the wheel hub and align the matchmarks on the driveshaft with the output shaft. Install the flange fasteners and torque them to 39–47 ft. lbs. (53–63 Nm).

12. Connect the lateral link and torque the mounting bolt to 69–86 ft. lbs. Connect the trailing link to the crossmember and torque the mounting bolt to 9–13 ft. lbs.

13. Install the driveshaft and torque the flange bolts to 20–22 ft. lbs.

14. Mount the wheels and lower the vehicle.

15. Fill the differential to the proper level (see Capacities Chart) and install the drain plug.

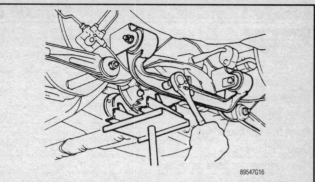

89547G16

Fig. 56 With the differential properly supported, remove its mounting bolts

Pinion Seal

➡This procedure applies to 4-wheel drive models only.

REMOVAL & INSTALLATION

1. Raise and support the front end on jackstands.
2. Matchmark and remove the driveshaft.
3. Remove the wheels and brake calipers.
4. Using an in. lbs. torque wrench on the companion flange nut, measure the rotational torque of the differential and note the reading.
5. Hold the companion flange from turning and remove the locknut.
6. Using a puller, remove the companion flange.
7. Using a center punch to deform the seal and pry it out of the bore.

To install:

8. Coat the outer edge of the new seal with sealer and drive it into place with a seal driver.
9. Coat the seal lip with clean gear oil.
10. Coat the companion flange with chassis lube and install it.
11. Install the nut and tighten it until the previously noted rotational torque is achieved. Torque on the nut should not exceed 130 ft. lbs.
12. Install the driveshaft.
13. Replace any lost gear oil.

TORQUE SPECIFICATIONS

Components	Ft. Lbs.	Nm
Clutch master cylinder bolts		
MX-3	8.7 ft. lb.s	12 Nm
Except MX-3	18 ft. lbs.	25 Nm
Clutch release cylinder bolt	12-17 ft. lbs.	16-23 Nm
Drain plug	36 ft. lbs.	49 Nm
Front half shaft lock nut	173-235 ft. lbs.	235-318 Nm
Gear shift rod bolts	10-14 ft. lbs.	14-19 Nm
Rear diffferential housing bolts		
Front bolts	33-49 ft. lbs.	45-67 Nm
Rear bolts	68-86 ft. lbs.	93-116 Nm
Rear half shaft lock nut	173-235 ft. lbs.	235-318 Nm
Rear halfshaft flange nuts	39-47 ft. lbs.	53-63 Nm
Speedometer driven gear bolt	69-104 inch lbs.	8-12 Nm
Transaxle-to-engine bolts	47-66 ft. lbs.	64-89 Nm

89547C01

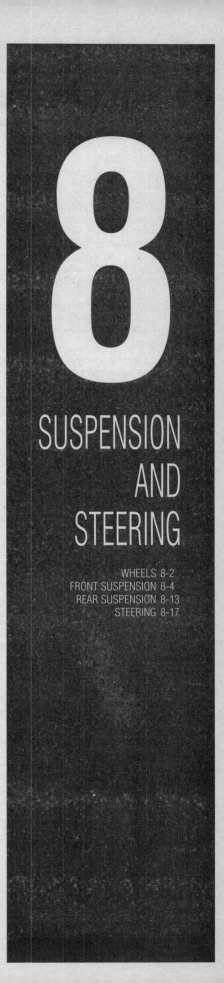

8

SUSPENSION AND STEERING

WHEELS

Wheel Assembly

REMOVAL & INSTALLATION

▶ **See Figure 1**

1. Park the vehicle on a level surface.
2. Remove the jack, tire iron and, if necessary, the spare tire from their storage compartments.
3. Check the owner's manual or refer to Section 1 of this manual for the jacking points on your vehicle. Then, place the jack in the proper position.
4. If equipped with lug nut trim caps, remove them by either unscrewing or pulling them off the lug nuts, as appropriate. Consult the owner's manual, if necessary.
5. If equipped with a wheel cover or hub cap, insert the tapered end of the tire iron in the groove and pry off the cover.
6. Apply the parking brake and block the diagonally opposite wheel with a wheel chock or two.

➡**Wheel chocks may be purchased at your local auto parts store, or a block of wood cut into wedges may be used. If possible, keep one or two of the chocks in your tire storage compartment, in case any of the tires has to be removed on the side of the road.**

7. If equipped with an automatic transmission/transaxle, place the selector lever in **P** or Park; with a manual transmission/transaxle, place the shifter in Reverse.
8. With the tires still on the ground, use the tire iron/wrench to break the lug nuts loose.

➡**If a nut is stuck, never use heat to loosen it or damage to the wheel and bearings may occur. If the nuts are seized, one or two heavy hammer blows directly on the end of the bolt usually loosens the rust. Be careful, as continued pounding will likely damage the brake drum or rotor.**

9. Using the jack, raise the vehicle until the tire is clear of the ground. Support the vehicle safely using jackstands.
10. Remove the lug nuts, then remove the tire and wheel assembly.

To install:

11. Make sure the wheel and hub mating surfaces, as well as the wheel lug studs, are clean and free of all foreign material. Always remove rust from the wheel mounting surface and the brake rotor or drum. Failure to do so may cause the lug nuts to loosen in service.
12. Install the tire and wheel assembly and hand-tighten the lug nuts.
13. Using the tire wrench, tighten all the lug nuts, in a crisscross pattern, until they are snug.
14. Raise the vehicle and withdraw the jackstand, then lower the vehicle.
15. Using a torque wrench, tighten the lug nuts in a crisscross pattern to 87 ft. lbs. (118 Nm). Check your owner's manual or refer to Section 1 of this manual for the proper tightening sequence.

✳✳ WARNING

Do not overtighten the lug nuts, as this may cause the wheel studs to stretch or the brake disc (rotor) to warp.

16. If so equipped, install the wheel cover or hub cap. Make sure the valve stem protrudes through the proper opening before tapping the wheel cover into position.
17. If equipped, install the lug nut trim caps by pushing them or screwing them on, as applicable.
18. Remove the jack from under the vehicle, and place the jack and tire iron/wrench in their storage compartments. Remove the wheel chock(s).
19. If you have removed a flat or damaged tire, place it in the storage compartment of the vehicle and take it to your local repair station to have it fixed or replaced as soon as possible.

INSPECTION

Inspect the tires for lacerations, puncture marks, nails and other sharp objects. Repair or replace as necessary. Also check the tires for treadwear and air pressure as outlined in Section 1 of this manual.

Check the wheel assemblies for dents, cracks, rust and metal fatigue. Repair or replace as necessary.

Wheel Lug Studs

REMOVAL & INSTALLATION

With Disc Brakes

▶ **See Figures 2, 3 and 4**

1. Raise and support the appropriate end of the vehicle safely using jackstands, then remove the wheel.
2. Remove the brake pads and caliper. Support the caliper aside using wire or a coat hanger. For details, please refer to Section 9 of this manual.
3. Remove the outer wheel bearing and lift off the rotor. For details on wheel bearing removal, installation and adjustment, please refer to Section 1 of this manual.
4. Properly support the rotor using press bars, then drive the stud out using an arbor press.

➡**If a press is not available, CAREFULLY drive the old stud out using a blunt drift. MAKE SURE the rotor is properly and evenly supported or it may be damaged.**

To install:

5. Clean the stud hole with a wire brush and start the new stud with a hammer and drift pin. Do not use any lubricant or thread sealer.
6. Finish installing the stud with the press.

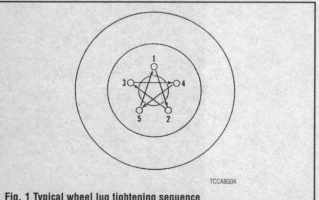

Fig. 1 Typical wheel lug tightening sequence

TCCA8G04

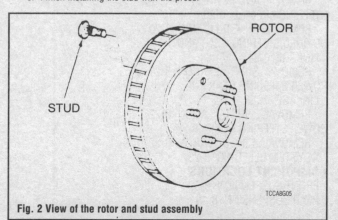

Fig. 2 View of the rotor and stud assembly

TCCA8G05

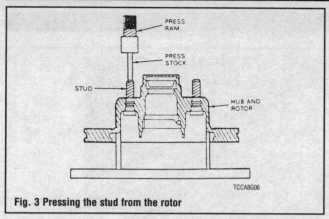

Fig. 3 Pressing the stud from the rotor

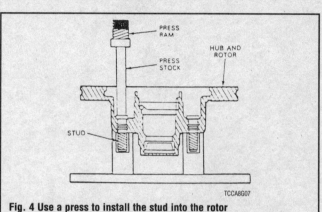

Fig. 4 Use a press to install the stud into the rotor

➡️If a press is not available, start the lug stud through the bore in the hub, then position about 4 flat washers over the stud and thread the lug nut. Hold the hub/rotor while tightening the lug nut, and the stud should be drawn into position. MAKE SURE THE STUD IS FULLY SEATED, then remove the lug nut and washers.

7. Install the rotor and adjust the wheel bearings.
8. Install the brake caliper and pads.
9. Install the wheel, then remove the jackstands and carefully lower the vehicle.
10. Tighten the lug nuts to the proper torque.

With Drum Brakes

▶ See Figures 5, 6 and 7

1. Raise the vehicle and safely support it with jackstands, then remove the wheel.
2. Remove the brake drum.
3. If necessary to provide clearance, remove the brake shoes, as outlined in Section 9 of this manual.
4. Using a large C-clamp and socket, press the stud from the axle flange.
5. Coat the serrated part of the stud with liquid soap and place it into the hole.

To install:
6. Position about 4 flat washers over the stud and thread the lug nut. Hold the flange while tightening the lug nut, and the stud should be drawn into posi-

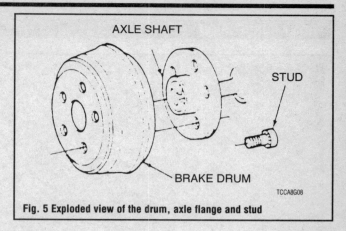

Fig. 5 Exploded view of the drum, axle flange and stud

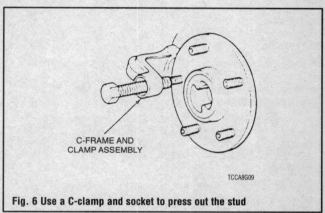

Fig. 6 Use a C-clamp and socket to press out the stud

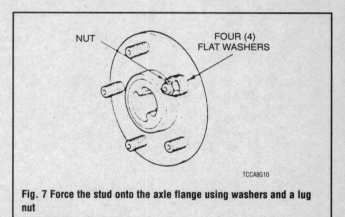

Fig. 7 Force the stud onto the axle flange using washers and a lug nut

tion. MAKE SURE THE STUD IS FULLY SEATED, then remove the lug nut and washers.
7. If applicable, install the brake shoes.
8. Install the brake drum.
9. Install the wheel, then remove the jackstands and carefully lower the vehicle.
10. Tighten the lug nuts to the proper torque.

FRONT SUSPENSION

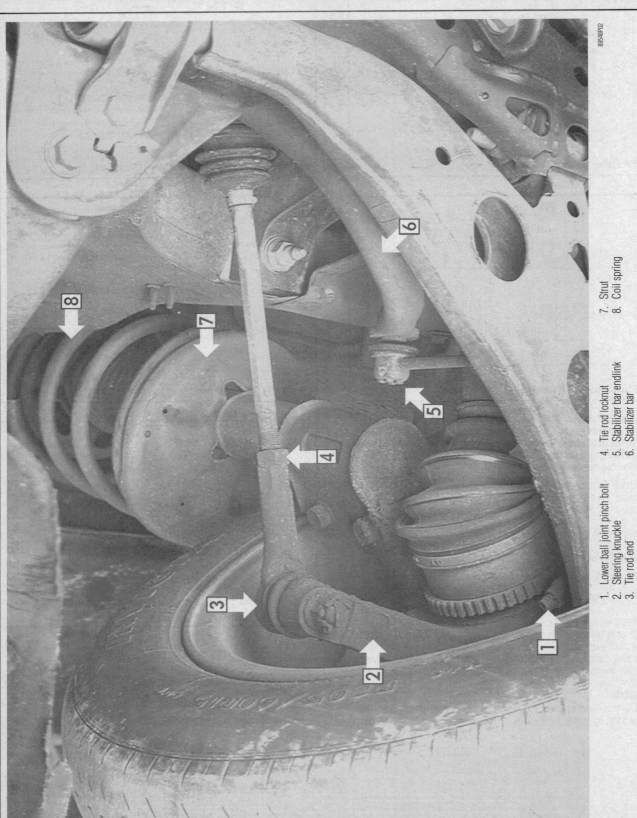

89548P02

1. Lower ball joint pinch bolt
2. Steering knuckle
3. Tie rod end
4. Tie rod locknut
5. Stabilizer bar endlink
6. Stabilizer bar
7. Strut
8. Coil spring

Fig. 8 Close-up view of the front suspension and steering components

FRONT SUSPENSION COMPONENT LOCATIONS

1. Strut assembly
2. Lower control arm
3. Control arm through bolt
4. Control arm rear bushing bracket

MacPherson Struts

REMOVAL & INSTALLATION

♦ See Figures 9 thru 17

1. Raise and safely support the vehicle. Remove the wheel and tire assembly.
2. Support the lower control arm with a jack.
3. Remove the bolts or clips attaching the brake hose and/or ABS sensor harness to the strut.
4. On vehicles equipped with the Automatic Adjusting Suspension (AAS), unplug the electrical connector and remove the actuator from the top of the strut.
5. On 1990–92 626/MX-6, when removing the left side strut, remove the ignition coil bracket.

6. Paint alignment marks on the upper strut mounting block and strut tower, and on the lower strut mount-to-steering knuckle so the strut can be reinstalled in the same position.
7. Remove the upper strut mounting block nuts and the strut-to-knuckle bolts and remove the strut assembly.

To install:

8. Install the strut into the strut tower, aligning the paint marks made during removal. Install the mounting nuts and tighten to specifications.
9. Install the strut-to-knuckle bolts and tighten to specifications.
10. If equipped with AAS, install the actuator and engage the electrical connector.
11. Install the clips or bolts attaching the brake hose and/or ABS sensor harness.
12. Install the wheel and tire assembly and lower the vehicle. Check the front end alignment.

Fig. 9 To remove the front strut, first unfasten the brake hose and/or ABS sensor wires from the strut housing

Fig. 10 Paint matchmarks on the upper strut mount-to-tower assembly . . .

Fig. 11 . . . and on the lower strut-to-steering knuckle mounting point. This will help preserve your alignment settings

Fig. 12 Remove the upper strut mounting nuts . . .

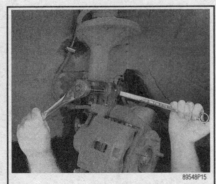

Fig. 13 . . . then loosen the lower strut-to-knuckle through-bolts . . .

Fig. 14 . . . and remove them. If the bolts seem stuck, try rocking the assembly slightly while pulling outward on the bolt

Fig. 15 Separate the steering knuckle from the strut. Support the steering knuckle to avoid stressing the brake hose (arrow)

Fig. 16 Remove the strut assembly from the vehicle

Fig. 17 If necessary, replace the upper mount-to-strut tower gasket

OVERHAUL

♦ **See Figures 18, 19 and 20**

1. Remove the strut from the vehicle.
2. If the vehicle is not equipped with AAS, remove the cap from the top of the strut.
3. Install the strut securely in a vise with either aluminum or copper plates to protect the strut.
4. Loosen the piston rod upper nut several turns but DO NOT REMOVE IT.

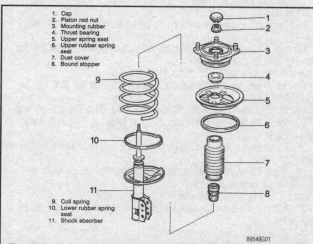

1. Cap
2. Piston rod nut
3. Mounting rubber
4. Thrust bearing
5. Upper spring seat
6. Upper rubber spring seat
7. Dust cover
8. Bound stopper
9. Coil spring
10. Lower rubber spring seat
11. Shock absorber

89548G01

Fig. 18 Exploded view of the front strut assembly. Rear strut is similar

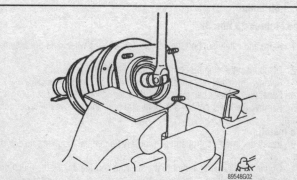

89548G02

Fig. 19 Secure the upper strut mount in a vise and loosen the piston rod nut several turns but DO NOT REMOVE IT!

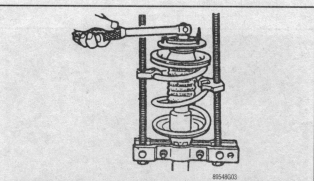

89548G03

Fig. 20 Use a coil spring compressor and relieve the spring tension from the upper mount, then remove the piston rod nut

5. Install the lower end of the strut in the vise and install a coil spring compressor. Compress the coil spring and remove the upper nut.

✳✳ CAUTION

Failure to fully compress the spring and hold it securely can be extremely dangerous.

6. Slowly release the coil spring tension.
7. Remove the suspension support, dust seal, spring seat, spring insulators, coil spring and bumper.
8. While pushing on the piston rod, make sure that the pull stroke is even and that there is no unusual noise or resistance. Also inspect for any oil leakage around the piston rod.
9. Push the piston rod in and then release it. Make sure that the return rate is constant.
10. If the shock absorber does not operate as described, replace it.

To assemble:

11. Install the strut assembly into a vise.
12. Install the bound stopper and dust boot onto the piston rod.
13. Install the coil spring and compress the coil spring with the spring compressor.
14. Install the rubber seat, the spring upper seat, the bearing and the mounting block. Make sure that the spring upper seat notched portion is facing inward and tighten the piston rod upper nut.
15. Remove the spring compressor from the strut. Secure the upper mounting block in the vise. Tighten the nut to specification.
16. Make sure that the spring is well seated in the upper seats.
17. Install the strut to the vehicle.

Lower Ball Joints

INSPECTION

1. Disconnect the lower ball joint from the knuckle or spindle.
2. Shake and rotate the ball joint stud several times.
3. Attach a suitable pull scale to the ball joint stud and measure the preload.
4. While the ball stud is rotating, the pull scale reading should be as follows:
   - 323, Protege, MX-3, 1990–92 626/MX-6: 4.4–7.7 lbs.
   - 1993–98 626/MX-6/Probe: 2.2–11.0 lbs.
   - Millenia: 0.7–6.6 lbs.
5. If the pull scale reading is not as specified, replace the ball joint or lower control arm, as required.

REMOVAL & INSTALLATION

Except MX-3, 323, Protege and Millenia

The lower ball joint is an integral part of the lower control and cannot be replaced separately. If the lower ball joint is defective, the entire lower control arm must be replaced.

MX-3, 323, Protege and Millenia

♦ **See Figure 21**

1. Raise and safely support the vehicle. Remove the wheel and tire assembly.
2. Remove the ball joint stud pinch bolt and nut from the steering knuckle. Pry the lower control arm down from the knuckle, and separate the ball joint from the knuckle.
3. Remove the bolt and nut and remove the ball joint from the lower control arm.
4. Installation is the reverse of the removal procedure. Tighten the ball joint-to-lower control arm bolt and nut to 86 ft. lbs. (117 Nm). Tighten the ball joint pinch bolt and nut to 43 ft. lbs. (59 Nm). Check the front wheel alignment.

1. Stabilizer nut
2. Retainer, bushing and spacer
3. Stabilizer bolt
4. Bolt, washer
5. Bolt
6. Bolt, nut
7. Nut
8. Washer
9. Lower control arm bushing (rear)
10. Nut
11. Bolt
12. Lower arm ball joint
13. Ball joint dust boot
14. Lower arm bushing (front)
15. Lower arm

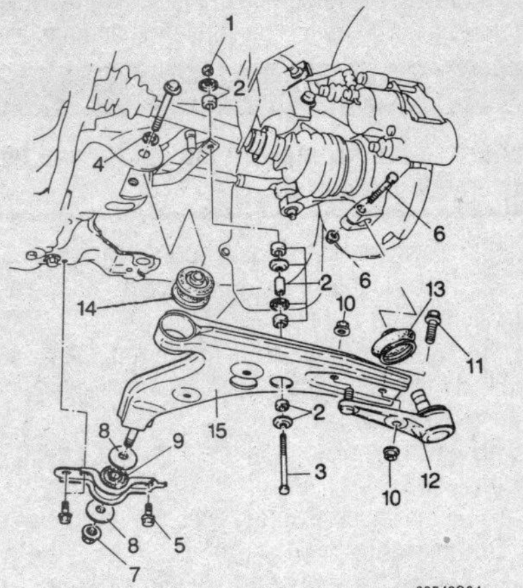

89548G04

Fig. 21 Exploded view of a common lower control arm with replaceable ball joint

Lower Control Arms

REMOVAL & INSTALLATION

Millenia

▶ See Figure 22

1. Raise and safely support the vehicle.
2. Remove the transverse member.
3. Disconnect the power steering return hose and pressure pipe.
4. Remove the intermediate steering shaft bolt.
5. Support the engine from the top and remove the engine mount member.
6. Remove the bolts for engine mount No. 1.
7. Remove the lower strut mounting bolt.
8. Disconnect the tie-rod end from the steering knuckle.

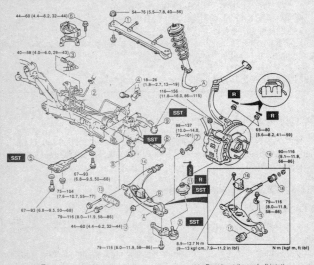

1. Transverse member
2. Return hose (power steering)
3. Pressure pipe (power steering)
4. Bolt (intermediate shaft)
5. Engine mount member
6. Bolts (No.1 engine mount)
7. Bolts (shock absorber and spring)
8. Tie rod end ball joint
9. Upper lateral link ball joint
10. Lower ball joint
11. Dust boot (lower ball joint)
12. Nut (stabilizer control link)
13. Gusset
14. Lower arm
15. Bracket (stabilizer)
16. Dynamic damper
17. Lower arm bushing (front)
18. Lower arm bushing (rear)

89548G05

Fig. 22 Exploded view of the Millenia front suspension assembly

9. Remove the upper lateral link ball joint.
10. Remove the lower ball joint.
11. Remove the stabilizer control link nut.
12. Remove the gusset.
13. Support the crossmember using a jack and remove the crossmember mounting nuts. Lower the crossmember to gain clearance and remove the lower arm assembly.

To install:

14. Replace the lower arm assembly to the vehicle and install the crossmember mounting bolts.
15. Install the gusset, torque the gusset mount bolts to 58–86 ft. lbs. (79–116 Nm).
16. Connect the stabilizer control link, torque the nut to 32–44 ft. lbs. (44–60 Nm).
17. Install the lower ball joint, torque the mounting bolts to 58–86 ft. lbs. (79–116 Nm). Torque the retaining
nut at the knuckle to 86–115 ft. lbs. (116–156 Nm).
18. Install the upper lateral link nut and bolt, torque to 58–86 ft. lbs. (79–116 Nm).
19. Connect the tie-rod end, torque the nut to 41–59 ft. lbs. (55–80 Nm).
20. Install the strut lower mounting bolt and torque to 73–101 ft. lbs. (98–137 Nm).
21. Install the No. 1 engine mount bolts and torque to 32–44 ft. lbs. (44–60 Nm).
22. Install the engine mount member, torque the bolts to 50–68 ft. lbs. (67–93 Nm) and the nuts to 55–77.3
ft. lbs. (75–104 Nm). Remove the engine support tool.
23. Install the intermediate steering shaft bolt, torque to 14–19 ft. lbs. (18–26 Nm).
24. Connect the power steering pressure pipe and return hose.
25. Install the transverse member.
26. Lower the vehicle. Check the power steering fluid and fill to proper level, bleed if necessary. Check the front end alignment.

Except Millenia

▶ See Figures 23 thru 32

1. Raise and safely support the vehicle. Remove the wheel and tire assembly.
2. Disconnect the stabilizer bar link from the lower control arm.
3. Remove the lower ball joint pinch bolt from the steering knuckle.
4. Seperate the lower ball joint from the steering knuckle.
5. Remove the lower control arm bolts and nuts and remove the lower control arm.

To install:

6. Install the lower control arm and loosely tighten the mounting nuts and bolts.
7. Connect the lower ball joint to the steering knuckle. Install the pinch bolt and tighten to specifications.
8. Connect the stabilizer link to the lower control arm.
9. Install the wheel and tire assembly and lower the vehicle. With the vehicle at normal ride height, tighten the lower control arm mounting bolts.
10. Check the front wheel alignment.

89548P22

Fig. 23 To remove the control arm, first, raise and support the vehicle then remove the wheel. Loosen the stabilizer bar end link nut . . .

Fig. 24 . . . and detach the end link from the control arm

Fig. 25 Loosen the lower ball joint pinch bolt . . .

Fig. 26 . . . remove the bolt and nut from the steering knuckle . . .

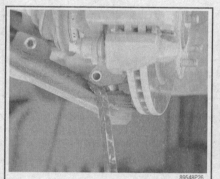

Fig. 27 . . . and disengage the lower ball joint from the steering knuckle

Fig. 28 Loosen the rear control arm bushing bracket retaining bolts . . .

Fig. 29 . . . and remove them. Note that the bolts are of different length so mark them to ensure proper installation

Fig. 30 Loosen the front control arm through-bolt . . .

Fig. 31 . . . then withdraw the bolt. Some gentle tapping with a hammer and drift pin may be necessary

Fig. 32 Remove the control arm from the vehicle

CONTROL ARM BUSHING REPLACEMENT

♦ See Figures 33 and 34

1. For the front bushing, cut away the projecting rubber portion of the bushing with a knife.

2. Install the control arm in a vise and install Mazda bushing removal tool 49 G034 2A0 or equivalent to the control arm. Remove the old bushing by tightening the nut on the tool.

3. To install a new bushing, apply soapy water to the new bushing and use Mazda tool 49 G034 2A0 or equivalent and pull the new bushing into place.

4. For the rear bushing, remove the retaining nut on the control arm and slide the bushing, complete with bracket, from the control arm.

5. Installation is the reverse of the removal procedure.

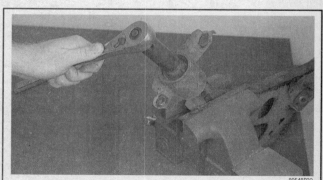

Fig. 33 Remove the rear control arm bushing by loosening the rear bushing retaining nut . . .

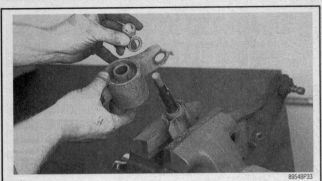

Fig. 34 . . . then remove the nut, lockwasher and bushing assembly from the control arm

Stabilizer Bar

REMOVAL & INSTALLATION

1990–92 626/MX-6 and 1990–94 323, Protege

▶ See Figure 35

1. Raise and support the vehicle safely. Remove the front wheels.
2. Remove the 2 stabilizer nuts and remove the upper bushing.
3. Remove the stabilizer bolt, bushing and retainer.
4. Remove the bushing, retainer and spacer.
5. Remove the stabilizer center bushings and bracket and remove the stabilizer bar from the vehicle. Examine the insulators (bushings) carefully for any sign of wear and replace them if necessary.

➡ **Check the bushings inside the brackets for wear or deformation. A worn bushing can cause a distinct noise as the bar twists during cornering operation.**

To install:

6. Install stabilizer bar bushings in the correct position.
7. Temporarily install stabilizer bar brackets. Install the stabilizer bar center bracket bolts and tighten to 27–40 ft. lbs. (38–54 Nm).

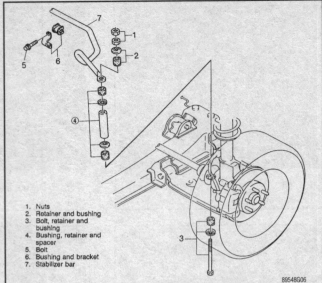

1. Nuts
2. Retainer and bushing
3. Bolt, retainer and bushing
4. Bushing, retainer and spacer
5. Bolt
6. Bushing and bracket
7. Stabilizer bar

Fig. 35 Exploded view of the front stabilizer bar for the 1990–92 626/MX-6 and 1990–94 323, Protege

8. Install the bushing retainers and spacers. Install the bolt retainer and bushing.
9. Install the upper link nuts. Tighten the link nuts so that there is 0.71–0.87 inches (18.1–22.1mm) of thread exposed.
10. Torque the top link nut to 12–17 ft. lbs. (16–23 Nm).
11. Install front wheels and lower the vehicle.
12. Check front wheel alignment.

Except 1990–92 626/MX-6 and 1990–94 323, Protege

▶ See Figure 36

1. Raise and safely support the vehicle. Remove the front tire/wheels.
2. Remove the engine undercover.
3. Install an engine support device, such as Mazda tool number 49 G017 5A0 or equivalent, to the vehicle.

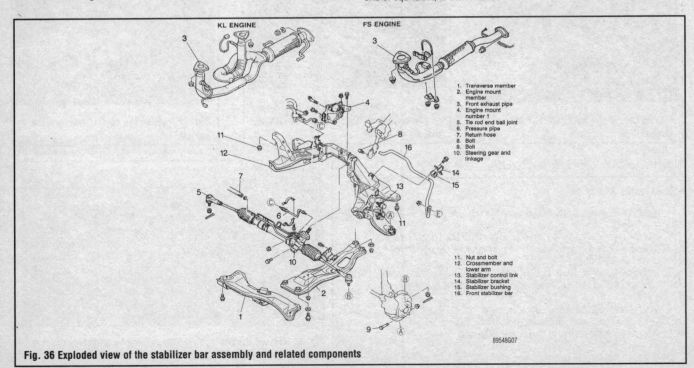

1. Transverse member
2. Engine mount member
3. Front exhaust pipe
4. Engine mount number 1
5. Tie rod end ball joint
6. Pressure pipe
7. Return hose
8. Bolt
9. Bolt
10. Steering gear and linkage

11. Nut and bolt
12. Crossmember and lower arm
13. Stabilizer control link
14. Stabilizer bracket
15. Stabilizer bushing
16. Front stabilizer bar

Fig. 36 Exploded view of the stabilizer bar assembly and related components

4. Remove the tie rod end /steering knuckle assembly.

5. Remove the transverse member from under the engine.

6. Remove the engine mount member.

7. Disconnect the oxygen sensor connectors and remove the front exhaust pipe from the manifold.

8. Remove the stabilizer nuts and insulator pad.

9. Disconnect the steering lines and plug. Remove the steering gear and linkage assembly.

10. Remove the lower arm and front crossmember assembly bolts and remove the assembly from the vehicle.

11. Remove the remaining stabilizer bar bolts and remove the stabilizer bar.

To install:

12. Install the stabilizer bar to the vehicle and install the mounting bolts. If the mounting bushings were removed, make sure that they are replaced to the original positions and that the bushings are aligned with the marks on the bar. Tighten the stabilizer bar bolts to 32–43 ft. lbs. (43–59 Nm).

13. Install the lower arm and front crossmember assembly to the vehicle. Tighten the mounting bolts to 69–93 ft. lbs. (93–127 Nm).

14. Install the steering gear and linkage. Tighten the mounting nuts to 27–38 ft. lbs. (37–52 Nm) and connect the lines to the steering gear and linkage.

15. Install the insulator plate and install the stabilizer nuts. Tighten the stabilizer nuts to 32–45 ft. lbs. (43–61 Nm).

16. Replace the exhaust pipe gaskets and tighten the nuts to 27–38 ft. lbs. (37–52 Nm).

17. Install the engine mount member.

18. Install the transverse member.

19. Connect the tie rod end to the steering knuckle. Replace the cotter pin.

20. Remove the engine support device and install the under engine cover.

21. Install the wheels and lower the vehicle.

Steering Knuckle

REMOVAL & INSTALLATION

Millenia

♦ **See Figure 22**

1. Raise and safely support the vehicle.

2. Lock the hub by having a helper apply the brakes firmly. Remove the locknut.

3. Remove the brake caliper assembly and disc plate.

4. Disconnect the ABS wheel speed sensor cable mounting bolts.

5. Disconnect the tie-rod end, upper leading link and upper lateral link.

6. Remove the lower arm ball joint.

7. Remove the front wheel hub and steering knuckle as an assembly.

To install:

8. Replace the knuckle/hub assembly to the vehicle and install the lower arm ball joint. Torque the ball joint mounting bolts to 58–86 ft. lbs. (79–116 Nm). Torque the ball joint nut to 86–115 ft. lbs. (116–156 Nm).

9. Connect the upper lateral link ball joint and torque the nut to 41–59 ft. lbs. (55–80 Nm).

10. Connect the upper leading link ball joint and torque the nut to 28–38 ft. lbs. (38–51 Nm).

11. Connect the tie-rod end and torque the nut to 41–59 ft. lbs. (55–80 Nm).

12. Install the ABS wheel speed sensor and torque the bolts to 14–18 ft. lbs. (19–25 Nm).

13. Install the disc plate and caliper assembly.

14. Install a NEW locknut and torque to 174–235 ft. lbs. (236–318 Nm).

Except Millenia

♦ **See Figure 37**

1. Raise and safely support the vehicle. Remove the front wheel and tire assemblies.

2. Uncrimp the tab on the center locknut and remove the locknut. Discard the old locknut.

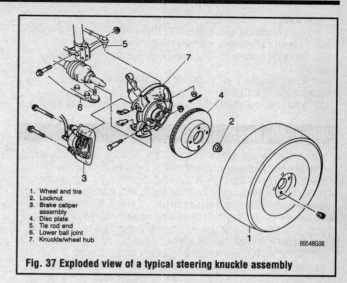

1. Wheel and tire
2. Locknut
3. Brake caliper assembly
4. Disc plate
5. Tie rod end
6. Lower ball joint
7. Knuckle/wheel hub

89548G08

Fig. 37 Exploded view of a typical steering knuckle assembly

3. Remove the caliper assembly from the knuckle. Do not disconnect the brake lines. Support the caliper with a piece of wire. Do not allow the caliper to hang by the hose at any time. Remove the brake disc.

4. Remove the tie rod end from the steering knuckle.

5. Remove the stabilizer upper nuts and remove the stabilizer link bolt.

6. Remove the lower ball joint pinch bolt and nut. Separate the ball joint from the knuckle assembly.

7. Remove the ABS speed sensor if so equipped.

8. Using a plastic mallet, tap the driveshaft free of the knuckle assembly. Remove the knuckle assembly.

To install:

9. Install the bearing/hub and knuckle assembly in place. Loosely tighten the knuckle to shock absorber bolt.

10. Install the lower arm ball joint to the knuckle and tighten the pinch bolt.

11. Install the driveshaft to the knuckle assembly.

12. Install the stabilizer control link.

13. If equipped with ABS, install the wheel speed sensor and tighten the bolts to 12–17 ft. lbs. (16–23Nm).

14. Connect the tie rod ends to the knuckle. Replace the cotter pins.

15. Install a new wheel hub lock nut and tighten the locknut to 174–235 ft. lbs. (235–319 Nm).

16. Check the end play of the wheel bearing by installing a dial indicator against the wheel hub and try to move the hub back and forth. There should be no more than 0.0079 inch (0.2mm) of free play present.

17. Stake the locknut into place by bending it into the groove.

18. Install the brake caliper(s).

19. Install the front wheels and lower the vehicle.

20. With the vehicle lowered check all of the bolts and re-torque as necessary.

21. Inspect the front end alignment and adjust as necessary.

Front Hub and Bearing

REMOVAL & INSTALLATION

1. Remove the steering knuckle from the vehicle.

2. Clamp the knuckle in a vise with protected jaws.

3. Remove the inner oil seal from the knuckle.

4. Use Mazda hub puller tools 49 G033 102, 49 G033 104 and 49 G033 105 or equivalent, and remove the front wheel hub from the knuckle assembly.

5. Remove the bearing inner race from the front wheel hub.

6. Remove the retaining ring from within the knuckle and using the hub puller tools, press the front wheel bearing from the knuckle.

7. Remove the brake dust shield.

8. Clean and inspect all parts but do not wash or clean the wheel bearing. The bearing must be replaced.

To install:

9. Using Mazda press tools 49 G033 107 and 49 H026 103 or equivalent, install a new dust shield cover assembly to the knuckle.

10. Using the press tools, press a new wheel bearing into the knuckle assembly.

11. Install the wheel bearing retaining ring, and install a new oil seal using installation tool 49 V001 795.

12. Install the front wheel hub by using the Mazda press tools or equivalent.

Wheel Alignment

If the tires are worn unevenly, if the vehicle is not stable on the highway or if the handling seems uneven in spirited driving, the wheel alignment should be checked. If an alignment problem is suspected, first check for improper tire inflation and other possible causes. These can be worn suspension or steering components, accident damage or even unmatched tires. If any worn or damaged components are found, they must be replaced before the wheels can be properly aligned. Wheel alignment requires very expensive equipment and involves minute adjustments which must be accurate; it should only be performed by a trained technician. Take your vehicle to a properly equipped shop.

Following is a description of the alignment angles which are adjustable on most vehicles and how they affect vehicle handling. Although these angles can apply to both the front and rear wheels, usually only the front suspension is adjustable.

CASTER

▶ **See Figure 38**

Looking at a vehicle from the side, caster angle describes the steering axis rather than a wheel angle. The steering knuckle is attached to a control arm or strut at the top and a control arm at the bottom. The wheel pivots around the line between these points to steer the vehicle. When the upper point is tilted back, this is described as positive caster. Having a positive caster tends to make the wheels self-centering, increasing directional stability. Excessive positive caster makes the wheels hard to steer, while an uneven caster will cause a pull to one side. Overloading the vehicle or sagging rear springs will affect caster, as will raising the rear of the vehicle. If the rear of the vehicle is lower than normal, the caster becomes more positive.

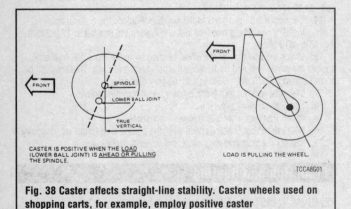

Fig. 38 Caster affects straight-line stability. Caster wheels used on shopping carts, for example, employ positive caster

CAMBER

▶ **See Figure 39**

Looking from the front of the vehicle, camber is the inward or outward tilt of the top of wheels. When the tops of the wheels are tilted in, this is negative camber; if they are tilted out, it is positive. In a turn, a slight amount of negative

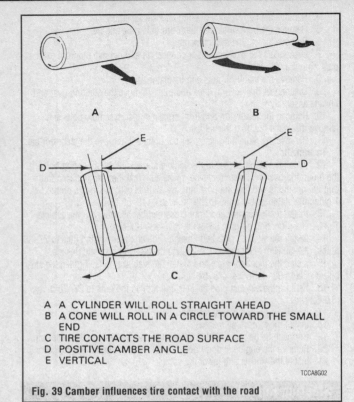

A A CYLINDER WILL ROLL STRAIGHT AHEAD
B A CONE WILL ROLL IN A CIRCLE TOWARD THE SMALL END
C TIRE CONTACTS THE ROAD SURFACE
D POSITIVE CAMBER ANGLE
E VERTICAL

Fig. 39 Camber influences tire contact with the road

camber helps maximize contact of the tire with the road. However, too much negative camber compromises straight-line stability, increases bump steer and torque steer.

TOE

▶ **See Figure 40**

Looking down at the wheels from above the vehicle, toe angle is the distance between the front of the wheels, relative to the distance between the back of the wheels. If the wheels are closer at the front, they are said to be toed-in or to have negative toe. A small amount of negative toe enhances directional stability and provides a smoother ride on the highway.

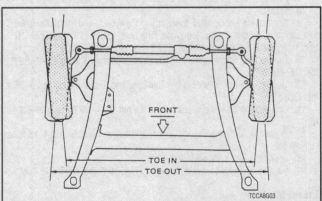

Fig. 40 With toe-in, the distance between the wheels is closer at the front than at the rear

REAR SUSPENSION

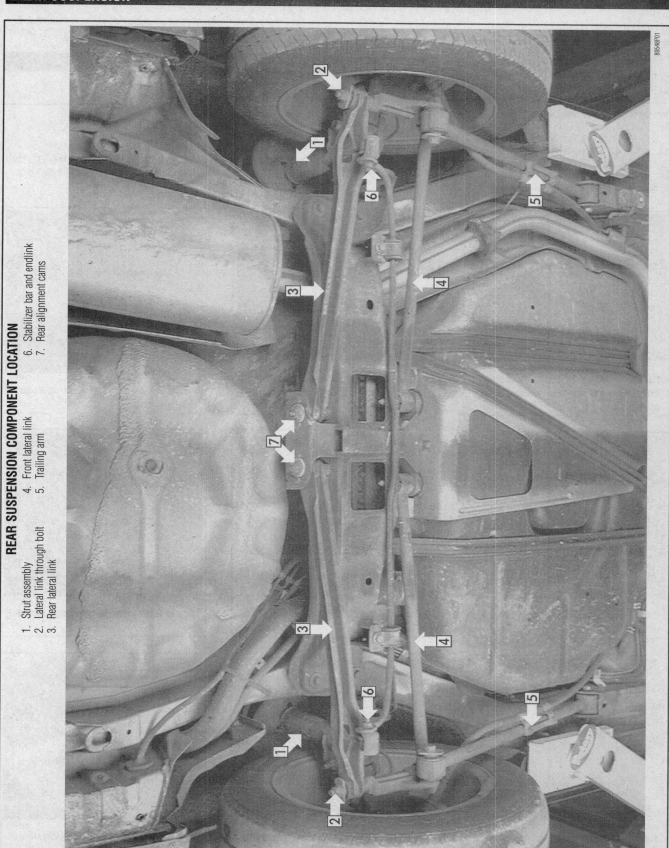

REAR SUSPENSION COMPONENT LOCATION

1. Strut assembly
2. Lateral link through bolt
3. Rear lateral link
4. Front lateral link
5. Trailing arm
6. Stabilizer bar and endlink
7. Rear alignment cams

MacPherson Strut

REMOVAL & INSTALLATION

▶ **See Figures 41 thru 50**

1. As required, remove the side trim panels from the inside of the trunk or the rear seat and trim.

2. If equipped with Automatic Adjusting Suspension (AAS) system, disconnect the wiring and remove the cap. Loosen and remove the top mounting nuts from the strut mounting block assembly.

3. Raise and safely support the vehicle and remove the rear wheels. The suspension will drop when the weight lifts off the wheels.

4. Unclip the brake line or wiring retainers as required and unbolt the bottom strut mount. Remove the strut.

5. Installation is the reverse of removal.

OVERHAUL

Overhaul procedures for the rear strut assembly are identical to the front strut overhaul procedures. Refer to front suspension strut overhaul found in this section.

Rear Control Arms and Links

REMOVAL & INSTALLATION

323/Protege, MX-3 and 1990–92 MX6, 626

1. Raise and safely support the vehicle and remove the wheels.

2. Before disconnecting the stabilizer bar link, on all except MX-3, measure the length of the threads protruding above the locknut. Remove the nuts and through bolt to disconnect the stabilizer bar.

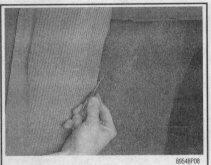

Fig. 41 To remove the rear strut assembly, first remove any trim fasteners inside the trunk . . .

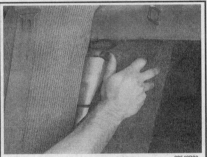

Fig. 42 . . . and move the trim aside to gain access to the upper strut mount retaining nuts

Fig. 43 Loosen and remove the upper strut mounting nuts

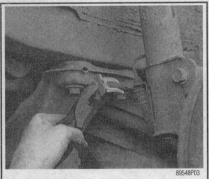

Fig. 44 Remove the brake line-to-strut retaining clip . . .

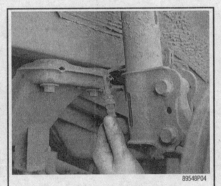

Fig. 45 . . . and detach the brake line from the strut

Fig. 46 Matchmark the lower strut mounting . . .

Fig. 47 . . . then loosen the lower mounting through-bolts . . .

Fig. 48 . . . and remove them. Make sure to support the strut assembly

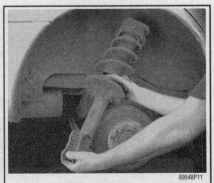

Fig. 49 Remove the strut assembly from the vehicle

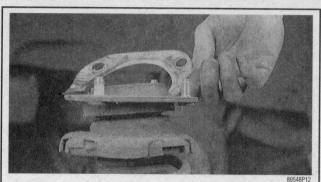

Fig. 50 If necessary, replace the upper strut mount gasket when installing

3. Remove the nuts and bolts as required and remove the control arms.

4. Installation is the reverse of removal. Make sure to properly adjust the stabilizer bar before tightening the locknuts and check rear wheel alignment.

Millenia and 1993–98 626/MX-6/Probe

♦ See Figures 51 thru 59

1. Raise and safely support the vehicle. Remove the wheel and tire assemblies.

2. Remove the access cap from the underside of the rear crossmember.

3. Remove the bolts and nuts and remove the lateral links and trailing link. If removing the rear lateral link, paint an alignment mark on the cam plate and crossmember for assembly reference.

4. Installation is the reverse of the removal procedure.

5. Do not final tighten the bolts until the vehicle is on the ground and at normal ride height.

Fig. 51 To remove the trailing arm, first unbolt any brackets (such as for brake cables) which are attached to the arm . . .

Fig. 52 . . . and position them out of the way

Fig. 53 Remove the trailing arm-to-wheel mount attaching bolt and disengage the arm

Fig. 54 Remove the trailing arm-to-chassis through-bolt . . .

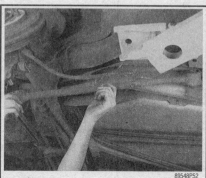

Fig. 55 . . . and pull the trailing arm backwards and remove it from the vehicle

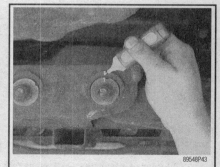

Fig. 56 To remove a lateral link, first matchmark any alignment cams to ensure proper installation . . .

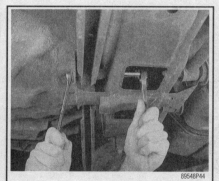

Fig. 57 . . . then loosen the link-to-center chassis attaching bolt . . .

Fig. 58 . . . and remove the bolt, nut and alignment cam

Fig. 59 Remove the lateral link-to-wheel mount through-bolt, then detach the link and remove it from the vehicle

Rear Stabilizer Bar

REMOVAL & INSTALLATION

323/Protege

♦ See Figure 60

1. Raise and safely support the rear of the vehicle.
2. Remove the rear wheels from the vehicle.
3. Remove the upper stabilizer nut, bushing, retainer and spacer.
4. Remove the stabilizer bolt and the remaining bushings, retainers and spacers.
5. Remove the stabilizer bracket bolts and remove the stabilizer bar.
6. Installation is the reverse of the removal procedure. Align the stabilizer bushing with the marks painted on the bar.

MX-3

♦ See Figure 60

1. Raise and safely support the rear of the vehicle.
2. Remove the rear wheels from the vehicle.
3. Remove the stabilizer bar to link mounting nut and protectors.
4. Remove the stabilizer bracket and remove the stabilizer bar. Remove the stabilizer bushings and inspect the bushing for deterioration or wear. Replace if necessary.
5. Installation is the reverse of the removal procedure.

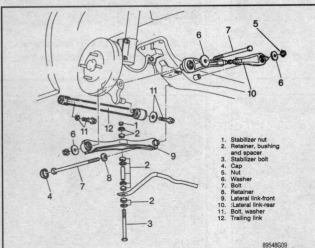

1. Stabilizer nut
2. Retainer, bushing and spacer
3. Stabilizer bolt
4. Cap
5. Nut
6. Washer
7. Bolt
8. Retainer
9. Lateral link-front
10. Lateral link-rear
11. Bolt, washer
12. Trailing link

Fig. 60 Exploded view of the 323/Protege rear stabilizer bar assembly and related components. MX-3 is similar

1990–92 626/MX-6

1. Raise and safely support the rear of the vehicle.
2. Remove the rear wheels from the vehicle.
3. Remove the upper stabilizer nut, bushing, retainer and spacer.
4. Remove the stabilizer bolt and the remaining bushings, retainers and spacers.
5. Remove the stabilizer bracket bolts and remove the stabilizer bar.
6. Installation is the reverse of the removal procedure. Align the stabilizer bushing with the marks painted on the bar.
7. Tighten the stabilizer bracket bolts to 27–40 ft. lbs. (36–54 Nm). Tighten the top stabilizer nut so that there is approximately 0.41 inch (10.4mm) of thread exposed at the end of the bolt.

Millenia and 1993–98 626/MX-6

♦ See Figures 61 and 62

1. Raise and safely support the rear of the vehicle.
2. Remove the rear wheels from the vehicle.

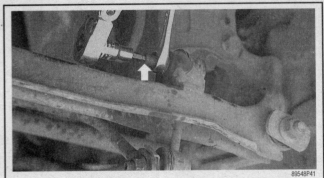

Fig. 61 When removing the rear stabilizer end links, you may need to hold the shaft with an Allen wrench (arrow). Loosen the nut . . .

Fig. 62 . . . then remove it and detach the stabilizer end link from the lateral link

3. Remove the stabilizer bar to link mounting nut and protectors.
4. Remove the stabilizer bracket and remove the stabilizer bar. Remove the stabilizer bushings and inspect the bushing for deterioration or wear. Replace if necessary.
5. Installation is the reverse of the removal procedure.

Rear Wheel Bearings

REMOVAL & INSTALLATION

♦ See Figures 63 and 64

1. Loosen the lug nuts on the rear wheels.
2. Block the front wheels, then raise and safely support the rear of the vehicle securely on jackstands.
3. Remove the rear wheels.

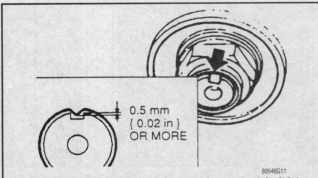

0.5 mm
(0.02 in)
OR MORE

Fig. 63 When installing the new hub nut, make sure to stake it into the notch on the spindle

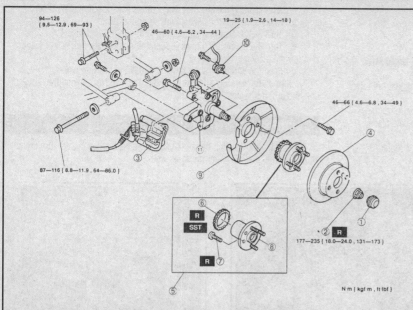

94—126
{ 9.5—12.9 , 69—93 }

19—25 { 1.9—2.6 , 14—18 }

46—60 { 4.6—6.2 , 34—44 }

46—66 { 4.6—6.8 , 34—49 }

87—116 { 8.8—11.9 , 64—86.0 }

177—235 { 18.0—24.0 , 131—173 }

N·m { kgf·m , ft·lbf }

1. Hub cap
2. Locknut
3. Brake caliper assembly
4. Disc plate
5. Wheel hub assembly
   Inspect for damage
   Inspect bearing for damage and rough
   rotation
6. ABS sensor rotor
7. Hub bolt
8. Wheel hub
9. Dust cover
   Inspect for damage and cracks
10. ABS wheel-speed sensor
11. Hub spindle
    Inspect for damage and cracks

89548G10

Fig. 64 Exploded view of the rear wheel hub and bearing assembly (disc brake model shown, drum is similar)

4. If equipped with drum brakes, remove the drum.
5. If equipped with disc brakes, remove the caliper and the rotor assembly from the hub.
6. Remove the hub dust cover.
7. Raise the staked portion of the hub retaining nut with a hammer and chisel. Remove and discard the nut.

8. Pull the hub and bearing assembly from the spindle.
9. The wheel bearings are not serviceable. If the bearings are bad, a new hub/bearing assembly must be installed.
10. Installation is the reverse of the removal procedure. If necessary, adjust the brake assembly.

STEERING

Steering Wheel

✳✳ CAUTION

Some models covered by this manual may be equipped with a Supplemental Restraint System (SRS), which uses an air bag. Whenever working near any of the SRS components, such as the impact sensors, the air bag module, steering column and instrument panel, disable the SRS, as described in Section 6.

REMOVAL & INSTALLATION

Without Air Bag

▶ See Figure 65

1. Disconnect the negative battery cable. Remove the horn pad button fasteners. If equipped with a 4 spoke steering wheel, pull the center cap toward the wheel top.
2. Detach the wire harness connectors for the horn and/or cruise control switches from the horn pad. Remove the pad.
3. Make matchmarks on the steering wheel and steering shaft. Never strike the steering shaft with a hammer, as damage to the column may result.
4. Remove the wheel using a suitable puller.
5. Installation is the reverse of removal. Torque the steering wheel nut to 36 ft. lbs. (49 Nm).

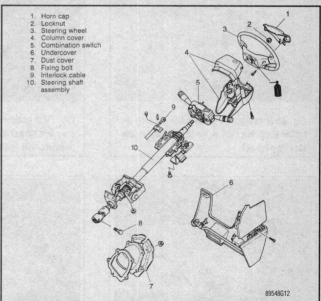

1. Horn cap
2. Locknut
3. Steering wheel
4. Column cover
5. Combination switch
6. Undercover
7. Dust cover
8. Fixing bolt
9. Interlock cable
10. Steering shaft
    assembly

89548G12

Fig. 65 Exploded view of a typical, non-air bag equipped steering column assembly

With Air Bag

▶ **See Figures 66 thru 76**

1. Disarm the air bag.

2. Turn the steering wheel to position the wheels in a straight-ahead position.

3. At the back of the steering wheel hub, remove the nuts/bolts that hold the air bag assembly and tilt the top of the air bag outward.

4. Detach the wire harness connectors for the air bag, horn and/or cruise control switches. Remove the air bag module and place the it in a safe place, pad side up.

5. Matchmark the wheel to the shaft and remove the nut. Use a puller to remove the wheel.

6. When installing the steering wheel, the clockspring must be reset.

   a. Make sure the front wheels are straight-ahead.

   b. Turn the clockspring all the way to the right (clockwise).

   c. Turn the clockspring back (counterclockwise) about 2¾ turns and align the marks.

   d. Feed the wiring through the and install the steering wheel.

7. Torque the steering wheel nut to 36 ft. lbs. (49 Nm). Install the air bag unit and arm the system.

Combination Switch

The combination switch houses the controls for the headlights, turn signals and, on some models, wiper motor as well.

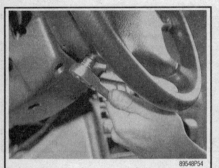

Fig. 66 To remove the steering wheel, first disarm the air bag, then loosen the air bag module-to-steering wheel fasteners . . .

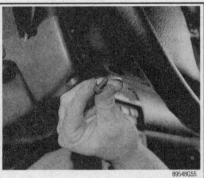

Fig. 67 . . . and remove them from the steering wheel

Fig. 68 Tilt the top of the air bag module outwards and detach the module, horn and/or cruise control wire harness connections

Fig. 69 If equipped, unhook the air bag tether from the cast in hook (arrow) on the steering wheel

Fig. 70 If necessary, detach any wire-to-steering wheel clips. Ensure that no components will inhibit wheel removal

Fig. 71 Loosen the steering wheel retaining nut . . .

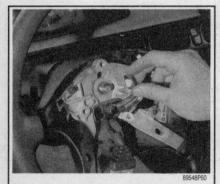

Fig. 72 . . . then remove the nut from the shaft

Fig. 73 Matchmark the steering wheel to the shaft. This will ensure proper installation

Fig. 74 Assemble a puller to the steering wheel and tighten the puller's center bolt to loosen the wheel from the steering shaft

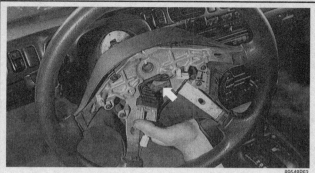

Fig. 75 Remove the puller and separate the wheel from the steering shaft. Guide the wire through the access hole in the wheel (arrow)

Fig. 76 Before installing the wheel, make sure to reset the clock-spring, following the directions given, and align the marks (arrow)

REMOVAL & INSTALLATION

▶ See Figure 77

❊❊ CAUTION

Some models covered by this manual may be equipped with a Supplemental Restraint System (SRS), which uses an air bag. Whenever working near any of the SRS components, such as the impact sensors, the air bag module, steering column and instrument panel, disable the SRS, as described in Section 6. Always carry an air bag assembly, with the bag and trim cover, away from your body. Store the assembly facing upward; never place the assembly face down on any surface.

1990–94 323, MX3 and 1990–97 Protege

1. Disconnect the negative battery cable.
2. Remove the horn cap.
3. Remove the steering wheel.
4. Remove the 2 column cover screws and remove the cover.
5. Disconnect the electrical connections from the combination switch.
6. Remove the combination switch as an assembly.
7. Installation is the reverse of the removal procedure. Check the switch operation.

1995 MX3

1. Remove the driver-side side and lower panels.
2. Disconnect the negative battery cable, and disarm the air bag.
3. Remove the steering wheel.
4. Remove the 2 column cover screws and remove the cover.
5. Disconnect the electrical connections from the combination switch.
6. Remove the combination switch as an assembly.

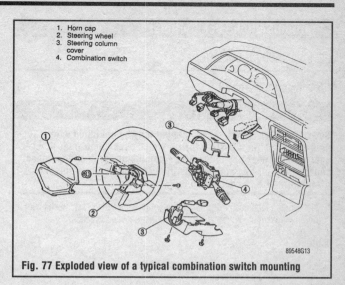

1. Horn cap
2. Steering wheel
3. Steering column cover
4. Combination switch

Fig. 77 Exploded view of a typical combination switch mounting

7. Installation is the reverse of the removal procedure. Check the switch operation.

1990–92 626/MX-6

1. Disconnect the negative battery cable.
2. Remove the horn cap.
3. Remove the steering wheel.
4. Remove the 2 column cover screws and remove the cover.
5. Disconnect the electrical connections from the combination switch.
6. Remove the combination switch as an assembly.
7. Installation is the reverse of the removal procedure. Check the switch operation.

1993–98 626 and MX6

WITHOUT AIR BAG

1. Disconnect the negative battery cable.
2. Remove the steering wheel.
3. Remove the steering column covers.
4. Disconnect the electrical connectors.
5. Remove the stop ring from the shaft.
6. Remove the switch retaining screws. Remove the combination switch from its mounting.
7. Installation is the reverse of the removal procedure.

WITH AIR BAG

1. Disconnect the negative battery cable and disarm the air bag system.
2. Remove the driver-side side panel and lower panel. Disconnect the clock spring connector.
3. Remove the steering wheel and the column covers.
4. Disconnect the wiring and remove the screws for the combination switch. Remove the combination switch.
5. Installation of the switch is the reverse of removal. To install the steering wheel, the clock-spring must be reset:
   a. Make sure the front wheels are straight ahead.
   b. Turn the clock-spring connector clockwise until it stops. Don't force it.
   c. Turn the clock-spring back about 2.75 turns and align the marks on the clock spring connector to the marks on the outer housing.
   d. Connect the wiring and install the steering wheel.

Millenia

1. Disconnect the negative battery cable and disarm the air bag.
2. Remove the air bag module and the steering wheel.
3. Remove the steering column cover.
4. Remove the electrical connectors and mounting screws, then remove the combination switch.
5. Installation is the reverse of removal.

Ignition Switch/Lock Cylinder

REMOVAL AND INSTALLATION

▶ **See Figures 78 and 79**

✳✳ CAUTION

Some models covered by this manual may be equipped with a Supplemental Restraint System (SRS), which uses an air bag. Whenever working near any of the SRS components, such as the impact sensors, the air bag module, steering column and instrument panel, disable the SRS, as described in Section 6.

The ignition lock is an integral component of the steering lock mechanism. If the ignition lock must be replaced, perform the following procedure.

Millenia

1. Disconnect the negative battery cable.
2. Properly disarm the air bag system.
3. Remove the rear console box, brake boot and center panel (disconnect the harness connectors).
4. Remove the rear console.
5. Remove the undercover, glove compartment and compartment cover.
6. Remove the upper and lower steering column covers.
7. Tilt the steering shaft down. Remove the cap and panel light control switch. Remove the meter hood mounting screws. Pull the meter hood forward to disengage the clips.
8. Remove the instrument cluster.
9. Remove the drivers side air bag and the steering wheel.
10. Remove the combination switch.
11. Remove the passenger side air bag mounting bolts, electrical connector and remove the air bag module.

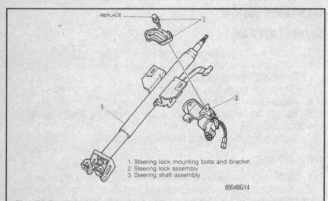

1. Steering lock mounting bolts and bracket
2. Steering lock assembly
3. Steering shaft assembly

89548G14

Fig. 78 Exploded view of the ignition switch/lock cylinder assembly

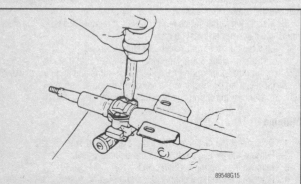

89548G15

Fig. 79 Remove the break-off head retaining bolts by chiseling a slot in the bolt, then removing them with a screwdriver

12. Remove the hood panel release lever. Pull the side panel forward to disengage the clips, remove the side panel.
13. Remove the side covers.
14. Remove the dashboard mounting bolts, pull the dashboard up and forward and remove.
15. Remove the steering shaft.
16. Remove the screw and the ignition switch and disconnect the ignition switch connector.
17. Using a chisel and a hammer make a groove in the heads of the steering lock mounting bolts. Remove the bolts and the steering lock assembly.
To install:
18. Install the steering lock mechanism to the steering column jacket. Make sure that the lock operates correctly. Install new mounting bolts and tighten the bolts till the heads break off.
19. Reconnect the ignition switch connector to the ignition switch and install the ignition switch to the steering lock mechanism with the screw.
20. Replace the dashboard close to its mounts and connect all harness connectors. Install all mounting bolts. Torque to 14–18 ft. lbs. (19–25 Nm).
21. Install the side covers.
22. Instal the side panels.
23. Install the steering shaft and torque the mounting bolts to 12–16 ft. lbs. (16–22 Nm).
24. Connect the passenger side air bag module electrical connector and replace the module to the dash and install the mounting bolts.
25. Install the combination switch on the steering column.
26. Install the steering wheel and drivers side air bag module.
27. Install the instrument cluster.
28. Install the meter hood.
29. Install the upper and lower steering column covers.
30. Install the glove compartment cover, compartment and the undercover.
31. Install the rear console, bracket, center panel, brake lever boot and the rear console box.
32. Reconnect the negative battery cable,
33. Place the steering column securely on a workbench. Use a chisel and hammer to make slots in the head of the lock screws. Remove the screws.

Except Millenia

1. Disconnect the negative battery cable.
2. If equipped, disarm and remove the air bag.
3. Remove the steering wheel and the combination switch.
4. Remove the steering column by performing the following:
   a. Remove the driver's side under dash covers.
   b. If equipped, disconnect the key interlock cable from the steering column.
   c. Detach any remaining electrical wire harness connectors from the column.
   d. Remove the upper column-to-dash mounting bolts. Support the steering column.
   e. Remove the intermediate shaft-to-steering column shaft coupling bolt and remove the steering column-to-firewall bracket bolts/nuts.
   f. Remove the steering column from the vehicle.
5. Place the steering column securely on a workbench. Use a chisel and hammer to make slots in the head of the lock screws. Remove the screws.
6. Remove the ignition lock assembly.
To install:
7. Position the ignition lock and bracket on the steering column.
8. Install the new screws until the head twists off. Make sure the lock operates properly while tightening the new locking screws.
9. The remainder of the installation is the reverse of the removal procedure.

Steering Linkage

REMOVAL & INSTALLATION

Tie Rod Ends

▶ **See Figures 80 thru 86**

1. Raise and support the vehicle safely. Remove the wheel and tire assembly.
2. Loosen the jam nut and thread it back along the linkage shaft. Ensure that the linkage shaft does not turn.

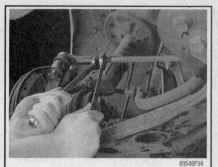

Fig. 80 To remove the tie rod end, first loosen the jam nut and thread it back along the linkage shaft

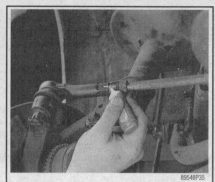

Fig. 81 Paint a matchmark on the tie rod end and the linkage shaft

Fig. 82 Remove the tie rod end nut cotter pin . . .

Fig. 83 . . . then loosen, but do not remove, the tie rod-to-steering knuckle nut

Fig. 84 Using the nut to protect the tie rod end threads, press the end from the steering knuckle

Fig. 85 Remove the nut and detach the tie rod end from the steering knuckle

Fig. 86 Unscrew the tie rod end from the steering linkage shaft

3. Paint a reference mark across the tie rod and shaft.

4. Remove the cotter pin and loosen the nut on the tie rod end ball stud. With the nut protecting the ball stud, press the stud from the knuckle using press tool 49 0118 850C or equivalent. Remove the nut and the tie rod end from the knuckle.

5. Unscrew the tie rod end from the shaft.

To install:

6. Thread the tie rod onto the shaft and align the marks made during removal. If installing a new tie rod end, try to assemble it in the same position as the old one.

7. Install the tie rod end into the knuckle. Install the nut and tighten specification.

8. Install a new cotter pin. If the cotter pin cannot be installed because the ball stud hole and the nut castellation do not align, tighten the nut further until the cotter pin can be installed. Never loosen the nut to install the cotter pin.

9. Tighten the jam nut.

10. Install the wheel and tire assembly and lower the vehicle. Check the front wheel alignment.

Manual Steering Gear and Linkage

REMOVAL & INSTALLATION

♦ See Figure 87

✳✳ CAUTION

Some models covered by this manual may be equipped with a Supplemental Restraint System (SRS), which uses an air bag. Whenever working near any of the SRS components, such as the impact sensors, the air bag module, steering column and instrument panel, disable the SRS, as described in Section 6.

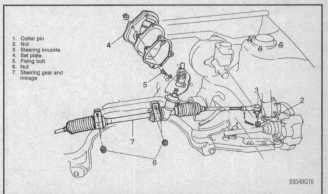

1. Cotter pin
2. Nut
3. Steering knuckle
4. Set plate
5. Fixing bolt
6. Nut
7. Steering gear and linkage

Fig. 87 Exploded view of the manual steering gear assembly

1. Raise and safely support the vehicle. Disconnect the negative battery cable and remove the front wheels.

2. Remove the cotter pins from both steering tie rod ends and remove the nuts.

3. Use Mazda special tie rod press tool 49 0118 850C or equivalent and press the tie rod out of the knuckle arm.

4. Remove the set plate from the firewall.

5. Remove the fixing bolt from the steering shaft to steering gear pinion shaft and separate the shaft from the steering gear.

6. Remove the steering gear mounting nuts and remove the steering gear to the right of the vehicle.

To install:

7. Install the steering gear to the vehicle and install the mounting nuts in the order shown. Tighten the nuts to 28–38 ft. lbs. (37–52Nm).

8. Connect the steering shaft to the steering gear pinion shaft. Tighten the bolt/nut to 13–20 ft. lbs. (18–27Nm).

9. Install the set plate to the firewall.

10. Install the tie rod ends to the knuckle arm and tighten the nuts to 31–42 ft. lbs. (42–57Nm). Install the cotter pins.

11. Install the wheels to the vehicle, lower the vehicle and connect the negative battery cable. Check the front end alignment.

Power Steering Gear and Linkage

REMOVAL & INSTALLATION

♦ **See Figure 88**

✳✳ CAUTION

Some models covered by this manual may be equipped with a Supplemental Restraint System (SRS), which uses an air bag. Whenever working near any of the SRS components, such as the impact sensors, the air bag module, steering column and instrument panel, disable the SRS, as described in Section 6.

1. Raise and safely support the vehicle. Disconnect the negative battery cable and remove the front wheels.

2. Remove the cotter pins from both steering tie rod ends and remove the nuts.

3. Use Mazda special tie rod press tool 49 0118 850C or equivalent and press the tie rod out of the knuckle arm.

4. Disconnect the pressure line and return pipe from the steering gear. Remove the set plate from the firewall.

5. Remove the fixing bolt from the steering shaft to steering gear pinion shaft and separate the shaft from the steering gear.

6. Disconnect the manual trans shifter linkage if necessary.

7. Remove the steering gear mounting nuts and remove the steering gear to the right of the vehicle.

To install:

8. Install the steering gear to the vehicle and install the mounting nuts/bolts. Tighten the nuts to 28–38 ft. lbs. (37–52Nm).

9. Connect the steering shaft to the steering gear pinion shaft. Tighten the bolt/nut to the specified torque.

10. Connect the manual trans shift linkage if disconnected. Install the set plate to the firewall.

11. Connect the pressure line and return hose to the steering gear.

12. Install the tie rod ends to the knuckle arm and tighten the nuts to 31–42 ft. lbs. (42–57Nm). Install the cotter pins.

13. Install the wheels to the vehicle, lower the vehicle and connect the negative battery cable. Bleed the power steering system and check the front end alignment.

Power Steering Pump

REMOVAL & INSTALLATION

♦ **See Figures 89 and 90**

1. Disconnect the negative battery cable. Disconnect and plug the hoses at the pump. If equipped,
disconnect the pressure switch connector.

2. Remove the pump drive belt.

3. On all except 323, Protege and MX-3, it is necessary to remove the pump pulley before removing the pump. Hold the pulley with tool 49 W023 585A or equivalent, or if possible, insert a small prybar through 1 of the holes in the pulley to hold it. Remove the pulley nut and pulley.

4. Support the pump, remove the mounting bolts and lift out the pump.

5. Installation is the reverse of removal. Tighten the pulley nut to 43 ft. lbs. (58 Nm). Adjust the belt tension and fill and bleed the system.

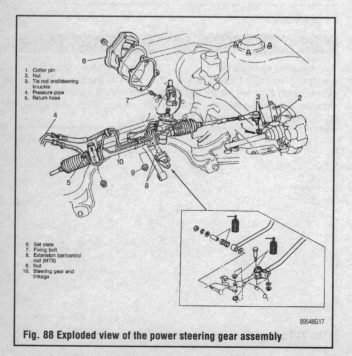

1. Cotter pin
2. Nut
3. Tie rod end/steering knuckle
4. Pressure pipe
5. Return hose
6. Set plate
7. Fixing bolt
8. Extension bar/control rod (MTX)
9. Nut
10. Steering gear and linkage

89548G17

Fig. 88 Exploded view of the power steering gear assembly

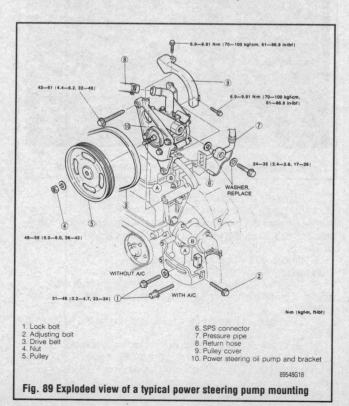

6.9–9.81 N·m [70–100 kgf-cm, 61–86.8 in-lbf]

43–61 [4.4–6.2, 32–45]

6.9–9.81 N·m [70–100 kgf-cm, 61–86.8 in-lbf]

24–35 [2.4–3.6, 17–26]

WASHER, REPLACE

49–59 [5.0–6.0, 36–43]

WITHOUT A/C

WITH A/C

31–46 [3.2–4.7, 23–34]

N·m [kgf-m, ft-lbf]

1. Lock bolt
2. Adjusting bolt
3. Drive belt
4. Nut
5. Pulley
6. SPS connector
7. Pressure pipe
8. Return hose
9. Pulley cover
10. Power steering oil pump and bracket

89548G18

Fig. 89 Exploded view of a typical power steering pump mounting

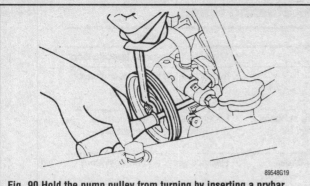

89548G19

Fig. 90 Hold the pump pulley from turning by inserting a prybar through a pulley hole, then loosen the retaining nut

SYSTEM BLEEDING

1. Check the fluid level. Add fluid, as required.
2. Raise and safely support the vehicle.
3. Turn the steering wheel full cycle, in both directions, 5 times with the engine **OFF.**
4. Recheck the fluid level again and add, as required.
5. Repeat Steps 3 and 4 until the fluid level stabilizes.
6. Lower the vehicle.
7. Start the engine and allow to warm up at idle. Turn the steering wheel full cycle, in both directions, 5 times with the engine running.
8. Check that the fluid is not foamy and the level has not dropped.
9. Add fluid, if necessary and repeat Steps 7 and 8.

TORQUE SPECIFICATIONS

Components	Ft. Lbs.	Nm
Front Suspension		
Front lower control arm through bolt	69-78	94-105
Lower ball joint pinch bolt and nut	32-43	44-58
Rear lower control arm bushing bracket-to-body bolts	69-96	94-131
Stabilizer bar end link nut	32-44	44-60
Stabilizer bar-to-body strap bolts	32-44	44-60
Steering gear-to-chassis bolts/nuts	27-39	37-53
Steering shaft-to-gear set bolt	14-19	18-26
Strut shaft-to-upper mount nut	58-81	79-109
Strut-to-steering knuckle bolts	76-93	103-126
Tie rod locknut	26-36	35-50
Tie rod-to-steering knuckle nut	32-41	43-56
Upper strut mount-to-body nuts	34-46	47-62
Rear Suspension		
Front lateral link-to- center chassis	64-70	87-95
Lateral link-to-axle through bolt	64-86	87-116
Lower strut mounting bolts	69-93	94-126
Rear lateral link-to-center chassis		
Except 1995-98 Protege	58-70	79-95
1995-98 Protege	26-39	35-53
Stabilizer bar end link nuts	32-44	44-60
Strut shaft-to-upper mount nut	41-49	55-67
Trailing arm-to-axle bolt	69-93	94-126
Trailing arm-to-body bolt	55-69	75-93
Upper strut mount-to-body nuts	34-46	47-62
Wheels		
Wheel lug nuts	87	118

89548C01

Troubleshooting the Power Steering Pump

Problem	Cause	Solution
Chirp noise in steering pump	• Loose belt	• Adjust belt tension to specification
Belt squeal (particularly noticeable at full wheel travel and stand still parking)	• Loose belt	• Adjust belt tension to specification
Growl noise in steering pump	• Excessive back pressure in hoses or steering gear caused by restriction	• Locate restriction and correct. Replace part if necessary.
Growl noise in steering pump (particularly noticeable at stand still parking)	• Scored pressure plates, thrust plate or rotor • Extreme wear of cam ring	• Replace parts and flush system • Replace parts
Groan noise in steering pump	• Low oil level • Air in the oil. Poor pressure hose connection.	• Fill reservoir to proper level • Tighten connector to specified torque. Bleed system by operating steering from right to left—full turn.
Rattle noise in steering pump	• Vanes not installed properly • Vanes sticking in rotor slots	• Install properly • Free up by removing burrs, varnish, or dirt
Swish noise in steering pump	• Defective flow control valve	• Replace part
Whine noise in steering pump	• Pump shaft bearing scored	• Replace housing and shaft. Flush system.
Hard steering or lack of assist	• Loose pump belt • Low oil level in reservoir **NOTE:** Low oil level will also result in excessive pump noise • Steering gear to column misalignment • Lower coupling flange rubbing against steering gear adjuster plug • Tires not properly inflated	• Adjust belt tension to specification • Fill to proper level. If excessively low, check all lines and joints for evidence of external leakage. Tighten loose connectors. • Align steering column • Loosen pinch bolt and assemble properly • Inflate to recommended pressure
Foaming milky power steering fluid, low fluid level and possible low pressure	• Air in the fluid, and loss of fluid due to internal pump leakage causing overflow	• Check for leaks and correct. Bleed system. Extremely cold temperatures will cause system aeration should the oil level be low. If oil level is correct and pump still foams, remove pump from vehicle and separate reservoir from body. Check welsh plug and body for cracks. If plug is loose or body is cracked, replace body.
Low pump pressure	• Flow control valve stuck or inoperative • Pressure plate not flat against cam ring	• Remove burrs or dirt or replace. Flush system. • Correct
Momentary increase in effort when turning wheel fast to right or left	• Low oil level in pump • Pump belt slipping • High internal leakage	• Add power steering fluid as required • Tighten or replace belt • Check pump pressure. (See pressure test)
Steering wheel surges or jerks when turning with engine running especially during parking	• Low oil level • Loose pump belt • Steering linkage hitting engine oil pan at full turn • Insufficient pump pressure	• Fill as required • Adjust tension to specification • Correct clearance • Check pump pressure. (See pressure test). Replace flow control valve if defective.

90918C02

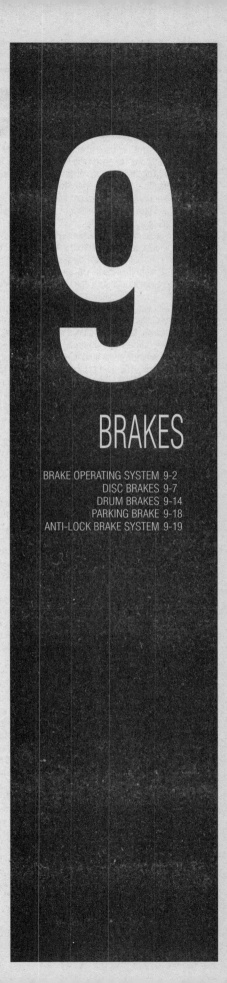

9

BRAKES

BRAKE OPERATING SYSTEM

Basic Operating Principles

Hydraulic systems are used to actuate the brakes of all modern automobiles. The system transports the power required to force the frictional surfaces of the braking system together from the pedal to the individual brake units at each wheel. A hydraulic system is used for two reasons.

First, fluid under pressure can be carried to all parts of an automobile by small pipes and flexible hoses without taking up a significant amount of room or posing routing problems.

Second, a great mechanical advantage can be given to the brake pedal end of the system, and the foot pressure required to actuate the brakes can be reduced by making the surface area of the master cylinder pistons smaller than that of any of the pistons in the wheel cylinders or calipers.

The master cylinder consists of a fluid reservoir along with a double cylinder and piston assembly. Double type master cylinders are designed to separate the front and rear braking systems hydraulically in case of a leak. The master cylinder coverts mechanical motion from the pedal into hydraulic pressure within the lines. This pressure is translated back into mechanical motion at the wheels by either the wheel cylinder (drum brakes) or the caliper (disc brakes).

Steel lines carry the brake fluid to a point on the vehicle's frame near each of the vehicle's wheels. The fluid is then carried to the calipers and wheel cylinders by flexible tubes in order to allow for suspension and steering movements.

In drum brake systems, each wheel cylinder contains two pistons, one at either end, which push outward in opposite directions and force the brake shoe into contact with the drum.

In disc brake systems, the cylinders are part of the calipers. At least one cylinder in each caliper is used to force the brake pads against the disc.

All pistons employ some type of seal, usually made of rubber, to minimize fluid leakage. A rubber dust boot seals the outer end of the cylinder against dust and dirt. The boot fits around the outer end of the piston on disc brake calipers, and around the brake actuating rod on wheel cylinders.

The hydraulic system operates as follows: When at rest, the entire system, from the piston(s) in the master cylinder to those in the wheel cylinders or calipers, is full of brake fluid. Upon application of the brake pedal, fluid trapped in front of the master cylinder piston(s) is forced through the lines to the wheel cylinders. Here, it forces the pistons outward, in the case of drum brakes, and inward toward the disc, in the case of disc brakes. The motion of the pistons is opposed by return springs mounted outside the cylinders in drum brakes, and by spring seals, in disc brakes.

Upon release of the brake pedal, a spring located inside the master cylinder immediately returns the master cylinder pistons to the normal position. The pistons contain check valves and the master cylinder has compensating ports drilled in it. These are uncovered as the pistons reach their normal position. The piston check valves allow fluid to flow toward the wheel cylinders or calipers as the pistons withdraw. Then, as the return springs force the brake pads or shoes into the released position, the excess fluid reservoir through the compensating ports. It is during the time the pedal is in the released position that any fluid that has leaked out of the system will be replaced through the compensating ports.

Dual circuit master cylinders employ two pistons, located one behind the other, in the same cylinder. The primary piston is actuated directly by mechanical linkage from the brake pedal through the power booster. The secondary piston is actuated by fluid trapped between the two pistons. If a leak develops in front of the secondary piston, it moves forward until it bottoms against the front of the master cylinder, and the fluid trapped between the pistons will operate the rear brakes. If the rear brakes develop a leak, the primary piston will move forward until direct contact with the secondary piston takes place, and it will force the secondary piston to actuate the front brakes. In either case, the brake pedal moves farther when the brakes are applied, and less braking power is available.

All dual circuit systems use a switch to warn the driver when only half of the brake system is operational. This switch is usually located in a valve body which is mounted on the firewall or the frame below the master cylinder. A hydraulic piston receives pressure from both circuits, each circuit's pressure being applied to one end of the piston. When the pressures are in balance, the piston remains stationary. When one circuit has a leak, however, the greater pressure in that circuit during application of the brakes will push the piston to one side, closing the switch and activating the brake warning light.

In disc brake systems, this valve body also contains a metering valve and, in some cases, a proportioning valve. The metering valve keeps pressure from traveling to the disc brakes on the front wheels until the brake shoes on the rear wheels have contacted the drums, ensuring that the front brakes will never be used alone. The proportioning valve controls the pressure to the rear brakes to lessen the chance of rear wheel lock-up during very hard braking.

Warning lights may be tested by depressing the brake pedal and holding it while opening one of the wheel cylinder bleeder screws. If this does not cause the light to go on, substitute a new lamp, make continuity checks, and, finally, replace the switch as necessary.

The hydraulic system may be checked for leaks by applying pressure to the pedal gradually and steadily. If the pedal sinks very slowly to the floor, the system has a leak. This is not to be confused with a springy or spongy feel due to the compression of air within the lines. If the system leaks, there will be a gradual change in the position of the pedal with a constant pressure.

Check for leaks along all lines and at wheel cylinders. If no external leaks are apparent, the problem is inside the master cylinder.

DISC BRAKES

Instead of the traditional expanding brakes that press outward against a circular drum, disc brake systems utilize a disc (rotor) with brake pads positioned on either side of it. An easily-seen analogy is the hand brake arrangement on a bicycle. The pads squeeze onto the rim of the bike wheel, slowing its motion. Automobile disc brakes use the identical principle but apply the braking effort to a separate disc instead of the wheel.

The disc (rotor) is a casting, usually equipped with cooling fins between the two braking surfaces. This enables air to circulate between the braking surfaces making them less sensitive to heat buildup and more resistant to fade. Dirt and water do not drastically affect braking action since contaminants are thrown off by the centrifugal action of the rotor or scraped off the by the pads. Also, the equal clamping action of the two brake pads tends to ensure uniform, straight line stops. Disc brakes are inherently self-adjusting. There are three general types of disc brake:

1. A fixed caliper.
2. A floating caliper.
3. A sliding caliper.

The fixed caliper design uses two pistons mounted on either side of the rotor (in each side of the caliper). The caliper is mounted rigidly and does not move.

The sliding and floating designs are quite similar. In fact, these two types are often lumped together. In both designs, the pad on the inside of the rotor is moved into contact with the rotor by hydraulic force. The caliper, which is not held in a fixed position, moves slightly, bringing the outside pad into contact with the rotor. There are various methods of attaching floating calipers. Some pivot at the bottom or top, and some slide on mounting bolts. In any event, the end result is the same.

DRUM BRAKES

Drum brakes employ two brake shoes mounted on a stationary backing plate. These shoes are positioned inside a circular drum which rotates with the wheel assembly. The shoes are held in place by springs. This allows them to slide toward the drums (when they are applied) while keeping the linings and drums in alignment. The shoes are actuated by a wheel cylinder which is mounted at the top of the backing plate. When the brakes are applied, hydraulic pressure forces the wheel cylinder's actuating links outward. Since these links bear directly against the top of the brake shoes, the tops of the shoes are then forced against the inner side of the drum. This action forces the bottoms of the two shoes to contact the brake drum by rotating the entire assembly slightly (known as servo action). When pressure within the wheel cylinder is relaxed, return springs pull the shoes back away from the drum.

Most modern drum brakes are designed to self-adjust themselves during application when the vehicle is moving in reverse. This motion causes both shoes to rotate very slightly with the drum, rocking an adjusting lever, thereby causing rotation of the adjusting screw. Some drum brake systems are designed to self-adjust during application whenever the brakes are applied. This on-board adjustment system reduces the need for maintenance adjustments and keeps both the brake function and pedal feel satisfactory.

POWER BOOSTERS

Virtually all modern vehicles use a vacuum assisted power brake system to multiply the braking force and reduce pedal effort. Since vacuum is always available when the engine is operating, the system is simple and efficient. A vacuum diaphragm is located on the front of the master cylinder and assists the driver in applying the brakes, reducing both the effort and travel he must put into moving the brake pedal.

The vacuum diaphragm housing is normally connected to the intake manifold by a vacuum hose. A check valve is placed at the point where the hose enters the diaphragm housing, so that during periods of low manifold vacuum brakes assist will not be lost.

Depressing the brake pedal closes off the vacuum source and allows atmospheric pressure to enter on one side of the diaphragm. This causes the master cylinder pistons to move and apply the brakes. When the brake pedal is released, vacuum is applied to both sides of the diaphragm and springs return the diaphragm and master cylinder pistons to the released position.

If the vacuum supply fails, the brake pedal rod will contact the end of the master cylinder actuator rod and the system will apply the brakes without any power assistance. The driver will notice that much higher pedal effort is needed to stop the car and that the pedal feels harder than usual.

Vacuum Leak Test

1. Operate the engine at idle without touching the brake pedal for at least one minute.
2. Turn off the engine and wait one minute.
3. Test for the presence of assist vacuum by depressing the brake pedal and releasing it several times. If vacuum is present in the system, light application will produce less and less pedal travel. If there is no vacuum, air is leaking into the system.

System Operation Test

1. With the engine **OFF**, pump the brake pedal until the supply vacuum is entirely gone.
2. Put light, steady pressure on the brake pedal.
3. Start the engine and let it idle. If the system is operating correctly, the brake pedal should fall toward the floor if the constant pressure is maintained.

Power brake systems may be tested for hydraulic leaks just as ordinary systems are tested.

Adjustment

DISC BRAKES

Mazda disc brakes are self adjusting. Periodic adjustment of disc brakes is not required. When new disc brake pads have been installed, the brake pedal must be pumped to seat the pads against the rotors, prior to moving the vehicle. If the pads are not seated before the vehicle is put into gear or driving the vehicle, the brake pedal will have to be applied a number of times before any braking action will be achieved.

BRAKE PEDAL HEIGHT

◆ See Figure 1

Measure the brake pedal height from the floor of the vehicle to the upper surface of the brake pedal. The distance should be 6.73–7.13 in. (171–181mm). If the brake pedal height is incorrect, adjust as follows:

1. Unplug the stop lamp switch connector.
2. Loosen the locknut on the base of the stop light switch and move the switch to a position where it does not contact the brake pedal .

    a. Loosen the operating rod locknut. Adjust the height of the brake pedal by turning the operating rod using pliers. Once the desired pedal height is obtained, tighten the locknut on the operating rod.

    b. Screw the stop light switch until the it contacts the brake pedal stopper. Turn switch in until the brake pedal just starts to move. At this point, return (loosen) the stoplight switch ½–1 turn and secure in this position by tightening the locknut.

    c. Connect the electrical connector to the stop light switch.

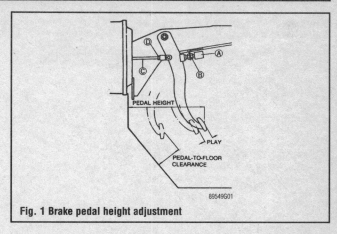

Fig. 1 Brake pedal height adjustment

    d. Check to be sure that the stop lights are not illuminated with no pressure on the brake pedal.

    e. Without starting the vehicle, depress the brake pedal. If the brake light switch is properly connected, the brake lights will illuminate.

BRAKE PEDAL FREE-PLAY

1. With the engine off, depress the brake pedal fully several times to evacuate the vacuum in the booster.
2. Once all the vacuum assist has been eliminated, press the brake pedal down by hand and confirm that the amount of movement before resistance is felt is within 0.16–0.28 in. (4–7mm).
3. If the free-play is less than desired, confirm that the brake light switch is in proper adjustment.
4. If there is excessive free-play, look for wear or play in the clevis pin and brake pedal arm. Replace worn parts as required and recheck brake pedal free-play.

Brake Light Switch

REMOVAL & INSTALLATION

1. Disconnect the negative battery cable.
2. Disconnect the stop lamp switch electrical harness connector.
3. Loosen the locknut holding the switch to the bracket. Remove the locknut and the switch.

To install:
4. Install the new switch and install the locknut, tightening it just snug.
5. Reposition the brake light switch so that the distance between the outer case of the switch and the pedal is 0.02–0.04 in. (0.5–1.0mm). Note that the switch plunger must press against the pedal to keep the brake lights off. As the pedal moves away from the switch, the plunger extends and closes the switch, which turns on the stop lights.
6. Hold the switch in the correct position and tighten the locknut.
7. Connect the wiring to the switch.
8. Check the operation of the switch. Turn the ignition key to the **ON** position but do not start the engine. Have an assistant observe the brake lights at the rear of the vehicle while you push on the brake pedal. The lights should come on just as the brake pedal passes the point of free-play.
9. Adjust the brake light switch as necessary. The small amount of free-play in the pedal should not trigger the brake lights; if the switch is set incorrectly, the brake lights will flicker due to pedal vibration on road bumps.

Master Cylinder

REMOVAL & INSTALLATION

◆ See Figures 2, 3, 4, 5 and 6

1. Disconnect the negative battery cable.
2. Disconnect the fluid level sensor connector.

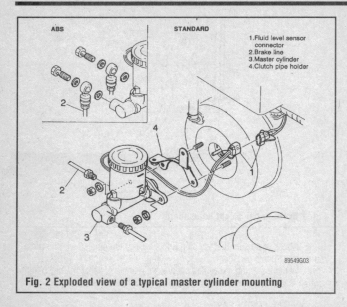

ABS	STANDARD

1. Fluid level sensor connector
2. Brake line
3. Master cylinder
4. Clutch pipe holder

89549G03

Fig. 2 Exploded view of a typical master cylinder mounting

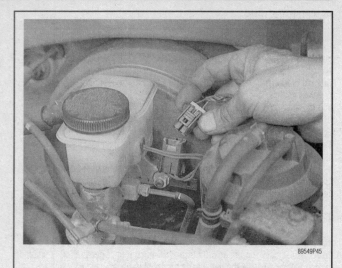

89549P45

Fig. 3 Unplug the electrical connector from the master cylinder

89549P46

Fig. 4 Use a flare nut wrench to loosen the lines from the cylinder

89549P48

Fig. 5 An extension is helpful for reaching the master cylinder mounting bolts

89549P49

Fig. 6 Once the bolts are removed, the master cylinder can be removed from the booster

3. Disconnect the brake lines from the master cylinder. Wrap the lines with a rag and plug the lines to prevent drainage.

4. Remove the 2 nuts securing the master cylinder to the brake booster.

5. Remove the proportioning bypass valve and bracket.

6. Remove the master cylinder, and on ABS equipped vehicles remove the O-ring.

To install:

7. Replace the O-ring, if equipped.

8. Position the master cylinder and the proportioning bypass valve onto the mounting studs and install the mounting nuts. Tighten mounting nuts to specifications as follows;

   a. 1990–94 323, 626, MX3, MX6 and Protege: 7–12 ft. lbs. (10–16 Nm).

   b. 1995 MX3: 9–12 ft. lbs. (12–16 Nm).

   c. 1995–98 Protege: 7–11 ft. lbs. (10–16 Nm).

   d. 1995–98 Millenia, 626 and MX6: 87–138 in. lbs. (9–15 Nm)

9. Fill the reservoir to the proper level with clean DOT 3 brake fluid. Bleed the master cylinder.

10. Replace the brake line washers. Install the brake lines to the master cylinder and tighten to specifications as follows;

   a. 1990–94 323, 626, MX3, MX6 and Protege: 9–16 ft. lbs. (13–22 Nm).

   b. 1995 MX3 1.8L engine: 15–21 ft. lbs. (20–29 Nm).

   c. 1995 MX3 1.6L engine: 10–16 ft. lbs. (13–21 Nm).

   d. 1995–98 Protege: 9–15 ft. lbs. (13–21 Nm).

   e. 1995–98 Millenia, 626 and MX6: 113–190 in. lbs. (9–15 Nm).

11. Apply the brake pedal and check for firmness. If the pedal is spongy, air is present in the system. If air remains in the system, the entire system must be bled.

12. Connect the negative battery cable and the fluid level sensor connector. Check the brakes for proper operation and leaks.

Power Brake Booster

REMOVAL & INSTALLATION

▶ See Figure 7

1. Disconnect the negative battery cable. Siphon the brake fluid from the master cylinder reservoir.

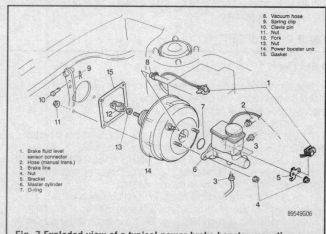

8. Vacuum hose
9. Spring clip
10. Clevis pin
11. Nut
12. Fork
13. Nut
14. Power booster unit
15. Gasket

1. Brake fluid level sensor connector
2. Hose (manual trans.)
3. Brake line
4. Nut
5. Bracket
6. Master cylinder
7. O-ring

89549G06

Fig. 7 Exploded view of a typical power brake booster mounting

2. Unplug the fluid level sensor connector, if so equipped.

3. Disconnect the brake lines from the master cylinder.

4. Remove the nuts attaching the master cylinder to the booster and remove the master cylinder.

5. Disconnect the vacuum hose and check valve from the power brake booster.

6. From inside the passenger compartment, remove the cotter pin and clevis pin that secures the booster pushrod to the brake pedal.

7. Lower or remove the steering column.

8. From inside the vehicle, remove the nuts that attach the booster to the dash panel. Remove the brake booster from the engine compartment.

To install:

9. Install the brake booster to the dash panel. From inside the vehicle, install the attaching nuts and tighten to 14–19 ft. lbs.(19–25 Nm).

10. Install the steering column.

11. Apply grease to the clevis pin and install with washers in place. Install new cotter pin and bend to secure in place.

12. Install the vacuum hose to the booster fitting.

13. Install the master cylinder assembly to the mounting studs on the brake booster. Install the master cylinder mounting nuts and tighten. Engage the electrical connector to the brake fluid level sensor.

14. Connect the negative battery cable and add fluid to the brake fluid reservoir as required. Bleed the master cylinder. If after bleeding the master cylinder the brake pedal feels soft, bleed the brake system at all wheels.

15. Check the brake system for proper operation.

Proportioning Valve

REMOVAL & INSTALLATION

▶ **See Figure 8**

1. Disconnect the negative battery cable. Drain the brake fluid from the brake system.

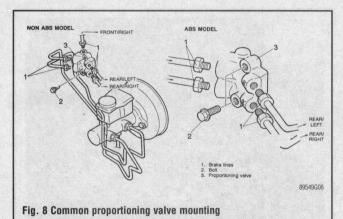

Fig. 8 Common proportioning valve mounting

2. Label and disconnect the brake lines at the proportioning valve.

3. Remove the proportioning valve mounting bolt and the valve from the engine compartment.

➡**Do not disassemble the proportioning valve because its performance depends on the set load of the spring inside the valve. If defective, replace the proportioning valve.**

4. Installation is the reverse of the removal procedure. Tighten the proportioning valve mounting bolt to 14–17 ft. lbs. (19–23 Nm). Bleed the brake system once the valve is installed.

Brake Hoses and Lines

Metal lines and rubber brake hoses should be checked frequently for leaks and external damage. Metal lines are particularly prone to crushing and kinking under the vehicle. Any such deformation can restrict the proper flow of fluid and therefore impair braking at the wheels. Rubber hoses should be checked for cracking or scraping; such damage can create a weak spot in the hose and it could fail under pressure.

Any time the lines are removed or disconnected, extreme cleanliness must be observed. Clean all joints and connections before disassembly (use a stiff bristle brush and clean brake fluid); be sure to plug the lines and ports as soon as they are opened. New lines and hoses should be flushed clean with brake fluid before installation to remove any contamination.

REMOVAL & INSTALLATION

▶ **See Figures 9 thru 14**

1. Disconnect the negative battery cable.

2. Raise and safely support the vehicle on jackstands.

3. Remove any wheel and tire assemblies necessary for access to the particular line you are removing.

4. Thoroughly clean the surrounding area at the joints to be disconnected.

5. Place a suitable catch pan under the joint to be disconnected.

6. Using two wrenches (one to hold the joint and one to turn the fitting), disconnect the hose or line to be replaced.

7. Disconnect the other end of the line or hose, moving the drain pan if necessary. Always use a back-up wrench to avoid damaging the fitting.

8. Disconnect any retaining clips or brackets holding the line and remove the line from the vehicle.

➡**If the brake system is to remain open for more time than it takes to swap lines, tape or plug each remaining clip and port to keep contaminants out and fluid in.**

To install:

9. Install the new line or hose, starting with the end farthest from the master cylinder. Connect the other end, then confirm that both fittings are correctly threaded and turn smoothly using finger pressure. Make sure the new line will not rub against any other part. Brake lines must be at least 1/2 in. (13mm) from the steering column and other moving parts. Any protective shielding or insulators must be reinstalled in the original location.

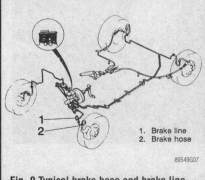

Fig. 9 Typical brake hose and brake line layout

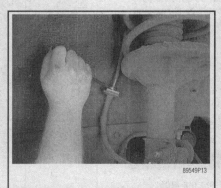

Fig. 10 Use a flare nut wrench to loosen the brake hose fitting

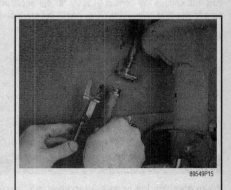

Fig. 11 Remove the securing clamp, then pull the hose down

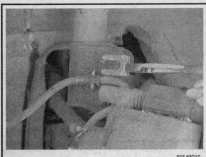

Fig. 12 Remove the clamp securing the hose to the strut

Fig. 13 The union bolt securing the hose to the caliper can now be removed

Fig. 14 Remove the hose from the vehicle. Always replace the sealing washers with new ones

※※ WARNING

Make sure the hose is NOT kinked or touching any part of the frame or suspension after installation. These conditions may cause the hose to fail prematurely.

10. Using two wrenches as before, tighten each fitting.
11. Install any retaining clips or brackets on the lines.
12. If removed, install the wheel and tire assemblies, then carefully lower the vehicle to the ground.
13. Refill the brake master cylinder reservoir with clean, fresh brake fluid, meeting DOT 3 specifications. Properly bleed the brake system.
14. Connect the negative battery cable.

Brake System Bleeding

※※ WARNING

Clean, high quality brake fluid is essential to the safe and proper operation of the brake system. You should always buy the highest quality brake fluid that is available. If the brake fluid becomes contaminated, drain and flush the system, then refill the master cylinder with new fluid. Never reuse any brake fluid. Any brake fluid that is removed from the system should be discarded.

Bleeding the brake system is required anytime the normally closed system has been opened to the atmosphere. When bleeding the system, keep the brake fluid level in the master cylinder reservoir above ½ full. If the reservoir is empty, air will be pushed through the system. If equipped with ABS, refer to the ABS portion later in this section for the bleeding procedure.

PROCEDURE

➡**If using a pressure bleeder, follow the instructions furnished with the unit and choose the correct adapter for the application. Do not substitute an adapter that "almost fits" as it will not work and could be dangerous.**

Master Cylinder

Due to the location of the fluid reservoir, bench bleeding of the master cylinder is not recommended. The master cylinder is to be bled while mounted on the brake booster. If the fluid reservoir runs dry, bleeding of the entire system will be necessary. Two people will be required to bleed the brake system.

1. Fill the brake fluid reservoir with clean brake fluid. Disconnect the brake tube from the master cylinder.
2. Have a helper slowly depress the brake pedal. Once depressed, hold it in that position. Brake fluid will be expelled from the master cylinder.

※※ CAUTION

When bleeding the brakes, keep your face away from the area. Spraying fluid may cause facial and/or visual damage. Do not allow brake fluid to spill on the car's finish; it will remove the paint.

3. While the pedal is held down, use a finger to close the outlet port of the master cylinder. While the port is closed, have the helper release the brake pedal.
4. Repeat this procedure until all air is bled from the master cylinder. Check the brake fluid in the reservoir every 4–5 times, making sure the reservoir does not run dry. Add clean DOT 3 brake fluid to the reservoir as needed. All air is bled from the master cylinder when the fluid expelled from the port is free of bubbles.
5. Connect the brake tube to the port on the master cylinder. Add clean fluid to fill the reservoir to the appropriate level.

Calipers and Wheel Cylinders

♦ See Figures 15 and 16

1. Fill the master cylinder with fresh brake fluid. Check the level often during this procedure. Raise and safely support the vehicle.
2. Starting with the wheel furthest from the master cylinder, remove the pro-

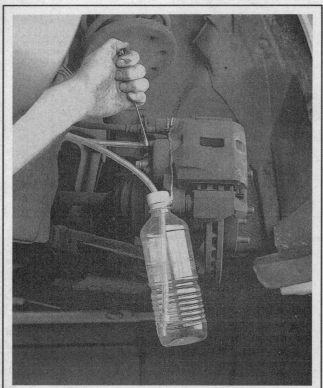

Fig. 15 Submerge the hose in a clear container of clean brake fluid—front caliper shown

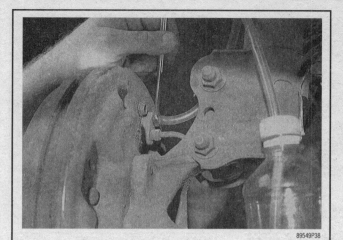

Fig. 16 The wheel cylinders are also equipped with a bleeder screw

tective cap from the bleeder and place where it will not be lost. Clean the bleeder screw.

3. Start the engine and run at idle.

> **⁎⁑⁎ CAUTION**
>
> **When bleeding the brakes, keep face away from the brake area. Spewing fluid may cause physical and/or visual damage. Do not allow brake fluid to spill on the car's finish; it will remove the paint.**

DISC BRAKES

> **⁎⁑⁎ CAUTION**
>
> **Brake pads and shoes may contain asbestos, which has been determined to be a cancer causing agent. Never clean the brake surfaces with compressed air! Avoid inhaling any dust from brake surfaces! When cleaning brakes, use commercially available brake cleaning fluids.**

Brake Pads

REMOVAL & INSTALLATION

▶ See Figures 17 and 18

1990–94 323, 626, MX3, MX6 and Protege

FRONT

▶ See Figures 19 thru 24

1. Remove some of the brake fluid from the master cylinder reservoir. The reservoir should be no more than ½ full. When the pistons are depressed into the calipers, excess fluid will flow up into the reservoir.
2. Raise the vehicle and support safely.
3. Remove the appropriate tire and wheel assemblies.
4. If equipped with 1 lower caliper mounting bolt, remove the caliper lower mounting bolt and pivot the caliper up and support it. If equipped with 2 caliper mounting bolts, remove both and support the caliper with mechanics wire. Do not kink the brake line or allow the caliper to hang by the brake line.
5. Remove the brake pads, shims and if so equipped, pins. Take note of positioning to aid installation.
6. If the caliper is single piston design, push the caliper back into the bore with a C-clamp or other suitable tool. If the caliper is a 4 piston type caliper, use Mazda tool 49-0221-600C or equivalent and the old inner brake pad, push the caliper piston(s) into the caliper bore.

4. If the system is empty, the most efficient way to get fluid down to the wheel is to loosen the bleeder about ½–¾ turn, place a finger firmly over the bleeder and have a helper pump the brakes slowly until fluid comes out the bleeder. Once fluid is at the bleeder, close it before the pedal is released inside the vehicle.

➡**If the pedal is pumped rapidly, the fluid will churn and create small air bubbles, which are almost impossible to remove from the system. These air bubbles will accumulate and a spongy pedal will result.**

5. Once fluid has been pumped to the caliper, open the bleed screw again, have the helper press the brake pedal to the floor, lock the bleeder and have the helper slowly release the pedal. Wait 15 seconds and repeat the procedure (including the 15 second wait) until no more air comes out of the bleeder upon application of the brake pedal. Remember to close the bleeder before the pedal is released inside the vehicle each time the bleeder is opened. If not, air will be introduced into the system.
6. If a helper is not available, connect a small hose to the bleeder, place the end in a container of brake fluid and proceed to pump the pedal from inside the vehicle until no more air comes out the bleeder. The hose will prevent air from entering the system.
7. Repeat the procedure on the remaining calipers in the following order:
   a. Left front
   b. Left rear
   c. Right front
8. Hydraulic brake systems must be totally flushed if the fluid becomes contaminated with water, dirt or other corrosive chemicals. To flush, bleed the entire system until all fluid has been replaced with the correct type of new fluid.
9. Install the bleeder cap on the bleeder to keep dirt out. Always road test the vehicle after brake work of any kind is done.

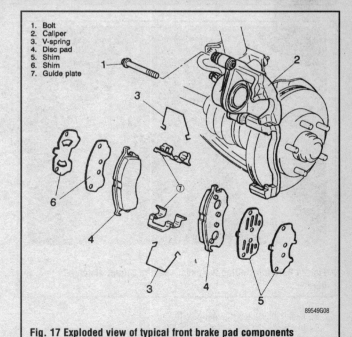

1. Bolt
2. Caliper
3. V-spring
4. Disc pad
5. Shim
6. Shim
7. Guide plate

Fig. 17 Exploded view of typical front brake pad components

To install:

7. Install the brake pads and shims to the caliper support. Install the caliper over the brake pads.

➡**Be careful that the piston boot does not become caught when lowering the caliper onto the support. Do not twist the brake hose during caliper installation.**

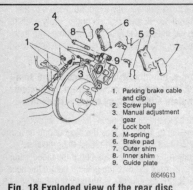

1. Parking brake cable and clip
2. Screw plug
3. Manual adjustment gear
4. Lock bolt
5. M-spring
6. Brake pad
7. Outer shim
8. Inner shim
9. Guide plate

89549G13

Fig. 18 Exploded view of the rear disc brake pad components

89549P07

Fig. 19 Loosen the lower guide pin . . .

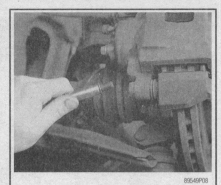

89549P08

Fig. 20 . . . then remove it from the caliper

89549P09

Fig. 21 Rotate the caliper upwards to access the pads

89549P10

Fig. 22 The pads can now be removed from the caliper mounting support

89549P11

Fig. 23 Remove and inspect the guide plates. Replace if damaged

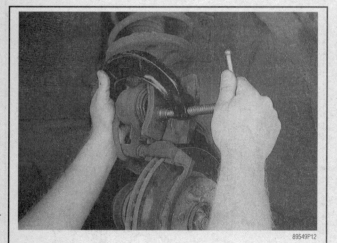

89549P12

Fig. 24 Before installing the pads, seat the caliper piston into its bore

8. Install the caliper mounting bolt(s).
9. Install the tire and wheel assemblies.
10. Lower the vehicle and test the brakes for proper operation.

REAR

1. Remove some of the brake fluid from the master cylinder reservoir. The reservoir should be no more than ½ full. When the pistons are depressed into the calipers, excess fluid will flow up into the reservoir.
2. Raise the vehicle and support safely.
3. Remove the appropriate tire and wheel assemblies. Loosen the parking brake cable adjustment from inside the vehicle.

4. Disconnect the parking brake cable from the cable bracket and the operating lever.
5. Remove the upper caliper mounting bolt and pivot the caliper downward off of the pads. Do not allow the caliper to hang by the brake line.
6. Remove the brake pads and spring clips from the caliper support. Take note of positioning of each to aid in installation.

   To install:
7. Install the brake pads, shims and spring clips to the caliper support. Pivot the caliper over the brake pads.

➡ **Be careful that the piston boot does not become caught when pivoting the caliper onto the support. Do not twist the brake hose during caliper installation.**

8. Lubricate and install the top caliper mounting bolt. Tighten the bolt to 12–17 ft. lbs. (16–23 Nm). Attach the parking brake cable to the operating lever and tighten the locknut to 12–17 ft. lbs. (16–23 Nm).
9. Start the engine and forcefully depress the brake pedal 5–6 times. Apply the parking brake and make sure the adjustment is within specifications. Adjust the parking brake cable, as required.
10. Check the disc brake drag by applying the brakes several times and then rotating the wheels to check for excessive dragging.
11. Install the tire and wheel assemblies. Lower the vehicle.
12. Test the brakes for proper operation.

1995–98 Protege

FRONT

1. Remove some of the brake fluid from the master cylinder reservoir. The reservoir should be no more than ½ full. When the pistons are depressed into the calipers, excess fluid will flow up into the reservoir.
2. Raise the vehicle and support safely.
3. Remove the appropriate tire and wheel assemblies.
4. Remove the spring and the pin.
5. Remove the two pad pins from the brake pads.

6. Remove the brake pads and shim. Take note of positioning to aid installation.

7. Push the caliper piston into the caliper bore.

To install:

8. Install the brake pads and shims to the caliper.

9. Insert the pad pins and spring.

10. Install the tire and wheel assemblies.

11. Lower the vehicle and test the brakes for proper operation.

REAR

1. Remove some of the brake fluid from the master cylinder reservoir. The reservoir should be no more than ½ full. When the pistons are depressed into the calipers, excess fluid will flow up into the reservoir.

2. Raise the vehicle and support safely.

3. Remove the wheels. Loosen the parking brake cable adjustment from inside the vehicle.

4. Disconnect the parking brake cable from the cable bracket and the operating lever. Remove the screw plug. Turn the manual adjustment gear counterclockwise with an Allen wrench to pull the brake caliper piston inward (turn until it stops).

5. Remove the upper caliper mounting bolt and pivot the caliper upward off of the pads.

6. Remove the brake pads and spring clips from the caliper support. Take note of positioning of each to aid in installation.

To install:

7. Install the brake pads, shims and spring clips to the caliper support. Pivot the caliper over the brake pads.

➡**Be careful that the piston boot does not become caught when pivoting the caliper onto the support. Do not twist the brake hose during caliper installation.**

8. Lubricate and install the bottom caliper mounting bolt. Tighten the bolt to 33–44 ft. lbs. (46–60 Nm). Attach the parking brake cable to the operating lever and tighten the screw plug to 9–11 ft. lbs. (12–15 Nm).

9. Start the engine and forcefully depress the brake pedal 5–6 times. Apply the parking brake and make sure the adjustment is within specifications. Adjust the parking brake cable, as required.

10. Check the disc brake drag by applying the brakes several times and then rotating the wheels to check for excessive dragging.

11. Install the tire and wheel assemblies. Lower the vehicle.

12. Test the brakes for proper operation.

1995 MX3

FRONT

1. Remove some of the brake fluid from the master cylinder reservoir. The reservoir should be no more than ½ full. When the pistons are depressed into the calipers, excess fluid will flow up into the reservoir.

2. Raise the vehicle and support safely.

3. Remove the appropriate tire and wheel assemblies.

4. Remove the spring and the pin.

5. Remove the two pad pins from the brake pads.

6. Remove the brake pads and shim. Take note of positioning to aid installation.

7. Using Mazda tool 49-0221-600C or equivalent and the old inner brake pad, push the caliper piston into the caliper bore.

To install:

8. Install the brake pads and shims to the caliper.

9. Insert the pad pins and spring.

10. Install the tire and wheel assemblies.

11. Lower the vehicle and test the brakes for proper operation.

REAR

1. Remove some of the brake fluid from the master cylinder reservoir. The reservoir should be no more than ½ full. When the pistons are depressed into the calipers, excess fluid will flow up into the reservoir.

2. Raise the vehicle and support safely.

3. Remove the wheels. Loosen the parking brake cable adjustment from inside the vehicle.

4. Disconnect the parking brake cable from the cable bracket and the operating lever. Remove the screw plug.

5. Remove the upper caliper mounting bolt and pivot the caliper downward off of the pads. Do not allow the caliper to hang by the brake line.

6. Remove the brake pads and spring clips from the caliper support. Take note of positioning of each to aid in installation.

To install:

7. Install the brake pads, shims and spring clips to the caliper support. Pivot the caliper over the brake pads.

➡**Be careful that the piston boot does not become caught when pivoting the caliper onto the support. Do not twist the brake hose during caliper installation.**

8. Lubricate and install the top caliper mounting bolt. Tighten the bolt to 12–17 ft. lbs. (16–24 Nm). Attach the parking brake cable to the operating lever and tighten the screw plug to 105–138 inch lbs. (12–16 Nm).

9. Start the engine and forcefully depress the brake pedal 5–6 times. Apply the parking brake and make sure the adjustment is within specifications. Adjust the parking brake cable, as required.

10. Check the disc brake drag by applying the brakes several times and then rotating the wheels to check for excessive dragging.

11. Install the tire and wheel assemblies. Lower the vehicle.

12. Test the brakes for proper operation.

1995–98 626 and MX6

FRONT

1. Remove some of the brake fluid from the master cylinder reservoir. The reservoir should be no more than ½ full. When the pistons are depressed into the calipers, excess fluid will flow up into the reservoir.

2. Raise the vehicle and support safely.

3. Remove the appropriate wheel assemblies.

4. Remove the caliper lower mounting bolt and pivot the caliper up and support it. Do not kink the brake line.

5. Remove the brake pads, shims and pin. Take note of positioning to aid installation.

6. Using Mazda tool 49-0221-600C or equivalent and the old inner brake pad, push the caliper piston into the caliper bore.

To install:

7. Install the brake pads and shims to the caliper support. Install the caliper over the brake pads.

➡**Be careful that the piston boot does not become caught when lowering the caliper onto the support. Do not twist the brake hose during caliper installation.**

8. Install the caliper mounting bolt and torque to 22–29 ft. lbs. (30–40 Nm).

9. Install the tire and wheel assemblies.

10. Lower the vehicle and test the brakes for proper operation.

REAR

1. Remove some of the brake fluid from the master cylinder reservoir. The reservoir should be no more than ½ full. When the pistons are depressed into the calipers, excess fluid will flow up into the reservoir.

2. Raise the vehicle and support safely.

3. Remove the appropriate tire and wheel assemblies. Loosen the parking brake cable adjustment from inside the vehicle.

4. Disconnect the parking brake cable from the cable bracket and the operating lever. Remove the screw plug.

5. Remove the upper caliper mounting bolt and pivot the caliper downward off of the pads. Do not allow the caliper to hang by the brake line.

6. Remove the brake pads and spring clips from the caliper support. Take note of positioning of each to aid in installation.

To install:

7. Install the brake pads, shims and spring clips to the caliper support. Pivot the caliper over the brake pads.

➡**Be careful that the piston boot does not become caught when pivoting the caliper onto the support. Do not twist the brake hose during caliper installation.**

8. Lubricate and install the top caliper mounting bolt. Tighten the bolt to 26–28 ft. lbs. (35–39 Nm). Attach the parking brake cable to the operating lever and tighten the screw plug to 105–138 inch lbs. (11.8–15.6 Nm).

9. Start the engine and forcefully depress the brake pedal 5–6 times. Apply the parking brake and make sure the adjustment is within specifications. Adjust the parking brake cable, as required.

10. Check the disc brake drag by applying the brakes several times and then rotating the wheels to check for excessive dragging.

11. Install the tire and wheel assemblies. Lower the vehicle.

12. Test the brakes for proper operation.

1995–98 Millenia

FRONT

1. Raise and safely support the vehicle.
2. Remove the wheels.
3. Remove the bottom caliper lock pin and swing the caliper upwards.
4. Remove the V-springs and remove the pads and shims.
5. Press the caliper pistons back into their cylinders. Installation is the reverse of removal. Torque the lock pin to 47–62 ft. lbs. (63–84 Nm). Bleed the brake system if necessary.

REAR

1. Raise and safely support the vehicle.
2. Remove the wheels.
3. Remove the lock pin and rotate the caliper upwards.
4. Remove the V-springs and remove the pads. Remove the shims from the pads.
5. Press the caliper piston back into the cylinder. Installation is the reverse of removal. Torque the lock pin to 37–50 ft. lbs. (50–68 Nm). Bleed the brake system if necessary.

INSPECTION

The front brake pads have built in wear indicators that contact the brake disc when the brake pad thickness becomes too thin and emit a squealing sound to warn the driver.

Inspect the thickness of the brake linings by looking through the brake caliper body check port. The thickness limit of the lining is 0.08 in. (2.0mm) except on 1995–98 626, MX6, Millenia. On 1995–98 626, MX6, Millenia, the limit is 0.04 in. (1.0mm).

When the limit is exceeded, replace the pads on both sides of the brake disc and also the brake pads on the wheel on the opposite side of the vehicle. Do not replace just one pad on a side without replacing the other pad on the same wheel as well as the brake pads on the other front wheel.

If there is a significant difference in the thickness of the pads on the left and right sides, check the sliding condition of the piston, lock pin sleeve and guide pin sleeve.

Brake Caliper

REMOVAL & INSTALLATION

▶ See Figures 25 and 26

1990–94 323, 626, MX3, MX6 and Protege

FRONT

▶ See Figures 27, 28 and 29

1. Raise the vehicle and support safely.
2. Remove the appropriate tire and wheel assembly.
3. If necessary, disconnect the flexible brake hose from the caliper.
4. If equipped with one caliper mounting bolt, remove the lower caliper bolt and pivot the caliper upward. Slide the top of the caliper off of the top pin and remove it from the vehicle (or support it with wire). If equipped with two caliper mounting bolts, remove both bolts and remove the caliper (or support it out of the way with wire).
   To install:
5. If equipped with one mounting bolt, lubricate the caliper pin and slide the caliper onto the guide pin. Pivot the caliper over the brake pads. Install the

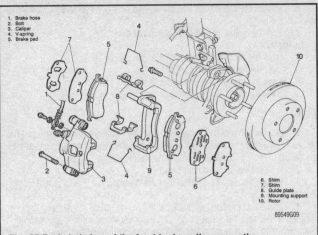

Fig. 25 Exploded view of the front brake caliper mounting

1. Brake hose
2. Bolt
3. Caliper
4. V-spring
5. Brake pad
6. Shim
7. Shim
8. Guide plate
9. Mounting support
10. Rotor

89549G09

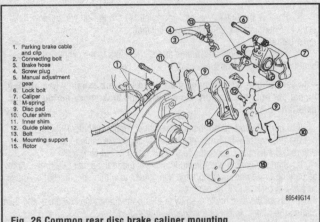

Fig. 26 Common rear disc brake caliper mounting

1. Parking brake cable and clip
2. Connecting bolt
3. Brake hose
4. Screw plug
5. Manual adjustment gear
6. Lock bolt
7. Caliper
8. M-spring
9. Disc pad
10. Outer shim
11. Inner shim
12. Guide plate
13. Bolt
14. Mounting support
15. Rotor

89549G14

mounting bolt. If equipped with two bolts, position the caliper and install the bolts.

6. Connect the brake hose to the caliper.

7. Bleed the brake system and inspect the brake system for proper operation.

8. Install the wheel and lower the vehicle. Connect the negative battery cable.

REAR

1. Raise the vehicle and support safely.
2. Remove the appropriate tire and wheel assemblies. Loosen the parking brake cable adjustment from inside the vehicle.
3. Disconnect the parking brake cable from the cable bracket and the operating lever.
4. Disconnect the flexible brake line from the caliper assembly.
5. Remove the caliper upper mounting bolt and pivot the caliper downward. Slide the caliper off of the guide pin. Remove the caliper from the vehicle.
   To install:
6. Lubricate the caliper pin and slide the caliper onto the guide pin. Pivot the caliper over the brake pads.
7. Connect the brake hose to the caliper and tighten the hose nut to 16–20 ft. lbs. (22–26 Nm).
8. Install the upper caliper mounting bolt and tighten the bolt to 33–49 ft. lbs. (45–67 Nm).
9. Bleed the brake system and inspect the brake system for proper operation.
10. Install the wheel and lower the vehicle. Connect the negative battery cable.

Fig. 27 Use a short extension to help reach the caliper mounting bolts

Fig. 28 Remove the mounting bolts and inspect for damaged threads. Replace if necessary

Fig. 29 Lift the caliper from the knuckle and support it with wire

1995–98 Protege

FRONT

1. Raise the vehicle and support safely.
2. Remove the appropriate tire and wheel assembly.
3. Disconnect the flexible brake hose from the caliper.
4. Remove the disc pad retaining pins. Remove the brake pads.
5. Remove the upper and lower caliper bolts. Remove the caliper from the vehicle.

To install:

6. Position the caliper on the brake disc. Install the caliper mounting bolts and tighten the bolts to 29–36 ft. lbs. (40–49 Nm).
7. Install the disc pad and retaining pins.
8. Replace the washers for the brake line. Connect the brake hose to the caliper and tighten the hose nut to 16–21 ft. lbs. (22–29 Nm).
9. Bleed the brake system and inspect the brake system for proper operation.
10. Install the wheel and lower the vehicle.

REAR

1. Raise the vehicle and support safely. Remove the wheels.
2. Disconnect the parking brake cable from the cable bracket and the operating lever.
3. Disconnect the flexible brake line from the caliper assembly.
4. Turn the manual adjustment gear counterclockwise with an Allen wrench to pull the caliper piston inward (turn until it stops).
5. Remove the caliper mounting bolts. Remove the caliper from the vehicle.
6. Installation is reverse of removal. Torque the caliper mount bolts to 34–44 ft. lbs. (46–60 Nm). Torque the brake hose line bolt to 16–22 ft. lbs. (22–30 Nm). Properly bleed the brake system.

1995 MX3

FRONT

1. Raise the vehicle and support safely.
2. Remove the appropriate tire and wheel assembly.
3. Disconnect the flexible brake hose from the caliper.
4. Remove the disc pad retaining pins. Remove the brake pads.
5. Remove the upper and lower caliper bolts. Remove the caliper from the vehicle.

To install:

6. Position the caliper on the brake disc. Install the caliper mounting bolts and tighten the bolts to 29–36 ft. lbs. (40–49 Nm).
7. Install the disc pad and retaining pins.
8. Replace the washers for the brake line. Connect the brake hose to the caliper and tighten the hose nut to 16–21 ft. lbs. (22–29 Nm).
9. Bleed the brake system and inspect the brake system for proper operation.
10. Install the wheel and lower the vehicle. Connect the negative battery cable.

REAR

1. Raise the vehicle and support safely.
2. Remove the wheels. Loosen the parking brake cable adjustment from inside the vehicle.
3. Disconnect the parking brake cable from the cable bracket and the operating lever.
4. Disconnect the flexible brake line from the caliper assembly.
5. Remove the caliper upper mounting bolt and pivot the caliper downward. Slide the caliper off of the guide pin. Remove the caliper from the vehicle.

To install:

6. Lubricate the caliper pin and slide the caliper onto the guide pin. Pivot the caliper over the brake pads.
7. Connect the brake hose to the caliper and tighten the hose nut to 16–21 ft. lbs. (22–29 Nm).
8. Install the upper caliper mounting bolt and tighten the bolt to 12–17 ft. lbs. (16–24 Nm).
9. Connect the parking brake cable to the cable bracket and the operating lever.
10. Bleed the brake system and inspect the brake system, including the parking brake, for proper operation.
11. Install the wheel and lower the vehicle. Connect the negative battery cable.

1995–98 626 and MX6

FRONT

1. Raise the vehicle and support safely.
2. Remove the appropriate tire and wheel assembly.
3. Disconnect the flexible brake hose from the caliper.
4. Remove the lower caliper bolt and pivot the caliper upward. Slide the top of the caliper off of the top pin and remove it from the vehicle.

To install:

5. Lubricate the caliper pin and slide the caliper onto the guide pin. Pivot the caliper over the brake pads.
6. Connect the brake hose to the caliper and tighten the hose nut to 16–21 ft. lbs. (22–29 Nm).
7. Install the caliper mounting bolt and tighten the bolt to 22–29 ft. lbs. (30–40 Nm).
8. Bleed the brake system and inspect the brake system for proper operation.
9. Install the wheel and lower the vehicle. Connect the negative battery cable.

REAR

1. Disconnect the battery negative cable.
2. Raise the vehicle and support safely.
3. Remove the appropriate tire and wheel assemblies. Loosen the parking brake cable adjustment from inside the vehicle.
4. Disconnect the parking brake cable from the cable bracket and the operating lever.

5. Disconnect the flexible brake line from the caliper assembly.

6. Remove the caliper upper mounting bolt and pivot the caliper downward. Slide the caliper off of the guide pin. Remove the caliper from the vehicle.

To install:

7. Lubricate the caliper pin and slide the caliper onto the guide pin. Pivot the caliper over the brake pads.

8. Connect the brake hose to the caliper and tighten the hose nut to 16–21 ft. lbs. (22–29 Nm).

9. Install the upper caliper mounting bolt and tighten the bolt to 26–28 ft. lbs. (35–39 Nm).

10. Connect the parking brake cable to the cable bracket and the operating lever.

11. Bleed the brake system and inspect the brake system, including the parking brake, for proper operation.

12. Install the wheel and lower the vehicle. Connect the negative battery cable.

1995–98 Millenia

FRONT

1. Raise and safely support the vehicle.
2. Remove the wheels.
3. Disconnect the brake hose and brake pipe. Cap the ends to prevent contamination.
4. Remove the caliper mounting bolts and remove the caliper. Remove the brake rotor.
5. Installation is the reverse of removal. Torque the caliper mounting bolts to 47–62 ft. lbs. (63–84 Nm). Add fluid and properly bleed the brake system.

REAR

1. Raise and safely support the vehicle.
2. Remove the wheels.
3. Disconnect the brake hose and cap the end to prevent contamination.
4. Remove the caliper bracket mounting bolts and remove the caliper. Remove the rotor.
5. Installation is the reverse of removal. Torque the caliper mounting bolts to 12–17 ft. lbs. (16–23 Nm).

OVERHAUL

▶ **See Figures 30 thru 39**

➡ Some vehicles may be equipped dual piston calipers. The procedure to overhaul the caliper is essentially the same with the exception of multiple pistons, O-rings and dust boots.

1. Remove the caliper from the vehicle and place on a clean workbench.

❊❊ CAUTION

NEVER place your fingers in front of the pistons in an attempt to catch or protect the pistons when applying compressed air. This could result in personal injury!

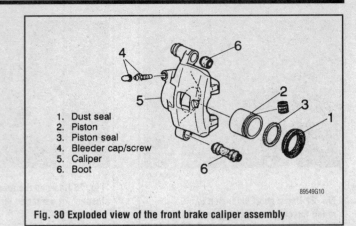

1. Dust seal
2. Piston
3. Piston seal
4. Bleeder cap/screw
5. Caliper
6. Boot

89549G10

Fig. 30 Exploded view of the front brake caliper assembly

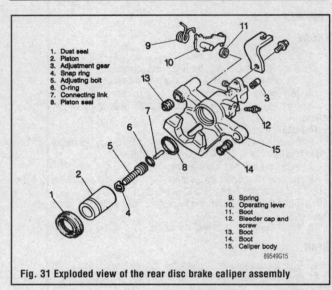

1. Dust seal
2. Piston
3. Adjustment gear
4. Snap ring
5. Adjusting bolt
6. O-ring
7. Connecting link
8. Piston seal
9. Spring
10. Operating lever
11. Boot
12. Bleeder cap and screw
13. Boot
14. Boot
15. Caliper body

89549G15

Fig. 31 Exploded view of the rear disc brake caliper assembly

➡ Depending upon the vehicle, there are two different ways to remove the piston from the caliper. Refer to the brake pad replacement procedure to make sure you have the correct procedure for your vehicle.

2. The first method is as follows:

a. Stuff a shop towel or a block of wood into the caliper to catch the piston.

b. Remove the caliper piston using compressed air applied into the caliper inlet hole. Inspect the piston for scoring, nicks, corrosion and/or worn or damaged chrome plating. The piston must be replaced if any of these conditions are found.

3. For the second method, you must rotate the piston to retract it from the caliper.

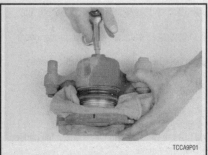

TCCA9P01

Fig. 32 For some types of calipers, use compressed air to drive the piston out of the caliper, but make sure to keep your fingers clear

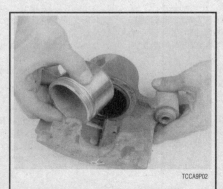

TCCA9P02

Fig. 33 Withdraw the piston from the caliper bore

TCCA9P03

Fig. 34 On some vehicles, you must remove the anti-rattle clip

Fig. 35 Use a prytool to carefully pry around the edge of the boot . . .

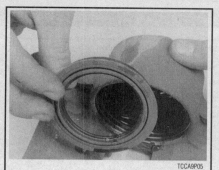

Fig. 36 . . . then remove the boot from the caliper housing, taking care not to score or damage the bore

Fig. 37 Use extreme caution when removing the piston seal; DO NOT scratch the caliper bore

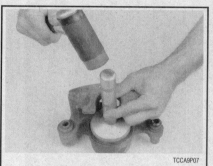

Fig. 38 Use the proper size driving tool and a mallet to properly seal the boots in the caliper housing

Fig. 39 There are tools, such as this Mighty-Vac, available to assist in proper brake system bleeding

Fig. 40 Remove the caliper and support it out of the way with wire

4. If equipped, remove the anti-rattle clip.

5. Use a prytool to remove the caliper boot, being careful not to scratch the housing bore.

6. Remove the piston seals from the groove in the caliper bore.

7. Carefully loosen the brake bleeder valve cap and valve from the caliper housing.

8. Inspect the caliper bores, pistons and mounting threads for scoring or excessive wear.

9. Use crocus cloth to polish out light corrosion from the piston and bore.

10. Clean all parts with denatured alcohol and dry with compressed air.

To assemble:

11. Lubricate and install the bleeder valve and cap.

12. Install the new seals into the caliper bore grooves, making sure they are not twisted.

13. Lubricate the piston bore.

14. Install the pistons and boots into the bores of the calipers and push to the bottom of the bores.

15. Use a suitable driving tool to seat the boots in the housing.

16. Install the caliper in the vehicle.

17. Install the wheel and tire assembly, then carefully lower the vehicle.

18. Properly bleed the brake system.

Brake Disc (Rotor)

REMOVAL & INSTALLATION

▶ **See Figures 40 and 41**

1. Raise the vehicle and support safely. Remove appropriate wheel assembly.

2. Remove the caliper and brake pads. Support the caliper out of the way using wire.

3. The rotor on most models is held to the hub by 2 small threaded screws. Remove screws, if equipped, and pull off the rotor.

4. Installation is the reverse of the removal process.

Fig. 41 The rotor can now be pulled from the hub

INSPECTION

Using a micrometer, measure the disc thickness in at least eight positions, approximately 45 degrees apart and 0.39 in. (10mm) in from the outer edge of the disc. The minimum thickness is 0.87 in. (22mm), with a maximum thickness variation of 0.0006 in. (0.015mm).

If the disc is below limits for thickness, remove it and install a new one. If the thickness variation exceeds the specifications, replace the disc or turn rotor with on the car type brake lathe.

DRUM BRAKES

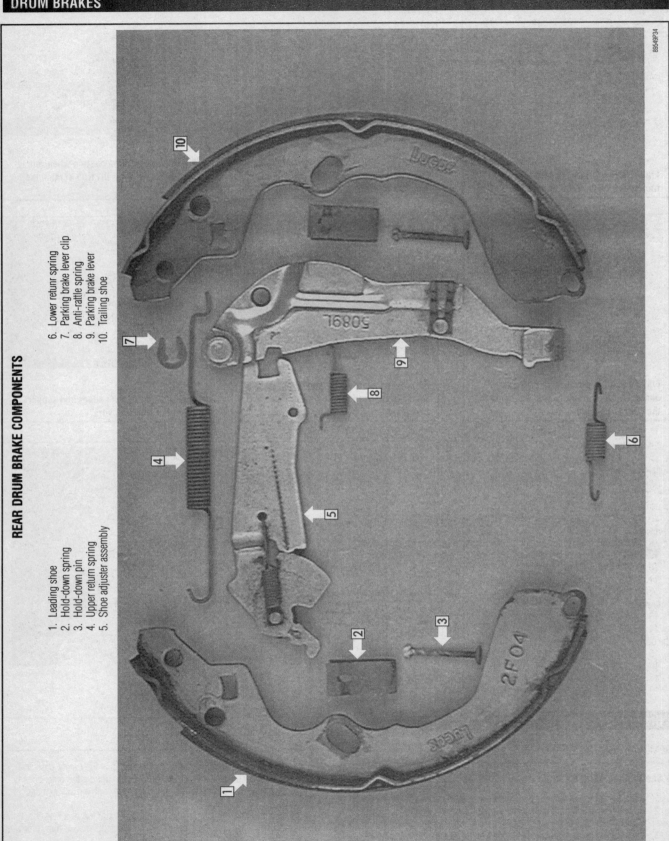

REAR DRUM BRAKE COMPONENTS

1. Leading shoe
2. Hold-down spring
3. Hold-down pin
4. Upper return spring
5. Shoe adjuster assembly
6. Lower retunr spring
7. Parking brake lever clip
8. Anti-rattle spring
9. Parking brake lever
10. Trailing shoe

Brake Drums

REMOVAL AND INSTALLATION

▶ **See Figures 42 and 43**

1. Disconnect the negative battery cable.
2. Loosen the rear wheel lug nuts. Raise and safely support the vehicle.
3. Remove the rear wheel and remove the center hub cap (if equipped). If equipped, uncrimp the locknut and remove it.
4. If the drum is secured the to hub by screws, remove them.
5. Pull the brake drum outward to remove. If the brake drum is difficult to remove, push the operating lever stopper at the backing plate upward to release the operating lever and to increase the shoe clearance.

Fig. 42 If the drum is secured the to hub by screws, remove them

Fig. 43 Pull the drum outward to remove it

6. Installation is the reverse of the removal procedure. If equipped, install a new locknut and tighten it to 72–130 ft. lbs. (98–177Nm). Crimp the locknut. If equipped with screws, tighten them until snug.

INSPECTION

Inspect the brake drum for any abnormal scratches, uneven or abnormal wear. Minor items may be corrected by sanding lightly. Refer to the brake specifications chart for wear limits.

Brake Shoes

INSPECTION

Inspect the brake shoes for peeling, cracking or extremely uneven wear of the brake shoe lining. Measure the brake shoe lining thickness. The minimum thickness is 0.04 inch (1.0 mm).

REMOVAL & INSTALLATION

▶ **See Figures 44 thru 51**

1. Remove the brake drum as previously described.
2. If accessible, disconnect the parking brake cable from the backside of the brake backing plate.
3. Using a prytool, release the pressure from the brake shoe adjuster.
4. Remove the upper and lower return springs.
5. Remove the hold pins and springs.
6. Remove the lower (leading side) brake shoe.
7. If applicable, remove the parking brake cable from the actuating lever.
8. Remove the upper (trailing side) brake shoe.
9. If necessary, remove the clip securing the actuating lever to the shoe, then remove the lever. Transfer the lever to the new shoe and secure with a new retaining clip.

To install:

10. Install the upper (trailing side) brake shoe to the operating lever and then to the wheel cylinder and backing plate. Install the brake shoe hold spring and hold pin.
11. Install the anti-rattle spring.
12. Install the lower return spring to both brake shoes.
13. Install the leading side brake shoe to the operating lever and then to the wheel cylinder and anchor plate.
14. Install the hold spring and hold pin to the leading side brake shoe.

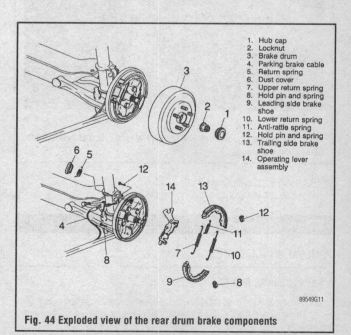

1. Hub cap
2. Locknut
3. Brake drum
4. Parking brake cable
5. Return spring
6. Dust cover
7. Upper return spring
8. Hold pin and spring
9. Leading side brake shoe
10. Lower return spring
11. Anti-rattle spring
12. Hold pin and spring
13. Trailing side brake shoe
14. Operating lever assembly

Fig. 44 Exploded view of the rear drum brake components

Fig. 45 Release the pressure on the adjuster assembly with a prytool

Fig. 46 Remove the upper . . .

Fig. 47 . . . and the lower return springs

Fig. 48 Remove the hold-down springs and pins

Fig. 49 Remove the leading side brake shoe

Fig. 50 If applicable, detach the parking brake cable from the actuating lever

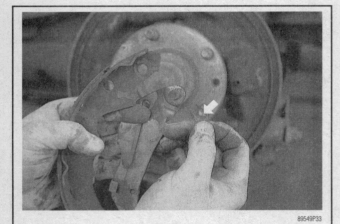

Fig. 51 If necessary, remove the lever retaining clip and remove the lever from the shoe

15. Install the upper return spring.
16. Install the brake drum as previously described.

Wheel Cylinders

REMOVAL & INSTALLATION

▶ See Figures 52 thru 57

1. Remove the brake drum(s) and brake shoes as previously described.
2. Disconnect the brake line from the back of the backing plate with a line type wrench.

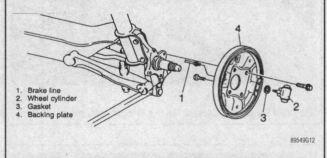

1. Brake line
2. Wheel cylinder
3. Gasket
4. Backing plate

Fig. 52 Rear drum brake backing plate assembly and wheel cylinder

3. Remove the wheel cylinder mounting bolt(s) and remove the wheel cylinder from the backing plate.
4. Installation is the reverse of the removal procedure. Replace the wheel cylinder to backing plate gasket. Tighten the wheel cylinder bolt(s) to 7–9 ft. lbs. (10–13 Nm).
5. Bleed the brake system and check operation.

OVERHAUL

▶ See Figures 58 thru 67

Wheel cylinder overhaul kits may be available, but often at little or no savings over a reconditioned wheel cylinder. It often makes sense with these components to substitute a new or reconditioned part instead of attempting an overhaul.

If no replacement is available, or you would prefer to overhaul your wheel cylinders, the following procedure may be used. When rebuilding and installing wheel cylinders, avoid getting any contaminants into the system. Always use clean, new, high quality brake fluid. If dirty or improper fluid has

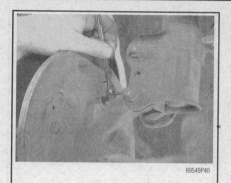

Fig. 53 Loosen the brake line fitting with a flare nut wrench . . .

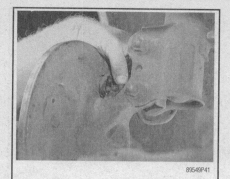

Fig. 54 . . . then carefully pull it away from the wheel cylinder

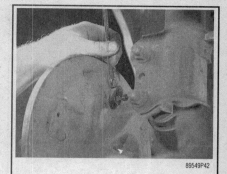

Fig. 55 Remove the bolt(s) securing the cylinder to the backing plate

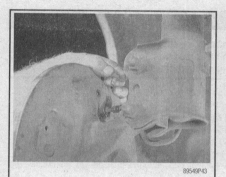

Fig. 56 Inspect the threads for damage and replace if necessary

Fig. 57 Remove the wheel cylinder and gasket from the backing plate

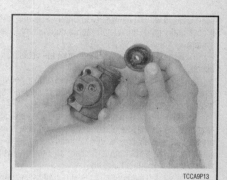

Fig. 58 Remove the outer boots from the wheel cylinder

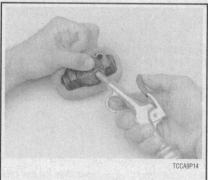

Fig. 59 Compressed air can be used to remove the pistons and seals

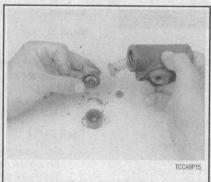

Fig. 60 Remove the pistons, cup seals and spring from the cylinder

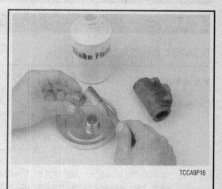

Fig. 61 Use brake fluid and a soft brush to clean the pistons . . .

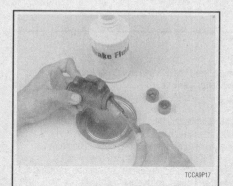

Fig. 62 . . . and the bore of the wheel cylinder

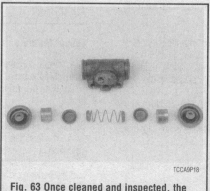

Fig. 63 Once cleaned and inspected, the wheel cylinder is ready for assembly

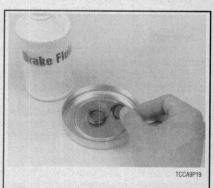

Fig. 64 Lubricate the cup seals with brake fluid

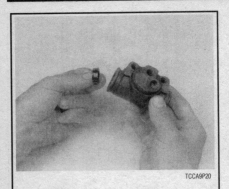

Fig. 65 Install the spring, then the cup seals in the bore

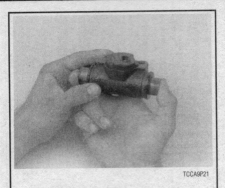

Fig. 66 Lightly lubricate the pistons, then install them

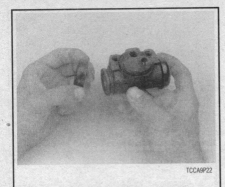

Fig. 67 The boots can now be installed over the wheel cylinder ends

been used, it will be necessary to drain the entire system, flush the system with proper brake fluid, replace all rubber components, then refill and bleed the system.

1. Remove the wheel cylinder from the vehicle and place on a clean workbench.

2. First remove and discard the old rubber boots, then withdraw the pistons. Piston cylinders are equipped with seals and a spring assembly, all located behind the pistons in the cylinder bore.

3. Remove the remaining inner components, seals and spring assembly. Compressed air may be useful in removing these components. If no compressed air is available, be VERY careful not to score the wheel cylinder bore when removing parts from it. Discard all components for which replacements were supplied in the rebuild kit.

4. Wash the cylinder and metal parts in denatured alcohol or clean brake fluid.

✳✳ WARNING

Never use a mineral-based solvent such as gasoline, kerosene or paint thinner for cleaning purposes. These solvents will swell rubber components and quickly deteriorate them.

5. Allow the parts to air dry or use compressed air. Do not use rags for cleaning, since lint will remain in the cylinder bore.

6. Inspect the piston and replace it if it shows scratches.

7. Lubricate the cylinder bore and seals using clean brake fluid.

8. Position the spring assembly.

9. Install the inner seals, then the pistons.

10. Insert the new boots into the counterbores by hand. Do not lubricate the boots.

11. Install the wheel cylinder.

PARKING BRAKE

Cables

REMOVAL & INSTALLATION

▶ **See Figure 68**

Except Millenia

1. Disconnect the negative battery cable.

2. Remove the rear center console as follows:

  a. Remove the screw plugs in the side covers. Remove the retainer screws and the side covers from the vehicle.

  b. Remove the mounting bolts and the floor console from the vehicle.

3. Loosen the cable adjusting nut at the parking brake handle. Disconnect the brake cable from the handle and remove the retaining spring.

4. Raise the vehicle and support safely. Remove the parking brake cable mounting bolts. Disconnect the cable end from the parking brake assembly.

5. Unfasten any remaining frame retainers and remove the cables from the vehicle.

To install:

6. Install the cable to the rear actuator. Secure in place with the parking brake cable mounting bolts.

7. Reattach the parking brake cables to the parking brake handle inside the vehicle. Tighten the adjusting nut until the proper tension is placed on the cable.

8. Secure all cable retainers tightening to 14–18 ft. lbs. (19–25 Nm). Apply and release the parking brake a number of times once all adjustments have been made. With the rear wheels raised, make sure the parking brake is not causing drag on the rear wheels.

9. Install the rear center console assembly.

10. Road test the vehicle and check for proper brake operation. Check that the parking brake holds the vehicle on an incline.

Millenia

FRONT CABLE

1. Remove the console around the parking brake lever.

2. Remove the nut securing the front parking brake cable to the lever.

3. Raise and support the vehicle safely.

4. Disconnect the rear parking brake cables from the equalizer.

5. Installation is reverse of removal. Torque the front parking cable nut to 14–18 ft. lbs. (19–25 Nm).

REAR CABLE

1. Disconnect the front cable from the rear cables.

2. Remove the clips and mounting bolts and remove the cables.

3. The rear parking brake shoe assembly must be removed for the rear cable to be disconnected and removed.

4. Installation is the reverse of removal. Torque the mounting screws to 14–18 ft. lbs. (19–25 Nm).

ADJUSTMENT

Except Millenia

1. Make sure the parking brake cable is free and is not frozen or sticking. Make sure the brake shoes are properly adjusted.

2. With the engine running, forcefully depress the brake pedal 5–6 times.

3. Apply the parking brake while counting the number of notches. Check the desired parking brake stroke; it should be 5–7 notches.

4. If adjustment is required, remove the adjusting nut clip and turn the adjusting nut which is located at the front of the parking brake cable.

5. After adjustment, check there is no looseness between the adjusting nut and the parking brake lever, then tighten the locknut.

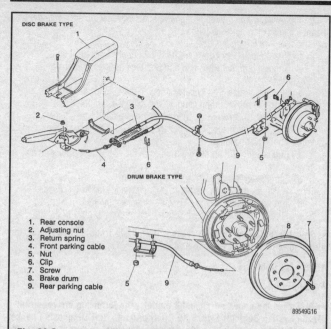

DISC BRAKE TYPE

DRUM BRAKE TYPE

1. Rear console
2. Adjusting nut
3. Return spring
4. Front parking cable
5. Nut
6. Clip
7. Screw
8. Brake drum
9. Rear parking cable

89549G16

Fig. 68 Common parking brake cable routing used by models covered in this manual

➡ **Do not adjust the parking brake too tight. If the number of notches is less than specification, the cable has been pulled too much and the automatic adjuster will fail or the brakes will drag.**

6. After adjusting the lever stroke, raise the rear of the vehicle and safely support. With the parking brake lever in the released position, turn the rear wheels to confirm that the rear brakes are not dragging.
7. Check that the parking brake holds the vehicle on an incline.

Millenia

1. Make sure the parking brake cable is free and is not frozen or sticking. Make sure the brake shoes are properly adjusted.
2. Raise and safely support the rear wheels.
3. Apply the parking brake while counting the number of notches. Check the desired parking brake stroke; it should be 7–9 notches.
4. If adjustment is required, remove the adjusting nut cover and turn the adjusting nut located at the front of the parking brake cable.
5. After adjustment, check there is no looseness between the adjusting nut and the parking brake lever, then tighten the locknut.

➡ **Do not adjust the parking brake too tight. If the number of notches is less than specification, the cable has been pulled too much and the automatic adjuster will fail or the brakes will drag.**

6. With the parking brake lever in the released position, turn the rear wheels to confirm that the rear brakes are not dragging.
7. Lower the vehicle.
8. Check that the parking brake holds the vehicle on an incline.

ANTI-LOCK BRAKE SYSTEM

General Description

Anti-lock braking systems are designed to prevent locked-wheel skidding during hard braking or during braking on slippery surfaces. The front wheels of a vehicle cannot apply steering force if they are locked and sliding; the vehicle will continue in its previous direction of travel. The four wheel anti-lock brake systems found on Mazda vehicles holds the individual wheels just below the point of locking, which in turn allows some steering response and prevents the rear of the vehicle from sliding sideways.

Electrical signals are sent from the wheel speed sensors to the ABS control unit; when the system detects impending lock-up at any wheel, solenoid valves within the hydraulic unit cycle to control the line pressure as needed. The systems employ normal master cylinder and vacuum booster arrangements; no hydraulic accumulator is used, nor is any high pressure fluid stored within the system. The system employs a conventional master cylinder and vacuum booster arrangements; no hydraulic accumulator is used, nor is any high pressure fluid stored within the system.

SYSTEM OPERATION

The ABS system monitors and compares wheel speed based on the inputs from the wheel speed sensors. The brake pressure is controlled according to the impending lock-up computations of the ABS control unit.

If either front wheel approaches lock-up, the controller actuates the individual solenoid for that wheel, reducing pressure in the line. Impending lock-up at either rear wheel will engage the rear control solenoid; hydraulic pressure is reduced equally to both rear wheels, reducing the tendency of the rear to skid sideways under braking.

SYSTEM PRECAUTIONS

• Certain components within the ABS system are not intended to be serviced or repaired individually. Only those components with removal and installation procedures should be serviced.
• Do not use rubber hoses or other parts not specifically specified for the ABS system. When using repair kits, replace all parts included in the kit. Partial or incorrect repair may lead to functional problems and require the replacement of components.

• Lubricate rubber parts with clean, fresh brake fluid to ease assembly. Do not use lubricated shop air to clean parts; damage to rubber components may result.
• Use only DOT 3 brake fluid from an unopened container.
• If any hydraulic component or line is removed or replaced, it may be necessary to bleed the entire system.
• A clean repair area is essential. Always clean the reservoir and cap thoroughly before removing the cap. The slightest amount of dirt in the fluid may plug an orifice and impair the system function. Perform repairs after components have been thoroughly cleaned; use only denatured alcohol to clean components. Do not allow ABS components to come into contact with any substance containing mineral oil; this includes used shop rags.
• The Anti-Lock control unit is a microprocessor similar to other computer units in the vehicle. Ensure that the ignition switch is **OFF** before removing or installing controller harnesses. Avoid static electricity discharge at or near the controller.
• If any arc welding is to be done on the vehicle, the ALCU connectors should be disconnected before welding operations begin.

Diagnosis and Testing

The ABS warning light is located in the instrument cluster. The lamp warns the operator of a possible fault in the system.

When the system is operating correctly, the ABS warning lamp will flash when the ignition switch is initially turned **ON** , then the lamp will turn **OFF** . During the lamp illumination the control unit checks the valve relays for proper function. When the ignition is turned to **START** , power to the ABS controller is interrupted and the warning lamp stays **ON** . Once the ignition returns to the **ON** position, power is restored and the system re-checks itself. The warning lamp goes out and should stay off during operation of the vehicle.

READING & CLEARING CODES

1990—91 Vehicles

▶ **See Figures 69, 70 and 71**

1. Turn the ignition switch **ON** and **OFF** several times and observe the ABS warning lamp.

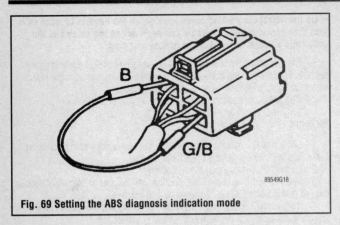

Fig. 69 Setting the ABS diagnosis indication mode

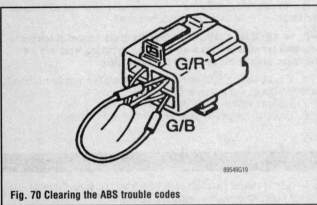

Fig. 70 Clearing the ABS trouble codes

2. If the ABS warning lamp illuminates constantly, set the system to the diagnosis indication mode as follows:

   a. Remove the drivers seat.

   b. Unplug the check connector from the under seat control unit.

   c. Connect terminal wires G/B and B at the check connector with a jumper wire.

   d. Start the engine. The system is now in the diagnosis mode.

3. Observe the ABS warning lamp. Count the flashes of the lamp.

4. Refer to the corresponding chart and correct the indicated item.

5. After repairs are made or components replaced, cancel the trouble code by following the steps below:

   a. Connect the G/R and G/B terminals of the check connector with a jumper wire.

   b. Turn the ignition switch to the ON position.

   c. Watch for the warning lamp to illuminate and wait 1–2 seconds.

   d. Turn the ignition switch OFF and disconnect the jumper wire.

   e. Start the engine and make sure the warning lamp goes OFF.

➡**Only 1 trouble code will be erased, if multiple trouble codes exist, the above procedure must be repeated.**

1992—98 Vehicles

◆ **See Figure 72**

➡**To access the codes on 1992–98 models, the following are required: Mazda System Selector Switch 49-BO19-9A0 and Self-Diagnosis Checker 49-HO18-9A1 or a scan tool. If a scan tool is used, be sure it is capable of pulling codes from ABS systems. Not all scan tools have this ability.**

1. Connect the Mazda system selector switch and the self-diagnosis checker or a scan tool to the underhood data link connector and to a ground. Set the select switch on the checker to A and the system selector knob to position 3. On scan tools, access the ABS menu. Follow the menu on the scan tool to access the codes. If any codes are present it will display the code number and the corresponding circuit or component.

2. Turn the ignition switch **ON** and observe the checker display. Initially, code 88 should appear. If code 88 does not appear check the connections between the checker and the selector. After code 88 appears, watch for and record any other trouble codes.

3. After the proper repairs are made, the codes must be erased by doing the following:

   a. At the data link connector under the hood, connect the TBS terminal to GND.

   b. Turn the ignition switch to the **ON** position.

   c. Output all of the memorized trouble codes.

   d. After the first trouble code repeats itself, depress the brake pedal 10 times at intervals of less than 1 second. This will clear all trouble codes.

Diagnosis indication		Possible failure
Warning lamp	Voltmeter	
ON / OFF	12V / 0V	Right front wheel-speed sensor
	⊓⊓	Left front wheel-speed sensor
	⊓⊓⊓	Rear wheel-speed sensor
	⊓⊓⊓⊓	Right front sensor rotor
	⊓⊓⊓⊓⊓	Left front sensor rotor
	⊓⊓⊓⊓⊓⊓	Right rear sensor rotor
	⊓⊓⊓⊓⊓⊓⊓	Left rear sensor rotor
⊓ / ⊓⊓⊓⊓⊓	⊓	Hydraulic unit / Harness / Control unit connector (11-pin)
⊓ / ⊓⊓⊓⊓⊓	⊓⊓	
⊓ / ⊓⊓⊓⊓⊓	⊓⊓⊓	Relay box / Hydraulic unit / Harness
⊓ / ⊓⊓⊓⊓⊓	⊓⊓⊓⊓	Hydraulic unit / Harness / Control unit
⊓ / ⊓⊓⊓⊓⊓	⊓⊓⊓⊓⊓	Control unit
⊓	No signal; failure conditions not stored in memory	Control unit / Control unit connector (17-pin) / Battery capacity / Alternator output voltage / Wiring harness (warning light—control unit—check connector)
		No problem

Several rows showing warning lamp and voltmeter waveform patterns with corresponding possible failures.

Fig. 71 ABS trouble codes

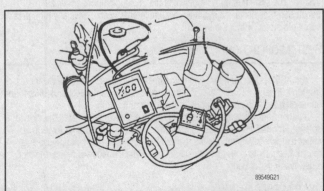

Fig. 72 Connecting the ABS system selector and self-diagnosis checker to the 1992–98 vehicles

VISUAL INSPECTION

Remember to first determine if the problem is related to the anti-lock system or not. The anti-lock system is made up of 2 basic sub-systems:

1. The hydraulic system, which may be diagnosed and serviced using nor-

mal brake system procedures, however, there is a need to determine whether the problem is related to the ABS components or not.

2. The electrical system which may be diagnosed using the charts and diagnostic tools.

Before diagnosing an apparent ABS problem, make absolutely certain that the normal braking system is in correct working order. Many common brake problems (dragging lining, seepage, etc.) will affect the ABS system. A visual check of specific system components may reveal problems creating an apparent ABS malfunction. Performing this inspection may reveal a simple failure, thus eliminating extended diagnostic time.

3. Inspect the brake fluid level in the reservoir.

4. Inspect brake lines, hoses, master cylinder assembly, and brake calipers for leakage.

5. Visually check brake lines and hoses for excessive wear, heat damage, punctures, contact with other parts, missing clips or holders, blockage or crimping.

6. Check the calipers for rust or corrosion. Check for proper sliding action if applicable.

7. Check the caliper pistons for freedom of motion during application and release.

8. Inspect the wheel speed sensors for proper mounting and connections.

9. Inspect the toothed wheels for broken teeth or poor mounting.

10. Inspect the wheels and tires on the vehicle. They must be of the same size and type to generate accurate speed signals. Check also for approximately equal tire pressures.

11. Confirm the fault occurrence with the operator. Certain driver induced faults may cause dash warning lamps to light. Excessive wheel spin on low-traction surfaces or high speed acceleration may also set fault codes and trigger a warning lamp. These induced faults are not system failures but examples of vehicle performance outside the parameters of the controller.

12. The most common cause of intermittent faults is not a failed sensor but a loose, corroded or dirty connector. Incorrect installation of the wheel speed sensor will cause a loss of wheel speed signal. Check harness and component connectors carefully.

➡ **If the battery on the vehicle has been completely drained, always recharge the battery before driving. If the vehicle is driven immediately after jump starting, the ABS self–check may draw enough current to make the engine run improperly. An alternate solution is to disconnect the ABS connector at the hydraulic unit. This will disable the ABS and illuminate the dash warning lamp. Reconnect the ABS when the battery is sufficiently charged.**

Control Unit

REMOVAL & INSTALLATION

▶ **See Figure 73**

1. Disconnect the negative battery cable.
2. Unplug the electrical connectors from the ABS control unit.

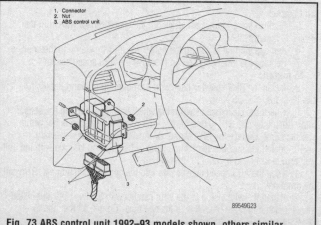

1. Connector
2. Nut
3. ABS control unit

89549G23

Fig. 73 ABS control unit 1992–93 models shown, others similar

3. Remove the ABS control unit mounting bolts and remove the ABS control unit.

4. Installation is the reverse of the removal procedure.

Hydraulic Unit

The hydraulic unit is located in the engine compartment. It contains the solenoid valves and the pump/motor assembly which provides pressurized fluid for the anti-lock system when necessary. Hydraulic units are not interchangeable on any vehicles. Neither unit is serviceable; if any fault occurs within the hydraulic unit, the entire unit must be replaced.

REMOVAL & INSTALLATION

▶ **See Figure 74**

1. Disconnect the negative battery cable. Use a syringe or similar device to remove as much fluid as possible from the reservoir. Some fluid will be spilled from lines during removal of the hydraulic unit; protect adjacent painted surfaces.

2. If necessary, remove the fuel filter and igniter mounting nuts and move them out of the way.

3. Remove the charcoal canister from the vehicle and if the vehicle is equipped with cruise control, remove the cruise control actuator.

4. Disconnect the brake lines from the hydraulic unit. Correct reassembly is critical. Label or identify the lines before removal. Plug each line immediately after removal.

5. Disconnect the electrical harness connectors to the hydraulic unit.

6. Remove the 2 nuts holding the hydraulic unit. Remove the unit upwards.

➡**The hydraulic unit is heavy; use care when removing it. The unit must remain in the upright position at all times and be protected from impact and shock.**

7. Set the unit upright supported by blocks on the workbench. The hydraulic unit must not be tilted or turned upside down. No component of the hydraulic unit should be loosened or disassembled.

8. The bracket assemblies may be removed if desired.

To install:

9. Install the brackets if removed.

10. Install the hydraulic unit into the vehicle, keeping it upright at all times.

11. Install the retaining nuts and tighten.

12. Connect the electrical connectors.

13. Connect each brake line to the proper port and double check the placement. Tighten each line to 113–190 inch lbs. (12.9–21.5 Nm).

14. Fill the reservoir to the MAX line with brake fluid.

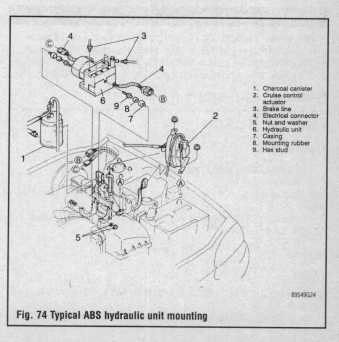

1. Charcoal canister
2. Cruise control actuator
3. Brake line
4. Electrical connector
5. Nut and washer
6. Hydraulic unit
7. Casing
8. Mounting rubber
9. Hex stud

89549G24

Fig. 74 Typical ABS hydraulic unit mounting

15. Bleed the master cylinder, then bleed the brake lines.
16. If removed, install the cruise control actuator and the charcoal canister.

ABS Relay

REMOVAL AND INSTALLATION

▶ **See Figure 75**

1. Remove the underhood fuse box cover.
2. Remove the diagnosis connector attaching bolt and move the connector to the side.
3. Remove the underhood fuse panel mounting nuts and move the fuse panel to the side.
4. Remove the ABS relay mounting bolt and unplug the relay electrical connector. Remove the relay.
5. Installation is the reverse of the removal procedure.

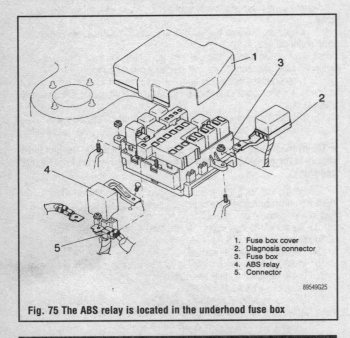

1.	Fuse box cover
2.	Diagnosis connector
3.	Fuse box
4.	ABS relay
5.	Connector

89549G25

Fig. 75 The ABS relay is located in the underhood fuse box

Wheel Speed Sensors

Each wheel is equipped with a magnetic sensor mounted a fixed distance from a toothed ring which rotates with the wheel. The sensors are replaceable but not interchangeable; each must be fitted to its correct location. The toothed rings are replaceable although disassembly of the hub or axle shaft is required.

REMOVAL & INSTALLATION

▶ **See Figures 76 and 77**

Except Millenia

1. Raise and safely support the vehicle.
2. Remove the wheel.
3. Unplug the connector. Remove the mounting bolts/nuts and remove the sensor.
4. Installation is the reverse of removal. Tighten the bolts at the sensor to 12–16 ft. lbs. (16–22 Nm).

Millenia

FRONT

1. Working from under the hood, unplug the ABS speed sensor electrical connector.
2. Raise and safely support the vehicle and remove the tire and wheel.

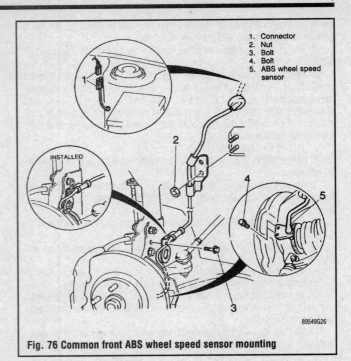

1.	Connector
2.	Nut
3.	Bolt
4.	Bolt
5.	ABS wheel speed sensor

89549G26

Fig. 76 Common front ABS wheel speed sensor mounting

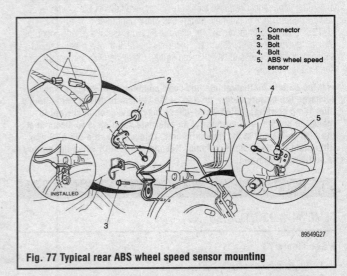

1.	Connector
2.	Bolt
3.	Bolt
4.	Bolt
5.	ABS wheel speed sensor

89549G27

Fig. 77 Typical rear ABS wheel speed sensor mounting

3. Remove the two nuts and the ABS sensor wire bracket from the body.
4. Remove the two nuts and remove the speed sensor wire clamp from the strut bracket.
5. Remove the grommet and draw out the speed sensor wire from the engine compartment.
6. Remove the bolt attaching the speed sensor wire clamp to the knuckle.
7. Remove the mounting bolt and remove the ABS speed sensor.

To install:

8. Install the ABS speed sensor with its mounting bolt and tighten to 14–18 ft. lbs. (19–25 Nm).
9. Check the clearance between the wheel speed sensor and the sensor rotor. Clearance is 0.012–0.043 in. (0.3–1.1 mm). If clearance is not within specifications, replace the ABS sensor or the sensor rotor as necessary.
10. Install the speed sensor wire clamp to the steering knuckle with the bolt. Bolt torque is 14–18 ft. lbs. (19–25 Nm).
11. Feed the ABS speed sensor wire into the engine compartment. Reinstall the grommet.
12. Install the wire clamp to the strut bracket with the two nuts and install the wire clamp to body bracket with the two nuts. Tighten all the nuts to 70–95.4 in. lbs. (7.9–10.7 Nm).

13. Reinstall the tire and wheel and safely lower the vehicle.
14. Engage the speed sensor electrical connector.

REAR

1. Unplug the speed sensor electrical connector.
2. Remove the bolts attaching the sensor wire clamps to the body and the strut assembly.
3. Remove the speed sensor mounting bolt and remove the sensor.
4. Installation is the reverse of removal. Mounting bolt and wire clamp mounting bolts are tightened to 14–18 ft. lbs. (19–25 Nm).

Filling the ABS System

The brake fluid reservoir is part of the normal brake system and is filled or checked in the usual manner. Always clean the reservoir cap and surrounding area thoroughly before removing the cap. Fill the reservoir only to the FULL mark; do not overfill. Use only fresh DOT 3 brake fluid from unopened containers. Do not use any fluid containing a petroleum base. Do not use any fluid which has been exposed to water or moisture. Failure to use the correct fluid will affect system function and component life.

Bleeding the ABS System

MASTER CYLINDER

If the master cylinder has been emptied of fluid or replaced, it must be bled separately from the rest of the system. Since the cylinder has no check valve, air can become trapped within it. To bleed the brake master cylinder after it has been drained, proceed as follows:

1. Disconnect the 2 brake lines from the master cylinder. Plug the lines immediately. The brake fluid reservoir should be in place and connected to the master cylinder. Check the fluid level before beginning.
2. An assistant should slowly depress and hold the brake pedal.
3. With the pedal held down, use 2 fingers to plug each outlet port on the master cylinder and release the brake pedal.

4. Repeat Steps 2 and 3 three or four times. The air will be bled from the cylinder.
5. Connect the brake lines to the master cylinder and tighten the fittings.
6. Start the engine, allowing the system to pressurize and self–check. Shut the ignition OFF and bleed the brake lines.

LINES & CALIPERS

The brake system must be bled any time a line, hose or component is loosened or removed. Any air trapped within the lines can affect pedal feel and system function. Bleeding the system is performed in the usual manner with an assistant in the car to pump the brake pedal. Make certain the fluid level in the reservoir is maintained at or near correct levels during bleeding operations.

The individual lines may be bled manually at each wheel using the traditional 2 person method.

1. The ignition must remain OFF throughout the bleeding procedure.
2. The system should be bled in the following order: Right rear, left front, left rear and right front.
3. Connect a transparent hose to the caliper bleed screw. Submerge the other end of the hose in clean brake fluid in a clear glass container.
4. Slowly pump the brake pedal several times. Use full strokes of the pedal and allow 5 seconds between strokes. After 2 or 3 strokes, hold pressure on the pedal keeping it at the bottom of its travel.
5. With pressure held on the pedal, open the bleed screw ½–¾ turn. Leave the bleed screw open until fluid stops flowing from the hose. Tighten the bleed screw and release the pedal.
6. Repeat Steps 3 and 4 until air-free fluid flows from the hose. Tighten the caliper bleed screw to 7.5 ft. lbs. (10 Nm).
7. Repeat the sequence at each remaining wheel.

➡ **Check the fluid level in the reservoir frequently and maintain it near the full level.**

8. When bleeding is complete, bring fluid level in the reservoir to the correct level. Install the reservoir cap.

BRAKE SPECIFICATIONS
All measurements in inches unless noted

Year	Model	Master Cylinder Bore	Brake Disc			Brake Drum Diameter			Minimum Lining Thickness	
			Original Thickness	Minimum Thickness	Maximum Runout	Original Inside Diameter	Max. Wear Limit	Max. Machine Diameter	Front	Rear
1990	323/Protege	0.875	0.870	0.790	0.004	9.000	9.040	—	0.080	0.040
	Rear Disc	—	0.350	0.280	0.004	—	—	—	—	0.040
	626/MX-6	0.875	0.940	0.870	0.004	9.000	9.060	—	—	0.040
	Rear Disc	—	0.390	0.310	0.004	—	—	—	—	0.040
1991	323/Protege	0.875	0.870	0.790	0.004	9.000	9.040	—	0.080	0.040
	Rear Disc	—	0.350	0.280	0.004	—	—	—	—	0.040
	626/MX-6	0.875	0.940	0.870	0.004	9.000	9.060	—	0.080	0.040
	Rear Disc	—	0.390	0.310	0.004	—	—	—	—	0.040
1992	323/Protege	0.875	0.870	0.790	0.004	7.870	7.910	—	0.080	0.040
	Rear Disc	—	0.350	0.280	0.004	—	—	—	—	0.040
	MX-3	0.875	0.870	0.790	0.004	7.870	7.910	—	0.080	0.040
	Rear Disc	0.937	0.350	0.310	0.004	—	—	—	—	0.040
	626/MX-6	0.875	0.940	0.870	0.004	9.000	9.060	—	0.080	0.040
	Rear Disc	—	0.390	0.310	0.004	—	—	—	—	0.040
1993	323/Protege	0.875	0.870	0.790	0.004	7.870	7.910	—	0.080	0.040
	Rear Disc	—	0.350	0.280	0.004	—	—	—	—	0.040
	MX-3	0.875	0.870	0.790	0.004	7.870	7.910	—	0.080	0.040
	Rear Disc	0.937	0.350	0.310	0.004	—	—	—	—	0.040
	626/MX-6/Probe	0.937	0.940	0.870	0.004	9.000	9.060	—	0.080	0.040
	Rear Disc	—	0.390	0.310	0.004	—	—	—	—	0.040
1994	323/Protege	0.875	0.870	0.790	0.004	7.870	7.910	—	0.080	0.040
	Rear Disc	—	0.350	0.280	0.004	—	—	—	—	0.040
	MX-3	0.875	0.870	0.790	0.004	7.870	7.910	—	0.080	0.040
	Rear Disc	0.937	0.350	0.310	0.004	—	—	—	—	0.040
	626/MX-6/Probe	0.937	0.940	0.870	0.004	9.000	9.060	—	0.080	0.040
	Rear Disc	—	0.390	0.310	0.004	—	—	—	—	0.040

89549C20

BRAKE SPECIFICATIONS
All measurements in inches unless noted

Year	Model	Master Cylinder Bore	Brake Disc			Brake Drum Diameter			Minimum Lining Thickness	
			Original Thickness	Minimum Thickness	Maximum Runout	Original Inside Diameter	Max. Wear Limit	Max. Machine Diameter	Front	Rear
1995	Protege	0.875	0.870	0.790	0.002	7.870	7.933	—	0.039	0.039
	Rear Disc	—	0.350	0.275	0.002	—	—	—	—	0.039
	MX-3	0.875	0.870	0.790	0.004	7.870	7.910	—	0.080	0.040
	Rear Disc	0.937	0.350	0.310	0.004	—	—	—	—	0.040
	626/MX-6/Probe	0.937	0.940	0.870	0.004	9.000	9.060	—	0.080	0.040
	Rear Disc	—	0.390	0.310	0.004	—	—	—	—	0.040
	Millenia	1.000	1.100	1.020	0.004	7.480	7.520	—	0.080	0.080
	Rear Disc	—	0.370	0.290	0.004	—	—	—	—	0.080
1996	Protege	0.875	0.870	0.790	0.002	7.870	7.933	—	0.039	0.039
	Rear Disc	—	0.350	0.275	0.002	—	—	—	—	0.039
	626/MX-6/Probe	0.937	0.940	0.870	0.004	9.000	9.060	—	0.080	0.040
	Rear Disc	—	0.390	0.310	0.004	—	—	—	—	0.040
	Millenia	1.000	1.100	1.020	0.002	7.480	7.520	—	0.080	0.080
	Rear Disc	—	0.370	0.290	0.002	—	—	—	—	0.080
1997	Protege	0.875	0.870	0.790	0.002	7.870	7.933	—	0.039	0.039
	Rear Disc	—	0.350	0.275	0.002	—	—	—	—	0.039
	626/MX-6/Probe	0.937	0.940	0.870	0.004	9.000	9.060	—	0.080	0.040
	Rear Disc	—	0.390	0.310	0.004	—	—	—	—	0.040
	Millenia	1.000	1.100	1.020	0.002	7.480	7.520	—	0.080	0.080
	Rear Disc	—	0.370	0.290	0.002	—	—	—	—	0.080
1998	Protege	0.875	0.870	0.790	0.002	7.870	7.933	—	0.039	0.039
	Rear Disc	—	0.350	0.275	0.002	—	—	—	—	0.039
	626	0.937	0.940	0.870	0.004	9.000	9.060	—	0.080	0.040
	Rear Disc	—	0.390	0.310	0.004	—	—	—	—	0.040
	Millenia	1.000	1.100	1.020	0.002	7.480	7.520	—	0.080	0.080
	Rear Disc	—	0.370	0.290	0.002	—	—	—	—	0.080

89549C21

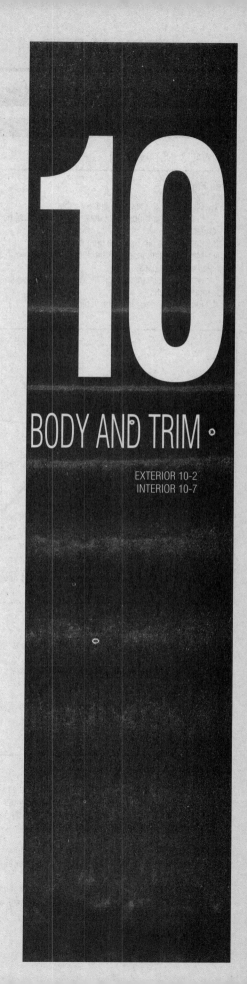

10

BODY AND TRIM

EXTERIOR

Doors

REMOVAL & INSTALLATION

▶ See Figure 1

1. Disconnect the negative battery cable.
2. Pull back the rubber boot covering the electrical harness then unplug the connector.
3. Remove the pin from the door check strap.
4. Mark the relationship of the door to the hinge with a crayon or marker for installation purposes.
5. Have an assistant support the door and remove the upper and lower hinge mounting bolts.
6. Remove the door from the vehicle.

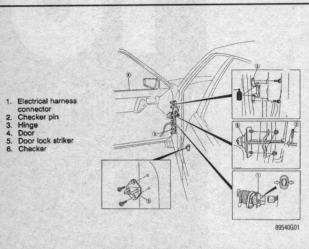

1. Electrical harness connector
2. Checker pin
3. Hinge
4. Door
5. Door lock striker
6. Checker

89540G01

Fig. 1 Common door mounting used on models covered by this manual

To install:

7. Have an assistant support the door in place and install the mounting bolts.
8. Align the hinge and the door with the previously made marks. Tighten the hinge bolts to 13–22 ft. lbs. (18–29 Nm).
9. Install the pin to the door check strap.
10. Engage the electrical connector then install the rubber boot.
11. Connect the negative battery cable.

ADJUSTMENT

▶ See Figure 2

The door latch striker can be adjusted laterally and vertically as well as fore and aft. The striker should not be adjusted to correct door sag.

1. Loosen the striker attaching screws and move the striker as required.
2. Tighten the attaching screws and check the door for fit. Repeat the procedure if necessary.

The door hinges provide sufficient adjustment latitude to correct most door misalignment conditions. Do not cover up a poor door alignment with the door latch striker adjustment.

3. Loosen the hinge attaching bolts and move the hinge as required.
4. Tighten the attaching bolts and check the door for fit. Repeat the procedure if necessary.

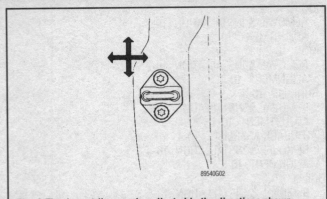

89540G02

Fig. 2 The door striker can be adjusted in the directions shown

Hood

REMOVAL & INSTALLATION

▶ See Figures 3, 4 and 5

1. Open the hood and support it securely. Mark the hinge location on the hood. If so equipped, disconnect the windshield washer hose from its retaining clamp.
2. Have an assistant hold the hood in the up position. Remove the hood support and remove the hinge-to-hood bolts.
3. Remove the hood from the vehicle.

To install:

4. Position the hood against the hinges, using the marks made previously on the hood to help with alignment.
5. Have an assistant hold the hood. Install the hinge-to-hood bolts, the hood support and the hood support bolts. If so equipped, install the washer hose.
6. Tighten all bolts securely and check the hood for proper alignment.

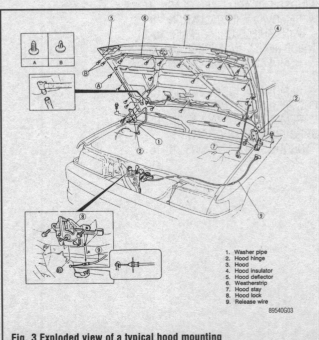

1. Washer pipe
2. Hood hinge
3. Hood
4. Hood insulator
5. Hood deflector
6. Weatherstrip
7. Hood stay
8. Hood lock
9. Release wire

89540G03

Fig. 3 Exploded view of a typical hood mounting

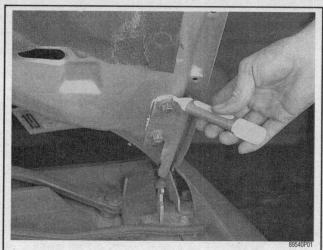
Fig. 4 Matchmark the position of the hood before removing the retaining bolts

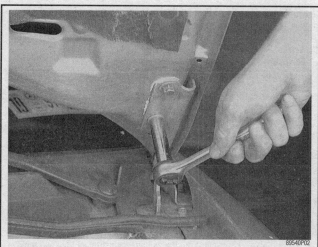
Fig. 5 Have an assistant secure the hood, then remove the retaining bolts

ALIGNMENT

Hood

The hood is provided with up-and-down and side-to-side adjustments.
1. To make the side-to-side adjustments:
  a. Loosen the hood attaching bolts and move the hood to the proper position, then tighten the attaching bolts.
  b. Repeat the procedure if necessary.
2. To make the up-and-down adjustment (at the rear of the hood):
  a. Loosen the hood stop bolts.
  b. Using a screwdriver, turn the hood stop screws clockwise to lower the hood and counterclockwise to raise the hood. Hood is at the proper height when it is flush with the fenders.
  c. Tighten the hood stop bolts.
  d. Repeat the procedure if necessary.

Hood Latch

▶ **See Figure 6**

1. Make sure that the hood is properly aligned.
2. Remove the hood latch attaching bolts. Move them as necessary to align with the latch dowel. Tighten the attaching bolts.

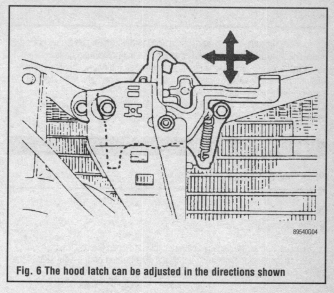
Fig. 6 The hood latch can be adjusted in the directions shown

3. Remove the locknut on the hood latch dowel, and turn the dowel clockwise to pull the hood tighter and counterclockwise to loosen it. The proper height is when the top of the hood is flush with the fenders.
4. Tighten the dowel locknut after the proper adjustment has been obtained.

Trunk Lid

REMOVAL & INSTALLATION

▶ **See Figure 7**

1. Open and support the trunk lid securely.
2. Mark the position of the trunk lid hinge in relation to the trunk lid. Disconnect the trunk lid stay from its mounting bracket, if so equipped.
3. Remove the two bolts attaching the hinge to the trunk lid.
4. Remove the trunk lid from the vehicle.
To install:
5. Align the marks on the trunk lid with the hinges.
6. Install the hinge-to-trunk lid bolts.
7. Tighten the trunk lid bolts and adjust if necessary.

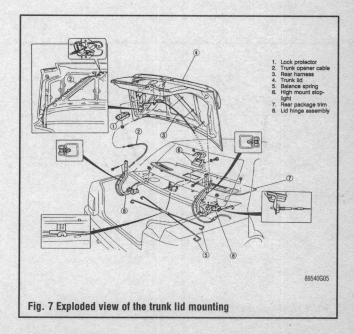

1. Lock protector
2. Trunk opener cable
3. Rear harness
4. Trunk lid
5. Balance spring
6. High mount stop-light
7. Rear package trim
8. Lid hinge assembly

Fig. 7 Exploded view of the trunk lid mounting

ADJUSTMENT

To make the side-to-side adjustment, loosen the trunk lid attaching bolts and move the trunk lid as necessary. Tighten the trunk lid attaching bolts.

To make the up-and-down adjustment, loosen the hinge-to-hinge support attaching bolts and raise or lower the hinge as necessary. The trunk lid is at the correct height when it is flush with the trunk deck.

To adjust the trunk lid lock, loosen the striker attaching bolts, and move the striker as required, then tighten the attaching bolts.

Hatchback Assembly

REMOVAL & INSTALLATION

323

▶ See Figure 8

1. Disconnect the negative battery cable and open the hatch fully.
2. Disconnect the electrical harness that is located on the right side of the hatch. Feed the harness out of the channel.
3. Disconnect the rear window washer hose from the rear hatch.
4. Matchmark the position of the hinges to the hatch.
5. Have an assistant support the rear hatch and remove the strut/damper supports from both sides.
6. From under the hatch lip, remove the hatch hinge mounting bolts and lift the hatch away from the vehicle.
   To install:
7. Lower the hatch into place, aligning with the matchmarks made earlier. Install the hatch hinge mounting bolts and tighten to 78–113 inch lbs. (9–13 Nm).
8. Install the strut/damper assemblies. Tighten the bolts to 69–104 inch lbs. (8–12 Nm).
9. Connect the rear window washer hose.
10. Feed the electrical harness through the hatch channel and engage the electrical connector.
11. Connect the negative battery cable.

MX-3

▶ See Figure 9

1. Open the hatch fully and disconnect the negative battery cable.
2. Remove the inside hatch trim panel clips and remove the trim panels.
3. Unplug the rear window washer hose and the electrical connector from the rear hatch.
4. Matchmark the position of the hinges to the hatch.

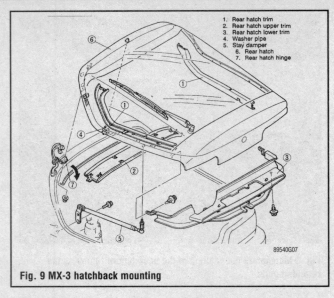

Fig. 9 MX-3 hatchback mounting

5. Support the hatch. Remove the strut/stay damper assembly bolts and remove the assemblies from the hatch.
6. Remove the hatch mounting nuts and remove the hatch assembly from the vehicle.
   To install:
7. Install the hatch to the vehicle and tighten the mounting nuts to 69–104 inch lbs. (8–12 Nm). Be sure the matchmarks are aligned.
8. Install the strut/stay damper assemblies. Tighten the mounting bolts to 13–16 ft. lbs. (18–22 Nm).
9. Connect the rear window washer hose and the electrical harness to the hatch.
10. Install the inside trim panels and the trim clips.
11. Connect the negative battery cable.

626/MX-6/Probe

▶ See Figure 10

1. Disconnect the negative battery cable and remove the trim that surrounds the rear hatch.
2. Unplug the connector from the luggage compartment light and remove the light from its socket.
3. Remove the rear hatch screen. Be careful not to rip or tear the screen when removing it.

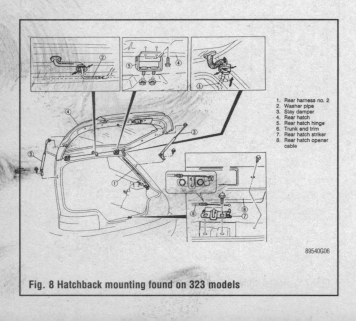

Fig. 8 Hatchback mounting found on 323 models

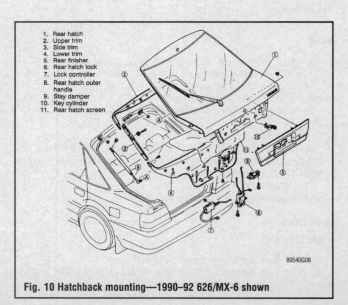

Fig. 10 Hatchback mounting—1990–92 626/MX-6 shown

Fig. 11 Remove any push-pins securing the shields . . .

Fig. 12 . . . then remove the shields from the vehicle

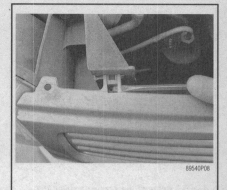

Fig. 13 Disengage the securing tabs . . .

Fig. 14 . . . then pull then grille back slightly

Fig. 15 After all the tabs have been disengaged and any screws removed, lift the grille from the vehicle

Fig. 16 Remove the cap covering the lever screw

4. Locate the rear defroster and wiper motor electrical connectors and unplug them. Pull the wiring through the rear hatch.

5. Matchmark the position of the hinges to the hatch.

6. Remove the stay damper mounting bolts and disconnect the rear washer hose.

7. Remove the wiring harness and route it off to the side.

8. Have an assistant grasp and support the rear hatch and remove the rear hatch-to-hinge mounting bolts. Remove the hatch.

To install:

9. Install the rear hatch assembly and install the hatch-to-hinge bolts. Be sure to align it with the marks made earlier.

10. Route the wiring harness to the side of the hatch.

11. Connect the rear washer hose and install the stay damper mounting bolts.

12. Engage the rear defroster and rear windshield wiper electrical connector.

13. Install the rear hatch screen.

14. Install the luggage compartment light and install the rear trim panels.

15. Connect the negative battery cable.

ALIGNMENT

1. To align the side to side position of the door, loosen the hinge attaching bolts on both the hatch and the body.

2. To adjust the door for the up and down position, loosen the hinge attaching bolts on the hatch side, the lock attaching bolts, and the striker attaching bolts.

3. Adjust the rear for closing, by moving the lock and striker.

4. Make all necessary adjustments by moving the rear hatch in the appropriate directions for the desired adjustments and tighten the attaching bolts. Open and close the hatch several times to ensure proper operation.

Grille

REMOVAL & INSTALLATION

▶ See Figures 11 thru 15

Note that on some models the grille is integral with the bumper fascia and is not removable.

1. Open the hood and remove any shields covering the top of the grille.

2. Remove any screws securing the grille. Some of these are hidden so be sure to check carefully.

3. Disengage the securing tabs of the grille using a small prytool. After all the tabs have been disengaged, remove the grille from the vehicle.

4. To install, position the grille and align the fastener holes with the holes in the body. Once they are aligned, press the fasteners into place and install any securing screws. Install the grille shields (if applicable) and close the hood.

Outside Mirrors

REMOVAL & INSTALLATION

▶ See Figures 16, 17, 18, 19 and 20

1. Disconnect the negative battery cable.

2. Remove the trim panel from inside the mirror.

3. Remove the mirror mounting screws and pull the mirror away from the door. On power mirrors, unplug the connector. Remove the mirror from the vehicle.

4. Installation is the reverse of the removal procedure.

Fig. 17 Remove the screw securing the lever then remove the lever

Fig. 18 Remove the trim cover

Fig. 19 The mirror attaching screws can now be accessed

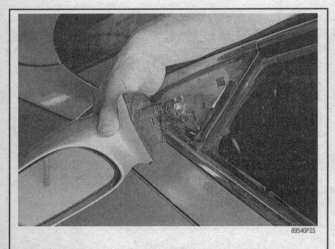

Fig. 20 Pull the mirror from the door once the screws are removed

Antenna

REPLACEMENT

Pillar Mounted

MANUAL

1. Remove the kick panel and disconnect the antenna feeder from the retaining clips.

2. Remove the screws that attach the antenna base and pull the antenna and feeder assembly from the front pillar. On vehicles equipped with a sunroof, the sunroof drain pipe will come out with the antenna assembly.

3. To install, insert the antenna feeder and drain pipe (if so equipped) into the front pillar opening and attach the feeder wire to the mounting clips. Install the antenna base retaining screws.

POWER

1. Remove the front side trim.

2. Remove the undercover and loosen the nut and remove the hood release knob.

3. Disconnect the negative battery cable. Locate the central processing unit which is part of the joint box. The joint box is attached to the driver's side wheel well in the engine compartment across from the brake power booster. Disconnect the connectors from the CPU. Release the locking clip using moderate finger pressure pull the unit from the joint box. Unplug the harness connectors from the joint box. Remove the joint box mounting bracket nut. Release the lock at the back of the joint box and remove the joint box.

5. Below the steering column and air duct, you will find the antenna feeder connector. Disconnect the feeder wire from the plug. Disconnect the connector from the antenna motor.

6. Remove the motor mounting bracket bolt and screws, and remove the antenna motor with the antenna mast. Slide the joint sleeve upward to disengage the motor from the mast.

7. Connect a 12 volt battery and a ground wire to the **R** and **W** terminals of the motor service connector to operate the motor. Connect the negative cable to the **W** terminal and the positive cable to the **R** terminal. Carefully pull the cable from the motor housing with the motor running.

➡**Even if the mast is broken or missing, make sure that all the cable is fed from the motor.**

8. Remove the antenna base mounting screws and withdraw the antenna from the front pillar.

9. A temporary protective cover is attached with tape to each new mast kit. The cover is there to protect the plastic rack cable and to make the installation easier. Before beginning the installation, extend the mast fully.

10. Take the plastic protective cover and install it over the base of the mast to protect the plastic cable. Use the tape provided in the kit to hold the tube in place.

11. Tape the antenna plug to the tip of the protector tube so that it will not be damaged or catch on body during installation.

12. Insert the antenna mast into the roof opening and carefully and slowly feed it down at the same angle as the windshield pillar. When the mast is fully inserted into the windshield pillar, remove the plastic tube and pull the antenna lead inside the passenger compartment. Carefully feed the plastic rack cable into the motor housing. The serrated side of the cable must face toward the motor as shown in the illustration.

13. Using the 12 volt battery, connect the positive lead to the **W** terminal and the negative lead to the **R** terminal on the antenna motor service connector. Operate the motor until all of the new cable is reeled into the motor housing.

14. Push the mast base into the motor housing joint. When the mast is locked properly, a faint click will be heard. Jiggle the mast base back and forth a few times to verify that the base is locked properly.

15. Check the operation of the antenna mast. The cable slack can be self adjusted by operating the motor a few times until the mast is fully extended. Complete the installation of the remaining components by reversing the removal procedure.

Fender Mounted

1. Disconnect the negative battery cable.

2. Remove the trunk panel or wheelhouse liner as appropriate.

3. Disconnect the antenna wire. On some models this may need to be done from the back of the radio. Route the wire through the vehicle if necessary.

4. Remove the mounting nut on top of the antenna. On some models this nut is recessed; a special tool is needed (a deep socket with two prongs for engaging the tangs on the nut).

5. Remove the antenna mounting screws and remove the antenna from the vehicle.

6. Installation is the reverse of the removal procedure.

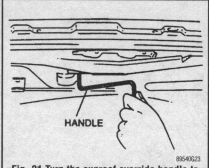

Fig. 21 Turn the sunroof override handle to move the sunshade to the rear for sunroof removal

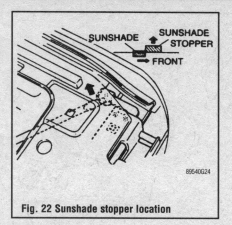

Fig. 22 Sunshade stopper location

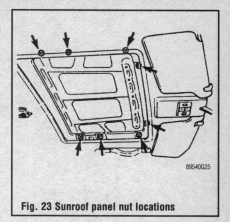

Fig. 23 Sunroof panel nut locations

Fenders

REMOVAL & INSTALLATION

1. Remove the grille and headlight assemblies.
2. Remove the front corner turn signal assemblies.
3. If attached to the fender, remove the front bumper assembly.
4. Remove the front mud guard and the inner fender plastic liner.
5. Remove the fender mounting bolts and remove the fender assembly.
6. Installation is the reverse of the removal procedure. Tighten the fender mounting bolts to 61–87 inch lbs. (7–10 Nm).

Power Sunroof

REMOVAL & INSTALLATION

▶ **See Figures 21, 22, 23, 24 and 25**

1. Slide the sunshade all the way to the rear position.
2. Fully close the glass sliding panel.
3. Remove the left, the right and the lower trim covers from around the sunroof perimeter.
4. Remove the installation nuts from around the sliding sunroof panel and the lower panel.
5. Remove the sliding panel by pushing it upward from inside the vehicle.
6. Fully close the sunshade. Insert the manual operation handle and move the sunshade so that it is to the rear approximately 0.19–0.39 inch (5–10 mm).
7. Using a prytool, lift the sunshade stopper, located at the rear of the cable holder and then release the stopper. Move the sunshade toward the front.
8. Turn the handle and fully open the lower panel. Leave the sunshade fully closed.
9. Open the sunshade halfway and remove the set plate cap. Pull the sunshade out from the set plate notch and remove it from the vehicle.

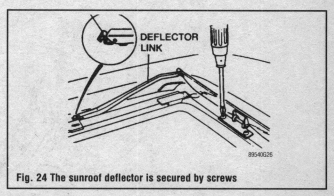

Fig. 24 The sunroof deflector is secured by screws

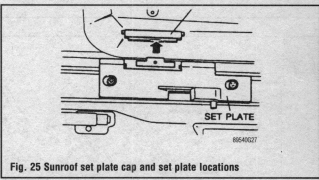

Fig. 25 Sunroof set plate cap and set plate locations

To install:

10. Install the slide panel to the lower panel and securely tighten the mounting screws.
11. Install the set plate cap.
12. Install the surrounding trim panels. Check operation of the sunroof and adjust as is necessary.

INTERIOR

Instrument Panel and Pad

REMOVAL & INSTALLATION

▶ **See Figures 26 thru 34**

1. Disconnect the negative battery cable and disable the air bag system (if equipped).
2. Remove the gearshift knob and remove the front console assembly.
3. Remove the front console side covers.
4. Remove the dashboard undercover plates.

5. Lower the steering column assembly. Be careful no to damage the column or stress any wiring harnesses.
6. Remove the garnish strip or caps along the windshield concealing the mounting screws.
7. Remove the dashboard side panels, if equipped.
8. Remove the hood release knob from its mounting point on the dashboard.
9. Remove the instrument cluster assembly.
10. Remove the radio.
11. Remove the glove box door.
12. Remove the center trim panel from around the heater controls, if equipped.

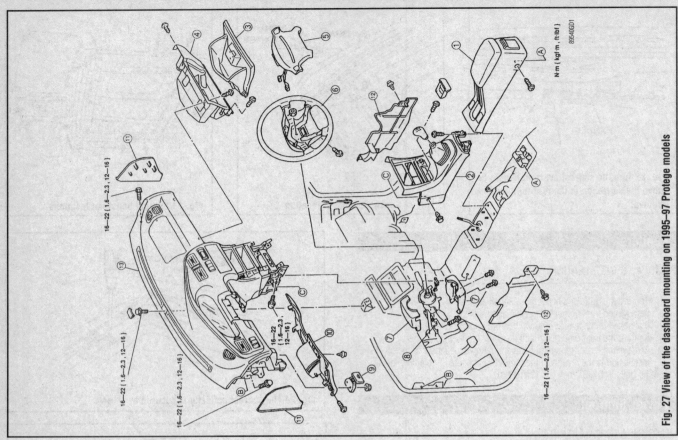

Fig. 27 View of the dashboard mounting on 1995–97 Protege models

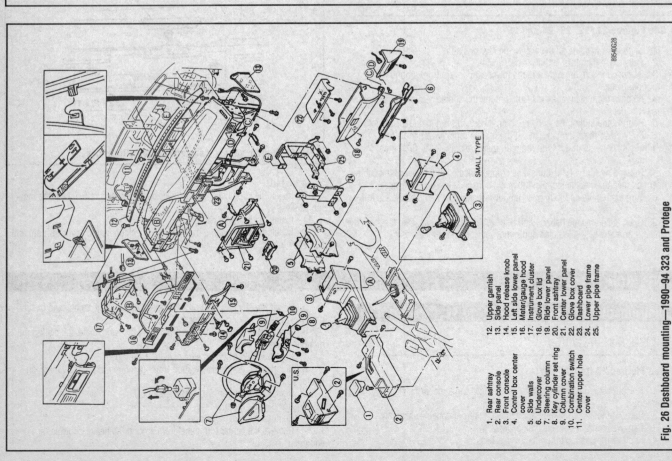

1. Rear ashtray
2. Rear console
3. Front console
4. Control box center cover
5. Side walls
6. Undercover
7. Steering column
8. Key cylinder set ring
9. Column cover
10. Combination switch
11. Center upper hole cover
12. Upper garnish
13. Side panel
14. Hood release knob
15. Left side side lower panel
16. Meter/gauge hood
17. Instrument cluster
18. Glove box lid
19. Ride lower panel
20. Front ashtray
21. Center lower panel
22. Glove box cover
23. Dashboard
24. Lower pipe frame
25. Upper pipe frame

Fig. 26 Dashboard mounting—1990–94 323 and Protege

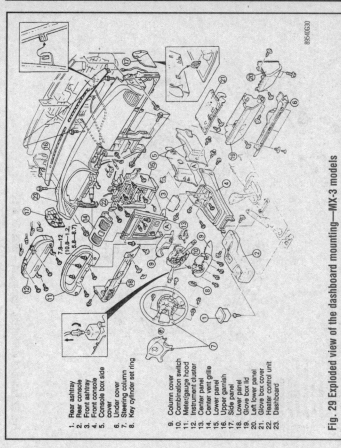

Fig. 29 Exploded view of the dashboard mounting—MX-3 models

1. Rear ashtray
2. Rear console
3. Front ashtray
4. Console box side cover
5. Under cover
6. Steering column
7. Key cylinder set ring
8. Column cover
9. Combination switch
10. Meter/gauge hood
11. Instrument cluster
12. Center panel
13. Center vent grille
14. Lower panel
15. Upper garnish
16. Side panel
17. Lower panel
18. Glove box lid
19. Left lower panel
20. Glove box cover
21. Heater control unit
22. Dashboard

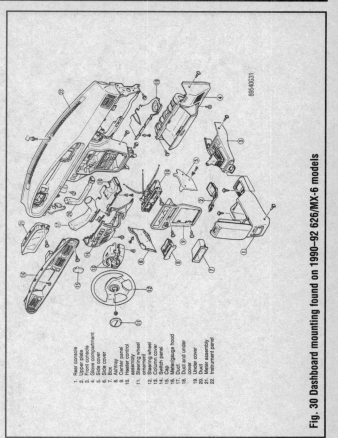

Fig. 30 Dashboard mounting found on 1990-92 626/MX-6 models

1. Rear console
2. Upper plate
3. Front console
4. Glove compartment
5. Side cover
6. Box
7. Ashtray
8. Center panel
9. Heater control assembly
10. Steering wheel ornament
11. Steering wheel
12. Column cover
13. Switch panel
14. Cap
15. Meter/gauge hood
16. Duct and under cover
17. Under cover
18. Duct
19. Meter assembly
20. Instrument panel

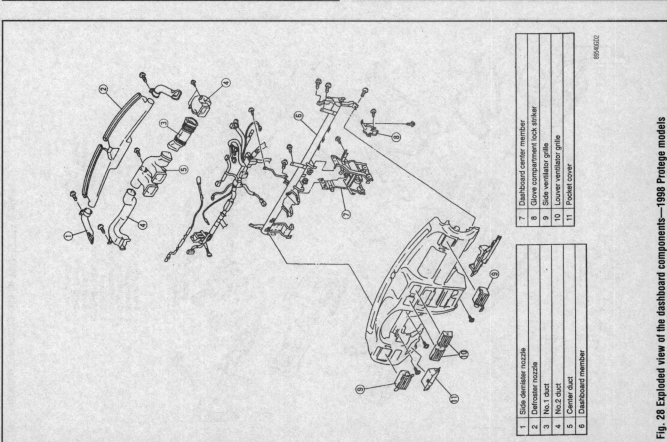

Fig. 28 Exploded view of the dashboard components—1998 Protege models

1. Side demister nozzle
2. Defroster nozzle
3. No.1 duct
4. No.2 duct
5. Center duct
6. Dashboard member
7. Dashboard center member
8. Glove compartment lock striker
9. Side ventilator grille
10. Louver ventilator grille
11. Pocket cover

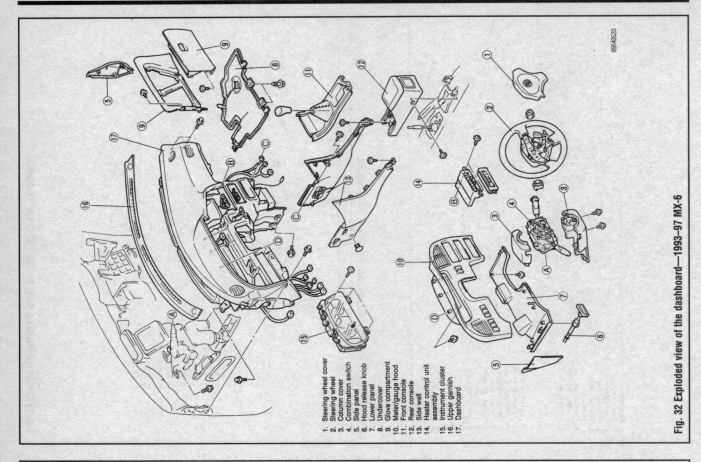

Fig. 32 Exploded view of the dashboard—1993–97 MX-6

1. Steering wheel cover
2. Steering wheel
3. Column cover
4. Combination switch
5. Side panel
6. Hood release knob
7. Lower panel
8. Undercover
9. Glove compartment
10. Meter/gauge hood
11. Front console
12. Rear console
13. Side wall
14. Heater control unit assembly
15. Instrument cluster
16. Upper garnish
17. Dashboard

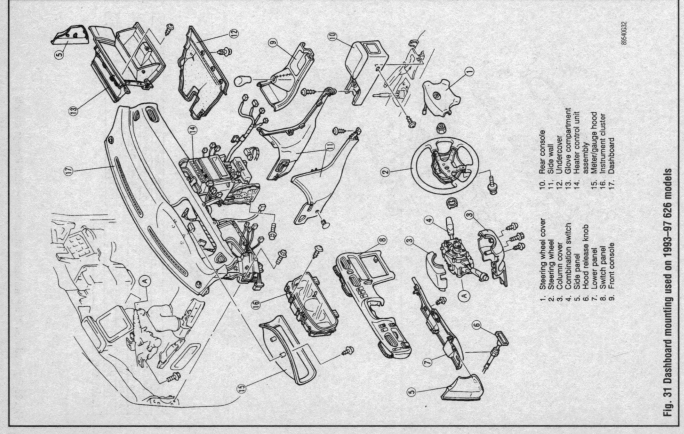

Fig. 31 Dashboard mounting used on 1993–97 626 models

1. Steering wheel cover
2. Steering wheel
3. Column cover
4. Combination switch
5. Side panel
6. Hood release knob
7. Lower panel
8. Switch panel
9. Front console
10. Rear console
11. Side wall
12. Undercover
13. Glove compartment
14. Heater control unit assembly
15. Meter/gauge hood
16. Instrument cluster
17. Dashboard

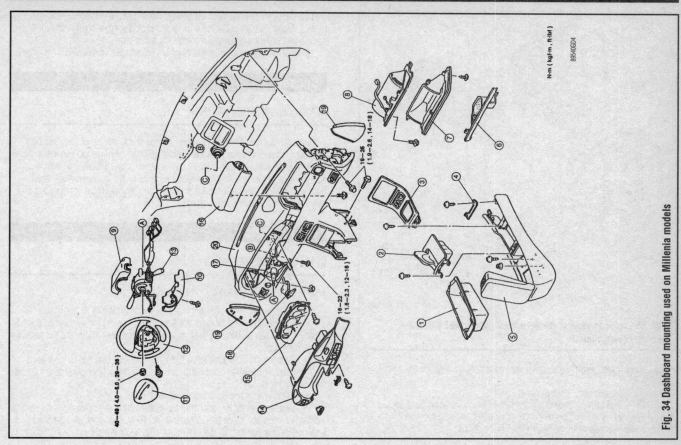

N·m (kgf·m , ft/lbf)

89540G04

16—25
(1.6—2.6 , 14—18)

16—22
(1.6—2.3 , 12—16)

40—49 (4.0—5.0 , 29—38)

Fig. 34 Dashboard mounting used on Millenia models

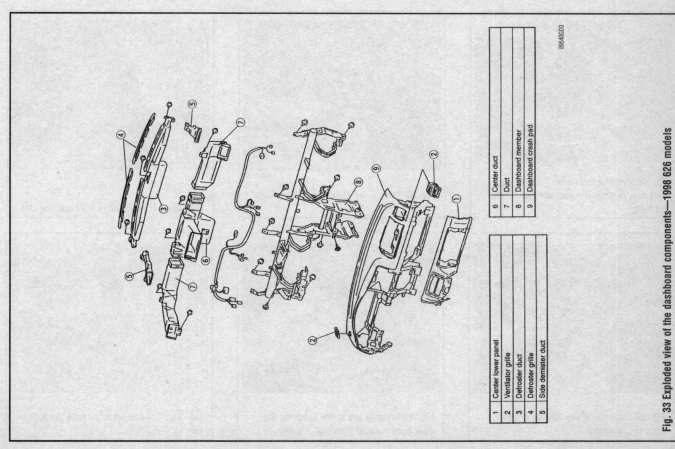

89540G03

1	Center lower panel	6	Center duct
2	Ventilator grille	7	Duct
3	Defroster duct	8	Dashboard member
4	Defroster grille	9	Dashboard crash pad
5	Side demister duct		

Fig. 33 Exploded view of the dashboard components—1998 626 models

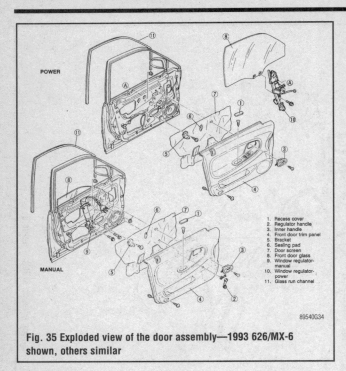

Fig. 35 Exploded view of the door assembly—1993 626/MX-6 shown, others similar

1. Recess cover
2. Regulator handle
3. Inner handle
4. Front door trim panel
5. Bracket
6. Sealing pad
7. Door screen
8. Front door glass
9. Window regulator-manual
10. Window regulator-power
11. Glass run channel

89540G34

13. If equipped, remove the center vent assembly from above the heater controls.

14. Remove the heater control panel.

15. Label and unplug and wiring harnesses which can now be accessed.

16. Remove all of the mounting screws or bolts. Be sure to make a note as to where each type came from. Refer to the illustrations.

17. Carefully pull the dash away from the vehicle. If it seems stuck, don't force it. Make sure all of the fasteners and harnesses have been released. If additional clearance is needed, remove the pillar trim.

18. Installation is the reverse of removal. Refer to the illustrations if necessary.

Console

REMOVAL & INSTALLATION

Removal of the console is fairly easy, once you locate all of the mounting fasteners. These are usually hidden under ashtrays or protected by plastic caps. The shifter handle will also need to be removed. Some are retained with a set screw, while others are simply twisted off. Once all the fasteners have been removed, lift the console from the floor. Unplug any electrical connections and remove the console from the vehicle.

Door Panels

REMOVAL & INSTALLATION

▶ **See Figures 35 thru 45**

1. Remove the armrest or the screw in the armrest cup as applicable.

2. Remove the window regulator handle, on non-power window equipped vehicles. This can be done by sliding a rag between the handle and the panel to release the clip.

3. Remove the door lock knob if it interferes with removal of the panel.

4. Remove the inner door handle cover. Pull the cover outwards are release the lock rod clip.

5. Remove any screws along the door panel.

6. Gently separate the door trim panel clips from the door. A special tool is available to do this. If this tool is not available, use a prytool with the blade wrapped in tape (be careful not to break the panel or the clips).

Fig. 36 Remove the screw from the armrest cup. A magnetic screwdriver is helpful here

89540P12

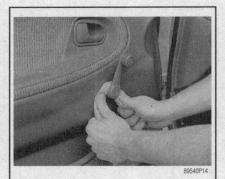

Fig. 37 Slide a rag between the panel and handle . . .

89540P14

Fig. 38 . . . to dislodge the retaining clip

89540P15

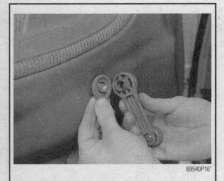

Fig. 39 The handle can now be pulled from the regulator

89540P16

Fig. 40 Remove the screw securing the door handle cover then pull it away . . .

89540P18

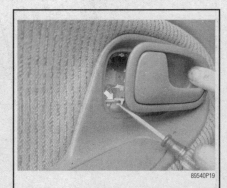

Fig. 41 . . . enough to release the lock rod

89540P19

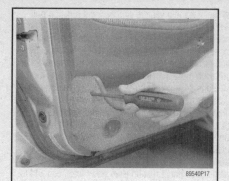

Fig. 42 Remove any screws securing the door panel . . .

Fig. 43 . . . then pull the panel away. . .

Fig. 44 . . . and unplug any electrical connections

7. Unplug and electrical connections necessary, then remove the door trim panel.

To install:

8. Engage the electrical connections, then place the trim panel into position on the door.

9. Apply pressure to the trim panel in the areas where the trim panel clips attach to the door.

10. Install the inner door handle cover, door lock knob and the armrest.

11. If equipped, install the regulator handle.

Door Locks

REMOVAL & INSTALLATION

1. Disconnect the negative battery cable.
2. Remove the inner door panel and remove the inner door screening.
3. If the locks are power, disconnect the power lock controller from the lock assembly.
4. Remove the door lock mounting screws and disconnect the linkage. Remove the lock assembly from the door.
5. Installation is the reverse of the removal procedure. Tighten the door lock mounting screw(s) to 37–55 inch lbs. (4.2–6.2 Nm).

Door Glass and Regulator

REMOVAL & INSTALLATION

▶ **See Figures 46, 47 and 48**

1. Lower the window glass and remove the inner handle cover, door lock knob (if necessary), the window regulator handle and the door trim panel.

➡**On vehicles with power windows, disconnect the wiring couplings.**

2. Carefully peel off the door screen so that it can be reused.
3. Replace the window regulator handle and position the door glass so that the door glass installation bolts can be removed from the service hole.
4. Remove the door glass installation bolts.
5. Remove the door glass. Remove the regulator installation bolts, and then remove the regulator through the service access hole. Remove the window motor mounting bolts and separate the motor from the regulator.
6. Installation is the reverse of the removal procedure. If the vehicle is equipped with power windows, connect the leads of the motor to a battery and run the regulator to the down position before installing the motor. Cycle the window several times to make sure that everything is in good working order.

Electric Window Motor

REMOVAL & INSTALLATION

1. Disconnect the negative battery cable.
2. Remove the door panel and the inner door shielding from the door.
3. Unplug the power window motor electrical connector from inside the door.
4. Prop the window in the up position and remove the window motor mounting bolts from the door. Remove the window motor from the door.
5. Installation is the reverse of the removal procedure. Tighten the motor mounting bolts to 61–87 inch lbs. (6.9–9.8 Nm).

Windshield and Fixed Glass

REMOVAL & INSTALLATION

If your windshield, or other fixed window, is cracked or chipped, you may decide to replace it with a new one yourself. However, there are two main reasons why replacement windshields and other window glass should be

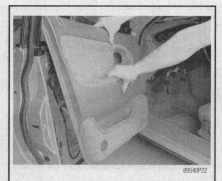

Fig. 45 The panel can now be removed from the door

Fig. 46 The door glass retaining bolts can be removed through the access hole

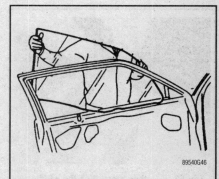

Fig. 47 Remove the glass up and out of the door as shown

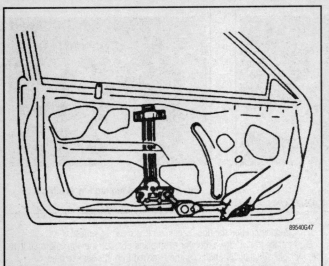

Fig. 48 The window regulator is secured to the door by bolts

installed only by a professional automotive glass technician: safety and cost.

The most important reason a professional should install automotive glass is for safety. The glass in the vehicle, especially the windshield, is designed with safety in mind in case of a collision. The windshield is specially manufactured from two panes of specially-tempered glass with a thin layer of transparent plastic between them. This construction allows the glass to "give" in the event that a part of your body hits the windshield during the collision, and prevents the glass from shattering, which could cause lacerations, blinding and other harm to passengers of the vehicle. The other fixed windows are designed to be tempered so that if they break during a collision, they shatter in such a way that there are no large pointed glass pieces. The professional automotive glass tech-

nician knows how to install the glass in a vehicle so that it will function optimally during a collision. Without the proper experience, knowledge and tools, installing a piece of automotive glass yourself could lead to additional harm if an accident should ever occur.

Cost is also a factor when deciding to install automotive glass yourself. Performing this could cost you much more than a professional may charge for the same job. Since the windshield is designed to break under stress, an often life saving characteristic, windshields tend to break VERY easily when an inexperienced person attempts to install one. Do-it-yourselfers buying two, three or even four windshields from a salvage yard because they have broken them during installation are common stories. Also, since the automotive glass is designed to prevent the outside elements from entering your vehicle, improper installation can lead to water and air leaks. Annoying whining noises at highway speeds from air leaks or inside body panel rusting from water leaks can add to your stress level and subtract from your wallet. After buying two or three windshields, installing them and ending up with a leak that produces a noise while driving and water damage during rainstorms, the cost of having a professional do it correctly the first time may be much more alluring. We here at Chilton, therefore, advise that you have a professional automotive glass technician service any broken glass on your vehicle.

WINDSHIELD CHIP REPAIR

♦ See Figures 49 thru 63

➡**Check with your state and local authorities on the laws for state safety inspection. Some states or municipalities may not allow chip repair as a viable option for correcting stone damage to your windshield.**

Although severely cracked or damaged windshields must be replaced, there is something that you can do to prolong or even prevent the need for replacement of a chipped windshield. There are many companies which offer windshield chip repair products, such as Loctite's® Bullseye™ windshield repair kit. These kits usually consist of a syringe, pedestal and a sealing adhesive. The syringe is mounted on the pedestal and is used to create a vacuum which pulls the plastic layer against the glass. This helps make the chip transparent. The

Fig. 49 Small chips on your windshield can be fixed with an aftermarket repair kit, such as the one from Loctite®

Fig. 50 To repair a chip, clean the windshield with glass cleaner and dry it completely

Fig. 51 Remove the center from the adhesive disc and peel off the backing from one side of the disc . . .

Fig. 52 . . . then press it on the windshield so that the chip is centered in the hole

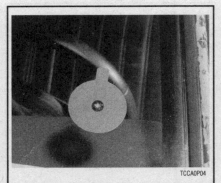

Fig. 53 Be sure that the tab points upward on the windshield

Fig. 54 Peel the backing off the exposed side of the adhesive disc . . .

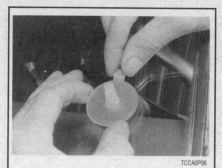

Fig. 55 . . . then position the plastic pedestal on the adhesive disc, ensuring that the tabs are aligned

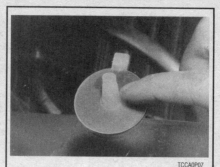

Fig. 56 Press the pedestal firmly on the adhesive disc to create an adequate seal . . .

Fig. 57 . . . then install the applicator syringe nipple in the pedestal's hole

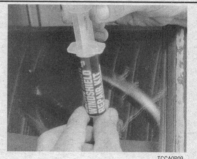

Fig. 58 Hold the syringe with one hand while pulling the plunger back with the other hand

Fig. 59 After applying the solution, allow the entire assembly to sit until it has set completely

Fig. 60 After the solution has set, remove the syringe from the pedestal . . .

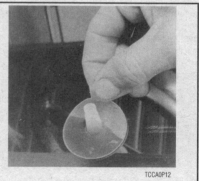

Fig. 61 . . . then peel the pedestal off of the adhesive disc . . .

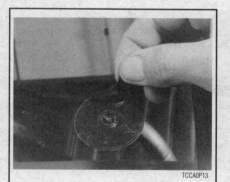

Fig. 62 . . . and peel the adhesive disc off of the windshield

Fig. 63 The chip will still be slightly visible, but it should be filled with the hardened solution

adhesive is then injected which seals the chip and helps to prevent further stress cracks from developing. Refer to the sequence of photos to get a general idea of what windshield chip repair involves.

➡ Always follow the specific manufacturer's instructions.

Inside Rear View Mirror

REMOVAL & INSTALLATION

Removal of the rearview mirror is simply a matter of removing the mounting screws and removing the mirror assembly. Installation is the reverse of the removal procedure.

Seats

REMOVAL & INSTALLATION

Front

▶ See Figure 64

1. If the vehicle is equipped with passive shoulder belt type seat belts, disconnect the buckle switch electrical connector from under the seat.
2. Remove the seat slide rear covers.
3. Slide the seat forward and remove the rear mounting bolts.
4. Slide the seat to the rear and remove the front mounting bolts.
5. Remove the seat(s) from the vehicle.

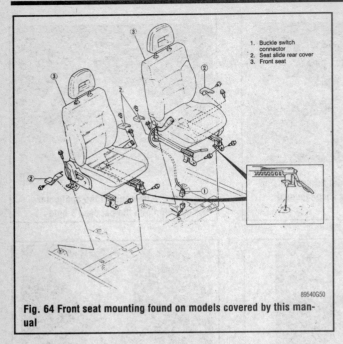

1. Buckle switch connector
2. Seat slide rear cover
3. Front seat

89540G50

Fig. 64 Front seat mounting found on models covered by this manual

6. Installation is the reverse of the removal procedure. Tighten the mounting bolts to 28–38 ft. lbs. (38–51 Nm).

Rear

▶ **See Figure 65**

1. From under the front of the rear seat bottom cushion, release the seat cushion locks.
2. If the vehicle has the folding rear seat, remove the side cushion pieces first by removing the bolts and lifting up.
3. Remove the bolts and/or nuts from the base of the back cushion(s) and lift the back cushion up and off of the fastening hooks.
4. Installation is the reverse of the removal procedure. Tighten the seat back bolts to 12–17 ft. lbs. (16–23 Nm).

Power Seat Motor

REMOVAL & INSTALLATION

1. Remove the driver's seat from the vehicle and set it on a clean, flat surface.

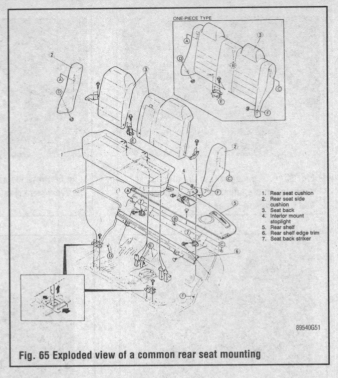

ONE-PIECE TYPE

1. Rear seat cushion
2. Rear seat side cushion
3. Seat back
4. Interior mount stoplight
5. Rear shelf
6. Rear shelf edge trim
7. Seat back striker

89540G51

Fig. 65 Exploded view of a common rear seat mounting

2. To remove and install the sliding and reclining motor, perform the following:
  a. Unscrew the cable from the motor using pliers.
  b. Remove the retaining screws and remove the motor from its mounting.
  c. Position the motor onto the mounting and install the attaching screws.
  d. Connect the cable to the motor and tighten it properly.
3. To remove and install the reclining motor, perform the following:
  a. Pull the head rest and the two headrest mounting poles from the seat.
  b. Remove the bolts from the front part of the reclining knuckles.
  c. Loosen but do not remove the rear reclining knuckle bolts.
  d. Remove the seat back cushion from the seat back frame.
  e. Unbolt and remove the reclining knuckle (3 bolts).
  f. Remove the three attaching screws and remove the motor from the reclining knuckle.
  g. Unscrew and remove the bracket from the motor. Transfer the existing bracket to the new motor.
  h. Complete the installation in reverse of the removal procedure.
4. Installation is the reverse of removal. Make sure that all the motors are functioning properly.

TORQUE SPECIFICATIONS

Components		English	Metric
Door		13-22 ft. lbs	18-29 Nm
Rear Hatch			
	323	78-113 inch lbs.	9-13 Nm
	MX-3	69-104 inch lbs.	8-12 Nm
Hatch Struts			
	323	69-109 inch lbs.	9-13 Nm
	MX-3	13-16 ft. lbs.	18-22 Nm
Fender		61-87 inch lbs.	7-10 Nm
Door Lock Screws		37-55 inch lbs.	4.2-6.2 Nm
Power Window Motor		61-87 inch lbs.	6.9-9.8 Nm
Seats			
	Front	28-38 ft. lbs.	38-51 Nm
	Rear	12-17 ft. lbs.	16-23 Nm

89540C01

GLOSSARY

AIR/FUEL RATIO: The ratio of air-to-gasoline by weight in the fuel mixture drawn into the engine.

AIR INJECTION: One method of reducing harmful exhaust emissions by injecting air into each of the exhaust ports of an engine. The fresh air entering the hot exhaust manifold causes any remaining fuel to be burned before it can exit the tailpipe.

ALTERNATOR: A device used for converting mechanical energy into electrical energy.

AMMETER: An instrument, calibrated in amperes, used to measure the flow of an electrical current in a circuit. Ammeters are always connected in series with the circuit being tested.

AMPERE: The rate of flow of electrical current present when one volt of electrical pressure is applied against one ohm of electrical resistance.

ANALOG COMPUTER: Any microprocessor that uses similar (analogous) electrical signals to make its calculations.

ARMATURE: A laminated, soft iron core wrapped by a wire that converts electrical energy to mechanical energy as in a motor or relay. When rotated in a magnetic field, it changes mechanical energy into electrical energy as in a generator.

ATMOSPHERIC PRESSURE: The pressure on the Earth's surface caused by the weight of the air in the atmosphere. At sea level, this pressure is 14.7 psi at 32°F (101 kPa at 0°C).

ATOMIZATION: The breaking down of a liquid into a fine mist that can be suspended in air.

AXIAL PLAY: Movement parallel to a shaft or bearing bore.

BACKFIRE: The sudden combustion of gases in the intake or exhaust system that results in a loud explosion.

BACKLASH: The clearance or play between two parts, such as meshed gears.

BACKPRESSURE: Restrictions in the exhaust system that slow the exit of exhaust gases from the combustion chamber.

BAKELITE: A heat resistant, plastic insulator material commonly used in printed circuit boards and transistorized components.

BALL BEARING: A bearing made up of hardened inner and outer races between which hardened steel balls roll.

BALLAST RESISTOR: A resistor in the primary ignition circuit that lowers voltage after the engine is started to reduce wear on ignition components.

BEARING: A friction reducing, supportive device usually located between a stationary part and a moving part.

BIMETAL TEMPERATURE SENSOR: Any sensor or switch made of two dissimilar types of metal that bend when heated or cooled due to the different expansion rates of the alloys. These types of sensors usually function as an on/off switch.

BLOWBY: Combustion gases, composed of water vapor and unburned fuel, that leak past the piston rings into the crankcase during normal engine operation. These gases are removed by the PCV system to prevent the buildup of harmful acids in the crankcase.

BRAKE PAD: A brake shoe and lining assembly used with disc brakes.

BRAKE SHOE: The backing for the brake lining. The term is, however, usually applied to the assembly of the brake backing and lining.

BUSHING: A liner, usually removable, for a bearing; an anti-friction liner used in place of a bearing.

CALIPER: A hydraulically activated device in a disc brake system, which is mounted straddling the brake rotor (disc). The caliper contains at least one piston and two brake pads. Hydraulic pressure on the piston(s) forces the pads against the rotor.

CAMSHAFT: A shaft in the engine on which are the lobes (cams) which operate the valves. The camshaft is driven by the crankshaft, via a belt, chain or gears, at one half the crankshaft speed.

CAPACITOR: A device which stores an electrical charge.

CARBON MONOXIDE (CO): A colorless, odorless gas given off as a normal byproduct of combustion. It is poisonous and extremely dangerous in confined areas, building up slowly to toxic levels without warning if adequate ventilation is not available.

CARBURETOR: A device, usually mounted on the intake manifold of an engine, which mixes the air and fuel in the proper proportion to allow even combustion.

CATALYTIC CONVERTER: A device installed in the exhaust system, like a muffler, that converts harmful byproducts of combustion into carbon dioxide and water vapor by means of a heat-producing chemical reaction.

CENTRIFUGAL ADVANCE: A mechanical method of advancing the spark timing by using flyweights in the distributor that react to centrifugal force generated by the distributor shaft rotation.

CHECK VALVE: Any one-way valve installed to permit the flow of air, fuel or vacuum in one direction only.

CHOKE: A device, usually a moveable valve, placed in the intake path of a carburetor to restrict the flow of air.

CIRCUIT: Any unbroken path through which an electrical current can flow. Also used to describe fuel flow in some instances.

CIRCUIT BREAKER: A switch which protects an electrical circuit from overload by opening the circuit when the current flow exceeds a predetermined level. Some circuit breakers must be reset manually, while most reset automatically.

COIL (IGNITION): A transformer in the ignition circuit which steps up the voltage provided to the spark plugs.

COMBINATION MANIFOLD: An assembly which includes both the intake and exhaust manifolds in one casting.

COMBINATION VALVE: A device used in some fuel systems that routes fuel vapors to a charcoal storage canister instead of venting them into the atmosphere. The valve relieves fuel tank pressure and allows fresh air into the tank as the fuel level drops to prevent a vapor lock situation.

COMPRESSION RATIO: The comparison of the total volume of the cylinder and combustion chamber with the piston at BDC and the piston at TDC.

CONDENSER: 1. An electrical device which acts to store an electrical charge, preventing voltage surges. 2. A radiator-like device in the air conditioning system in which refrigerant gas condenses into a liquid, giving off heat.

CONDUCTOR: Any material through which an electrical current can be transmitted easily.

CONTINUITY: Continuous or complete circuit. Can be checked with an ohmmeter.

COUNTERSHAFT: An intermediate shaft which is rotated by a mainshaft and transmits, in turn, that rotation to a working part.

CRANKCASE: The lower part of an engine in which the crankshaft and related parts operate.

CRANKSHAFT: The main driving shaft of an engine which receives reciprocating motion from the pistons and converts it to rotary motion.

CYLINDER: In an engine, the round hole in the engine block in which the piston(s) ride.

CYLINDER BLOCK: The main structural member of an engine in which is found the cylinders, crankshaft and other principal parts.

CYLINDER HEAD: The detachable portion of the engine, usually fastened to the top of the cylinder block and containing all or most of the combustion chambers. On overhead valve engines, it contains the valves and their operating parts. On overhead cam engines, it contains the camshaft as well.

DEAD CENTER: The extreme top or bottom of the piston stroke.

DETONATION: An unwanted explosion of the air/fuel mixture in the combustion chamber caused by excess heat and compression, advanced timing, or an overly lean mixture. Also referred to as "ping".

DIAPHRAGM: A thin, flexible wall separating two cavities, such as in a vacuum advance unit.

DIESELING: A condition in which hot spots in the combustion chamber cause the engine to run on after the key is turned off.

DIFFERENTIAL: A geared assembly which allows the transmission of motion between drive axles, giving one axle the ability to turn faster than the other.

DIODE: An electrical device that will allow current to flow in one direction only.

DISC BRAKE: A hydraulic braking assembly consisting of a brake disc, or rotor, mounted on an axle, and a caliper assembly containing, usually two brake pads which are activated by hydraulic pressure. The pads are forced against the sides of the disc, creating friction which slows the vehicle.

DISTRIBUTOR: A mechanically driven device on an engine which is responsible for electrically firing the spark plug at a predetermined point of the piston stroke.

DOWEL PIN: A pin, inserted in mating holes in two different parts allowing those parts to maintain a fixed relationship.

DRUM BRAKE: A braking system which consists of two brake shoes and one or two wheel cylinders, mounted on a fixed backing plate, and a brake drum, mounted on an axle, which revolves around the assembly.

DWELL: The rate, measured in degrees of shaft rotation, at which an electrical circuit cycles on and off.

ELECTRONIC CONTROL UNIT (ECU): Ignition module, module, amplifier or igniter. See Module for definition.

ELECTRONIC IGNITION: A system in which the timing and firing of the spark plugs is controlled by an electronic control unit, usually called a module. These systems have no points or condenser.

END-PLAY: The measured amount of axial movement in a shaft.

ENGINE: A device that converts heat into mechanical energy.

EXHAUST MANIFOLD: A set of cast passages or pipes which conduct exhaust gases from the engine.

FEELER GAUGE: A blade, usually metal, or precisely predetermined thickness, used to measure the clearance between two parts.

FIRING ORDER: The order in which combustion occurs in the cylinders of an engine. Also the order in which spark is distributed to the plugs by the distributor.

FLOODING: The presence of too much fuel in the intake manifold and combustion chamber which prevents the air/fuel mixture from firing, thereby causing a no-start situation.

FLYWHEEL: A disc shaped part bolted to the rear end of the crankshaft. Around the outer perimeter is affixed the ring gear. The starter drive engages the ring gear, turning the flywheel, which rotates the crankshaft, imparting the initial starting motion to the engine.

FOOT POUND (ft. lbs. or sometimes, ft.lb.): The amount of energy or work needed to raise an item weighing one pound, a distance of one foot.

FUSE: A protective device in a circuit which prevents circuit overload by breaking the circuit when a specific amperage is present. The device is constructed around a strip or wire of a lower amperage rating than the circuit it is designed to protect. When an amperage higher than that stamped on the fuse is present in the circuit, the strip or wire melts, opening the circuit.

GEAR RATIO: The ratio between the number of teeth on meshing gears.

GENERATOR: A device which converts mechanical energy into electrical energy.

HEAT RANGE: The measure of a spark plug's ability to dissipate heat from its firing end. The higher the heat range, the hotter the plug fires.

HUB: The center part of a wheel or gear.

HYDROCARBON (HC): Any chemical compound made up of hydrogen and carbon. A major pollutant formed by the engine as a byproduct of combustion.

HYDROMETER: An instrument used to measure the specific gravity of a solution.

INCH POUND (inch lbs.; sometimes in.lb. or in. lbs.): One twelfth of a foot pound.

INDUCTION: A means of transferring electrical energy in the form of a magnetic field. Principle used in the ignition coil to increase voltage.

INJECTOR: A device which receives metered fuel under relatively low pressure and is activated to inject the fuel into the engine under relatively high pressure at a predetermined time.

INPUT SHAFT: The shaft to which torque is applied, usually carrying the driving gear or gears.

INTAKE MANIFOLD: A casting of passages or pipes used to conduct air or a fuel/air mixture to the cylinders.

JOURNAL: The bearing surface within which a shaft operates.

KEY: A small block usually fitted in a notch between a shaft and a hub to prevent slippage of the two parts.

MANIFOLD: A casting of passages or set of pipes which connect the cylinders to an inlet or outlet source.

MANIFOLD VACUUM: Low pressure in an engine intake manifold formed just below the throttle plates. Manifold vacuum is highest at idle and drops under acceleration.

MASTER CYLINDER: The primary fluid pressurizing device in a hydraulic system. In automotive use, it is found in brake and hydraulic clutch systems and is pedal activated, either directly or, in a power brake system, through the power booster.

MODULE: Electronic control unit, amplifier or igniter of solid state or integrated design which controls the current flow in the ignition primary circuit based on input from the pick-up coil. When the module opens the primary circuit, high secondary voltage is induced in the coil.

NEEDLE BEARING: A bearing which consists of a number (usually a large number) of long, thin rollers.

OHM: (Ω) The unit used to measure the resistance of conductor-to-electrical flow. One ohm is the amount of resistance that limits current flow to one ampere in a circuit with one volt of pressure.

OHMMETER: An instrument used for measuring the resistance, in ohms, in an electrical circuit.

OUTPUT SHAFT: The shaft which transmits torque from a device, such as a transmission.

OVERDRIVE: A gear assembly which produces more shaft revolutions than that transmitted to it.

OVERHEAD CAMSHAFT (OHC): An engine configuration in which the camshaft is mounted on top of the cylinder head and operates the valve either directly or by means of rocker arms.

OVERHEAD VALVE (OHV): An engine configuration in which all of the valves are located in the cylinder head and the camshaft is located in the cylinder block. The camshaft operates the valves via lifters and pushrods.

OXIDES OF NITROGEN (NOx): Chemical compounds of nitrogen produced as a byproduct of combustion. They combine with hydrocarbons to produce smog.

OXYGEN SENSOR: Use with the feedback system to sense the presence of oxygen in the exhaust gas and signal the computer which can reference the voltage signal to an air/fuel ratio.

PINION: The smaller of two meshing gears.

PISTON RING: An open-ended ring with fits into a groove on the outer diameter of the piston. Its chief function is to form a seal between the piston and cylinder wall. Most automotive pistons have three rings: two for compression sealing; one for oil sealing.

PRELOAD: A predetermined load placed on a bearing during assembly or by adjustment.

PRIMARY CIRCUIT: the low voltage side of the ignition system which consists of the ignition switch, ballast resistor or resistance wire, bypass, coil, electronic control unit and pick-up coil as well as the connecting wires and harnesses.

PRESS FIT: The mating of two parts under pressure, due to the inner diameter of one being smaller than the outer diameter of the other, or vice versa; an interference fit.

RACE: The surface on the inner or outer ring of a bearing on which the balls, needles or rollers move.

REGULATOR: A device which maintains the amperage and/or voltage levels of a circuit at predetermined values.

RELAY: A switch which automatically opens and/or closes a circuit.

RESISTANCE: The opposition to the flow of current through a circuit or electrical device, and is measured in ohms. Resistance is equal to the voltage divided by the amperage.

RESISTOR: A device, usually made of wire, which offers a preset amount of resistance in an electrical circuit.

RING GEAR: The name given to a ring-shaped gear attached to a differential case, or affixed to a flywheel or as part of a planetary gear set.

ROLLER BEARING: A bearing made up of hardened inner and outer races between which hardened steel rollers move.

ROTOR: 1. The disc-shaped part of a disc brake assembly, upon which the brake pads bear; also called, brake disc. 2. The device mounted atop the distributor shaft, which passes current to the distributor cap tower contacts.

SECONDARY CIRCUIT: The high voltage side of the ignition system, usually above 20,000 volts. The secondary includes the ignition coil, coil wire, distributor cap and rotor, spark plug wires and spark plugs.

SENDING UNIT: A mechanical, electrical, hydraulic or electro-magnetic device which transmits information to a gauge.

SENSOR: Any device designed to measure engine operating conditions or ambient pressures and temperatures. Usually electronic in nature and designed to send a voltage signal to an on-board computer, some sensors may operate as a simple on/off switch or they may provide a variable voltage signal (like a potentiometer) as conditions or measured parameters change.

SHIM: Spacers of precise, predetermined thickness used between parts to establish a proper working relationship.

SLAVE CYLINDER: In automotive use, a device in the hydraulic clutch system which is activated by hydraulic force, disengaging the clutch.

SOLENOID: A coil used to produce a magnetic field, the effect of which is to produce work.

SPARK PLUG: A device screwed into the combustion chamber of a spark ignition engine. The basic construction is a conductive core inside of a ceramic insulator, mounted in an outer conductive base. An electrical charge from the spark plug wire travels along the conductive core and jumps a preset air gap to a grounding point or points at the end of the conductive base. The resultant spark ignites the fuel/air mixture in the combustion chamber.

SPLINES: Ridges machined or cast onto the outer diameter of a shaft or inner diameter of a bore to enable parts to mate without rotation.

TACHOMETER: A device used to measure the rotary speed of an engine, shaft, gear, etc., usually in rotations per minute.

THERMOSTAT: A valve, located in the cooling system of an engine, which is closed when cold and opens gradually in response to engine heating, controlling the temperature of the coolant and rate of coolant flow.

TOP DEAD CENTER (TDC): The point at which the piston reaches the top of its travel on the compression stroke.

TORQUE: The twisting force applied to an object.

TORQUE CONVERTER: A turbine used to transmit power from a driving member to a driven member via hydraulic action, providing changes in drive ratio and torque. In automotive use, it links the driveplate at the rear of the engine to the automatic transmission.

TRANSDUCER: A device used to change a force into an electrical signal.

TRANSISTOR: A semi-conductor component which can be actuated by a small voltage to perform an electrical switching function.

TUNE-UP: A regular maintenance function, usually associated with the replacement and adjustment of parts and components in the electrical and fuel systems of a vehicle for the purpose of attaining optimum performance.

TURBOCHARGER: An exhaust driven pump which compresses intake air and forces it into the combustion chambers at higher than atmospheric pressures. The increased air pressure allows more fuel to be burned and results in increased horsepower being produced.

VACUUM ADVANCE: A device which advances the ignition timing in response to increased engine vacuum.

VACUUM GAUGE: An instrument used to measure the presence of vacuum in a chamber.

VALVE: A device which control the pressure, direction of flow or rate of flow of a liquid or gas.

VALVE CLEARANCE: The measured gap between the end of the valve stem and the rocker arm, cam lobe or follower that activates the valve.

VISCOSITY: The rating of a liquid's internal resistance to flow.

VOLTMETER: An instrument used for measuring electrical force in units called volts. Voltmeters are always connected parallel with the circuit being tested.

WHEEL CYLINDER: Found in the automotive drum brake assembly, it is a device, actuated by hydraulic pressure, which, through internal pistons, pushes the brake shoes outward against the drums.

MASTER
INDEX